Production
management

THE IRWIN SERIES IN MANAGEMENT
and
THE BEHAVIORAL SCIENCES

L. L. CUMMINGS and E. KIRBY WARREN   CONSULTING EDITORS

JOHN F. MEE, ADVISORY EDITOR

Sixth edition

Production management

FRANKLIN G. MOORE, Ph.D.
Professor of Management
The University of Michigan

1973

RICHARD D. IRWIN, INC. *Homewood, Illinois 60430*

IRWIN-DORSEY LIMITED *Georgetown, Ontario L7G 4B3*

Sixth Edition

First Printing, January 1973
Second Printing, July 1973
Third Printing, February 1974
Fourth Printing, January 1975
Fifth Printing, May 1975
Sixth Printing, November 1975
Seventh Printing, January 1976
Eighth Printing, August 1976
Ninth Printing, November 1976

Previous editions published under the title
Manufacturing Management

ISBN 0-256-01393-4
Library of Congress Catalog Card No. 72–86622
Printed in the United States of America

Foreword to students

THE PURPOSE of a course in production and operations management is to provide you with an insight into how production is brought about. And it is the purpose of this book to give you a background in this subject. This book tries to portray the conditions under which production takes place and the part managers and workers play in effecting production.

The book will also call your attention to many of the problems faced by managers and to the merits of the different courses of action which are open to them. Emphasis is put on managers as decision makers who continually face alternatives, each having certain advantages, yet at the same time having disadvantages.

The subject material in this book supplies descriptive material to provide you with the background necessary for understanding the concepts and appreciating the managerial problems presented. Quantitative materials and problems are introduced frequently. These follow the trend in the last several years toward quantifying more and more of the areas of decision making in production areas. These problems are confined to small ones of the kind which can be presented and solved in the text. Difficult mathematical calculations have been avoided.

There may be times when you will wish for a definite answer and recommendation in some matter, and find none in the text. This may not be fully satisfying, yet this is how it often is in the real world. If you fly, you generally arrive at your destination quickly but you don't see the countryside. If you drive on the superhighway, you go more slowly and see more. And if you go on the back roads, you go still more slowly and see much more. Which is best? The answer depends on what you want. The text frequently points out the good and bad things about alternative actions without categorically choosing one as best.

This is the way the world operates. Sometimes it is hard for a manager, even with a considerable array of facts before him, to choose which action will prove to be the best. So don't feel annoyed if the text sometimes weighs pros and cons and does not make a choice. Often the matter being discussed is a little like trying to answer such questions as, "Should I buy a house or rent one?" or "Should I choose this college or that college?" There isn't any one answer which is best for everyone. There *are* two or more sides to many problems and these promote our understanding and help us make better decisions if we are aware of them, even if it does make choosing more difficult.

At the end of every chapter you will find several aids which will help you to understand what was presented in the chapter. First, there are review questions. These questions are about matters which you should be able to answer from having read the chapter. If you cannot answer them, it may be well to reread the text discussion on the subject.

It is well to familiarize yourself with new terms introduced in the chapter. If there is any question about the meaning of certain terms, you should consult the index at the end of the book. There you will find references to the pages where the terms are discussed and explained. By referring to the text discussion you will get a better explanation of the term than could be supplied in an abbreviated glossary.

Next are discussion questions. These questions relate to the subject of the chapter but often they go beyond it. They have to do with difficult problems and how to apply the ideas in the chapters to actual situations. Many of these questions have been taken from executive training programs. They are questions about how to apply the ideas presented, which mature men in training classes have asked.

Following the discussion questions are problems or cases or both, depending on the chapter. The problems allow you to apply the techniques introduced in the text to other similar problems to help you fix the method in your mind. The cases are like the discussion questions in that they relate to the subject of the chapter in a general way, although they are frequently even more far reaching. These cases, too, are often real life cases brought up in executive training classes.

Students as well as teachers may want to do further research on the subject of a chapter. For this purpose, a short bibliography is provided at the end of each chapter. These are sources where you will find a more thorough treatment of the material. Sometimes these sources will bring up different points of view from those expressed in the text and sometimes they will deal with different aspects of the subjects.

All of these study aids are presented as aids to learning. In a very real sense, a text does not teach, it only helps you to learn.

Preface

PAST USERS of this book will recognize the change in title to *Production Management*. This is in line with general thinking that production should not be thought of as being restricted to making products. The production of services is also production. This change is more than a change in title only. Rather, throughout the book, the concept of production is regarded as embracing the work of both manufacturing and service organizations.

Nonetheless most of the attention in this book is devoted to manufacturing organizations. The manufacturing firm is a particularly useful model in that it not only represents a large segment of our working population, but it is also the most complex type of firm. Similarly the making of automobiles is used as the illustrative example in several places. This is because the product is familiar to us all and it is easy for students to relate the concept being discussed to its real-life setting when the illustration is of a familiar product.

In this edition, a considerable amount of descriptive material has been eliminated in order to provide more space for conceptual matters and to allow for still more emphasis on managerial decision making. Enough descriptive material has been retained, however, to provide a background of information so that students without industrial work experience will not have to discuss concepts and cases in a vacuum. Quantitative materials have been retained but the emphasis is in the direction of acquainting the student with the methods and making him aware of the existence and availability of such methods. The purpose has not been to develop in him a high degree of manipulative skill in quantitative areas.

In order to emphasize the managerial decision-making viewpoint, general information is first presented. Following this is a discussion of the problems that managers face in each subject area. Alternative courses of action are considered along with the pros and cons of each. This gives the student both an acquaintance with the various subject areas and their problems, and a feel for the appropriate managerial actions. We have tried to lead the reader along the road to problem solutions so that he, himself, may better develop skill in this area.

In several cases the quantitative problems at the ends of the chapters are given "in series." A first problem illustrates the method, then a second and a third problem follow which change the problem a little. Solving these follow-up problems further acquaints the student with the method and also shows him how managers can use these techniques to help them solve problems. Managers often need to ask: Suppose that the situation is different, then what? They can find out how sensitive results are to changes in the input factors which bear on the problem and then determine the best course of action.

The whole book has been extensively rewritten and the text tightened up. Reductions in space were made in many places in order to allow for needed expansion elsewhere. Because other college courses usually consider personnel matters and wages, the space devoted to these subjects has been greatly reduced.

The book has been divided into ten general subject areas, each covering several chapters. The reviewers of this text offered helpful suggestions about the general format of the book, although the final grouping of subjects and the sequence in which subjects are presented is a compromise because there was not full agreement on this matter. Most teachers have personal preferences for the sequence in which they like to take up subordinate subjects. It is suggested that where the instructor prefers a different sequence, he adopt the one he likes. Most of the chapters are self-contained enough to allow for their being put into a different order to suit individual teachers.

The aids to the teacher in the classroom have been strengthened. First, at the end of each chapter, some review questions are presented. These allow the student to test his own understanding of the subject of the chapter and they can be used in the classroom to further clarify the text material.

Next, some discussion questions are presented. These relate to the subject of the chapter but often go beyond it. They are often difficult questions which may have no exact answer. Rather they are intended to generate classroom discussion. Most of these are questions originally brought up by mature men taking executive training programs. They provide an opportunity to relate the subject of the chapter to real-world settings. Usually they generate lively classroom participation, which in turn helps develop a better understanding of the subject.

Each chapter has its own problems or cases or both, as may be appropriate. The problems are related to the subject of the chapter and often are similar to the problems explained in the text. It is helpful to have the student work out such problems since it often happens that a student's reading about how to do a problem leaves him with less than full understanding. Working out problems gives him a better appreciation and a fuller understanding of how the technique operates.

Some subjects, however, are better explained through cases rather than computational problems. To serve this purpose, cases, some short and some long, are provided at the end of appropriate chapters.

The practice of putting short bibliographies at the end of each chapter, instead of one large bibliography at the end of the book, has been continued. Only recent sources are listed since contemporary authors usually incorporate in their books the best of the thinking of earlier writers.

I want to thank the many teachers who have written to me from time to time offering helpful suggestions. Particularly helpful in his capacity as a reviewer of the manuscript was Vincent G. Reuter. These suggestions help keep me aware of trends and directions in which the subject of production management is moving, and so help me to write a better book.

December 1972   FRANKLIN G. MOORE

Contents

Element precedence. Man requirements. Subassembly lines. Problems with lines. Fixed-position assembly.

Section ten
MANAGEMENT TOMORROW   671

section one
American industry

PRODUCTION MANAGEMENT as it operates today in America is largely a development since World War II. Yet this is not wholly so because the first consequential thinking about management as such started 100 years ago, shortly after the end of the American Civil War. It is perhaps surprising that such thinking did not start earlier because the Industrial Revolution itself got under way 100 years earlier yet—at, as it happened, the same time as the American Revolutionary War.

Chapter 1 recounts briefly these historical roots of production management as it operates today. Attention is also called to recent trends and to the most pertinent problem areas in which today's managers must operate. Most of these matters will be discussed more fully in later chapters.

1

American industry

OUR WESTERN industrialized civilization seems so firmly rooted that it is hard to believe that, even today, it is only 200 years old. In the long history of man that is but yesterday. George Washington would have fitted better into the world of Julius Caesar than into today's world—so great has been the change since his time and so little before.

Like Caesar, Washington traveled on horseback, in a carriage, or in a rowboat or sailing ship. He would, no doubt, have preferred to go by steamship, train, automobile, or airplane, but they had not been invented yet. Abraham Lincoln read books by firelight, candlelight, or lamplight. He, too, no doubt, would have preferred something better. But electricity and electric lights came later. Automobiles, airplanes, and radio came in the present century. Television, air-conditioning, penicillin, and computers are hardly 25 years old. And moon space ships, atomic fuel, and sea-water desalting plants are even newer.

All this flood of products coming out of today's factories is the result of the Industrial Revolution, the introduction of machinery to do work, and the growth and application of scientific knowledge.

The Industrial Revolution started in England at about the time of the American Revolutionary War—in the 1770s and 1780s. During this period machines were invented to spin thread and weave cloth. They made better thread and cloth than men could make and they did it faster and at less cost. During this same period James Watt developed a workable steam engine. This combination—machines to do the work at low cost and power to run the machines—spread to other industries and set off the Industrial Revolution.

It took a hundred years, however, for people to get interested in management. This time the change came in America instead of England. By the 1880s companies with several hundred employees were common in the United States and Frederick Taylor became the apostle of better management. Taylor was mostly interested in improving shop operations and is the father of time study. Before his time there was widespread interest in making labor-saving machines and some interest in the advancement of scientific knowledge but little interest in management.

The idea of progress

After the American Civil War, in the first half of the 1870s, interest in management methods awakened. Perhaps it grew out of the difficulties encountered in operating bigger factories. Perhaps it grew out of a new philosophical idea that caught the fancy of Western civilization—the idea of progress.

Important discoveries had been made in chemistry and physics. People began to believe that we live in a world governed by physical laws, and that once we know the laws we can apply them and use them to better our living conditions. Most of the laws of nature discovered in the scientific field came to light as a result of experiments—consciously directed experiments aimed at finding nature's laws. People began to have confidence in science and scientific inquiry into problems.

"Progress" is the end idea of a three-step analysis: (1) There are natural laws for everything; (2) We can learn nature's laws by experimentation; and (3) We can apply the laws and improve our well-being. Step 3 is the progress idea. Always we will know as much as we knew yesterday plus what we have learned today, so every new day should be an improvement over the day before.

But we must use step 2 to get to step 3. We must have an inquiring mind; we must experiment and search for nature's laws. If we do this we can expect to improve our lot. These ideas took hold in manufacturing— first in product design and process and machine development and then in management.

Frederick W. Taylor

The time was ripe and the stage was set for just such a man as Frederick W. Taylor. With him came the period of rapid development in the emerging subject of production management.

Taylor was probably the most important man in the development of shop management techniques. Born in 1856, he died in 1915. After having served a machinist's apprenticeship at the Cramp Shipyard in Philadelphia, he came to the Midvale Steel Company in 1878, where he worked for the next twelve years.

Many of Taylor's ideas grew out of practices he observed at Midvale. William Sellers, Midvale's president, was also owner of William Sellers and Company, manufacturers of machinery, and was at that time the leading machine designing engineer in the country. Sellers' machines were among the best in the world. They were noted for the precise work they could do and for being designed to save the time of the machine operators. An English writer, seeing them exhibited at the Vienna machinery exhibition in 1873, said: "No opportunity is lost to save a useless step, an unnecessary motion. Writers on this subject remark that Americans [as evidenced by the Sellers' machines] try to arrange their machines so as to make them the most convenient for the workmen."[1]

Taylor was fortunate in having an opportunity to work at Midvale. He gave Sellers credit for much of what he learned there. The ideas of experimentation, of finding better methods, of saving human movements, all were favored at Midvale before Taylor's arrival, having been introduced by Sellers in 1873 when he came in to head what was then virtually a bankrupt company. The friendship between Taylor's family and the E. W. Clark family, who owned a majority of the Midvale stock, probably helped his early advancement in the company. Though he started as a laborer, he was made a gang boss two years later, and then after four more years, when he just was 28 years old, he was appointed chief engineer.

Taylor is sometimes referred to as the father of scientific management, but to credit him with originating it is claiming too much. He certainly did a great deal to develop the field of management into a scientific study, but his greatest contribution was to develop and dramatically publicize the field of management. He was the movement's catalytic agent. His imagination and zeal in carrying through his investigations were perhaps equal to the task of originating the ideas. The fact is, however, that he arrived too late on the scene to be credited with doing the whole job.

The shoveling experiment. Taylor had a flair for the dramatic and received widespread attention for some of the things he did. In the late 1890s, while working for the Bethlehem Steel Company, he conducted

---

[1] Quoted from *The Engineering Magazine* (London) in the *Journal of the Franklin Institute*, November 1873, p. 352.

two historic experiments with the yard labor gang, the first of which dealt with their various shoveling jobs. Taylor wasn't the first to study shoveling, but his study made the headlines. He found that each man in the gang furnished his own shovel and that the shovels were of various sizes. Sometimes the yard laborers had to shovel coal, sometimes iron ore, sometimes ashes. Hence the weight per shovelful varied considerably, depending on the material lifted as well as the size of the shovel. By experiment Taylor found that the most work was done when a load of about 21 pounds per shovelful was moved. He had the company buy a stock of shovels of various sizes. No matter what the material shoveled, the appropriate size shovel could be furnished to the workers. Large shovels were used for ashes, small shovels for iron ore, etc. In that way the load was always about 21 pounds. As a result, the work done per worker increased and costs were reduced.

Pig iron handling.   Taylor's second experiment, which became a classic example of job improvement, was with a pig iron handler named Schmidt. Taylor decided after watching his men load pig iron into freight cars from the storage yard that they weren't doing it the best way. He thought that they used the wrong motions and that they worked too hard and too long, became overtired, and then had to rest too long. He believed that the work would be less tiring if the workers did the work differently and took frequent short rest periods.

The men were paid $1.15 a day and they loaded an average of 12½ tons of pig iron per man per day. Schmidt, one of the group, was offered the opportunity to earn more money if he would follow directions on how to pick up, carry, and put down the pigs of iron, and if he would take frequent short rests. Taylor believed that in this way Schmidt could load more pig iron. Schmidt followed the directions, loaded 47 tons in one day, earned $1.85, and continued to do so thereafter. Some of the workers couldn't handle that much pig iron, but the company soon had many applicants for the $1.85 job.

In speeches and articles Taylor later described both the shoveling and the pig iron handling incidents. They created considerable interest and comment (not all favorable) and caused many industrial leaders to become interested in his methods.

Taylor's other activities.   Although Taylor is best known for his work in trying to improve work done in factories, he was also the leading researcher of his time in the art of cutting metals. In experiments at Bethlehem Steel and at Midvale Steel he, together with colleague Maunsel White, in the late 1890s developed high speed cutting steel. This development revolutionized metal cutting procedures all over the world because metal cutting machines could run twice as fast and turn out twice as much as the carbon steel cutting tools then in use were able to do.

Taylor also developed a special piece rate system which he thought would motivate workers more. It consisted of two piece rates for every job. There was a low rate per piece for all production if a man did not produce as much as standard output, and a high piece rate to be paid for all units produced if the man did produce standard or more. The system never became popular but it set off the thinking of other men along these lines. Quite a few other piece rate methods of pay then grew up. Today almost none of them remain in use.

The Taylor image today has a Simon Legree coloration. It is true that he was a strict disciplinarian, but he was also a very human person. He and Mrs. Taylor adopted and raised three children. As a young man, Taylor played tennis and was one of the national doubles team champions of the United States in 1878. Later on he took up golf and as a player had a handicap of 8. He experimented for years with golf greens construction and wrote a book on the subject. He was not wholly and only an apostle for better factory operations.

Other pioneers in the management movement

Some pioneers in the management movement, such as Henry L. Gantt and Carl B. Barth, worked with Taylor. Others, such as Henry R. Towne and Frederick A. Halsey, were active contributors before and, to some extent, during Taylor's time. Still others, among them Frank B. and Lillian M. Gilbreth, worked independently and into a later period. (Mrs. Gilbreth died in 1971 at the age of 93 and was active in management work almost to the end of her life.)

Gantt is best known as an author and an engineer. An early colleague of Taylor, he later installed "scientific" management procedures in several companies. He developed an incentive wage payment plan which was used by some companies. And he developed a type of bar chart which helped control manufacturing operations. Such charts, known as Gantt charts, are still used occasionally today.

Carl Barth is best remembered as the inventor of slide rules with which the proper machine speeds, feeds, and depth of cut for metal cutting machines could be calculated.

Frank B. and Lillian M. Gilbreth did important pioneer work in motion study. Taylor and his predecessors had made some progress in motion study but did not carry it as far as the Gilbreths did. They introduced charts and moving pictures (or "micromotion" study) to help analyze, study, and improve jobs. Gilbreth, a bricklayer by trade, became an outstanding industrial engineer in the decade before his death in 1924. Mrs. Gilbreth, a psychologist by training, worked with her husband during his lifetime and after his death continued the practice of industrial engineering.

The two Gilbreths did very important pioneer work in fatigue analysis as well as motion study. They also developed the idea that all human work is composed of various combinations of basic human movements, which they called "therbligs." Although their work was done many years ago, only since World War II has their therblig idea been taken up by industrial engineers generally. Today many leading industrial engineers think it offers a valuable approach both to improving jobs and to setting time standards.

The current scene

In the hundred years since Taylor first came on the scene America has changed to an industrialized society. Today we have more than 400 manufacturing companies and more than 50 nonmanufacturing companies with more than 10,000 employees. And there are perhaps almost as many more large companies in the rest of the world.

How to manage such giant companies with widely dispersed operations has long been the subject of an extensive literature. Researchers continually delve into men's motivations and reactions, trying to learn how better to control and direct these huge organizations. Mathematicians and operations researchers, using computers, try to develop new and to improve old techniques to help managers make the best economic decisions. For companies which need more direct help, management consultants stand ready to make recommendations or to do the work.

Training in management is now widespread both in the United States and in the whole world. Management courses are offered by colleges all over the country, and indeed in various parts of the world, both to regular students and, in short summer courses, to businessmen. Private organizations, such as the American Management Association, conduct hundreds of short seminars on management problems. Companies conduct training courses of their own and see to it that their young men get varied experience and coaching from experienced administrators.

As we progress into the 1970s a whole new dimension is being introduced into management. This is the growing feeling, on the part of society, concerning the responsibilities and obligations of all organizations, business organizations included. There are many facets to this new social atmosphere. Nondiscrimination, responsibility to employees, consumerism, honesty in advertising, safety, antipollution and antinoise programs, and ecology are all part of the total picture.

So far as managers are concerned, all of these matters have one element in common. They constitute constraints on their former freedom to manage as they see fit. And most of these new constraints cost extra money and make it harder for managers to keep costs down.

The area of "production" management

"Production" management, the subject of this book, concerns production in the same way an economist refers to production. To an economist, production has to do with the production of *goods* and *services,* and *not* just how a factory should operate. Service organizations, merchandising companies, railroads, hospitals, insurance companies, governments, etc., all are also engaged in production even though their end products are services and not physical products. The fundamentals of how best to *produce* have many elements which are common to service as well as to manufacturing organizations.

Most of the examples used in this text will, however, be from manufacturing because this is by far the biggest single area of production. Many more people work at producing products than at any other kind of production.

Figure 1–1 is a typical pattern of a manufacturing organization. The big main departments are the manufacturing and sales departments. They make and sell the products which are the company's reason for being.

Line and staff departments. In Figure 1–1 there are quite a few other

FIGURE 1–1. Organization chart of a typical manufacturing company

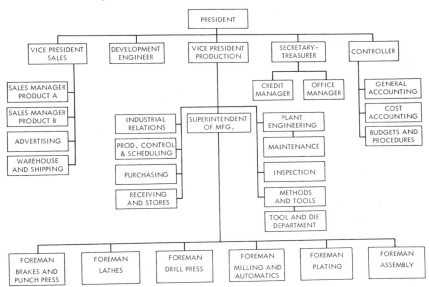

departments (such as advertising, credit and collection, personnel, and engineering) which neither make nor sell products. They are "staff" departments whose "production" is in the nature of the help they give to other departments.

Staff departments are those which advise or serve other departments. Some of these departments, such as the legal, economic, public relations, and part of the personnel department, are advisory. Some, such as industrial engineering, personnel, credit, costs and budgets, and accounting and auditing largely do control work. Normally they have authority to see that their functions are properly carried out throughout the organization.

Some departments are designed to provide service as such. These include the research and development, engineering, maintenance, purchasing, inventory control, traffic, tax, and insurance departments. Still other departments, such as order and distribution and planning and production control, do work which helps other departments coordinate their work.

Relationships between line and staff departments are usually harmonious, but occasionally this is not so. Departments receiving help and those giving it do not always agree. Staff groups may find that their work is sometimes neither appreciated nor wanted, nor is their advice always followed. And sometimes line men feel that staffs try to boss them and that they have too many bosses. Or they feel that staffs are sometimes too pushy and give either poor service or advice at too high a cost.

These differences of opinion do not come up often, and when they do they usually are not serious. Yet, because they might come up, managers need to work continually at building good interdepartmental relations so that effective operations will result.

Functional and divisional organizations. With the coming of giant companies, most of which are manufacturing companies, there has come a change in organizational structures, from "functional" to "divisional." A functional manufacturing organization has one sales department and one manufacturing department, each of which handles all of the company's products. In contrast, in a divisional company the major subsections are usually based on product lines, although they can be based on geographical areas, customer groups, or the nature of the technology.

The Aluminum Company of America is largely a functional company, with one large sales department and one large manufacturing group, whereas General Electric is divisional. GE has no company-wide sales or manufacturing department. Instead it has a lamp, household appliance, jet engine, and other divisions, each with its own sales and manufacturing department and its own profit-making responsibility. A functional company has only one profit center, the central office.

This distinction has far-reaching implications. In divisional companies, decisions relating to each division are delegated to it. Divisionalization helps push profit-making thinking down a little further in the organization than is possible in functionalization. Usually this is an advantage, but it works well only if the company has capable divisional managers who are able to make major decisions on their own. Some companies have tried divisionalization and have got poor results because they lacked capable divisional managers.

Capable divisional managers can, however, be developed only over a period of time. Once good men have been developed, divisional management, operating with considerable freedom yet within the corporate restraints set by the central office, seems to be the best way to administer large companies.

Management and organization fundamentals

Although there is widespread interest in management and organization, people do not agree on how best to manage. No one has yet developed a set of rules or fundamentals which is universally acceptable and applicable.

Part of the trouble is in differing viewpoints about which causes produce which effects in situations where several factors interact. This makes it hard to draw conclusions about what rules one ought to follow. Another part of the trouble is in the inherent conflict among the factors which operate in any given situation. Still another factor is that, in order to have widespread applicability, generalizations often become *so* general that they are not very helpful. And, lastly, organizations are made up of people who do not always react according to the rules.

Yet, having said this (that there seem to be no rules which are universally valid), it may well be worthwhile to list certain statements which seem to be both valid and helpful. The following nine generalizations surely have widespread applicability:

1. The proper kind of organization depends on what it is to do. If it is not set up on the basis of what it has to do, it will do poorly. A bank and a manufacturing company should not have the same kind of organization.

2. Organizations should have departments and structural arrangements that are set up in a logical way; for example, work of like nature or work that is closely related should be assigned to the same department.

3. Every organization should have *one* man at the top who is responsible for its performance. And it is desirable that nowhere in the organization should men have two or more superiors.

4. Top men cannot do all of the work themselves, so they have to assign work to others. They must delegate responsibility, authority, and decision-making power. Subordinates need to be given instructions, and at the same time some freedom.

5. No superior can directly supervise the work of many subordinates. He has a limited "span of control" even though reliable specific numbers cannot be set.

6. Superiors should check on what their subordinates do. Delegation should not be abdication.

7. Superiors should ask subordinates for their ideas and let them participate in decisions affecting their work wherever it is reasonably possible.

8. Managers must staff the organization both for today and for the future. In the long run, developing good managers is as important as making and selling goods or services.
9. Specialization usually is more effective than nonspecialization.

Because space limits us, we cannot go into these matters more fully. This list, however, suggests the kinds of subjects dealt with in the literature of management and organization.

The management of people

In the early days, and even up to World War II, many managers were rather autocratic and gave little thought to their employees as people. But this has changed and today most managers are more human relations minded. Subordinates, particularly middle-level managers, are brought more into the decision-making processes. They get a chance to make suggestions and to have a voice in decisions which will affect them. And they are given considerable authority to make their own decisions in the spheres of their work. A more democratic atmosphere prevails.

This does not mean that top managers abdicate their overall responsibility. Subordinates still have to produce and to coordinate their work with the work of other departments, but superiors and subordinates work more as team members. This change in managerial thinking has been fostered by the work of social or "behavioral" scientists, whose research findings have pointed up the need to recognize that subordinates are people. They behave and react like people and do not always do what managers want and tell them to do.

Possibly managers would have become more human relations conscious even without social scientists because superiors cannot treat today's employees arbitrarily, be they hourly paid blue-collar workers or middle-level managers. Today's subordinates are well educated, enjoy high standards of living, and expect reasonable treatment.

In the case of blue-collar workers, both our laws and unions give them added protection against unsympathetic supervision. And furthermore, most employees can easily get well-paying jobs elsewhere if they do not like it where they are. So it happens that a combination of circumstances reinforces the social scientists' conclusions that managers need to be human relations conscious. This, in turn, seems to result in managers' having less confidence in "principles" or rules.

The growth of fixed costs

One of today's particularly difficult managerial problems is how to manage in the face of higher fixed costs. Year by year fixed costs, as opposed to variable costs, take a larger share of the sales dollar.

In the factory, mechanization and automation cause part of this increase. When machines are substituted for men, direct labor costs, which are variable costs, are reduced, but depreciation charges, which are fixed costs, go up. This is true even though the newly added depreciation charges are less than the old labor costs. But whatever their size, they are additions to fixed costs and they replace variable costs. And since companies keep growing bigger all the time, so do the fixed costs.

But more important than mechanization is the growth of service-type organizations and white-collar workers in both manufacturing and service organizations. Fully one fourth, and sometimes up to one half, of manufacturing company employees are salaried office workers.[2] And in service organizations, office workers make up an even larger fraction of the total. The costs of office people are relatively resistant to reduction in any short period of time, and in the long run they seem always to go up.

Managing the production of office workers and service workers, in both manufacturing and service industries, is most difficult. Only rarely is it possible to set production standards and to measure the work done. Yet, somehow, managers have to try to manage this work and to see that production occurs. Budgets are often used here, although—as we shall see in Chapter 17—they are far from perfect for such jobs.

Most of the office worker expansion in manufacturing has come from the expansion of staff departments—those which help other departments. But regardless of the fact that they help, they are substantial blocs of relatively fixed costs.

Blue-collar cost, too, is tending to become fixed. Unions press for guaranteed annual wages and large unemployment payments. Some companies, among them Procter & Gamble, have for years had wage guarantees which make factory labor costs more fixed than variable. Motorola and Texas Instruments pay factory workers a salary. Tomorrow's managers will surely have to manage with more rigid cost structures.

Companies having heavy fixed costs have to operate differently from those whose costs are largely variable. It becomes very important to operate both steadily and at high-capacity/use ratios. This is even more important in service organizations than in production organizations.

Operating steadily becomes increasingly difficult inasmuch as technological changes seem to come more frequently than ever while at the same time it takes longer than ever to bring new products to the marketplace. Black and white TV's bonanza period lasted hardly 10 years, whereas TV's predecessor, radio, had a 25-year boom. To compound this difficulty, it takes 3 years to bring a new automobile to the market, 5 years for an airplane, and up to 10 years for a new drug.

Customers and competitors do not help the situation because their demands are not related to the production capacities of companies, or to

---

[2] In 1971, 6 million of the 19.5 million people employed by manufacturing companies in the United States were office workers.

their fixed overhead costs. The demand for Ford's Mustang, when it first appeared a decade ago, was four times the company's expectations and four times Ford's initial capacity to make Mustangs. Several years earlier, in contrast, customers' demand for Edsels had been far below the company's expectations and production capacity.

In the mid-1960s, customer demand for color television sets was nearly double the industry's expectations and more than double the available manufacturing capacity. Then, beginning in 1967, fickle as consumers are they bought *fewer* color TVs than expected, leaving the industry operating at only 75 percent of its new higher-level capacity.

The aluminum and the chemical industries suffered a different fate in the late 1950s and the 1960s, when competition caused the trouble. In each of these two industries, lured by forecasts of increased usage, most companies expanded their capacity. The forecasts proved correct: industry sales went up; but because of too many factories the result was short hours for everyone. Because of the new and high fixed costs, profits for aluminum and chemical companies all but vanished for a decade. The same sequence of events hurt the fertilizer industry in the late 1960s and early 1970s.

Managers have difficult jobs indeed when they operate under these conditions. Saddled with rather rigid high fixed costs, they may have to increase (or decrease) production as much as 25 to 50 percent (or more) in a few months. In other cases, and in spite of cost rigidities, they may have to reduce costs quickly and drastically. In service industries, such as airlines, this is a very serious problem.

Such severe changes cause convulsive changes inside companies. In order to have as few such crises as possible, management needs to have good forecasts so that their companies will not be caught off base too often.

Research costs

The last 20 years have seen a tremendous upsurge in research work. Some $20 billion or more has been spent annually, which has amounted to roughly 2 percent of our national income. A good bit of this has been spent on space ships and military products; but many companies spend from 1 to 2 percent of their gross income (in a few industries, as will be brought out in Chapter 11, companies spend much more than this) on developing new products, materials, and processes for their regular business.

Today, managers accept as a fact of life that most products are likely to be superseded by newer products. They believe, therefore, that they need continually to bring on new products to replace old ones. Managers have to make their own products obsolete before someone else does. And because a new product comes only out of research, there is great emphasis on research.

Managing researchers and research expenditures and incorporating research findings into profitable products is one of management's most difficult new jobs. The cost of research is one of those big semifrozen blocks of overhead which are so hard to manage and control. And because so much research has been done in the last decade, big payoff discoveries are becoming fewer. Today, research expenditures are both bigger and more hazardous than they were only a few years ago.

Systems

Along with the coming of computers several years ago has come the idea that all minor flows of information within an organization are parts of larger, more complete "systems." Actually, several quite different ideas lay claim to being called systems. But the most important idea seems to be that all flows of information are, or ought to be, viewed as parts of an overall, single, unified information flow system. These various views are the subject of Chapter 22.

Operations research

Managers today have a number of mathematical techniques available called "operations research." Those which are the most useful in production management are probability theory, queuing theory, simulation, the transportation method, the assignment method, the simplex method, decision trees, and Bayesian analyses. All of these are explained together with examples of their use, in later chapters.

Operations research procedures always require that things be put into numbers, even things which are not fundamentally quantifiable. This need rules out the use of operations research in some cases. In other cases it means that the answers must be used with care since they do not rest on a base of exact numbers.

Review questions

1. What part did the idea of progress play in the development of managerial thinking?
2. What did Frederick W. Taylor do and what contribution did he make to early managerial thinking?
3. How can line and staff departments be distinguished, one from the other? Why is it that occasionally there is conflict between the two?
4. How does a "functional" organization differ from a "divisional" organization? When should each be used?
5. Since organizations are made up of people and people differ, is it possible to have organization principles?
6. How does the growth of fixed costs make the managerial job more difficult?

Discussion questions

1. "Lines do, staffs advise." Suppose, however, that staffs give orders to the line. Would this make any difference?
2. In a divisional company, each division has its own staffs. But in most cases there is a home office staff too. What does this home office staff do?
3. Suppose that General Motors' Pontiac division put in a computer and went through a lengthy and costly period of debugging its programs, after which the programs worked fine and, in fact, boosted Pontiac's profits by 5 percent. The Buick head wants to copy the programs and thus save all of this expense at Buick, but the Pontiac head objects. Why should he object? What should the head of General Motors do? If he lets Buick use the programs, how can he justify it to the Pontiac head in a way which will be satisfactory to the latter?
4. Is it not logical to believe that management principles exist? And that, if so, they can be learned, and managers who follow them will do better than if they did not know about them? Yet, if the answer is yes, doesn't this imply that once men have learned the principles, they can learn no more since they know all there is to know? Yet this conclusion hardly seems logical. Discuss.
5. Admittedly, managers today are more human relations minded than their predecessors 50 years ago. Most people regard this as good. In fact, many people feel that even more human relations orientation would be better. Assuming that we accept this position, where does this lead us? Is there an ultimate best or final degree of human relations consciousness? And where does one go after he arrives at that degree? Discuss.
6. European companies characteristically operate with smaller staffs than American companies, and this is one of several reasons why their costs are often lower than those of American companies. Should we take a lesson from them and reduce our staffs by, say, half? Discuss.
7. Can operations research be of any value in cases where it is not possible to have exact numbers for everything? Justify your answer.

Recent references

Athos, Anthony G., "Is the Corporation Next to Fall?" *Harvard Business Review,* January–February 1970

Davis, Keith, and Robert L. Blomstrom, *Business, Society, and Environment,* New York: McGraw-Hill, 1971

Drucker, Peter F., *Technology, Management and Society,* New York: Harper & Row, 1970

George, Claude, *The History of Management Thought,* Englewood Cliffs, N.J.: Prentice-Hall, 1968

McDonald, John, "How Social Responsibility Fits the Game of Business," *Fortune,* December 1970

Samuelson, P. A., "Businessmen's Shrinking Prerequisites," *Management Review,* March 1972

section two

Production investment economics

PRODUCTION in both manufacturing and service organizations almost always requires a considerable investment in facilities in the form of buildings, machinery, equipment, and inventories. In each of these areas managers face choice alternatives. They can choose to invest more, and so own the facilities, or they can choose to rent facilities, or they can choose to buy products and services, thus shifting the ownership of facilities back to the suppliers.

Chapters 2, 3, and 4 consider the economic implications inherent in these alternatives. As a rule, it is more risky to own most of the required facilities because, in the event of failure, it often is not possible to recover all of the resources. Yet, at the same time, owning can be, and usually is, the most rewarding choice. More of the economic returns from operating the enterprise accrue to the owner of the facilities.

Chapter 2 considers the break-even point in operations. This is the critical point in the scale of operations because long-continued operations at lower volumes will result in bankruptcy. Chapter 2 shows how various investment inputs need to be related to expected outputs in order to allow for continued operations above the break-even point.

Chapter 2 also considers problems of establishing balance points between conflicting costs. The costs from having excess capacity as insurance are compared to the costs from production losses when equipment breaks down. Queuing and Monte Carlo simulation as methods for making these comparisons are explained.

Chapter 3 investigates capital investment policies and the conceptual philosophy behind the choices made in capital investment decisions. This chapter also considers the differing accounting practices for depreciation and the impact of their differences on income taxes and on final decisions.

In Chapter 4 the main methods for weighing individual capital expenditure proposals against each other are presented. These include return on investment, payback, discounted cash flow, and others. The Bayesian method and decision trees, and how they can help in capital investment decisions, are also explained.

2

Basic economic concepts

THE BREAK-EVEN CHART is a helpful tool in analyzing managerial economic problems. Such a chart shows how much business a company needs to do in order to break even financially. And it shows how much profit and how much loss the company would earn or suffer at various business volumes above and below the break-even point. Probably most manufacturing companies must operate at above 60 percent of their capacity to break even. Normally, most companies operate at a little over 85 percent of their capacity, although they would like to operate at about 92 or 93 percent. At above 92 or 93 percent efficiency usually drops off.

In order to calculate break-even points it is necessary to know the fixed and variable costs associated with the problem. Fixed costs are those which remain constant regardless of volume, whereas variable costs are those whose total changes with changes in volume. When break-even charts are used in machinery buying decisions, the fixed costs are normally the costs of the machine's depreciation, insurance, and such items. Variable costs are almost wholly made up of materials and direct labor costs. Variable costs are sometimes also referred to as "incremental" costs, meaning that for each unit of product there is an increment of costs.

Break-even charts are "if" charts. They say that *if* the sales volume is this, then the costs and profits will be that. They show the costs and profits and losses in prospect for various sales volumes.

Calculating break-even points

To calculate a company's break-even point it is necessary to know its fixed costs, its total variable costs, and its sales volume. Then the break-even point can be calculated by using this formula:

$$\text{BEP} = \frac{\text{Total fixed costs}}{1 - \dfrac{\text{Variable costs}}{\text{Sales}}}$$

This can also be expressed as:

$$\text{Gross profit margin}$$

A company might, for example, have sales of 1 million units at $1 each. At this level its variable costs are $700,000 and its fixed costs are $200,000. This makes the calculation of its break-even point:

$$\text{BEP} = \frac{\$200,000}{1 - \dfrac{\$700,000}{\$1,000,000}} = \$667,000 \text{ (or in this case units, since the price is \$1 per unit)}$$

The BEP can also be calculated another way. On every break-even chart there is an income and an outgo line, each of which can be expressed in formula form. The income line's formula for every break-even chart is $0 + \$1x$, and the outgo line for our example is $\$200,000 + \$.7x$. Setting these two equal to each other and solving for x gives the break-even point:

$$0 + \$1x = \$200,000 + \$.7x$$
$$\$.3x = \$200,000$$
$$x = \$667,000$$

Contribution ratios or profit variations

For some purposes it is well to know the "contribution ratio," or as it is sometimes called the "profit variation," of different products. This is the amount that each sales dollar contributes to carrying fixed costs or profits. The contribution ratio is simply the difference between income and variable costs expressed as a percentage. In our example, the $1 million of sales cost $700,000 in variable costs, so the remaining $300,000, or 30 percent of the sales income, was available to carry fixed costs, or, after fixed costs have been recovered, as profits. The contribution ratio is 30 percent. Every sales dollar pays its own variable costs and contributes $.30 more.

This sort of analysis can be helpful in evaluating the worth of individual products. Some products have a high contribution ratio, others contribute less. Once a manager knows the contribution ratios of his products he can concentrate on the ones which contribute the most. Such ratios can also help him decide whether to take on jobs at prices which cover variable costs but not all the prospective order's share of fixed costs.

An example will illustrate how important different contribution ratios can be in determining overall results. Suppose that a company makes three models of typewriters, each of which has a different contribution ratio, as follows:

	Total sales	*Contri-bution ratio*	*Contribution*	*Fixed costs*	*Profit*
Portable manual....	$1,000,000	25%	$ 250,000	$200,000	$ 50,000
Portable electric.....	1,000,000	35	350,000	200,000	150,000
Regular electric.....	1,000,000	45	450,000	200,000	250,000
Total...........	$3,000,000		$1,050,000	$600,000	$450,000

If a sales increase of $1 million, or 25 percent, came from selling more portable manual typewriters, this would increase profits only $250,000. But if a $1 million sales increase came from selling more regular electric models, it would add $450,000 to profits. Obviously, the greater sales effort should go into selling regular electric typewriters.

Often it is more meaningful to express contributed value on a per man-hour basis. In our example it might be that portable manual typewriters sell for $100 each and take 10 man-hours of labor. Portable electrics might cost $200 each and take 15 man-hours while regular electrics sell for $300 each and take 25 hours of labor. Unit sales in our example would be 10,000, 5,000, and 3,333, respectively. The contribution per unit is $25, $70, and $135. The contribution per man-hour comes to $2.50, $4.67, and $5.40 respectively. This bears out the conclusion (above) that regular electric typewriters should be pushed; but it would not always come out this way. If, for example, it took 35 man-hours for each regular electric typewriter, the contribution per man-hour would be $3.86. In such a case it would pay to push portable electrics instead.

Break-even charts and decision making

Mechanization decisions. Figure 2–1 is a break-even chart for a company that does not have much machinery and whose fixed costs are small. Most of its total costs are variable and go up and down with changes in volume. These are chiefly for labor and materials. This company's break-even point is one fourth of its capacity volume, so even when it operates at only 50 percent of capacity it will earn a small profit. But it will never earn a big profit, even if it operates at close to top capacity.

FIGURE 2–1

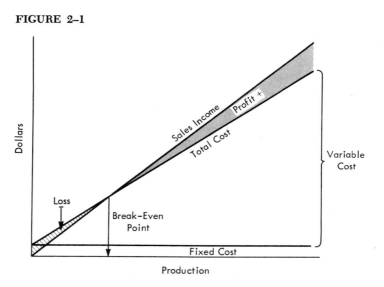

Figure 2–2 could be the situation in the same company after it bought several labor saving machines. Because of heavier depreciation charges, its fixed costs would go up and the company would need more business to break even. As we have drawn it, its new break-even point is at 60 percent of capacity. But because the company's variable costs are now very low, profits would be high at *high production levels.*

Break-even charts can be used in managerial decision making concerning whether to mechanize, as Figures 2–1 and 2–2 show. Suppose, for example, that a one-product company, doing work largely by hand, is considering mechanizing some of its operations and wants to know at what volume it would be better off. (It would have to be at some higher volume than the new break-even point because at the new break-even volume point the old method produced profits.)

In order to calculate the point where the profits are equal, it is necessary to have cost and profit figures. We will assume that the company now has $12,000 in fixed charges, variable costs of $.40 per unit and a selling price of $1. Its present break-even point is 20,000 (obtained by solving for x as follows: $0 + 1x = 12,000 + .4x; .6x = 12,000; x = 20,000$).

FIGURE 2-2

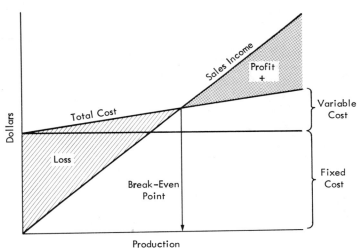

The mechanization program would increase fixed charges to $15,000 but would reduce variable costs to $.30 per unit. The selling price would still be $1. The new break-even point would be 21,429 units ($0 + 1x = 15,000 + .3x; .7x = 15,000; x = 21,429$).

The point of equal profits can be found by setting the costs of these two alternatives as equal to each other and solving for x:

$$12,000 + .4x = 15,000 + .3x$$
$$.1x = 3,000$$
$$x = 30,000$$

This equation is just like the "crossover" equations explained below. X, the volume at which the profits are equal, in the example above, to be 30,000. If future volumes are likely to be greater than 30,000, the company will be better off to mechanize, otherwise not.

Choices among processing alternatives. Break-even charts can also be used to aid in making choices from among alternative processes by comparing the different ways of doing work. In a factory, for example, methods requiring simple machines are usually easy to set up but slow

and costly to operate. Bigger quantities allow for the use of faster machines, which are costly to set up but which, once set up, are much less
costly to operate. Often there are several alternative methods, each of
which is the most economical for a certain volume range. (It has a "domain" or volume range for which it is the best method.) The method
which should be used depends on the expected volume, and Figure 2–3
shows how this would work.

FIGURE 2–3

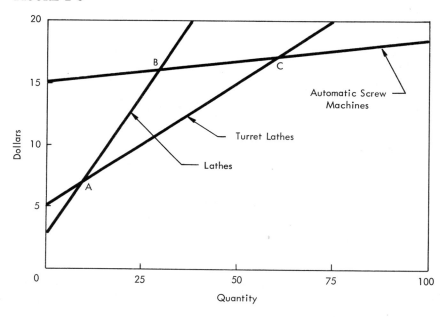

The lines in Figure 2–3 compare methods for making a small bushing
on three kinds of machines. Each of the three lines in the figure shows
what it would cost to make these bushings on one kind of machine. Lathes
are general-purpose machines, and are easy to set up for new jobs,[1] but
they are not very efficient in production. Turret lathes require more setup
time but produce at lower unit costs once they are set up. Neither of
these machines is "in it," however, with automatic screw machines when
volume begins to mount. Automatic screw machines produce at low unit
costs. Unfortunately, it takes hours to set up such machines, so setup
costs are high.

In Figure 2–3 the lines all start with certain costs before production
starts. These starting amounts ($2.50, $5, and $15) are the setup costs.

---

[1] Setup costs cover the costs of getting the machine ready (installing the tools
and the holding clamps to hold the bushings in place). These figures also include
the later tear-down time, taking the tools and holding clamps off the machine.

The lines in Figure 2–3 are all straight lines, which go up steadily. This shows the effect of operating costs, which, once operations start, are constant per unit of product. These costs, $.45, $.20, and $.04, cover the cost of the machines' operations, including labor, electricity, depreciation, and all other costs, *on a unit cost basis.*

Sometimes a chart is all that is needed for deciding which machine to use for a job because the size of an order is not close to a crossover point on the chart. But if it is necessary to know the exact crossover points (points A, B, and C in Figure 2–3), these can be calculated by using simple formulas. In our example the formulas for the three cost lines (with x equal to the quantity) are:

Machine	*Cost formula*
Lathes............................	$ 2.50 + $.45x
Turret lathes......................	5.00 + .20x
Automatic screw machines...........	15.00 + .04x

The crossover points A, B, and C can be found by setting pairs of equations equal to each other and solving for *x:*

1. Lathes versus turret lathes:

$$\$2.50 + \$.45x = \$5 + \$.20x$$
$$\$.25x = \$2.50$$
$$X, \text{point } A \text{ on Fig. 2–3, } = 10 \text{ units}$$

2. Lathes versus automatic screw machines:

$$\$2.50 + \$.45x = \$15 + \$.04x$$
$$\$.41x = \$12.50$$
$$X, \text{point } B \text{ on Fig. 2–3, } = 30 \text{ units}$$

3. Turret lathes versus automatic screw machines:

$$\$5 + \$.20x = \$15 + \$.04x$$
$$\$.16x = \$10$$
$$X, \text{point } C \text{ on Fig. 2–3, } = 63 \text{ units}$$

Equation 1 shows that for orders of 10 units (or fewer) lathes should be used. Above 10 units, turret lathes should be used. But if all the turret lathes are in use and not available, it is necessary to go to equation 2. This shows that, in this case, lathes should continue to be used for orders up to 30 units. For orders calling for more than 30 units should be shifted to automatic screw machines. But if turret lathes are available, they should be used for all orders for more than 10 and up to 63 units. Equation 3 shows that all orders for more than 63 units should be put on automatics.

Crossover charts can also be used in new equipment purchase choices. The lines on the chart would compare the costs of doing the work in the present way against what they would be if a machine were bought.

Make-buy decisions. When a plant is not busy, a make-buy decision need consider only variable "make" costs as contrasted to the purchase cost per unit.[2] Fixed costs other than job setup costs do not have to be considered because "making" would use capacity which is already owned but not in use. In such a case the decision would frequently be to make because a customer company's variable costs ought almost always be less than a vendor's price, which includes his variable costs and a share of his fixed costs as well. However, such decisions to make should be reviewed when business picks up, lest it prove that the item is causing its own share of overheads which might push its costs up to more than the buying price.

Figure 2–4 shows how these relationships might work out. (The costs of the paper work involved in making out purchase orders and shop

FIGURE 2–4

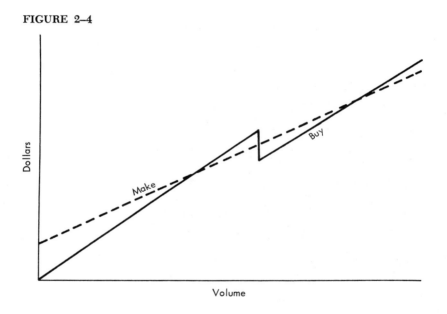

orders for making products are assumed to be equal and so are omitted in this example.) Setting up factory machines is, however, an extra which must be paid for if the decision is to make. Figure 2–4 shows how this would work out if buying costs $1.55 a unit for up to 10,000 units and $1.30 a unit for orders of more than 10,000 units. Making is assumed to cost $3,500 for setting up the machines and the variable cost is $1 per unit.

---

[2] Make-buy decisions and leasing decisions are discussed more fully in Chapter 23 on Purchasing.

The numerical scales have been omitted from Figure 2–4—and in any case the diagram is too small to read off exact values. Actually, it pays to buy quantities up to 7,778 and then to make the items, up to 9,000 units. From 9,000 to 10,000 it costs less to make than to buy, but, because of the operation of the quantity discount, it would pay to buy 10,000 at the reduced discount price, even if the excess over 9,000 were to be thrown away. At the 10,000 mark it still pays to buy, and on up to 15,000. If more than 15,000 are wanted, it will pay to make them.

Pricing decisions. Price changes are sometimes part of competitive strategy. If demand is strong, it may be possible to increase prices and yet not lose very much business. Break-even charts tell managers how big a sales decline they can stand yet still be as well off if they increase prices. This is shown in Figure 2–5, as is the extra volume which a price cut would need to generate. A similar chart could be drawn to show the effects of a price cut if that were being considered.

FIGURE 2–5

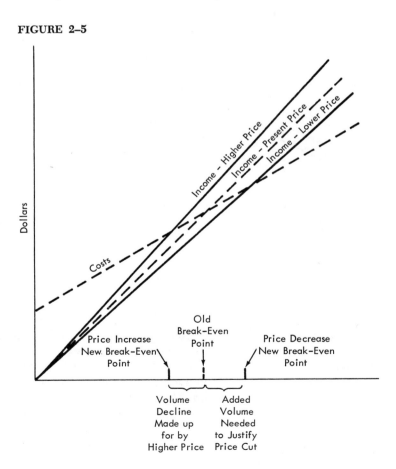

Advertising decisions. Similar calculations can be made and similar charts could be drawn up to show the effects of other actions. If more is spent for advertising, for example, costs would go up and the break-even point would move to the right. But, because of the advertising, volume would also go up. Break-even calculations can be made to show how far up the volume would need to go in order to justify the expenditure. Figure 2–6 shows how this would operate.

FIGURE 2–6

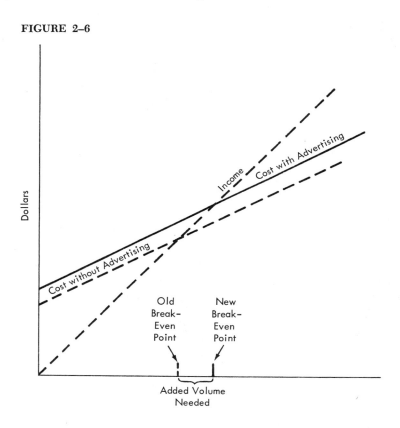

Use of overtime. Sometimes business is very good, and extra volume is there to be had, but the plant is already busy and so the added volume would have to be produced at overtime labor rates (time and a half pay for all overtime hours worked by the men). In this case the variable cost line changes its slope at the point where the overtime commences, and it goes up more steeply from there on. The profits from high volume are less than they would appear to be on ordinary break-even charts. Figure 2–7 shows how this works out.

Variable fixed costs. Although most conceptual break-even diagrams

FIGURE 2–7

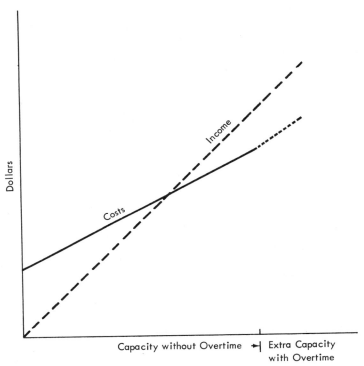

regard fixed costs as fixed for all volume levels, this is an oversimplifica-
tion that has been adopted to allow for emphasis of the main points. Part
of the fixed costs are the costs of supervisors, which obviously have to be
changed if volumes change a great deal. Yet they will not change in a
steady, consistent way. If a second shift is added, a whole set of additional supervisors must be provided. This will make a step up in the
fixed cost line. Figure 2–8 shows how such steps would operate.

Break-even analyses and decision making under uncertainty

In the example on page 23 we said that it would pay to mechanize if
the sales volume would go above a specified sales mark. But whether sales
will actually go above this mark is uncertain, and this brings probability
into the matter. Every company faces probability problems all the time.

American automobile companies, for example, sell some 9 million or
more domestically made passenger cars a year, but how likely is next
year to be a 7-million-car year? Surely it is highly improbable. Perhaps a
manager would feel safe in saying about 1 chance in 50, or a probability
of .02. It is also possible for next year to be a 10-million-car year, but how

FIGURE 2–8

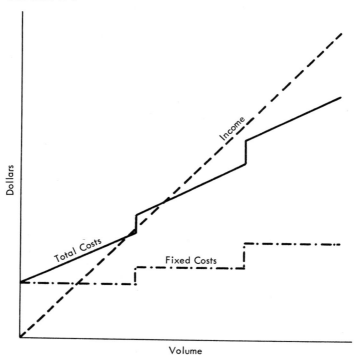

likely is this possibility? Perhaps the same manager would say 1 chance in 5, or a probability of .20. Makers of milk bottles, suits of clothes, and all kinds of products have similar problems. They have to think of different levels of future business, some of which are more probable than others.

Probability analysis can be helpful here. Suppose, for example, that the figures plotted in Figures 2–1 and 2–2 are the same as those shown in Figure 2–9. By adding a probability column, a manager can come up with an estimate of how well off his company is likely to be if it mechanizes.

Columns 2 and 3 are "if" figures. *If* sales are 30, 40, 50, or whatever, *then* the resulting profits will be those shown in columns 2 and 3. Column 4 shows probabilities. These figures show that low volumes are highly unlikely and that there is a high probability that volume will be in the 70 to 90 range.

Columns 5 and 6 are obtained by multiplying each possible profit result by its probability. These, when summed up, show which action is likely to be the best. In our example, mechanizing will—on the average—pay off better than not mechaninzing. If this company's managers faced such a decision 100 times and always chose not to mechanize, the average

FIGURE 2–9

Volume (thousands of units)	Profit (millions of dollars)		Probability of this volume	Probability times profit (millions of dollars)	
	Old method	New method		Old method	New method
1	2	3	4	5	6
0...............	$−5.0	$−60.0	.00	$ 0.0	$ 0.0
10...............	−2.5	−50.0	.00	0.0	0.0
20...............	0	−40.0	.00	0.0	0.0
30...............	2.5	−30.0	.01	0.0	−0.3
40...............	5.0	−20.0	.03	0.2	−0.6
50...............	7.5	−10.0	.06	0.5	−0.6
60...............	10.0	0	.10	1.0	0.0
70...............	12.5	10.0	.20	2.5	2.0
80...............	15.0	20.0	.25	3.8	5.0
90...............	17.5	30.0	.25	4.4	7.5
100...............	20.0	40.0	.10	2.0	4.0
110...............	22.5	50.0	.00	0.0	0.0
Total............			1.00	$14.4	$ 17.0

profit would be $14.4 million, as against $17 million from mechanizing.

The probability numbers, however, are open to question because they are just the managers' thinking put into numbers. In our example, the managers believed that low volumes would be unlikely and that the actual volume would most likely be in the 70 to 90 volume range. So, since probability analysis is based on judgment, it does not insure certainty of expected results. But it does provide a method for incorporating managers' expectations about the future into their calculations.

Weaknesses of break-even charts

If a company wants to construct a break-even chart, it starts with two points: today's costs and today's income. From here on, someone, probably the controller, studies the various cost accounts and separates them into fixed and variable costs. It is then assumed that variable costs go up and down with sales and that fixed costs stay fixed regardless of production and sales levels.

The controller's job is not all this easy, however. The fluidity of variable costs and their responses to changes in output levels are not always on a one-to-one basis. Some variable costs are somewhat variable but not wholly so. Similarly, some fixed costs are fixed only over limited volume ranges. If volume goes up very much, some of the fixed costs, such as those for machines, may also have to be increased. The controller no doubt will try to estimate as best he can what all of these costs would be for volumes above and below the present level.

One thing he should not do, however, is to assume that if volume were to slide off to what it was a few years ago, costs will go down to their former levels. Not only is the company bigger, and therefore has larger fixed costs, but quite a few variable costs are quite sticky on the going down side. They prove to be not wholly variable and to be hard to reduce. Furthermore, inflation is not reversible, so today's costs of doing business at yesterday's levels will be higher than formerly.

Stepped up lines.   Some people object to break-even chart makers' drawing income and cost lines as straight lines because, in fact, probably neither the income nor the cost line is truly a straight line. Particularly is this true of the cost line. If production goes up beyond a certain point, a company may have to go to overtime, and production above that point will cost considerably more per unit. Or perhaps it will have to put on a second shift and add more foremen and so boost costs a good bit all at once. Cost changes are more pronounced at some points than at others, so the cost line on a break-even chart ought to be an upward sloping line, but it should go up more steeply in some areas than in others. Possibly the line should even have an occasional upward step. This objection is more a quibble with simplified book examples than with the break-even charts as they might be used in practice. If, in practice, a stepped up line would better represent the true situation, the company ought to draw in a stepped up line (as we did in Figure 2–8) and not a straight line.

Lines or zones.   The lines on break-even charts really ought to be bands or zones extending across the chart and not just thin lines. This is because such charts are "if" charts. They purport to show what the results would be for a whole continuum of possible circumstances. *If* production were 20 percent higher, such and such results would come about. Or *if* production were 30 percent lower, such and such results would come about. "If" charts are loaded with forecasts and should be used with discretion. If sales really do go up or down, managers will have to do things to bring about the cost changes the charts indicate for the new volume; the projected costs do not come about automatically. A department store has fewer sales clerks in January than it had for the Christmas rush in December because it has laid off all the extras. They didn't all just resign. Management has to do something to try to produce the result shown on the chart. Maybe its efforts in trying to produce the expected costs will be successful, but maybe not.

The cost part of break-even charts is also only half the story. Income, the other half, is also in a state of constant flux. Break-even charts show how sales volume goes up and down if prices and the product mix don't change, but prices and the product mix *do* change. If sales shift from low-profit-margin items to high-profit items, a company would have more profits even though the total sales volume stands still. Also, general price changes would make the income line angle up or down.

Valuable though break-even charts are, they must be used with discretion. The lines are really wide bands and not thin lines. Perhaps the break-even point should even be thought of as a blob on a chart and not as a point.

Minimizing the costs of opposing factors

The preceding discussion of break-even and other crossover charts was actually about examples of a whole family of problems where the object is to select the optimum balance point between the costs of two or more factors which work in opposite directions or in the same direction but at differing rates.

The second of the two Monte Carlo simulation examples, which follow in this chapter, illustrates this selection. When men service machines, they represent a cost. So do machines that are waiting for men. Many service men mean high costs from the wasteful use of men. Very few service men mean high costs from excessive machine waiting time. At some point the cost of man power waits and machine waits are equal and the sum of these two costs is less than for any other combination.

This conceptual idea, of minimizing conflicting costs by finding the optimal balance point, will appear at several places in future chapters. It comes up in maintenance, where we discuss the worth of having standby equipment to hold down production delays that result from equipment failures.

The major use of this conceptual idea, however, is in inventory control, where it is the essence of the "economic order quantity" idea. In this chapter we want only to note that this fundamental concept of balancing conflicting costs at their minimum total point has many applications.

Queuing or waiting lines

In one sense, the whole factory is a service facility upon which calls for service are made. In this light, a plant's capacity can be viewed as the capabilities of a facility upon which irregular calls for service are made. It can be thought of as a queuing problem. It is desirable to balance out the system's capabilities against the irregular demands so as to minimize the costs caused by the factory's inability to serve (the costs would largely be lost sales) and the costs from underuse of the facilities (these costs would be those associated with partially idle plants).

Queuing theory, however, cannot be applied to *total* demand—*total* resource problems. Queuing theory applies only to specific situations. Within production organizations there are frequently places where there is need to balance resources against demands and where queuing theory can be advantageously applied. These queuing situations are essentially of the same kind that we are all familiar with when we get in line to pay at the supermarket check-out counter.

In factories queuing occurs at stock rooms, tool rooms, receiving docks, shipping rooms, and other places where there is sometimes imbalance between a service resource and the calls for service. Similar imbalances occur in machine repair work. If too many machines need repairs, some will have to wait until the repair man can get to them. They form a queue. Or if there are not enough repair jobs to keep the men busy, the men have to wait, and thus the men form a queue.

Queuing problems can sometimes be worked out mathematically. If they are too complex for this, Monte Carlo simulation can be used.

We will take up queuing formulas first and use two examples to illustrate how these formulas can help in a factory. The first will be a single-channel example, meaning that there is only one service facility to fill the service need.

Suppose that 1 maintenance man serves 25 machines in a department. He sets up all of the jobs done on these machines and also repairs them and keeps them operating. Their calls for service time average 12 per day and the service time averages 30 minutes each time. A simple average shows that this amounts to 6 hours of work in the man's 8-hour day. He would be idle one quarter of his time. If the service calls were spread out evenly—1 every 40 minutes—and if they always took him 30 minutes, machines would never have to wait for the man. He would have 10 idle minutes between jobs.

Both service calls and service time are, however, variable. There may be more or fewer than 3 *calls* every 2 hours. And the service *time* may be more or less than 30 minutes. Queuing theory formulas require only that the analyst know the *average* number of calls per hour and the *average* time each takes. The formulas allows for variations above and below the average. (The formulas assume Poisson arrivals and negative exponential service times.)[3]

We will not take text space for presenting queuing formulas since they are somewhat complex. (These formulas and calculations of answers for our examples are given in Appendix A.)

In our example, it is likely that a manager would want to know several

---

[3] Poisson arrivals and negative exponential service times are explained in statistics books. Briefly, Poisson arrivals assumes that the time between arrivals does not follow a normal distribution curve. This is because long intervals between arrivals can be much longer than the average interval but shorter intervals cannot be much shorter. If arrivals average every 5 minutes, the shortest possible time is zero, or 5 minutes less than the average. But longer intervals could go up to 15 or 20 minutes more than the average. Poisson curves thus have longer tails on the right than on the left.

Negative exponential service times assume that the greatest number of service times will be very short and that there is a rapid drop in the frequencies of longer service times.

things so that he can decide how much capacity to provide in the service facility—in our case, how many repair men to have. He would probably want to know, if one service man is provided, how many machines will, on the average, be waiting for service. This proves to be 2.25 machines. And how many machines will be in the system on average, either waiting or being served? This will be 3 machines. It proves, too, that the average waiting time per waiting machine is 1.5 hours, while the average time machines spend waiting and being served is 2 hours. (So far as the service man is concerned, the inequalities of arrivals and service time are irrelevant. He averages 30 minutes of work every 40 minutes of time and is therefore idle one quarter of his time.)

With these figures, a manager can apply cost data and find out how costly it is to operate with one service man.

We now change to a multichannel problem. We will say that we have 2 service men who service 50 machines which generate 24 service calls a day. The service time still averages 30 minutes. The mathematics of multichannel problems, even with only 2 channels, is considerably more complicated than for single-channel problems, so again the calculations have been put in Appendix A.

The answers to this 2-channel queuing problem are:

Average number of idle machines waiting for sevice: .97.

Average number of idle machines either waiting or being serviced: 2.47.

Average idle time of machines waiting for service: .32 hours.

Average idle time of machines waiting and being serviced: .82 hours.

Average idle time of the service men: 25 percent.

The purpose of getting all these figures is to provide a basis for answering the really important questions: Is 2 the right number of service men? Would it be better to have 3 service men?

To answer these questions we start by calculating the money cost for the 2-man arrangement. If idle machines cost $10 per idle machine-hour in the value of lost work, the average cost of .97 machines idle all of the time is $9.70 per hour.

Besides the machines' idle time, the service men are idle one fourth of their time. If each man costs $5 an hour ($10 for two men), we seem to have wasted $2.50 in labor cost, but this is not so in practice. An idle setup man or repairman does not do nothing, he applies himself to standby work worth perhaps $3 an hour. So his "idle" time really costs $2 an hour, not $5. The loss from these 2 men not being kept busy on repair or setup work is, therefore, a fourth of $4, or $1.

Add this to the $9.70 cost for idle machines and we find that the waste costs incurred with 2 service men is $10.70 per hour.

Now we go through the whole calculation again with 3 men and get the costs (which we have worked out in Appendix A). It turned out that the idle-man cost came to $3 per hour. Idle machine cost came to $.80, so the total was $3.80. In this example it will pay to add the third service man.

Use of charts in queuing problems.   It is actually not necessary to calculate queuing problems. TRW Company found that queuing-type problems came up from time to time but that its people did not calculate answers because the formulas looked too forbidding. TRW solved this problem by developing charts, based on the formulas, from which they could read off answers to most questions.

Figure 2–10 is a chart used by TRW to give answers to various waiting-line questions merely by reading them from the chart.[4] The horizontal

FIGURE 2–10

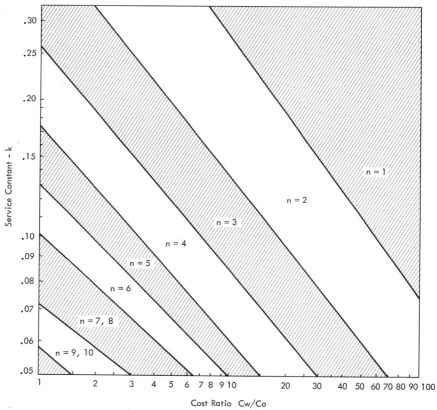

Cw—Cost of an activity waiting per unit time
Co—Cost of a service facility per unit time
$$k = \frac{\text{Servicing time}}{\text{Running time}}$$

---

[4] This chart is one of several presented in *Waiting Line Pamphlet* (Cleveland, Ohio: TRW Inc.), pp. 11–20.

scale is a scale of ratios. To find the ratio to use for any specific problem, the cost per hour of an idle machine is divided by the cost per hour of an idle service man. Suppose we say that this is $15 divided by $4, or a ratio of 3.75.

The vertical scale is another scale of ratios. This time it is the average repair or service time divided by the time the machine runs. If service time averages half an hour per day per machine and if the machines' average operating time is 7 hours a day (including the service time), the ratio is .5 divided by 7, or .071. (During the other hour of the day the machines are not operating because the next job is not ready, or the operator is away from his machine, or for other reasons not related to this calculation.) If the analyst reads across the bottom scale in Figure 2–10 to 3.75 and then goes up to .071, he will find that he is in the 6 area. This means that the best answer is to have each man service 6 machines. If the company has 24 machines, it needs 4 service men.

This chart does not, however, provide answers to all waiting-line questions. To get answers to other questions, such as how many jobs will normally have to wait if there is 1 service man, 2 service men, etc., the analyst will have to go back to using queuing formulas. Or else he would have to make other charts similar to Figure 2–10.

TRW has such a second chart to use for tool crib waiting-line problems similar to our example problem. Suppose that factory operators come to tool cribs in random fashion and it takes tool crib men variable amounts of time to take care of them. Figure 2–11 tells how many tool crib attendants will be needed. Again, the horizontal scale is a ratio scale. This time it is the cost per hour of the machinists who may have to wait divided by the hourly cost of tool room attendants who, at other times, may have to wait.

Suppose that machine operators' idleness (while waiting) costs $6 an hour and that tool room attendants cost $3 an hour. $6 divided by $3 equals 2, which is the ratio to use on the horizontal scale. Suppose that 12 men an hour arrive and ask for tools and that, on the average, it takes a tool crib attendant 5 minutes (or .08 hours) to get and issue the tools. Multiplying 12 by .08 we get .96, the number to use on the vertical scale.

The number to use when reading the vertical scale is the answer obtained by multiplying the average arrival rate by the average service time. To use the chart, the analyst reads over on the bottom scale to 2 and then goes up to .96. He is in the 2 zone. So 2 crib attendants is the proper number to have.

It may be possible, however, to give the tool crib attendants some other work to do (grinding tools, cleaning or repairing returned tools, putting a protective covering of oil on them, etc.) when they are not busy serving factory operators. Such odd jobs might salvage a good bit of their idle time, so that the loss would really be only $1.50 an hour when they are idle. In this case the first ratio is 4, so it is necessary to go across to 4 and read up to .96. Now we are just barely in the 3 zone, so probably there should be 3 tool crib attendants. Their "extra" idleness is not so important because some value is realized from this "idle" time.

Sometimes waiting-line-type problems become very complex and are impractical to solve mathematically. This would happen, for example, if a company has, say, 3 baking-enamel ovens whose heating elements some-

FIGURE 2–11

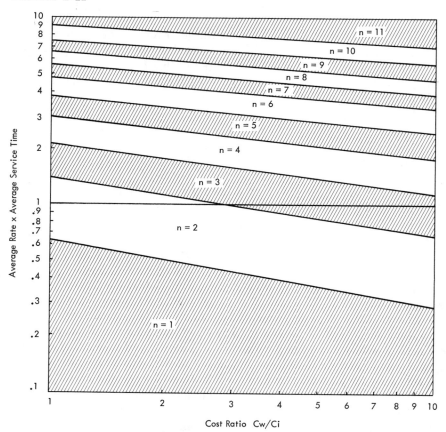

Cw—Cost of an activity waiting per unit time
Ci—Cost of an idle service facility per unit time

times burn out and cause extensive downtime. The question might be: Should the company put in all-new heating elements every time one burns out? Or should it replace only the burned-out element? Or should it replace the others at the same time if they have been in use for 6 months? Or should some other policy be followed? Such a problem is too complex for reasonable mathematical solution. It can, however, be handled quite satisfactorily by Monte Carlo simulation, which is explained in the next few pages.

Monte Carlo simulation

Monte Carlo simulation does not use formulas. Instead, it is a happenstance trial method for seeing what would happen if certain events, normal or abnormal—as one chooses—were to occur.

Monte Carlo simulation is a conscious attempt to imitate a business situation so managers can test and evaluate various policies. It is a technique whereby a system and its associated possible sequences of events are produced on a make-believe basis. This is usually done by a computer which is programmed to act like the system being studied. Simulation of this sort allows managers to investigate changes in systems and results without incurring the costs of manipulating real systems. It also helps decision makers develop an understanding of how systems react to certain stimuli.

U.S. Steel uses Monte Carlo to simulate the operation of coal mines, loading and unloading docks, and the movements of barges and boats on various routes under conditions of ice, fog, and high water. In one such simulation, even though it took 40 computer runs to investigate all of the possibilities, the managers had every possible result run off for study in less than 1 hour's time.[5]

Two examples will illustrate how Monte Carlo simulation works:

Example 1. The ABC Company is considering giving up leasing 12 delivery trucks. If it does, it will have to buy 12 trucks right away and then buy replacement trucks in the future, one by one, as the old ones wear out. The question ABC's managers want to answer is how many trucks they may have to buy during the next 5 years (including the initial 12 trucks) in order to keep 12 trucks in operation all the time. At the moment, ABC's managers are not concerned with the fact that at the end of 5 years they will have 12 trucks on hand, some of which will be old and some of which will be relatively new. The only question is how many will have to be bought. (The answer is *not* 29, which would be the answer obtained from finding the average truck life, which is 21 months, and dividing it into the 600 months of truck life to be used up in 5 years. Such a calculation would overlook the leftover lives of the 12 trucks still on hand at the end of 5 years.)

Without using a computer, it is possible to carry this simulation forward by using a random number table such as the one on page 686. First, though, it is necessary to know how long trucks usually last. Figure 2–12 shows how long past experience has shown that they will last:

---

[5] Monte Carlo simulations of complex situations where many factors interact are themselves quite complex. Normally, such simulations are run off on computers.

FIGURE 2–12

Time (months)	Percentage of trucks which will wear out
12	5
15	10
18	20
21	25
24	30
27	5
30	5

Next, random numbers are assigned to expected truck lives (the numbers in the random number table on page 686 go from 1 to 1,000). Since 5 percent of the trucks will wear out in 12 months, the numbers 1 to 50 are assigned as representing 12-month lives. The next 10 percent of the trucks will last 15 months, so random numbers 51 to 150 are assigned to 15-month lives. The next 20 percent of the numbers, 151 to 350, are for 18-month lives, etc.

The simulation process can now proceed. The best way to use a random number table is to start at some point in the table and read numbers consecutively from the starting number in some consistent sequence. To illustrate, we might start on the table on page 686 at the upper left and read across horizontally. The first five numbers are: *217, 590, 735, 965,* and *276,* which would translate into truck lives of 18, 21, 24, 30, and 18

FIGURE 2–13

Truck	Month when unit wears out			
	1	2	3	4
1	18	36	60	
2	21	42	66	
3	24	45	66	
4	30	51	72	
5	18	36	57	78
6	12	27	51	72
7	24	48	69	
8	18	39	63	
9	18	39	57	75
10	21	45	72	
11	24	45	63	
12	21	42	63	

months. This process would then be continued until the complete simulated history of 5 years of truck use was developed. Figure 2–13 shows the result for this problem using Monte Carlo with random numbers.

This simulation indicates that a total of 39 trucks—the original 12 plus 27 replacements—will have to be bought.

How reliable are these figures? It is never possible to say exactly how reliable any simulation answer is since no one can know exactly what sequence of events (in our case the lives of specific trucks) will occur. But if the distribution of events being simulated is accurate, extended simulations give quick and good pictures of what will happen in real life. In our example, if the life expectancy table we used is accurate, then most of the time, in an actual case, 26 to 28 replacement trucks would have to be bought.

Example 2. At the ABC Company, setup men are required to set up jobs and its managers want to know how many setup men to use. The length of job runs on machines vary, as do setup times, and there are 10 machines. The times vary as follows:

Length of job		Setup time	
Hours	*Instances*	*Hours*	*Instances*
4	20%	2	50%
8	30	4	20
16	20	8	15
24	20	12	10
40	10	20	5

This problem also is solved by using simulation and random numbers and we will start this problem's solution by assuming that all jobs have just been set up. We then refer to the random number table for numbers to tell us how long the jobs on the machine will take (numbers 1 to 200 mean a 4-hour job, numbers 201 to 500 an 8-hour job, etc.). Ten random numbers provide the job times for the 10 machines. These simulated times are listed in Figure 2–14 in the first column, the *J* column of numbers—the 4, 8, etc.

After the first round of assigning jobs to machines is completed, the process is repeated and random numbers are used to get setup times for the next jobs on each machine (numbers 1 to 500 mean a 2-hour setup time, 501 to 700 a 4-hour setup time, etc.). Then another round of random numbers is used for each machine's second job, then the second setups, then the third jobs, etc.

These operating and setup times are all shown in Figure 2–14, where the lower half is a summation, left to right, of the use of each machine's time. The simulation was carried forward for 80 hours, or 2 weeks' work time. Then the first week was discarded because it might be distorted by the unnatural effect from having all machines start their jobs at the same time—at the start of the problem.

The use of the machines during the second week, hours 41 to 80, were plotted in Figure 2–15 in 2-hour blocks of time. Thus 20 2-hour blocks of machine use time were plotted.

FIGURE 2–14

Machine	J*	S*	J	S	J	S	J	S	J	S	J
				Actual times							
1................	4	2	8	4	24	8	24	8			
2................	8	2	16	4	40	2	16				
3................	16	12	4	2	4	12	40				
4................	16	4	4	12	24	2	8	2	4	2	8
5................	16	2	40	2	4	8	4	12			
6................	24	8	24	4	40						
7................	4	2	8	4	24	2	4	4	24	2	4
8................	4	2	24	8	24	2	24				
9................	40	12	40								
10...............	24	12	8	2	8	2	8	4	24		
				Cumulated times							
1................	4	6	14	18	42	50	74	84			
2................	8	10	26	30	70	72	88				
3................	16	28	32	34	38	50	90				
4................	16	20	24	36	60	62	70	72	76	78	86
5................	16	18	58	60	64	72	76	88			
6................	24	32	56	60	100						
7................	4	6	14	18	42	44	48	52	76	78	82
8................	4	6	30	38	62	64	88				
9................	40	52	92								
10...............	24	36	44	46	54	56	64	68	92		

* J and S mean "job" and "setup." The numbers shown as actual times are determined by using random numbers. The cumulated times show the use of each machine for 80 hours.

It is possible now, by looking at Figure 2–15, to count and see how many setup men would be required at different times. This count shows the following requirements:

Number of men	Number of instances
0......................	2
1......................	6
2......................	6
3......................	2
4......................	4

These requirements average out to 2 men all the time. But with 2 men there will be some idle machine time because more than 2 men are sometimes needed. The chart shows, for example, that from hours 43 to 46, 4 men are needed. But, having only 2 men, 2 machines will have to wait. And since the 2 men are also busy during hours 47 to 48, at least a 4-hour delay for some machine is in prospect. In fact, having only 2 men, they get behind almost at the start of our simulated week and don't catch up until late in the week. Then they have a little slack time, but they get behind again by the time our simulation week finishes. In total, quite a few lost machine hours are in prospect.

FIGURE 2–15

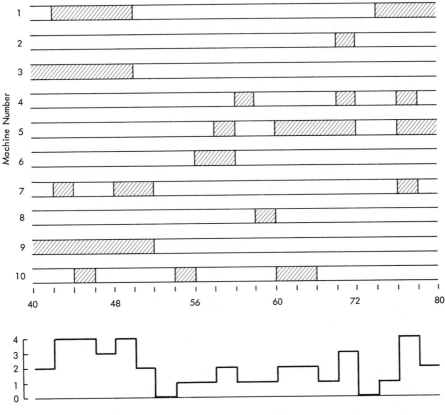

Number of Setup Men

Using Monte Carlo simulation, decision makers can study the effects of various courses of action (such as what will happen if there are 3 repair men, or even 4), and they can even try out various alternative actions.

We will not pursue this Monte Carlo example any further inasmuch as the two examples illustrate the method. We should note, however, that the method implies the assumption that it is based on realistic data. If these data have come from past experience, they should be applicable to the future if the results are to be valid.

Review questions

1. Explain how the contribution ratio and the break-even point are related.
2. List the ways that managerial decisions might change the break-even point and show how it would be changed.

3. How can a manager incorporate uncertainty into his calculations concerning break-even points and thus make more intelligent decisions?

4. If a service man's calls for service average 5 calls per hour and 10 minutes each, would there ever be times when a facility that needs service would have to wait? Why is this?

6. Explain the way to use random number tables to help develop simulated results in Monte Carlo simulation problems.

7. Is it necessary to have actual experience figures upon which to base Monte Carlo simulations? Explain.

Discussion questions

1. How can the break-even volume be calculated for specific products?

2. The president looks at the break-even chart which his controller has just constructed and asks: "How can we lower the break-even point?" How should the controller answer him?

3. Is a break-even chart reliable enough as a managerial tool for a manager to rely on it in making a major business decision? Discuss.

4. Would the cost line on a break-even chart provide a reliable projection of costs if volume decreased by, say, one third? Justify your answer.

5. Suppose that some variable costs prove not to be wholly variable, particularly on the going down side, and some fixed costs prove not to stay wholly fixed, particularly when volume goes up. What would this do to break-even analyses? How often are either of these possibilities actual factors in real situations?

6. How can "probability" have any significance in a situation where there is one and only one decision to make? There just aren't going to be 100 cases over which to average out results.

7. Would you rather have $1,000 or a 50–50 chance to have $2,000? Is your answer the same if we say $1 million versus a 50–50 chance of having $2 million? What, if anything, does your answer have to do with managerial decision making relating to break-even points and capital investments?

8. "Although Monte Carlo methods are useful to help managers see what average conditions will be like, they are of little help to a manager who is interested in extremes." Discuss this statement.

Problems

1. At a volume of $125,000, a company's variable costs are $60,000, fixed costs are $50,000, and profits are $15,000. What is its break-even point? How much sales volume does it take to produce profits equal to a cost reduction of $500?

2. A company has capacity to produce 600,000 units of a product per year. At present it is operating at 65 percent of capacity and has an annual income of $425,000. Fixed costs are $200,000. Variable costs are $.60 per unit. What

is the company's profit or loss? What is its break-even point? What will it earn at 80 percent of capacity?

3. Variable costs are 40 percent of the sales price of $10 per unit. With fixed costs of $200,000, what is the break-even point? Assuming that sales have been exactly at the break-even volume, should the company cut the price to $8 if this would boost sales volume to 50,000 units?

4. Fixed costs are $20,000 and variable costs are $50 per unit. In order to improve profits, it has been proposed that the company spend $30,000 plus $50 per unit to improve the product, and change the price as well. The marketing staff has made the following estimate of the effects of these actions:

Price per unit	Annual sales without improvement	Annual sales with improvement
$400.	5	40
350.	15	125
300.	40	200
250.	100	375
200.	250	600
150.	500	1,000
100.	900	2,000

What action will yield the greatest profit?

5. Plant A, with a capacity of 50,000 units per year, has fixed costs of $240,000 and variable costs of $3 per unit. Plant B makes the same products. It has a capacity of 75,000 units per year, fixed costs of $260,000, and variable costs of $4 per unit. The present production rates are Plant A, 22,000 units, and Plant B, 45,000 units a year.

a) What are the unit costs of production in each plant at present production levels?

b) What would they be at capacity?

c) For most economical production costs, how should the present 67,000 units be divided between the two factories?

d) Assuming that sales will, in the future, come to 75,000 units a year, how should this production be divided between the two plants?

6. Using one-shift operation, the company is selling its maximum output except for overtime) of 4,000 units at $175 each. Fixed costs are $300,000 and variable costs are $360,000 for capacity operation.

It would be possible, however, to boost sales to 4,500 units by using overtime. This would increase variable costs to $400,000. (Some of the variable costs do not go up and down in direct proportion to output.) It is also possible to raise prices to $180 and still sell 4,100 units.

For greatest profit, what should be done?

7. For the past period, the ABC Company has operated at capacity with the following distribution between products:

Product	Volume (units)	Contri- bution per unit	Labor hours	Contribution
A..............	10,000	$10	10,000	$ 30,000
B..............	12,000	12	20,000	35,000
C..............	6,000	20	20,000	30,000
D..............	4,000	10	15,000	20,000
E..............	3,500	25	17,500	30,000
			82,500	$145,000

Business is expected to be 10 percent better in the next period, but it will not be possible to expand labor beyond 85,000 hours. What products should ABC push? What should the product distribution be to use the 85,000 hours to best advantage?

8. A plant with a capacity of 200,000 units per year has fixed costs of $450,000 and variable costs of $3 per unit. It can probably sell 100,000 units in its home market at $13 each. It can probably sell the other 100,000 units it could make in foreign markets at $7 per unit. What are the profits prospects from the home market alone? What might they be if the company produced at capacity and sold the second 100,000 abroad?

9. At the present time a part for product A is being made on general-purpose machines at a cost of $20 per unit. The problem concerns only the next 3 years, after which product A will be replaced by a new model.

It is possible to put in new tooling attachments at a cost of $30,000, which will reduce the cost of making the part to $19. (The tooling is durable and should easily last 3 years, although—because it would be special—it would have little or no salvage value at any time.) Taxes, interest, and insurance come to 18 percent.

It is also possible to put in new machines, costing $300,000, which will reduce the cost to $12. (However, these machines, at the end of the 3 years will be worth 50 percent of their cost.)

a) For 10,000 pieces per year, which method should be chosen? For 12,000?

b) What is the crossover volume point (the volume where the two methods would cost the same)?

10. The X Company, a large chain store company, makes the following proposal to a vendor. X proposes to pay $4 for each product. Labor and machine costs come to $7.50 per hour for the vendor. Factory overhead is 125 percent of labor and machinery costs. General and administration costs are equal to 20 percent of factory costs. Materials cost will be $.50 per unit. The cost of tooling may be neglected since X Company will pay separately for it.

For small quantities, the total product time for men and machines is 10 minutes per unit for up to 1,000 units. This production time will be reduced by 10 percent by the time 5,000 are produced, 12 percent at 10,000, and 15 percent at 50,000.

a) What should the supplier's price be if his profits are to be 10 percent of the selling price—for 1,000, 5,000, and 50,000 units?

b) At what point will the $4 price allow the vendor to earn $.40 on each unit?

11. With fixed costs of $30,000 and variable costs of $4 per unit, a company has been selling 6,000 units at $10 each. What profit has it been earning? Would it be wise for it to spend $10,000 for advertising if advertising would raise the volume to 7,500 units? Assuming that the advertising has no carry-over benefits into future periods, how much better or worse off will the company be if it spends the $10,000?

12. Continuing problem 11, suppose that the company believes that a $5,000 advertising expenditure would raise the volume to 7,500 units, but its managers don't feel very sure about this. They feel that a $5,000 expenditure for advertising will be likely to increase volume as follows:

Volume	Probability
6,300	.05
6,600	.10
6,900	.15
7,200	.18
7,500	.25
7,800	.17
8,100	.10

Should the company advertise? What is the probable payoff (or loss)?

13. In the text on page 25, suppose that the cost lines were changed to lathes, $2 + $.75x, turret lathes, $6 + $.15x, and automatics, $12 + $.07x. For what volumes should each method be used? What are the crossover points?

14. Suppose that the company that owns the 3 kinds of machines referred to on page 25 got an order for 100 products. As we saw on page 25, this work should be done on automatic screw machines, but the automatics are busy, so the work has to be done on turret lathes or regular lathes. How much extra would it cost to do this work on either of the two less efficient kinds of machines?

15. Experience with fork lift trucks shows the following record of repairs (they cost $10,000 new):

Year after purchase	Operating expenses during year (including interest)	Trade-in value at end of year
1.	$2,000	$6,000
2.	2,200	3,600
3.	2,500	2,000
4.	3,000	1,300
5.	3,800	900
6.	5,000	600
7.	7,000	400

When should the company trade in its old trucks? In answering this question, should the choice be in the single year of lowest cost or the low point of the average accumulated costs to date? Why?

16. An automatic screw machine department has 23 machines. The service needs of these machines are random and Poisson in pattern. Service times follow a negative exponential pattern. On the average, each machine needs

some kind of adjustment or service every 3 hours, and service times average 25 minutes.

a) How many machines would be running if there were 4 service men? Five service men? (Solve by using queuing formulas.)

b) At $8 an hour, what will be the cost of machine downtime with 4 service men? With 5 service men?

17. Using the information given in problem 16, and using the TRW diagram (Figure 2–10), determine the most economical number of service men to have. Service men cost $5 an hour. Assume that, except for service time, the machines are in operation.

18. A battery of 16 machines is serviced by 4 men who are combined setup and repair men. These men are able to give good service and keep the machines running almost all of the time, but the men themselves are not always busy. Machine time is worth $10 an hour and the men cost $6 an hour. But if they are not busy there is standby work for them, so that half of their wage loss is salvaged. A work-sampling study showed that the machines typically were in operation 80 percent of the time, were serviced 10 percent of the time, and were idle from lack of orders 10 percent of the time.

How many service men should be on this assignment in order to hold costs to a minimum?

19. How many service men should there be at a tool crib which serves machinists who arrive at a rate of 20 an hour and whose service times average 10 minutes? Both arrival times and service times are irregular.

The machinists cost $12 an hour (including the cost of their idle machine while they are at the tool crib) whereas tool crib attendants cost $5 an hour. When tool crib men are not serving the men at the issue window, they spend their time cleaning tooling that was previously returned. This work is regarded as saving two thirds of the cost of what would otherwise be idle time.

Would the answer to this problem be any different if the men who come to the window were $4.50 machinist helpers whose time at the tool crib did not cause any machines to be idle?

20. Records of 100 truck loads of finished jobs arriving in a department's check-out area show the following: Checking out time takes 5 minutes and the checker takes care of only 1 truck at a time.

Minutes between arrivals	Number of cases
1	1
2	4
3	7
4	17
5	31
6	23
7	7
8	5
9	3
10	2
	100

As soon as the jobs are checked out, the truck drivers take them to the next departments. Using Monte Carlo simulation, determine (a) what percent of the time there is no load at all at the check-out station, (b) what is the average waiting time, and (c) what is likely to be the longest wait.

21. The Standard Automobile Company's home plant can, when everything goes perfectly, turn out 1,000 cars a day. But even when sales are high and the schedule calls for 1,000 a day, production varies because of interruptions. Here is the record during past peak seasons when 1,000 cars were actually scheduled (the problem concerns only the 100-day peak period; there's no problem during the rest of the year):

Production	Percent of the time
750	3
800	7
850	15
875	25
900	23
925	14
950	9
975	3
1,000	1
	100

Standard has a contract with the Truckaway Company to haul out up to 900 cars a day. (This is all that Truckaway's equipment can handle from March through May, the company's peak period.) If there are fewer than 875 cars to be hauled away in any one day, Standard pays a penalty charge of $1 per car short of this amount. If there are more than 900 to be removed, the excess go into a parking lot (storage cost $.50 per car per day) until they can be taken away.

a) What will be Standard's combined cost for penalties and parking charges for 100 days of operation? What will be the largest number of cars in the parking lot at any one time? (In order to reduce the problem solving time, carry through a simulation for 25 days only and then multiply the costs by four in order to get a reasonable approximation of the costs for 100 days.)

b) Will it pay Standard to buy a parking lot which will hold 50 cars if the cost of operating the lot will be $300 a year? (The 100 days in our problem is the only time that the lot would be used.)

c) Truckaway has proposed a new contract covering this peak period. This contract would reduce the trucking cost $.10 per car for all cars hauled away but would call for 925 cars a day to be hauled away with a penalty charge of $1 for every empty space below 925. Should Standard accept this proposal?
Suggestion: Use the Monte Carlo method to solve this problem.

Recent references

Barish, Norman M., *Economic Analysis for Engineering and Managerial Decision-Making*, New York: McGraw-Hill, 1972

Gordon, Geoffery, *System Simulation,* Englewood Cliffs, N.J.: Prentice-Hall, 1969

Hansmann, Fred, *Operations Research Techniques for Capital Investment,* New York: John Wiley, 1968

Maxwell, T., "Queuing Theory, What It Is and How It Works," *Administrative Management,* December 1971

Nelson, R. T., "Simulation of Labor Efficiency and Centralized Assignment in a Production Model," *Management Science,* October 1970

Panico, J. A., *Queuing Theory: A Study of Waiting Lines for Business, Economics and Science,* Englewood Cliffs, N.J.: Prentice-Hall, 1969

Schmidt, J. W., and Taylor, R. E., *Simulation and Analysis of Industrial Systems,* Homewood, Ill.: Richard D. Irwin, 1970

Singhui, S. S., "Determination of a Cut-Off Rate for New Investment Decisions," *Management Advisor,* January 1972

Yechiali, U., and Naor, P., "Queuing Problems with Heterogeneous Arrivals and Service," *Operations Research,* May 1971

3

Capital investment policies

51

AMERICAN factory workers are the most productive workers in the world, but this is not because they work harder or are more skillful than workers in other countries. It is because they, plus their machines, turn out more products. In American manufacturing companies it takes a $25,000 investment to make a job for one worker. Much of this investment is in machines and production facilities.

In order to maintain the physical plant needed and to provide for expansion in a growing economy, American business corporations usually invest something over $80 billion a year in plant and equipment. The larger part of this goes to replace old, worn-out assets, but a considerable fraction goes into paying for expansion. But whichever it is in any given case, capital investment decisions are of utmost importance to every large company.

Policies and capital expenditures

The managers of all organizations have to make their guideline decisions. Many of these have far-reaching capital expenditure implications. What activities is the organization to engage in? What businesses? Where will it operate? Such decisions determine the configuration of the organization and the areas of activities in which it will and will not take part.

In a manufacturing company, the managers need to decide the question of ownership of assets. Almost all of the needed assets could be owned, or they could be rented. Or ownership could be avoided by buying items instead of making them. Generally, the more a company owns, the bigger will be both the investment and the earnings. Not owning, but buying parts or renting assets, is generally less risky and less profitable.

The question of integration is closely related. Should a company own its sources of supply? Or, on the other side, should it own its ultimate outlets to consumers? If the decision is in favor of vertical integration, more capital investment will be required. Another alternative is horizontal integration, where a company owns a chain of stores. And again, if integration is chosen, more investment will be required. Also, conglomerate-type expansion takes more investment—except that in this case the company's many different operating units may have little relation to each other.

The need for capital expenditures

The need for capital expenditures comes from two sources. First, fixed assets (other than land) are continually wearing out. Machines are always figuratively marching down the road to the junk heap, and some reach the end of the road every year. Sometimes the end of the road is economic; a machine is obsolete even though it may still be operable.

The first and usually the biggest need for capital investment is to keep the production facilities operating efficiently. Existing machines and equipment can be overhauled, rebuilt, or renovated, or they can be replaced. In all of these cases the capital expenditure is made only if it will save money relative to the cost of today's methods. Most capital expenditures are for the purpose of saving money.

The second need for money is expansion. Our country is growing, and most companies grow year after year, so they have to keep buying more plants and equipment year after year. Growth needs may, however, be somewhat iregular, and normally are smaller in amount than expenditures made more directly to reduce costs.

A third need is for money for socially desirable projects, such as equipment to reduce air and water pollution and to carry forward other activities for the benefit of society. In a similar way, costly equipment sometimes has to be installed for worker safety and health. Usually the money needs for such projects are much less than those for projects needed to continue to operate economically and for expansion.

A fourth need might be said to be sustaining projects, such as a new vault for keeping records.

The money a company has (from its cash flow) and the money it needs don't always match. Almost always, the total cost of requested projects exceeds the money available. Robert Tyson, a long time U.S. Steel chairman of the finance committee of the board of directors, once said that he had to make up his annual $500 million capital expenditure program out of department heads' "Christmas lists," which usually asked for more than double what was available.

Top managers should not, however, regard money-saving proposals of their subordinates as "Christmas lists," nor should they start with the notion of how much money is available. Rather, these men should consider how essential the new equipment is and, if they are money-saving proposals, how much money they can save. Individual projects should be studied on their own merits, regardless of how much money they take . and how much money is available.

A decision about what to do should be made only after all of the promising proposals have been looked over. Probably a priority list of projects should be set up. Ordinarily, only as many projects as can be paid for will be approved, but a company might approve more proposals if they look so good as to justify borrowing money or selling more stock. Or possibly the equipment could be leased or bought on the installment plan. In 1970 U.S. Steel spent $70 million more on capital investment than its cash flow provided. (U.S. Steel got most of this money by borrowing.)

Although it is not generally considered, selling unproductive or low-producing assets is another possible source of money. U.S. Steel raised $10 million this way in 1970.

Discovering machine needs. When does a machine need replacing? When does an old automobile need replacing? Neither machines nor automobiles are like the one-hoss shay. They don't wear out all at once, in which case people would know for certain when they need replacing. Actually, it is possible to keep old machines or old automobiles running for years by continuing to repair and rebuild them. But repair costs are usually high for old machines, as well as old automobiles. Obsolescence, too, occurs. Every new and more efficient model of a machine makes it a little less economical to continue to operate the old one.

The point is that uneconomical operations have to be searched out. Lower managers have to watch for the point of uneconomical operations of old machines. Single-spindle lathes that are 40 years old can turn out considerable quantities of products which would cost less if they were made on newer automatic screw machines. The fact that an old machine still operates and can be kept busy does not necessarily mean that it is economical to keep it busy. It is also necessary to search out places where money needs to be spent to reduce noise, smoke, or water pollution, as well as to make conditions safer for workers.

Most companies rely on the foreman or the machine operator to tell them when machines can no longer hold tolerances or when they need continual repairs. And it is true that these men know the most about what shape the machines are in, but they seldom know how economical it might be to use new machines, which could be bought or made. Relying on superintendents and master mechanics is a little better but is still a haphazard way to unearth cost-saving opportunities. Probably, however, it will be up to the safety engineer and the personnel department to unearth working-condition improvement needs which do not directly save money.

Major projects.   In contrast to what we have been saying about discovering machinery replacement needs, major project proposals do not come from the shop. Minor shop projects start near the bottom and go up to the front office for review, but the need for whole new factories or for million-dollar projects is first seen in the front office. Often such projects are so big that special task forces of high-level people are set up to do the planning and later to oversee the project.

Cash budgets.   Not only do a company's officials have to pay attention to how much money approved projects will require, they have to pay attention to *when* the money will be needed. If, in November, they approve spending money, it is one thing if the money has to be paid out right away, but it is quite another thing if the money will not have to be paid out until August. By August the company may be able to get the money from profits and depreciation cash which is not yet in hand.

A cash budget is needed. It shows, by month, and for the months ahead, how much cash the company will have—how much will come in and how much will go out. Without a cash budget, a manager might not realize far enough ahead that the outgo will sometimes come first and the income second. Thus the company could get into a financial jam. Small companies frequently get into financial difficulties because of poor financial planning.

The forward look and capital investment

Capital expenditures should be wholly forward looking. The past is nothing except as it helps one foresee the future. The point is that a company is not just replacing machines; it is not like a man buying a new automobile who is really just replacing an old one. Seldom does a company replace a worn-out machine in the sense that it buys a new one which is like the old one. It buys new and different machines to make the products that customers will buy in the future. Both the products and the machines are likely to be different from yesterday's products and machines.

Choice of projects

Since there are nearly always many more profitable projects and more socially desirable projects than a company has money for, its managers have to choose among them. Normally, the projects which promise the highest rate of return on the investment are approved. But this should not be the only guide. No-rate-of-return, socially desirable "must" projects and sustaining projects needed to carry on the business also get a share of the money.

In addition, various projects which are not very certain to pay off might be approved if they might some day pay off very well. An electric power company, for example, may build a power plant to use atomic fuel. Perhaps this particular plant is not expected to pay very well but is expected to serve as a pilot project which will help pave the way for a better paying atomic power plant in the future. The probability of high later payoffs might be introduced into analyses of the prospects.

Capital expenditure decisions are not always clear and distinct from operating decisions. For example, should a company spend cash for research and for advertising? Or should it save on research and advertising and buy more machines? Top managers often must choose between operating costs and capital investments.

Approval of capital spending plans usually means that the company will go ahead and complete the project, but not always. Suppose that a project hardly gets started when business turns down—unexpectedly. This calls for a reappraisal. Promising projects now look less promising and urgent projects become less urgent. In such a case most companies apply the ax freely, and project after project is canceled or postponed even if this means losing the costs of the groundwork already laid. Managers don't hesitate to stop half-finished projects if the crisis is bad enough. Of course, this doesn't happen often, but it is far from rare. Or, conversely, if

FIGURE 3–1.   Typical large company capital expenditure decision-making model

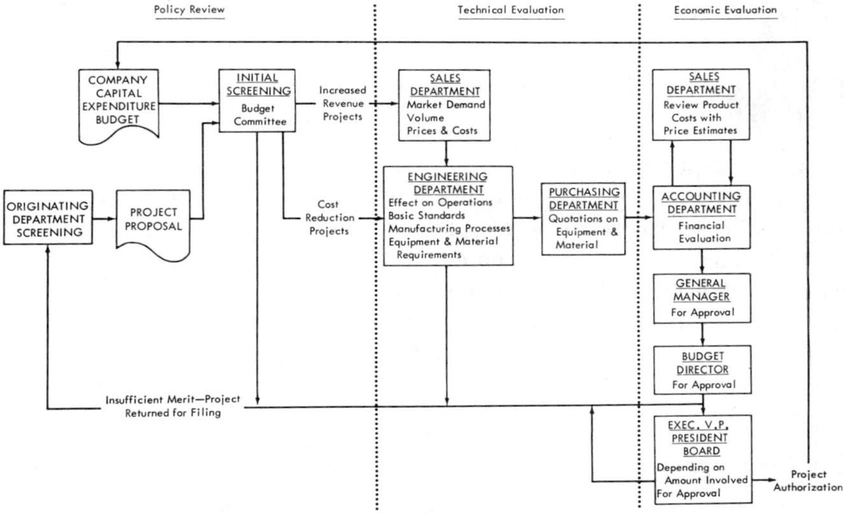

Source: American Management Association.

sales boom, new-capacity projects are pushed ahead despite the high costs of Saturday and Sunday overtime and extra construction crews.

Marginal returns and opportunity costs

Sometimes one project might be chosen over another because of marginal differences which might be called "opportunity cost" situations. (When there are two or more ways to do something which will cost different amounts or which will yield different returns, there is an opportunity to save money by using the least costly way or by investing in the most advantageous way.)

Suppose, for example, that project A will return 15 percent on an investment of $50,000 and project B will yield 18 percent and would cost $40,000. If the decision were to invest in A, its extra $10,000 investment would produce a little extra income in spite of the lower rate, but the extra contribution would not be large. Project A's total return would be $7,500, B's would be $7,200; so the extra $10,000 invested in project A would bring in only $300, or 3 percent. But if B were a 12 percent project, B would bring in only $4,800 against A's $7,500. This time the extra $10,000 required for A would produce $2,700, or 27 percent, on the extra investment.

A manager probably would not use the opportunity cost idea when comparing two projects such as these because the choice is so obvious. The opportunity cost idea could, however, be very important if C, a

completely unrelated project, required $10,000 and would yield 20 per-
cent. Suppose, for example, that there is only $50,000 to invest and only
these three projects to consider. The best choice would be to choose B
and C, the two highest returning projects. But if B were a 12 percent
project, the choice should be A with its 15 percent rate, even though this
means forgoing both B and C—in spite of C's being a 20 percent project.
A will yield $7,500; B and C combined will yield $6,000. Here is a case
where a manager ought to pass up a 20 percent project in favor of a
15 percent project.

Savings and alternatives

It costs money to buy machines and buildings, and it costs money to
use them. Yet we speak of their "saving" money. How can costs be
savings? How is money saved by spending it?

This, again, is an "opportunity cost" situation. Nearly always it is possible to do things several ways—there are alternatives. All ways cost
money, but some cost less than others. One way is said to save money
when it costs less than another way. It is always a matter of choosing cost
opportunities from among alternatives.

Curiously, a project's savings depend not only upon its own cost of
operation but also on the cost of the existing method. So the worse the
present method, the more a new project can save. If a situation is bad, a
company can always save even more money, a year later, by letting the
situation deteriorate further. Actually, any time a new project will save
a great deal, the improvement probably should have been made earlier.
Costs have been allowed to creep up higher than should have been permitted.

Overhead savings. Capital investment project analysts should be quite
conservative in claiming savings in overhead costs. Overhead charges, as
calculated by the accounting department, are rarely less than 100 percent
of direct labor, and they may be 250 percent or more of the labor cost.

Almost never should a project's prospective savings estimate include
saving that much overhead, because savings in direct labor seldom cut
overhead expenses very much. Every project should be credited with
saving any overhead that it really will save, but most capital investment
projects don't, in fact, save much overhead. On the contrary, because
they create more depreciation, they may cause overhead to go up.

Make or buy in capital investment

To make or buy parts is often a capital investment problem because if
a company decides to make things itself, it will have to buy the necessary
machines.

It would seem that make-buy decisions would be few, that once a company decides to buy an item instead of making it, it has settled the problem. But the picture may change. Usually, as a company grows, its purchases of outside items also grow. Sometimes it finds itself buying perhaps millions of dollars worth of one or more items every year. Since the seller normally makes a profit on his sales, the buyer begins to think about making the product himself.

Make-buy decisions need not be permanent, but if a company decides to make instead of to buy, it usually has to buy some machines, and this becomes a capital investment matter. Furthermore, decisions to buy, as far as big items are concerned, are usually reversible whereas decisions to make are less so. It is easier to install the required new facilities in order to make than to dispose of a no longer wanted factory when the decision changes to buy.

Cash flow

Most of the money to pay for new machines, new equipment, and new buildings comes from companies' cash flows, although companies sometimes also sell stock or borrow money.

A company cash flow is the money it could have left over each year (assuming that it doesn't have to use it to pay off mortgages). This is not, however, the same as a company's profits for the year. When customers buy products and pay their bills, a company has a gross cash income. The customers are, in effect, paying all of the company's bills. They are giving it—today—money to cover the payments the company made some time ago for the electricity bill, the tax bill, the pay of employees, the cost of materials, the wearing out of the machines and buildings, everything—and probably a little more which is left over as profit. Normally, most of every company's gross cash inflow goes right out again as it is used to pay today's bills for electricity, taxes, and so on.

The gross cash flow not only pays all of a company's day-to-day expenses but also includes money to recover the decline in the value of machines and buildings because of their wearing out. A company's net cash flow, then, is equal to retained profits after taxes and dividends, plus depreciation on machines, equipment, and buildings, plus any income from the sale of fixed assets.

This does not mean that a company will have all of its net cash flow left over at the end of a year. A good bit of this cash, or maybe all of it, will be spent for new machines or other new capital investment projects as the year goes along. The company will never have all of it in hand at any one time. The point is, however, that during the year certain monies, free of immediate commitment to current bills, come into the company and it gets to decide how to use them.

Since the net cash flow provides the money used for capital projects, its size has much to do with capital investment decisions. The part of the cash flow that comes from depreciation provides most of the money for machinery *replacement* purposes. It ought to provide all of the money needed for replacement machines but today's new machines always seem to cost more than the ones they replace, so companies sometimes have to use part of their profits for replacement projects. And, of course, all of the money for *expansion* has to come out of the profits part of the cash flow, unless the company sells more stock or borrows money.

Cash flow is usually equal to more than 15 percent of a company's fixed assets, and sometimes it goes up to 25 percent or more. In 1970 General Motors' net cash flow of $1.4 billion amounted to 26 percent of its $5.4 billion of fixed assets. More than half, $820 million, of GM's cash flow

FIGURE 3-2.   Cash flow system of a manufacturing organization

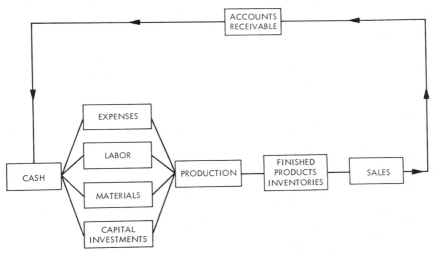

came from depreciation. This was equal to 15 percent of GM's equipment and plant value. U.S. Steel's 1970 depreciation of $295 million was 8 percent of its $3.92 billion investment in equipment and plant. Besides this, retained profits in U.S. Steel produced another $145 million, so its cash flow came to $440 million, or 11 percent of its fixed assets.

Perhaps most people don't think of having cash as being a problem, but inasmuch as idle cash produces nothing, managers have to put it to work. Capital investment is therefore a two-sided affair. On the one hand, there is need for machines and buildings; on the other hand, there is need to put spare cash to work.

Depreciation

Depreciation cash. It has been shown that depreciation produces part of a company's cash flow. But accountants don't like the word *produces* because the company is not any richer because of it. Nor do accountants like the word *generates,* although both words are used in *The Wall Street Journal,* in *Fortune,* and sometimes in companies' annual statements.

Perhaps either the word *releases* or *recovers* is more descriptive. After a year's operation, and if a company did not buy any more machines or buildings, the effect of depreciation would be to move money from the machines and buildings accounts into the cash account. As we saw, in 1970 depreciation released $820 million of cash from General Motors' fixed asset accounts. And for U.S. Steel in 1970, depreciation released $295 million in cash from its fixed asset accounts.

It has also been said that depreciation cash probably never turns up in full in the cash account at the end of the year because every company has to keep buying new machines and buildings all the time. But when it buys new machines and buildings it gets to make choices about how much to spend and what for.

In 1970 General Motors spent $1.13 billion for plant and equipment, so it spent all of the $820 million depreciation money and $310 million of retained profits. U.S. Steel spent $515 million for plant and equipment, so it spent more than its net cash flow of $440 million. In both cases depreciation provided most of the money.

Reinvested depreciation cash does not necessarily go into the same kind of assets that it came from. In fact it usually goes into different kinds of machines and equipment—those which will be most useful in the future.

Depreciation semantics. There are several ways to figure how much depreciation amounts to, and, in the short run, each method gives a different answer and yields a different cash flow. But first a word about the ambiguous nature of depreciation.

The word *depreciation* has several meanings. When a man speaks of depreciation he may mean the loss in value between a machine's cost and its present value. Or he may be referring to the physical wearing out rather than the decline in value. Or he might mean the proportion of its total benefits that has been used up. And he may also be referring to the total depreciation since the item was bought, or be talking about just this year's decline in value or this year's physical wear.

Besides all these uses of *depreciation* there is also the connotation of the related word *obsolescence*—meaning that old machines have been outdated by new machines. Value declines are not always wholly depreciation. Obsolescence, as an idea, is easy enough to understand, but it is hard to know what to do about it in the accounting record.

Suppose that this year a new and better machine is brought out. It is better than the one a company bought last year—but the company does not buy one of the new machines. If a man does not sell his last year's car when this year's new models come out, has he suffered any obsolescence? Suppose he drives his old car for ten years, and during these ten years its values goes down; is this loss in value obsolescence or depreciation? It is not easy to separate these two causes of the decline in value. Similar problems occur in factories in the decline in value of machines. If a company uses a new machine for years, even though newer and better machines become available, there is a question as to whether the machine's loss in value should be called depreciation or obsolescence.

A purist would probably say that the moment a new and better machine comes out it "obsolesces" all the old ones—not making them worthless but *worth less*. The purist would say that this sudden loss in value is obsolescence and that it should be put into the company's records that way as a present loss. From this point on, the machine should be valued at a smaller amount (perhaps its market price if sold now) and future depreciation charges should be based on that amount.

In practice, businessmen don't try to separate obsolescence and depreciation unless something drastic happens. This would occur if a pharmaceutical company builds a factory to make penicillin from plant mold and then someone discovers how to synthesize it artificially by another process, and at far less cost, the company soon loses a great deal of money. (This actually happened to Merck Company in the early days of penicillin.) In such a case the loss on the new factory and its processing equipment is nearly all obsolescence, with only a little of it being depreciation. Except for extreme cases, however, businessmen call all the decline in value "depreciation," even though they know that part of it is obsolescence.

Value. Obsolescence is not the only concept that complicates a discussion of depreciation; "value" is another complication. Depreciation, from a bookkeeping standpoint, is loss in value, but to find the extent of the decline a company needs to know today's value of every machine. What the machine cost when it was new is known, but what is its value today? If this cannot be established, a company cannot tell how much depreciation has occurred.

Using the current market value would seem to be a good idea, but this doesn't always work out very well because there is no good market value for every used machine and piece of equipment a company owns. What, for example, is the value of 10 drill presses which were bought 5 years ago? They cost $30,000 and still run well. How much are the 50 file cases in the offices worth? Some are old and some not so old; they are of several kinds and were bought over the years at different prices. Also, prices are higher today than when most of them were bought. Or how much is an oxygen process furnace for making steel worth? Not as much to someone who would have to dismantle it and haul it away as it is to the company which owns and operates it.

The trouble is that it is not possible to get a good value figure. For many items, a man from the purchasing department could go to used-machinery dealers and get prices, but this would be a difficult job. And for other items, it is not possible to get a good estimate of market price at all. Besides, this would have to be done every year to see how much each year's added depreciation comes to. If prices in general went up, there might be no decline in value, or possibly even an increase. This would happen if the machines were worth more at the year's end in spite of their being a year older and more worn. Or if prices in general went down, there might be a year with three or four times the usual depreciation. Such irregularities would make annual profit figures meaningless.

Besides all the reasons given above for not using market value, the federal government will not allow companies to handle depreciation this way when they make out their profit-and-loss statements for income taxes.

Depreciation methods

Pointing out that depreciation is complicated solves no business problems. Businessmen still have to show on their accounts a money value figure for depreciation every year. And the way that businessmen keep their accounts must satisfy the U.S. Internal Revenue Service. This is because of the tie-in between the calculation of costs (including depreciation), profits, and income taxes.

The Internal Revenue Service wants everyone to depreciate everything over its full life. But because no one really knows how long equipment will last, business practice is to write machinery investments off on a minimum —not a maximum—life expectancy. This means claiming that machines will not last very long and claiming full depreciation in just a few years. If a company doesn't do this, it will sometimes end up showing an asset on its books—as still being worth money—when in fact it is valueless. The explanation is that not every machine lasts as long as was expected.

Straight-line method. Historically, the straight-line method has been much the most common method for figuring depreciation. This method starts with a machine's installed cost, minus its expected scrap value at the end of its expected useful life. This number is divided by the number of years it will be used. A $10,000 machine, expected to last 10 years and then to be worth $1,000 as scrap, will have a $900 depreciation every year.

Declining balance method. In the declining balance method, an item is depreciated by a certain *percentage* of the balance every year. A $10,000 machine which is expected to last 10 years can be depreciated at a 20 percent depreciation rate. Twenty percent of $10,000, or $2,000, is the first year's depreciation. At the beginning of the second year, the machine is carried on the books at $8,000. Twenty percent of that, $1,600, is the second year's depreciation. The third year's depreciation is 20 percent of $6,400, and so on.

The declining balance method allows for heavy depreciation in the early years of an asset's life and then less and less as time goes on. This method never depletes all the values, so users of this method, near the end of an item's life, switch over to straight-line depreciation.

The examples above used 10 percent of the expected loss in value for straight-line depreciation and 20 percent of the remaining value for the declining balance method. In general, a company can use, as the declining balance rate, a rate double that of the straight-line method, except that it is not allowed to go over 20 percent, and in the case of some classes of assets the allowable limit is less than double the straight-line rate. So, in our example, the company could not go over 20 percent, but it could

FIGURE 3–3. Comparison of straight-line, declining balance, and sum-of-the-years'-digits depreciation methods

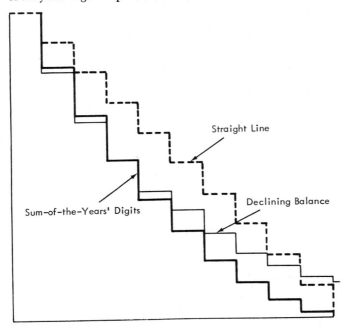

use any other lower percentage if its managers cared to. A company does not have to depreciate at the highest allowable rate.

Sum-of-the-years'-digits. Another method is the sum-of-the-years' digits. If we take a 5-year-life item and add $5 + 4 + 3 + 2 + 1$, we get 15. In the first year we depreciate the item $\frac{5}{15}$ of its cost, next year $\frac{4}{15}$, and so on. For a 10-year item the sum of the digits is 55, so the first year's depreciation would be $\frac{10}{55}$ of its cost. Although it is not particularly complicated, this method is not commonly used.

Variable or unit depreciation. Variable or unit depreciation is becoming more popular. This method requires an estimate of the number of units a machine will produce during its lifetime (these units can also be expressed as hours of operation). Depreciation is then figured on a unit basis and charged to accounting periods according to the number of units produced in the period. The amount charged to any period, therefore, depends on the asset's use in the period. Many accountants feel that this method gives a better picture of the amount of depreciation which should be charged than do other methods.

Group depreciation. In practice, probably no big company depreciates every machine separately. Instead, except for big items where considerable money is involved, machinery investments are grouped into life groups. All machines with 10-year life expectancies are put into one class in the company's accounts. Every time a new 10-year-life machine is bought, its cost is added to the total for all 10-year-life machines. Every year 10 percent of this total is charged off as depreciation.

This makes it necessary to have separate accounts for several life classes: 5 years, 10 years, 15 years, and so on. But there is no need for thousands of separate depreciation accounts—one for every machine. The effect of depreciating by groups is to put depreciation largely on a straight-line method of depreciation which neglects salvage value.

Other methods. There are still other methods of depreciation, but the four that have been described here are the only ones commonly used by manufacturing companies. The sinking-fund method, for example, sometimes used by utilities and railroads, is probably unknown in manufacturing.

Inflation

Inflation complicates normal depreciation practices. An example of this might be a machine that was bought in 1970 for $10,000 (with an expected 10-year life). Suppose a company sets aside the $1,000 depreciation cash every year. By 1980 the machine will be worn out and the company will have its $10,000 for a replacement machine. By 1980, however, the replacement machine may cost $20,000. Thus the company had better have laid aside some extra money because it will have to have $20,000 to buy another machine. Part of the apparent profits over the years has disappeared.

Some years ago, when U.S. Steel wanted to replace a 25-year-old open-hearth steel mill which had cost $10 million, it found that it would cost $64 million to put in a new open-hearth mill. Today this old mill would not be replaced by a new open-hearth mill but by oxygen process equipment at an even much higher cost.

Because of continual inflation, companies would like to depreciate on the *replacement cost* of a machine, but the government says no. Actually, even depreciating on a replacement-cost basis fails to recover enough cash. Suppose that, in the example above, the replacement machine's price went up $1,000 every year and that the government allowed depreciation on a replacement-cost basis. Depreciation cash would have been $1,000 for the first year, $1,100 for the second, and so on. But this practice, if carried on for 10 years, produces only $14,500, not $20,000.

Borderline decisions. If, in the long run, it appears to be a toss-up as to whether to put in new machines or not, it is often better to install them. There are several reasons for this.

First, the quality of the product is usually improved. This gain, though real, is not measurable, and therefore is usually left out when figuring savings.

Second, new machines usually make jobs simpler, thus reducing the skill required and simplifying employee training. This, too, is not in the calculations.

Third, some companies calculate wage savings as if wages would not go up very much in the future. But wages somehow go up even more than expected, and thus it is easy to underestimate future labor cost savings.

A fourth reason is the short life of the machine that is assumed in the calculations. Nearly all machines last longer than the life expectancy used in the calculations, and very few have to be thrown away sooner because of obsolescence. Most calculations of savings are biased to show more depreciation and less savings than will actually occur.

The arguments in favor of mechanizing when the figures show it to be of borderline merit therefore seem strong, but there is a negative side. First, the machines cost money. So even if they show promise of producing considerable savings, it is necessary to produce the money before spending it for the machines.

Second, there is an increase in fixed costs. Investments in machinery increase depreciation costs and raise the company's break-even point. It takes more business volume to break even after buying machines than it did before.

Third, because of the heavier fixed costs and the higher break-even point, the company is more vulnerable to loss. Low sales volume results in greater losses than would have taken place without mechanization.

Still another bad thing—and this in spite of the claims made above—is that new machines don't always come up to expectations. Of course, no one expects them to do as well as the machinery maker says they will, but even after allowing for that, new machines sometimes produce less than was expected. They get out of order too often, turn out too many poor products, need more repairs, wear out tools faster, and so on, than was expected. Particularly, there is likely to be trouble at the start, and it takes time to debug new equipment. Because all these things add to the cost, such extra costs should be put into estimates, but often not enough is allowed for.

Knowing these things, officials sometimes turn down projects which—on paper—show considerable promise. They do not always go ahead and buy machines even in promising situations, to say nothing of toss-up situations.

Income tax considerations

Federal income taxes are high for companies which make much money. In 1970 General Motors earned $1.47 billion but paid $860 million of it to Uncle Sam. (And 1970 was, because of a long strike, a poor year for General Motors.) No one is required to carry on his business in such a way as to pay the utmost in taxes, so when there are choices, as occurs with depreciation methods, the tax angle ought to be considered.

In the case of depreciation, all machines ultimately become fully depreciated no matter what method is used. Yet the depreciation method that is used affects *when* taxes are paid. Some methods allow a company to retain more cash earlier in an asset's life than other methods. If the company can put this money to work profitably right away, this is an advantage.

We can use a one-machine factory, the ABC company, as an example to show how the straight-line, declining balance, and sum-of-the-years'-digits depreciation methods operate. Straight-line depreciation is a slow depreciation method whereas both of the other two methods recover depreciation faster.

ABC has a newly bought machine that cost $10,000 and has an expected life of 10 years and an expected resale value at the end of that time of $1,000. This machine reduces operating costs by $2,000 a year, in addition to recovering the $900 of depreciation claimed to have occurred in the straight-line depreciation method. The machine thus produces a pretax relative cash flow of $2,900.

Here is how taxes and cash retention would work out in the first year with these three methods of depreciation:

	Straight line	Declining balance	Sum-of-years' digits
Claimed depreciation..................	$ 900	$2,000	$1,636
Savings (or pretax profits).............	2,000	900	1,264
Income taxes (48% of profits).........	960	432	607
Cash retention.......................	1,940	2,468	2,293

By using declining balance rather than straight-line depreciation, the company gets to keep $528 more in the business for the time being. The sum-of-the-years'-digits method lets it keep $353 more than with straight line.

One could wonder why the government allows the use of fast depreciation when this deprives it of taxes for the time being. The government allows it because it wants to encourage, rather than discourage, new machinery purchases since this increases the nation's productive capacity. Also, later on, as the machine gets old, the remaining depreciation is small and taxes will be higher. The effect is to change the timing of paying the tax. Businesses gain because they can put the retained extra cash to work. In billion-dollar companies the extra retention amounts to millions of dollars. Fast depreciation also provides protection against unexpected obsolescence.

Capital investment tax credit.   In order to encourage investment in capital projects the government sometimes gives a special tax credit in investments in items eligible for the credit.

Such credit allowances change frequently as Congress changes the law to encourage or discourage greater investment at given times. Often the allowance is a reduction in taxes, amounting to 7 percent of a company's new investments in eligible projects.

Income tax considerations in other areas.   Maintenance is another area where taxes affect decisions. During lean years with no profits, a company probably will not fix or repair anything it doesn't have to. It would probably decide upon this course just to conserve cash, regardless of income taxes. But income taxes are another reason for undermaintenance in bad years, because all maintenance costs in years when a company loses money come out of the company's pocket. But in good years, if money is not spent, it takes the form of profits and the government takes half of it. So it is well to do maintenance work in good years because half of the expense is saved in taxes.

The Internal Revenue Service knows this, of course, and will not let a company charge big expenses all to one year. A new roof on a factory building, for example, cannot be charged in full to the one good year when the company is in a high tax bracket. The new roof is a "betterment," and it has to be shown as an asset and be depreciated over several years. But in spite of IRS restrictions a company can, in profitable years, take care of many little things in the way of maintenance and do it with "cheap" dollars. On the other hand, if a company makes money every year, it doesn't matter much when maintenance and improvements are done.

Many research costs are similar to those for maintenance. In good years a company might proceed with research which may not pay off, but it should not go ahead with this kind of research in bad years.

There is not space here to go into all the angles of how income taxes influence management decisions, but the years when a company loses money should be mentioned. If a company makes money some years and not others, the tax laws are relaxed a little. A company can, to a limited extent, average out the figures, offsetting good and bad years, and so pay less in taxes. There are strict rules about how and when this can be done, but if a company qualifies it can save on taxes.

Review questions

1. Where do the needs for capital investments come from? What kinds of projects are there?
2. Who in an organization should normally see the need for a capital expenditure project and so originate a request?
3. If there is not enough money for all requests for capital expenditure projects, what priority rules should a manager follow as he decides which projects to carry forward?
4. Which is better: to limit capital expenditures to the money available or to approve all good projects, regardless of how much money they take, and then to raise capital outside? Explain.
5. What is a company's cash flow? What is it made of? How is it related to capital expenditures?
6. Why is depreciation important in a company's capital investment program?
7. Explain the most commonly used depreciation methods. Which recover the investment the quickest? Which the slowest?
8. Does inflation make it easier or harder to buy new machines? Why?

Discussion questions

1. Under what conditions should a company *not* own all the assets it needs to carry on its business? What particular assets should it not own? Why?
2. Should companies engage in the manufacture of ancillary products that are outside their main line of production? Ford Motor Company, for example, is the only automaker which makes its own steel. And most steelmakers sell certain industrial chemicals produced in their coke-making operations. They don't make these chemicals into end products. What factors would seem to govern a company's entering into ancillary production?
3. What good does it do to have divisional and central-office staff groups study machinery buying proposals carefully? How can they, 1,000 miles away, tell if the proposals are sound or not?
4. Division heads know their new machine needs best. Why not let them have the final say on what they get?
5. The manager of the wire drawing mill has been able to keep several old, fully depreciated machines in operation. Should he be praised for this? Why?
6. The employees have been complaining about poor locker room facilities. Explain how to calculate the rate of return on the prospective investment required to modernize these facilities.
7. Should the analyst always, sometimes, or never include overhead and sales and administrative costs in the calculation of break-even points for individual projects, such as one machine? Why? If sometimes, when and why?

8. Should an investor prefer to own stock in a company with a big cash flow but low profits or in one that has more profits and a smaller cash flow? Explain how this could happen and then answer the question.

9. Some people say that it is impossible for a company to increase its cash account in years when it loses money. Can it? Explain.

10. Why would anyone ever want to recover depreciation slowly?

11. Conglomerate companies often use accelerated depreciation in their accounts on which they base their profits when they calculate their income taxes. Then they use a second set of books and straight-line depreciation when they calculate the profits for the reports they publish for the public. Why should they do this?

12. Will using the sum-of-the-years'-digits depreciation method instead of straight-line depreciation give a company more or less protection against inflation? (This relates to the matter of normal depreciation providing inadequate funds to buy replacement machines.)

13. Isn't group depreciation about the same as the declining balance method? How are they alike and how are they different?

14. How can sum-of-the-years'-digits depreciation be handled by a company using group depreciation?

15. The text says to mechanize if the figures show it to be a toss-up so far as saving money is concerned. What justification is given? Is this sound? Discuss.

16. Do income taxes encourage or discourage the making of capital investments? Why?

Problems

1. If there is $100,000 to invest, which of the following projects should be chosen? Project A requires $30,000 and will return 23 percent, B requires $30,000 and will yield 20 percent; C requires $60,000 and will return 14 percent; D requires $80,000 and will yield 18 percent; E requires $20,000 and will yield 10 percent. Idle cash yields 4 percent.

2. Suppose that $500,000 is available for investment in capital projects. Which projects from among the following shall be chosen?

a) Which projects should be chosen and what would be the average rate of return?

b) In this solution has any project been selected which has a lower return

Project	Capital requirement	Expected rate of return
A	$300,000	18%
B	50,000	25
C	350,000	15
D	175,000	15
E	100,000	20
F	100,000	30
G	Invest excess in 5% bonds	5

than any omitted project? If so, what would be the effective rate of the high-return project if it were put into the list of approvals at the expense of dropping a project to make room for it?

c) If the company could borrow $50,000 more at 15 percent, should this be done? What projects should be approved and what would their average rate of return be? (Do not forget the interest charge as an offset to the income.)

3. Suppose that a machine which cost $28,000 installed is expected to last 15 years, at which time it is expected to have a salvage value of $4,000. Assume that the machine recovers an amount equivalent to straight-line depreciation and saves $2,000 a year besides. Profits are taxed at 50 percent. Cash retained yields 20 percent pretax profits per year. Compare the position after seven years from using straight-line, declining balance, and sum-of-the-years'-digits depreciation methods.

Which method puts the company in the best cash position? How much better is it than the others?

4. A company buys a machine for $6,000 and uses a 20 percent declining balance method of depreciation. Maintenance costs are expected to be $300 in each of the first two years and then to go up annually as follows: $500, $700, $1,000, $1,400, $1,900, $2,500. When should this machine be replaced?

5. A $10,000 asset has been depreciated by the declining balance method. Its normal life is 10 years. The company can earn 15 percent on depreciation cash and is free to change to straight-line depreciation for the last few years, when it cares to. When should the change be made?

6. Some years ago TRW bought a Warner & Swasey lathe for $18,000. It was depreciated on a 12-year basis. Last year, at the close of the 12th year, it was fully depreciated on TRW's books and the $18,000 had been recovered. The lathe, although practically worn out, still had a resale value of $2,000. A replacement lathe to do the same work is priced at $34,000, but since today's work is more exacting the proper lathe to buy (attachments included) costs $48,000.

If, over the 12 years, the depreciation cash had been put to work each year earning 15 percent and if income taxes were 50 percent of profits:

a) How much extra money would TRW now have to find in order to replace the machine with the $48,000 machine?

b) How much extra sales would it have taken to generate this extra amount of money (TRW would get a pretax profit of 20 percent of the sales price on these products)?

c) Suggest a solution to the problem that TRW faces.

Case 3–1

The ABC Company has been considering several capital investment projects on which various rates of return appear to be in prospect. The accountant who has prepared the figures has been careful to point out that the anticipated returns have been reduced to half because of income taxes. (If projects save money, presumably it will show up as a profit and be taxed at 50 percent.)

There has been a question about how to evaluate the cost of borrowed capital. The bank will lend money at 8 percent. The accountant carried this cost in the calculations at the full 8 percent. This had the effect of reducing the effective rate to 4 percent since, if the company were to use its own money, the whole 8 percent would show up in profits and be taxed at 50 percent. Since this is the normal situation, it is therefore customary to regard the true cost of borrowed capital as half of the stated interest rate.

The ABC Company has earned no profits during the last two years and therefore has paid no income taxes. The question the president raised with his accountant is about this matter of considering the interest on borrowed money as costing only half of its actual rate, considering the fact that ABC is currently paying no income taxes.

The president saw even more to this problem, however. He asked: "If it is proper to say that costs associated with capital equipment investments ought to be thought of as costing only half because of income taxes, then why should we not say the same about labor and materials? These costs, too, are deductible for tax purposes, so let's consider them to have a net cost of only half of their actual cost."

There seems to be some kind of a problem here. What is it? Is there usually something wrong in considering interest to cost only half of its rate? What *is* the true interest rate?

Recent references

Anderson, H. R., and Schwartz, R. P., "Capital Facility Decisions," *Management Accounting*, February 1971

Carter, E. E., "Simulation Approach to Investment Decisions," *California Management Review*, Summer 1971

Hackamack, Lawrence C., *Making Equipment-Replacement Decisions*, New York: American Management Association, 1969

Hertz, David B., "Investment Policies That Pay Off," *Harvard Business Review*, January–February 1968

Laughhunn, D. J., "Capital Expenditure Programming and Some Alternative Approaches to Risk," *Management Science*, January 1971

Meyer, R. A., "Equipment Replacement under Uncertainty," *Management Science*, July 1971

Murdick, Robert C., and Deming, Donald D., *The Management of Capital Expenditures*, New York: McGraw-Hill, 1968

4

Capital investment analysis methods

BECAUSE CAPITAL investment is wholly a forward-looking matter, it is highly important to try to calculate how productive new facilities will be and how much it will cost to operate them. But since these matters lie in the future, they, like all forecasts, are likely to be somewhat inaccurate. No method for analyzing capital expenditure proposals, whether elegant and sophisticated or not, will insure good decisions. It is like a man trying to figure out whether he ought to trade in his old car this year. There is no way to tell for sure that one decision is better than other decisions. Yet, because today's machinery and equipment is more specialized and consequently less flexible, good analyses are more critical than ever.

To complicate matters in capital investment decisions, normal cost accounting records rarely supply all of the figures needed for the calculations. Few companies, for example, make records, by machine, of machine-hours worked, amount of spoiled work, machine downtime, costs of supplies and tools, and repair costs.[1] And when companies don't have such records, they can't know very much about what it will cost to keep an old machine operating.

Actually, most companies use one or all of the following three methods in their calculations for capital equipment buying decisions:

1. Return on investment
2. Payback
3. Discounted cash flow

None of these methods is perfect. Return on investment and payback are easy to figure but are not very incisive. Discounted cash flow requires more involved calculations but more truly reflects the relative merits of alternative choices.

Before we consider these methods individually, one fundamental difficulty inherent in all methods should be pointed out. Whether a new machine should or should not be bought depends upon what it will cost compared to what it will save. But what it will save depends upon a company's present methods. Thus, in replacement problems, there can never be any absolute measure of the profitability of the investment. It depends as much on how bad the present method is as on how good the proposed method is.

Investment and income flow patterns

Capital equipment projects always cost money during their construction period. As construction moves along, more and more money is paid out. Then, when a project comes on line (which is, for a steel mill, perhaps three years after getting started), it starts to generate an income flow. After an early shakedown period, during which minor troubles keep costs high, and which may last for several months, the flow of savings usually is high for several years. Thereafter, as the project "ages," its savings flow lessens.

The pattern of total money going out and coming back is likely to be something like that depicted in Figure 4–1. The money keeps flowing out until the project comes on line. Thereafter the savings flow first recoups the investment and then produces a net earning. First, the project breaks even currently, and later it recovers all of the earlier negative cash flows and produces net earnings.

---

[1] A study made by the Machinery and Allied Products Institute of its member companies found that although 80 percent had records of machine repairs, only 50 percent had most of the other records. Since MAPI members include most of the nation's best companies, it seems probable that only a minority of all companies have such records.

Sometimes, however, prospective savings flows have different patterns. This would happen if a company builds more capacity than it needs in the near future. Even after such a project comes on line, its savings or income flow will start out small and grow later, as the excess capacity begins to be used. In the mid-1960s, for example, the John Deere Company built a farm equipment machinery factory in France even though

FIGURE 4–1.   Typical life history of a capital investment project's outgo and income flows

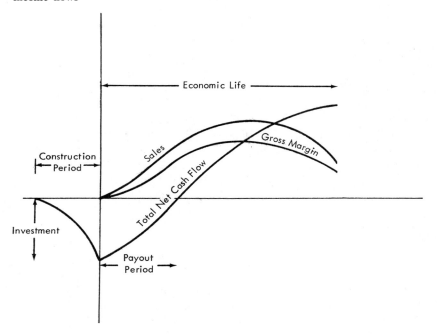

the company expected to lose money for five years before sales would be enough to generate profits. Even after the factory was built, operating losses were expected for some time. Such an outflow and income flow pattern would be unusual but is not unknown. No doubt, too, Deere's analysts also considered both optimistic and pessimistic estimates, and how probable each was, before they selected the estimates they used.

In any case, in profitability calculations the analyst should use whatever income flow pattern the project is likely to generate because the time and shape of earnings streams have much to do with a project's profitability. For simplicity's sake, in the examples used below a regular, even flow for all the years of a machine's life will be assumed. This is common practice, and it is, in fact, just about as good a forecast as can be made in most cases.

Depreciation and rates of return

In Chapter 3 it was shown that a company's depreciation method affects cash retention. The depreciation method also affects the apparent savings and the calculated rate of return on investments. On page 66 the apparent savings from a project ranged from $900 to $2,000 in its first year, depending on the depreciation method used.

Fast depreciation always results in lowering the apparent rate of return while slow depreciation works in the opposite direction and makes a project appear to yield a higher rate. In the example on page 66 the high rate was more than double the low rate. Calculated rates of return are, particularly in the near future, extremely sensitive to the depreciation method. Over longer periods the differences between methods diminish.

Return on investment

Some companies call their method for judging an investment's probable return the "return on investment" method. In fact, according to a Conference Board study, this method is commonly used.[2] Yet there is really no one method called the "return on investment" method.

First-year return. Companies which call their method "return on investment" (ROI) sometimes look only one year ahead and compare a prospective machine's savings to its required investment. They divide its first year's after-tax savings by the average investment for the year and get its rate of return on the investment.

Full-life return. On bigger projects, companies divide the average annual after-tax savings expected during the future years of a project's life by the average investment. Again, the answer is regarded as the return on investment.

Calculating the return on investment this way is not a good way for long-life projects because it puts distant years' profits on the same basis as the profits of near-future years. In fact, however, near-future profits are worth much more than distant-future profits. Using full-life expected income in this way does not consider the time-value of money. Not only are near-future profits worth more (they can be reinvested so as to earn more), they are more certain than the distant future's possible profits. On the other hand, this method considers the total benefits from an investment over its full life, something that payback doesn't do.

Payback

The payback or payout method of analyzing capital investment projects tells how long it takes to get the investment back. Payback is widely used.

[2] *Managing Capital Expenditures,* by Norman E. Pflomm (New York: National Industrial Conference Board, 1963).

Most executives seem to want to know every new project's payback period before they approve it. The payback period should always, of course, be much shorter than the asset's expected life. Managers should try to protect against any possibility that a machine will wear out before they get their money back.

The calculation to get the payback period is one of finding out how long it will be until a project's gross after-tax cash flow equals its investment.[3] If the prospective cash flow is constant year after year, the calculation is to divide the investment by the annual cash flow and get the payment period expressed in years. Sometimes, however, the cash flow changes over the years. When this is expected to be the case, it is only necessary to add up the expected flow until it equals the investment. Then the company will have got its money back and it will have found the payback period.

In payback, all interest is centered on the near-future cash flows of the project and not on its ultimate profits or long-term cash flows. Payback pays attention to how long the investment is at risk and, as a method, overemphasizes liquidity.

Actually, however, no one buys machines just to get his money back. The idea is to get back more money over the years than was put in and to earn money on the investment. Payback pays no attention to the economic life of the asset beyond the payback period, nor to its salvage value or its post-payback cash flows. Thus it neglects the most important part: how much a company will end up earning on the investment.

Some companies follow short payback policies and turn down projects which will not pay off quickly. As a policy, this is probably unwise because it may result in a company's becoming very inefficient before it mechanizes. A new project can pay off in two or three years only if the present method is quite bad. Mostly, companies should not wait until present methods become so inefficient.

Yet because the amounts involved are small, most minor tooling and cost-saving devices are approved only if they will pay out in a year or so. Small machines, where neither costs nor savings are great, are allowed two or three years. Large, expensive, heavy-duty, durable machines may be allowed more time. This could occasionally take up to five years or more.

Businessmen do not, however, apply payback yardsticks blindly, and they change them up or down sometimes, depending on how much money they have and how good business promises to be. Often, too, payback is used in conjunction with the more sophisticated discounted cash flow method for analyzing the worth of projects.

---

[3] In these calculations the cash flow is the project's savings, minus the income tax on the savings, plus depreciation. This differs from a company's overall net cash flow because this cash flow is not diminished by any dividends paid out.

Discounted cash flow

The discontinued cash flow (sometimes also called "discounted rate of return," "investors' method," "profitability index," "yield to maturity," or "present value") method for analyzing capital equipment expenditures is widely used.

The essence of the discounted cash flow method is simple. All expected future costs and all incomes expected to be generated by a project are reduced to their present value and compared. Discounted cash flow more or less assumes that all the savings a machine will make in the future are available to the company right now, but discounted to their present value. And it assumes that—right now—it pays fully for the project and for all its future expenses (again discounted to their present value), including repairs and income taxes on the machine's savings. Then the method compares the totals to see how profitable the project may be.

Although the discounted cash flow idea is simple, its calculation is a little complicated because of the need to express future incomes and outgoes in today's dollars. A second complication comes from the fact that a project's savings are savings only as they are compared to something else (probably to continuing to use a machine the company already owns). Complications arise when the present machine will last fewer years than the proposed new one. It is not really possible to speak about savings beyond the life of the present machine.

To explain the method we start with the matter of discounting everything to the present. If a 1980 expense is paid in 1975, less money will need to be paid than if the payment has not been made until 1980, because the recipient can earn interest on it for five years. So the method starts with compound interest.

One dollar put at interest of 10 percent and compounded annually will grow to $2.594 in 10 years. Or, expressed as a discount, $2.594 in 10 years has a present value of $1 or 38.55 percent of its 10 years' later value.[4]

---

[4] To get the future value of money for other interest rates and other periods of time, this formula for each single year can be used.

$$F = P(1 + i)^n$$

F is the future value, P the present amount, i the interest rate, and n the number of years.

To get the present value of a future amount of money the formula can be restated as:

$$P = \frac{F}{(1 + .i)^n}$$

Appendix C is a precomputed discount table. All transactions are considered to be completed at the end of the year.

The formula for the sum of the present values of an equal series of annual payment is:

$$P = R \frac{(1 + i)^n - 1}{i(1 + i)^n}$$

In this formula, R is the amount of the payment made every year.

Discounted value in machine economy studies.   Discounting lets everything be put on a current-dollar basis. If a company buys a 10-year-life machine today at $10,000, its cost is in 100-cent dollars. During the first year it gets back $1,000 depreciation. To simplify the problem it will be assumed that the company gets no depreciation money back until the end of the year, and then it gets the whole $1,000.

Getting $1,000 a year from now is the same as having $952, or $900, or $870, or $833 (or some other figure) now; it depends on the interest rate. Actually, businesses usually use 20, 25, or 30 percent in their calculations. This seems high, but things don't always work out well. There are risks. Also, machines may become obsolete before they wear out. And if new machines save money, there will be more profits, half of which will go into income taxes.

Before applying the discounting idea to a problem it is well to see how the problem works out if no attention is paid to discounting. We will consider two alternatives:

Proposal A	*Proposal B*
1 machine	2 machines
$20,000 installed cost	$10,000 installed cost ($5,000 each)
8 years of life	10 years of life
No scrap value	No scrap value
$5,000 per year to operate, including labor, repairs, and all other items (*but not depreciation*)	$7,000 per year to operate

Since the life of proposal A is only 8 years, the comparison will be made only for 8 years even though the machines in proposal B will last 10 years.

Proposal A		*Proposal B*	
Depreciation in 8 years	$20,000	Depreciation in 8 years	$ 8,000
Operating costs for 8 years	40,000	Operating costs for 8 years	56,000
Total cost	60,000	Total cost	64,000
Average cost per year	7,500	Average cost per year	8,000

On the basis of this analysis the company should purchase the machine in proposal A rather than the 2 machines in B. A final decision should wait, though, until the answer obtained from the discounted cash flow method is available.

In using the discounted cash flow method, everything is reduced to today's dollars. Starting with proposal A (see Figure 4–2), we see that this machine is paid for with 20,000 of today's dollars. There is no discount on today's dollars; thus today's value of this payment is $20,000.

Next, it will cost $5,000 to run the machine for 1 year. Rather than get-

FIGURE 4-2

	A One machine	B Two machines	Discount factor at 20%	Present value	
				A	B
First cost......................	$20,000	$10,000	1.000	$20,000	$10,000
Operating cost during: Year					
1............................	5,000	7,000	0.833	4,165	5,831
2............................	5,000	7,000	0.694	3,470	4,858
3............................	5,000	7,000	0.578	2,890	4,046
4............................	5,000	7,000	0.482	2,410	3,374
5............................	5,000	7,000	0.402	2,010	2,814
6............................	5,000	7,000	0.335	1,675	2,345
7............................	5,000	7,000	0.279	1,395	1,953
8............................	5,000	7,000	0.233	1,165	1,631
Credit for remaining value of machines at end of 8 years................		2,000	0.233		467
Total......				$39,180	$36,385
Average......				$ 4,898	$ 4,548

ting mixed up with some costs coming soon and some late within the year, we will assume that none of the $5,000 is paid until the year end and then it is all paid at once. A 20 percent discount rate is used.

Appendix C, in the 20 percent interest rate column, shows that $1,000 a year from now—at 20 percent—has a present value of $833. So $5,000 a year from now is worth, today, .833 × $5,000, or $4,165.

Similar calculations are carried through for other years. The present value of all cash outflows for project A is $39,180, or an average of $4,898 per year. Similar calculations for B show that the present value of its 8-year costs comes to $36,385, or an average of $4,548 per year.

This time, then, the choice is B, and by a margin of $350 per year ($182 after taxes). On page 78 it looked as if A were better, but the analysis that uses regular dollars gives too little consideration to the fact that choosing A would require the paying out of $10,000 extra, and right away. The discounted rate of return analysis shows that the company will be better off not to invest that extra money in proposal A—that is, if a 20 percent return is desired. The added investment in proposal A will not produce a 20 percent return.

Calculating the rate of return. But, one might ask, what rate of return will the extra $10,000 investment in A produce? To find this it is necessary to try different discount rates until the present value totals for A and B are equal. When they are equal, the rate of return used for discounting is the rate that the extra investment needed for project A will yield.

In the example above we used 20 percent in the original comparison and found that the extra investment in A would not produce this much. We then recalculated the example, using 16, 12, and finally 8 percent before finding out how much the extra investment in A would yield. It proved to be a 9.3 percent return. If the company wants a higher rate than 9.3 percent, it should choose B and invest the extra $10,000 elsewhere. (Furthermore, we have not yet considered income taxes, which would reduce the 9.3 rate to 4.8 percent.)

The way to find the exact rate (the 9.3 percent in this case) is to try two or three trial calculations, as is illustrated in Figure 4–3. Such trial calculations will reveal interest rates above and below the actual rate. The actual rate can then be found by interpolation.

To work this out it is necessary to set the problem up as is done in Figure 4–3, whose data columns and numbers are different from those in

FIGURE 4–3

		1st trial		2d trial		3d trial	
		Present value at 16%		Present value at 12%		Present value at 8%	
	Cash (outflow		of cash		of cash		of cash
Year	or inflow)	of $1	flows	of $1	flows	of $1	flows
0..............	($10,000)	1.000	($10,000)	1.000	($10,000)	1.000	($10,000)
1..............	2,000	.862	1,724	.893	1,786	.926	1,852
2..............	2,000	.741	1,482	.800	1,600	.855	1,710
3..............	2,000	.641	1,282	.714	1,428	.794	1,588
4..............	2,000	.552	1,104	.637	1,274	.735	1,470
5..............	2,000	.476	952	.568	1,136	.680	1,360
6..............	2,000	.410	820	.508	1,016	.629	1,258
7..............	2,000	.353	706	.452	904	.585	1,170
8..............	2,000	.305	610	.405	810	.541	1,082
Remaining value of project B after 8 years	2,000	.305	(610)	.405	(810)	.541	(1,082)
			−1,930		−856		+408

$$8\% + (4 \times 408 \div 1264) = \text{actual rate}$$
$$8\% + (4 \times .323) = \text{actual rate}$$
$$8\% + 1.3\% = 9.3\%$$

Figure 4–2. The cash flow column in Figure 4–3 is wholly a comparison of proposal A with B. A takes $10,000 more starting cash than B, so this shows as a negative cash inflow at the beginning of year 1 (shown in Figure 4–3 as the end of year 0). A operates at a $2,000 lower cost per year than B, so it yields a comparative cash inflow every year of $2,000.

Next comes trial-and-error discounting. The inflow column was first discounted at 16 percent and then was added up. The total was −$1,930, so the project will not pay back the extra $10,000 in 8 years plus 16 percent return. It falls $1,930 short of doing this. The next trial was 12 percent, and again there was a negative number: −$856. The extra investment in A will not yield 12 percent. Then 8 percent was tried. This time there was a positive answer, +$408; so A's extra investment will yield 8 percent and more.

From here on, the actual rate of return can be found by interpolation. The present value, calculated at 8 percent, differs from the 12 percent figure by $1,264, and it differs from 8 percent by $408. So the actual rate is 408 divided by 1,264 of the 4-point spread between 8 and 12 percent. The calculation in Figure 4–3 shows that this comes (pretax) to 9.3 percent.

Probably it would be a good idea in capital investment calculations to use, as a discount rate, the interest rate available on other investments. Then, if a project's return is positive, it shows that the project promises to yield the usual percentage and more. And it shows how much more. If the sum is negative, the project will not yield the usual rate of return.

MAPI

Over the years the Machinery and Allied Products Institute (MAPI) has studied methods for evaluating machinery replacement and has developed a quite sophisticated method for judging the merits of projects. The method is basically quite complex but has been reduced to a simplified form for general use. Among other things, it considers all current tax regulations (such as those which allow for fast depreciation or tax credits) and therefore is frequently changed in accord with changes in the regulations of the Internal Revenue Service.[5]

The MAPI method is less widely used than the payback and discounted cash flow methods, perhaps because of its complexity. (MAPI actually offers three slightly different methods to cover different situations). There are also certain built-in assumptions which may not suit all users. MAPI's method assumes, for example, that part of the money to be invested will be borrowed and that interest will be paid. It also assumes increasing repairs with age. And it assumes that the advantages that a machine will have over others decreases over the years as newer and better machines become available for use. Those assumptions appear to be logical yet they may not always be appropriate; hence they might be reasons for not using this method.

Book value of old machines

Some people see the book value or "sunk costs" of old machines as a problem in machine economy studies. Sunk costs are expenditures already made and not directly returnable. They represent past decisions which are irreversible and therefore not relevant to the present decision.

A company may, for example, buy a 10-year-life machine for $20,000, use it for 6 years, depreciating it on its books at $2,000 a year, and then

---

[5] A full description of MAPI's method is given in *Business Investment Management,* by George Terborgh (Washington, D.C.: Machinery and Allied Products Institute, 1967).

consider replacing it. The accounts show it still to be worth $8,000. Suppose that it has a value today of $3,000 if sold and that it will probably be worthless in 4 more years.

At this point there is a proposal to buy a new machine. In the analysis comparing continuing to use the old machine against buying the new one, should the costs of using the old machine include $2,000 of depreciation for each of the next 4 years? One might say, of course, that this is consistent with what the company has been doing. It is what the government requires for tax computing purposes. It is what would be done if there had never been any thought of buying a new machine.

Why even think of not listing $2,000 depreciation every year? The reason is that the machine is actually worth only $3,000, not $8,000. From here on—in machine economy studies—the depreciation every year should be $750 (one fourth of $3,000), not $2,000 (one fourth of $8,000). The past should not be considered with the future, and accounting practices should not be allowed to confuse the issue. Past depreciation charges have, in fact, been too low, and this produces a wrong picture of the future if these past mistakes are carried into machine economy studies.

The hard point to accept is that if a new machine is not bought, the regular depreciation schedule of $2,000 per year carries on, and in 4 years $8,000 of depreciation is recovered. There seems not to have been a loss of $5,000. Yet if a new machine is bought and the old one is sold for $3,000, this would establish a $5,000 loss on the company's books. What has happened, though, is that the company has already suffered an unrecognized loss of $5,000. If it does not buy the new machine and it continues to recover $2,000 "depreciation" annually, it is actually recovering $750 of depreciation and $1,250 of unrecognized profits. In the next 4 years this unrecognized profit will total $5,000 and will offset the $5,000 unrecognized loss that the company has already suffered. Normal depreciation practices cover up all of this, and since it washes out in the end, it goes unseen.

Writing down the old asset to its present used-machine value makes it hard for a new machine to make a good showing. The old machine's future depreciation is now shown to be very low ($750 in our example instead of $2,000); this holds down the calculated cost of keeping it in operation.

Book life of old machines

Just as the analyst should not use the book value of old machines in machine economy studies, neither should he use book life. If the accounts say that a machine has 3 more years of life but it now appears that it will last 5 more years, by all means the 5-year figure should be used in the calculation.

Bayesian analyses

Bayesian analysis is a method which helps in capital equipment investment decision making by bringing probability into the calculations. A Bayesian analysis allows managers to convert nebulous and vague intuitive judgments into quantitative numbers which can be more precisely analyzed, equated, and compared.

Managers make many such decisions all the time but they do it intuitively. If a manager is asked, for example, if he will approve the spending of an extra $100 to get a delayed order shipped on time, he will say yes or he will say no. Yet if he says yes, he might have said no if the request was for $1,000. He has some kind of a value calculus of a money-time relationship in his mind.

A Bayesian analysis can help him refine his judgment by taking his information about alternatives and adding his intuitive calculus, thus putting the problem into a logical form for mathematical solution. An example will illustrate the process.

Assume that the ABC Company is bringing out a new product but its managers are in doubt about how well it will catch on. Almost surely it will sell a satisfactory minimum quantity, and it might sell very well indeed. ABC cannot manufacture this new product in its present plant and so will have to build an addition to the plant to house the new operations. The question is how big an addition to build. ABC would like, of course, to build a big enough addition to handle all of the sales, but no bigger.

A Bayesian analysis starts with several alternative forecasts of the product's possible sales. In Figure 4–4 are listed four forecasts of prospec-

FIGURE 4–4.   Profit prospects (thousands of dollars)

Plant addition	High	Near high	Moderate	Low
		Sales forecast		
Very large.	310	220	−20	−290
Extensive.	280	240	80	−180
Moderate.	150	130	70	−90
Small.	70	60	50	−20

tive sales volumes: *High, Near High, Moderate,* and *Low.* In practice, all of these estimates would be expressed as quantities.

Next are listed the several factory-addition-size possibilities that are being considered. If the sales demand proves to be *high,* ABC's managers would like to have built a *very large* addition. But this would be uneconomical if the sales demand turned out to be *low.* So they want to consider several plant-addition-size possibilities: *Very Large, Extensive, Moderate,* and *Small.*

The body of Figure 4–4 is then filled with payoff numbers. If ABC were to build a *very large* addition and if sales demand proved to be *high,* ABC would make $310,000 of profits. But if sales reached only the *near high* level, ABC would, if it had constructed a very large addition, earn only $220,000 of profits. Should sales be *low,* it would lose $290,000. Or ABC could build an *extensive* addition, in which case, if the sales proved to be *high,* earnings would be only $280,000 because it could not fill all the demand except by producing at costly overtime.

All told, 16 combinations of high and low sales are combined with big and little plant additions. And for each combination there is a prospective profit or payoff figure. These 16 payoff figures make up the body of the table or matrix in Figure 4–4. This payoff matrix shows that the *very large* plant can be the most profitable, or can cause the most loss, depending on sales. And the *small* addition will yield the smallest profits if sales demand is *high, near high,* or *moderate;* yet it holds the possible loss to the smallest figure if sales prove disappointing.

The payoff matrix does not, however, tell ABC's managers what to do. It only says that if they do this, and if sales are such-and-such, this is how they will fare. Figure 4–4 gives them 16 "if" answers.

FIGURE 4–5.   Profits for each choice (thousands of dollars)

Plant addition	Sales Forecast				Expected monetary value
	High .06*	Near high .43*	Moderate .36*	Low .15*	
Very large....................	18.6	94.6	−7.2	−43.5	62.5
Extensive.....................	16.8	103.2	28.8	−27.0	121.8
Moderate.....................	9.0	55.9	25.2	−13.5	76.6
Small........................	4.2	25.8	18.0	−3.0	45.0

* Probability

A Bayesian analysis then proceeds as in Figure 4–5, in which a probability is assigned to each of the 4 sales forecasts. If ABC's managers believe there is only a small chance that *high* sales will materialize, they assign this forecast a low probability (we used .06). But if they think there is a much greater chance that sales will reach the *near high* sales projection, this column should be given a higher figure. (We used .43 for *near high* sales demand and .36 and .15 for the lower sales possibilities. The probabilities have to add up to 1 because, collectively, they have to cover all the possibilities.) In Figure 4–5 the probability of each sales level is shown at the top of its column.

The next step is to multiply the probability by the payoff and get a set of "expected monetary value" figures—those in the body of Figure 4–5. The *18.6* figure, for example, comes from multiplying *.06* (the probability of the *high* sales demand) and $310,000 (the payoff if ABC builds a *very large* addition and if sales are *high*). Similar payoff figures are calculated for all 16 combinations of sales and plant size.

Next, the 4 expected monetary value figures for the different sales levels are added (horizontally) to get a total. In the ABC example, the total expected monetary value of building a *very large* plant is *$62,500*. But there is a much higher probable payoff, *$121,800,* if ABC constructs an *extensive* instead of a *very large* addition. In fact, putting up a still smaller addition, of *moderate* size (with its *$76,600* figure), is better than putting up a *very large* addition.

The *$121,800* should not, however, be interpreted as the profit that ABC will almost surely make if it puts up an *extensive* addition. How much it will earn will depend upon actual sales, but they will be some specific number—not an average. If sales demand is *high,* ABC will get a payoff of $280,000; if sales are *moderate,* it will get $80,000; etc. The actual payoff will be one of the numbers in Figure 4–4 (or between-column numbers) and not those in the right-hand column (the expected monetary value column) of Figure 4–5.

As in an earlier example that used probability, ABC's managers should think of these figures as showing average results—as if they were looking ahead at 100 instances. If there were 100 new products, each requiring a plant addition, and if in each case ABC built an *extensive* addition, payoffs would average *$121,800.* Considering the information ABC's managers now have about the future, and in spite of their not having an opportunity to make 100 decisions, their best choice in this instance is to choose the action which would produce, were there 100 choices to make, the highest average return. In this case, ABC should build an *extensive* addition.

Weaknesses of Bayesian analyses. The example above deals with a capital expenditure project. The actual payoff figures that ABC will realize from its decision in a real-life situation, might depend a good bit upon factors which were not included in the above analysis. The analysis did not, for example, pay any attention to whether ABC has, or can easily get, the money to pay for the plant additions. Nor did it concern itself about the possibility of building a small addition first and then making it bigger if it were necessary to expand it. And it did not consider the possibility of ABC's buying extra parts outside if it gets into a jam. There are probably other omissions as well.

All of these factors could be put into a more complicated Bayesian analysis; that is, they do not have to be neglected. Sometimes, however, it is not possible to get good quantitative data for every pertinent factor, so some have to be omitted. Whenever this is the case, the answers obtained have to be used with considerable discretion because not everything was included.

Decision trees

When a man comes to a Y in the road, he has to choose which branch to take. Having chosen one, it opens up a whole set of possibilities while cutting off another set. And having chosen one road and pursued it for a distance, this man comes to another Y. Again he has to choose, and again he opens up certain possibilities while closing off others.

Businessmen often have to make similar decisions. They do something or they don't. Take a manufacturer of television sets, for example, who is considering the manufacture of color sets. He has to decide to make them or not to make them. If he makes the sets, there is high probability of his being able to make them at less cost than if he buys them. Whichever choice he makes causes him to do certain things and not to do certain other things. And he accomplishes certain results and not others. Yet, although the probability of success is high, it is not certain.

But his decision chain does not stop with one decision. If he decides to make color sets and does so successfully for some time, he may then ask himself, "Should I make my own color tubes?" (He already makes black and white tubes.) Again, a yes or no. And again his choice opens some doors and closes others. And again there is a probability of his being successful and a small possibility of his losing money because his costs are too high.

But all this still goes on. He decides yes, and his color tubes operate very well. Now another question comes up: Should he make color tubes only for his own needs or should he sell color tubes to competitors too? This process could be continued to show that such decision chains go on and on.

"Decision trees" provide a technique for analyzing such action sequence–type situations and the various probabilities of expected payoffs when the planning is still at the beginning stage. Decision trees differ from Bayesian analyses in that they portray the possible consequences of two or more successive sets of decisions, some of which will be made later on and not at the outset.

Bayesian analyses are usually limited to analyzing the alternatives upon which one initial decision, and one decision only, will be made. Decision trees help a manager evaluate the various alternatives when the first decisions may have to be followed by second and even third decisions. They give him some idea about when decisions will need to be made and they let him consider the probability that each of the various events will occur and their value if they should occur.

An example will illustrate the decision tree process. The ABC Chemical Company has developed a new product that has an expected market life of 10 years before other new products will probably take its place and force it off the market. ABC's president has to decide whether to build a big plant to produce the new product or a small plant which can be added to if the demand proves to be high.[6]

Figure 4–6 shows the possible decisions, and where they will lead, and it shows when decisions will have to be made. The decision tree in Figure 4–6 is not, however, in a very helpful form because it does not include cost, payoff, and probability figures. These figures have been added in Figure 4–7.

FIGURE 4–6. Decision tree showing possible end results

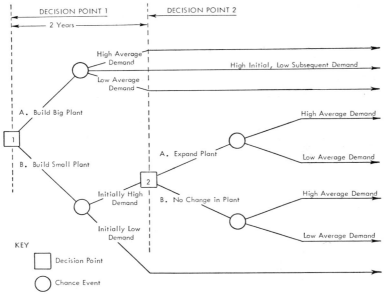

Source: John F. Magee and *Harvard Business Review.*

Figure 4–7 shows that a big plant (requiring a $3 million investment) and high demand promises to yield $1 million a year for 10 years. But a big plant will probably yield only $100,000 a year if demand is low. Demand might also start high and bring in $1 million during each of the first 2 years, and then drop off and bring in only $100,000 a year for the remaining 8 years.

A small plant would require an original investment of $1.3 million and

---

[6] This shortened example was originally presented at greater length in "Decision Trees for Decision-Making," by John F. Magee, in the *Harvard Business Review* for July–August 1964 (pp. 126–35).

FIGURE 4–7. Decision tree with end results and payoff possibilities

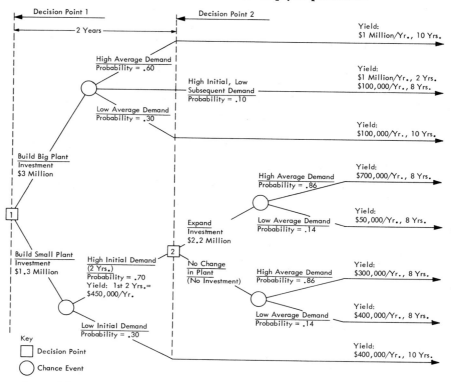

Source: John F. Magee and *Harvard Business Review.*

would yield $400,000 per year if the demand is low. But if ABC builds a small plant and then finds that demand is high, it will make $450,000 for each of the first 2 years. By the end of 2 years ABC will have to make another decision. It can invest an additional $2.2 million to expand its small plant into a large plant. If it does, and if the demand continues high, ABC can expect to earn $700,000 a year for the remaining 8 years. On the other hand, the demand might drop, and if this happens ABC will earn only $50,000 a year for the remaining 8 years.

There is still one more set of events which needs to be considered. If ABC builds a small plant and finds a high demand (which continues for the full 10 years) and chooses not to expand, its competitors *will* expand, so ABC will earn only $300,000 a year for the last 8 years. The competitors will not expand, however, if demand starts high and then drops off. In that case, ABC's not expanding will yield $400,000 a year for the last 8 years.

Figure 4–7 shows ABC forecasters' estimates of the probability of each situation. They think there is a 60 percent probability that sales will start off high and continue high for the whole 10 years. They believe there is a 10 percent chance that the demand will start out high but after 2 years will drop off and be low. And they think there is a 30 percent probability that sales will start low and stay that way. They think there is no chance at all that demand will start low and then pick up.

Now ABC's managers can use the numbers shown on the decision tree to see how each possible action will work out.

What should the managers do? At this point, as they look ahead 10 years, they can build either a large plant or a small one. If they build a large plant they face these prospects:

Demand	Return in 10 years		Probability	Expected monetary value
High	$10,000,000	× .60	=	$6,000,000
High first, lower later	2,800,000	× .10	=	280,000
Low	1,000,000	× .30	=	300,000
				$6,580,000
Less investment.....................				$3,000,000
Net..........................				$3,580,000

If ABC builds a small plant, the results for the first 2 years will be as follows:

	Return	Proba-bility		Expected monetary value
High demand $450,000 × 2 =	$900,000 ×	.70	=	$ 630,000
Low demand 400,000 × 2 =	800,000 ×	.30	=	240,000
				$ 870,000
Less investment........................				$1,300,000
Net after 2 years.......................				−$ 430,000

The analysis for the next 8 years has to consider several possibilities, depending on whether or not an addition is built. If no addition is built, these are the prospects for the next 8 years:

Demand continues high	$300,000 × 8 = $2,400,000 × .60 = $1,440,000
Demand falls off	400,000 × 8 = 3,200,000 × .10 = 320,000
Demand starts low, stays low	400,000 × 8 = 3,200,000 × .30 = 960,000
Total	$2,720,000
Add net for first 2 years	−$ 430,000
Net for 10 years	$2,290,000

After 2 years, however, should ABC build an addition, it faces this prospect:

Demand continues high $700,000 × 8 =	$5,600,000 × .86 =	$4,816,000
Demand falls off	50,000 × 8 =	400,000 × .14 =	56,000
Total			$4,872,000
Less cost of addition			$2,200,000
Net for 8 years			$2,672,000
Add net for first 2 years			−$ 430,000
Net for 10 years			$2,242,000

In summary, if ABC chooses, right away, to build a large plant, the expected monetary value above all costs will come to $3.58 million in the 10 years. If ABC first builds a small plant, then, after 2 years, its managers must choose between putting up an addition or not. If they choose not to do so, and to continue for the whole 10 years with the small plant, the expected monetary value is $2.29 million for the whole 10 years. If they decide to build an addition, they face an expected monetary value of 2.24 million for the whole 10 years. ABC, therefore, should build the large plant. But if it decides not to do so, it should not build an addition 2 years later, even if the product is selling well.

Review questions

1. How do the return on investment and payback methods differ from each other?
2. Is the return on investment method better than payback in its ability to reveal the ultimate long-range merits of a proposal?
3. Explain how the discounted cash flow method operates.
4. Explain how to find the actual rate of return a company would get on the extra capital invested when one project requires more investment than another.
5. How should the book value of old machines be handled in capital investment comparisons among projects?
6. Explain how the "expected monetary value" column in a Bayesian analysis is arrived at. How is it used?
7. How do decision trees differ from Bayesian analyses? When would a decision tree probably be better?

Discussion questions

1. Calculating the rate of return by comparing a new method to an existing method makes the new method look good or bad, depending on how bad the old method was. How can the badness of the old method properly have anything to do with the goodness of a new method? Why not do away with comparisons to the past and calculate the absolute rate of return on new proposals?
2. "The future's not ours to see." Try to forecast the number of miles you will drive your car next year and the amount you will spend on gasoline and

repair bills. What is the good of trying to forecast a machine's productivity and operating costs?

3. Is it true that return on investment studies implicitly assume that the cash flow will automatically be reinvested at the project's rate of return? And if this is true, doesn't this result in wrong answers because other new investment projects, undertaken later, will also claim credit for these new gains? Doesn't this method claim credit two or three times for the same savings? Discuss.

4. Why do discounted-dollar calculations use extremely high interest rates? What does this do to the results?

5. Some people say that in cost saving calculations made when comparing new machines with old machines, the prospective loss in book value of old machines to be discarded if a new machine is bought should be disregarded. Do you agree or disagree? Why?

6. Postconstruction audits to see if the expected gains from investments in projects actually came up to those claimed in the proposals are rarely made. It is difficult to do this, and doing it is somewhat fruitless since the decision was made and the money spent for the project selected. Suppose, however, that there is plenty of time and money for making a postconstruction audit. Part of the comparison should be with alternative projects that were not selected. How might an analyst go about appraising how a forgone project might have worked out?

7. Aren't decision trees rather worthless in that the organization finally ends up going down one and only one path? What good does it do to know all about what might have been?

Problems

1. Compare the following two alternatives:

	Machine A	Machine B
Installed cost.	$8,500	$14,000
Estimated life.	10 yrs.	12 yrs.
Salvage value at end of estimated life.	$2,500	$ 1,000
Annual operating cost.	$3,500	$ 2,000
Interest cost.	15%	15%

a) Using first-year costs only, which investment is better?

b) Is the answer to (a) influenced by the depreciation method used? Show the figures for straight-line, sum-of-the-years'-digits, and declining balance methods for the first year.

2. The question is whether to replace an existing machine with a new machine. The new machine will cost $12,000 and will have an expected life of 12 years, with an expected salvage value of $1,500 at the end of 12 years. This machine will recover its straight-line depreciation each year, and when compared to using the old machine will show a $2,500 pretax savings besides. The

company is in the 50 percent tax bracket and can earn 15 percent (pretax) on alternative investments.

Should this machine be bought, and if it should, what is its payback period?

3. A man laying out a casting for a hole-drilling operation has to measure carefully and use a center punch so that the drilled hole will be in the right place. He costs $6 an hour and can do 3 pieces a minute. For $50 a drill jig can be made which will allow a $5-an-hour man to do 9 pieces a minute.

What are the costs of the two methods for 3,000 pieces? At what volume will the jig pay for itself?

4. Because of the lack of sensitivity of the weigher, a company's automatic coffee can-filling machine is set to put 16¼ ounces of coffee into the cans so that no can will contain less than 16 ounces.

This weigher cost $3,000 five years ago and ought to last for 10 more years. The machinery salesman offers a new, more sensitive weigher which could be set at 16⅛ ounces. He will allow a $400 trade-in on the old weigher against the new machine's purchase price of $8,000. The new machine ought to last 10 years. Neither it nor the present weigher will have any final salvage value. Coffee cost $.80 a pound. Interest is 10 percent.

How many 1-pound cans of coffee must be sold per year to pay for the new weigher?

5. Assume the following data:

Cost of a new tool..............................	$800
Expected life of new tool........................	5 yr.
Interest rate on invested funds..................	10%
Insurance and repairs per year...................	$80
Number of times used per year....................	10
Setup cost per time used.........................	$10
Estimated labor cost savings per unit from using new tool.......................................	$.05
Increased material cost per unit................	$.015

Using the first-year performance method:

a) Compute the volume required to break even (include a savings in overhead at 100 percent of direct labor).

b) What would the break-even volume be if the overhead savings were omitted?

c) What would the true break-even point probably be?

6. A heavy duty 10-ton truck can be bought for $15,000. It should last 8 years, at which time its salvage value ought to be $2,000. Maintenance will probably cost $1,200 a year. Besides these costs there are other costs, exclusive of the driver, of $30 a day. A similar truck can be rented for $55 a day (without a driver). Interest is 10 percent. How many days a year will the truck have to be used in order to justify buying instead of renting one?

7. Using the data given on page 78 for proposals A and B, assume that because of annual wage increases and inflation the costs of operations will go up 4 percent a year. Using the discounted cash flow method, compare these proposals.

8. Suppose that proposal B on page 78 has an installed cost of $13,000 and that proposal A has a 12-year life (all other figures remain the same). What is the answer this time? Comparing this answer to the one in the book, should one say that this model is very sensitive to changes in the investment required or to changes in the expected life of the assets?

9. Suppose that we are doubtful about our estimates of the machines' salvage values (on page 78). What effect will it have on the calculations and the answer if, at the end of 8 years, all the machines prove to be worth ten percent of their original installed cost? Show the figures. From this analysis, how sensitive should we say this model is to changes in salvage values?

10. There are two proposals for making new products. Method A equipment costs $250,000, will last 10 years, and will have a salvage value of $25,000. Method B equipment costs $450,000, will last 15 years, and is expected to have a salvage value of $45,000. Each method should produce a $150,000 annual revenue.

Besides the original investment, method A will cost $90,000 a year. Method B has annual added costs of $60,000. The company wants to get 15 percent on this kind of project.

a) How big a rate of return will method A yield?
b) How big a rate of return will method B yield?
c) What rate of return will the extra investment in B yield?

11. Suppose that in the example of the Bayesian method on page 84 the probability figures are changed to *high sales*, .15; *near high*, .30; *moderate*, .45; and *low*, .10. What will the best decision be? How much extra will this action earn or lose as compared to the example in the text?

12. According to Bayesian analysis, which action will be best in the following case? An all-out cost reduction program will produce a gain of $500,000 if it is highly successful, $200,000 if it is moderately successful, or will lose $100,000 if it works out poorly. A less extensive program would produce $250,000 or $75,000, or lose $25,000. On a business-as-usual basis, the prospects are $100,000, $25,000, and 0. The chances of excellent results are .30, mediocre results, .55, and poor results, .15. Which action should be taken?

13. The ABC Company has developed a new product which it can either market itself or license other companies to make and sell. ABC's market research staff has estimated that there is a 30 percent chance that sales will be high, a 50 percent chance that they will be mediocre, and a 20 percent chance that they will be low.

If ABC installs its own facilities for making the item and does not license it out, ABC will earn $1 million if the product is received well, $300,000, if sales are mediocre, and will lose $250,000 if the product is poorly received. If ABC licenses it, the company stands to earn $500,000, $175,000, and $100,000 respectively, according to sales.

The prospective licensees are willing to sign contracts which allow ABC to buy back the patent rights for a penalty charge of $100,000. In this case ABC could wait to see how well the product sells and then decide whether to buy back its patents. If they do buy back the patent rights, 20 percent of the profit opportunities will already have been lost.

Use a decision tree-type analysis to determine what ABC should do.

Case 4–1

Companies A, B, and C each invested $100,000 in a project which would yield a post-tax profit of $10,000 each year. Each company used straight-line depreciation, which came to $10,000 a year. After 5 years these companies reviewed their performance and found that their expectations had been fully realized. Each had $50,000 in post-tax profits and $50,000 in cash returned from the investment via depreciation.

Business was good, so each of these three companies bought a second, identical machine. Inflation, however, made this machine cost $125,000, so its depreciation came to $12,500 per year. Post-tax profits were still expected to come to $10,000 a year, as in the case of the first machine. Again, business proved to be as good as was hoped. At the end of 10 years the profits from unit 1 were $100,000 and from unit 2, $50,000—for a total of $150,000. The net book value of unit 1 was 0, and $62,500 for unit 2.

At this point all of the companies considered buying a third machine, which now, because of inflation, would cost $175,000. So each paused to calculate the rate of return on the investment.

The company A controller figured that the company had invested $225,000 and that the profits for the past year were $20,000, a return of 8.9 percent. The company B controller figured that the book value for unit 1 was $10,000 at the beginning of the year and 0 at the end, an average of $5,000. For unit 2, the value at the start of the year was $75,000 and $62,500 at the end, or an average of $68,750. The 2 units combined had an average investment of $73,750, so the $20,000 return was 27 percent on the investment. The company C controller decided that replacement machines, which now cost $175,000, should be the basis of the calculation, so he divided $20,000 by $350,000 and got a 5.7 percent rate of return.

None of these companies did anything immediately. In fact, all three waited a year and then recalculated. In all three companies unit 1, though old and requiring $2,000 for repairs, did its usual work. But since there was no longer any depreciation on it, it showed an after-tax profit of $18,000. This, added to unit 2's profit, made the total $28,000. In company A the $28,000, when divided by $225,000, showed a 12.5 percent return. In B the $28,000 divided by the average investment of $56,250 produced a 50 percent return. In C the $28,000 divided by $350,000 showed an 8 percent return.

A therefore decided that a third machine would be a good investment and bought a third unit. B thought it was a wonderful investment and bought 2 more machines. C decided the risk was too great and did not buy a third machine.

Discuss the merits of each approach in the calculation of rate of return.

Case 4–2

The Daisy Company has asked for a review of its practice of making its own gunstocks (the part of the gun which fits against the shoulder) out of wood or whether it should buy gunstocks made out of plastic. Historically, all were made from wood and all were made by Daisy. In recent years, plastic gunstocks have become available at a price of $1 each and have been used in increasing number on low-price BB guns.

Daisy figured that it made a $.30 profit on each wooden gunstock it made and $.10 on each plastic gunstock it bought. The volume of purchased plastic gunstocks has grown to 1 million a year. It is expected that this volume will grow steadily to 2 million in 5 years and hold steady at that level for the next 5 years. This analysis is to concern only the next 10 years.

Daisy is considering several choices: (1) continuing the present practice and buying all plastic gunstocks, (2) continuing to buy for 5 years and then change to making, (3) buying enough plastic-making equipment to make 1 million gunstocks a year, (4) after 5 years expanding this plastics operation to an annual capacity of 2 million gunstocks.

Alternative 2 will require an investment at the end of 5 years of $3 million, which will have to be written off in the next 5 years. There is a 20 percent chance that operating costs will be $2 million in the first year and $600,000 per year for the last 4 years. There is an 80 percent chance that first-year operating costs will be $1.2 million, and $600,000 per year for the last 4 years.

Alternative 3 will require the immediate purchase of $2 million worth of equipment (which will be worthless at the end of 10 years). There is a 75 percent chance that the first year's operating costs will be $1.5 million, and $700,000 a year for the remaining 9 years. There is a 25 percent chance that operating costs will be $1.2 million the first year, and $600,000 a year for the remaining 9 years.

Alternative 4 will cost another $1 million at the start of the sixth year. Additional operating costs associated with operating the expanded operations have a 60 percent chance of being $700,000 a year for all 5 remaining years and a 40 percent chance of being $500,000 a year.

What should Daisy do? Why? What profits prospects do the various alternatives offer?

Case 4–3

The Flash Plating Company quoted prices to 4 different companies for new electroplating equipment. The installations were so nearly identical that the same kind of equipment would serve all 4 companies, so all were quoted the same price. All 4 companies accepted the bids, and the Flash Company put in the equipment.

A year later the sales manager was preparing some advertising material and wanted to quote rate of return figures from users of Flash equipment, so he wrote letters to these 4 customers asking them what rate of return they were getting.

Company A was quite satisfied and reported a 35 percent return. B was also satisfied, reporting that the equipment did the work well and yielded a 25 percent return on the investment. C and D also reported satisfactory performance, but they were getting rates of return of only 15 and 10 percent respectively.

The sales manager called in his own company's equipment analyst. "Carl," he said, "I want to use these rate of return figures in an advertisement, but they are so different that I don't know which figure I can safely use. Will you go over to these customers' plants and see why the figures are so different?"

Carl came back in a few days and reported to the sales manager. "I found out the trouble," he said. "These companies are doing the same kind of work, paying their men the same wages, and keeping the equipment busy about equally. The whole difference is in the equipment replaced. At company A our equipment replaced a 40-year-old installation which was very inefficient. At B, the old equipment was a 20-year-old Eclipse unit which never was any good. C and D took out our own 1960 model equipment, so neither one of them could show such big savings."

"I think that I understand," said the sales manager, "yet it doesn't seem right that the same equipment used under the same conditions could yield such different rates. Would you mind running through that once again? I don't quite understand what the method these companies used to use has to do with the rate our equipment is earning for them today. Maybe we should donate some old, very inefficient equipment to prospective customers. Then they will always get a high rate of return when they replace it with our new equipment."

How can 4 different rates be right? Should old, inefficient methods have any place in calculations of rate of return? If a new method is compared to an old way of doing something, why should the analyst limit himself to any particular inefficient way? Why not consider other ways even though they are not used? How should an analyst go about calculating the proper rate of return in the above situation?

Recent references

Brown, R. V., "Do Managers Find Decision Theory Useful?" *Harvard Business Review,* May–June 1970

Flinn, R. A., and E. Turban, "Decision Tree Analysis for Industrial Research," *Research Management,* May 1970

Henrici, Stanley B., "Eyeing the ROI," *Harvard Business Review,* May–June 1968

Horowitz, Ira, *An Introduction to Quantitative Business Analysis,* 2d ed., New York: McGraw-Hill, 1972

Moskowitz, Herbert, *A Dynamic and Parametric Linear Programming Approach for Analyzing Decision Tree in Normal Form,* Lafayette, Ind.: Institute for Research in the Behavioral, Economic, and Management Sciences, Purdue University, 1971

Newman, Joseph W., *Management Applications of Decision Theory,* New York: Harper & Row, 1971

Raiffa, Howard, *Decision Analysis,* Reading, Mass.: Addison-Wesley, 1968

Reitman, Julian, *Computer Simulation Applications,* New York: John Wiley, 1971

section three

Production facilities

EVERY KIND of production requires physical facilities in the form of buildings, machines, and equipment. These have to be so designed and arranged as to allow for the economical production of products and services.

These facilities should be located advantageously, considering the sources of the company's physical inputs, such as materials, labor, and other costs, and its outputs, considering freight costs and the location of markets. Chapter 5 considers locations and the interactions of the various factors which bear upon the proper location of an organization's production facilities.

Chapter 6 introduces the concept of capacity and relates the productive capacity provided to the capacity which future operations seem likely to call for. Methods for calculating the capacity of a production facility are discussed. So also is the matter of men's work hours and their probable output as it relates to the hours of work. The effect of the learning curve as it changes capacity is considered.

The buildings which house operations need to be so designed as to facilitate economical production. They need to provide for housing the facilities used directly to produce values and to keep these assets in operable condition. Chapter 7 deals with the kinds of buildings and their internal services. It also considers the whole subject of the maintenance of productive facilities. Here, too, are places where cost trade-offs need to be considered in order to arrive at the best balance between spending money for preventive maintenance as against spending less money for prevention while expecting somewhat higher costs from breakdowns.

The arrangement of production facilities within a factory to allow for economical production is the subject of Chapter 8. The merits of various layout patterns are presented. Methods for moving products from operation to operation are also considered.

Chapter 9 continues the study of arrangements of machines and equipment so that production will be facilitated and carried on in the most economical way. Chapter 9 also considers the nature of metal working operations. Then it turns to the possibility of using lines of machines, and then to the advantages and disadvantages of using lines of machines.

Chapter 10 continues the discussion of the overall designing of factory operations for economical production. This chapter is devoted to the designing of manual jobs along assembly lines—the kind of work we all associate with mass production. This is where large numbers of workers have adjacent work stations through which products pass from one to the next until the products emerge at the end of the line as finished products.

5

Location of facilities

CONTRARY to what we might intuitively think, a plant's exact location is not always of great importance. Nearly all giant companies have production facilities in many locations around the country and all are relatively equal in efficiency.

Yet there are differences, and there may be advantages or disadvantages because of location factors. It is even possible for negative factors to be critically important. Several years ago the National Seating and Dimension Company went to Varney, West Virginia, for low labor rates but went bankrupt trying to train coal miners to be good wood workers. And over the last half century, most New England textile companies which did not move South, where costs are less, went bankrupt. Most furniture companies, too, have had to move South in order to remain competitive. So although a plant's location is often not highly important, there are cases where it is very important.

Some locations are better, sometimes decidedly better, than other locations, yet good locations are not scarce. Otherwise, how can one explain the spreadout nature of American industry? Steel mills are found in Pennsylvania, Ohio, Indiana, Illinois, Alabama, California, and other states. There are shoe factories in Massachusetts, New York, Maryland, Ohio, Illinois, Wisconsin, Missouri, and California. Many other industries show similar dispersion.

FIGURE 5–1. Location of steel production facilities in the United States

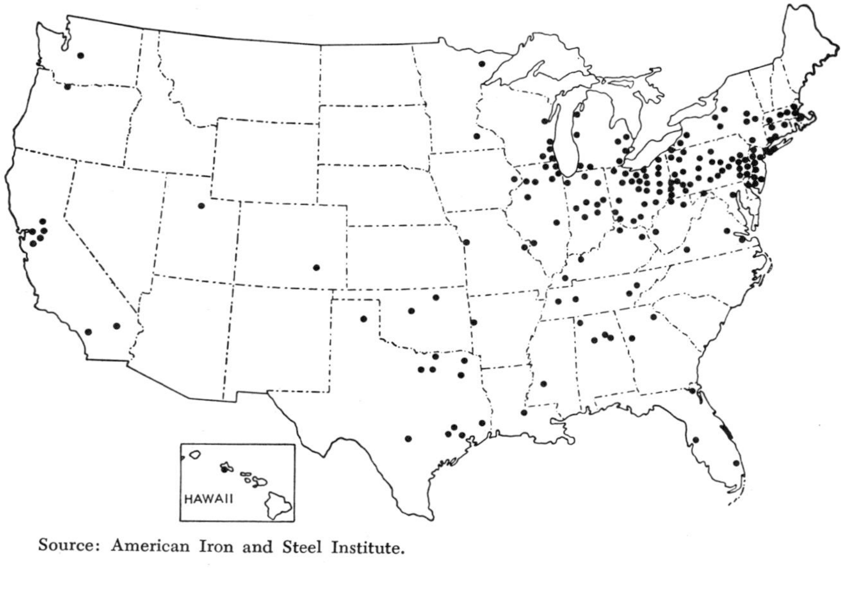

Source: American Iron and Steel Institute.

There are other examples. Years ago General Electric built its Appliance Park (for household appliance manufacture) at Louisville. Why Louisville, instead of Cincinnati, St. Louis, or Indianapolis? Many other companies have built plants in those cities. And years ago General Motors built its Electro-Motive Division (diesel-electric locomotives) at La-Grange, Illinois. Why? We could go further: Why autos in Detroit? Tires in Akron? Airplanes in Los Angeles? Eastman Kodak in Rochester? General Electric in Schenectady? National Cash Register in Dayton? In most of these cases the original choice to locate, many years ago, was pure happenstance.

Pitfalls in location choices. Companies sometimes make mistakes in choosing locations. One firm accepted a community's offer of a free site, then found that subsoil conditions were so bad that it had to spend several times a good site's cost on foundations. Another put up its building and then asked for a railroad siding, and found that it had to tear out a corner of its new building to make room for the spur because railroad tracks can't make sharp turns.

A third company turned down an in-town site at $15,000 an acre, bought outlying land at $3,000 an acre, then ran into two years of zoning problems and had to buy two extra lots for "protection," only to have sewer troubles. It finally cost $20,000 an acre, plus the delay.

A fourth company accepted a town's claims that glossed over a poor labor picture, and six months after it moved in it had labor trouble. A fifth firm bought 120 acres, then found too much subsurface water and couldn't use the site at all. A sixth company located where there was only one means of transportation—whose charges promptly went up because of the lack of competition. A seventh located in a nice industrial park, then found that it was 4 miles out of the free city pick-up and delivery zone. It is paying a penalty of more than $40,000 a year for this oversight. An eighth put up a $15 million paper mill but didn't buy much space for the disposal of waste chemicals. Now its 5-acre lake of waste liquid is filling up, and there is no more land for reservoirs.

Plant location specialists have no end of such stories. The common thread is that some one thing, overlooked, turned out to be seriously disadvantageous. Location choice is perhaps as much avoiding all seriously negative features as it is choosing the most positive factors.

Rarely does a company locate a new plant today without careful study. Every attempt is made to choose the best location and, in particular, avoid faux pas. When Chrysler was choosing a place to put a new $50 million assembly plant (which opened a few years ago in Belvidere, Illinois), it went through a computer analysis of 20 locations. Among the considerations were inbound and outbound freight rates; direct and indirect labor costs; the anticipated percentage of sales in each of 459 economic zones all over the United States for 3 years and 5 years hence, and other variables designed to yield a dollars-and-cents fix on such unknowns as freight backhauling versus overtime operation.

Location as an individualized matter

The examples just given of unfortunate location choices would have been unfortunate for any company. In total, such mistakes are probably few. Many more times, however, it is probable that a location is good or poor because of the circumstances and the way they relate to the particular company concerned.

A location is good or bad depending on how it fills the need of the particular company. A good location will be close to *this company's* customers and to *this company's* sources of supply. It needs to have transportation facilities and a labor supply of the kind needed by *this company*.

This is perhaps by far the biggest reason why companies choose such varied locations. *Their* needs differ, so it takes different locations to meet these different needs. So although the discussion in the remainder of this chapter is in general terms, each company needs its own optimum combination of factors. A good location is an individualized matter.

Ecology and environmental values

Manufacturing plants often produce waste in the form of polluted water, air, or solid wastes, and they are sometimes noisy. For the most part noise is within the plant, so its reduction is related to worker safety and not to community well-being.

Not many years ago, polluted air and water were accepted as facts of life about which nothing need be done, and indeed as things about which nothing *could* be done. But not today. Public sentiment, backed by federal and local laws, is putting pressure on managers to improve these conditions. (The ecology wave is not confined to the United States; Sweden, Japan, Russia, and many other countries also have antipollution laws.)

Federal law prohibits any company from dumping waste into navigable waterways without a permit, and such permits are now almost impossible to obtain. Companies which have been dumping effluents now have to clean up. The contaminants are of many kinds. A steel mill, for example, routinely flushes cyanides, phenols, sulfide, and ammonia into adjacent rivers. Electric power and many others plants return hot water to rivers (thermal pollution). There is apparently no good way to get rid of heat except by means of expensive and gigantic cooling towers. The law says that warm water discharged into a river may not raise the stream's temperature by more than 5°, or above 87° in any case. (The sun does better than 87° in many places.) Sometimes this water contains too much oxygen and is harmful to fish. Steel plants usually emit sooty smoke and sulfur dioxide fumes into the air.

The job of cleaning up is by no means easy, nor can it be done at low cost. Union Carbide, for example, spends $40 million a year trying to stop its air and water pollution in West Virginia. And even at this rate it will take several years to do the job well. Riegel Paper Company spends $10 million a year on cleaning up.

It has been estimated by the President's Council on Environmental

Quality that it will cost some $5 billion annually throughout the 1970s to reduce emissions and solid wastes to a satisfactory level. Some 20 percent of the cost will be required for air pollution control, 40 percent for water pollution control, and the other 40 percent for solid waste disposal. Industry will not have to pay all of this cost, however, since sewage, waste, and trash disposal are included in the figures and these are largely costs to local city governments.

Managers of some factories say—perhaps correctly—that the costliness of meeting all the antipollution standards is too great and that they will have to close down some operations. No doubt such statements are for the most part exaggerations, but nonetheless they will prove to be true in some cases.

If, in an individual case, it comes to relaxing the standards or closing down, some communities seem ready to let the factory close down and do without the industry and its jobs. More likely, however, the men who work and live there would rather have jobs and dirty air or water than clean air and water but no jobs.

Yet the choice may not be theirs to make. On the one hand, a company may decide to close down an old factory rather than even try to clean up. In such a case the desires of employees may not count since the company is obeying the law. Furthermore, some of the most stringent antipollution laws are state and federal laws. Individual communities may not have the power, even if they have the will, to relax the standards and allow their communities to tolerate the bad conditions.

Industry gets some tax relief in alleviating pollution situations. The costs of antipollution equipment receive special tax consideration (in both federal and state income taxes) in the form of faster write-offs and tax reductions so as to offset part of the expense. And local tax rates on the value of antipollution equipment are often very low or are eliminated altogether. And there may be one more offset to the cost. The recovered effluent itself, particularly from chemical plants, is worth enough to offset a quarter or more of the cost of staying clean.

Besides these positive incentives to clean up, a number of possibly punitive actions face polluters. Penalties that would deny government contracts to polluters seem likely to be enacted into law. Also, if managers of plants are held to be guilty of pollution, they can be held liable as individuals and fined or even jailed. And lastly there is a slight possibility that individuals will be allowed to sue polluters.

Because of all this, a consequential anti-ecology backlash is building up. Employees, and frequently their unions, are objecting to the severity of restraints which may result in their losing their jobs. Furthermore, some of the biggest problems are faced by city governments which have to contend with sewage and trash disposal. A great many communities just don't have the money to build the facilities needed to meet the state and federal standards.

Relocation

Several years ago PPG (formerly Pittsburgh Plate Glass Company) built a mile-long modern addition to its glass plant outside Cumberland, Maryland. It was built to use a new process which floated molten glass on a bed of molten tin, a process that was developed in England for producing plate glass at low costs. When the new plant came into production, the company's old Ford City, Pennsylvania, plant went on short hours. Essentially, PPG relocated its production and moved it from Ford City to Cumberland.

Whenever a company does anything about location, it relocates—because it has a plant which is already located. Its managers "live with" this location, reaping advantages if it is good and enduring disadvantages if it is bad. Probably the company's officials spend little time thinking about the matter.

But if business gets better and the company has to expand, its managers have to decide where to build the added facilities. Or if business gets worse, maybe the poor location is an important cause. There are also other reasons for moving. PPG would have liked to build its new glass factory at Ford City (it did not want to move) but the union at Ford City wouldn't allow this process there, hence the expansion at Cumberland.

Actually, plant relocations probably should be more common than they are. Many plants are in locations which get poorer every year, yet each year their managers put off moving. Sometimes they even expand production facilities in wrong locations because they are already there. They really have a relocation problem but they don't recognize it, or they don't have the courage to face the cost of building a new plant.

The community viewpoint

Most communities are anxious to attract industry because of the jobs and the money industry brings into the community. Besides this, the taxes industry pays helps lower the burden on individuals. Men need jobs, and communities without businesses are rarely prosperous. The United States Chamber of Commerce says that 100 new factory workers in a community will make 110 new households and will create 75 more jobs in the community in other lines. One hundred new factory workers in a community also mean nearly a million and a half dollars more in personal income and a million dollars more in bank deposits in the community.

In fact, so many communities want industry that even a minor objection by anyone in one community can be enough to cause a company to choose another community. Several years ago Columbus lost a new Ford Mercury factory to Lorain, Ohio, because a professor objected to the rezoning of a small part of the site.

On the other hand, most communities are quite demanding. They want industry, but they want it to be nondefense, odorless, noiseless, and underground. They want it to be staffed entirely with high-paid childless executives. It is not easy to satisfy all their demands.

Furthermore, in the 1970s the ecology and antipollution wave has dampened the enthusiasm for new industry in some areas. In 1970 residents of the small town of Congers, New York, picketed the site of a future $3 million Reynolds Metal Company plant. They were afraid it would pollute a nearby state park, and the plant went elsewhere. In 1970 the people of Beaufort, South Carolina, demonstrated against a proposed $100 million chemical plant to be built by BASF, a large German chemical company. They were afraid it would cause air and water pollution. This plant, too, was not built.

However, people are not united in such viewpoints. In 1971 the Sierra Club, the United Automobile Workers, and several other groups objected to the building of an atomic power plant in Midland, Michigan, whereupon 15,000 Midland citizens held a football-style rally supporting its construction.

In all three of these cases the unemployment rate was probably 5 to 6 percent at the time. Turning away new jobs is surely not what everyone wants.

Such opposition to new industry (and there have been other such cases) would never have occurred a decade earlier. But in recent years people have become so conscious of pollution of all kinds that this consciousness is often a major factor in plant location choices. It has been so strong, in fact, that pollution of any kind is unacceptable anywhere. Even if a company goes into remote rural areas, a new factory must plan to be clean in every way.

Communities as places to live. Over the years, companies planning new factories are also paying increasing attention to the nature of the community as a place to live. Employees, and company executives as well, probably do better work when the community is a pleasant place in which to live. Adequate schools are part of this picture. On the other hand, companies avoid many big-city suburbs if they are only residential because taxes will probably be high there.

Community domination

Most companies prefer not to put a plant anywhere where it would dominate the community. General Electric does not like to put a plant anywhere where it will hire more than one eighth of the people working in the area. GE has more than 100 factories, so this policy would rule out many locations where GE already is, including Schenectady. And these policies are in agreement with most community objectives; they too do not want single-company or single-industry domination. Another GE policy is not to locate a small plant in a big metropolitan area where its corporate voice would be muffled or lost.

Still another policy is not to put plants too close together. Ford Motor Company likes to have its plants 15 miles or more apart (although its Detroit plants are not that far apart). Westinghouse says 20 miles. These reasons are tied in with the above reasons, but a company also avoids having two of its plants drawing from and competing for the same labor pool.

Labor laws and relocation

When a company relocates and closes down its old plant it may have a legal obligation to offer jobs in the new location to employees in the closed-down plant. Laws and court decisions are ambiguous on this matter, but they are moving in the direction of giving employees in a plant that is being closed down a vested right in a similar job in the new plant.

Some companies forestall the question by spelling out in their labor contracts what, if any, obligation they have in case of plant relocations. Usually this means that they agree to offer either (1) employment in the new plant, and possibly some expense money for moving, or (2) substantial severance pay to employees who are not offered jobs in the new location. Retraining programs are also sometimes set up for severed employees. Also, employees near retirement age can retire early on liberal pensions.

If employees are given a chance to move with the relocation, the number of employees who accept drops off sharply with the distance of the move, and even more sharply if the new plant's pay rates will be less. Several years ago, when Armour closed its Sioux City, Iowa, meat packing plant (1,200 employees), it gave 3 months' notice and set up both an employment and retraining office. One hundred displaced workers who were more than 55 years old and had 20 years' service retired. Six hundred others took severance pay equal to about $125 per year of service. Only 400 asked to be transferred to Armour jobs elsewhere. And at an earlier plant closing at Fort Worth, Texas, only 155 out of 1,000 asked for transfers.

Labor

Wherever a company goes, it must have employees, so an ample supply of labor is essential. It helps if the available labor is already skilled, but for most companies this is not necessary. Most companies expect to train new employees because the jobs are so varied and so highly specialized. A company will never find very many new employees who already know how to do most of its jobs.

For regular factory or office jobs the work habits and attitudes of prospective workers are much more important than the skills they already have. Men in some areas are just better workers than men in some other areas. Absentee rates differ, and so does the willingness to work.

If a company moves to a new location, it may have to move a few of its skilled workers and some foremen, but it will recruit most of its new work force from the area of the new plant. If it moves to a lower wage area, this can make problems about what pay rate to use for the trans- ferred workers. If they are paid their old, high rate, they are out of line with the new workers. But if they are to get the local area rate, they take a pay cut, which of course they do not like.

A good new labor force cannot be recruited quickly. When a factory moves into a community, therefore, it will take time to build up a work force of good workers. Good men are not out looking for jobs in great numbers. At first every new factory has to get along with more than its share of marginal people: drifters and generally poor men. In fact, it may be well to plan to build up employment slowly in order to be choosy.

One should also pay attention to quantity and distance. The personnel planners for a new factory should not plan to hire more than 5 percent of the people in the area, or 20 percent of the eligible labor force. Nor should they plan to recruit beyond 20 miles from the new plant. If there are not enough men to fill the factory's needs within 20 miles, it will probably have trouble finding employees.

Freight costs

Freight costs don't amount to much for companies making small, high- value products such as watches or cameras. Their freight costs amount to only 1 or 2 percent of their total costs. So, as far as freight costs are concerned, it doesn't matter where they locate. But for larger, heavier products it matters more. In rare cases (cement, plaster, gypsum), freight costs are much higher. Johns-Manville and U.S. Gypsum spend close to 20 percent of their sales dollars for freight.

For most companies, freight cost differentials are not as important as wage differences. If wages in one location are noticeably lower than in another, it will pay to go there even if freight costs are a little higher.

So far as freight costs are concerned, a plant should be located where the sum total of freight costs is the least. But this is easy to say and hard to do. Companies buy thousands of different raw materials from suppliers in many locations. And they sell nationwide. It is hard to discover the center where freight cost is least. Besides, in 10 years' time suppliers will not all be where they are today, nor will a company's customers. So the rule to locate where freight costs are the least is not too helpful.

Freight costs can't be eliminated no matter where a factory is located. In one form or another, the product has to be hauled all the way from the raw material producer to the final user; thus a factory can be located anywhere between the raw material source and the market. Locating near raw materials reduces raw materials freight, but freight costs for delivering products go up. Locating near the market saves on finished products freight, but loses on raw materials freight. Being near the supply source, however, is not always important becaue vendors often "equalize" or absorb freight differences. They pay all freight costs above the cost from the customer's nearest competitive supplier. Sometimes they pay all the freight costs, in which case a company might as well locate its factory near its market.

Nearness to market

Being near the market lets a company give better service to customers and it saves on freight costs. Of these two advantages, giving better service is usually the more important.

But, as we have noted, a factory can't always be near its market—its whole market—because this market is too widespread. It may be nationwide. Large companies with nationwide markets put plants in many parts of the country. This way they get close to most markets.

Smaller companies must either give up the idea of being close to all their customers or must concentrate their selling in the area near their factory so that they can be close to their market. Small plants in New England serve the northeastern states; those on the West Coast serve the Pacific states. Most small plants are started close to the owner's home, and as they grow they develop their market nearby. Probably the location of a plant determines its market area more than the market area determines the plant location.

Nearness to raw materials

Being near its raw materials allows a company to get better service and to save on incoming freight. But—like being close to its market—this is not always possible. No one factory can be close to 5,000 suppliers. General Motors buys from 50,000 suppliers in at least 1,000 different locations. On the other hand, no matter where a factory is located it can probably find nearby suppliers for most of the things it buys, so every factory can be near many of its suppliers. General Motors' buying is so spread out partly because its own manufacturing is spread out. Its plants are near most of their suppliers.

Companies that use iron ore or other materials which make lots of waste often locate near their raw materials so they don't have to haul the heavy, bulky waste very far (at least not very far on land because the freight costs are so high). Similarly, where finished products are heavy, bulky, and of low value, freight costs limit the area the companies can serve. Cement plants, for example, mostly serve local areas and are found in many parts of the country.

Nearness to other plants and warehouses

Companies always try to place new plants where they will complement sister plants and warehouses. The best location for a factory therefore depends on where its other factories are. The location should fill a hole where the company has no factory and where its markets are now served by long-distance hauls.

The location of competitors' plants and warehouses also need to be considered. Each company tries to put its new facilities where they will have the advantage over competitors both in freight costs and fast customer service.

Water

Some companies need a great deal of water—more than there is in some places. U.S. Steel's Fairless Works uses 250 million gallons of water a day, and only a big river (the Delaware) could supply so much.

For industries that need lots of water, locations without plenty of water are out. Such industries include paper, sugar refining, steel, rubber, leather, chemical, rayon, food processing, and others. Making a ton of synthetic rubber requires 60,000 gallons of water, a ton of aluminum takes 300,000 gallons, a ton of rayon 200,000 gallons, and steel 40,000 gallons per ton. Water is used directly in the processes, or for cooling products or machines, or for condensing steam, or for washing, cleaning, quenching, and air-conditioning.

Companies that use lots of water need to be very sure that future supplies will be ample for their needs. This becomes a more critical factor in plant location year by year because the use of water is increasing so rapidly.

Factory-used water is often contaminated or hot after its use and needs to be decontaminated or cooled before it can be returned to rivers or lakes. Because nearly all cities and states have laws against dumping waste of a harmful nature into waterways, it is unlikely that any one location has much advantage over the other locations in this respect.

Land costs

Land costs and local taxes are sometimes deciding factors in factory location, although on the whole they are relatively unimportant. The total cost of a site, including taxes and landscaping, may be as little as

3 percent, and is usually less than 10 percent, of the total cost of a factory. Of this total, the land itself is often less than half. Since it is only a one-time cost, it usually figures but little in the choice of a location.

Local taxes

Local real estate and property taxes also are usually relatively un-important, and except where other considerations are nearly equal, neither should be the deciding factor in the choice of a location. Most manufacturing companies have investments in plant and equipment and inventory of $10,000 or more per employee. (General Electric's investment in plant and inventories is $8,500 per employee, National Cash Register's is $11,000, General Motors' is $15,000.)

Big cities usually have tax rates of from 2 to 6 percent of the value of property, so it would seem that taxes might be anywhere from $200 to $600 (or more) per year per employee. But rarely are taxes as high as, say, 6 percent because assets are almost never appraised at their full value (although legally, they are usually supposed to be appraised at full value). A company usually ends up paying perhaps 2 percent of its assets' real value. This comes to somewhere around $200 per employee, with differences between areas rarely being more than $100 per employee per year. This could be important, but taken by itself it is seldom a decisive factor, particularly since low tax rates often don't stay low.

This generalization, that taxes should count but little in location choice, does not always apply, however. U.S. Steel has investments in plant, equipment, and inventories of $24,000 per employee. DuPont's total plant, equipment, and inventory investment comes to $22,000 per employee. To them, even small tax rate differences are of consequence.

Communities that furnish free sites or even rent- and tax-free buildings to new companies for a period of years usually get new companies. Generally these "handouts" are for limited periods, after which a company pays regular rent and taxes (or even more to support free handouts for others). Companies should not allow temporary inducements to over-shadow the basic merits of alternative locations. If they do, they may find themselves located where, in the long run, overall costs are high.

Most big companies regard free handouts as a relatively minor factor. By no means, however, are they opposed to accepting such offers, and they frequently accept them. They do so, however, only where the other factors for alternative locations are just about equal.

Foreign locations

With domestic production costs going sky high and foreign markets expanding rapidly, many American companies are putting up plants abroad. Most of these are primarily to supply foreign markets. The movement is slowing down, however, because wages in almost every part of the world have gone up faster in recent years than in the United States.

The main attraction, of course, is low wage rates. Even Sweden's and West Germany's rates (and they are among the highest outside the United States) are not much over one half of U.S. rates. Other countries vary—all the way down to rates of a few cents an hour in underdeveloped countries.

In spite of the many difficulties in learning local customs and complying with local laws, and the tremendous distances, the wage savings overseas are so great that it is likely that most heavy-labor content items will be made abroad in the years ahead.

On the other hand, wage costs are not so low as they appear. In Italy, fringe benefit costs amounts to 75 percent extra, above and beyond employees' direct pay. In France the extras add 50 percent, and in West Germany 40 percent. And the continuing inflation of all costs, including wages, is greater in most other countries than in the United States. Overseas costs are catching up with ours.

Urban, suburban, and small-town locations

The rush away from the cities is still on so far as factory locations are concerned. Today there is hardly a small town that does not have one or two factories. But—and this is sometimes not appreciated—most manu- facturing is still done, and most new buildings are still being built, close to cities. Today's trend is to moderately small factories, so small towns with small labor pools are suitable. But new plants, large and small, are also being built on the outskirts of big cities.

Wage rates in small towns are usually a little lower than in cities, although not so much lower as they used to be. Even so, they are sometimes as much as one fifth lower. Often, too, labor relations are better in small towns since they are less influenced by other companies' troubles.

Small towns have some disadvantages, but most of them are minor. It takes a good while—possibly a year or two—to train unaccustomed new workers to get used to factory ways. Inventory investments are likely to be larger, particularly for spare parts for maintenance. And the company will need to have a fairly complete maintenance department because it cannot draw on outsiders. Fire insurance rates may be higher. Absenteeism during hunting season will be greater.

Many companies, wishing to leave congested city locations, go only as far as the suburbs, and not to rural locations. If they move to a nearby suburb they don't have to hire very many new employees. And in suburban locations a company gets most of the advantages of both city and country. Labor is plentiful and the plant is not far from the market provided by the city, which, in the case of small plants, is often its main market. Plenty of land for present and future needs is usually available at reasonable prices and taxes are generally a little lower than in cities.

Suburbs usually have better rail and truck connections than small towns—almost as good, in fact, as those of cities. Suburban plants are close to service industries. Located in a suburb, a company does not need to have so many of its own repair men—electricians, plumbers, and so on—as it would in a small town.

Organized industrial districts

Factories, stores, and houses don't mix very well; they ought to be in separate areas. Factories need railroads and superhighways, and they create truck traffic. Among other things, they need high-power electric lines. All these things are bad or undesirable in residential areas. Whole industrial districts—of factories and only factories—constitute a happy solution to the problem of mixed areas. To meet this need, some 2,000 industrial parks have been set up in the last 20 years.

The advantages of industrial parks include lower construction costs, because preliminary site work is done, and site preparation pitfalls are few because the land is already prepared. Financial and transportation services are close. The site is already favorably zoned, and it is in a prestige area where land values are likely to go up because of the controlled programs.

On the bad side is the small acreage available for expansion (usually 5 acres and rarely more than 25 acres). The factory also becomes part of a community and may have to submit to control of its architecture, design, and construction, or even to using a "suggested" contractor. It has close neighbors whose labor troubles may spill over and become one's own troubles too. Traffic flow in and out of the park and from and onto roads and highways may be congested during rush periods.

Space requirements. Inasmuch as the amount of floor space needed in a new plant varies a great deal between industries, a company's old operations will suggest how much space is needed. Here are some general guides: compact operations, not much extra space anywhere, and 200 square feet per worker (this includes all floor space, not just the space at a man's workplace). Ordinary manufacturing, with ample aisles and storage areas, needs perhaps 500 to 700 square feet per worker. Spread-out manufacturing might require up to 1,500 square feet per worker.

When a company is going into a project so big as building a new factory, it should also prepare for the future and choose a site with more space than it needs for the present. Westinghouse Electric uses a 5-to-1 or 50-acre rule, whichever is greater. It tries to get a site 5 times as big as its present-building floor space requirements, or at least 50 acres. Some companies use even a 10-to-1 ratio. Even if they end up not wanting all the land, they may want to control the land next to their new factory.

Otherwise it will soon be built up with hot-dog stands, bars, loan companies, gasoline stations, and small stores, which look bad and add to the traffic congestion.

Most companies acquire enough land to let them double their initial capacity. Actually, a 4-to-1 ratio will often provide enough land for this much expansion.

Sites

Choosing the area is the real job in selecting a location, but the site within the area must also be suitable. It must have, to some extent, all of the characteristics already discussed. Besides, it should be near a residential area where workers can live. And it should be near main streets or roads. Often land that has been zoned for industrial use is the poorest available; it is sited on an old dump, or it is swampy or subject to floods, or it is inaccessible.

Land for a site should be dry and able to carry the building's weight without much settling. The site must be zoned for industrial use, and it needs to have good police and fire protection.

If the factory's operations make smoke or fumes, it should choose a site so that the prevailing winds will carry them toward the open country—although a company may have to put in anti-airpollution equipment to stop smoke and fumes even in rural locations. If the plant's processes produce large quantities of waste which have to be carried away by water (common in chemical companies), the site must be next to a river or some other large body of water. And again, antipollution regulations also must be met.

The cost of alternative sites will be important only if there is a great difference in the prices and little difference in the merits. Besides the charge for the land, some sites will require more filling, grading, and expensive foundations, or more costly connections to utilities, than other locations.

It is desirable to have a railroad siding and a truck dock, and for some companies a dock for ships. Being near a superhighway is also very desirable and may be more important than being near a railroad. (Half of everything Ford buys comes in in trucks and half of Ford's finished cars leave by truck.)

There should be enough room for the present buildings, for future expansion, and for parking employees' automobiles. In size, the parking lot may approximate the total area of the plant itself.

Any company that is planning to build a new factory should not look only at communities that are aggressively going after new industry. Communities that are not actively seeking industries may have greater advantages than those which try to attract new plants. And both "active" and "passive" communities will often, if asked, make concessions equal to those offered by other places. Parke-Davis wanted to build a research facility in Ann Arbor, Michigan, on a site which would require new sewer construction, and when the company objected to bearing the nearly $100,000 charge, the city cut it to less than half. When Chicago Pneumatic Tool Company was thinking of moving from its Cleveland plant, Utica, New York, was its choice until the company found that New York tax laws were unfavorable. When Utica's city fathers went to Albany and in two days got the laws changed, Chicago Pneumatic found the new laws satisfactory and moved to Utica.

When the search for a new location gets down to picking the exact site, it is well to have either expert consultants or real estate brokers do the final investigating of good and bad points of different sites. Better yet, they should first get an option on the most likely site. The point is that the company needs to keep its identity secret. Any time a well-known company gets interested in a plot of ground and people find out about it, its price skyrockets. Options protect a company against price gouges.

The operations research transportation method[1]

The transportation operations research technique can be helpful in making factory and warehouse location decisions. When a company has

---

[1] Technically, transportation problems are special cases of linear programming problems (described on pages 457–62). They belong to the same family. Some books also describe an alternative method for solving transportation problems called the modified distribution method (MODI). This latter method is a little more complicated to work out, but on big problems usually gets to the best solution more quickly than the more usual method, the one we describe. (Vogel's approximation method (VAM) is another method for solving this type of problem. Both of these methods are described in operations research books.)

Stated in mathematical terms, the transportation method is as follows: There are m plants and n warehouses to which a given commodity is to be shipped. The ith plant has an amount, s_i, of the commodity $(i = 1, \ldots, m)$ and the requirements are such that the jth warehouse will get the amount r_j $(j = 1, \ldots, n)$. X_{ij} is the quantity of the commodity to be shipped from plant i to warehouse j. C_{ij} is the cost of shipping one unit of the commodity from plant i to warehouse j. The problem becomes:

$$\text{Minimize} \sum_{i=1}^{m} \sum_{j=1}^{n} c_{ij} x_{ij}$$

Subject to

$$(1) \quad \sum_{j=1}^{n} x_{ij} \leq s_i$$

$$(2) \quad \sum_{i=1}^{m} x_{ij} \geq r_j$$

$$(3) \quad x_{ij} \geq 0 \text{ for all } i,j$$

It is assumed also that $c_{ij} > 0$, $r_j > 0$, $s_i > 0$ and $\sum_j r_j \leq \sum_i s_i$.

several plants and several warehouses and is thinking either of putting
in added capacity in one place or another, or of reallocating the territories
served by each factory, this method can be used.

It is easier to understand the transportation method if we start with a
reallocation problem, where it must be determined which factories should
supply which warehouses and in what quantities. The assumption here is
that both factories and warehouses are already in existence. Later the
method can be switched to the question of whether or not to build new
facilities and where.

In its initial form, the transportation method assumes that each warehouse should be supplied from the nearest factory. There will be times,
however, when nearby plant capacities and nearby warehouse needs
don't match up and shipments have to be made from more distant plants.
The transportation method will show the most economical pairing up of
capacities and demands.

The transportation method is suitable both for small and large problems. A company such as H. J. Heinz, for example, might use it to control
tomato canning and the shipment of canned tomatoes. Heinz could find
out from which canning factory it should ship and to which of its many
warehouses, or from which of its many warehouses to customer companies.

The transportation method is a stepping-stone technique. It does not,
at first, produce the optimal answer. Rather, it first produces a feasible
answer and then improves it until the best solution is found. Often, transportation method problems consider only relative freight costs, but if
different factories produce at different costs, then the two (factory costs
and freight costs) can be added together to get relative delivered costs
for use in the problem.

To illustrate this we will assume that the ABC Company has 4 plants
and 5 warehouses and is concerned with only 1 product. Any plant can
ship to any warehouse, but the costs are different. The costs used in this
example include each factory's unit costs and the freight costs per unit
for shipping products to each warehouse. Plant capacities and warehouse
needs are shown in Figure 5–2.

When a problem of this kind is solved manually and without a com-

FIGURE 5–2

Plant	Capacity	Warehouse	Quantity needed
A.	200	1.	150
B.	100	2.	300
C.	400	3.	100
D.	400	4.	200
		5.	300
Total	1,100		1,050

puter (big problems would always go on a computer), the first step normally undertaken is to subtract the least cost figure ($20 in Figure 5–3) from every cost figure, thus producing Figure 5–4. This is not an

FIGURE 5–3

From plant	To warehouse				
	1	*2*	*3*	*4*	*5*
A	$22	$30	$25	$20	$24
B	20	29	21	25	20
C	24	30	24	24	24
D	23	28	24	22	23

essential step and is taken only to make the numbers small (so that the analyst can see the differences more readily) and to hold down the size of the numbers used in later manipulations.

FIGURE 5–4

From plant	To warehouse				
	1	*2*	*3*	*4*	*5*
A	2	10	5	0	4
B	0	9	1	5	0
C	4	10	4	4	4
D	3	8	4	2	3

Partial matrix A is then made up. The cost differences are put into little boxes in the upper right corner of each box in partial matrix A. A column to show the plant capacities is added at the right. Similarly, a row showing total warehouse needs is added at the bottom (the added column and row figures are sometimes called "rim conditions").

Partial matrix A also contains an added column for "warehouse 6" because of the fact that the 4 factories can supply more product units than are needed. Warehouse 6 is a make-believe warehouse, which would get the 50 units the 4 factories can produce but which are not needed. In the final allocation of orders to factories, one of the plants will not have to supply all the products it could. This will show up as an allocation of 50 units of its capacity to (imaginary) warehouse 6.

The solution of the problem begins by arbitrarily allocating warehouse needs to plants. Starting at the upper left, plant A is first assigned 150 units from warehouse 1. This is all that warehouse 1 needs. So the remaining 50 units of plant A's capacity go to warehouse 2. But warehouse 2 needs 300 units altogether. So plant B's capacity of 100 is also allocated to warehouse 2. Warehouse 2's remaining needs, then, are to be furnished

Partial matrix A

From plant	To warehouse						Supply
	1	*2*	*3*	*4*	*5*	*6*	*Supply*
A	2	10	5	0	4		200
B	0	9	1	5	0		100
C	4	10	4	4	4		400
D	3	8	4	2	3		400
Demand	150	300	100	200	300	50	1,100 Total

by plant C. This arbitarary allocation process goes on until everything needed is allocated.

This process is called the "northwest corner method" because it starts in the upper left corner (the northwest corner of a map). With this allocation, matrix A is complete. Demands and capacities are matched in a feasible way.

Matrix A

From plant	To warehouse						Supply
	1	*2*	*3*	*4*	*5*	*6*	*Supply*
A	2 / 150	10 / 50	5 / 0	0 / 0	4 / 0	0	200
B	0 / 0	9 / 100	1 / 0	5 / 0	0 / 0	0	100
C	4 / 0	10 / 150	4 / 100	4 / 150	4 / 0	0	400
D	3 / 0	8 / 0	4 / 0	2 / 50	3 / 300	50	400
Demand	150	300	100	200	300	50	1,100 Total

So far no attention has been paid to the costs of this allocation, so the next step is to multiply the cost differentials in each little corner box by the quantity allocated and then add them up. The calculation is $150 \times 2 + 50 \times 10 + 100 \times 9 + 150 \times 10 + 100 \times 4 + 150 \times 4 + 50 \times 2 + 300 \times 3 = 5,200$. This allocation therefore entails total costs of $5,200 in excess of the base $21,000, which would be the inescapable minimum if all allocations could have been made to the original $20 blocks.

It is obvious from looking at matrix A that some allocations have been made to high-cost blocks whereas lower-cost blocks are available. So the next step is to set about improving this first tentative allocation.

Looking first at plant A's allocations, can we see any shifts that can be made that would save costs? It costs zero excess to ship from plant A to warehouse 4, whereas this initial allocation of plant A's capacity to warehouses 1 and 2 entails excess costs of $2 and $10 respectively. Is it possible to ship warehouse 2's allocation of 50 units to warehouse 4 instead and save $10 excess costs per unit? Yes, this can be done by transferring either 50 units of plant C's warehouse 4 allocation to warehouse 2 or 50 units of plant D's warehouse 4 allocation to warehouse 2. Either transfer would, in itself, lose $6 per unit transferred, but the $10 savings from shifting plant A's allocation to warehouse 4 would result in a net savings of $4 for every unit so shifted. Accordingly, the 50 units from plant A are shifted to warehouse 4 and 50 units from plant C are shifted from warehouse 4 to warehouse 2.

Matrix B can now be made by incorporating these changes in the original allocations.

Matrix B

From plant	To warehouse						
	1	2	3	4	5	6	Supply
A	2 150	10 0	5 0	0 50	4 0	0	200
B	0 0	9 100	1 0	5 0	0 0	0	100
C	4 0	10 200	4 100	4 100	4 0	0	400
D	3 0	8 0	4 0	2 50	3 300	50	400
Demand	150	300	100	200	300	50	1,100 Total

Since 50 units were shifted, at a savings of $4 each, the total costs are reduced $200.

From here on, the procedure repeats. Are there any possible changes in matrix B allocations which would further reduce costs? Yes, if factory B's 100 units for warehouse 2 were instead sent to warehouse 5, there would be a $9 savings per unit. This can be done by shifting 100 of factory D's allocation to warehouse 2 at a loss of $5 per unit. There is a net gain of $4 per unit shifted.

There are other changes which will still further reduce the costs. The intermediate matrices are not shown, but in due time the final matrix emerges. This matrix reduces the total cost to $4,100 above the $21,000 inescapable minimum.

Final matrix

From plant	To warehouse						Supply
	1	2	3	4	5	6	
A	2 0	10 0	5 0	0 200	4 0	0	200
B	0 100	9 0	1 0	5 0	0 0	0	100
C	4 0	10 0	4 100	4 0	4 250	50	400
D	3 50	8 300	4 0	2 0	3 50	0	400
Demand	150	300	100	200	300	50	1,100 Total

This solution shows that plant C, with a capacity of 400 units, will actually ship only 350, and will either not produce the other 50 that it could produce or will put them in its own stock room for the time being.

Had the warehouses needed more than the factories could produce, we would have had to put in plant E, a make-believe factory, instead of imaginary v arehouse 6. Allocations of products to be shipped from plant E would actually be shortages and would tell us which warehouse would have to do without and how many units it would be short of its total needs.

Our example of how to use the transportation method has been confined to how best to use existing facilities. This same method can also be used to weigh the merits of expanding one plant as against another.

All that is necessary is to work out the problem as if the expanded capacity were already in existence and to use cost figures that are appropriate to what the actual costs would be.

The transportation method can also be used to weigh the merits of building a new factory versus not building but instead expanding some existing facility.

Finally, it can also compare building new factories in different locations. All that is necessary is to work through the calculations as if the new facilities were in existence and operating at their probable costs.

Review questions

1. How stringent are antipollution laws? Will they, in fact, cause companies to do anything which they would not otherwise do if there were no regulations?

2. What part do labor laws and union contracts play in factory relocation decisions?

3. Both nearness to good transportation and the availability of an adequate labor supply are almost always listed as musts in discussions about location. Yet if these are so important, how does it happen that industry is so spread out across the United States?

4. How important are local taxes in the choice of locations? How much do they come to in total?

5. What advantages should a company expect to gain if it locates in an industrial park? What bad features might there be?

6. What characteristics should an ideal site have? What should the relationship be between the size of the building and the size of the site?

7. When they build a new factory, many companies buy 50 acres or more of land. Why do they waste money buying so much land they don't need?

8. Could the operations research transportation method be used if demands exceed capacity? How? Could it be used to help decide whether or not to put up a new factory? How?

Discussion questions

1. How could a company go about picking a location which would be good over the years? Explain.

2. How can one location be much better than others if it takes a computer to figure out which one is better?

3. Each year *Factory* magazine surveys new plant construction in the United States; the results of its studies are reported in the May issue each year. As part of this activity the reporters ask company officials why they put their new factories where they did. There is no general agreement, and the most popular reasons given one year shift a bit from those of the year before. Why do experts differ so widely on the relative importance of location factors?

4. If a company moves to a lower wage area, should it offer its former wages to employees who are invited to move or should those who are invited to move be offered wages comparable to those in the area where the new operations will be located?

5. If a company happens to locate in an area where the labor attitude is poor, is there anything its managers can do about it?

6. How can location be so important if a college professor's objections are enough to cause a company to choose a location 150 miles away? (See page 104.)

7. Why the movement by industry out of big cities? Are there any losses in moving away from big cities?

8. If a small town gave a company a free site and tax exemption for 10 years, should the company accept? Discuss fully.

9. A small toy manufacturer, who sells nationally and is located in the Chicago area, is thinking of moving his plant to Fayetteville, Arkansas. Advise him and support your position.

10. A location consulting firm has produced the following analysis comparing 6 alternative locations for a company which will have 1,000 employees.

	A	B	C	D	E	F
Hourly cost of labor....	Low	Moderate	Very low	Moderate	High	High
Productivity of labor...	Moderate	Moderate	Moderate	Low	Moderate	Moderate
Freight cost..........	High	Moderate	High	Moderate	Moderate	Low
Labor supply.........	Adequate	Adequate	Plentiful	Plentiful	Adequate	Plentiful
Union activity........	Moderate	Active	Negligible	Active	Active	Significant
Living conditions......	Good	Very good	Rural	Very good	Excellent	Good

If the company were to choose on the basis of this evidence, which location should be chosen? Why? If more information is really needed, what information?

Problems

1. Minimize the shipping costs in the following situation. The numbers in the body of the table are the shipping costs per unit.

	To warehouse				
From factory	D	E	F	G	Factory production
A................	$9	$12	$5	$ 9	300
B................	8	8	6	12	400
C................	6	11	8	6	500
Warehouse needs.........	200	600	100	300	1,200

2. Suppose that in problem 1 (above) competition between trucks and railroads reduces shipment costs from plant C to $4, $8, $6, and $4 respectively. What is the solution to the problem?

3. Suppose that in problem 1 the factory costs were $25, $24, and $27 respectively for plants A, B, and C. Now what is the best solution?

4. The ABC Company has plants in Cleveland, Chicago, Houston, San Francisco, and Seattle. It ships product A from these plants to warehouses in Los Angeles, Denver, Omaha, St. Louis, and Atlanta. In the table below are given the freight costs per unit for shipping product A from each plant to each warehouse.

	Warehouse					
Plant	*Los Angeles*	*Denver*	*Omaha*	*St. Louis*	*Atlanta*	*Quantity available*
Cleveland..................	$14	$10	$9	$ 7	$ 7	800
Chicago....................	12	8	5	5	7	200
Houston...................	9	7	8	6	6	600
San Francisco..............	4	7	9	9	15	100
Seattle....................	8	9	9	10	16	400
Quantity needed...........	300	500	300	400	600	2,100

From which plant should products be shipped to each warehouse? What is the total freight bill?

5. If, in problem 4, ABC enlarged its Chicago factory so that it had a capacity of 500, how should the shipment pattern change? How much freight costs would ABC save? If these were weekly savings, how long would it take freight savings alone to pay for the Chicago factory's $5,000 expansion cost?

6. Sales have been increasing in areas distant from ABC's present plants in Chicago and New York, so the company is considering putting a third plant in Denver or Dallas. After study it has reduced the pertinent remaining data to the following:

	Distribution costs per unit				*Expected annual demand units*
	From existing plants		*From proposed plant*		
To warehouses	*Chicago*	*New York*	*Denver*	*Dallas*	
Washington..................	$ 1.62	$ .92	$ 2.71	$ 2.51	24,000
Atlanta......................	1.78	1.95	2.12	1.72	18,000
New Orleans.................	2.05	2.41	1.93	1.17	27,000
San Francisco................	3.22	4.69	1.67	2.14	17,000
Los Angeles..................	3.32	4.78	2.25	2.38	22,000
Plant capacity (units).........	40,000	45,000	25,000	25,000	
Production cost per unit........	$ 3.66	$ 3.79	$ 4.19	$ 4.13	

Where, on the basis of these figures, should ABC put the new plant, in Denver or Dallas?

7. A company has been considering building a second factory and has the following figures to look at. It now has only one plant, located in Cleveland. With heavy overtime, it is supplying 1.5 million units a year. But after the

new plant, which will have a capacity of 1 million units, comes on line, Cleveland's production rate will fall back to 1 million units a year.

Three alternative locations are being considered: Chicago, St. Louis, and San Francisco. Manufacturing costs will differ between these plants. Costs in Chicago will be the same as in Cleveland; costs in St. Louis will be $.05 per unit less, and costs in San Francisco will be $.20 per unit higher.

Transportation costs from these sources to the company's warehouses are as follows:

| | Freight costs per unit from | | | | Prospective |
To	Cleveland	Chicago	St. Louis	San Francisco	volume units
New York..............	$ .84	$1.03	$1.24	$3.60	400,000
Chicago...............	.63	.17	.47	2.61	500,000
New Orleans..........	1.17	1.09	.81	2.74	200,000
Denver...............	3.02	1.84	1.62	1.71	200,000
San Francisco.........	3.40	2.61	2.43	.22	400,000
Seattle...............	3.40	2.65	2.53	.65	300,000

Assuming that selling prices are the same all over the United States, and using the above figures, where should the company put its new plant? Show the supporting figures.

Case 5–1

The Costello Company, with 1,500 employees and located in Terre Haute, Indiana, makes hinges for all kinds of doors, from house doors to automobile doors. It also makes related hardware items such as door latches and catches. Business has been good and the company has to expand. Several members of the board of directors favor moving all automobile parts to a site near Detroit in Mt. Clemens, Michigan. Several key personnel men, however, don't want to move their families to or near a big city.

They propose, instead, moving to Jackson, Michigan—75 miles from Detroit. Labor rates would be 10 percent lower, but extra freight costs would offset half of this gain. Also favoring Jackson is relative freedom from labor troubles. Satisfactory sites and ample labor supplies are available both in Mt. Clemens and Jackson. Transportation is also satisfactory in both places.

What should be done? Why?

Case 5–2

A few years ago the Fisher Body Division of General Motors decided that it needed to put up a factory east of Chicago, west of Pittsburgh, and north of the Ohio River. This was to be Fisher's 10th and, at the time, largest factory.

Fisher picked Kalamazoo, Michigan—150 miles east of Chicago and 150 miles west of Detroit. At the time the head of Fisher said that Kalamazoo was picked because of "its progressive business climate. We took a good look at Kalamazoo and its people, and we liked what we saw."

What characteristics give a community a "progressive business climate"?

How might a mayor of a city go about helping to create a climate which will attract business? Could a company's management *create* a favorable attitude in its new employees? What makes a community appeal to a prospective employer so that he "likes what he sees"?

Case 5–3

In the past decade the movement out of big cities has extended to large-company home offices as well as factories. Literally hundreds of major companies have deserted the U.S. major cities for surrounding suburban areas. Among others, for example, American Can and U.S. Tobacco, have moved to Greenwich, Connecticut and Pepsico has moved to Purchase, New York, Olin Corporation to Stamford, Connecticut, and American Cyanamid to Wayne, New Jersey.

Yet all is not well, and now a different tune is often played. Working in suburbia is not all it was cracked up to be. Executives miss the excitement and stimulating contacts of the city. They complain about being company captives and smothering in a cocoon of paternalism in suburbia. "You get awfully tired of seeing those same faces every day and all day, and evenings too."

Once many large home offices move into a small town, it soon begins to develop big-city problems. Crime rates rise, 5 P.M. traffic jams develop, pollution often becomes a problem, and green trees and open spaces turn into parking spaces and big buildings. The local labor supply is frequently inadequate, and almost always the company has to hire almost a whole new office staff since its former staff people will neither commute to a distant new location nor will they sell their houses and move to the new location. Should they want to move, their problem is made worse by the high housing costs in nice suburbs.

The company officials too are somewhat isolated. They are not close to lawyers, bankers, accountants, consultants, and advertising agencies.

As a result of all these factors working together and at the same time, there has been a slowing of the exodus, and in fact a slight reversal of the outward movement. This has been stimulated by rising office rental rates in suburban locations and lower rates in the big cities.

Yet Caterpillar operates successfully in Peoria, Illinois. The same is true of Maytag in Newton, Iowa, and Kellogg in Battle Creek, Michigan.

Discuss the merits of being located "where the action is."

Case 5–4

According to *The Wall Street Journal* of May 18, 1972, the town of Blackwell, Oklahoma (1960 population: 9,600; 1970: 8,500), was torn between two factions. A plant belonging to the American Metal Climax Company had just announced that it was closing its old zinc smelter. This was a victory for the local forces that were fighting pollution, but it meant that 800 men, whose annual payroll came to $6 million, would lose their jobs. The antipollution group—35 people, members of 16 families, and mostly farmers—had filed suit to force the company to clean up the air. They also asked for $4.8 million ($300,000 per family) in damages.

The smelter was an old facility and was at best a marginal operation. So when confronted with the need to spend large amounts of money which would not make its operations more economical, the company decided against spending the money.

Fumes from the operation of the smelter were sometimes, apparently, a real problem to the farmers. It depended on the wind. Once in a while the fumes withered the farmers' alfalfa and the zinc that settled on the ground stunted the growth of wheat. In one case, in 1971, the company paid a farmer $12,500 in compensation for injury to his crop.

After the request for an injunction was filed to prohibit the company from polluting the air, the plaintiffs found that they had many fewer friends. Most of those with full- or part-time jobs at the smelter lost their jobs. The manager of the local IGA store said, concerning the closing of the smelter: "There won't be much town left."

Discuss this situation.

Recent references

Buggie, Frederick D., and Gurman, Richard, *Toward Effective and Equitable Pollution Control Regulation,* American Management Association, 1972

Carruth, E., "Big Move to Small Towns," *Fortune,* September 1971

Factory. Usually the May issue is devoted to new factory construction and location choices.

Fulton, Maurice, "New Factors in Plant Location," *Harvard Business Review,* May–June 1971

"Industrial Development and Plant Location." Reported annually in the October issue of *Business Management.*

Karaska, Gerald J., and Bramhall, D. F., *Locational Analysis for Manufacturing,* Cambridge, Mass.: M.I.T. Press, 1969

Khumawala, B. M., and Whybark, D. C., "A Comparison of Some Recent Warehouse Location Techniques," *Logistics Review,* July 1971

Lund, Herbert F., ed., *Industrial Pollution Handbook,* New York: McGraw-Hill, 1970

Plant Movement, Transfer, and Relocation Allowances, Washington, D.C.: U.S. Bureau of Labor Statistics, 1969

Speir, W. B., "Pollution and Plant Site Selection," *Factory,* July 1971

6

Capacity planning

WHEN FLORSHEIM builds a plant to produce shoes, it has some idea of the number of pairs of shoes the plant will turn out. When General Motors builds an automobile assembly plant, it has certain expectations concerning the number of cars the plant will produce. These plants are built to a size that will have certain "capacities."

The concept of capacity

The capacity of a factory is an ambiguous concept. It is not like the capacity of a milk bottle, which will hold one quart of milk and no more, under any circumstances.

Capacity is a *rate* of output, a quantity of output in a given *time,* and it is the highest quantity of output that is possible during that time. But there is more to the matter than this simple statement suggests. Capacity is a dynamic concept which is subject to being changed and managed. To some extent, it can be adjusted to meet the fluctuating rates needed to meet market demands.

The unit of output. One problem with the concept is the unit of output. A shoe factory turns out shoes, but shoes come in many varieties. A shoe factory can turn out more of some kinds and sizes of shoes than other kinds and sizes. So its capacity when expressed only in "pairs of shoes" is ambiguous.

In a one-product factory there would not be this ambiguity, but single-product factories are almost unknown. Even a Kellogg's corn flake factory turns out several kinds of breakfast cereals. Oil refineries turn out different kinds of gasolines and oils. Book printing companies turn out big books and little books and in various quantities. It is possible to express a refinery's capacity as so many barrels or gallons of oil or gasoline, and it is possible to express a book printer's capacity as so many books, but neither figure would be wholly accurate because the number would differ according to the mix of the kinds of products being made. The units of production are not homogeneous.

The matter of product mix is important when planning for the future. Sometimes, when a company's top administrators approve plans to spend money for added capacity, they express the new capacity only in terms of dollars' worth of sales. They leave it to the industrial and process engineers to develop a prospective product-mix breakdown. After doing this, these same engineers proceed to calculate the kind and number of machines needed to produce the stated dollar volume for the mix they anticipate.

Time. Time poses another problem. A man who is talking about capacity is talking about a quantity of output in a given time, but how much time? Some kinds of manufacturing processes require continuous operation. A steel mill must operate continuously, 24 hours a day, or not at all. When it it is not operating, the furnaces cool down (unless extra money is spent to keep them hot though idle) and they must be relined with new fire bricks at high cost. The only way a steel mill can change its scale of operation is to open up or close down furnaces. When talking about the capacity of a steel mill, a manager probably would be thinking about the total amount of steel it can turn out while operating all of its furnaces 24 hours a day, 7 days a week.

Most factory operations are not like this; instead, they operate from 8 to 5 daily, Monday through Friday. Their capacity is regarded as being their normal output in a 40-hour work week. But a 40-hour week is not their maximum capacity; it is just normal capacity. It is usually possible to work more hours a day or more days a week. Often it is also possible to put on a second or third shift and operate machines 24 hours a day. So in most cases the top capacity is a good bit more than the 40-hour output.

Effectiveness of operation.   The concept of capacity is also related to the productivity of workers. It assumes that men work and turn out products at an expected and consistent rate per hour. Ordinarily this rate is known from past operations and can be counted on. But if a plant goes on long hours, there will be a decline in hourly output because of fatigue unless the men are paced by machines. This will change the plant's hourly capacity.

Break-even charts and capacity

When a factory is operating at or below capacity, the relationships among costs, sales, and profits are as they are shown in the break-even charts in Figures 2–1 and 2–2 (pp. 22 and 23).

But there are times when demand exceeds capacity, so that managers have a problem. If such an excess demand appears to be temporary, probably they should try to expand their capacity and to meet the demand by working overtime in spite of the extra costs. Such a company's break-even chart would change from that shown in Figure 2–2 to that shown in Figure 6–1. So long as the new profit spread, "*A*" in Figure 6–1 exceeds the old "*B*" profits in Figure 6–1, this would be a paying action.

Should, however, the greater demand appear to be permanent, then perhaps the capacity should be genuinely expanded by adding more machines rather than just stretched by overtime. Such a change would result in a new break-even chart: Figure 6–2. The new, higher level of fixed costs would move the break-even point a little to the right (a higher volume would now be required). But since considerably higher volume is expected, the profit spread should be greater than before.

Even if today's beyond-normal-capacity demand is only seasonal, it may still pay to make the permanent additions to capacity indicated in Figure 6–2. This would be true, for example, if the extra amount of available profits, even though available for only part of a year, were greater than the reduction in profits during the rest of the year when operations return to the old capacity level. Whether or not such permanent capacity should be added can be calculated.

FIGURE 6–1

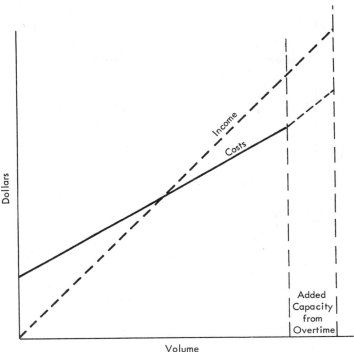

Let us say that:

Old profits at old capacity are P_o.

New profits at new capacity are P_n.

Profits with new capacity but at old capacity levels are P_r.

The fraction of the year when operations will be at new capacity are F_1.

The fraction of the year when operations will be at old capacity are F_2.

Then the new capacity should be installed any time that

$$(P_n \times F_1) + (P_r \times F_2) > P_o.$$

Possibly it would not often be wise, but still another choice is open to managers when demand exceeds capacity, and that is to raise prices and so hold volume down. Such an action would raise the income line but would decrease the volume and would lead to the situation shown on page 27 in Figure 2–5. Again, the proper decision would depend on the expected profits at the two different volume levels.

Capacity, inventories, and steady production

Capacity should never be considered by itself but rather as part of a bigger picture. Sometimes, for example, because of sales ups and downs,

FIGURE 6–2

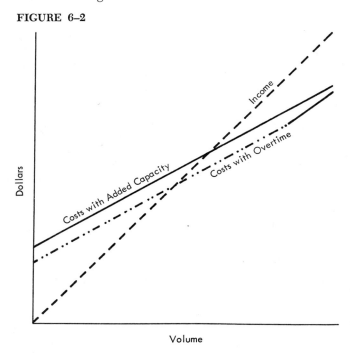

a company has to choose between increasing or decreasing its production levels or carrying inventories, both of which are costly. Christmas is a time of big sales in department stores, spring is a big period for automobiles, and bathing suits sell well in the summer. But sales dip a good bit in off seasons. Such ups and downs make it hard to run a factory efficiently, yet factory products have big seasonal fluctuations in sales.

If a factory's managers were to expand and contract production with sales, their plant's capacity would have to be big enough to take care of peak sales, but the plant would not work at top capacity very much of the time. Operating this way would almost surely be wasteful. Besides, it is impossible to keep an efficient work force with off-and-on employment. A factory's normal production capacity probably should be set at a point well below its peak needs.

Operating steadily is fine from the production point of view, but if sales are irregular, a factory is hard put to operate efficiently. Its managers could choose to produce at low volumes continually and pass up the extra sales during high sales periods. This would, however, be a costly solution to the problem because of the sales which would be lost. Steady production at a higher level would also be possible if inventories were built up during slack periods. But carrying inventories also costs a great deal of money.

In the case of automobiles, for example, the late fall and winter months are low months; then sales pick up. It would be very expensive for Chevrolet to make 50,000 extra cars in October, November, and December just to keep producing steadily. By the end of December it would have 150,000 extra cars on hand. Even at $1,500 each, $225 million would be needed to carry the inventory. By the first of April the inventory would be up to 300,000 cars and $450 million. Whole farms would be needed as parking lots for all of these cars, and some of them would surely be in bad condition by the time the last of them were sold in the summer.

Besides the staggering investments, there is a danger of a poor sales year. If car sales in the spring did not come up to what was expected, production would have to be cut back, and even then it would take months to clear the inventory. Such miscalculations can bankrupt companies. Stockpiling finished products is dangerous because no company knows for sure just what volume it will sell in the future.

There are, however, some things a company can do to regularize production. It can change its capacity by increasing or decreasing shop work hours. It can change its capacity by hiring extra men or laying men off as sales go up and down. And it can change its capacity by farming out extra work during peak periods and doing all the work itself in slack periods. It can also do a little stockpiling and try to stimulate sales in off seasons. Possibly, too, it can try to hold back some peak-season business, promising later delivery and hoping that business will not be lost.

No one of these measures can be carried far enough to take care of the whole problem by itself. A little of each, however, carried on at the same time, will allow for quite a bit of leveling out in production.

Before leaving the subject of conflicting pressures from trying to operate at economic capacity levels, it is well to note that idle plant capacity is a tremendous spur to trying to sell more. It might produce sufficient extra sales effort to generate enough sales to alleviate much of the problem.

Planning production levels

In order to adjust a factory's capacity up and down to respond to the demands of the market place, it is highly desirable to forecast sales expectations and to plan for the needed capacity changes. Otherwise changes are too likely to be sudden and drastic—if indeed such adjustments can be made economically at all.

Forecasting is particularly important where products are made to be stocked rather than to fill customers' orders already on hand. Almost all makers of products that are sold to final consumers make them to stock. Products are made for expected sale, but they are neither ordered nor sold until after they are made and put into finished goods stock. Here it is necessary to forecast, product by product and month by month, the sales of every important product and of groups and classes of minor products. This has to be done in order to tell the factory what to make and to check the future capacity demands against the capacity available. The problem is to foresee what and how many products the customers will buy, and customers are an unpredictable lot. This is a big area where computers have done a good job.

Aside from the unreliability of forecasts are the equally important irregularities of sales loads. It could easily be, for example, that a sales forecast shows that product A's sales for the next 3 months will probably be 15,000, 25,000, and 10,000. It would be most uneconomical to make the necessary capacity adjustments in order to jump production up and down like that. At 25,000, maybe the plant would be on a 10-hour, 6-day week. But at 10,000 it would be on short hours, would have some men laid off, and the plant would be half idle. Managers must try to operate more steadily than this.

Yet if operations are carried on more steadily, this will mean that there will be times when more products will be produced than are being sold, and inventories will build up. There will be other times when the reverse happens. Sales will exceed production, and if there are inventories, they will be drawn upon. Or if there are no inventories, sales will be lost.

This means that, besides forecasting sales peaks and valleys, it is necessary to decouple production and sales by building up inventories during low periods and then filling orders out of stock during peak periods. Inventories cushion the difference between productive capacities and market place demands. This is one place where optimizing one factor, in this case inventories, should not occur. Optimal inventories, considered by themselves, are small inventories. But holding down inventories neglects the total picture, and would sometimes be poor inventory control from the total operations viewpoint.

Forecasting.   Forecasting is sometimes done by a "top-down" method. In other cases the reverse, a "bottom-up" method, is used.

The top-down method starts with forecasts of general business conditions from economists in the government and large companies and universities. Such forecasts appear frequently in newspapers and magazines. The experts may say, for example, that next year's gross national product will be $1,000 billion. In a company making kitchen stoves, refrigerators, disposals, dishwashers, and the like the question then becomes: How will this affect us? The forecaster in the company must first translate this general forecast into terms of his industry's future business. Then he needs to estimate his company's share, and finally how many of each product are needed, and how many the company will be able to sell each month.

The bottom-up method starts with individual product expectations. How many of each product does it seem the company will sell next year? The forecaster gets estimates from salesmen and dealers. Finally, he adds up the different product forecasts and gets a total, which is the forecast.

Actually, most companies use both the top-down and the bottom-up method at the same time and combine the resulting projections into a single forecast. But before settling on a final forecast, they probably also use the "jury of executive opinion" idea. They adjust the numbers up or down according to what a company's top men think about the future.

Forecasting revisions.   Unfortunately, forecasting operates in a dynamic economy and is therefore never perfect. As weeks and months pass, actual sales figures become available, and they almost never follow forecasts perfectly. This introduces a new variable. How then, should the departures of sales from forecasts be interpreted? At first, departures of sales from forecasts result in inventories' being different from those planned. An important question is: Should such differences be continued? Or should production levels be changed instead? A new forecast is needed, and this new forecast may justify the making of new inventory plans and new production schedules.

To illustrate the problem, suppose that the forecast and sales of product A for the first 4 months of the year are as shown in Figure 6–3. It is now May 1.

FIGURE 6–3

	Sales		Inventory (end of month)	
Month	*Forecast*	*Actual*	*Forecast*	*Actual*
January..................	30	10	30	50
February...............	30	25	60	85
March..................	40	55	100	110
April...................	120	160	60	30
Total................	220	250		

The sales forecasters now have the problem of figuring out what to do next. How should they interpret the April sales running way over the forecast? Was there a strike at a competitor's plant? Did customers just buy earlier this year? If either of these things caused the sales upsurge, there may be no need to change production schedules because lower sales levels may lie ahead. Or have the forecasters underguessed the market? If this is the case, production schedules should be revised upward right away. Already the inventory is down 30,000 below the plan. The stock will be way behind if the top sales months still ahead also run ahead of the original forecast.

What to do is a factory capacity problem, a scheduling problem, and an inventory control problem. Up to now (through April) the schedulers let the first production schedule stand and let the inventory come out differently from the plan. Now, though, with sales catching fire and the best months still ahead, maybe production should be boosted to the limit (150,000) right away. Otherwise product A will soon be out of stock.

We won't decide the answer here, but this is one of the problems of controlling capacities, schedules, and inventories. To appreciate the problem, it should be remembered that it exists with every one of a company's many finished product lines. Also, its effects reach all the way back to raw materials stores. If production schedules are increased or are cut back, this upsets all the raw materials inventory plans, and even purchase order delivery schedules and supplier plant production schedules.

Capacity as a lower-limit constraint. The discussion so far has emphasized how a factory's lack of capacity sets top limits to production schedules. But a factory's capacity also serves as a lower-level constraint. During slow sales periods it is almost always desirable to produce more products than are currently being sold because it is so uneconomical to reduce capacity drastically when it is highly probable that sales will soon require more capacity.

Capacity as a limiting constraint to production schedules at the low end is different from the way it works at the upper end. At high levels it becomes a very positive limiting factor. No more can be produced. At the low end it is a managerial decision constraint. Physically, it is possible to stop production altogether, but this would be so uneconomical that managers impose a managerial decision constraint requiring a certain amount of production even when some of the production has to go into inventories.

Specific item forecasting

It is fine to make forecasts of general prosperity and then refine them for specific items or to find out from customers what they think people will buy. But neither of these methods helps much for the thousands of small items that some companies make. Consider, for example, the sales prospects at Singer for 6-inch scissors, or at Black and Decker for 1/4-inch drills, or at Eli Lilly for aspirin sold in 5-grain pills in 100-pill bottles. Neither top-down nor bottom-up forecasting tells the sales forecasters how many of these individual items will be sold next month. It is not practicable to spend much money making careful forecasts for each of the thousands of such items. Yet these companies have to manufacture these items, so they have to decide how many to make.

This is an area where computers have taken over a good bit of the work. And this is the area dealt with by books on statistical inventory control. It is a big area because in many companies it covers tens of thousands of items. If a programmer gives a computer rules to go by, it will make forecasts of sales for all of these items and it will tell the inventory controller when he needs to order new supplies and how many to order. How computers do this will be taken up in Chapter 25.

Overtime for expanding capacity

Although workers in the automobile industry almost always work short hours in the winter, in the spring they are almost always on overtime. Management plans it this way. Yet when we say that management plans it this way we do not mean that management wants the short hours. We mean that companies plan for overtime in the spring so they won't have to hire large numbers of extra men who would soon have to be laid off.

Planned overtime to meet seasonal peaks has many advantages. It boosts the men's pay and usually more than offsets the small checks of the short hours during seasonal lulls, so most of the men like it. It minimizes the need for hiring more men and laying them off later. Jumping employment up and down would result in poor production from new men and would boost unemployment taxes when the men were laid off. And often a company cannot find enough men to hire anyway.

Furthermore, in autos, steel, and many other industries full work crews are needed. It is not possible to get, say, 10 percent more output by adding 10 percent more men. Overtime for regular crews is the only way to get 10 percent more output. Also, much of the work is paced by conveyors; consequently, fatigue does not result in lower output, which would run up the labor costs.

Overtime is not, however, without its problems. One is that workers' income goes up and down because the overtime is not regular and continued. Another problem is the lowered production pace when the work is not done along fixed-speed conveyors. On page 143 we will go into the costs of products made on overtime going up because of lower productivity from fatigue. But if production drops off drastically, labor costs during overtime hours become prohibitive.

Important, too, is the crimp in a man's pay when overtime stops. A cut from a 50-hour week to a 40-hour week pares off 28 percent of a man's pay (from the equivalent of 55 hours' pay to 40). Men don't like 28 percent pay cuts, so if they have any notion that operations are going down to 40 hours, and if they are not machine paced, they may drag out their work. Then it may be necessary to keep on with the overtime just to get a normal 40 hours of work done. It may be a struggle to go back to 40 hours of production at the same time.

Overtime decisions are not wholly management's decisions; the men often have a voice in it, too. Today's labor contracts often give operators a right to refuse to work overtime unless they are told ahead of time and unless the whole department works extra hours. This has a curious effect on assembly line work. If there are several lines and it is decided on short notice to work one of them overtime, some of the men say no. Then the foreman has to recruit members from other work crews for the overtime hours on this line. The foreman ends up with a mixed crew of men, some of whom are on jobs strange to them. Yet production goes right along. One wonders if there is anything at all to the notion that men need training or that men need to be put on jobs that suit them.

Inventory and production planning

Inventories fit into all of this by cushioning the difference between irregular sales and steady production. Here is one company's procedure, and it is typical; we will call it the Jones Company. The Jones Company makes toys—mostly of the music box type which have rubber belts with molded-on bumps to play the tunes. The music boxes are put into all kinds of toys and play tunes when a handle is cranked. It is a highly seasonal business, with Christmas being the big selling peak. For the Jones Company this means an August and September production peak, as retail stores do most of their Christmas buying way ahead.

Jones's problem is not to lose sales in its peak period yet to level out production as much as it can without carrying large inventories. Also, it doesn't want to get caught with Mickey Mouse products after Mickey has had his day. (Most toys have only a one-year sale period; then they are dead.)

Jones first makes a sales forecast for an item month by month for 12 months—for example, a toy banjo (model A) with a crank-up music box inside. Figures 6–4 and 6–5 show its expected monthly sales and cumula-

FIGURE 6–4. Expected sales of model A toy banjo (in thousands)

Month	Sales	Accumulated sales	Production	Accumulated production	Inventory at end of month
January..............	30	30	60	60	30
February............	30	60	60	120	60
March...............	40	100	80	200	100
April................	120	220	80	280	60
May.................	80	300	120	400	100
June.................	60	360	150	550	190
July.................	140	500	150	700	200
August..............	300	800	150	850	50
September...........	250	1,050	150	1,000	−50
October.............	80	1,130	130	1,130	0
November...........	40	1,170	40	1,170	0
December...........	30	1,200	30	1,200	0

tive sales for a year. Figure 6–5 also shows a first attempt to project what the production levels should be. The 12 months' total comes to 1,200,000 toy banjos, but the peak sales month, August (with 300,000 expected sales), has 10 times the volume of the poorest months, December and January (with 30,000 expected sales per month). The thin line in Figure 6–5 is the expected sales line.

The production controller begins by taking the sales figures and trying to develop a reasonable production schedule. His proposed production schedule (the heavy line in Figure 6–5) is much flatter than the sales line. The top production of 150,000 banjos per month from June through September is only half of the August sales peak. From the factory's point of view, this is a big improvement over the extreme irregularities in the

FIGURE 6–5.   First attempt to develop a production schedule to make toy banjos so as to meet the following sales peak

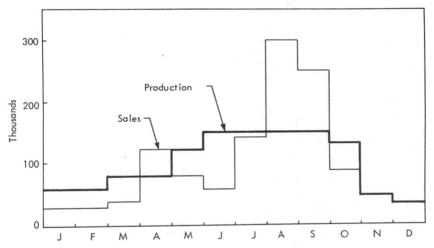

expected sales. It is not perfect, however, because peak production is still more than double normal off-season production. But even this much production leveling can be done only by building up inventories during the slack season.

Figure 6–6 shows Jones's forecasted inventory of the toy banjo. It shows that the inventory will reach a peak of 200,000 banjos at the end of July. Yet the average inventory for the whole year is only 75,000, or less than 3 weeks' average monthly sales.

Figure 6–6 shows a negative inventory at the end of September— although there can't really be a negative inventory. The minus figure just means that, for a week or so at the end of September, Jones will not be able to fill all of the expected orders off the shelf. Jones's managers hope it won't lose any sales if it gets those orders filled early in October. By then it will be caught up.

Our example uses only one item: model A banjos. But Jones has to do the same thing for all its main items, one by one. For lesser items, Jones will probably forecast for groups at a time—perhaps using only sales dollar figures. After making forecasts, production schedules, and inventory projections for the items separately, Jones will combine them into overall figures—probably just in dollars since it can't add Mickey Mouse water pistols to model A banjos. Here—in this chapter—we are concerned with the factory's capacity and how capacity can be adjusted to respond to sales needs.

FIGURE 6–6. Planned inventory levels needed to take care of sales needs while allowing the factory to produce on a somewhat more even basis

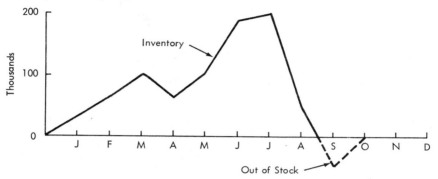

Manpower capacity. Manpower, as a resource, is not nearly such a fixed capacity resource as it might seem. Substantial adjustments can be made without having to resort either to hiring more men or laying men off.

Suppose, for example, that a company's proposed production schedule calls for men as follows:

> January.................. 300
> February................. 400
> March.................... 600
> April.................... 450
> May..................... 400

The manpower load in March is double that of January. Actually, however, the figures on the number of men needed are for "equivalent men." There is a need for the work that this number of men would do in a 40-hour week. But the hours per week can be changed, and so can the amount of work sent outside. And by doing a little stockpiling, some of the work from peak months can be transferred to earlier months. Here is a feasible plan for factory work hours to take care of the sales needs while holding the work force constant:

Month	Number of men	Hours a week	Equivalent men contracted outside
January.............	350	34	—
February............	350	46	—
March.............	350	58	92
April..............	350	51	—
May...............	350	46	—

Whether to go to overtime, or to vary the work force more, or to send out more work, or to build inventories are obviously managerial decisions. But in any case a factory's capacity, so far as manpower is concerned, is very susceptible to change by managerial action, yet without either hiring more men or laying men off.

Manpower planning has many more minor facets which need to be allowed for. First, all months are not alike, and may have as few as 20 and as many as 23 work days, so a given man-hour load is not the same man load in different months. Absences also figure in. It takes perhaps 105 men on the payroll to keep 100 men on the job, and it takes even more in the summer when men take vacations. Labor turnover may also need to be considered. There is always a loss in production when a man leaves and is replaced, so if there is a significant turnover it needs to be allowed for.

Indirect labor to support the work of direct workers needs to be planned just as much, and perhaps more, than direct labor. This is partly because some "indirect" men are technical men and are hard to find and partly because it is hard to know just how many indirect workers are needed. Most companies try to get an idea of how many indirect workers they need by using some kind of a ratio of indirect workers or to the factory's work load. They do not, however, continually raise and lower indirect employment in proportion to factory work load changes.

Individual machine capacity

The discussion so far has been about capacity in broad terms, but in the final analysis capacity comes down to individual machines. Whenever a work load calls for more than one machine can turn out, a company needs to have two or more machines. How many are needed is no problem when it is only a matter of adding one machine here or there in response to current needs.

But when a company tools up to make new models in large volumes, it may have to get whole lineups of machines. This requires calculating how many of each will be needed. To do this it is first necessary to figure each operation's cycle time. This calculation starts with the bare machining time required per unit of product; then the time it takes the operator to put a product into the machine and later to take it out is added in. Then some more time is added to cover the usual minor interruptions operators always have. The sum of these times yields the operation's complete average cycle time. Next, it is necessary to multiply the average cycle time by the quantity of product wanted in, say, one week and get the weekly load of work. And if this kind of machine is to be used for two or more operations or for other products, then all of their loads are combined to get the total weekly load.

Next there is need to consider the machines' probable "use ratio." In job-lot shops, machines are actually in operation only about half of the time (or less) because of setup time and sometimes lack of work. In line production, higher ratios prevail, sometimes up into the 90s. In any case, the final step is to divide the total machine work load by the number of hours a machine is likely to work in a week, and not by 40. If the machines are actually in operation only half the time, then the work load should be divided by 20, not by 40. This answer is the number of machines needed.

The accuracy of the estimated machine-use ratio is often quite important. Several years ago, when Ford built an automatic foundry to make engine blocks, no one knew just how it would work. It was set up to supply the expected needs while running at 80 percent utilization. But when it started up it ran at 40 percent and produced only half as many engine blocks as had been planned. It took months to raise the percentage. To make matters even worse, the sales forecast turned out to be too low. More engines were wanted than had been expected. All in all, the mistake was serious, but this is the kind of situation—where no one really knows just how things will work out—that companies face when they introduce whole sequences of new mechanical operations.

Capacity and the 40-hour week

A small plant, operated day and night, can turn out as much as a larger plant operating only one shift. So when a company plans its operations it can choose whether to put up a small plant and use it intensively or a larger plant and use it less intensively.

Most manufacturing companies can operate 8, 16, or 24 hours a day. A plant operating 8 hours a day needs to be nearly 3 times as large as one in 24-hour operation in order to produce the same daily output. Similarly, operations can be carried on for 5, 6, or 7 days a week. The fewer hours worked, the bigger the plant needed for a given output.

At first, operating a small plant long hours looks like the best arrangement because the overhead costs per unit of product are reduced. Most of the time, however, it costs less to operate a larger plant fewer hours. Common practice is to have a plant big enough to take care of normal needs when it operates 8 hours a day and 5 days a week.

Although single-shift production requires a bigger plant and more machines than 24-hours-a-day production, equipment depreciation costs per unit of product may, in the long run, be about the same either way. Three-shift operations permit 1 machine to produce almost as much as 3 machines would produce in 1 shift, but a machine that is used 24 hours a day lasts only about one third as long as a machine that is used 8 hours a day. Over the years, a company will have to buy about the same number of machines in either case.

Many overhead expenses, such as building depreciation, insurance, taxes, interest on investment, and obsolescence of machinery, are reduced when a small plant is used intensively. But three-shift operation has costly disadvantages which often more than offset the gains. Second- and third-shift employees get higher hourly pay rates (possibly as much as 5 percent extra). And unless they are paced by production lines, night-shift men are a little less productive than first-shift workers. Night shifts often have more new men than day shifts because most men like the day shift and use their seniority to transfer to first-shift work. There is also usually a little more turnover and more absenteeism among night-shift workers. Also, night-shift men often do too many things during the day and come to work tired, and so are less productive.

In any case, and as a consequence of all these factors, night-shift workers may be no more than 90 percent as efficient as day-shift men. Products made on the night shift are likely to cost at least 10 percent more than products made on the day shift.

Maintenance is also easier with 1-shift, 5-day operation than with 3-shift, 7-day operation. In the former case, most repairs can be done in off hours with no interference to production. Less intensive use of the plant also permits production to be expanded during peak periods with little increase in overhead costs because adequate plant capacity is already available.

Many companies use parts of their plants intensively (16 or 24 hours a day) and other parts extensively (8 hours a day) at the same time. They buy the smallest possible number of very expensive machines and operate them two or three shifts, while other machines work only the normal first shift.

Detroit's "big three," GM, Ford, and Chrysler, usually plan that their automobile assembly factories will operate at a normal maximum capacity when operating 53 hours a week (five 9-hour days plus one 8-hour day). They do not plan to use second shifts even during seasonal peaks because there are just too many problems and costs involved in hiring large numbers of people for short periods of time. And the auto companies have found that work weeks of more than 53 hours cause too much absenteeism. Men just don't show up for work.

Automobile companies do not, however, put in enough capacity to handle their *peak* needs in a 53-hour week. Rather, they set top capacity at 75 to 80 percent of their peak sales needs. This means they are not able to fill all orders quickly during sales peaks. During peak seasons, some customers have to wait. To avoid losing too many sales, the companies do a little stockpiling ahead of the peaks and try to get their dealers to do a little stockpiling as well. By setting capacity below their peak needs, they can operate at capacity a good bit of the time.

Yet everybody has seen automobile plants lighted up and operating at night, so there is obviously some second-shift operation. This, however, is usually confined to parts-making departments, where machines are costly. In such cases normal parts-making "capacity" is the output of 2 shifts. The capacity of 2-shift parts-making plants equals the 1-shift needs of the assembly plants.

Hours of work and operating efficiency. Long work weeks are fatiguing, and gains in output from long hours (except when machines pace the workers and except where the workers normally work at a leisurely pace) are not proportional to the extra hours because hourly output slides off. The output declines which normally result, coupled with extra overtime costs for working more than 40 hours a week, make long work weeks quite costly. (Often, however, there is no consequential output decline when long hours are first instituted; such declines set in later. It may take two weeks or more before output declines reach their lowest levels.)

No studies seem to have been made in recent years of the effects of long hours on productivity; however, scattered reports from industry support the results reported in two studies made several years ago.[1] This is what these studies found:

Hours per week	Hours, percent of 40	Percent of 40-hour production	Index of hourly production
40	100	100	100.0
48	120	117	97.5
56	140	121	86.4

These figures are of course only approximate and cannot be used as exact relationships. The actual decline in any specific case would depend on a great many things. The decline is worse on heavy work than on light work, worse for women than men, worse after weeks of overtime than at

---

[1] *Hours of Work and Output* (Bulletin No. 917) (Washington, D.C.: U.S. Department of Labor, Bureau of Labor Statistics), and "The Facts about Hours of Work and Output," *Factory Management and Maintenance* (February 1951).

first, worse on man-paced work than on machine-paced work, and worse when men are paid by the hour than when they are on piece work. Absenteeism and accidents also increase a little with continued long hours, and this adds to the costliness.

For men (according to the two studies), total output reaches its peak at about 56 hours (less on heavy jobs). Above 56 hours, the drop-off in hourly output from fatigue more than offsets the production in the added hours, so total production goes down. For women, somewhere around 52 hours is tops for total quantity.

For low labor costs per unit, a company should stick to 40 hours, and Figure 6–7 shows how very costly long hours can be. It shows that by going from 40 to 48 hours a week, total production (in a hypothetical case) might be expected to go from 4,000 units to 4,656; but because of overtime costs and slightly lowered hourly output, the unit costs for the extra units are much higher.

FIGURE 6–7

Hours per week	Production per hour	Total production in week	Labor cost: $5.00/hr. regular $7.50/hr. overtime	Average cost per unit	Extra production	Extra costs	Cost per unit for extra products
40	100	4,000	$200	$.050	0	0	0
48	97	4,656	260	.056	656	$ 60	$.091
56	86	4,816	320	.066	816	120	.147

The extra 656 units produced by going from 40 to 48 hours cost $.096 each (direct labor costs only), or nearly double the $.05 unit cost for production in a 40-hour week. And the extra 816 units produced by working 56 hours are obtained at a labor cost of $.147 each, nearly 3 times the labor cost of the units produced in 40-hour weeks.

It is small wonder that most companies work a 40-hour week, particularly in situations where labor costs are a big part of total costs. (Total labor costs, including fringe-item costs, however, go up a little less because several fringe-item costs are not increased by the extra hours a man works.)

This might change in the future. Unions are talking of shorter work weeks, but should they get down to 35 hours or fewer, a new problem arises. A man's regular job would leave him so much free time that he may become a "moonlighter" and take a second job in another company.[2] It has been estimated that some 4 million people already hold two jobs (but most of them work only 10 or 12 hours a week on their second jobs). A few moonlighters have two regular full-time jobs. During the last

---

[2] In Italy, where it is customary to give full pay to absentees, Fiat automobile company had trouble with "daylighting." The men did not go to their regular jobs, because they got paid anyway, and they worked at another job for "extra" pay.

decade moonlighting has become fairly common, yet it does not seem to be a fast-growing practice.

It is possible that working long hours today will not cause as much decline in productivity as was found in the older studies cited above. The pace of work in today's factories is less demanding than it used to be. Affluent workers, who can easily get jobs elsewhere, do not push themselves very hard. Absentee rates, for example, are double what they used to be, and even go to 10 and 12 percent on Mondays and Fridays. When this is so, the work pace during the regular 40 hours may be leisurely enough that long hours will not necessarily result in a large reduction in hourly output.

In fact it is now customary for factory departments to have a few extra "floater" employees to fill in for absentees. It is not unknown for such men to come to work and be kindly told to "get lost." They are not sent home, lest they quit, but on days of excellent attendance there is simply nothing for them to do.

The 4-day work week

Two surveys of the 4-day work week, made in 1971, reported that this idea, though it was getting considerable publicity, had not got very far.[3] Some evidence was found that small, nonunion service companies were trying out 4-day work weeks, usually in the form of four 10-hour days, with pay for 40 hours. One third of the reporting companies were considering going to a 4-day, 40-hour week.

Curiously, there seem to be more labor leaders who oppose than favor the 4-day, 40-hour week. Presumably their objection is to the lack of time-and-a-half pay for the ninth and tenth hours each day.

Points in favor of the short week are the extra day of leisure for workers and fewer trips to work. Against it is the fear on the part of managers that hourly output will slide off because of the long hours and thus increase unit costs.

So far there is little good evidence concerning such productivity and costs. All the reported cases of 4-day weeks were in small companies, and they were most often in service industries where productivity is hard to appraise and where the work pace is often not wearing. In the cases reported, absences went down and more than half of the companies reported that productivity went up a little. Meeting customer delivery schedules was, however, more difficult because business was conducted on only four days.

Should 4-day work weeks become common, both the matter of productivity and of scheduling work would become more important to manu-

---

[3] Kenneth E. Wheeler, Richard Gurman, and Dale Tornowieski, *The Four-Day Week* (New York: American Management Association, 1972), and a survey by the Bureau of National Affairs reported in *Factory* (April 1972), p. 9.

facturing companies. If the productivity per work hour were to decline, then the 10-hour days would reduce the factory's capacity.

Capacity balance

For companies that make varied products, the mix of products shifts all the time, and this places unequal demands on different machines and departments. Also, some machines are slower than others; consequently, some equipment will always be working full time while other equipment is sometimes idle. And some departments work overtime while others are on short hours.

Long-time trends cause part of the problem because yesterday's products often required machines which are not needed much today. At the same time, today's products call for heavy use of certain other machines. About all that can be done is to add more machines where today's demand consistently requires costly overtime work and where this demand seems likely to continue. Old machines—those no longer used—can be retired. By making such changes all the time, a reasonable balance of capacity for doing various kinds of work can be maintained.

It is also possible to work on the demand side. If some department is not busy, the salesmen can try harder for the kind of business which will use its machines. Or if departmental capacities are out of balance, jobs formerly sent out can be brought back. Similarly, work in overloaded departments can be sent out.

Bottleneck limitations. When machine capacities are out of balance with needs, it is the bottlenecks which hurt because they limit what can be done. Often a bottleneck can be loosened by "quick and dirty" improvisations which expand the capacity of bottleneck machines. They can be operated through the lunch period and they can be worked overtime. Normal overhauls can be postponed by running the machines until they stop. Often they can be speeded up and run as fast as they will go, even if this is hard on the machines and on tools. Two or three men, instead of one man, can be put on setups and repairs to speed them up.

The foreman can also try to get men who operate bottleneck machines to hold down their coffee breaks. And if a man has to be away from the machine during the day, the foreman can have someone else keep the machine running. Finally, it may be possible to supplement the bottleneck machine's capacity by doing some of the work on older, less efficient machines. Or perhaps part of the work can be sent out to the other companies.

Most of these improvisations are only expediencies, however, and they do not solve imbalances between operations permanently. And because individual machines' capacities differ and the work loads generated by sales keep shifting, there will always be a few bottleneck spots.

A plant's capacity is therefore limited by the capacity of its bottleneck operation. If this operation can be changed, this single change affects the capacity of the whole plant or department. It may even be economical to redesign the bottleneck machine so that it will run faster, or maybe a second machine of this kind should be bought.

The gain in total capacity, however, may not be equivalent to the improvement in the bottleneck operation. If the latter's capacity is increased by 25 percent, the increase in a department's capacity might come to, say, only 5 percent, because now some other operation becomes a bottleneck. Capacity expansion, therefore, becomes a matter of handling a succession of bottlenecks. To increase total capacity substantially, it is usually necessary to add machines for successive bottleneck operations.

The learning curve in defense work

The learning curve assumes that practice leads to improvement: men need fewer man-hours for producing a given quantity of work. Learning, with its reduced man-hour input implications, is always at work in manufacturing. More experience at making anything can always lead to more economical methods.

Airplane and electronics manufacturers have found that the learning curve operates when they make products in large numbers. Knowing about the curve and expected rates of improvement allows their managers to project the need for fewer man-hours per unit of product as well as lower costs per unit. All airplane and electronics makers therefore use the learning curve (on all government contracts, in fact, the government requires them to expect lower costs per unit as quantities mount) in estimating the cost of direct labor and in scheduling, manpower planning, budgeting, purchasing, and pricing.

Mostly these companies use an 80 percent curve, or something very close to it. An 80 percent curve means that every time the production quantity doubles, the average amount of direct labor for all units produced up to that point goes down to 80 percent of its former level. This is an average for all units and not just the direct labor hours put into the last unit. Thus if the first 10 units require an average of 100 direct labor man-hours per product, the first 20 units (including the first 10) will average 80 man-hours per unit of product. Airplane companies plot their figures on double-logarithmic graph paper, which makes the curve become a straight line.[4]

Learning curves in decision making. An example will illustrate how the learning curve can help in managerial decision making. The ABC Company has a contract for 1,000 units of product A. Labor is $5 an hour,

---

[4] The formula for the line is

$$\log Y = S \cdot X + \log C$$

where S is the slope, X is the number of units of product, and C is the direct labor and the contract was taken with the idea that the labor cost should average out at 10 hours or $50 per unit.

ABC has now been producing for 6 months on this contract and the president asks for a report. He wants to know (1) What is the average labor cost per unit for all of the products to date? (2) What did the last unit produced cost? (3) At what volume will the labor cost go down to $50 per unit? (4) Will the company make or lose money on the labor part of the contract? And how much? (5) What learning curve percentage is operating and what is its slope?

Here are the production records:

Month	Units produced	Direct labor man-hours
March	14	410
April	9	191
May	14	244
June	18	284
July	20	238
August	38	401

First it is necessary to figure the cumulative production, the cumulative man-hours, and the average man-hours per product.

Month	Total production to date	Total man-hours to date	Average man-hours per unit
March	14	410	29.3
April	23	601	26.1
May	37	845	22.8
June	55	1,129	20.5
July	75	1,367	18.2
August	113	1,768	15.6

The easiest way to get answers to the president's questions is to start by plotting the average man-hours per unit on a double-log chart, as is

---

man-hours required by the first product. Y is the average number of man-hours. The formula for the slope of the line is

$$\text{Slope} = \frac{\log \% - 2}{\log \text{ of } 2}.$$

For an 80 percent curve the formula becomes $\dfrac{\log 80 - 2}{\log 2}$

$$\frac{1.90309 - 2}{.30103}$$

$$-.322$$

The slope of the line is always minus since costs go down as volume goes up. To get the slope of any other percent than 80, the procedure is the same.

done in Figure 6–8. The horizontal scale is the accumulated production and the vertical scale is the average man-hours per unit. After plotting the points, the next thing is to draw a straight line that best fits the location of the dots. (Usually this can be drawn by inspection, but such a line could be calculated by the least squares method.) This line is the learning curve that is operating.

FIGURE 6–8

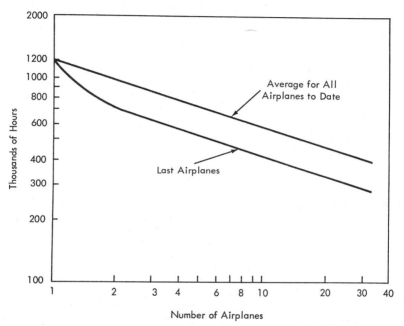

Number of Airplanes

Most of the president's questions can be answered by looking at this line of best fit. What is the average labor cost for all of the production to date? To answer this, it is not necessary to use the chart at all since the actual data are available and were used in calculating the average man-hours figures. As of the end of August the products have averaged 15.6 hours; so, up to now, the direct labor cost has averaged $78 per unit.

At what volume will the average labor cost go down to $50, or 10 hours? To answer this question, it is necessary to extend the line in Figure 6–8 to the right and read the quantity below the point where the curve crosses the 10-hours line. Although this is too fine a measure to read off such a small chart as Figure 6–9, the answer is actually 604 units. Will ABC make or lose money on the labor content of the contract? At 1,000 units, and at the rate it is improving, labor will be down to 8.65 hours, or $43.25 per unit. So ABC stands to make $6.75 per unit, or $6,750 in total, on the labor part of the contract. This is in addition to the profit originally expected and included in the price for each unit of product.

ABC's analysts were also asked for the slope of the line. To find this they should insert (in Figure 6–9) a point 0 anywhere below the curve. Then they should measure from point 0 horizontally to the right to where it intersects the learning curve line (in Figure 6–9 this measures 1.75 inches). Next they should measure vertically up to the curve (49 inches on Figure 6–9). The next step is to divide the vertical measurement by the horizontal measurement and thus get the slope of the line. In our example this slope proves to be −.28.

FIGURE 6–9

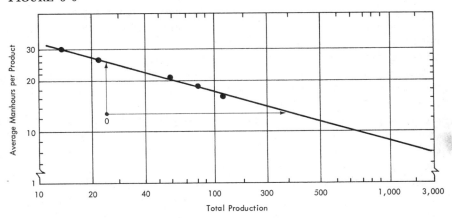

ABC's president also asked the percent at which the improvement curve is operating. The analysts can get this by doubling any quantity and reading off the gain. For example, at 20 units the curve shows 26.6 man-hours; at 40 it is 21.8 man-hours. Dividing 21.8 by 26.6 shows that doubling the quantity reduced the man-hours to 82 percent of their former level. So this is an 82 percent curve. Both the slope of the line and the curve's percent can also be calculated more accurately mathematically.

Still one other relationship can be established: the relationship between the cost of the last individual product and the average cost. This relationship is always the average cost multiplied by 1 minus the slope of the line. In this case it is 1 − .28 or .72. Since the average time of all units produced to date is 15.6 hours, the last individual unit uses .72 × 15.6 hours, or 11.23 hours of labor, which cost $56.15.

Learning curves in nondefense industries. Outside the airplane and electronics industries, learning curves are rarely used because of certain limitations. One weakness pertains to carryover knowledge, because new products usually are not wholly new. Even new airplanes are not wholly unlike earlier models. And each year's new automobiles are much like last year's. Even a new industry, such as television was in 1950, depended on electronic tubes and circuitry which were familiar to radio makers. When manufacturers turned to making TVs they already knew a good bit about how to make them. Such carryover knowledge makes it difficult to set a starting point for learning curve calculations.

Another limitation is that the curves are concerned only with manual work. Where machines are involved, an 80 percent curve calls for more improvement than can be realized, and it may be necessary to use an 85 or 90 percent curve. The problem is deciding, for the case at hand, what curve to expect—80? 85? 90? or what?

Still another problem is that curves somewhat exaggerate the savings. In order to achieve reductions in direct labor costs it is necessary to put industrial engineers, tool engineers, supervisors, and others to work trying to make improvements. But these men are indirect labor and their costs are not shown as offsets against the gains in direct labor costs.

Still one more difficulty is that companies that are not used to using the curve are likely to get wrong ideas about the expected savings unless they change the way they keep their cost records. To use the curve correctly, setup and preparatory costs incurred before the contract starts should be kept apart and excluded from the calculation. If these are charged to the contract and later incorporated into a cost calculation for the first units produced, the first units will appear to cost a great deal.

Similarly, all work hours should be charged to the products that get the benefit of the work. If some of the hours worked in March are put on units of products to be finished in April or May, these hours should not be charged to the products that were finished in March. Proper charging is easy for giant, complex products such as airplanes but is less feasible for stoves and refrigerators. If a company's regular cost records are not separated this way, it will have to change them so that they provide the proper data.

Review questions

1. Why is it so difficult to know the capacity of a production facility?
2. What helpful adjustments can production schedule planners make in order to bring the capacity needed to meet sales demands into reasonable balance?
3. Compare top-down, bottom-up, and the jury-of-executive-opinion methods of forecasting. Which should a manager use, and why?
4. Should sales forecasts be expressed in terms of money or of physical units? Why? If money, who translates them into units, and when? Is this more important in continuous production or in job-lot work? Why?
5. What has the problem of evaluating sales to do with inventory control? Explain.

6. Overtime is commonly used as a way of temporarily expanding capacity. How costly is it?

7. What is a reasonable machine-use ratio? Show how this ratio is important in determining capacity.

8. How much reduction in direct labor cost per unit should an airplane company expect if it produced 100 airplanes instead of 50 and if an 80 percent curve were in operation? Explain how this concept operates.

9. When the learning curve is used, what is the relationship between the direct labor cost required for the last individual unit and the average for all units to date? Is this relationship always the same?

10. If companies that make household appliances were to try to use the learning curve, what adjustments would they need to make in their accounting procedures? Why?

Discussion questions

1. The president of a company asks his analyst to make up an "index of capacity" for the plant. He wants the analyst to reduce the company's various products to some kind of common denominator so that he can compare the capacity requirements of schedules to the plant's capacity to produce. How should the analyst go about making some kind of a measure of "standard units" output which would serve this purpose?

2. The analyst has just reported to the general manager that his figures show that the company should not expand its capacity right now because this would mean idle capacity during future low periods. The president decides to expand anyway. He says that an idle plant is a tremendous spur to the sales department to get out and sell. Discuss.

3. If shorter work weeks boost hourly production and cut unit costs, why not work only 30 hours instead of 40? Discuss.

4. "It is illogical for the learning curve line to go down forever." Discuss.

Problems

1. A company with a capacity of 1,000 units a month has fixed costs of $2,000 a month and labor costs of $6 a unit. Materials costs are $2 per unit. The company has been producing at 80 percent of capacity and selling its product for $12. What is its net income? What would it be at 100 percent of capacity?

What would its net income be at 120 percent of capacity if it is assumed that 20 percent more products could be produced on overtime at an extra $3 labor cost per unit for all production above 100 percent? What would the net income be if production declines by 2 percent per hour because of the long hours? Should the company accept a contract which will call for 120 percent capacity for an extended period of time if the price is $12 and if the company could not otherwise operate at 100 percent of capacity?

2. The Home Appliance Company has been developing a new line of washing machines and expects to have them on the market by November. The company has installed enough capacity to make 4,500 units per month. First-year sales are expected to be:

January...................	4,000	July......................	5,500
February.................	3,500	August...................	7,500
March....................	2,500	September................	6,000
April.....................	2,000	October..................	4,500
May......................	3,500	November................	5,000
June.....................	4,500	December................	5,500
			54,000

a) The personnel director wants level and stable production throughout the year. If the plant were to produce steadily, what would the inventory level be at the end of each month? And what would inventory carrying charges be at $3 per machine on the quantity in inventory at the end of each month?

b) The treasurer is worried about inventory carrying costs and suggests considering an increase of capacity at a cost of $60 per unit of added capacity. If the personnel manager's viewpoint can be neglected and if production can be raised or lowered, should any new capacity be added? How much capacity? Show the new production schedule and the inventories in prospect at the end of each month. (For purposes of this calculation, any costs incurred because of changing production levels can be neglected.)

3. The forecast of sales during the first 4 months of the year for product A was 22,000, 18,000, 35,000, and 50,000. Actual sales have been 16,000, 19,000, 41,000, and 61,000. This leaves the April month-end inventory 12,000 under the expected figure, although there are still 30,000 units in inventory.

Production has been at the rate of 40,000 per month for several months, and can go as high as 60,000. The earlier sales forecasts anticipated sales of 70,000 per month for May through September.

What schedule changes should be made right now, if any. Why? Make a forecast of sales, production, and inventories at each month-end for the next 5 months.

4. There are 5 products to be made on 6 types of equipment. The table below shows the operating times (in decimal hours) and the job setup times for each operation. In each block there are 2 times: the upper number is the job setup time and the lower number is the operating time per unit.

Omitting a consideration of machine-use rates, how many of each kind of machine will be needed if the plant works a 40-hour week?

Equipment	*Job number*				
	1	2	3	4	5
Mult-Au-Matic	.670		.761		.073
	.036		.078		.097
Vertical mill		.543	.790		.870
		.097	.102		.105
Turret lathe		.732			.839
		.019			.021
Forging machine	.521	.434			.768
	.017	.049			.057
Centerless			.087	.161	
grinder			.036	.016	
Simplex mill	.617	.614	.911	.658	
	.053	.073	.081	.077	
Quantity needed per month	700	2,300	1,400	100	300
Manufacturing lot size	300	200	500	200	400

5. The production schedule for a certain part calls for manufacturing 1,500 units per week. While there is some fluctuation in this requirement, the fluctuation is very small. Production of the part calls for 5 operations performed on 5 different machines. The time requirements for each of these operations are as follows:

Machine	Time per unit (hours)	Machine-use ratio	Operator efficiency
1.........................	.045	.84	110
2.........................	.101	.77	130
3.........................	.089	.91	90
4.........................	.049	.69	105
5.........................	.050	.81	130

Calculate the number of machines required for these operations if the plant works 40 hours a week. (See Chapter 15 for a discussion of operator efficiency.) If you feel that more information is needed before it is possible to decide how many machines will be needed, what information is lacking?

6. Machines A, B, and C characteristically lose .3, .7, and .2 hours each day for maintenance. Besides, frequent rush orders have in the past taken up

.5 hours each on these machines. In planning work it is necessary to allow for such orders. The department works 8 hours a day. Operators on these machines are usually 110, 135, and 120 percent efficient respectively.

How many hours will it take for an order to be produced which calls for 20, 15, and 25 standard hours of work on each machine, respectively?

7. In the following example, should 1 machine be bought and operated 24 hours a day or should 3 machines be bought and operated 8 hours? The machines cost $100,000 each and have a normal life of 10 years with no salvage value. Interest on investment is figured at 20 percent a year.

Twenty-four-hour operation is really only 21 hours because of lunch periods and the loss of production at shift changes. But it is necessary to pay for 24 hours of operator time. First-shift operators get $5, second-shift operators $5.20, and third-shift operators $5.25 per hour. Production on the second and third shifts is only 98 percent of the first shift.

With regular 1-shift production the company does not pay for lunch periods, and it gets 8 hours' work for 8 hours' pay. Since the plan is to work only 5 days a week, there is plenty of time in either arrangement for major repairs, so this matter need not be considered.

8. What would the answer be in the problem above if the machines cost $25,000, would last 10 years (with no salvage value), and required operators at $4.50 on the first shift and $4.80 on the second and third shifts, with both second- and third-shift men being only 90 percent as efficient as the first-shift men?

9. It is required to make 3,000 units a month of a part which requires grinding machine time. The standard time for this operation is .17 hours per unit.

a) How many machines will be needed if they work 8 hours a day for 20 days a month at 100 percent efficiency and there were no scrap losses or lost machine time?

b) What is the answer if the company gets only 80 percent machine utilization from the machines and the operators are 105 percent efficient?

c) How many items should be started into production if the scrap rate is .07? And how many machines (using the production expectations arrived at in [b]) will be needed?

10. The up-to-date figures on the ABC Company's contract for making 500 small airplanes show the following:

Number of airplanes	Direct man-hours per pound
10	21.0
15	19.5
25	18.9
35	16.2
50	15.8
100	15.3
150	14.3
200	13.9
250	13.2
350	12.3
450	11.9

The contract price anticipates that the average direct labor man-hours per pound will be down to 10.5 by the time the contract ends.

a) Will the average be down to 10.5 at the end of the contract?

b) Suppose the contract includes an expected $5 per man-hour cost (the airplanes weigh 3 tons each), $300,000 for materials and bought components, $400,000 overhead, and 8 percent on all costs for profit. What is the price per airplane?

c) What is the cost of the last airplane?

d) At the rate things are going, how much profit will the company make or lose on this contract?

e) Negotiations are being started for a second contract for 100 more of these airplanes. What should the new price be if all arrangements are carried over from the first contract but the achievements to date of the learning curve are recognized?

11. We are working on a contract for 10,000 units of product and are now looking at the following record. The remaining units are to be made in equal quantities in the next 4 months.

Period	Man-hours	Finished units
January.	2,583	366
February.	2,384	290
March.	2,710	892
April.	2,718	920
May.	2,797	865
June.	2,248	770
July.	2,166	937

a) How many man-hours will this contract require, month by month, until we finish the contract?

b) Our price is based on an average labor content (for the whole 10,000 units) of 3 hours per unit. Figuring labor at $5 an hour, how will we do on this part of the contract? Will we make or lose money on the labor part of our estimate, and how much?

c) At what volume will labor get down to 3 hours per unit?

d) What is the slope of this learning curve?

e) Our selling price of $30 includes a prospective profit of $2 per unit. When was it or when will it be reached? When did we or when will we start to make profits on labor, having recovered all the out-of-pocket losses?

f) In bidding for another contract for 10,000 more units of this product, what labor cost should we estimate, assuming that we could continue on with the new quantity without any interruption to production?

Case 6–1

The production manager of the ABC Company was considering the unusually large backlog of orders with early promise dates. Quite a few of the company's best customers were wanting quick delivery.

Just then he got a call from the sales manager about one of these orders. The sales department had promised delivery last Friday, but because of the factory's heavy load it had not been shipped—and was, in fact, not finished on Tuesday, when the sales manager made his call.

"I thought that order went out days ago. I promised that we would get it to them by last Friday. What is happening? What can I tell them now? Tomorrow for sure?"

"Wait until I check on today's reports. According to my reports, that order won't get shipped until Friday of this week. We've got a 'rush' tag on it, but everything that has to go through the gear hobbing machines is rush, so a good many orders are going to get behind. And you want all of those other orders, too, don't you?"

"Yes, we do; it has taken us a long time to land two or three of those new orders and it is very important for us to give good service if we are to get any more orders from them. And we can't let our regular customers down either; they depend on us. I think you ought to be working overtime."

"Well, I asked about that for last Saturday and the superintendent turned me down. He said no—that you had to bid pretty low to get most of those jobs and the price just won't stand the added cost of overtime work. I'll ask him again, and maybe you ought to call him too. If he still says no, then maybe we can send a few jobs out to other shops. That would help the schedule, but we don't make much money sending work out."

"OK, but how about giving me a call tomorrow morning so I can tell the customer something? And something he can rely on, too."

Almost immediately, another call came through to the production manager— from the general manager. He, too, wanted to know about one of the late orders because he had had a call about it from the customer company's president.

Discuss this case.

Recent references

Baloff, N., "Extension of the Learning Curve—Some Empirical Results," *Operations Research Quarterly*, December 1971

Burack, Elmer H., *Manpower Planning and Programming*, Boston: Allyn & Bacon, 1972

Ehrenberg, Ronald G., "Absenteeism and the Overtime Decision," *American Economic Review*, June 1970

Morcrombe, V. J., "Straightening Out Learning Curves," *Personnel Management*, June 1970

Poor, Riva, *4 Days, 40 Hours*, Bursk & Poor, 1970

Thomopoulos, N. T., "The Mixed Model Learning Curve," *American Institute of Industrial Engineers Transactions*, June 1969

Wheeler, Kenneth E., Richard Gurman, and Dale Tarnowieski, *The Four-Day Week*, New York: American Management Association, 1972

7

Facilities provision and maintenance

THE MANAGEMENT of production includes providing and maintaining the buildings and services needed to house and serve the men and machines used to make products. Most of the time buildings and services are probably regarded as merely being present and not needing managerial effort. Yet they constitute part of the productive asset base of every manufacturing company and require a great deal of managerial input when they are constructed. And they continue to call for a considerable amount of ongoing managerial attention to keep them operating so that they contribute to effective operations.

The main job of factory buildings is to house the manufacturing operations. But they must also house a multitude of supporting services, which may take up to half of the total space.

There need to be aisles, elevators, stairways, offices, a cafeteria, a dispensary, stock rooms, tool rooms, dispatching stations, timecard racks, locker rooms, washrooms, and toilets. There is need for telephones, intercom systems, computer data input and print-out stations, electricity of various voltages, hot and cold purified water, unpurified water for processes, compressed air, high- and low-pressure steam, natural gas, lights, heat, ventilation, and probably air-conditioning. Some of these services need wires, pipes, or ducts. Out of doors there is need for shipping and receiving docks for both rail cars and trucks. Also needed are a parking lot for cars and storage space for coal or other materials. This list is long.

Factory services are much like services in a house—no one thinks much about them so long as they work well. But let them be poorly arranged, or get out of order, and they become very important. Factory buildings and their services are sometimes so poorly arranged as to interfere with efficient operations. High buildings with several floors, or weak floors, low ceilings, columns too close, elevators off in corners, and so on all interfere with efficient production and boost material handling costs.

Factories should be flexible and easily adaptable to changes in operations. Built-in flexibility is the best way to make changes easily. Some things which help are: (1) wide bays (open areas between rows of posts or walls); (2) ceilings high enough for overhead conveyors, or mezzanines, whether they are needed now or not; (3) space (or put-in wires) for high-voltage electricity for areas that do not need it today; (4) heavy duty floors; and possibly (5) machines (in some areas) on easily detachable mounts so that departments can easily expand.

Types of buildings

Single-story buildings. Single-story buildings are the most common kind today. They can be as wide or long as needed and can easily be expanded. Single-story buildings have no stairs, elevators, elevator wells, or ramps to connect floors. There are not many posts to interfere with overhead cranes or to cut off light. It is easy and inexpensive to move materials from job to job because all the moving is horizontal, not up and down. Heavy equipment can be put on separate foundations.

There are some bad features, though. Single-story buildings require a good bit of ground space. Also, if there is a flat roof and no glass skylights, it is necessary to use artificial light all the time in most of the plant. Besides, a forced ventilation or air conditioning system will be required.

Architecture and styling. There has been a trend for some time now toward campus-type layouts. Characterized by well-kept lawns, patios, and even pools, and by several buildings rather than one, campus-type factories have a pleasant, leisurely feel. However, campus-type factories need ample ground space and they are expensive to build. This kind of plant is best suited for light, highly engineered products. And they are more suitable in warm, dry climates, although there are several such plants in other parts of the country. There is also a trend, even in non-campus-type factories, toward putting in interior patios, and often with a pool that is surrounded by outdoor lounging areas for use during lunch time and coffee breaks.

Prefabs of one sort or another continue to be popular. Sometimes a prefab is a whole prefabricated steel building and sometimes only interior components, as when movable office partitions have been prefabricated. They can be designed as modular units that can be put together in varied ways to give variety in shape and form. The units are made to blend well with masonry, brick, and glass. The metal panels of prefabs come prepainted in various colors, so there can be attractive combinations. Not only are prefabs low in initial cost, but usually they can be expanded easily or disassembled and moved to other places.

Building costs

A new factory's cost depends on what is wanted. In 1973 a simple building with a 10-foot ceiling might be built for maybe $12 a square foot. But it would be necessary to go above $20 a foot to get very many "trimmings." Costs vary, of course, in different parts of the country. Size also affects the square-foot unit cost. Big factories cost a little less per square foot than small factories. Worker density also affects the costs. Less space per worker means more machines per foot, more electrical connections, and more of all of the accessories that go with men (locker rooms, cafeterias, entrance ways, etc.) and machines. These things boost the cost per square foot.

How much should a building cost per year? This can easily be worked out as a quick estimate. Let us say that the initial investment is for 400 square feet per employee at $15 per foot, or $6,000 per employee. Depreciation probably ought to be figured on a 40-year basis, so depreciation will be about $150 a year. Interest at 7 percent of $6,000 comes to $420.

So depreciation and interest will probably approximate $570 per year for near-future years. Taxes, insurance, and other costs will probably bring the total cost to $800 per employee per year. This would be not far from 10 percent of the payroll, or a little more than 3 percent of the sales dollar. A company ought to save more than this from the economies it incorporates into the new plant.

How does renting stack up against buying? One year's rent is likely to cost more than one tenth of the total cost of a new building (including land), or probably well above the $800 per year per employee in the example above. Normally it costs more to rent than to own.

Companies that build new plants always try to build improvements into their new plants. Almost always they end up with lower costs for (1) handling (down 20 percent or so), (2) supervision, (3) maintenance, (4) inventory, (5) shipping, and (6) insurance. Lighting usually is improved so much that it costs a little more. Employee morale and product quality both go up. Output per man-hour nearly always goes up, so labor costs per unit of product go down.

Communications systems in the plant

The factory, though normally a beehive of activity, would stop the minute communications stopped. Men talk to each other, giving and receiving directions, and they send and receive written directions and reports. Besides the internal telephone system, most companies also have public address systems with speakers in all departments so they can page anyone. And if papers have to be sent back and forth, there might also be pneumatic tubes. Electrically transmitted facsimile reproduction is also found occasionally. Work orders, documents, and drawings can be sent by wire from one department, or even from one plant, to another.

Computers may also be wired directly to various reporting stations. Men who have finished jobs on their machines insert their job cards into card reporting boxes which tell the computer that these jobs are completed. The same thing happens with stock withdrawals from storerooms, or with inspectors' reports. The computer then updates its records and, if need be, prints out a report. This instantaneous reporting keeps the computer's records up to the minute.

On-line consoles for computers are now the rule in big factories. Consoles with direct input and output access to the central computer are located in various departments around the plant. Thus each department can have immediate computer use.

Radio and television are sometimes used. Radio is very good for directing men, such as truck drivers and maintenance men, who usually are away from their home departments. Television (not broadcast TV but closed-circuit TV) is in a class by itself as a way of seeing what goes on at impossible-to-watch spots—say inside a furnace, or to watch freight yards, plant fences, or emissions from smoke stacks. And videoscopes of processes in operation can be studied at leisure, or even in slow motion. General Electric, in one of its plants, televises drawings to assemblers who are doing complex wiring jobs. Hughes Aircraft has a complete closed-circuit TV system so that its people can not only talk to each other but can see each other. TV is also used for sales meetings. Men from the West Coast do not have to be brought to New York; they can get together in West Coast cities and be part of a two-way TV meeting.

Security

Factories have always needed fences and a certain amount of outdoor floodlighting to hold down thievery and vandalism. This need has become greater in recent years since crime rates, bomb scares, and the possibility of civil outbreaks are greater. Visitors are no longer allowed to wander around inside the premises, and even outside service repair men are escorted to and from their work and their tool boxes are inspected before they leave.

Television has proved to be a great help here. From a central location, it is possible to monitor parking lots, loading docks, storage yards, fences, and entrances. Television cameras also help discourage vandalism and illegal harassment during strikes. Troublemakers are often reluctant to make trouble if they know they are being photographed in the act. Pictures become irrefutable evidence of offenses.

Electric-eye systems with alarms and scanning moving picture cameras have been added in interior areas that are vulnerable to theft or sabotage. It helps, too, to put up signs warning people of such security measures. Seeing these signs, only the most dedicated troublemakers will not be dissuaded. More locks and barred windows and fewer entry and exit doors are now provided. Records are kept of those who have keys to security doors.

Worker safety

Worker safety should always be high on the list of factors to consider in job design. Fast-moving machinery, heavy loads and products, high electrical voltage, extremely high temperatures, and noxious chemicals and fumes are present at times and present hazards to employees. In fact, they cause thousands of accidents to workers every year.

So long as there is even one accident which causes human suffering, it is too many. Yet, on a relative basis, factories are fairly safe places to work. Statistically speaking, life is safer on the job than off—people get hurt more at home and on the roads. On the average, there is only 1 lost-time accident per year for every 40 men, and the death rate is only 1 in 10,000. These rates are much less than in farming, transportation, construction, and mining.

Besides the losses in suffering and wages to a man who is injured, the company also suffers losses when injuries occur. These include medical costs and the cost of maintaining first-aid facilities, as well as the costs associated with investigating and reporting accidents. Besides these are the costs of damage to machines, lost production, and possibly damaged products. In total, these costs are substantial.

Accidents happen because of hazardous conditions and the carelessness of the worker. Managers must always keep working at reducing the hazards and trying to get workers to work carefully.

Hazards can be reduced by covering or screening off fast-moving machine parts, sharp cutting tools, gears, belts, and noxious liquids and fumes and by keeping men away from molten materials and high-voltage electrical currents. Men who have to work close to such conditions can be supplied with mechanical handling devices and protective coverings so they won't get hurt. All heavy work has been mechanized so that the physical hazards from lifting have been eliminated.

The possibility of worn machines or equipment causing accidents can be reduced by regular inspection and lubrication and preventive repairs. Pipes, valves, and fire protection equipment also need periodic checking and maintaining. So do material-handling devices, conveyors, over-head cranes, lift trucks, automotive equipment, and elevators.

But the human element, which is the *big* element, can never be wholly eliminated. (Goodyear reports that 92 percent of its accidents result from unsafe acts and only 8 percent from unsafe conditions.) It seems to be human nature always to expect accidents to happen to someone else, so it is hard to instill a safety attitude in men. Young men who drive lift trucks often drive them at full speed when there is no need and where doing this creates a hazard. And men who operate machines often won't wear their protective equipment unless they are made to.

Safety campaigns, safety committees, and bulletin board posters all help in this respect, but—above all—the foreman has to be safety-conscious.

Workers sometimes get hurt through their own fault, but this in no way reduces the employer's liability. Men who are injured on the job, no matter how, receive workmen's compensation according to the severity of their injury and the duration of the time they have to miss work. If there are many such claims, the employer's tax rate goes up.

Today's federal safety law, the Occupational Safety and Health Act, passed in 1970, goes farther, however. This law covers many hazards and requires employers to meet more rigid safety standards than were ever required before. Should these standards not be met, a company can be fined and it is even possible for the Secretary of Labor to order a factory to close down. Enforcement by inspectors is further strengthened by a provision that employees can file complaints charging unsafe conditions.

Noise

One safety area, however—noise—remains a problem. Industry has not been unaware of noise as a problem, and factory designers have done much to reduce it, but most factories are still noisy places. In the 1970s noise reduction became part of the spillover from the new emphasis on environmental improvement.

Interestingly, noise is not always considered disagreeable. Many young men like the loud roar from their motorcycles or automobiles. They like the feeling of power that seems to go with it. And indeed, rock music concerts have sometimes been measured at 125 decibels.[1]

Although we know that long exposure to excessive noise will ultimately impair a man's hearing, we don't know very much about the levels of noise that do harm. Noise affects some people more than others. Also, most people's hearing deteriorates as they get older even when they have not been overly exposed to noise. And, unfortunately, the harm which might be caused in a young man working in noisy surroundings does not show up until he gets older. There are no bad effects when he is young.

The law now regards long-time exposure to noise levels of 90 decibels or over as probably injurious to most people. It does not prohibit high noise-intensity levels but limits a man's exposure to them. Figure 7–1 lists the restrictions and relates them to familiar noise levels.

Companies must limit noise exposure to the levels indicated in Figure

FIGURE 7–1

Source of noise	*Decibels above the start of hearing*	*Maximum daily exposure (hours)*
Painful noise	130	0
Jet engine at passenger ramp	115	¼
Riveting, chipper, planer, circular saw	110	½
Textile loom, screw machine, subway train passing station	105	1
Noisy factory, punch press, blast furnace	100	2
Jack hammer, grinder	95	4
Lathe, motorcycle, Niagara Falls	90	8
Very loud radio in home, spinner, lathes	80	—
Average street or factory noise	70	—
Typical office	60	—
Quiet office	50	—
Quiet home	40	—

---

[1] Noise is expressed in terms of decibels, which are a measure of sound intensity; but sound intensity differences are so great that numerical differences are not just arithmetic differences. A sound of 70 decibels is 10 times as loud as one of 60 decibels. Eighty decibels is 10 times as loud as 70 decibels; etc.

7–2 or else supply workers with ear plugs or ear muffs or reduce the time exposure. (Workers, however, often refuse to wear plugs or muffs.)

Company interest in noise reduction is being spurred by occasionally successful lawsuits for damages by employees who have suffered hearing

FIGURE 7–2. **Legally permissible noise limits for employee exposure**

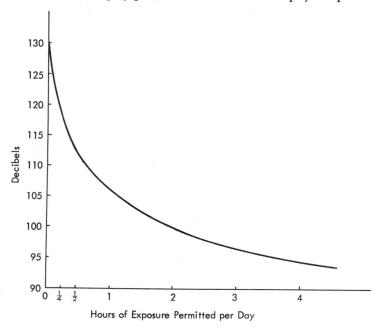

Hours of Exposure Permitted per Day

impairments they claim were caused by working on a noisy job. Labor unions are also taking more interest in noise reduction than they used to.

Maintenance

Because machines and buildings are wearing out all the time, they need repairs. On machines, wear on shafts, bearings, gears, belts, and other parts makes repair necessary. Electric motors must be serviced. Transportation facilities, too—elevators, conveyors, gasoline- and electric-powered trucks, hand trucks, hoists, and cranes—all need continual lubrication and repairs. Plant services—electric power, light, gas, water, compressed air and steam lines, washrooms, sewers, pumps, fire protection equipment, and heating systems—all need occasional upkeep. So do the buildings themselves—the roofs, windows, walls, floors, and foundations. In total, keeping everything going often costs more than one tenth of all a company's operating costs.

The maintenance department and its duties

Generally, maintenance is assigned to the plant engineer, who is under the general direction of the chief engineer. The plant engineer often has two main departments: a machine shop and a plant maintenance department.

The machine shop keeps the factory's machines and equipment in working order. Its employees include millwrights (general mechanics and men who move machines), machinists who can operate most machines and others who can run only one or two kinds of machines, sheet metal workers, welders, and others who repair machines and keep trucks and conveyors operating.

The plant maintenance group specializes in the building and the building's services. Its employees are electricians, tinsmiths, welders, pipefitters, steamfitters, bricklayers, steeplejacks, painters, glaziers, carpenters, millwrights, oilers, window washers, janitors, charwomen, helpers, and laborers. Also, the maintenance department usually operates its own stock room since it decides on and orders the materials used on repair jobs.

Besides repairing machines and equipment, the maintenance department in most factories does all the company's minor remodeling and relayout work. It tears down or puts up partitions between departments, builds new concrete foundations for equipment, and makes mountings for machines and motors. Since some of this work requires construction drawings, the department should include one or more construction engineers who are acquainted with building codes and safety regulations.

The maintenance department has to keep all fire prevention equipment in operating order at all times. To do this, the department must periodically inspect the sprinkler systems, valves, fire pumps, elevated tanks, portable extinguishers, fire doors, and sirens. The maintenance department also takes care of the premises outside the building. It maintains all truck and rail sidings, storage yards, parking lots, and fences, and it mows the grass.

Inside versus outside maintenance

Normally a company staffs its maintenance department with enough men with the necessary skills to do all of its day-to-day repair work except where a very high level of technical competence is required and where the needs are irregular.

Most companies do not, for example, repair their own elevators or telephones or computers. Nor do they do any but minor construction work, because bigger projects impose heavy extra work loads. Sometimes, too, such jobs as window washing and lawn care are contracted out. And sometimes the garage work on company cars is done outside on a contract basis.

Trouble sometimes arises over matters of inside versus outside maintenance. If a serious breakdown requires a good bit of extra work, the inside men want to do it all because it will require considerable overtime at high overtime pay rates. They object to the company's bringing in outsiders. The same thing happens on not-so-minor construction projects: the inside men can do them, but because so much extra work is involved they can do them only on overtime. Again, they object to letting this work to an outside contractor. In still a third situation, trouble again arises: when the company decides to discontinue certain work that was formerly done by its inside men and to contract it out permanently.

Labor contracts need careful formulation to cover the company's right or lack of right to use outsiders in any of these cases. If the contract is not clear, arbitrators and courts will usually hold that the company cannot make such decisions without bargaining over them with the union. This is a decision which managers are not wholly free to make on their own.

The inherent inefficiency of maintenance work

A considerable amount of maintenance work must be done to take care of breakdowns—the fix-it-now jobs. Such demands for service are irregular and impose variable work-load demands on the maintenance department. The department must maintain the capability of serving at a high technological level although such high-level service is not often required.

Such irregularities force the maintenance department to operate at less than its peak efficiency. Maintenance men can give good service only if there are enough of them to answer calls quickly, but they can do this only if they are not very busy. If they are always fully occupied, they cannot give the best service. This is seldom a serious problem, however, because there are usually a few necessary but not urgent jobs for them to do. They work on them when they are not otherwise busy, and they drop such work to attend to more urgent calls.

This is a case where it is necessary to forgo optimizing the work of one department in the interest of optimizing the whole enterprise.

Preventive maintenance

Just fixing things up is not good maintenance; *good* maintenance *prevents* breakdowns. The biggest cost of maintenance is usually *not* the cost of repairing, even if it is done at high overtime labor rates; more often the big cost is the "down for repairs" cost. Breakdowns, even when repairs are made quickly, stop production for at least a while. Men and machines are idle, production is lost, and orders fall behind schedule. Finally, getting the delayed orders back on schedule may entail overtime.

Breakdown repair jobs are almost always bigger than preventive repair jobs. It costs something to fix a loose front wheel on a car, but it costs more to fix the car after the wheel comes loose on the road. Then the owner (or his heirs) has to pay for a car wreck.

Preventive maintenance means *preventing* breakdowns. Putting new spark plugs in an automobile before winter comes is preventive maintenance. It anticipates likely difficulties and does the expected needed repairs at a convenient time, *before* the repairs are actually needed. Preventive maintenance depends upon knowledge from the past that certain wearing parts will need replacement after a normal interval of use.

In the case of factory equipment, the maintenance needs are sufficiently irregular that it does not always pay to try to anticipate trouble and overhaul equipment which doesn't need it badly. Preventive maintenance should be undertaken only if there seems to be need for it. Machine operators and foremen pay close attention to their machines and ask for repairs before parts get too worn to do the work. On unusual items, such as air-conditioning equipment or elevator motors and cables, the maintenance department inspects on a cyclic basis and watches for wear.

Maintenance prevention. Another and quite different kind of preventive maintenance can better be called *maintenance prevention*. Maintenance prevention is concerned with designing machines which will be both trouble free and easily repaired.

Lubricants and hard-to-get-at bearings for today's machines are designed to operate without attention for up to five years. Temperature detectors and gages also reveal trouble spots (they usually get hot) before failures occur. And replacement units are modular so that they are as simple to replace as a light bulb. When a part goes bad, the whole unit of which it is part can be taken out and a new one can be plugged in. Designing machines with replaceable units is particularly helpful in maintaining their electrical control parts, which are so complex that in many cases maintenance men cannot repair them. All they can do is replace the module.

Preventive maintenance economics

In general, preventive maintenance wastes the remaining life value of the worn parts that are removed during repairs. The repair man takes out worn but still operating parts and puts in new ones before the old ones wear out completely. This is wasteful, and so are the extra and more frequent repairs; however, the maintenance repair jobs are done at low cost and they reduce the number of more costly breakdown repair jobs.

The operation of the whole production system is optimized, albeit at the cost of not maximizing the life of parts and not minimizing the number of repair jobs.

If a company's maintenance men spend as little as 25 percent of their time on emergencies and "crash" work, they probably are doing a good job of preventive maintenance. Normally, without preventive maintenance, they will almost surely spend much more of their time on fix-it-now work. If they spend most of their time on emergency jobs, the company is surely suffering too many costly production hold-ups and has to do too much work on overtime. Preventive maintenance expenditures should probably be increased.

Preventive maintenance is, however, like so many other good things; it can be carried too far. A machine doesn't need an overhaul every time a bearing wears out. If a car owner lets the garage man fix everything he says the car needs, the owner will have a big bill—and it will include things the car doesn't need very badly. Still worse is the possibility that the repair man, in fixing something that does not need fixing badly, unintentionally damages something else and makes more trouble than there was.

In some cases a preventive program is hardly necessary because a breakdown policy is reasonably satisfactory. This would be so when there is little need for immediate repair and little harm will be done by waiting. If the automatic ice defroster on a home refrigerator starts to build up ice, it needs fixing, but the housewife can turn off the refrigerator and defrost it herself. Or if her automatic dishwasher is out of order, the dishes can be washed by hand. Repairs are needed in such cases but they don't have to be made on a rush basis at high overtime pay rates. Nor is their need depriving anyone of anything important. Not all breakdowns are as critical as a furnace failure in zero weather.

In a factory, a minor production facility may even be used wastefully in the interest of maximizing the whole. Suppose, for example, that a $500 electric motor will be ruined if it is kept running, but a whole production line will shut down—with a loss of $2,500—if it stops. By all means the motor should be kept running. Meanwhile, everything possible should be done to get another motor before the production-line motor burns out.

Extras as replacements

Preventive maintenance is not nearly so important when production is at low levels as when production is high. At low levels there is excess capacity except where a machine is the only one of its kind. When there are several machines, it doesn't matter much if one machine breaks down. Production can be transferred to other machines and no hold-up will occur. The machine that needs repairs can be repaired at the convenience of the maintenance men without suffering any penalty or cost because of the breakdown. Excess capacity operates, in a sense, in lieu of preventive maintenance.

This same idea can be incorporated into a preventive maintenance program when operations are at high levels. Excess standby capacity can be provided and thrown into the breach should trouble occur. This excess capacity can be whole machines or it can be major parts or components which ordinarily take time to get. Whether or not to do this is a matter of cost tradeoffs. It costs money to carry the extras, but they reduce the costs of breakdown interruptions.

Suppose that it is necessary to keep a fleet of 20 fork lift trucks in operation and it costs $40 a day to own each idle truck. If only 1 or 2 of the

FIGURE 7–3

Number out of order	Cost	Probability	Expected costs (no extras)	Costs with 1 extra	Expected costs	Costs with 2 extras	Expected costs	Costs with 3 extras	Expected costs
0	$ 0	.09	$ 0	$ 0	$ 0	$ 0	$ 0	$ 0	$ 0
1	50	.30	15	0	0	0	0	0	0
2	100	.25	25	50	13	0	0	0	0
3	200	.15	30	100	5	50	8	0	0
4	300	.10	30	200	20	100	10	50	5
5	400	.05	20	300	15	200	10	100	5
6	900	.03	27	400	12	300	9	200	6
7	1,400	.02	28	900	18	400	8	300	6
8	1,900	.01	19	1,400	14	900	9	400	4
		1.00	$194		$ 97		$ 54		$ 26
Add cost of extras............			0		40		80		120
Total....................			$194		$137		$134		$146

20 trucks are not in operation, the work can still be done by men with hand trucks, but at an extra cost of $50 for each fork lift truck not operating. But if 3, 4, or 5 of the trucks are out of order, this is too much; the hand truckers can't handle the work. There will be production holdups during the day and overtime costs at night as the remaining fork lift trucks catch up on the work. Thus the costs are $100 per day for each extra fork lift truck out of order. If more than 5 are out of order at any one time, certain production work will be seriously affected and the cost will be $500 for each truck (over 5) out of use.

Figure 7–3 shows how these various costs balance out. Its column of probability figures is based on the record of how often fork lift trucks have been out of order in the past. To make the calculation, the cost columns are multiplied, in turn, by the probability figure in that column. The vertical summation of each expected cost column shows the average cost for trucks being out of operation over a period of time. These totals go down markedly with more and more standby trucks. But when the cost

FIGURE 7–4.   Cost effects of having standby trucks available

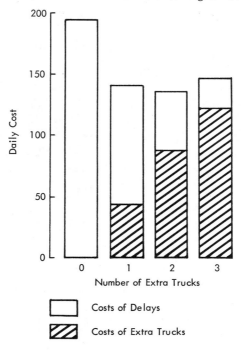

of the extra standby trucks is added in, as is shown in Figure 7–4, there soon comes a time when this cost more than offsets the losses from trucks being out of operation. In this example, it will pay to own a fleet of 22 fork lift trucks, recognizing that occasionally more and occasionally fewer than 3 will be out of order.

Preventive maintenance repairs

Sometimes preventive maintenance is a matter of overhauling whole groups of machines rather than letting them operate until they break down. Here, too, it is possible to calculate which policy is best to use.

Suppose, for example, there are 50 machines to keep in service and they can be overhauled on a preventive basis at a cost of $200 per overhaul. Such a policy will prevent most, but not all, breakdowns. On the other hand, it would be possible to wait until machines break down. Breakdown repairs, however, cost $700. Experience shows that breakdowns will occur in the manner shown in Figure 7–5.

There are two questions to ask and answer. First, should a preventive overhaul policy be followed? Second, if it should be followed, how often should the machines be overhauled?

FIGURE 7–5

Months after overhaul or repair	Probability of breakdown	Cumulative probability of breakdown
1	.05	.05
2	.02	.07
3	.03	.10
4	.04	.14
5	.04	.18
6	.05	.23
7	.08	.31
8	.11	.42
9	.13	.55
10	.14	.69
11	.15	.84
12	.16	1.00

The first step is to find out what a breakdown and repair policy will cost. The average expected time between breakdowns, T_e, can be obtained by using this formula:

$$T_e = \sum_{n}^{M} T_n(p_n)$$

in which T_n is the number of months after repair, p_n is the probability of a breakdown, n is the number of the month, and M is the total number of months (12 in the example we will use).

To get T_e we simply multiply column 1 and column 2 of Figure 7–5, and then add $1 \times .05 + 2 \times .02 + 3 \times .03 + 4 \times .04$, etc., and get 8.42 months. A breakdown and repair policy would therefore mean we would have to repair every machine every 8.42 months. This will cost $50 \times \$700$, or \$35,000, every 8.42 months—or \$4,157 per month.

In our example the probability of repair does not follow any mathematical formula or pattern, so the only way to calculate the cost of a preventive repair policy is to figure out its cost for each alternative policy. This example assumes that occasionally the repair work is not done well and that it has to be done over almost right away. If a repaired machine gets through the first month without needing more repairs there is little likelihood of its needing repair until it begins to wear out from use.

It is first necessary to calculate the probable number of breakdowns which would occur under each policy (overhaul every month, every 2 months, every 3 months, etc.). If every machine were overhauled every month, breakdown repairs would be limited to only the breakdowns which occur within 1 month after repair. But if every machine is overhauled every 2 months, there will be more breakdowns, both because another month's breakdowns will occur but also because a few of the machines that were repaired in the first month will break down again in the second month, before the scheduled overhaul. The formula for calculating the number of breakdowns, which is somewhat complicated, is given in Appendix D. So, also, are the calculations for our example.

The cost figures for each maintenance policy (preventive overhaul of every machine every month, or every 2 months, or every 3 months, etc.) are given in Figure 7–6. These figures, which are plotted in Fig 7–7,

FIGURE 7–6

Preventive maintenance every M *months*	*Total expected breakdowns in* M *months*	*Average number of breakdowns per month*	*Cost of breakdowns per month*	*Cost of preventive maintenance per month*	*Total cost of PM program, including $10,000 for periodic overhaul*
1	2.50	2.50	$1,750	$10,000	$11,750
2	3.63	1.82	1,274	5,000	6,274
3	5.23	1.74	1,218	3,333	4,551
4	7.44	1.86	1,302	2,500	3,802
5	9.68	1.94	1,358	2,000	3,358
6	12.54	2.09	1,463	1,667	3,130
7	17.03	2.43	1,701	1,433	3,134
8	23.28	2.91	2,037	1,250	3,287
9	30.90	3.43	2,401	1,111	3,512
10	39.44	3.94	2,758	1,000	3,758
11	48.93	4.45	3,115	909	4,024
12	59.62	4.97	3,479	833	4,312

show that preventive maintenance should be used. The machines should be overhauled every 6 or 7 months. Such a policy would entail monthly costs of $3,130 and would save $1,027 a month, compared to the $4,157 monthly cost of a breakdown and repair policy.

Simulation in preventive maintenance

Sometimes it is hardly possible to get good evidence about the merits of preventive maintenance—at least not by mathematical formulas, because the process is just too complex. Simulation can be used in such cases. Various policies and cost relationships can be tried out to see which combination will result in the least cost.

Centralization of maintenance

Big factories are so spread out (they may cover 100 acres or more) that it may take a long time for men to get from place to place. The managers of such factories therefore face the question of how much to centralize the maintenance department. Whether they centralize it or not, there is always a "central" maintenance department; but sometimes this department does more of the total work even though the maintenance has not been formally decentralized.

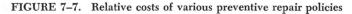

FIGURE 7–7. Relative costs of various preventive repair policies

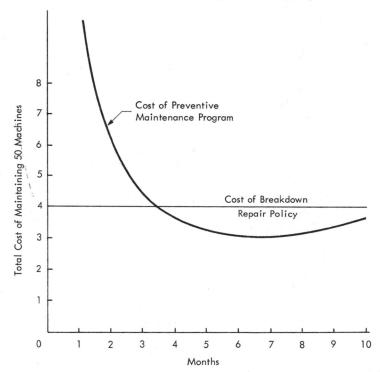

Area maintenance. In general, the closer that maintenance men are to the place where there will be need for their work, the better service they can give, but at a slightly extra cost, because they won't always be fully occupied at their highest skills. The waste in their not being fully utilized is usually less than the time wasted by men getting to jobs from central maintenance departments. Equipment duplication is also wasteful but this is usually only minor since it occurs only in small tools (most of the costly equipment is kept in the central office).

Decentralized area men are usually kept busy as members of fixed, small crews on routine maintenance. On bigger jobs they get extra help from the central department.

Area maintenance men feel more sense of responsibility for their own, limited areas, and they become more familiar with the equipment and with each other. Costs sometimes are better controlled when they are directly associated with a given area.

Central maintenance. Yet even with area maintenance there is still a central department. Since this is so, some companies—if they are not spread out too much over too big an area—prefer to have the central department do the whole job. In such a case, each area "cell" does not have to be fully equipped with men, tools, and supplies. Whereas area maintenance tends to be more costly (except where equipment needs constant surveillance), central maintenance makes it easier to adjust crew sizes and craft mixes to task needs. Crews' work assignments can be more specific and can utilize men's capabilities better.

In central maintenance the supervisors are craft oriented (an electrician foreman supervises the electricians, etc.), but in area maintenance the individual craftsmen seldom have much supervision. Area maintenance sometimes underutilizes particular men, who are nonetheless kept there rather than released to possibly more productive use in other areas.

The slight advantage which central maintenance seems to have over area maintenance disappears, however, when factories become giant in size. In giant factories the distances and travel time become too great and cause so much waste that such factories are almost compelled to go to area maintenance—yet with a central maintenance back-up group.

Repair or replace?

Should a maintenance man repair worn machine parts or replace the worn parts with new parts? The answer would seem to be whichever is less costly. When a person gets a small dent in his car fender he wants it straightened out, but if it is badly dented it pays to put on a new fender rather than straighten out the old one. It depends on costs.

But this is only half the story. Old automobiles and old machines that need repairs seem to keep on needing repairs. A person, or a manager, never knows how much added life he is buying when he repairs an old automobile or an old machine. It may not pay to commit oneself to successive repair bills. No one knows how soon more repairs will be needed or what the total final costs will come to.

Here, however, our concern is whether a repair man should repair a faulty part, thus making it operable, or discard and replace it with a new part. Often the problem is similar to that with automobiles. If the machine is old, the repair man probably should fix the part at the minimum cost so that it will operate a while longer (it won't have to last very long, in any case, since the machine will soon be worn out regardless of the part) rather than put in a new part which will outlast the machine.

Possibly, too, which a repair man in a factory should do (repair or replace) ought to depend on how busy he is. If the maintenance men are not busy, they may take the time to repair worn parts, but if they are very busy, they probably ought just to put in replacement parts. Today, maintenance labor costs are so high that there is a tendency (more than in the past) to replace worn parts with new parts rather than repair worn parts. Even though this costs more for new parts, it costs less for maintenance labor.

Maintenance in line production and automation

As was said in other context, line production in a factory operates like a large machine: everything operates or everything is idle, and even a few minutes' delay is expensive.

Preventive maintenance therefore becomes very important. It should start with the design of machines and equipment and thus truly be *maintenance prevention.* Machines should be designed to operate dependably, accurately, and steadily for long periods of time without breaking down. Some of them are designed with removable sections, which in emergencies can be replaced quickly with spare sections or parts. Also, in line production a maintenance man should be close at all times to take care of minor emergencies. Maintenance supervisors need to think in terms of maintaining production rather than maintaining machines. Maintenance men, rather than being on call to make repairs, should be on patrol to anticipate them.

Breakdowns are often caused by the tooling, not by the machines themselves. To prevent the tooling from wearing too much and breaking in use, all cutting and grinding tools should be inspected frequently. Some companies even attach counters to each tool (to show how many times it has performed its operation) so they can anticipate its wearing out and replace it before it fails or gets so dull or worn that it will make trouble.

Control-panel monitoring systems

Process industries (oil refineries, cement, chemicals, etc.) are usually highly automated. The processing is done in pressure vessels, vats, tanks, mixers, etc., that are automatically controlled. Materials are moved in enclosed pipes or ducts—again, all automatically.

In such cases the whole, integrated process is frequently controlled from a central monitoring office whose walls are covered with control gages, lights, meters, push buttons, and switches. Interruptions to operations, wherever they occur, are flashed immediately to the central control and maintenance men are dispatched by telephone or radio to the point of interruption.

Similar control consoles are sometimes used in other kinds of automated production, such as steel rolling mills, where twenty or thirty successive mills operate as a unit and are centrally monitored.

Budgeting maintenance costs

Most large companies—and some small companies as well—try to control maintenance costs by budgets. The expected costs of repairing and keeping production equipment in operation are allocated in separate budgets for each producing department. The foreman of each department is responsible for keeping his maintenance costs within the budgeted amount. Capital expenditures and big repair projects also are covered by separate budgets.

Unfortunately, however, budgets don't keep machines from wearing out: *maintenance costs can't be budgeted out of existence.* And if budgets are set too low, some things are not fixed which ought to be fixed. This might go on until heavy and costly repairs become necessary.

Actually, many maintenance costs *can* be postponed and money can be saved thereby—particularly in the case of such things as painting (which can be overdone). Some maintenance jobs are like car washing: a man doesn't *have* to get his car washed every month. In many cases, however, the apparent savings may be wiped out when a straw—so to speak—breaks the camel's back and a serious breakdown or accident occurs. For example, a man can wait only so long before he has to get new brakes or tires for his car. Maintenance should be postponed only as a calculated risk, and the risks should be properly evaluated.

Review questions

1. Obviously, a new factory is built only if it will allow for more effective operations. Where do these savings come from?
2. How far does a company's responsibility extend in the matter of safety for workers? Does it cover the men's being required to use safe methods? Or does it stop with the company's providing safe working conditions?
3. How can an employer get workers to do their work safely? What problems must be solved?
4. Which cause accidents, hazards or people? Discuss.
5. Does a man who gets hurt while disobeying company safety rules get workmen's compensation benefits? What is the logic behind this practice?
6. Why is it that inefficiency is inherent in maintenance work?
7. What is the difference between preventive maintenance and maintenance prevention?
8. Under what conditions is preventive maintenance *not* of considerable importance?
9. Is central or area maintenance better for (*a*) small factories, (*b*) very large factories?

Discussion questions

1. If a company's estimates show that it can probably save 10 percent of its direct labor costs if it builds a new factory, should it go ahead and build or not? Why?
2. When a company is planning to build a new factory, should it make improvements in the old plant or should it wait until it gets into the new plant?

3. "When my maintenance men have nothing to do, the plant is running well and we are doing a fine job." Comment on this statement.

4. Does the supervision of maintenance workers differ from the supervision of workers who work on the product? Are maintenance men of such high caliber that you don't need to watch them? What problems arise? How can they be solved?

5. If a plant closes down for two weeks in the summer for vacation, what does this do to or for maintenance work?

6. How should materials used by maintenance workers be charged? What ways are available? Discuss.

7. Some years ago, when the government made a check, it found that repairing airplanes at Norfolk, Virginia, and Alameda, California, cost just about the same. Looking into the figures, however, disclosed that Alameda's labor costs were much higher but its costs for materials and parts were much less than Norfolk's. Why might this be? Which distribution of expenditures is better? Discuss.

Problems

1. A company needs to expand and is considering a metal prefab, a wooden building, and a cinder-block building. The figures are as follows:

	Metal prefab	Wood building	Cinder-block building
Initial cost.	$10,000	$12,000	$25,000
Years of expected useful life.	10	20	30
Annual maintenance.	400	300	150
Carrying charges.	18%	18%	18%

Which type of construction should be chosen and how much will this type save as against the other methods?

2. What would it cost to build a factory for 750 workers who need 450 square feet of space each (service areas take additional space equal to 40 percent of the space needed per worker)? There is no need to build a building with many fancy trimmings, but on the other hand there is need for something better than the simplest construction.

3. Suppose, in problem 2, that land costs were extra and were $3,000 per acre (43,560 square feet) and that the company wants a 4-to-1 ratio (land-space total is 4 times the new-building space). What will the real estate tax be on the land and building (not including machinery or inventories) if appraisals come to about 40 percent of the costs and the rate is $3 per $100 of valuation?

4. Suppose, in problem 3, that land costs $6,000 an acre and the tax rate is $3.25 per $100 of valuation (valuation being 50 percent of true market value). Labor costs $5 an hour in both cases, but in the second case labor is more efficient. How much more efficient would labor have to be to make these two choices equal so far as taxes are concerned?

5. The company needs more space, and can add 3 floors on top of its present building at a cost of $500,000. If it does this, its taxes will go up $9,000 and its maintenance costs $8,000 a year. Or the company can buy the lot next door for $150,000 and build the same amount of space for $300,000, which would increase taxes by $16,000 and maintenance costs by $5,000. In both cases a 40-year life should be expected, after which time the value of the 3-story addition is expected to be $100,000 after 40 years. The next-door lot and building are expected to be worth $250,000. Interest and other charges are 20 percent.

Which alternative should be chosen? How much better is this choice than the rejected alternative?

6. The Carrier Company's studies show that air-conditioning costs about 1 percent of a year's payroll for each 100 square feet of air-conditioned floor space. Thus if a plant has 300 square feet per worker, air-conditioning will cost about 3 percent of its payroll. (These cost estimates include charges for the regular depreciation of the equipment.)

Will it pay to put in air-conditioning if workers, because of greater comfort, boost their productivity by 5 percent for the 6 warmest months of every year and if there are 200 square feet per worker? If there are 700 square feet per worker? Is the answer the same in both cases if it would be possible to achieve this productivity increase the whole year round?

7. An air-conditioning company estimates that it will cost $1 a square foot to install air-conditioning and $.60 per square foot a year to operate it on the days when it will be needed. The equipment will have a 10-year life. Money is worth 15 percent.

This company claims that air conditioning will cut labor turnover by half (it is now 25 percent per year and each turnover is estimated to cost $400). The air conditioning company also claims that labor productivity will go up 5 percent.

At the ABC Company the men earn $5 an hour and are provided with 350 square feet per worker. The men work 2,000 hours a year.

a) On the basis of these figures, should ABC put in air-conditioning?

b) ABC's managers suspect that the air-conditioning company is exaggerating and that the savings will come to only half of those claimed. If this were so, what should the answer be?

c) Suppose, on the other hand, that ABC's managers believe they will get the gains but that air-conditioning will cost 50 percent more than they have been told. Is the answer the same? Show the figures.

d) If the savings estimates are accepted but the turnover reductions are not believed, how much productivity gain will be required to break even on installing air-conditioning?

e) Because business is picking up, ABC is hiring more workers and expects soon to have 1 worker for every 250 square feet. What would the answer be for this worker density?

8. In trying to reduce maintenance costs, the maintenance inspector has tried inspecting all of the machines frequently and infrequently. Frequent inspection, followed by immediate repair of machines in need of repair, has reduced the number of emergency repairs. Results of the experiment showed:

Number of inspections per week	Number of emergency repairs	Number of preventive repairs
0...........................	37	0
1...........................	20	39
2...........................	14	44
3...........................	8	47
6...........................	2	52

Preventive repairs cost $15 each and emergency repairs cost $50. Inspection costs $1.50 each for the 75 machines in the department. How many inspections per week should be scheduled?

9. Using the text's example of keeping fork lift trucks in operation by having standby extras, suppose that the cost of standby trucks is $75 a day and the cost of out-of-service trucks is $100 per truck. In this case, however, this cost does not increase (per truck) if several trucks break down at the same time. What is the proper number of standby trucks to have and what will this minimum cost come to?

10. The ABC Company has 20 machines to keep in service. Preventive overhauls cost $100 each. Overhauls from breakdowns in service, however, cost $300. These machines are hard to get into adjustment, and often they need repairs again right after being repaired. If, however, they operate without trouble through the initial period, they usually operate a good while before needing repair again. The probability of breakdown since the last overhaul is as follows:

Months after overhaul	Probability of breakdown	Cumulative probability of breakdown
3..............................	.10	.10
6..............................	.02	.12
9..............................	.03	.15
12.............................	.04	.19
15.............................	.04	.23
18.............................	.05	.28
21.............................	.08	.36
24.............................	.12	.48
27.............................	.16	.64
30.............................	.22	.86
33.............................	.10	.96
36.............................	.04	1.00

What preventive maintenance policy should be followed?

Case 7–1

After a company appointed a safety engineer, accidents went up to a new high, so the personnel department interviewed the foremen with the worst records to see what was happening. Here are some of the answers. "Safety? That's not my job anymore." "Safety's the safety engineer's job. He'll get the credit, so let him work for it." What should be done at this point?

Case 7–2

A sheet metal shear at the Treadway Company had no guard on it and therefore was dangerous, making it possible for men to lose their fingers. The state safety inspector ordered Treadway to install a safety shield and control buttons so that the men could not operate the shear unless they had their hands out of danger.

A year and a half later, Bill Gott, an employee, lost three fingers in the still unprotected shear. The safety inspector had not been back in the interim, and in the ordinary course of events wouldn't have been back for at least six months more. Shortly after this visit, Jack Combs, a former machine operator, had been made foreman of the department. He said he'd never heard of the safety engineer's order.

What allows such things to happen? Suggest a remedy.

Case 7–3

The ABC Company (500 employees) has had a maintenance department of 50 employees but these men have not been very busy. There just is not a great deal of work requiring skilled maintenance men. Upon investigation, ABC has discovered that it can contract its maintenance work and have it done by the Jackson Services Company at a savings of $75,000 a year. The ABC Company accordingly has entered into a contract with Jackson and reduced its own group to a skeleton crew.

The union then files a grievance with the National Labor Relations Board accusing the company of engaging in an unfair labor practice. It claims that changing to contracting out the maintenance work is a bargainable issue and that the company should not be allowed to proceed with this action without bargaining about it.

Discuss this case.

Recent references

Accident Facts, Washington, D.C.: National Safety Council (annually)

Blanchard, B. B., Jr., and Edward E. Lowery, *Maintainability: Principles and Practice,* New York: McGraw-Hill, 1969

Gilmore, Charles L., *Accident Prevention and Loss Control,* New York: American Management Association, 1970

Gordon, James S., "We're Poisoning Ourselves with Noise," *Reader's Digest,* February 1970

"Incentives for Safety," *National Safety News,* September 1971

Lewis, Bernard R., *Developing Maintenance Time Standards,* Industrial Education Institution, 1968

Plant Engineering, Technical Publishing Co. (monthly)

Rose, M., "Computing the Expected End-Product Service Time Using Stochastic Item Delays," *Operations Research,* March 1971

Wilkinson, John J., "How to Manage Maintenance," *Harvard Business Review,* March–April 1968

8

Facilities design

A FACTORY'S EQUIPMENT should be designed so as to permit the economical movement of materials through processes and operations. Travel distances should be as short as possible, and picking up and putting down products or tools should be held to a minimum—as should paper work and instructions to operators and truckers. Hopefully, this will also result in the minimization of handling and transportation costs, as well as reducing inventories in process and machine idle time.

The never ending struggle to keep the productive capacity of operations in balance means constantly adding machines in some places and taking out old machines in other places. Mostly, because businesses grow, more machines are added than are removed. In any case, machine placement must be rearranged and materials handling systems must be redesigned.

Since the advantages of good layout are so great and so obvious, a person might wonder why any company would put up with any other kind. There are several reasons. One is that management doesn't always know that its layout is poor. In other cases the managers recognize that their layout is poor but it costs money to change it, so nothing is done.

Other reasons (and very important ones) why all companies don't have good layouts is that a good layout does not just happen, nor does a good layout, if unchanged, stay good very long. Most companies make many products, each of which follows different routes through the plant, and thus a good layout for one product is poor for another. Changes in the product mix sometimes change good layouts into poor layouts. Besides, there are design and process changes, which change the machines required, the space needed, and the arrangements. A good layout must therefore be a changing layout. It must be flexible enough to be changed quickly and with little expense and few holdups in operations.

Space requirements

Machine space. Machines need floor space plus space for their electric motors and control panels, as well as for their operators and conveyors (if they are used). And they need space for the storage of materials before and after the operations have been performed. There is also need to consider the shapes of the machines: some are long and narrow, others are round, and some are nearly square. Some go up in the air 10 feet or more above floor level; others go down several feet below floor level. Furthermore, maintenance and machine repair men need enough room to work.

In total, machines will always take up more space than the total of their separate space needs because these spaces never dovetail exactly. Storage spaces, however, rarely need to be of any particular shape, so they provide a certain amount of flexibility. The actual placing of machines is generally decided after experimentally placing machine templates (paper cutouts or even three-dimensional models made to scale) in position on a floor plan.

Product space. In most companies the space allowed for storage, machines, conveyors, and aisles provides enough room for products in process, but companies that make large assembled products, such as locomotives, freight cars, or airplanes, need big assembly or erection floors. Acres of floor space are needed, for example, for assembling airplanes.

Usually, big products are partially assembled in one part of the assembly area and then moved to another area where more work is done. Each area needs to be large enough to hold several products at a time. Probably, too, the space will need to be high and free from posts so that partially assembled products can be moved by an overhead crane.

For smaller products, it is usually necessary to provide point-of-use temporary storage areas next to the machines. In line production, it might be possible to make such spaces large enough so that material can be taken directly from the receiving point to the production line, thus saving its going into and out of storage.

Service area space. Service areas—washrooms, locker rooms, restaurants, medical facilities, offices, tool rooms, stock rooms, and storage areas, as well as weighing scales, elevators, stairs, and aisles—are secondary to manufacturing operations, but they are necessary. They should be close to work areas, where they can be most useful, yet where they are not in the way of production.

Some companies with unused overhead space put locker rooms and washrooms on balconies. But service areas should not be shunted off into leftover corners without regard to their proper functional location. Convenience is a part of the service. Utility services, such as power, light, water, and so on, also take up space, and the layout should put them where they are needed.

Overhead space. Overhead space, as well as floor space, should be considered in layouts. Using overhead space saves floor space and so saves money. Overhead conveyors and cranes can take materials directly to work places, which is something that trucks operating in aisles can't always do. Also, overhead conveyors are sometimes used for the temporary storage of materials between operations, which may save considerable in handling costs, and they free floor space at the machines.

Today's high-stacking lift trucks allow for the economical use of floor space. They can, despite narrow aisles, stack materials up to 20 or 30 feet at almost no cost above that of setting loads on the floor. Floor-space requirements are thereby reduced drastically.

Effects of materials handling equipment

The kinds of materials handling equipment that are used affect machine arrangements. Hand or powered trucks, for example, require wider aisles than are needed by conveyors. Fork lift trucks require wider aisles than other types of indoor trucks. Sloped ramps from one floor to the next may be needed if trucks are used and if elevator capacity is limited. Overhead cranes, on the other hand, require open spaces that are free from supporting columns.

Lot versus continuous production

Many companies make finished products which are assemblies of separate pieces or components. Raw materials are first made into parts which are later assembled into finished products. In this kind of manufacturing, products can be made continuously or in lots. This applies to individual parts as well as to finished products. A company uses "lot production" when it makes up, as one order, enough products or parts to meet the needs of, say, one month. Then it turns to other products, which also are made in lots. When the supply of one kind of part or final-assembled product is nearly used up, another lot is processed and the stock is replenished.

When parts or products are made in lots there are several decisions to make. How many units should be made at one time as one lot? Only a few at a time and frequently? Or larger lots less frequently? These are not idle questions because they result in different unit costs, depending on how many units are made at a time. The number that should be made in one lot to get the lowest unit cost is called the "economic lot" (which is discussed in Chapter 25).

Here we are not interested in the size of reorder lots, or with lots as such, but with the fact that lot production and continuous production need different layouts of facilities. Lot production needs a "process" layout whereas continuous production needs a "product" layout.

Layout patterns

There are three basic patterns of layout. "Process layout" refers to the grouping of similar machines into departments where only certain kinds of work are done. "Product layout" refers to the grouping of machines required to make certain products into lines down which the products move continuously. Departments are places where particular products are made. "Fixed position layout" calls for complex assembled products' being put together in one spot. Most companies use predominately one or the other of these layout patterns.

Departments making parts for assembled products do not need to use the same pattern as that of the assembly department. Parts are often made in process departments whereas subassembly and final assembly are more often arranged on a product basis.

Process layout

Process layout (sometimes called "functional" or "job lot" layout) is a grouping together of machines and men who do like work. Grinding is done in a grinding department, painting in a paint department, etc.

FIGURE 8–1. Probable cost relationships of different layout patterns for most manufactured products

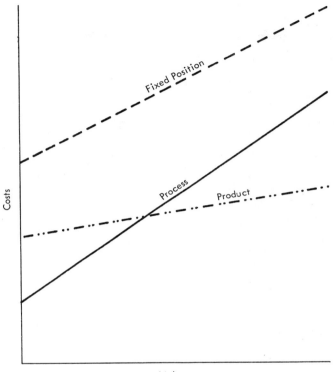

Advantages of process layout. Process layout (or functional departments) makes the best use of the specialization of machines and men. Functional departments are also flexible and are able to handle varied products. The machines are general-purpose machines, which are usually less costly than special-purpose machines. Products requiring diverse operations can easily follow diverse paths through the plant.

Process layout plants are less vulnerable to shutdowns than product layout plants. If a machine breaks down, its work can be transferred to a nearby machine, and the delay will rarely interfere with the progress of other orders through the plant. If the products are varied and made in small quantities, costs are lower with process layouts than with product layouts. And since the machines and men are somewhat independent of each other, this method is suitable for incentive pay systems.

Disadvantages of process layout. Process layout has certain bad features. General-purpose machines operate much more slowly than special-purpose machines, so the operation costs per unit are higher—often much higher. Work routing, scheduling, and cost accounting are costly because everything has to be done over again for every new order. Materials handling and transportation costs are high. Things go to so many places

FIGURE 8–2. Possible cost relationships of different layout patterns for large unwieldy manufactured products

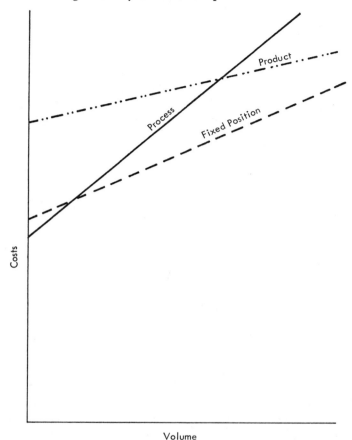

that it is not economical to use conveyors, and men have to haul them around instead.

Materials move slowly through the plant, consequently the inventories of materials in process are always high, and a good bit of storage space is needed. Orders sometimes get lost. It is also hard to keep a good balance of labor and equipment against needs. Process layouts are best for small volumes of a wide variety of products, and are not as good as product layouts for large volumes.

Product layout

Product layout means that the product's movement dominates and determines the layout. Products move, usually continuously, down a

FIGURE 8–3.   Process layout

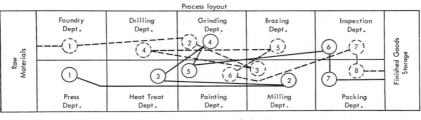

Process layout

———— Product A   – – – Product B

Source: Macmillan Co. (from James M. Moore, *Plant Layout and Design*).

conveyor line and past successive work stations where men or machines do work which ends up making the finished product.

Continuous production, where the product is always moving is the rule for small items that are made in big volume. Products are moved by a conveyor which moves steadily, or on a stop-and-go basis, from work station to work station. This is the way television sets, kitchen stoves, and automobiles are made. And it is also the way most of the parts for such products are made. At individual work stations the work may be manual, as it usually is in assembly work, or it may be machine work, as in the making of parts. This kind of line production is often called "straight-line layout," although the lines sometimes turn corners and go on to other work stations.

When the work is manual and requires tool assistance, the operator usually works with portable tools. These tools have limited capabilities, which can be a disadvantage. But continuous manufacture of parts usually requires big, expensive, special-purpose machines to stamp, forge, shear, drill, bore, tap threads, plane, grind, hone, or otherwise give a piece of metal the shape, size, contour, and surface it needs to have. (Product layout lines are the subject of Chapters 9 and 10.)

Advantages of product layout.   The main advantage of product layout of the continuous manufacturing kind is its low cost per unit, provided there is volume and standardization. Low costs come from the use of automatic, fast-production equipment, and because there are fixed routes for materials, almost everything can be moved, and moved fast, and at low cost by conveyors. Materials handling costs, travel distances, inventory in process, and storage space are all reduced materially. Production-control paper work is also simplified. And the comparatively simple machine-tending jobs make training new workers easy. Supervision is also easy since the jobs are routine and superiors can supervise large numbers of subordinates. In total, these advantages usually far outweigh the disadvantages of lines.

Disadvantages of product layout.   There are, however, several possible disadvantages. The big investment requires high volume in order to achieve low unit costs. Without volume, unit costs are very high. Furthermore, product layout with continuous manufacture is vulnerable to stoppages because the small supplies of products between operations are small. When work stops at any point, everything stops quickly. Also, the rate of output is quite inflexible. Usually it is possible to get more output only by working the whole unit more hours. And because product layouts are so inflexible, design changes are costly and may not be made as often as they should.

FIGURE 8–4. Product layout

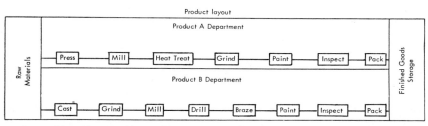

Source: Macmillan Co. (from James M. Moore, *Plant Layout and Design*).

Continuous production does not handle variety very well. Again, high volumes of the same product are needed for economical production. It is possible, however, to have some variety in trim and components provided they are interchangeable, as in the case of 6- and 8-cylinder engines for cars.

The capital investment is usually high in product layouts owing to the special-purpose machines and conveyors. Also, wherever a machine is needed part time it is necessary to put in a whole machine, even though similar machines are also used part time elsewhere in the plant. And because whole sets of operations are tied together, line production is not suitable for incentive pay systems.

There can be problems, too, with labor. The highly repetitive work along the line appeals to some workers but not to everybody. And most of the jobs are machine paced, which some workers find objectionable. Behind-the-scenes labor costs are high. The operators who tend the machines are relatively few, but they are only a part of the labor picture. Machine designers, setup men, repair men, methods engineers, materials supply men, and so on are the other part of the picture.

Fixed-position layout

Fixed-station layout is often used for large, complex products, such as factory machines themselves, hydroelectric turbines, locomotives, airplanes, and ships. The product may remain in one location for its full assembly period, as in the case of a ship, or else it stays in one area for a long time, perhaps several weeks, while considerable work is done on it. Then it is moved to another assembly area where more work is done. In total, it may be moved only four or five times.

There really are few advantages to the fixed-work station method except that it avoids the prohibitively high costs which would be entailed if the product were moved from one work station to another very often. Indeed, the fixed-station arrangement is the only feasible way to put the product together. Perhaps it is also possible to list as an advantage the pride that skilled men get out of doing big parts of the work themselves. This method is also flexible so far as design changes are concerned. And it is usually possible to shift the sequence of doing things if materials or tools don't arrive or if men are absent.

Its disadvantages are its high cost because of the slow pace of work by men who have to move around a great deal and have to work largely with portable hand tools as they put the product together on a more or less handcrafted custom basis.

Making a layout

Companies that plan to build new factories sometimes spend 2 or 3 years in preliminary work, part of which goes into hunting for improved methods to use in the new plant. Thus the building of a new plant provides an excellent opportunity to make far-reaching improvements. With a new layout, it is possible to get rid of old, wasteful practices. Suppose, for example, that in the present plant two men are operating a truck where one is enough, but dismissing one of the men would produce objections. In a new layout, a conveyor—using no men—can be put in, thus eliminating the problem and improving the method.

One way to go about making a layout is to start with an assembly diagram (or process chart) that shows the way the finished products are made from subassemblies and how the subassemblies, in turn, are made from parts. Then lists of the operations required to make the parts are obtained from the engineering department. These lists show the sequence of machines needed for successive operations. If the layout is to be product controlled, the lists provide a pattern for setting up work stations for the men and for placing machines.

A second way to start a new layout is to consider products from a materials handling point of view. Are the products heavy and dense (castings, forgings) or bulky and light (hollow sheet-metal items)? How about their shape? Are they long and slim, or floppy, or readily stackable? How about the risk of damage? Are they easily broken or marred, or dangerous or hard to contain (acids), or are they immune to harm (scrap iron)? Are they covered with oil and grease, or are they dry and clean?

Next, the quantities of each product need to be considered. If the volume in prospect will justify it, a product layout for the hard-to-handle items can be developed. But if the volume is small, it may be necessary to stay with a process arrangement. In any case, cutting the transportation cost of hard-to-handle items is an important consideration in layout.

A third way to start a re-layout is to start with floor-space drawings showing all permanently or semipermanently fixed items—everything that can't be changed or moved easily. Then all new machines and equipment can be marked in their ideal positions. Almost certainly, some permanently fixed features (posts, stairways, elevator wells, etc.) will be in the way; so it is necessary to make adjustments. Part of the ideal layout has to be given up as the proposed locations of machines are juggled around until a reasonably good layout, yet one which respects the fixed factors, is arrived at.

The travel chart or load-path matrix method

A quite different way to solve a layout problem is to focus largely on trying to reduce the transportation of materials in process from department to department.

The travel chart method tries to juxtapose departments between which there will be a heavy flow of products. A simple example will show how this works.[1] We assume that a factory that will make nuts and bolts is to be laid out and that, in total, the factory will produce 100,000 pounds of nuts and bolts every week.

First, it is necessary to construct a "from and to" matrix showing the flow of materials from department to department. These figures would come from order routing sheets and from projections of the quantities of products to be produced in the future. Figure 8–5 shows this expected volume of flow.

Next a schematic diagram is made up showing the sequence of departments through which the materials will have to move. Ideally, the ultimate solution should be the one where most materials would move along a line drawn directly from the first department to the last department. In Figure 8–6 (a first attempt to develop such a schematic diagram) the numbers in the circles are department numbers. The numbers along the connecting lines are the thousands of pounds of products which go from one department to the other. As can be seen, there are quite a few

---

[1] This method can be stated mathematically as one which minimizes $\sum_i \sum_j N_{ij} D_{ij}$, where i and j are the "to" and "from" departments. N_{ij} is the number of loads going from department to department and D_{ij} is the distance between departments i and j. For complex layout problems, computers can be programmed to carry through all of the necessary interaction calculations. Four somewhat different computerized programs that are available for arranging layouts are described in Thomas R. Hoffmann, *Production Management and Manufacturing Systems* (Belmont, Calif.: Wadsworth Publishing Co., 1971), pp. 242–46.

FIGURE 8–5

Thousands of pounds from departments	Thousands of pounds per week to departments											
	2	3	4	5	6	7	8	9	10	11	12	13
1	90									10		
2		75	15									
3				20	45	5					5	
4							13				2	
5									5	12	3	
6								35		10		
7									5			
8								3	5	5		
9									18	20		
10										33		
11												90
12												10

situations where material has to go past several departments to get to its destination. Whenever this happens it means a long and wasteful haul. The object is to reconstruct Figure 8–6 so as to minimize these wasteful long hauls and always to move materials to adjacent departments.

In an example as simple as this one an analyst can soon arrive, by trial and error, at a reasonably good arrangement of departments. It took us five stages of improved layouts to arrive at Figure 8–7, in which all solid lines are transportation routes to adjacent departments and are therefore short hauls. The dotted lines are wasteful long hauls. Figure 8–7 still

FIGURE 8–6

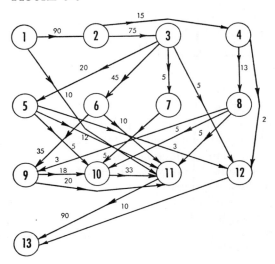

shows 35,000 pounds going by long hauls, but this is low compared to the 499,000 pounds going by short hauls.

Having arrived at the best schematic arrangement of departments, our next step is to consider each department's size. (In Figure 8–7 the size of the blocks is in accord with each department's required square footage.) Next, it is necessary to put the departments in an arrangement that

FIGURE 8–7

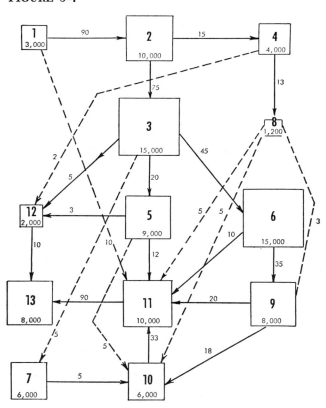

will fit the shape of the building (or possibly determine it). Figure 8–8 shows how the 13 departments might fit into a 560 by 700-foot floor plan.

The travel chart method does not consider all of the problems engineers face when doing layout work since it pays attention only to the flow of products *between* departments and not to transportation *within* departments. It also pays attention only to the material which has to be moved, but only as loads. And, implicitly, it assumes that distance and costs vary together. There may also be other things which are important,

FIGURE 8–8

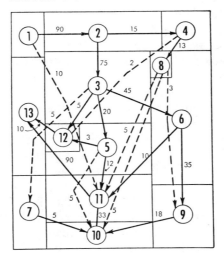

such as bulk, fragility, the need for departments to be close together in order to help coordination, and their need for common service and supporting facilities.

Materials handling and transportation

Every company is, in effect in the materials transporting or materials handling business, whether it wants to be or not. Materials have to be moved from the incoming freight car to "receiving inspection," and then on to raw materials storage. From there they go to the first operation, then to other operations, and to and from temporary storage points between operations, and to finished stores, to the shipping room, and finally to the outgoing freight car. During their trip through the plant they are picked up, moved, and put down many times. In and of itself, every kind of materials handling or transportation is waste in that it does not change the form of the product. Getting rid of any part of such movement is clear gain.

Companies that make materials handling equipment report that few companies spend less than 15 percent of their labor costs for handling materials. Most companies probably spend from 20 to 30 percent of their factory payroll for materials handling—or something well over $2,000 per employee per year! A company with 1,000 employees probably spends more than $2 million every year carrying things around! Giant companies spend *hundreds* of millions annually carrying things around.

Most companies don't know quite how big their materials handling costs are because accounting reports never show all of this cost. They know the cost of handlers and truckers, but, besides this, a great deal of materials handling (picking things up and putting them down) is done by machine operators and assemblers incidental to their work. These men are classified as production workers, and all of their pay is recorded as pay for productive work, ignoring the materials handling cost. And because the records don't show the amount of time direct production men spend picking things up and putting them down, no one realizes how much of this goes on. In addition, although neither stock room employees nor inspectors are classed as materials handlers, they too spend quite a bit of time picking things up and putting them down. Many companies, particularly small companies, never give handling costs the attention they deserve.

The best way to handle materials is *not* to handle them; but if this can't be done, then "hands off" handling is next best. Materials handling costs can be cut by (1) eliminating the handling whenever possible, (2) mechanizing—largely by conveyors and power-driven trucks—whatever handling still remains, and (3) making the necessary handling more efficient by reducing movement distances, keeping equipment well maintained, etc.

Sometimes there is a question of what to move—men, tools, or materials and products. In parts making, it is almost always more economical to move materials and parts to the men and their machines. But for large items such as airplanes, or ships, or locomotives it is more economical to do assembly work in one or only a few areas. The product remains stationary as men with portable tools assemble the product's components.

Getting parts to assembly stations

Getting parts to assembly stations is more than a matter of just moving them. In all, it is necessary to bring hundreds of different parts to dozens of assembly stations. Each part has to go to the station where it is attached to the product, yet, except for very small items, very few parts can be stored at these stations.

The object is to keep a steady, though small, stream of parts arriving at the assembly stations just before the assemblers need them, but to do it so that materials supply men are not carrying one and two parts all the time. This can be done economically by using service conveyors with pans or trays which are loaded in stock rooms and pass by the operators, who take what they need from them. Parts may also be gathered into sets in the stock room and, by conveyor or truck, taken in pans to the assemblers. The pans can have sections for separate parts so that assemblers do not have to fish around for the part they want next.

Small items (washers, cotter pins, etc.), however, should be stored in ample supply at the assembler's work stations. Doing this saves expensive stock room handling of many small, minor items.

Economics of manual handling

Often, when any big volume of products is to be handled, it is possible to calculate how best to do it. Suppose, for example, that incoming materials are typically received and stacked near the receiving point. Later they must be moved to another storage point closer to the operations. We will assume that there is a pile of cased products, each case weighing 30 pounds, and that they are to be moved and stacked again.

The various methods for moving them are (a) by hand, with a man carrying one case at a time; (b) manually, with a man pushing or pulling a two- or four-wheel truck; (c) manually and mechanically, by putting the cases on a pallet and then using a fork lift truck; (d) mechanically, by using a fork truck with the cases already on pallets; or (e) by using a conveyor.

At the moment, we are calculating only worker costs and are not concerned with equipment costs. The man costs $4.50 per hour, or $.075 per minute.

If a man carries the cases, he will take $\frac{1}{3}$ of a minute to get a case off the pile, will walk at the rate of 250 feet per minute, and will take another $\frac{1}{3}$ of a minute to put the case on the new pile. This costs $.025 per case for "unpiling," $.03 per 100 feet per case for carrying, and $.025 per case for piling—or $.05 plus $.03 per 100 feet per case.

Using a two-wheel truck requires the following: unpiling, $\frac{1}{3}$ minute; piling on truck, $\frac{1}{3}$ minute; travel at the rate of 200 feet per minute for a load of 5 cases; unpiling from truck, $\frac{1}{3}$ minute; and piling onto stack, $\frac{1}{3}$ minute. This comes to 1.33 minutes for handling each case plus .5 minute of travel per 5 cases. The cost is $.10 + 3.75 \div 5 = $.10 + $.0075 per 100 feet per case.

The four-wheel truck requires the same handling as the two-wheel truck, but travel is at the rate of 150 feet per minute for loads of 20 cases. The time requirements are 1.33 minutes' handling plus .666 minute per 100 feet per 20 cases. This costs $.10 + 5 \div 20 per 100 feet, or $.10 + $.0025 per 100 feet per case.

Using a fork lift truck requires unpiling the cases ($\frac{1}{3}$ minute each) and piling them on a pallet for the truck at another $\frac{1}{3}$ minute per case. They travel at the rate of 600 feet per minute in a 15-case load. At the depositing end, the fork truck puts a loaded pallet on the stack in $\frac{1}{2}$ minute. Handling at the beginning is $\frac{2}{3}$ minute per case; travel is $\frac{1}{6}$ of a minute per 100 feet per 15 cases; handling at the end is $\frac{1}{3}$ minute per case. In total, handling comes to $2\frac{1}{30}$, or .7, of a minute. This costs $.053. Travel costs are $.0125 per 15 cases, or $\frac{1}{12}$ of a cent per 100 feet per case.

The stacked cases could, however, already be on pallets. If this is so, getting the cases onto the truck would be reduced to $\frac{1}{2}$ minute per pallet, or $\frac{1}{30}$ minute per case. Handling at both ends would be $\frac{2}{30}$ of a minute, or $.007 per case. Travel would continue to cost $\frac{1}{12}$ of a cent per 100 feet per case.

If a conveyor were used instead of a fork lift truck, the travel cost for a man would be eliminated. Unpiling cases and putting them onto the conveyor would take ½ minute per case. Taking them off at the other end and piling them there would take another ½ minute. Handling time would then total 1 minute per case, at a cost of $.075 cents per case, with nothing extra added for distance.

Figure 8–9 shows how these alternatives compare. It shows (rather

FIGURE 8–9

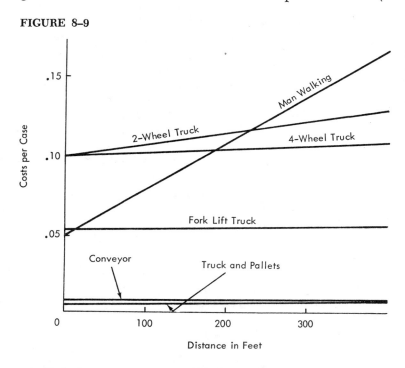

dramatically) the cost savings possible from using palletized loads, which reduces the costly handling of cases one by one. Figure 8–9 also shows that although the distance hauled adds to the cost, it is, at least for short distances, only a minor cost. The big cost is the manual handling at each end.

A summary of the relative costs of these methods shows these costs per case:

	Handling cost	*Travel cost per 100 feet*	*Total cost for*	
			100 feet	*300 feet*
Man walking....................	$.05	$.03	$.08	$.14
2-wheel truck...................	.10	.0075	.1075	.1225
4-wheel truck...................	.10	.0025	.1025	.1075
Fork truck.......................	.053	.00083	.0538	.0555
Truck & pallets..................	.007	.00083	.0078	.0095
Conveyor.......................	.075	.000	.075	.075

This example deals only with manual costs and assumes that the various kinds of equipment are already available at no extra cost. In a real-life problem the equipment cost would have to be included. The total volume of cases to be handled would also be a factor. For very low volumes it might pay to choose hand trucks rather than fork lift trucks and pallets.

Fixed versus varied path equipment

Equipment for moving materials may be divided into "fixed path" and "varied path" equipment. Varied path equipment handles material in separate lots whereas fixed path equipment usually handles material continuously. Varied path equipment is flexible and fixed path equipment is relatively inflexible. Fixed path equipment is more economical if large quantities of material follow the same path, but it is uneconomical if materials follow diverse paths. Varied path equipment must have portable power units for each piece of equipment or each piece of equipment must be hauled by a man. Fixed path equipment usually can be driven electrically, or, in the case of materials transported downward, by gravity.

Fixed path equipment "fixes" the path materials follow and, parts that are going to assembly don't go astray. Mostly, too, this gets rid of identification tags, separate work orders, and records of individual operations. Also, conveyors can be used to pace the worker; in assembly lines, workers must keep up with the work.

Fixed path equipment. Conveyors are the main kind of fixed path equipment for moving materials. Big plants, which often use several miles of conveyors, are heavily "conveyorized."

Conveyors can be put overhead, or at work level, or on the floor. Overhead conveyors generally operate by chain, cable, or connected links suspended from a monorail, and have separate pans, hooks, or carrying cradles in which or on which materials are placed. Overhead conveyors are used primarily for horizontal transportation, but they can also go up or down to other floors. Generally, they move continuously rather than stop and go.

Both overhead and work-level conveyors are frequently an integral part of the producing process, and operations are often performed automatically or by a worker as the conveyor moves the material along. Painting, baking, cooling, cleaning, degreasing, electroplating, washing, and many other operations can be done in this way.

Conveyors are also often used in raw materials stock rooms and warehouses, where materials are stored on sloping roller conveyors. As they are wanted, quantities are released automatically by computer and electronic controls—as orders come in. The quantity slides off the storage conveyor onto a collecting conveyor which moves the items to an order makeup area. The savings possibilities are great where large numbers of items are stored and the volumes received and issued are high.

Fixed path conveyors at floor level are often used in assembling large products—for example, automobiles and farm tractors. According to which kind of conveyor is used, the products may be set on the conveyor or they may be towed or dragged by cables arranged below the floor. Sometimes wheeled cradles are attached to a tow line and materials are put in them. In still other cases the frame of the product is fastened to the conveyor, and as it moves down the line, parts are added to the frame.

Automatic transfer machines, like the one depicted in Figure 9–5 (p. 216), use conveyors. Products are fastened in exact position to the conveyor at one end, which moves a fixed distance to the first machine and stops while the machine does its work. Then it takes the product to the next machine, where it stops again. This goes on until the product comes off at the other end all machined and ready to use. The conveyor is a very important part of this process, but it takes a back seat to all of the automatic machines that do the operations.

Cranes are a second type of fixed path equipment for handling materials. Overhead cranes, operating on tracks running the whole length of a work bay, are common. They can service any point in an area, whether at floor level or above and whether it is accessible from aisles or not. They carry materials by means of hooks, buckets, or magnets. Large overhead cranes are operated by a man in a suspended cage that is attached to the crane. Operators of smaller overhead cranes control them from the floor by means of suspended controls.

There are many other kinds of fixed path conveying equipment besides conveyors and cranes. Automatic and nonautomatic elevators are commonly used to move materials as well as men in multistory buildings. Chutes can frequently be used to advantage where material is moved downhill, but if the materials can be easily damaged the slope must be moderate. Pipes, ducts, and tubes are often used for bulk materials (particularly liquids). Air pressure and vacuum systems are used for dry bulk materials.

Varied path equipment. Practically all moving equipment which can follow a varied path is some kind of truck. Manually operated trucks are generally four-wheel platform trucks which also must be loaded and unloaded manually. One variety of hand truck, the lift truck, hoists already loaded skids and so eliminates the truck's being idle at loading and unloading points. Many variations of dolly trucks (a "dolly" is almost any kind of four-wheel carrying rack) and mobile racks are used. Some are especially designed for particular purposes and are generally used for short-distance moves. Even supermarket pushcarts are sometimes used. Today, most lift trucks that are used for heavy loads are powered, although they require a trucker to operate the controls and guide them.

Hand trucking is generally confined to short-distance hauls, perhaps from a machine to temporary storage. Trucks that are powered by gasoline motors or electric storage batteries and driven by truckers are faster and generally more economical for long hauls. Hand trucking is not only slow but, with heavy loads, somewhat unsafe. Truckers may try to pull overloads, or may start and stop heavily loaded trucks too quickly, and so may injure themselves. There is also more likelihood of damage to materials that are moved on hand trucks. Smooth and level floors are desirable for power trucking, but are absolutely necessary for hand trucking. If hand trucks are used, elevators must be large enough to hold the trucks so as to move them from floor to floor. If power trucks are used, ramps can connect the floors. Where the path of transportation varies, most plants use powered and driver-operated industrial trucks.

Most industrial trucks have power-driven pickup arrangements. The metal forks in front of fork lift trucks can be lowered almost to floor level and run under skids or pallets to hoist them and carry them to their destinations, then set them down on the floor or stack them on top of each other. This is all done mechanically, and fast. Although fork lift trucks are very common, they require 12-foot aisles, which is wider than the aisles in some plants. Walking fork lift trucks (where the trucker walks and guides the truck by a handle), being smaller and more maneuverable, require less room and can be used where aisles are narrower. One-way aisles can also be used.

Tractors and trailers are used by some companies for the transportation of materials. The trailers can be parked and left to be loaded or unloaded whenever it is convenient. When they are to be moved, a trucker hooks them, one behind the other, to a power-driven truck and hauls them to their destination.

Materials handling devices

The amount of materials handling for production operations is often reduced by mechanical lifting devices, such as jib cranes, chain hoists, compressed air hoists, block and tackles, and winches. Specialized devices at the machines include materials holding fixtures, magazine feeds, automatic product ejectors, welding positioners, elevating sheet-feed tables, and automatic scrap disposers. Robot fingers and arms are used wherever there is excessive heat, exposure to acid, or dangerous emissions of fumes or rays from processes or products.

Many kinds of devices are used to reduce the handling required to get materials on and off trucks and conveyors or transferred from one conveyor to another. They include up-enders, down-enders, turn-overs, rotators, transfer equipment, positioners for materials and platforms, regular and portable elevators, and conveyor unloaders. There are also many devices which permit the handling of loads rather than individual pieces. Tote boxes, skids, and pallets are universally used. Carrying cradles, wire baskets, collapsible wire containers, wire-bound wood slat containers, sacks, and movable racks also are used. Steel strapping is sometimes used to hold loads or packs on their pallets. Tote boxes, skids, pallets, and other types of materials holders should be "tierable" even if special corner posts have to be provided.

Review questions

1. What are the three basic layout patterns for factories? What are the advantages of each? When should each be used?
2. How should an analyst go about laying out a new plant to make sewing machines? Explain the steps. What information will he need and how will he use it?
3. How should a company's practice of producing by lots or continuously be related to the layout pattern used in the factory? Why?
4. How should a layout engineer go about devising a factory's layout if he uses the travel chart method?
5. How does it happen that a great many companies do not really know what it costs to move products around and to handle them?
6. Compare (give the good and bad points) of using fixed and varied path materials moving equipment.
7. In general, are costs higher for *moving* materials over considerable distances or for *handling* them at both ends of a move?
8. What are the pros and cons of using tractors and trailers to move materials? Where are they most suitable? Where are they poorly suited?

Discussion questions

1. The engineer for the construction company which wants to sell a company on building a new plant has just looked over the present layout. "Your layout is very poor and is no doubt resulting in your costs' being from 8 to 10 percent more than they should be," he tells the company president. How can anyone tell if the layout is poor?
2. If the engineer in question 1 says the present layout is quite inflexible as one piece of evidence that it is poor, how important is this? Does inflexibility matter today? He says that if his company were to build a new plant, it would build in flexibility. How does one "build in" flexibility?
3. Under what conditions should the layout be based on moving the men and not the products? What diseconomies would this method cause?
4. When, if ever, should a factory's offices be put on mezzanines rather than on the ground floor?
5. How should an analyst go about his task if he is told to produce an estimate of the costliness of a company's materials handling?
6. Suppose the analyst in question 5 is also asked to develop a program for reducing the costs of materials handling. How should he go about this assignment?
7. Should there be a central materials handling department or not? What would be the advantages and disadvantages of having such a department?

Problems

1. Experience shows that incoming trucks will arrive on the average of 1 every 25 minutes but that there is considerable irregularity in the intervals between arrivals. As it happens, the unloading time also averages 25 minutes per truck, so it would seem there is need to provide truck unloading space at the receiving dock for only 1 truck. Since it costs money to provide dock space, the company would like to provide only 1 space if this will not make too many problems. Experience figures on the time intervals between arrivals and on the irregularities in unloading times show the following:

Minutes between arrivals	Occurrences
5	1
10	2
15	4
20	8
25	9
30	5
35	5
40	2

Unloading time in minutes	Occurrences
15	4
20	6
25	13
30	10
35	2

a) Using Monte Carlo simulation, find the greatest number of trucks which will be waiting and for which parking space will have to be provided.

b) What fraction of all truck arrivals will have to wait as much as half an hour before their unloading starts?

2. Suppose that an extra man could be assigned to the unloading dock in problem 1. This man would speed up unloading time by one third. If he were to cost $4.50 per hour and idle truck waiting time is worth $15 an hour, should this extra man be put on?

3. The following departments are to be fitted into a 200 by 300-foot building which is being bought. The building has a railroad spur along the west side, the long side, of the building. Along the tracks is a loading platform for both rail and truck traffic. It is outside the building and not part of the space allocation problem. The layout has to meet the following space requirements inside the building:

	Department	*Space (sq. ft.)*
A	Receiving............................	750
B	Raw materials storeroom...................	1,500
C	Manufactured parts storeroom..............	1,250
D	Subassemblies storeroom...................	3,000
E	Finished products storeroom...............	3,750
F	Supplies storeroom.......................	1,000
G	Machine shop I..........................	200′ × 30′
H	Machine shop II.........................	150′ × 45′
J	Bench operation.........................	50′ × 45′
K	Subassembly I...........................	150′ × 45′
L	Subassembly II..........................	70′ × 50′
M	Final assembly*.........................	245′ × 50′
N	Packing and shipping.....................	2,500
P	Production & engineering office..............	1,200
Q	Factory manager's office....................	400
R	Cost accounting office.....................	1,700
S	General accounting office..................	1,700
T	General offices...........................	2,400
U	Secretary & treasurer's office...............	300
V	V.P. & general manager's office.............	400
W	President's office.........................	600
X	Sales office..............................	1,100
Y	Purchasing and traffic office................	825
Z	Personnel...............................	625
AA	Reception room for departments Y and Z.....	750

* Includes 3,000 sq. ft. for subassembly storeroom department D.

Lay out the departmental arrangement on a scale of 1 inch = 40 feet.

4. The new engineers, recently hired, are crowded for office space. It has been necessary to put them 5 to an office. Since the offices are only 16 by 20 feet, they are somewhat crowded. The average salary of these engineers is $14,000. More space can be built for $20 a square foot. Newly built space would have a life of 25 years and would then be worth 10 percent of its original cost. Taxes, insurance, maintenance, and interest cost 10 percent a year. Janitor service, heating, and lighting cost $1.50 per square foot.

How much would the productivity of the men have to increase to justify assigning 4, 3, 2, or 1 man to a 16 by 20-foot office?

5. Three alternative plans for a revised layout show the following expected results:

	A	B	C
Cost...................	$8,000	$10,000	$13,000
Annual saving.........	2,200	2,600	3,200

The new layout will probably be used for 5 years before it will be changed. Interest on investment is 12 percent.

a) Which plan should be chosen?

b) How much higher a rate of return will the selected plan yield than the other two alternatives?

6. The Stevenson Company needs a new layout which will meet the following conditions. The problem is to suggest a general pattern and arrangement of departments. Department sizes are to be approximately as follows:

Department	Size (sq. ft.)	Department	Size (sq. ft.)
A	3,000	D	2,500
B	7,500	E	3,500
C	6,000	F	4,500

On the average, the loads of work that go from one to the other department every day are as follows:

From	To	No. of loads	From	To	No. of loads
A	B	22	C	A	1
A	C	11	C	B	6
A	D	1	C	D	6
A	E	5	C	E	3
A	F	6	C	F	9
B	A	4	D	E	1
B	C	15	D	F	10
B	D	6	E	B	2
B	E	7	E	F	12
B	F	2	F	B	2
			F	C	3

Draw a proposed plant layout for a rectangular building that can be nearly square but should not be long and narrow.

Indicate how many loads will have to pass between nonadjacent departments. Don't, however, make departments into corkscrew shapes just so they will touch many other departments.

7. The analysis of work loads at the ABC Company has proceeded to the point where the area requirements for each work center have been established. These space needs are:

Work center	Department number	Square feet
Centering	1	1,000
Mill	2	5,000
Lathe	3	6,000
Drill	4	3,000
Arbor press	5	1,000
Grinder	6	2,000
Shaper	7	2,000
Heat treat	8	1,500
Paint	9	1,000
Bench assembly	10	1,000
Inspect	11	500
Pack	12	1,000

Production in those departments is confined to the following 7 products, which will move through these departments in the sequence shown:

Units per month	Units per load	Product	Sequence
500	2	A	4,7,8,10,11,12
500	100	B	1,3,8,4,6,2,11,3,10,12
1,600	40	C	1,2,4,6,3,11,10,12
1,200	40	D	4,10,2,12
400	100	E	4,6,10,5,12
800	100	F	3,9,10,12
400	2	G	1,2,3,4,5,6,7,8,9,10,11,12

Using the method described in this chapter, develop a proposed arrangement and layout of departments for the new plant expansion. Aim for a rectangular plant.

8. The ABC Company, to remove cases of bottled detergents from the end of the container line, has to build pallet loads for fork lift trucks. Cases may contain 9, 12, and 24 plastic or glass bottles. Because plastic and glass bottles differ in shape, they take different amounts of handling time. This information is available about the operation:

Container	Time (in hours) per 100 cases		Annual volume (thousand cases)		Cases per load	
	Plastic bottles	Glass bottles	Plastic	Glass	Plastic	Glass
9-bottle cases...........	.286	.536	1,125	130	75	45
12-bottle cases...........	.286	.386	2,500	550	84	50
24-bottle cases...........	.327	.410	2,400	410	70	42

The men who do this work get $4.40 per hour (plus fringe benefits costs of 25 percent more), and fork lift truck time (including pay for the trucker) is calculated as $8 an hour. It takes .078 hours per load to haul loads from the conveyor to the point of shipment.

There are two ways to mechanize this load-building work, and either method would eliminate the men now building truck loads. One is to use a 3-lane accumulating unit system capable of handling all kinds of plastic bottles and the 12- and 24-glass bottle cases (9-unit glass bottle cases would be continued as at present). The second alternative uses 4 accumulating lanes and can handle all 6 combinations. The automatic load accumulators would be located closer to the point of shipment and would reduce trucking time to .043 hours per load.

The automatic methods would require 1 man's full time (2,000 hours a year at $4.50 per hour) to attend each lane, and would cause the following additional costs annually:

	3 lanes	4 lanes
Maintenance....................	$9,300	$10,200
Extra insurance and taxes..........	1,080	1,200

The installed cost of the 3-lane arrangement is $312,000 and that of the 4-lane arrangement is $336,000. The equipment life is figured at 15 years, with no salvage value. Money costs 12 percent.

Should you put in either of the proposed automated load accumulators? What would be their rate of return on the investment?

9. A conveyor costing $3,500 to connect operations A and B would save half an hour a day of $4.30 an hour labor time. It would also boost the productivity of machines A and B by 5 percent. Machine operating time is worth $12 an hour. Will this conveyor pay for itself in one 2,000-hour (250-day) year? What rate of return will it yield on this investment?

10. The Sunbeam Company wants to know how many pallets to buy and whether to leave loads on them in storage, thus tieing them up, or to unload them and keep them in use. For the purpose of this calculation it is not necessary to consider whether the materials are to be kept in stock very long. It is to be assumed that, so far as pallets are concerned, this is a matter of buying more pallets versus unloading them. The relevant figures are:

Cost per pallet.	$5
Pallet life.	5 years
Pallet maintenance.	$.03 per use
Space costs.	$.08 per cubic foot per year
Pallet size when loaded.	48″ × 40″ × 6″ (a loaded pallet occupies 6.7 cubic ft.)
Cost to unload and load.	$.50
Total loads per year.	1,000

How many pallets should Sunbeam have? How much floor space will be needed? How long will the pallets stay in storage?

11. The Scanlon Company is changing to fork lift trucks and wants to know how many it is likely to have to buy in the next 5 years in order to maintain its fleet of 40 trucks. Experience shows the following life expectancy for such trucks.

Months of use before replacement	*Number of cases*
12.	4
16.	7
20.	13
24.	17
28.	27
32.	11
36.	7
40.	6
44.	5
48.	3

Suggestion: Use the Monte Carlo method.

Recent references

Improving Material Handling in Small Businesses, New York: Material Handling Institute, 1969

Levings, G. E., "Small Computers: Big Boost for Materials Handling," *Industry Week,* January 17, 1972

Muther, Richard, and Knut Haganas, *Systematic Handling Analysis,* Cahners, 1969

Muther, Richard, and Kenneth McPherson, "Four Approaches to Computerized Layout," *Industrial Engineering,* February 1970

Perlman, J. A., "Materials Handling: New Market for Computer Control," *Datamation,* May 1970

9

Production processes
and machine lines

YEAR BY YEAR, more and more work once done by men continues to be transferred to machines, machines are often better than men. They respond very quickly to control signals and can apply great force smoothly and precisely. They can do several operations at the same time and they can handle repetitive and routine tasks well. And more and more, machines are being developed to do things which men never did at all, such as to refine oil or to make chemicals or plastics. And in all such cases the equipment is becoming more fully automatic. (Machines are not good, however, at improvising or reasoning, or at exercising judgment, or at developing new methods.)

Today's more advanced equipment is being designed to include closed-loop feedback systems. Machines control themselves. They inspect their own output, and if they are turning out poor work, they reset themselves.

In order to do these things, they contain minicomputers which contain built-in memory units which allow them to remember what they are supposed to do, sensor units which monitor their output, reporting and judging systems which they use to compare the quality of the work they are turning out with what they are supposed to be turning out, and correction effectuators which reset the machine whenever this is needed. All of this is done quickly and accurately since the computer can store almost unlimited amounts of information and can calculate so fast as to be virtually instantaneous.

Automated process controls that use electronics are now the rule in oil refining, chemicals, steel making, and other process industries. Companies in these industries don't make products out of pieces of anything. Materials are processed inside tanks, vats, pressure vessels, and the like, and materials go from one processing step to another in pipes and ducts. The processing, the rates of flow, temperatures, mixture ratios, etc., are controlled largely by minicomputers.

FIGURE 9–1. A process control system

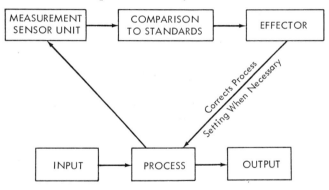

Several years .ago McLouth Steel Corporation, in Detroit, spent $3 million for a computer to control one of its hot strip steel rolling mills (which was already a highly automated facility). The computer takes, continually, some 200 separate readings of the texture of the moving strip, the different chemical composition, etc., all the while making whatever adjustments are needed.

The computer increased the mill's output by 2 percent through reducing wastes and shutdown time. Compared to the gains usually realized from computer control of processes, 2 percent sounds small, almost picayunish, but to McLouth it was worth $1.5 million a year. The computer paid for itself in two years. Besides its direct money savings, McLouth reports that the computer brought about more uniform output, faster production changeovers, and fewer mill jams.

② Least Exp. Pkg:-

FIGURE 9–2. Model of information flow from product design to production

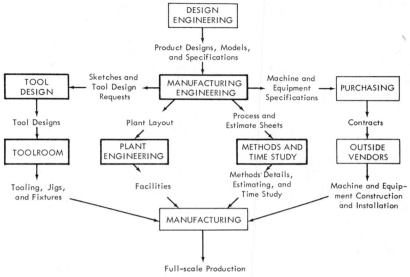

Source: Richard C. Vaughn.

B. F. Goodrich's chemical division uses a minicomputer to control the production of vinyl chloride and acrylonitrile. This computer calculates the best way to get production, considering equipment limitations and the availability and costs of various kinds of raw material. It reads and activates the devices that control the operations, automatically making whatever changes are necessary for optimum production. At first the mathematical model, which was supposed to maximize profits and minimize costs, was quite crude, but the computer periodically analyzes its own predictions and improves the statistical relationships it uses. It now does an excellent job.

Production processes

Every industry uses processes that are peculiar to it, but almost all machinery and equipment is made of metal, usually steel; so the processes used to form metal into end products for consumer use or for making the machines and equipment used to make other products are the most fundamental of all.

Often molten metal is first poured into ingots, which are later reheated, and, while hot, are rolled between squeezing rollers into billets, bars, sheets, or other standard forms. Or the metal can be extruded through orifices which give it various cross sections, such as are used in aluminum window or door frames.

Billets and bars can be cut by shearing, sawing, or flame cutting into smaller pieces which can be pounded into rough shape by forging. In forging, the metal is heated to a soft state and then pounded into final shape (the head of a hammer is made this way).

Metal can also be rolled out into sheets which can be sheared and then folded or bent into desired shapes (the outside of a stove or refrigerator is made this way). Pieces of sheet metal can also be "drawn," or pushed by main force between two dies, to make them take on the desired shape (an automobile fender is shaped this way).

Metal is sometimes made directly into its final shape by casting, which means pouring it, while molten, into molds, which usually are made of sand. Sometimes molten metal is forced into water-cooled metal molds of intricate shapes. This method, called die casting, is used to make many trim and decorative parts out of zinc or plastic. Knobs on television sets, the striking buttons on typewriters, electric plugs, and a host of other items are made this way.

There are also other less common processes, such as sintering, where powdered metal is compacted in a forming die to the desired shape. Later this compacted part is baked at close to the metal's melting point, which causes it to fuse into a solid piece. Or sheet metal can be "spun" (dished aluminum platters and bun warmers may be made this way). A flat piece of metal is put next to a semiround form and rotated, and, as it rotates, force is applied to push it bit by bit against the semiround. In the end, it will have taken the shape of the semiround form. Another somewhat uncommon process is "coining," where a forming-surface contour is forced against a piece of metal (our coins are made this way).

The big work in metal forming is, however, in starting with a rough piece which is too big and then removing the excess, much as a sculptor "exposes" a statue in a stone. The excess metal can be got off many ways. It can be ground off. Or it can be drilled out or, with thin metal, punched out. It can be chipped off, or sheared or shaved off.

Of these processes, shaving off the excess is much the most common. Except for grinding, which is done by an abrasive grinding wheel, the tool is almost always a steel tool with a carbaloy tip which is harder and tougher than the metal being cut. Almost always the process generates considerable heat and so requires that a stream of coolant liquid be directed at it constantly.

Sometimes the material being worked on is rotated against a stationary cutting tool, as in the case of lathes. One form of lathe is the turret lathe and another is the automatic screw machine. Both of these machines perform two or three operations on the part, one operation after the other. Sometimes the cutting tool is stationary, or else it rotates in a fixed spot and the material is passed back and forth against it as the tool shaves or chisels off a little more metal at each pass. Usually this would be called "milling," but some variations are called "shaping."

If the tool rotates and makes a hole, it is "drilling," but if the tool stands still and the work is rotated around it so as to make a hole, it is "boring." Sometimes a hole is first drilled to rough size and then finished to more exact size by using a "broach." A broach is a very slightly tapered mandrel with sharp ridges at each size expansion, and as it is pulled through the hole it enlarges it by gouging off the required amount of metal and so makes the hole the right size.

A quite different way to remove excess metal is by the use of chemicals, which eat away the unwanted metal. To control the process, the areas that are not to be thinned down are covered with a plastic coating. The chemical then eats away the exposed surfaces, leaving the wanted areas projecting above. Later the plastic is removed, and the piece has the high and low areas as planned.

Other important processes include heat treating parts for hardening. The parts are heated close to their melting point and then are quenched quickly in a cool liquid. This process hardens the surface. In other cases, just the reverse is done: castings are heated up close to their melting point and allowed to cool very slowly. This "annealing" process relieves the internal strain originally set up by thick and thin areas' cooling at different rates. The unequal cooling rates, by causing the castings to shrink unevenly, creates internal strain.

Speeds and feeds

When excess metal is to be removed by cutting or grinding, there is a question of how fast it should be removed. If a considerable amount is removed every time the work goes past the cutting tool, this requires a sturdy machine, strong fixtures to hold the material in place, and a sharp as well as a strong cutting tool. The process will generate a good bit of heat and so will require a substantial flow of coolant liquid. It will also produce a considerable quantity of chips or metal shavings which have to be removed.

If heavy cuts are used, the surface of the product will not be altogether smooth. To get a fine finish on the surface being machined, it is necessary to remove very little metal at each cut. Usually, if considerable metal is to be removed, it is better to do it in two stages. The first cuts can be heavy cuts, which remove a good bit of metal, whereas the last cuts need to be fine cuts which take off only a little metal and leave smooth surfaces, and which can be held to close measurements.

"Feeds and speeds" of machines has to do with how fast the cutting tools rotate or how fast the material passes the cutting edges of cutting tools, as well as with how deep and how wide the cut is at each pass. Years ago experienced machine operators decided what speeds and feeds to use, but now engineers almost always figure these out. Machinery manufacturers always supply general guidelines figures, but these guides can't provide optimal speeds and feeds for every operation.

A considerable part of the savings from using numerically controlled machines comes from the very careful determination of proper speeds and feeds, which is done when the N/C machine instruction tapes are made.

Depth of tooling and special-purpose machines

The best way to make a product depends upon how many are to be made, because machines can be designed to do most manual operations. Such machines sometimes are very costly, yet they are so productive that they cost very little per unit of product if a large volume is produced. So the prospective volume determines the proper "depth of tooling," or the extent to which managers should mechanize or automate. In fact, specialized machines are so costly that they are sometimes made in sections so that product model changes will obsolete only part of the whole machine. Automobile fenders, for example, are formed in huge presses that have removable dies. When models change, the companies take out the old model dies and put in the new. They still have a specialized machine, but they do not have to buy a whole new press for every model change.

For low volumes, the big investments in special-purpose machines cannot be justified, so general-purpose machines, which are designed to do one kind of work rather than one job, should be used. Usually these machines are not costly, and they are suitable for performing a wide range of operations. It takes highly skilled men to set them up and to operate them, and they are relatively slow in operation.

As volume goes up, it is possible to justify the use of specialized gadgetry attachments on a machine, such as magazine feeds, special tool guides, or material holding devices ("jigs and fixtures"). These items speed production and lower the operating costs.

Numerically controlled (N/C) machines

Today, the majority of metal cutting machines used to make parts are "numerically controlled." Instead of a man getting instructions to plane a surface, mill a slot, or drill a hole in each item of a lot of 50 steel castings, the directions go directly to the machine. The machine is told, by means of electronic tape or punched paper tape, to advance its planing tool to the surface of the casting and to plane its surface to a set thickness for a certain width. It is then told to change to a tool for cutting a slot, to cut the slot, and then to drill a hole, etc. Once a tape has been programmed and the machine set up with the proper tools in place, all the machine operator has to do is fasten the unfinished casting and remove it when the work is done.

The term "numerically controlled" comes from the fact that a machine's whole program is based on numbers in mathematical formulas which tell the machine how far to advance its tools, how many cuts to take, to what depth, etc. Where necessary, these directions cause the machine to make several coordinated motions at the same time. These directions come from each machine's own minicomputers, which may not always be wholly independent but may be satellites of a central computer and receive part of their instructions from the central computer. Local tape controls might even be eliminated in "direct numerical control" (DNC).

Numerically controlled machines do work much faster and more accurately than skilled operators in manual operation. And although it takes high skill to program a tape from a drawing and to design a machine's setup, once this is done, production is almost fully automatic and little labor is required. Both the tapes and the design of the machine setup can be kept for repeated use in the future.

Their high initial cost is against N/C machines; most of them cost $100,000 and over. And even as attachments put on older machines, numerical controls are likely to cost $50,000 or more. Machine programmers are also needed, and castings and forgings can't have as much variation as with conventional machines.

FIGURE 9–3. System for direct control of numerically controlled machines

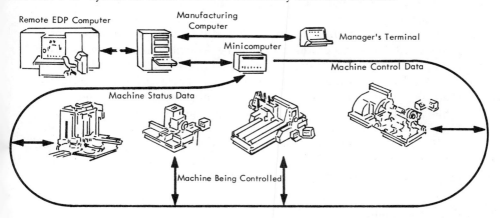

Also against N/C machines is complex and frequent maintenance. Because they operate so effectively, they remove metal a large part of the time they are running and consequently they wear out tools, as well as their own operating parts, more rapidly. Besides, in order to operate correctly they need to be in perfect adjustment. Their downtime is likely to run over 4 percent, which is higher than for less sophisticated machines.

All of these requirements mean that N/C machines require a good bit of maintenance—and highly sophisticated maintenance. Sometimes a job is so complicated that the machinery company's troubleshooters have to be called in.

Robotry

It is usually possible to develop mechanical robots to do most highly repetitive manual jobs. And only their cost stands in the way of more of them. Curiously, Japan (where labor pay rates are lower than in most other developed countries) apparently has gone further in this direction than any other country. Probably this is because its rapid industrial development in the 1960s created a severe labor shortage and more hands were needed, whether human or mechanical. Furthermore, Japanese forecasts anticipate a severe labor shortage in the late 1970s.

In the United States, robotry is somewhat uncommon. A robot costs from $15,000 to $30,000, and is considered economically worthwhile only if it can substitute for one man on each of two shifts, or where the work is particularly dangerous or arduous.[1] Operating costs, however, are usually low, running between only $1 and $2 an hour.

Robot makers estimate that ultimately they can make robots that can do half of the jobs done in factories by blue-collar workers.[2] Even after one discounts the probably optimistic estimates of robot makers, the possibilities are still enormous.

Robots are more general purpose in application than automated machines since the former can be reprogrammed rather easily. Robots are, however, both blind and stupid; they cannot do "scene analysis." If a robot is supposed to pick up something, it does so whether something is there or not. Parts and products have to be presented to them "just so," but if they are not, the robots don't know it and proceed to act as if they were.

Industrial robots are an important means for releasing human beings from dirty and painful labor. They eliminate drudgery. They don't take coffee breaks, don't belong to unions, and they work around the clock. They show up for work every day and quickly learn reasonably complex work. They don't get hurt, and never complain about dust, fumes, heat, or cold. And they can do a great variety of jobs with only a change in program and gripper hand (large mechanical tweezers).

Transfer machines

Automatic transfer machines have almost attained the automation stage in metal working (see Figure 9–5). An unfinished part, say a steel casting or a forging, is fastened to a conveyor which moves on a stop-and-go basis from one machine to the next. The part stops long enough at each machine to have one or more operations performed on it. Separate machines, performing successive operations, are lined up on each side of a conveyor

---

[1] See "The Hard Road to Soft Automation," by Tom Alexander, in *Fortune* (July 1971), p. 97.

[2] In General Motors' heavily automated Chevrolet Vega factory at Lordstown, Ohio, robots do 95 percent of the spot welding (there are over 9,000 spot welds in a Vega car body). At one point, two robots make 130 spot welds in 4½ seconds.

and as the conveyor stops, each machine automatically reaches out and performs its operation on the part. As the operating parts on the various machines move back and out of the way, the conveyor moves another step and the performance is repeated on the next units. The machines, though actually separate, operate together as if they were parts of a very complex single-purpose machine. Such machine groupings eliminate all product handling except the little that is needed before the first and after the last operation.

FIGURE 9–4. A mechanical robot spraying paint on automobile engines

An interesting problem arises when one operation takes considerably longer time than others. In such a case the operation must be considerably speeded up or else that particular operation must be broken into two parts. If it is a hole, one drill may drill it only part way and another drill, at another work station, may drill it the rest of the way. This allows individual operations to be in balance.

FIGURE 9–5   Schematic diagram of a transfer machine group

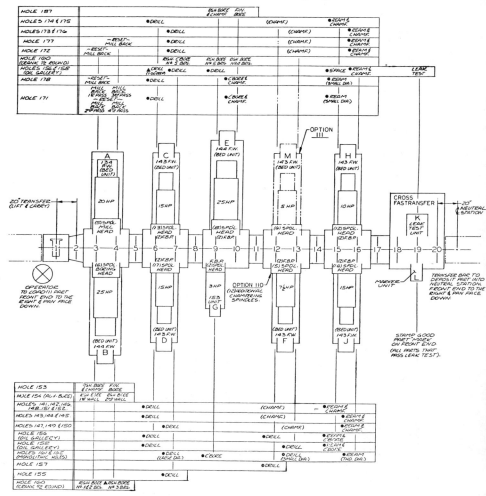

Source: The Cross Company.

Maldistribution curves and production methods

Most companies make many kinds of products, some of which sell in big volumes and others in small quantities. Such companies ought to use production lines for the high-volume products but not for the others.

It is possible to use a Pareto maldistribution curve to find out which products to make on lines. The idea is that, in many situations, there are "vital few" and "trivial many" groups of items. It is not uncommon for a company to find that 20 percent of its products are responsible for 80 percent of its volume. In fact, this idea is sometimes known as the 20–80 law.

To make a Pareto curve, the first step is to make a list of all a company's products and the sales volume of each. Next, they are ranked in order of their sales volume. Then the sales volumes are summed up cumulatively and the figures are converted into percentages of total sales. The same thing is done for the number of items. And then the paired percentages are plotted on a chart.

A simplified example will illustrate the development of a Pareto mal-distribution curve. Let us say that the ABC Company sells many kinds of products, of which the following 20 are representative. Their volumes (in thousands of dollars) are:

Annual volume	*Annual volume*
1,000	5,000
44	30
300	73
56	200
3,800	600
900	140
115	105
2,100	1,600
87	50
100	100

Sales in order of magnitude	*Cumulated sales*	*Percent of cumulated sales*	*Items*	*Percent of items*
5,000	5,000	30.5	1	5
3,800	8,800	53.7	2	10
2,100	10,900	66.5	3	15
1,600	12,500	76.2	4	20
1,000	13,500	82.3	5	25
900	14,400	87.8	6	30
600	15,000	91.5	7	35
300	15,300	93.3	8	40
200	15,500	94.5	9	45
140	15,640	95.4	10	50
115	15,755	96.1	11	55
105	15,860	96.7	12	60
100	15,960	97.3	13	65
100	16,060	97.9	14	70
87	16,147	98.5	15	75
73	16,220	98.9	16	80
56	16,276	99.2	17	85
50	16,326	99.5	18	90
44	16,370	99.8	19	95
30	16,400	100.0	20	100

When all of the paired percentages have been plotted and connected by a line as is done in Figure 9–6, they will make up a distribution curve (it is called a maldistribution curve because it departs so much from a diagonal line).

Figure 9–6 is curved a great deal, showing that the company's volume is heavily concentrated in a few of its products. If, in Figure 9–6, we read across the bottom scale to 20 percent and then go up to the curve and left to the vertical scale, we arrive at approximately the 75 percent mark. If we assume that our sample was representative of all the company's products, then the best-selling 20 percent of all of ABC's products produce 75 percent of the company's sales volume. These are its big bread-and-butter products. Reading across the bottom to 50 percent and going

FIGURE 9–6

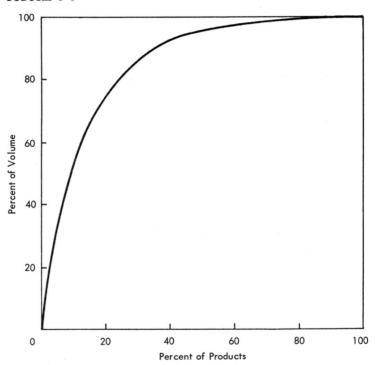

up to the curve, we find that the best 50 percent of the products produce 95 percent of the volume. The remaining 50 percent produce the remaining 5 percent of the volume, and thus don't amount to much.

This information can help a manager decide whether to go to line production by telling him where to look. If the company ought to go to line production for any products at all, those products will be in the 20 percent group that produces 75 percent of the business. Quite possibly, several of these big-selling items should be made by line production. Considering the other end of the chart, a company should surely not use line production methods for making the 50 percent of its products which bring in only 5 percent of the volume. Perhaps some kind of special production facilities, short of line production, would be best for the middle 30 percent of the products which produce 20 percent of the volume.

In a real-life analysis of this kind, the company involved, after seeing that its chart was quite dished, went to line production for its big-volume items, and saved 17 percent of its manufacturing costs.

Machine-use ratios

As was said in Chapter 6, owning a machine for 8 hours and getting 8 hours of work out of it are two different things. Setup time, repair time, operator personal time, not enough work to keep machines busy, and other causes all result in machine idle time. This reduces a machine's operating time and its realized capacity. It was also said that machines along production lines might be kept busy up to 90 percent of the time. But no one ever keeps machine-use ratios this high in such functional departments as the drill press, automatic screw machine, grinders, and similar departments which specialize in one kind of work.

In functional departments, 60 percent utilization of machine time (meaning that such a machine is actually running 288 minutes in a 480-minute day) is quite good and 40 percent is common. If it is assumed that machine use in functional departments is 50 percent, and if it would be possible (by installing a line) to get this up to 60 percent, the gain would be very worthwhile. The extra 20 percent in production would be free so far as extra machine investment is concerned.

An example will show how volume helps boost machine-use ratios. The discussion will assume that the line arrangement, where a whole line of machines is devoted to making one item, is responsible for the gains.

If a company has high volume and limited variety, it might be able to get reasonably high machine-use ratios even in functional departments. But with high volume and limited variety, it would probably be better to go to lines anyway so as to get the gains from low handling and low inventory costs. So high machine-use ratios and lines go together.

Differential housing production line example. This example assumes that a company makes a differential housing which is needed in large quantities and which requires 7 machining operations. Figure 9–7 lists the machines and each machine's hourly output.

Besides listing the machines, Figure 9–7 shows how many machines of each kind would be needed for various production levels. The company has to have 1 of each machine in order to turn out any products at all. And of course, the machines will not be very busy at low levels of output. As the quantities produced go up, the machines' use ratios go up until production gets to 40 units per hour, which is the internal grinder's output limit. At 40 units per hour, the internal grinder is operating at 100 percent of its capacity, and all 7 machines combined are averaging 58 percent.

FIGURE 9–7

					Units of output per hour				
		40	*57*	*62*	*63*	*79*	*80*	*114*	*120*
Kind of equipment	*Units per hour*	Percent of capacity of 1 machine at various production rates per hour							
Automatic screw machine..........	57	70	100	109	111	139	140	200	211
Surface grinder..................	156	26	37	40	40	51	51	73	77
Drill press......................	128	31	45	48	49	62	63	89	94
Centerless grinder...............	63	63	90	98	100	125	127	181	190
Polishing jack for exterior..........	62	65	92	100	102	127	129	184	194
Internal grinder..................	40	100	143	155	158	198	200	285	300
Polishing jack for interior..........	79	51	72	78	80	100	101	144	152
Total of percents......................		406	579	628	640	802	811	1,156	1,218
Number of machines (before adding one)....		7	8	9	10	11	12	13	14
Average utilization (percent)..............		58	72	70	64	73	68	89	87
Average utilization after buying next machine (percent)..................		51	64	63	58	67	62	83	81

If more than 40 units per hour are needed, the company will have to buy another grinder. Then it is all right up to 57 units per hour, at which time it will be necessary to get a second automatic screw machine. If the units climb to higher volumes, another bottleneck occurs at 62, at which point it will be necessary to get a second polishing jack for the exterior.

Figure 9–7 shows how, as production rates go up, one bottleneck after another arises. At each such point another machine will have to be bought. Figure 9–7 carries this example's analysis to 120 units an hour, by which time the company would have 2 or more of all but 2 kinds of machines.

In making up Figure 9–7, the percent use of each of the 7 kinds of machines was calculated for every production level at which it became necessary to buy another machine; hence the columns headed *40, 57, 62,* etc. In each column, the percent use of each kind of machine at that production level was listed. Then these use percentages were added and the total was divided by the number of machines.

At the first bottleneck point, where the production rate was 40 units an hour, the 7 machines' average use was 58 percent of the time. But buying a second internal grinder would make 8 machines, so the average machine-use rate would drop to 51 percent. Then no more machines would be needed until production got up to 57 units per hour. At 57 units, the average machine use is 72 percent. Then the company would have to buy a second automatic screw machine, and this would drop the average use ratio to 64 percent.

The use ratios in Figure 9–7 have been plotted on a chart, Figure 9–9. The line is jagged, but always moves upward toward the right, since the higher the volume, the greater the average use of all machines.

Theoretically, it is wrong to average the use rates of a $16,500 machine with those of $350 pieces of equipment. The real goal should be to get the greatest use from the *investment* in machines. So the attention should go to each machine's investment. High or low rates of use of expensive machines are more important than differences in the use of inexpensive machines.

We figured the investment-use ratios in Figure 9–8 and plotted them, along with the time-use ratios in Figure 9–9. It is surprising that the investment-use ratios are almost the same as the time-use ratios. Actually, these two ratios will almost always be close together if there are several machines. A simple ratio of the use of the machines' times proves reasonable after all.

FIGURE 9–8

	Installed cost of 1 machine	Units of output per hour							
		40	57	62	63	79	80	114	120
		Machine value used at various production rates per hour							
Automatic screw machine.........	$16,500	$11,550	$16,500	$18,000	$18,300	$22,950	$23,100	$33,000	$ 34,800
Surface grinder.......	8,275	2,150	3,050	3,300	3,300	4,200	4,200	6,050	6,350
Drill press..........	650	200	300	300	300	400	400	600	600
Centerless grinder.....	6,000	3,800	5,400	5,900	6,000	7,500	7,600	10,900	11,400
Polishing jack for exterior..........	350	200	300	350	350	450	450	650	700
Internal grinder......	8,700	8,700	12,450	13,500	13,750	17,250	17,400	24,800	26,100
Polishing jack for interior...........	350	200	250	250	300	350	350	500	550
Total value used............		26,800	38,250	41,600	42,300	53,100	53,500	76,500	80,500
Investment before adding 1 new machine.............		40,825	49,525	66,025	66,375	72,375	72,725	81,425	97,925
Investment utilization (percent).		66	77	63	64	73	74	94	82
Investment after adding new machine.................		49,525	66,025	66,375	72,375	72,725	81,425	97,925	106,625
Investment utilization (percent).		54	58	63	58	73	66	78	75

Lines and functional manufacture comparison. Now it is possible to turn to the question Should the company go to line production to make these differential housings or not? (The assumption is that high machine-use ratios mean that a line will be economical. And by "high use ratio" is meant anything higher than the 50 percent use that might be possible in functional departments.)

Figure 9–9 shows that the machines will be busy 50 percent of their time at a production rate of 35 units per hour. And 35 units an hour is 6,000 a month. So if volume is expected to stay above 6,000 a month, the company should go to line production because the machine–use ratios in prospect will be above 50 percent.

Putting in a line should save money, and to get an idea of how much a line might save, suppose that a sales volume of 13,000 gear casings a month (75 per hour) is assumed. The chart shows that at 75 units per hour, the machines will operate about 67 percent of the time. They will be $^{67}\!/_{50}$ as productive as the productivity usually obtained from machines in functional departments. In our example, it will take $70,000 worth of machines to turn out 75 units an hour. Were the machines in use only 50 percent of the time, the company would have to have $^{67}\!/_{50}$ as many machines, or $94,000 worth, to get this much output.

FIGURE 9–9

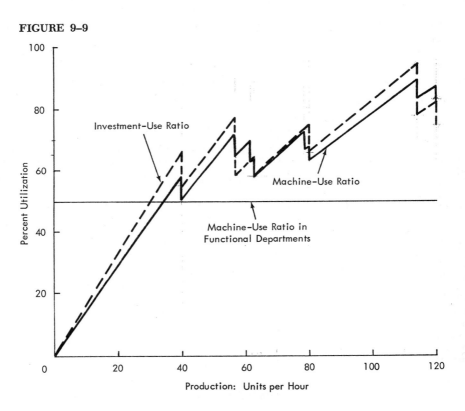

In this example, therefore, a line would save some part of the extra $24,000 investment in machines. How much would depend upon how high the company might be able to get the machines' use ratio in functional departments. Possibly, with a volume of 13,000 a month, even functional departments could get their ratio up halfway from 50 to 67 percent. If so, then the line would save the remaining half of the possible $24,000, or $12,000. Probably the savings in handling and inventory costs would be more important than this investment saving; yet a $12,000 savings in investment in machines is not trivial.

Vulnerability of lines to downtime

Lines almost eliminate the inventories of work in process. As soon as one operation is finished, the product moves to its next operation. The product deadtime between operations amounts to seconds, not hours, and only 1 or 2 items wait between operations—not 50 or 100 as in functional work arrangements.

Yet it is dangerous to have whole sequences of operations tied closely together. If one machine stops, they all stop, making it very costly.

Figure 9–10 shows how hooking successive operations together could work out. This example assumes 4 machines of equal capacity doing successive operations on a part made in large quantities. When the machines are operated individually, products slide down a chute at each machine into a tote box on the floor. When the box is full, the operator dumps it into the next machine's feed hopper.

FIGURE 9–10

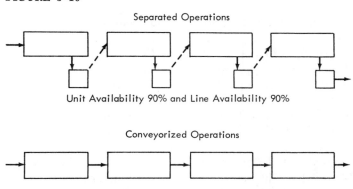

Separated Operations

Unit Availability 90% and Line Availability 90%

Conveyorized Operations

Unit Availability 90% and Line Availability 65%

Suppose that it is possible to hook these 4 machines together by adding, say, $800 worth of conveyors. Then each machine will dump its products onto a conveyor which takes them directly to the next machine's feed hopper. This saves labor, eliminates almost all the inventory of partly made products in process, and moves products through production faster.

This all sounds very good, but it may be unwise. Each machine has trouble sometimes, tools become worn or get out of adjustment, and the machines must be stopped in order to straighten things out. Suppose that each machine in Figure 9–10, when run separately, is down 10 percent of the time. This rarely holds up the others because of the between-machine supplies of products. So close to 90 percent utilization of the machine group can be achieved.

It would appear that if these four machines are connected, their utilization would be .90 raised to the fourth power, or .65. This is not so, however, since such a calculation implicitly assumes that any machine not in operation has the same likelihood of breaking down as it has while operating. To get the correct ratio it is first necessary to get a value for x by using the formula: $.90 = 1 \div (1 + x)$. In this case $x = 1 \div 9$. The formula for four machines hooked together is $1 \div (1 + 4x) = 9 \div 13 = .69$ (actually, production would be a little higher than 69 percent because the feed hoppers of each machine hold a few minutes' supply, so that very short stoppages of one machine would not stop the others).

Whether successive machines should be hooked together in this fashion depends a great deal on how much downtime each machine has. In Figure 9–10, for example, suppose that when the between-machines tote pans of material were eliminated, this cut the investment inventory by $400. At 20 percent a year, this saves $80 per year. And suppose that there will be additional savings of $1,000 worth of labor each year, which was formerly needed to put material into the next machine's feed hopper.

Against this should be set the $800 cost of installing the conveyors. So the proposed new arrangement seems to gain $280 the first year and $1,080 each year thereafter. So it would seem to pay well to install the conveyor.

But these figures have not considered the downtime. If each machine is worth $3 an hour in operation, the extra loss of 21 percent of one year's time (because the machines now run only 69 percent of the time instead of 90 percent) comes to 420 hours per machine, or 1,680 hours in total, and causes a loss of $5,040 per year. The company should surely not conveyorize and hook these machines together until this downtime can be reduced.

Automated installations of all kinds require that individual machines be highly reliable. Chrysler's Plymouth Division, for example, has a stretch of automated assembly line in its engine factory that uses 1,800 solenoid switches. If one goes off, merely finding which one is off is sometimes a big job. But whether the bad one is hard to find or not, such failures just cannot be allowed to happen often, or the losses will be staggering. (To keep this from happening, the equipment needs to be designed to be largely trouble free and parts need to be replaced before they fail.)

If a line stops when it should be operating, it idles all the machines and all the men, which is very costly. In a heavily automated steel mill, interferences which stop the mills are figured to cost $1,000 a minute and up. Production is lost, and possibly products or equipment are ruined. Such losses can easily occur in food production, chemicals, glass, rubber, and other industries. If a line stops during production, almost surely this will ruin both the products in process and the machinery. Besides these losses are the further losses from the cost of idle men.

Paradoxically, managers of highly mechanized production lines should be but little concerned about keeping the few men who serve such lines busy all the time. Quite the reverse. It pays to have some men standing around, doing little more than watching but instantly ready to fix anything that goes wrong. When things go well, these men have little to do.

Automatic assembly

In manufacturing, one of the last frontiers of handwork is assembly, and putting finished pieces together is still handwork in most industries. Assembly lines for putting shoes together, suits of clothes, automobiles, typewriters, adding machines, stoves, refrigerators, radios, television sets, and so on are characterized by *people* putting things together.

Nevertheless, automatic assembly is slowly becoming more common, although its high first cost and lack of flexibility stand in the way of faster acceptance. Automated assembly requires costly magazine feeds, indexing turn tables, robot fingers, hands, and arms, and all the electronic equipment (electric eyes, solenoid switches, electronic circuitry, etc.) that goes along with it. IBM assembles many of its electronic panel units automatically. Parker Pen assembles ball-point pens automatically. Gabriel Company assembles 2,000 valves an hour automatically. McGraw-Edison assembles 1,500 roller skate wheels an hour.

Here, in general, is how automatic assembly operates. A supply of every part is loaded into a hopper (or magazine feed) located above an assembling machine along a conveyor or around a Lazy Susan revolving table. The first assembling machine automatically picks out one of the frame parts of the product and fastens it on the conveyor. Then the conveyor "indexes" or moves it to the next work station (a foot or so away). There the next assembling machine puts its part into place in the frame. Then the conveyor indexes again and moves the frame to the next station, where part 2 is attached. Then more moves and more parts. Besides placing the parts, the machine fastens them, so that finished assemblies come off at the end of the line.

Here is what goes on at each of the 16 work stations of an IBM automatic machine for assembling wire contact relays:

Station 1 feeds molded plastic frames into the left side of a turret fixture. A vibrating feeder positions the frames, which move down inclined rolls to a loading platform. An air cylinder drives a horizontal reciprocating plunger, which pushes frames along a platform one at a time. Jaws lift a frame and place it in the left side of the fixture. A photoelectric cell watches the frames on rails and cuts off the feed if the frames back up. Frames pass through a fixture which stops those with misaligned or bent terminals. If one stops, the frames back up to a photoelectric detector.

Station 2 is the same as station 1 except that it feeds frames into the right side of the turret fixture. Between stations 2 and 3 an inspection device checks the loading of frames in their holding fixtures.

Station 3 probes for the presence and location of holes in the frames, and absence of dirt or "flash" in the holes. If the probe is impeded, work on the frames stops.

Station 4 countersinks holes in the frames for guide pins.

Station 5 taps holes for set screws.

Station 6 cleans chips from holes with an air blast.

Station 7 ejects frames found substandard at station 3. A memory pin, extended at station 3, closes an electric circuit at station 7, actuating rams that remove the frame from its work-holding fixture.

Station 8 examines tapped holes with photoelectric cells for broken taps. Clogged holes stop the light and this stops the machine. A signal light shows the operator the trouble spot.

Station 9 inserts rubber bumpers into threaded holes. Vibratory hoppers feed these bumpers in the correct position. Nozzles lift the bumpers by suction and transfer them to holes. When bumpers are seated in the frame, the air flow in nozzles automatically reverses from suction to pressure. Bumpers are released and pushed into position by air pressure.

Station 10 checks with photoelectric cells for the presence of bumpers. When a frame lacks one or both bumpers, the machine stops and a red light signals the operator.

Station 11 inserts a set screw into a tapped hole in the relay frame in the left side of the holding fixture. A vibratory feeder positions screws for driving. An automatic screwdriver sets screw at the right depth.

Station 12 inserts a set screw into frame in right side of the holding fixture.

Station 13 inserts guide pins into frames. A transfer arm picks up pins by vacuum and moves them by mechanical linkage to location where it inserts the pins into the frames.

Station 14 flares guide pins to secure them in frames.

Station 15 performs final inspection. It probes for guide pins and checks for high, low, or missing set screws.

Station 16 removes all relays. Those that have passed all inspections slide down a track into a container. Memory pins locate faulty relays, and when they find a faulty one they close an electric circuit, which shifts the track so that it drops the rejected relay into a reject box. This station also probes the fixtures to make sure all relays have been ejected.

So far, no one puts whole automobiles or any other big product together automatically, although General Motors' Lordstown, Ohio, factory approaches automated assembly. But small assemblies, yes. Probably industry will never assemble many whole, complex products automatically, but the possibilities are great for small electrical products, such as light bulbs, switches, telephone transmitters and receivers, transistors, radios, condensers, electric circuit panels, and the like. Also, small mechanical products, such as scissors, wrenches, staplers, can openers, and a host of others, could be assembled automatically.

Review questions

1. In metal cutting operations in factories is it, in general, better to have the material or the cutting tool move? Or is this not revelant? Why?
2. Is it possible to get the benefits of costly special-purpose machines, which

produce low unit costs for high-volume items, yet avoid most of the risks of loss if product designs change before the machines have fully paid for themselves? Explain.

3. Why do numerically controlled machines operate so economically?

4. How can the 20–80 law be helpful in decisions concerning the depth of tooling?

5. How much improvement in machine-use ratios ought to be achieved when a company changes from lot production to line production? What conditions would make this an economical move?

6. Is it more important, when comparing machine-use ratios of machines under different production situations, to compare the machines' hours of use ratio or dollars' investment-use ratio? Why?

7. Is there anything that managers can do to reduce either (a) the probability of a production line's having to stop or (b) the duration of the downtime when a stoppage occurs?

Discussion questions

1. Machine tool builders should know the capabilities of their machines better than anyone else, so their recommendations about speeds and feeds ought to be the best. Yet many companies feel that they can do better and so figure out their own speeds and feeds. Why is there this discrepancy? Discuss.

2. How can machine design engineers do a proper job of setting the most appropriate depth of tooling when market forecasts of sales volumes of products are often off by 50 percent or more?

3. Why is it that interest in robotry seems to be more general in Japan, where wages are low, than in the United States, where wages are high?

4. Since high volume makes it possible for a company to use production lines, which are so economical, how can companies with lower volumes get along?

5. If a company has several machines, each doing its job in sequence on the product, would conveyors probably cause production to go up or down? Why?

6. Isn't the maldistribution idea largely a textbook concept since every company ought to know which products are its biggest sellers? Discuss.

7. There is a good bit of acceptance of the Pareto maldistribution curve. Would its principle hold true for the products sold in a K-Mart or Sears store? If the answer is no, doesn't this suggest that maldistribution curves do not have such universal application?

Problems

1. Suppose that the following is a fair sample of the variety in sales volumes of all the items made by the ABC Company. Construct a maldistribution curve and read from it about what percent of the company's best-selling products produce 80 percent of its sales.

Product	Annual sales	Product	Annual sales	Product	Annual sales
1.........	$315,000	6.........	$ 60,000	11.........	$275,000
2.........	25,000	7.........	450,000	12.........	190,000
3.........	110,000	8.........	8,000	13.........	13,000
4.........	9,000	9.........	110,000	14.........	60,000
5.........	17,000	10.........	5,000	15.........	125,000

2. A company is introducing a new product which it plans to price at $100 per unit. It is considering 5 alternative ways to make this product, each having different tooling-up costs and different variable costs, as follows:

Method	Tooling cost	Variable cost per unit
A......................	$10,000	$75
B......................	15,000	50
C......................	25,000	30
D......................	40,000	20
E......................	50,000	16

The prospective volume estimates are:

Quantity	Probability
1,000.........................	.15
1,500.........................	.20
2,000.........................	.25
2,500.........................	.18
3,000.........................	.13
3,500.........................	.06
4,000.........................	.02
5,000.........................	.01

Which manufacturing process should be chosen?

3. The Lapperre Electric Company is primarily a producer of 110-volt AC fractional HP motors. It has a single factory, which is composed of a series of assembly lines surrounded by various subassembly departments. The company is at present scheduling an order for 10,000 ¼-hp. 110-volt universal motors. One phase of this scheduling is concerned with the armature winding operation. This winding is done by machine and has had a time standard of 6 minutes per armature set by time study methods. The standards are loose enough for the average machine operator to exceed the standard by 20 percent. The assembly line on which this lot of motors will be assembled has a capacity of 2 motors per minute. Actually, though, this line has an average downtime rate of 5 percent. The production control department has 4 winding machines which are, or will be, available for this job.

Will it be possible for the armatures to be wound continuously as an integral part of the assembly, or will it be necessary to wind and store some of them before the final assembly begins to insure uninterrupted assembly?

If it is necessary to wind and store some of the armatures, how many hours before assembly begins must the winding begin? (Assume that winding will continue during assembly, so that in the ideal case the finished armature will go directly from winding to assembly without storage.)

4. Suppose that in the example given in the text on line balancing (p. 223) the productivity figures are as follows:

Kind of equipment	Units per hour	Kind of equipment	Units per hour
Automatic screw machine....	22	Polishing jack for exterior ...	175
Surface grinder............	180	Internal grinder...........	75
Drill press................	90	Polishing jack for interior....	200
Centerless grinder.........	20		

Draw up a machine time-use chart similar to Figure 9–9. Should the company go to line production (assuming that this should be done at the point where the machines will be 55 percent busy on average) if production will be 10 units per hour? 20, 30, 40, 50 units? Where is the crossover point—where should the change be made to line production?

The company doesn't have a very good idea of what the demand for this product will be, but the market forecasters have made the following estimates:

Hourly output	Probability
10.........................	.05
20.........................	.15
30.........................	.20
40.........................	.30
50.........................	.20
60.........................	.05
70.........................	.05

Should a line arrangement or a functional arrangement be installed?

5. In the text's example of chaining successive machines together (p. 224) we found that the losses outweighed the gains. Suppose we had 6 machines with the following normal downtimes: .02, .06, .07, .03, .05, .10. This means that machine 1 runs 98 percent of the time, machine 2, 94 percent, etc. (The machines are of equal capacity.)

By spending $10,000 for equipment, which will last 5 years, we can reduce the inventory between operations by $3,000, and also save $10,000 in labor (in a year) picking up and putting down materials. Inventory carrying costs are figured at 20 percent per year. The plant operates 2,000 hours a year, and we'd like to keep these machines operating; in fact, we lose $8 an hour on every machine for every hour it does not operate.

Should we go ahead and mechanize? If we do, how much will we gain or lose?

6. The engineers have decided that volume is sufficient to justify setting up a small work center to work continuously at making part A. This particular job is a drilling operation, and 120 pieces per hour are wanted.

It takes ¼ minute to unload the drilling machine, ½ minute to load it, and 1½ minutes to drill the hole. The work is done by a machinist whose hourly rate is $6. But the unloading could be done by a $4 an hour helper. Machine time is calculated to be worth $10 an hour. During the 1½ minute of drilling time the machinist could be doing other work, such as loading another machine.

Set up this work station so as to minimize the costs of producing 120 pieces per hour.

Recent references

Alexander, T., "Hard Road to Soft Automation," *Fortune,* July 1971

Bennett, K. W., "Best Seller '72: Run, Robot, Run," *Iron Age,* December 23, 1971

Buzacott, J. A., "Prediction of the Efficiency of Production Systems without Internal Storage," *International Journal of Production Research,* London, 1968, Vol. 6, No. 3.

"Computer Controlled Machines," *Purchasing,* April 15, 1971

Dooley, A. R., and T. M. Stout, "Rise of the Blue-Collar Computer," *Harvard Business Review,* July–August 1971

Driscoll, Leo C., and John C. Kotelly, "Blue-Collar Robots," *Industrial Research,* October 1971

Ertell, Glenn G., *Numerical Control,* New York: John Wiley, 1969

Pritchard, H. S., "New Approaches to Computer Control of Conveyor Lines," *Factory,* November 1971

Sandford, J. E., "Increasing Output Is Job for Machine—Not People," *Iron Age,* February 10, 1972

10

Designing manual jobs along production lines

THE ASSEMBLY PART of making assembled products out of parts is largely manual. Men attach parts and components, doing it all manually or with the aid of simple, portable hand tools. As we said in an earlier chapter, production lines save labor because products are moved by conveyor and are not carried around by men. Also, the direct movement of products from one operation to another almost eliminates inventories in process. And it also eliminates a great deal of paper work because it is not necessary to tell production workers and material handlers what to do.

Perhaps the most important problem in line production is to align the jobs so that they all require almost identical times to perform. Thus the output of a line is determined by the work station which takes the most time. If one assignment takes more time than the others, its rate of output will determine the line's maximum production. Men at other work stations with shorter work assignments, will be underutilized. It becomes highly important, therefore, to try to develop equal work assignments for every work station.

Automobile assembly job design

In General Motors' Willow Run plant outside Detroit, Walter Jones, at work station 15, picks up a long, slender metal tube which is bent into an odd shape. Jones fastens this tube with four clips to the underside of a Chevrolet automobile body that is hanging from an overhead conveyor as it slowly passes over his head. The tube is part of the Chevrolet hydraulic brake system, and the bends in it allow it to follow the contours of the underside of the car.

Jones does not, however, fasten either end of the tube to anything because this is not part of his job. Fastening the ends is part of someone else's job, because either (1) Jones already has all the work he can handle (this is true in any case, because if Jones fastened the ends he would *not* do some of the other work he now does), or (2) the parts that the hydraulic tube is to be fastened to are not on the car yet, or (3) Jones's working position would make it hard or awkward for him to do the fastening, whereas this will not be so for some other worker farther down the line.

Jones has a collection of small tasks to perform on every car that comes along (at the rate of 1 a minute). His collection of tasks adds up to enough to keep him busy for about 1 minute (probably a little less, but not more than 1 minute).

Jones does not have the work station to himself, but this makes no problem because he works only on the left underside of Chevrolets. Jack Hamett, who works at the same station, works only on the right underside of Chevrolets.

Neither Jones nor Hamett is hurrying with his tasks, yet each works steadily. The duties which make up each man's 1-minute job package were selected to add up to almost 1 minute's work when he works steadily yet not at a rapid pace. (A relief man takes each man's place along the line for two 12-minute periods each shift. There is 1 relief man for every 20 regular men on the line.)

A visitor walking along this assembly line would find everybody working at about the same pace. At every work station men, sometimes 1, sometimes 2, perform their near 1-minute collection of tasks on the cars that keep coming along. And as the conveyor moves, the Chevrolet becomes more nearly a car as more parts are put on. Somewhere along the way, someone fastens one end of the hydraulic brake tube to the car's master brake cylinder, and someone else fastens the other end to the brake for a wheel.

Rate of output and number of work stations

The output of lines is high, not because they turn out 50 units often but because they turn out 1 unit *very* often. If, for example, there is need for 2,000 assembled products a week, they probably should be produced by the line production method. The line could be planned to turn out about 1 unit a minute. (There are 2,400 minutes in a 40-hour week, but some time is lost for rest breaks and starting and stopping each day.)

Both the men and the machines along the line would be geared to work 1 minute on each unit of product, so that the total work to be done would have to be broken up into 1-minute jobs. If, in total, it took 120 man-minutes to assemble a product, this work might well be divided into, say, 130 slightly less than 1-minute jobs. The plan, then, could be for a line with 130 work stations. (Each man's assignment would have to be for a little less than 1 minute's work because the bits and pieces of work won't come out even and because their work time will vary a little.)

The matter of line speed and job cycle time is discussed later in this chapter; here, however, it should be said that line production usually is not very satisfactory for low production—say 25 units per week. In such a case each man would have nearly an hour-and-a-half job assignment on every unit since he would produce 25 units in 40 hours. He could not become very proficient at doing all of the minute tasks he would have to do in his hour-and-a-half assignment, and he might even have trouble remembering them. Almost always, it would be better to use lot production for only 25 units a week.

A first step in determining work station assignments is to determine the work load of the line. The number of units wanted per hour, multiplied by the man-hours required per unit, gives the total man-hour work load per clock hour. And, as we said, if it takes a total of 2 man-hours, or 120 man-minutes of assembly time per unit of product, and 60 units an hour are wanted, something like 130 man-hours must be provided along the line every hour.

Cycle times and number of work stations. It is also necessary to determine the cycle-time and number-of-work-stations (or work zones) relationships. If 60 units an hour are wanted, 65 work stations through which 1 unit of product moves every minute would do the job. There would be 2 men at every work station. Thus almost 2 minutes of work will be done at every work station every minute.

But a 65-work-station arrangement is not the only alternative; the line could be set as 130 work stations with 1 man at each. Another choice would be to have 80 or 90 stations with 1 man at some stations and 2 men at others. Or the line could have 45 stations with 3 men at most of them. Or, if the men would not get in each other's way, there could be fewer stations with more men.

It is also possible to change the cycle time. There could be 2 lines with 30 units coming off each line per hour. This would double the amount of specialized equipment needed, but it would open up other possibilities of line speed, number of stations, and number of men at each station. In any case, there are many possible choices, and not just one or two.

When the cycle-time and number-of-work station relationships have been decided, this automatically sets both the line speed and the amount of space which will be needed along the line. If the products are automobiles and 1 per minute is wanted, it may be necessary to provide as much as 25 feet per work station along the conveyor. If so, then the conveyor will have to move at a rate of 25 feet per minute. And since all the men have close to 1-minute jobs, each station will have to be 25 feet long or longer. In total, at least 65 x 25 feet, or 1,625 feet of work space, will be needed for the work stations along the line. This is a minimum.

If a line normally moves 25 feet during the minute it takes a man to do his work, it is a good idea to allot a little more than 25 feet to the station. Then, if he sometimes needs to stay with the product a little longer, he can do so. This gives him a little latitude in balancing out his long and short work cycles. It also gives the job designer the opportunity to assign men work packages which contain almost a full minute's work instead of something less. Normally, since a man can stay with the product for only a minute, his work package has to be sufficiently less than 1 minute to care for his occasional long work cycle within a minute. This results in the underutilization of men.

More space can often be made available. In-between station space may also be needed to provide space for between-jobs storage banks or for other reasons. But if there are no such reasons, it is well to put a work station in as little space as is required—25 feet in our example.

The discussion so far has assumed that the number of work stations and the space required can be figured out ahead. This isn't quite the case, however, because the exact number of work stations and the number of men needed have to await the development of what we call "work packages" for each man. Possibly these can be developed so that on average they contain .85 minutes of work for each man. Or the average work content of each man's assignment could be higher or lower. But whatever it is, the final number of men and work stations is in part a result of how the computer manages to group minor bits of work into work packages. We will see (later in this chapter) that there can be variations in how this works out.

Desirability of a single line. It might seem that when a total assembly job is made up of a thousand or more small bits of work which add up to 120 man-minutes, there would be an almost limitless number of permutations and combinations of how these bits can be made into men's work assignments.

At one extreme, 1 man could do the whole job. In this case it would seem that 130 or so men could be working at the same time, each assembling a complete product. At the other extreme, 130 or so men could each be doing just about 1 minute's work on each product as it passes his work station. Between these extremes there could be millions of combinations. There could be, for example, 24 men each doing 5 minutes of work on every 24th product in one place along the line; there could be individual men, each doing 2 minutes work on every second unit somewhere else; or there could be only 40 men along a line, each doing 3 minutes work on every third product, etc.

A moment's thought, however, reveals how impractical almost every other possible combination is when compared to a line with each man doing 1 minute's work. Other arrangements multiply both materials handling costs and tooling costs.

FIGURE 10–1. A loop-type assembly conveyor and work stations

If 130 men each made whole products, supplies of the hundreds of parts would have to be brought to each of the 130 work stations. At each work station, therefore, the men would have to have supply bins for these hundreds of parts.

Each man would also need every tool that would be required for every bit and piece of the whole job. He would need nut and bolt tighteners, soldering irons, riveters, and everything else. If any operation needed special work area conditions, such as heat removal from welding, each work place would have to have this too. One hundred and thirty sets of everything would have to be provided.

Truckers would also have to truck away finished units: 1 every 2 hours from 130 different work stations, or else let them pile up. In any case, the inventories of parts and finished products and the materials handling costs would be exorbitant.

When all of these factors are considered, the economical choice is almost always *one* production line, with each man doing 1 part, and 1 part only, of the total work and doing it on every unit.

Heuristic line balancing

Years ago it was a tedious task for engineers to work out the neat balance between men's assignments along production lines so that they were equally busy and so that everything was kept moving evenly. The engineers had to make out long lists of minor parts ($\frac{5}{100}$ and $\frac{10}{100}$ of a minute parts, not 2- and 3-minute parts), called "elements," of the total task of assembling a car. Then, mindful of which things had to be done first and how long the minor tasks took, they developed work packages of close to 1-minute duration for the men who were to work along the line.

Today this method has not changed, but it is no longer the tedious task it used to be because computers do almost all of it. Computers do it faster and almost perfectly because they can, almost instantly, search out more combinations than the engineers could by using their slow, old, cut-and-dry methods.

Computers do not, however, search out every possible combination of the thousands of minor tasks before settling on certain collections of tasks that become the job assignments along the line. Instead, they search for near perfect bundles of duties for the men who do the first jobs along the assembly lines. When the computer finds a near perfect set of tasks, it sets these tasks apart as the man's job assignment for work station 1, then it does the same for work station 2, and so on down the line.

The computer does not just take the first duties it comes to which add up to less than the limit time. If these happen to add to .65 minute and the next element the computer comes to takes .40 minute, it would reject the .40-minute element (for the moment) because this element would make the work package exceed 1 minute. But neither does the computer "close" the package at .65 minute, because this would leave the man with .35 minute of idle time. Instead, the computer sets the .40-minute activity aside momentarily while it searches for other short-time activities to bring the work assignment for work station 1 up to .85 or .90 of a minute. Then it regards work station 1's assignment as complete and sets it aside. Next the computer comes back to the .40-minute activity and uses it as the first part of the assignment it will develop for work station 2.

FIGURE 10–2. Assembling refrigerators and freezers at Whirlpool, where the minor tasks add up to nearly full use of the men's time (average 82 percent)

(*a*) putting insulation on cold plate tubing (79.2%)

(*b*) driving 3 screws in shelf and liner (94.8%)

(*c*) installing crisper pan (85.5%)

(*d*) positioning suction line in clips (69.3%)

When the computer collects minor tasks this way and arranges them in sets that will become a man's assignment, it is doing it "heuristically." This is in contrast to doing it mathematically. Theoretically, the computer could, by mathematics, select the very best combination of tasks to make every man's assignment. But there are billions of possible combinations of these tasks, and it would take even a computer a long time to work out every combination and then pick the best.

In a heuristic procedure the computer is told to make logical decisions such as a man would make. The computer is given logical rules to follow, such as element A must come before B, work on the top of a car cannot be combined with work on the bottom, work on the frame must be done before the body shell goes on, the total time in a job assignment cannot add up to more than a minute, etc. The computer is given all of the restrictions it must respect and it is told to find combinations of duties which fit the restrictions.

The reason the computer may not arrange the minor tasks into the very best combinations is that once it puts a minor task into the package for job 1, the computer regards this as disposed of and does not consider it in its further searching. It removes the job 1 duties from its list of duties and goes on to search for a good set of duties for the next work station, and so may never find the absolutely perfect set of job assignments. (The perfect set might, for example, require withdrawing some of the duties put into job assignment 1 and reassigning them elsewhere, where they would fit even better.) This is only a quibble, however, because at relatively low cost, computers, using the method just described, do an excellent job of dividing work into almost exactly equal assignments for men along the line.

Yet, before going on, it should be said that when the computer is "told to follow logical rules," its job is made to sound too simple. This implies that a few elementary rules of logic can guide the computer. Yet these rules *can't* be too simple and too few. The computer can develop better sets of work packages if it gets several rules to follow as it selects packages of elements from among those which are eligible.

Policy decisions. Random selection by a computer of activities from among eligible activities, if based only on how long they take (the procedure described above), may not produce the best work packages. Fred Tonge, in an extensive heuristic simulation in which he tested several policies, found that indeed it did not. Tonge tested the following eight policies (as well as others which produced poorer results):[1]

1. Choose the activity with the longest time.
2. Choose the activity with the most immediate following tasks.
3. Choose activities randomly.
4. Choose activities which first became available for assignment.
5. Choose activities which last became available for assignment.
6. Choose activities with the most following tasks.
7. Choose activities with the greatest work time for following elements.
8. Choose activities with the lowest priority number (all tasks having been previously given priority numbers in approximate accord with their required sequence).

Using hypothetical figures and a large number of simulated computer runs (the original data were rearranged randomly after each run), Tonge tested these rules and found the computer produced a considerable variety of work packages for the list of activities in the problem he was testing. Except for one instance of 21 work stations, the computer distributed the tasks to 22, 23, and even 24 work stations.

Since each station requires 1 man, these differences represent differences in the efficiency of the use of men's time. Several of the rules always yielded 24-station assignments whereas others always yielded 22. Clearly, if a computer is told to follow only one policy, it should follow one of those which always found the 22-station combinations (this would be policy 1, or 4, or 7).

---

[1] This list is adapted from a list in Fred M. Tonge, "Assembly Line Balancing Using Probabilistic Combinations of Heuristics," *Management Science,* 11, No. 7 (May 1965), 727–35.

Rule: choose task	Number of work stations Percent of time listed			
	21	22	23	24
1. With largest time...................		100		
2. With most immediate followers.......		44	56	
3. Randomly.........................		3	65	32
4. Which became available first........		100		
5. Which became available last.........				100
6. With most followers................. 1		93	6	
7. With largest positional weight.......		100		
8. With highest distinct number........			100	
9. With highest positional number......			43	57
10. With least time....................				100
11. With fewest immediate followers.....		31	48	21
12. With fewest followers...............				100
13. With smallest positional weight......				100
14. With lowest distinct number.........			100	
15. With lowest positional number.......		17	83	

Tonge went further in his analysis and tried giving the computer pairs of rules, with the second to be used to break ties. This produced a noticeable improvement. Although 22- and 23-station work sets were still the most common, 24-station assignments were fewer. And 21-station assignments were common. In one combination, where policy 1 and policy 7 were used together, 21-station assignments turned up in 60 percent of the simulations.

It appears from Tonge's work that the quality of the computer's work depends on the quality of the rules given to it.

Rules	Number of work stations Percent of times listed			
	21	22	23	24
1 and 7.....................	60	40		
6 and 7.....................	31	69		
1 and 6.....................	24	76		
1 and 11....................	14	40	45	
1 and 9.....................	7	43	40	10
1 and 8.....................	1	39	55	5
1 and 15....................		69	31	
1 and 14....................		51	49	
1 and 10....................		17	71	12
8 and 9.....................		5	56	39
10 and 11...................			28	72

Information needed for job balancing

Before a computer can be used to balance work along assembly lines it is necessary to gather quite a bit of information. The kind of information needed is of the same kind whether the job is to assemble washing machines, television sets, automobiles, or whatever. But we will continue to use automobiles as an example.

First, it is necessary to make a list of every minor task required to assemble a car. By "minor" is meant tasks as short as $5/100$ or $10/100$ of a minute, not 2- or 3-minute tasks. This list may well run into thousands of minor tasks, which a time study man calls "elements." The list must also show how long it will take a man to perform each element. All these things need to be known *before* any cars have been assembled along the line.

Yet how can an industrial engineer know ahead of time what minor tasks have to be done in order to assemble a washing machine or an automobile? And how can he know, before a line is set up, just how long each element will take? Most of the engineers who do this work usually rely on past experience with similar products to supply this information because much of the work on, say, this year's cars is like that on last year's models.

If, however, a company is going into totally new kinds of work, the methods men will not be able to figure these things out too well. It would therefore be a good idea to assemble a few pilot items in an experimental area so they can learn as much as they can from seeing the work done.

In any case, the industrial engineers try to visualize how the work is going to be done along the line and develop the list of minor tasks it takes to do the whole job. Then they try to figure out about how long it will take to do each little part of the whole task. (Chapter 16 will show how industrial engineers do this, using catalogs of how long it takes to make basic human movements.)

Elements for line balancing purposes are generally different from those used by time study men in setting production standards. For line balancing they need to be "transferable work components"—minor activities which can be removed, if need be, from one place and put somewhere else without making extra work. Tightening a bolt is transferable from placing it. But tightening one bolt on a wheel of a car is not transferable from tightening another bolt on the same wheel because the worker has to pick up and put down a bolt tightener, and it is desirable to hold down tool handling time.

Element precedence

Element precedence matters also have to be determined before the computer can go to work. Some elements have to be done before others, whereas it doesn't matter with other elements. A man putting on his clothes in the morning has to put on his shirt before his tie, but it doesn't matter whether he combs his hair and then puts on his shoes or the other way around. And so it is with cars and television sets; sometimes the element sequence matters and sometimes it doesn't. A hole has to be drilled before it can be threaded and an automobile wheel has to be put on before the bolts that hold it can be put on. But it doesn't matter whether a storage battery is installed before or after the carburetor or whether a front wheel goes on before a back wheel. The order of sequence is sometimes "must do" and at other times it is "can do."

"Must do" is both a positive and a negative restraint at the same time. The wheel must be put on the car before its bolts can go on. Similarly, the bolts cannot be put on ("must not do") until the wheel is on.

All "can do" elements finally become "must do." It doesn't matter whether a front wheel goes on before a back wheel or the other way around; they are "can do" with respect to each other. And for a good while early in assembly, it doesn't matter when the steering wheel is put in. But finally, and well before the car is finished, the steering wheel has to go in. It is "can do" for a long time, but the time will come when it becomes "must do" with respect to the next element.

FIGURE 10–3. Zoning sketch indicating possible zones for assembly operations along a conveyor (conditions for a specific situation will determine "can do" for a given work element in several zones or "must do" in a particular zone)

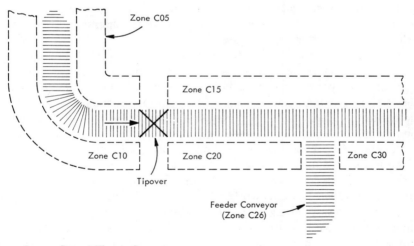

Source: General Electric Company.

Often it is a good idea to think of "must do," "must not do," and "can do" elements as they apply to zones or general areas along the line rather than as they relate to particular work stations. An element way well be "must not do" for early zones (a car can't be washed until it is put together); then it may become "can do" for several zones; and finally, if it has not been assigned earlier, it is "must do" for some particular zone.

Sometimes there are "must not do" constraints because of the nature of the work. Some elements are dirty whereas others are clean, and they should be kept apart. The car should not be greased, for example, adjacent to putting in the upholstery.

General Motors' engineers use a quality or priority index to help the computer slot elements into their most desirable work package. The quality index for each element, which is set by the industrial engineers, reflects their view of its overall priority in the assignments of elements to first jobs along the line.

Man requirements

Normally, work station assignments should not be used just as they come from the computer because a good methods man can improve them here and there. Maybe he can rearrange them and avoid having an operator work in an awkward position. He can move the awkward-position duty to the assignment of a man whose other duties have him in a better position.

Also, knowing the men's work assignments lets the methods man visualize where an operator will be standing and which direction he will be facing. He can then develop instructions for the people loading parts on parts-supply conveyors so that the operator does not have to turn things around. They would load suspension springs, axles, differentials, motors, doors, radios, etc., in the right position and save the operator's time. Computers cannot see these needs.

Besides the purely physical element-precedence matters, methods men need to consider how elements will combine into job packages for the men. The analyst should try to hold down extra "nonproductive" activities, such as picking up wrenches or having a man move from one side of the car to the other. And a man should not have to work under a car and then on top of it.

Nor should men walk while not working, except in a direction opposite to the line's movement. If a man is to have a 1-minute set of elements to perform while the product moves through his station, he has to work on a moving product. If all his work is done on the product at the same spot, he will have to walk along with it for 25 feet as the product moves along. Then he will have to walk back the same 25 feet to the start of his work station and again follow the next product through his station. He walks all day long. This actually happens, sometimes, in the assembly of automobiles, refrigerators, stoves, and television sets. Sometimes, however, the man rides along with the product on a floor-level conveyor and only walks back.

It might seem that it would be possible to cut out this waste (the nonproductive walking back the length of the work station), and one way to stop it is to use a stop-and-go conveyor and give each man a work package of elements which he can perform while remaining in one spot. Then workers could do all of their work without walking. But if a stop-and-go conveyor is used, everyone is idle during the time the conveyor is moving the product to the next station. And besides, if the man's work is partly on one end of the car and partly on the other end, he has to walk anyway.

Another possibility is to try to put together minor tasks so that they are done from front to back on the product. If it is an automobile, the analysts try to give the men certain tasks on the front of the car, then some on the middle, and then some on the rear end. Then the men can stand still and do their work.

Above all, men's tasks should not be in reverse. A man should not have to do work on the rear end of a car, followed by work in the middle, and finish with work on the front end. He would always have to chase the car in order to do the next part of his work. By the time he got to his last duties, he would be over in the next work station area, because that is where the front end of the car would be by then.

A methods man can also pay attention to "closed" and "open" work stations. In a closed station, all the work must be done in the regular area; nor can other work be done in this area. In an open station, a worker from the previous station could follow the product into the next area if he gets behind a little. His finishing his task would not disrupt the next station's work. Closed-area work packages must never take too long. Open-area packages could occasionally take longer than normal.

Try as one may, however, to foresee everything and to balance out the work, there will always be a good many bugs (unequal work loads, parts can't be fastened so quickly as was expected, quality troubles, etc.) to straighten out when a line starts production. There will be some rearranging to do.

Subassembly lines

The best way to make an assembled product is to make it out of subassemblies. Valves, pumps, generators, gear sets, and other components should first be put together as components and then assembled into the final products.

Figure 10–4 is a diagram of the way Western Electric puts telephones together, and is based on subassembly and final assembly being carried on as a single, coordinated activity. The output rates of subassembly lines and final assembly are the same, and, normally, subassemblies flow off their lines at the rate of the final assembly line's needs.

It often happens, however, that it is uneconomical to operate subassembly lines at exactly the same rate of the final assembly line. When this is so, they should be decoupled and each should operate at its most economical rate, with differences being compensated for by unlike work hours and small between operation balancing inventories wherever they are needed. Not only can subassembly lines operate different hours, they

FIGURE 10–4. Schematic diagram of sub- and final assembly of telephones

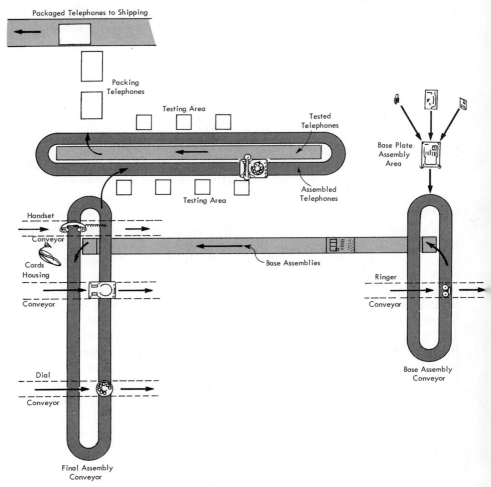

Source: Western Electric Company.

can be located in other departments, other plants, or even in other companies. Magnavox assembles television sets using color tubes it buys from RCA. Both the finished sets and the tubes are made on production lines, but the tube lines for Magnavox's TV sets are in RCA's factories.

Often, and aside from possibly differing output rates, it is best to do subassembly work in its own area, away from final assembly. Subassembled components usually need inspection and performance testing, so there is need for a break before final assembly. Furthermore, subassembly lines always have to produce more units than final lines use in order to supply repair components for sale—or, as in the case of RCA making tubes for Magnavox, for sale to other companies as well. Sometimes, too, and within the same company, one plant produces components for one or more sister plants, so that—again—the subassembly lines' output quantity is very different from its own plant's final-line needs.

Problems with lines

Lines create numerous problems, one of which is the matter of manning them. Lines usually need men at every work station, and if anyone is absent, someone else has to fill in for him. Not only this, but the substitute has to keep up with the line's pace although he may be quite unacquainted with the work. Fortunately, job assignments are usually so simple that men not experienced on particular jobs can step in with little preparation and yet hold up their end. Should this not be possible, it might be necessary to put two men on in order to keep production up.

Product variety introduces a second class of problems: lines can handle minor but not major variations in products. Similarly, some products require operations which are not needed for other products. In an automobile assembly line, four-door cars require men to work on the two rear doors—work which two-door cars don't need. In order to operate economically, a line's output must be confined to one main kind of product, with variations confined to minor differences. It would be quite uneconomical to assemble trucks on the same line with passenger cars; they are too unlike and require too many unlike operations.

In the case of line work on smaller items (radios, kitchen clocks, etc.), a great deal of flexibility in variety of products can be achieved by not fastening them to conveyors. The operators can stay at fixed work stations where they work on the products that come to them. If the products are not fastened to a conveyor, the operators can keep an inventory of two or three products on their work benches. Then, if some kinds of products require an operation which others don't need, those not needing it can go right on to their next operation. But if two or three products needing one operation come along at one time and if the operator might get behind, he just pulls them off the conveyor and lets them wait a few minutes until he gets to them.

Product-mix variations also make problems. Customer demands force some variety, so lines need to be flexible enough to handle a limited amount of change in product mix. Instead of one problem, this makes two: line balancing and model sequencing.

Such variety changes the bits and pieces of work done at the work stations along the line. They subtract from, or add to, a man's assignment and create imbalances here and there. A nominal amount of variety will not create undue imbalances, and this can be tolerated.

But if substantial product-mix variations seem to be permanent, or if they last for several weeks, it may be worthwhile to realign and reassign the work along the line. It is possible to have two or three alternative work assignment lists prepared ahead of time so that foremen can change the men's job assignments whenever the product mix changes and thus avoid excessive idle time.

Volume variation also makes problems. Normally, if there is need for less (or more) output from a line, the whole line works fewer (or more) hours. It would be possible, however, to use fewer men and to send products down the line at a slower rate. This would, of course, necessitate rearranging the bits and pieces of work and changing the work packages for the work stations.

Again, as in the case of product-mix variations, it is possible to pre-compute the worker-package assignments suitable for several production levels. The foreman then could use the assignment list which is appropriate for the volume. Changing is a big job, however, and is not often done.

Another problem is that average job performance times don't always average out in an offsetting way. If, for example, operation B follows operation A, and each averages 2 minutes but has some variation, then it will *not* be possible to get 1 product every 2 minutes from this combination.

Suppose that although each operation averages 2 minutes, each operation also takes as long as 2.25 minutes in 10 percent of the cases. So whenever A takes 2.25 minutes, B has to wait .25 minute. Then worker B goes ahead with his operation, which takes 2 minutes. But 4.25 minutes pass before the 2 operations are completed. The average time the product spends in these 2 operations is, in this example, 2.125 minutes per operation, not 2 minutes. In practice, the average time would be close to, but nevertheless *more* than, 2 minutes.

There would be no trouble if operations A's and B's long and short performance times always dovetailed and so offset each other, but this won't happen very often. The irregularities are bound to cause a certain amount of lost time. It is possible to take care of such variations, of course, by allowing for a small work-balancing stock of products between operations. This is not, however, a feasible solution to the problem of time variations along a line where the products are large and there are many work stations.

Multiple stations. Sometimes a particular job cannot be economically subdivided into 1-minute assignments and must be treated as a 2- or 3-minute job. If so, then 2 or 3 work stations will be needed and the man at each station will work on only every second or third product.

In order for this to work well, it would be desirable for the products coming down the line to split into 2 or 3 lines at such stations. Then each man can do his 2- or 3-minute job on his product. The product can then move on and resume its place in the regular flow to the following work stations. This is not absolutely necessary, however. The work station can be 2 or 3 times as long as usual and each man can take his second or third product in turn and walk along with it for 2 or 3 minutes as he performs his assignment. When he is finished, he can walk back past his 1 or 2 fellow workers to his next product.

Fixed-position assembly

Large products, such as certain factory machines or airplanes or loco-motives, are not put together along assembly lines in the usual sense. They are not assembled on the go. Instead, they are more or less *con-structed* in one spot in the assembly department. They are usually moved only occasionally from one assembly area to another.

In these cases the men come to the work, rather than have the work come to them. Often whole crews of men work possibly for days or weeks before their work is done. Then either the product is taken to the next general assembly area or the next work crew takes over.

Job design is very different from what it is along the more usual kind of assembly line. Instead of men having to perform a limited collection of minor job elements which add up to only a minute, in this case the men have general, overall job-accomplishment assignments. It is like a man painting a house or putting the electrical wiring in a house. The men themselves have to figure out the bits and pieces of work that need doing, and then do them. Usually they work with portable tools because the total number of any one product does not justify extremely specialized equipment. Furthermore, such specialized equipment, if used, would also need to be portable, since—except when it is being used—it would just be in the way.

Review questions

1. What is the fundamental relationship between the number of units per hour a line will turn out and the design of work stations along the line? How should an analyst determine the number of work stations and the length of time each man's work assignment should be?

2. When a computer is used to aid in setting up job packages for men along assembly lines, the process is often called heuristic. How does a computer do this work when it is doing it heuristically?

3. How are policy decisions concerning job element choices used in setting job assignments for men along assembly lines?

4. What kinds of information are required before a computer (or an analyst) can properly group bits of work into job assignments along a line? How can these job bits be determined?

5. How is element precedence established? How is it made effective in the process of setting up men's work packages?

6. What kinds of improvements can a good job analyst probably make in improving the collections of work elements as first set up by a computer?

Discussion questions

1. How finely should the analyst try to cut up job assignments along an assembly line? If the object is to get 450 units a day and if there are 450 man-minutes of work to be done on each unit, should there be 1 line with 450 men each having a 1-minute task? Or would it be better to have 5 lines, each turning out 1 unit every 5 minutes, and each line with 90 men who have 5-minute job packages? Or would some other combination be better? What factors enter into such decisions? Discuss.

2. Bill Parker, a newly hired man for an assembly line job, looked at the forever advancing line bringing him one more product as fast as he could finish the last one. When the foreman came by, Bill said to him: "I'm getting mighty tired of this job; when do we change to something else?" "Next year," said the foreman. "Next year!" said Bill. "Then I quit. I ain't never worked on a job that hasn't got any end." Discuss.

3. When Motorola redesigned a small radio receiver and reduced its number of parts from 210 to 80, it changed (in its Fort Lauderdale factory) from a regular repetitive assembly line back to individual product assembly. Each worker assembles the whole product. The result has been a great improvement in pride of work and quality and a reduction in absenteeism. Is there a "message" here?

4. Tom Manly had been a materials supply man in the stock room, a low paid job, for six months. When a higher-paying opening occurred along the assembly line, Tom asked for the job but the personnel department refused to recommend his transfer. The job was to work on the underside of cars passing overhead, which, because Tom was a short man, would mean quite a reach for him. He filed a grievance, claiming that he had been wrongly denied an opportunity to earn more pay. Should the personnel department's desire to put men on jobs for which they are well suited prevail in such a case?

5. Suppose that a company would like to operate an assembly line at different rates of output and use fewer or more men. Wouldn't it have to have different sets of work packages for each change? If so, wouldn't this make problems because the men would have to learn other sets of duties? Also, what would happen to work stations and sets of tools? Would the number of stations and the allocation of space along the line need to be changed? And what would happen if the output rate were changed in only a minor way, such as reducing it two or three units an hour? How big a change would it take to justify changing the number of men?

6. How can absenteeism be handled along assembly lines? Is there any way to avoid having men not accustomed to the work having to step in and try to keep up with the line?

Problems

1. The analyst is planning a 2-station sequence of work formerly done in different locations. Past records show the following distribution of operation time:

Time in	*Number of occurrences*	
minutes	*Operation A*	*Operation B*
.50.............................	1	0
.60.............................	4	2
.70.............................	5	7
.80.............................	10	13
.90.............................	20	18
1.00............................	32	23
1.10............................	27	16
1.20............................	17	11
1.30............................	12	6
1.40............................	6	3
1.50............................	1	1
Total......................	140	100
Average time................	1.00	1.00

Although we have more data for operation A, the 2 operations must be performed once on all products.

a) Assuming no storage bank of products between operations A and B (if A finishes a unit before B is ready for it, the A operator has to wait until B can start his operation on this unit), can we get 60 units per hour from this 2-job sequence? (Use Monte Carlo simulation.)

b) Suppose that it is possible to build up a supply bank between these operations; what will its average size have to be to allow production to average 1 unit per minute? What will the maximum bank size be?

2. It is necessary to set up an assembly line to assemble 3,000 units in a so-called 40-hour week. (Because of start-up and put-away time, as well as rest periods, the men will lose a half hour each day; so there are only 37.5 productive hours.) There are 6 operations to be done, whose operation times are 1, 1.35, .75, .80, 1.70, and 3 minutes respectively.

a) How many men will be needed if each job is done at a separate work station? Is it possible to have more than 1 man at a work station, although the men, if they are not fully busy, do not do anything else?

b) How much loss of man time because of lack of equal work assignments will this program entail?

c) How will this program be affected if it is possible to group operations in various ways, or to shift men around, or have men do 2 or 3 operations, and it is not required to use 6 work stations with everyone tied to his work station? How does this compare to the answers in (*a*) and (*b*)?

3. General Products Company is planning an assembly line for one of its small products. The plan is for a line which will turn out 75 units an hour, or at the rate of 1 every 48 seconds. Work elements may be grouped in any combination, provided only that the required preceding elements are done, even if in the same work package. They don't need to have been done at an earlier work station. Preceding elements can also be performed several work stations before a following element. The line operates 60 minutes per hour.

Using the work element information below, determine how many assemblers and how many work stations will be needed.

What average percent use of their time does the plan call for?

Work element	Time in seconds	Must follow	Work element	Time in seconds	Must follow	Work element	Time in seconds	Must follow
1	5	...	13	24	3,5	25	22	19
2	13	1	14	14	8,12	26	17	25
3	31	2	15	12	2	27	25	19
4	7	2	16	14	2	28	9	19
5	26	2	17	13	2	29	17	20
6	7	2	18	34	2	30	16	8,10,12
7	6	2	19	16	2	31	20	27
8	11	5	20	24	19	32	19	27
9	11	5	21	12	11,13	33	18	27
10	11	5	22	6	21	34	15	33
11	24	3,5	23	6	19	35	10	34
12	11	5	24	9	19	...	...	...

4. In problem 3, could the efficiency of the assembly line be improved by letting banks of work sometimes pile up between jobs? Which jobs? How much improvement in the use of labor could be expected by doing this?

5. Below are given times and precedence restrictions for 37 job elements for part of the work to be done along an assembly line. (Elements may be put into the same work package with other elements which they must precede or follow.)

Element number	Time in hundredths of a minute	Must Precede Element number	Must Follow Element number
1	5	3	...
2	80	17,18	...
3	13	7,16,17,18,19,21	1
4	31	12,14	3
5	7	12,14	3
6	26	9,10,11,13	3
7	7	...	2,3
8	6	...	3
9	11	15,32	6
10	11	...	6
11	11	32	6
12	24	23	4,5,6
13	11	15,32	6
14	24	23	4,5,6
15	14	...	9,11,13
16	12	...	2,3
17	14	...	2,3
18	13	...	2,3
19	34	...	2,3
20	29	22,29,30	3
21	16	25,26	3
22	24	31	21
23	12	24	12,14
24	6	34	23
25	6	...	21

Element number	Time in hundredths of a minute	Must Precede Element number	Must Follow Element number
26	9	...	21
27	22	21	24
28	17	...	27
29	25	35	21
30	9	...	21
31	17	...	22
32	16	...	9,13
33	20	...	29
34	19	...	24
35	18	36	29
36	15	37	35
37	10	...	36

Arrange these work elements into appropriate job jackages in order to turn out 100 finished products per hour. Show which elements go into which work assignments. Show also how much wasted man time this program's assignments contain because of the failure of job packages to even out perfectly. (Suggestion: Note that 100 units an hour means 1 unit every 36 seconds, or .60 minute. Try to develop work packages of a little less than .60 minute.)

6. Do the same for 150 finished products per hour. How much has the wasted man time been reduced?

7. Assume that, in problem 5, methods study men are able to put in improvements which reduce the time on all elements of $^{16}/_{100}$ of a minute and over by one fourth. Now what is the answer?

Recent references

Barkley, F., "Problems of an Assembly Line Supervisor," *Supervisory Management,* November 1970

"Point-of-Use Components Storage Transforms Plant Layout," *Factory,* November 1971

Thomopoulos, N. T., "Mixed Model Line Balancing with Smoothed Station Assignments," *Management Science,* May 1970

Thomopoulos, N. T., "Some Analytical Approaches to Assembly Line Problems," *Production Engineer,* July 1968

Tonge, F. M., "Assembly Line Balancing Using Probabilistic Combinations of Heuristics," *Management Science,* May 1965

section four

Product development

NEW PRODUCTS and new ways to serve people are being developed continually. Neither the managers of factories or service organizations can safely rest on their present products or methods of serving for their organizations' future well-being.

It is necessary to put resources into searching for new and better ways of doing things so that one's own company, rather than a competitor, will bring out the new product or introduce the new way of serving that will someday replace today's products and service methods.

Research and development, the subject of Chapter 11, differs from most of the other subjects in this book in that the work being discussed is not production in the usual sense. Often the end product is more knowledge. And sometimes it is not obvious how this new knowledge can be incorporated into the organization's products or services.

Chapter 11 considers research as the searching for new knowledge. Included is a discussion of how to choose areas of greatest promise. Then it turns to development, the means by which this knowledge is incorporated into improved products.

Development shades off into product design, the subject of Chapter 12. Designers, however, have to be more practical and earthier people than researchers. They have to work within two very important constraints. First, they have to consider customers and what the customers want and what they don't want. And second, there is always a cost parameter. Products must not cost too much, or else they will not sell.

In addition to these two constraints, which engineers have always had to be concerned with, there is one more, and where it applies it is of overriding importance. This is the need to comply with all laws and obligations to protect consumers and to meet all antipollution standards.

Besides these operating constraints, designers are concerned with such technical matters as explaining their designs to the factory (by means of drawings, specifications, and tolerances) and standardization and simplification.

11

Research and development

EVERYTHING in old movies looks out of date because it *is* out of date. Old products are continually redesigned and new products are continually developed. And inside factories new processing methods are continually developed. But few such changes would occur except as new research findings provide the basis for them and development incorporates the new findings into product designs.

Research is a conscious effort to find new and better ways to do things, and although small amounts of research have been done for many years, far and away the largest push has been in the last twenty years. During this time in the United States, research expenditures have probably averaged $20 billion a year, or between 2 and 3 percent of our national income. Most of this research has been government sponsored and has been related to space travel and defense, but industry and other groups have also done a great deal.

Such research has produced the scientific knowledge that lies behind the development of television, jet airplanes, electronic computers, sea-water desalting plants, nylon stockings, wonder drugs, the "pill," insecticides, nuclear power plants, laser beams, and thousands of other things. Nature never made any of these products. They are man made, and they exist because researchers were hired and put to work to try to find answers to problems and to unlock nature's secrets. And they exist, also, because engineers then used this new knowledge in product development.

The bloom is off the rose, however, so far as big, quick payoffs are concerned. New discoveries and innovations are harder to come by. Nevertheless, all large companies now do research, so everyone has to keep on doing it or be left behind. Because of lower payoffs and the greater risk of no payoff, today's research work needs more careful managing than formerly.

The problem is even more difficult because even though unusual new products are hard to come by, new scientific findings continue to be made. In some areas they come so fast that scientists and engineers find that their knowledge soon goes out of date. Indeed, in some areas technology advances so fast that today's knowledge has a "half life" of less than 10 years: half of what a scientist or engineer knows will be outdated in 10 years. Men in these fields have to go all out to keep up. Accordingly, their employers have to provide them the opportunity to read journals, go to meetings of scientists, and keep up with advances in their fields.

Product life cycles

Most new products that are introduced to the public go through a cycle. First, the products are very new, do not always work very well, and are high priced. Only the venturesome consumer buys at this stage. The market for the product has to be developed. Then comes the second stage: the product is improved and standardized, becomes dependable in use and lower in price, and customers buy it with little urging. It sells in enormous quantities as it comes into common use.

This is followed by a third stage. The product is mature, dependable in performance, reasonably stable in price, and does not change much from year to year. Sales volume may even fall off because everybody now owns one, and sales are dependent on population increase plus replacements. Automobiles, radios, television sets, and electric refrigerators all went through these stages. Industries based on important innovations seem to take up to 30 years to reach maturity.

Finally, most products come to the fourth stage, the end of the line. They are supplanted by new products. (Admittedly, this does not happen to all products. Scissors and paper clips have been around for a long time.

So have pork chops.) Because so many products keep coming to the end of the line, companies have to work continually at developing new products to take their places.

Merck Company usually gets 70 percent of its sales income from products that were nonexistent 10 years earlier. Year after year RCA consistently gets 80 percent of its sales income from products introduced in the previous 10 years. Bell & Howell reports that 90 percent of its sales in the photographic field comes from products newly developed in the last 10 years. This is the reason why so many companies spend so much on research and development.

Some products get out on the market too soon. It takes five years or more to perfect complicated products—to get all the bugs out—but venturesome customers don't want to wait. International Business Machines has always had orders for newly designed computers before they were ready to deliver them. Customers hear about new things and want them right away—long before they are fully developed.

But is it too soon after all? No product is ever fully engineered. It just isn't possible to wait until a product is perfect before starting to sell it. Sewing machines have been used for more than 100 years, but they keep changing for the better. And the automobiles and airplanes of 50 years ago were, by today's standards, not very fully engineered, but they were produced and sold and they rendered good service to the buyers.

The first ball-point pens didn't work very well, but the two companies which made them, Reynolds and Paper Mate, got rich. Parker and Sheaffer spent too long doing too good a development job and missed the boat. No one should wait for final, permanent designs before he offers his product to the public.

The question is: When is a product well enough developed to sell it? Somewhere along the line, it should be offered for sale, and at this point its design has to be "frozen"—so far as manufacturing is concerned—long enough to get some products made. Engineers never get to do as much improving as they would like before their product goes on the market. And after it goes to market, they keep trying to improve it more.

Pure and applied research

Some people like to distinguish between "pure" and "applied" research, depending on its purpose. Pure research is research into nature's basic laws, regardless of how that knowledge can be used. Applied research tries to solve a problem, a definite problem, and usually one that costs money or one which will make money for the company if it is solved. Naturally, almost all of industry's research is the applied kind. Universities and research foundations work more on basic research. Probably less than 10 percent of all research expenditure is for basic research and over 90 percent is for applied research.

FIGURE 11–1. Organization of the research department of Parke Davis & Company

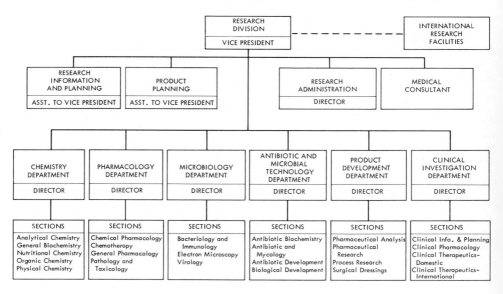

Research risks

Only after the research on a project is done and money spent can it begin to save money or produce income. RCA had $50 million invested in color TV before its color sets reached the American living room, and had $125 million invested in it before it began to pay off. In the years since, it has got its money back several times over. Unfortunately, however, research does not always pay off. Du Pont spent $25 million over 25 years developing Corfam (artificial leather) before it put Corfam on the market in 1964. Six years later, after losing $100 million in Corfam, Du Pont stopped making it.

Nor are the risks always limited to the research expenditures themselves. If a company does not do research, it risks losing out to its researching competitors. The dilemma is even worse, however, because competition is interindustry. Aluminum has taken over part of steel's tin can industry. Plastics have taken over part of paper's position in wrappings. And paper has taken away part of wood's market for containers. Nuclear power plants are cutting in on coal in electric-power generating plants.

Probably the biggest risk in research lies in the high mortality rate of research projects. RCA estimates that 90 percent of its research ideas are useless. Du Pont reports that one third of its chemical research projects flop while still in the laboratory. And even after succeeding in the laboratory, most of the rest prove impractical in production.

Even technical successes sometimes go sour. Plastic pipe, made from vinyl, styrene, and polyethylene, grew from nothing to a $100 million business some years ago. Plastic pipe was a great success, but everybody got into the act. By 1970 none of the 80 manufacturers of plastic pipe was making much money out of it because of price competition.

Yet if research is so hazardous and so few projects pay off, one might ask why everyone does it. Aside from having to research in order to keep up, it is still true that some of the successes pay for themselves many times over. In general and in total, research usually pays off.

And, of course, if a company does not do research, income taxes will take half of its profit dollars—half of everything left over—so tax savings carry half of the research costs. The question is not "Is research worth its cost?" but "Is research worth half its cost (or even less if any of the retained earnings would have been paid out in dividends)?"

Research subjects

Usually industrial companies carry on research to try to:

1. Search for basic chemical or physical relationships, particularly those having to do with their own products or processes.
2. Improve their products.
3. Find new uses for their present products.
4. Develop new products.
5. Reduce the cost of present products by improving their operations and processes.
6. Develop tests and specifications for operations and purchased materials.
7. Analyze competitors' products.
8. Find profitable uses for by-products.

Of this list of eight objectives of research, probably number 4, developing new products, is the most important because the ultimate possibilities of new products are sometimes so great. Once in a while such a new product can double or triple the organization's business, as computers did years ago for IBM, as copiers did for Xerox, and as instant-picture cameras did for Polaroid. Rarely can ordinary product improvement or cost-cutting innovations have such effect.

This is not, however, to suggest cutting out research aimed at minor improvements in products and cost reduction. Nor is there any intent to belittle the widespread but small-scale efforts that foremen and methods study men continually put into reducing costs. Design and tool engineers, too, are always making improvements. This work is usually not thought of as research, nor is its cost counted as a research expenditure, but it really is research and in total is quite worthwhile.

Process development. Research work goes into improving processes as well as products. The steel industry, for example, was revolutionized a decade ago by the introduction of the basic oxygen process, which makes steel better and at less cost than other processes. And to this has been added continuous steel casting and strip rolling, making steel processing very different from what it was only a decade ago. Machine tool builders, too, today make not only numerically controlled machines but electrochemical machinery as well, all new in the last decade. And in the electronics industry, microminiature integrated circuits are causing revolutionary changes in designs.

FIGURE 11–2. Schematic drawing of continuous strip rolling process for sheet metal

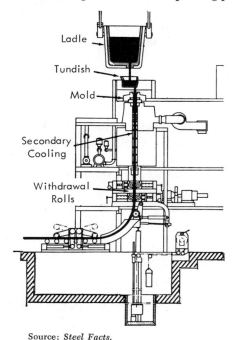

Source: *Steel Facts.*

Every industry has many stories to tell of equally impressive improvements in processes. Space will not be given to them here, however, because, in a very real sense, processes are products. Every bit of the equipment used in new processes in one company is some other company's product. So our discussion about product research and development is at the same time a discussion about process research and development.

Project evaluation

A research department almost always has more proposals than its budget will support, so a selection must be made. There is no one best way to select the best projects, but the selection process probably would be improved by using the discounted cash flow idea.

The problem here is not quite the same, however, as in machinery buying problems because the future worth of research projects is so much more a matter of guessing than are forecasts of machine costs and productivity. For example, it probably will be decades before we know the ultimate value of the oil shale research work in Colorado, which has been going on for 25 years and has cost millions of dollars. It has proved that we can get oil in large quantities from shale, but not at a cost to compete with regular oil. Up to now, this knowledge has not been worth its cost; yet if oil ever gets to be scarce, this knowledge may become very valuable.

A different situation exists when there is a real value but one which cannot be quantified. How valuable, for example, is automatic gear shifting in a car? This development has value, but no one knows how much. But when managers try to evaluate this kind of project, perhaps they should put some kind of value on it and then its cost should be judged against that value, just as with capital replacement projects.

Figure 11–3 shows how the present-value method could be used to

FIGURE 11–3*

Year	R & D costs	Profits from product	Pretax net	After-tax net	Discount factor at 15%	Discounted after-tax profit
1	100	0	−100	−50	.870	−44
2	200	0	−200	−100	.756	−76
3	250	10	−240	−120	.658	−79
4	300	50	−250	−125	.511	−64
5	200	200	0	0	.498	0
6	50	400	350	175	.433	76
7	0	600	600	300	.376	113
8	0	500	500	250	.327	82
9	0	400	400	200	.284	56
10	0	200	200	100	.247	24
Total						88

* Amounts are in thousands of dollars.

help evaluate research projects. This example assumes that all research expenditures are considered to be costs of current operations so far as income taxes are concerned. In this example, a 15 percent discount rate was used and it was assumed that the product being developed will not sell beyond 10 years.

The project promises to return all R & D expenditures plus a 15 percent after-tax yield, and the equivalent of $88,000 current dollars as well, so it would seem that it should be approved. But the risk has not yet been considered. The expected profits in Figure 11–3 can be considered to be only one of several possible streams of profits. We will call it stream A. In Figure 11–4, two other possible profits streams, B, and C, are shown.

FIGURE 11-4*

Year	R & D costs	Income pattern B		Income pattern C		Discount factor at 15%	Discounted after-tax profit	
		Profits	After-tax net	Profits	After-tax net		B	C
1	100	0	−50	0	−50	.870	−44	−44
2	200	100	−50	0	−100	.756	−38	−76
3	250	300	25	0	−125	.658	16	−82
4	300	300	0	50	−125	.511	0	−64
5	200	300	50	100	−50	.498	25	−25
6	50	300	125	400	175	.433	54	76
7	0	200	100	400	200	.376	38	75
8	0	200	100	600	300	.327	33	98
9	0	100	50	200	100	.284	14	28
10	0	100	50	100	50	.247	12	12
Total							110	−2

* Amounts are in thousands of dollars.

Each has been discounted, as was done with A in Figure 11–3. Pattern B yields a discounted present value of +$110,000; C shows a −$2,000 total.

Risks (probability) can now be considered. Probability factors are assigned to each of these possible income streams. This allows the expected monetary value of each stream to be calculated. Considering the three possible income streams and their likelihood, it turns out that this research project has an expected after-tax monetary value of 15 percent on the investment, plus $50,000 current dollars. It still appears wise to go ahead with the project, but it no longer looks quite as promising as it did with only income pattern A to look at.

FIGURE 11-5

Income pattern	Profit (thousands)	Probability	Col. 2 × Col. 3 (thousands)
A	$ 88	.45	$40
B	110	.10	11
C	−2	.45	−1
Overall expected monetary value			$50

Responsibilities to consumers

Consumer protectionism has grown explosively in the last decade. Many years ago it used to be "Let the buyer beware," but today it's "Let the seller beware." It used to be that society relied on the operation of the market place to reward producers of acceptable products and to penalize those who produced unacceptable products. No longer is this so.

Producers of goods may today be sued in court, and sometimes are successfully sued for the consequences of the failures and shortcomings of their products. Product liability lawsuits now number over 500,000 a year. The food industry alone has more than 50,000 such cases a year. Society is demanding that manufacturers give their product users greater protection against all possible harm. Unfortunately, too, consumerism is good politics, so that the merits of consumer issues are sometimes distorted by legislators and candidates for office in order to capitalize on them politically. In any case, the discipline of the market place is now being strongly reinforced by the law to protect consumers from inferior products.

Unfortunately, people who use various products sometimes hurt themselves—or they eat a particular food and get sick, or they buy this or that medicine and get sicker instead of well. Sometimes they abuse or misuse a product, and then, when it doesn't work or when they get hurt, they blame the company. And then they sue the company, perhaps for some huge amount of money, and sometimes they win.

Engineering and research must work together to develop the safest, most foolproof products possible. (In fact, however, reliability and safety are not quite the same thing. A toy cook stove may be reliable, but a little girl might burn herself.) Proper safety protection should be designed into products, which should be tested under all conditions of extreme use, misuse, and abuse. The company should know what its products can safely do and what they cannot do. Advertising and package labels should carry proper instructions and warnings although instructions for proper use are no longer enough. Warnings concerning the dangers from misuse must also be given. Labels on packaged foods and pharmaceuticals must be carefully drawn up. Mechanical products, especially, should be designed for safe operation. Repair men, too, should keep full records of their repairs and the reasons why they were made, lest they be charged with having been negligent.

An interesting facet of the whole liabilities matter is that proponents of consumerism appear to believe that the consumer is getting more protection free of cost. But a manufacturer has only one source of income, the consumer. One wonders if so many people would favor consumer protection (which adds to costs) so avidly if they recognized that they were paying the bills.

Warranties. It used to be that warranties were guarantees made by manufacturers to customers. They were written assurances that covered certain quality characteristics, together with promises to replace faulty parts or products free of charge. Besides these guarantees, whether verbal or in writing, our laws have always recognized certain implied warranties, such as fitness for expected use. If a man buys paint for his house, the paint should neither fade and change color nor peel off in two or three years.

Curiously but not surprisingly, whereas a decade ago manufacturers were outdoing each other in offering customers expanded warranties, today they are pulling back. Several years ago Chrysler offered a 5-year or 50,000-mile warranty on all power and drive systems in its cars. Later, the other car companies followed suit; but not today. Making good on such promises cost too much. Making good on warranties cost car companies over *half a billion dollars* a year in the late 1960s.

All of this is becoming more and more academic, however. The wave of consumerism, abetted by laws and court decisions, is taking the warranty option away from manufacturers. The latter, in fact, must act as if they had given warranties in every case. They have to guarantee reliability, often beyond what they would prefer, and sometimes beyond what a great many consumers really want.

Reliability

Sometimes as a man sits in his chair in the evening, reading the newspaper, the light bulb in the reading lamp suddenly burns out. Designers can never design, nor manufacturers make, products that will not finally fail; nor can they design or make products which will last for an exact length of time—no more, no less. Yet products must be reliable enough to give trouble-free service for a reasonable time.

How long a product will last is partly dependent upon its design, partly upon the degree of manufacturing perfection, partly upon its conditions of use, and partly on chance. And so far as a product's expected life is concerned, usually the longer it is supposed to last, the more costly it is to make.

Reliability is the probability that a part or a product will last a given length of time under normal conditions of use. So one aspect of reliability is the length of operating time, or expected life. In the case of a light bulb, the goal could be 1,000 hours. Or it could even be 2,000 hours. But ordinary light bulbs, though quite reliable for 1,000 hours, are not reliable for 2,000 hours. Because under normal use a light bulb ought almost certainly to last 1,000 hours, perhaps the reliability of its lasting 1,000 hours would be .98, meaning there are only 2 chances in 100 that a bulb will fail in less than 1,000 hours. Indeed, most such bulbs are supposed to last 1,250 hours, and the probability of their lasting 1,250 hours might be .90. But not many bulbs will last 2,000 hours, and the probability of this occurring might be .05. So anyone who wants 2,000 hours of life from light bulbs should not use regular bulbs because regular bulbs will rarely last that long. Instead, he will have to order special bulbs.

A second aspect of reliability is the condition of use. A light bulb of the usual design is very unlikely to last even 100 hours if it is continually bumped around. But a flashlight bulb is expected to be bumped around, so it is sturdier than a reading-lamp bulb; it is expected to work in spite of a few bumps. And sometimes, of course, the conditions of expected use are even more extreme: space ships have to operate at more than 200 degrees *above* and 200 degrees *below* zero.

Parts, therefore, need to be designed to have the desired reliability under their expected conditions of use. For most consumer products, conditions of use are not extreme, although automobiles are sometimes used hard. Probably the reliability of most consumer products is satisfactory to most users. On the other hand, most of us wish that the mufflers and storage batteries in our automobiles would last for more than two or three years.

Third, reliability has to do both with individual parts and whole products. Whole products fail when *any* critical part fails, so the reliability of whole products is much less than the reliability of individual parts, and

FIGURE 11–6. **System availability as a function of component reliability and the number of components**

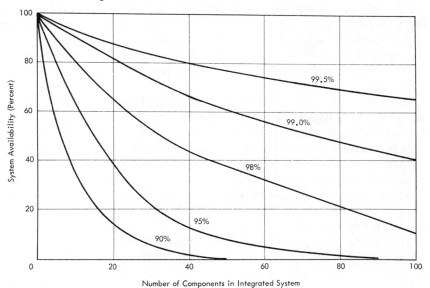

Number of Components in Integrated System

the more critical parts there are, the less is the reliability of the whole product. Sewing machines, power lawn mowers, automobiles, all have a good many parts whose failure, individually, would cause the product to fail. And computers, space ships, and other exotic products have thousands of parts whose operation is critical to the operation of the whole product. A decade ago it took the United States 13 tries to get a missile to take close-up pictures of the moon; the first 12 tries were failures. And several years ago, also, the United States submarine *Thresher* sank and 129 men lost their lives because one pipe joint—out of 8,000—failed.

A system of 100 interacting parts, each of which has .9999 (or 99.99 percent) reliability, has an overall reliability of .9900 (or 99 percent); a system with 1,000 interacting parts has 90 percent reliability; 3,000 parts have 75 percent; and 10,000 parts have 37 percent. The Telstar communications satellite has more than 10,000 electronic parts, and even though these parts do not all interact, and not all are of critical importance, extremely high reliability had to be built into Telstar's parts to get it to operate in the first place and to keep it operating in the years since it was orbited.

A fourth matter is how serious is failure? If an automobile steering mechanism fails, it can cause a wreck, but sometimes the failure of a part is not critical. If a lamp bulb in a reading lamp fails, little harm is done. Or if a person drops a telephone and the plastic casing cracks, the casing has "failed" but the telephone still works.

Point 5 is a corollary of point 4: How quickly can a part failure be fixed and how big a job is it to fix it? Indeed, the seriousness of a failure often depends upon how quickly it can be fixed. Quick maintenance gets the system back into operation right away so that little harm is done. When the light bulb in a lamp burns out, we can unscrew it and put in another. When replacement is simple and fast, product reliability is less important.

Unfortunately, points 4 and 5 sometimes don't apply because there is no chance to fix or replace a critical part that has failed. The United States missed taking pictures of the moon the first 12 tries because the parts that failed were critical and there was no fixing them out in space. And broken steering mechanisms on automobiles cause accidents before there is any chance to fix them. Faulty electronic components in computers cause wrong answers, and maybe no one will know they are wrong. In such cases a high degree of reliability is very important even if it costs a good bit of money.

A sixth point is that almost always the reliability of systems can be improved by making products out of more perfect parts, parts which are made to fit more exactly or which are made out of special materials. But always this is at extra cost; and the greater the reliability, the higher the cost. Again, this is particularly true when operations under extreme conditions may cause a costly failure.

Since added reliability almost always is achieved only at added cost, there is need to consider its cost and value. The high cost of extreme reliability may be fully justified by the serious cost of a failure; nonetheless, reliability engineering is not always a matter of making something better. Possibly, it might even be well to lower the reliability of a part, and lessen its life, because it does not need to last forever. If an automobile will last only 150,000 miles, it does not need a crankshaft which will last a million miles. Money could probably be saved by making lower-quality crankshafts which usually last only 175,000 miles.

Frequently, the higher the degree of quality required, the higher the price. Texas Instruments sold one kind of transistor for consumer and industrial use for $.25 each with no guarantee of its reliability. But for its use in military systems it had to give reliability guarantees, so the price was $.85 cents for the same (but more carefully processed and tested) transistor. But when it came to missile and spaceship use, its very careful manufacture and testing, which were required to insure its high reliability, shot the costs of this same transistor up to $10.

Fortunately, greater quality does not always cost very much more money. Parts which might fail can often be "overdesigned" at nominal cost. A handle or a hinge on a suitcase can easily be made far stronger than it needs to be at very little extra cost. So can a door hinge on an automobile. Added strength in these cases costs very little.

The discussion so far might lead one to think that reliability is a black-or-white matter: A product works or it doesn't. Often, however, failure is not like that. This leads to point 7, the degree of failure. If a television tube sometimes goes zigzag or gives snowy or fuzzy pictures, has it failed? Has there been a failure in an automobile if the brake pedal has to be pushed farther down than formerly? Poor performance is often a matter of degree, with absolute failure as the final stage. In a practical sense, failure occurs when performance is so poor that there is a decision to repair or replace the part.

There is also the question of performance expectations. When a television picture tube fails, the customer regards it as a failure, whereas if it lasted 10 years before failing, it is not—in the eyes of the manufacturer— a failure at all.

Point 8 is that reliability is closely tied to maintenance, particularly preventive maintenance. A reading lamp will probably never burn out while someone is reading if the old bulb is taken out and a new one is put in every 800 hours. Normally, preventive maintenance can result in high reliability for a product even where long-term reliability is not engineered into the parts of the product. It is only necessary to replace parts before they are old enough to become unreliable. If a man buys a new storage battery for his car every 2 years, the car will probably always start in the winter. Unfortunately, however, preventive maintenance costs money, so it is only a different (and usually a somewhat costly) way to increase the reliability of products.

We have said that sometimes the failure of a noncritical part often does not affect the whole product's operation very much. This is, in fact, often only a half truth because the failure of one part hastens the failure of other parts. A broken telephone case lets dust and dampness into its inside, and this will in due time probably make trouble. Or an automobile will run when one cylinder is not firing, but if it is continued in operation with one cylinder missing, it is hard on the car's bearings and will make them fail sooner.

Strength and stress analysis

It is sometimes possible to check mathematically to see if parts are strong enough to meet the stress demands called for. And this in spite of the fact that the strength of individual parts and the stress demands both vary.

A given part, for example, may be subjected to varied stresses which average 100 pounds per square inch. The analyst, however, also must be concerned with the variations in these stresses. For this analysis he will need to calculate their "standard deviation," a statistical measure which is found as follows.

FIGURE 11–7

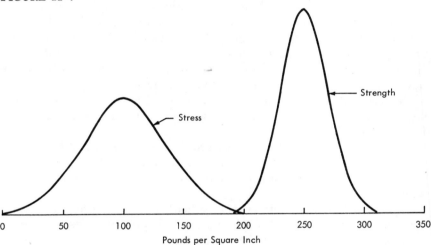

Calculate the average stress (the arithmetic mean) for all of the cases covered by the study; then calculate how much different each individual case is from the average. Square these differences, sum them up, divide by the number of cases, and take the square root of this quotient. The answer is the standard deviation in this group of measurements.

The standard deviation is helpful in many kinds of analyses and is much used in statistical quality control (the subject of Chapter 27). It is appropriately used whenever the data being analyzed are characterized by a middle point of concentration and fewer instances of much higher or much lower size. If the distribution has this bell-shape, symmetrical pattern, then the mean ±1 standard deviation (often symbolized as σ, the Greek *sigma*) gives measurements within which 68.26 percent of the individual items fall. The mean ±2σ gives limits between which 95.45 percent of the cases fall. ±3σ sets limits between which 99.73 percent, or virtually all, of the cases fall.

In the example at hand, we will assume that the mean of the stresses is 100 pounds per square inch and that the standard deviation of the variations is 35 pounds per square inch. Parts intended to meet this stress average to withstand successfully, 250 pounds per square inch. Their standard deviation is 20 pounds per square inch.

The question the analyst is to answer is: Are the parts strong enough? Will there be any cases of unusually great stress when the part is one of the few weak parts? Figure 11–7 shows that there is a small area of overlap between the two normal curves for the stresses and strengths, and this is shown on an enlarged scale in Figure 11–8. (The mathematics for

FIGURE 11–8

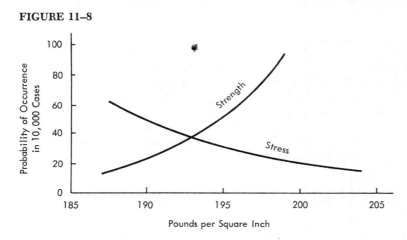

Pounds per Square Inch

calculating the chances of failure are quite complex and are not reproduced here.[1]

It turns out that the curves overlap at 192.9 pounds, which is 2.86 standard deviations less than the mean of the strengths and 2.63 standard deviations more than the average stress. The calculations in Appendix E show that the probability of inadequate strength to meet an unusually large stress is, in this case, in the order of 1 chance in 10,000.

The method just described sounds as if an analyst would end up with a pretty good idea of the chances of failure. But the description sounds better than the method really is because good stress data are almost impossible to obtain. In one case an automobile company found that customers who bought its trucks had an occasional failure of the rear axle. Yet the tests showed that the axles were much stronger than any stress they might be called upon to stand.

Investigation showed two faults in the data. The failures were not on new axles but on those which had been used a good while. It turned out that fatigue in the metal was reducing the axles' strength. At the same

---

[1] For a discussion of this point see "Prediction of Percent Failure from Stress/ Strength Interferences," by Charles Lipson and Narendra S. Sheth, a paper read at the Automotive Engineering Congress, Detroit, January 8, 1968, and published by the Society of Automotive Engineers as publication 680084.

time, the users were subjecting the axles to extreme stresses by dropping heavy loads on their trucks at loading docks and by driving fast on bumpy roads. Momentary but extreme impact stresses were being created in excess of the stress data used in the company's calculations.

In actual practice, designers usually try to avoid problems of the kind just described by overdesigning their products. If it is not too costly, they apply the typical "military fear factor" and make the part three times as strong as it needs to be. Then the curve overlaps are infinitesimal.

"Bathtub" curves

Unless final inspectors do a good job of screening, a plot of an item's length of life may have a shape like that of a bathtub silhouette. It is high on the left, then has a long, relatively flat and low middle section, and then goes back up on the right.

FIGURE 11–9.   The "bathtub" curve length-of-life pattern of many items

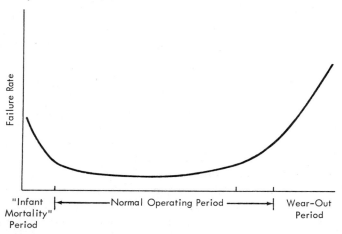

Some items will fail quickly. These are the truly faulty items which the screening should catch. Thereafter, failures should be rare until long use raises the failure rate again, as the items wear out. In cases where the manufacturing process cannot be improved enough to eliminate the bathtub effect, the supplying company may have to "age" the components by operating them on a test basis through the "infant mortality" period, thus screening out those that are initially defective. Items that survive this early period will then have a low mortality until old age is reached.

Bathtub curves sometimes do not have a chance to appear because items which fail are replaced, one by one as they fail, with new items. Ultimately, the failure rate levels off since some of the items in use are new and some are older, while some are near the end of their normal life.

The actual failures include the composite effects of many age curves, each in a different stage of its life cycle. The failure statistics are summations of failures from different age groups. Because of this there is no visible evidence of the operation of bathtub life-curves.

Redundancy

Where the failure of a part or subsystem is critically important yet a redundant part or system doesn't cost much, engineers often add such a redundant part or subsystem as insurance. It is like wearing a belt and suspenders at the same time. The extra part or subsystem is not used at all unless the regular part fails. Should the regular component fail, the total system automatically switches over and uses the standby extra.

This sounds wasteful, and like something no one would ever do, but every automobile, for instance, has a mechanical hand brake as well as its regular hydraulic brake system. If the foot brake fails, the driver is not without a brake. And today's big electronic computers have two sets of every subsystem whose failure is critical to their operation. Such redundancy is not wasteful in the long run.

In industry, we hear most about redundance in exotic products, such as moon spaceships, where, we are told, every critical subsystem is backed up by a second, emergency system. In a smaller way, however, the redundancy idea is used a good bit in everyday products. Men's shirts are

FIGURE 11–10

often sewn with double seams where one really ought to be enough. Or, in the factory, if two pieces of steel have been welded together with four spot welds and there has been trouble with the welded spots not holding, it is easy to specify six spot welds instead of four. Then it won't matter if one or two of them don't hold. This can be done wherever the extra cost of welding two extra spots is nominal.

Even nature believes in redundancy. We all start with two eyes, ears, lungs, and kidneys, but we can get along with one. Nature's redundancy, however, usually calls for the regular use of both components, whereas industry's redundancy is usually a first-unit-use, second-unit-standby arrangement.

Redundancy economics can be quite complex, but a simple problem will illustrate the principle. Suppose a system has two components, A and B, that operate as in Figure 11–10. The probability of A's being operative for as long as the normal life of the system is .90 and B's is .95. Since both have to operate, and either can fail, the system reliability is .90 × .95 = .855.

Suppose that a failure costs $1,000. The probability of failure during the system's normal life expectancy is therefore $1 - .855 = .145$ and the probable cost of failure is $.145 \times \$1,000 = \$145$.

To make the system more reliable, it is proposed to put in a second A unit, together with a switch, so that if the first A unit is inoperative, the second (A′) will switch on automatically—a system like that shown in Figure 11–11. Should such a redundant system be put in at a cost of $300 if the switch has a reliability of .98 and the reliability of unit A′ is .90?

If called into use, the redundant system will be operative $.98 \times .90 = .88$ of the time. The redundant system will then take care of 88 percent of the 10 percent failures of part A. So the reliability of the A-A′ part of

FIGURE 11–11

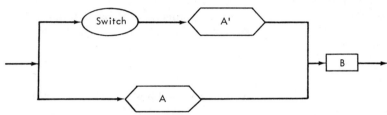

the system becomes $.90 + .10 \times .88 = .988$. B, however, has not been improved; so the whole system's reliability has now become $.988 \times .95 = .939$. The probability of failure is $1 - .939 = .061$. On the average, the failure cost will be $.061 \times \$1,000 = \$61$.

Average failure costs are now reduced to $61, but the protection cost $300, so the total cost is $361. Without the redundant system, the average expected cost of failures was $145; so the redundant system will not pay for itself. It would be better to take the 14.5 percent chance of having a $1,000 failure than to spend $300 to reduce the risk to a 6.1 percent chance of having a $1,000 failure.

Since the redundant system's cost is $216 too high, it would pay only if its cost could be reduced from $300 to $84.

Patents

Every inventor has two forms of protection, or umbrellas, to shield him against expropriation of his ideas by others. The first is simple security— keeping mum about valuable ideas and hoping that others won't find out about them or won't realize their value. This umbrella may develop leaks.

The second umbrella is a patent (which also may provide inadequate protection). Patents, which are issued by the U.S. Patent Office, give their owners the right to keep other people from using the patented ideas. Patents are good for 17 years and are not renewable. After 17 years they are in the public domain.

Patent protection.   The Patent Office will deny a request for a patent if it thinks that an idea is not new, but the Patent Office is not the court of final recourse. If it says no, a patent claimant can appeal to a special patent court or to a civil court. Either the Patent Office or the court can say yes, of course, but no matter how a man gets a patent, he—not the Patent Office—has to defend his patent in court if someone claims that his new patent infringes on the latter's earlier patent. Or he may want later to claim that a still newer patent infringes on *his* patent. It is well for an inventor to keep all records, applications, and correspondence on file against the day he may have to defend his patent in court or support his claim that someone has infringed on his patent.

Patents often do not give as much protection as they seem to. Often it is possible for a competitor to design something almost the same as a patented item and so defeat the exclusive right to use of the idea. Also, big companies often fight other people's patents in court, claiming that they are not new. (Sometimes, for example, a small part of the idea is new but most of it is not new.) Such lawsuits may cost thousands of dollars and take years to settle—which are beyond the means of many patent holders.

Furthermore, the idea in dispute can be used by everyone until the lawsuit is finally settled. Moreover, if a patent is infringed, it is up to the patent holder to discover this and then sue in court at his own expense. He may not find out about the infringement; and even if he does, he may not have the resources to sue; and even if he has the resources, he might not win.

Problems with patents.   There are many other problems with patents, and an important new problem area is computer programs. These are costly to develop, yet once developed they are usable by anyone. And since such programs are in regular computer languages, they are hard to patent. Perhaps the best way is to regard programs as trade secrets and expect to get protection against others using them by falling back on the laws against unfair competition.

Computer programs can be copyrighted if they are unusual, which allows protection under the copyright laws. A question here, however, is if one company develops a program, can another company be denied the right to develop a similar or even identical program for itself? Probably not.

Questions of ownership of patents occasionally arise between companies and employees. Employees sometimes claim they worked out their idea at home, and they patent it themselves. If this is really so, they usually own the patent; otherwise, if they developed the idea on company time, it belongs to the company, which paid them for the work they did.

The government's dominant position in the support of research often makes problems of the ownership of patents because patents often come out of government-supported research. The question is who owns the patents, the researching company or the government? Companies that do research for the Department of Defense are usually allowed to take out patents in their own name for the patentable results of their research. But this is not so for companies doing research for the National Aeronautics and Space Administration or the Atomic Energy Commission, which are required by law to own such patents themselves. They may license their use to the researching (or other) companies, or they may not. Companies that do research for NASA or AEC often prefer that patents not be taken out on their innovations lest they be denied their use.

There are also problems with patents in different countries—especially as many companies operate worldwide and in countries where patent laws are different. Italy, for example, does not have reciprocity in patents with the United States. France and the United States have reciprocity, but France's patent office grants patents "without search": the government makes no attempt to see if anyone else has patented an idea first. If a man already has a patent and someone else patents the same idea, the first man has to find out about it by himself and then sue for infringement.

Review questions

1. What is the "half life" idea so far as scientists and engineers are concerned? Of what importance is it and what can managers do about it?
2. Sometimes companies use the discounted cash flow method for evaluating research proposals. How does this method work?
3. Why do manufacturers offer fewer and more limited warranties than they used to? Discuss warranties.
4. Is it true that the wave of consumer protection has gone so far as to cause production cost increases as producers try to make more reliable products? How high a price are consumers probably willing to pay for greater reliability?
5. Designers are sometimes said to incorporate the "military fear factor" in their designs. What is this factor? Does it increase value to consumers in accord with its cost?
6. Why is the "bathtub" pattern of failure rates of products a relatively unknown idea?
7. Companies doing research for the government sometimes develop new and patentable ideas. Who should own such patents? Why?
8. What protection does a patent holder get from his patent? Discuss.

Discussion questions

1. Since a high proportion of research projects are failures, can most companies really justify spending 2 percent of their gross income on research? Discuss.
2. What does it mean when a company "expenses" its research costs? Does this not mean essentially that today's products have to be priced high enough

to pay for the research for both the failures and for tomorrow's products? And isn't this wrong, particularly for medicines?

3. If a company expenses its research won't this cause it to have higher prices than nonresearching companies and so make it vulnerable to price competition from nonresearching companies? Discuss.

4. An administrator says "Why can't technical people think less about abstractions and more about end products with real market potential?" What can an administrator do to develop a realistic attitude in the minds of his company's scientists?

5. Should research departments be set up according to fields of science (such as chemistry, metallurgy, etc.) or by product lines (such as automobiles, refrigerators, etc.), or on some other basis? Discuss the advantages and disadvantages of each procedure.

6. Without arriving at an exact number, tell how much effort an automobile company should put into trying to develop (*a*) an air-ride car that rides on a cushion of air blown out underneath the car, or (*b*) a gasoline turbine engine, or (*c*) a method for getting rid of the undesirable hump made by connecting the engine with the rear wheels in a car (yet without going to rear-engine drive because rear-engine-drive cars tend to weave a little on the road).

7. Electric automobiles have many advantages over gasoline-powered automobiles, although, with the present state of the art, gasoline is better. For several years Ford spent $3 million a year on research on electric automobiles. With no breakthrough in sight (it takes too many storage batteries to pack the wallop of a tank of gasoline), should Ford continue this expenditure?

8. A scientist develops an improvement for a carburetor. This improvement has value for cars and for the company. How might a top manager go about judging the value of this contribution from research?

9. An airplane crashes because its altimeter (a bought part for measuring how high up the airplane is) gave a wrong reading. Who is responsible? The altimeter manufacturer? The airplane maker? Suppose that the altimeter had been in use for a long time; does this affect the answer? Discuss.

Problems

1. ABC's laboratory has developed an antibiotic, B62, which safely and surely cures disease X in mice. A limited number of tests on human beings shows that it seems to be effective in the large majority of cases but not at all in a few cases. So far, no bad side effects have been discovered.

Before marketing the product on a large scale, more extensive research will have to be done, and the method and facilities for its production will have to be developed. Product B62 seems sure to reach the market ahead of any successful competing product and so will produce a good income for several years, possibly many years. In the long run, however, it is probable that competitive products will replace it.

Here are the expected figures:

	Additional costs necessary to get into production	Income if no competition develops	Likelihood of no competition
Next year.......................	$50,000	$ 10,000	1.00
Year 2.........................	75,000	30,000	1.00
3.........................	50,000	100,000	.90
4.........................	25,000	200,000	.90
5.........................	0	200,000	.80
6.........................	0	200,000	.60
7.........................	0	200,000	.40
8.........................	0	200,000	.30
9.........................	0	200,000	.25
10.........................	0	200,000	.20

Use the discounted cash flow method and a 20 percent rate of return. Should this project be carried forward? Over the next 10 years, how much will B62 be worth, or how much will ABC likely lose on it, if the firm goes ahead with this project? What is the actual rate of return in prospect?

2. Sales are $10 million a year. Fixed costs are $5 million (which includes $300,000 now being spent annually for research). Variable costs come to $4 million a year. The research director wants to double the research expenditures, claiming that this will boost sales. After talking it over with the sales department, the following estimate was arrived at concerning the sales probabilities if the research expenditures are doubled:

Sales (millions of dollars)	Probability
10............................	.50
11............................	.30
12............................	.10
13............................	.05
14............................	.03
15............................	.02

Should the research expenditures be doubled? On a nondiscounted basis, what is the answer? What would it be if future incomes were discounted at 15 percent?

3. The ABC Company finds that because a competitor has brought out a new product it is lagging behind, but it can probably catch up if it starts immediately on a crash design program. Doing this will probably get ABC's new product out in 6 months. Less expenditure will still produce results, but more slowly. A crash program will cost $1.5 million instead of the $800,000 a slower program would cost. The hurry-up job also opens the door to a .1 probability that the design will be faulty in which case another $300,000 will have to be spent and it will take 6 more months to correct the trouble.

If the cash program suceeds, ABC will not only catch up but its managers think that ABC will have a 6-month lead on its competitors. This will mean profits of $400,000 during that period. Besides this, there will very likely be a continuing advantage to ABC for the 5 remaining years of the product's life. The payoff prospects for the next 5 years in total are:

With crash program		Without crash program	
Profits	*Probability*	*Profits*	*Probability*
$2,000,000............	.50	$2,000,000............	.20
1,500,000.............	.30	1,500,000.............	.30
1,000,000.............	.15	1,000,000.............	.35
500,000............	.05	500,000............	.15

What action should be taken?

4. From what we hear, many television viewers resent loud and blatant commercials. The ABC Company, a television manufacturer with national distribution, has had an occasional request from a dealer for a remote control cutoff with an automatic timer. A viewer could push a button on the cutoff box and it would turn off the speaker (or the picture also, as the viewer chooses) for 1 minute. Then the program would turn on again automatically.

ABC's analysts estimate that it will cost $25,000 to develop such a "Hush Button" and $40,000 more to get it into production. Besides this, it will take a $50,000 advertising campaign to introduce the product to the market.

It is proposed, in the future, to supply Hush Buttons without added charge on all sets retailing for $250 and up. For lower price sets, it is to be available as an "extra" for $25. Owners of any make TV can buy a Hush Button and have their sets modified for its use for $40.

It is estimated that Hush Buttons will cost $3 each in variable costs to produce. Besides this there will be an extra fixed cost of $30,000 in the first year. It is proposed to sell Hush Button units to dealers for $20. It is expected that the Hush Button will boost the sales of sets priced at over $250 (where its cost will be included in the set's price at no extra charge) enough to offset the cost of providing it on all such sets.

With this cost-price structure, how many Hush Buttons will ABC need to sell in order to recover all its initial expenses out of profits during the first year?

5. The XYZ Company sells automobile batteries for $20 each and offers a 30-month-life guarantee. These batteries cost XYZ $12. The guarantee allows a credit of $29/30$ of the purchase price toward the purchase of a new battery within one month, $28/30$ for failure in the second month, etc. Will this guarantee cost as much as $.50 per battery sold if the failure rate corresponds to the following table and if the company has to make good on all failures in the first year but on only half of the failures thereafter? (People who have had a battery for more than one year don't always claim their guarantees when their batteries fail.) (You may disregard second failures; that is, having the replacement battery also fail and having to replace it.)

Months after purchase	Probability of failure Current	Cumulative
1	.005	.005
2	.001	.006
3	.001	.007
4	.001	.008
5	.001	.009
6	.001	.010
7	.001	.011
8	.001	.012
9	.001	.013
10	.002	.015
11	.002	.017
12	.002	.019
13	.002	.021
14	.002	.023
15	.003	.026
16	.003	.029
17	.003	.032
18	.004	.036
19	.004	.040
20	.005	.045
21	.006	.051
22	.006	.057
23	.007	.064
24	.008	.072
25	.009	.081
26	.012	.093
27	.017	.110
28	.025	.135
29	.035	.170
30	.050	.220
31	.070	.290
32	.090	.380
33	.115	.495
34	.140	.635
35	.165	.800
36	.200	1.000

6. The ABC Typewriter Company tests the strength of the metal stampings on which key faces are mounted. Below are the test results for samples from two different suppliers. These samples were pulled apart and their tensile strength recorded.

If ABC wants greater strength, which source should it buy from? It it wants consistency, which one? Is either difference very certain from these samples?

Source A*	Source B*
171.2	134.9
139.3	155.2
152.7	170.4
154.1	160.7
156.7	151.0
145.0	155.2
133.4	184.6
163.1	148.2
148.3	131.6
159.4	166.1

° *Tensile strength in thousands of pounds per square inch*

7. What risks of failure is a company taking if a part's strength averages 100 pounds per square inch with a standard deviation of 7 pounds when the stress demands upon it average 60 pounds per square inch with a standard deviation of 8 pounds? For this answer use the formula given in Appendix E.

8. If, in problem 7, failures cost $50 each, would it pay to increase the average strength to 105 pounds, with a standard deviation of 7 pounds, if the added strength costs $.01 for every part?

9. The Amrine Company offers to deliver 5 small machines for $1,700 each and guarantees a mean time between failures (MTBF) of 1,000 hours and a useful life of about 5,000 hours. The Phillips Company bid is $2,500 with a guaranteed MTBF of 1,500 hours and a useful life of about 7,500 hours. Breakdowns cost $50 each for repair time and lost production. Replacement parts of the kind needed for the Amrine machines will normally cost $25 per repair. Parts for Phillips machines come at $50.

   a) Which machines should be bought?

   b) How many machines of each kind would operate a year without a break-down? To answer this question, divide 2,000, the operating hours in a year, by the MTBF. Use the answer as an exponent and raise the fraction 1/2.72 to the power indicated. If, for example, the exponent is 1, then 1/2.72 is simply 0.37. This is the probability that 1 machine will operate for a year without failure. Multiply this probability by the number of machines to answer this question.

10. The ABC Company pays a royalty of $.60 a unit on a product it manufactures. Royalties are paid at the end of the year and will have to be paid for 5 more years before the patent runs out. Production for this year and the next 5 years is expected to be 7,000, 8,000, 10,000, 12,000, 12,000, and 11,000 respectively.

   The patent holder has offered ABC the opportunity to pay $25,000 in lieu of all future royalty payments.

   Assuming that money is worth 8 percent to ABC in other uses, what should it do? Show the figures.

11. In the case of the redundancy example in the text, what would the answer be if part A had a reliability of .94 and part B .92, with all other figures remaining the same?

Case 11–1

According to Peter Drucker, consumerism means that the consumer looks upon the manufacturer as "somebody who is interested but who doesn't really know what consumer realities are and who has not made the effort to find out." Perhaps Drucker is right, so far as what many consumers think. But whether this is what consumers think or not, consumerism seems to have gone even further. Manufacturers are often held liable for injuries even when consumers use products wrongly.

A woman bothered by bugs, bought a can of insecticide, but instead of spraying it on the furniture or in the air, she sprayed herself. She had a violent allergic reaction, and sued and collected from the manufacturer.

In another case, a man who was injured in an accident while riding in a 13-year-old car sued the manufacturer. When he was thrown against the gear shift, the knob on top broke apart, and he was impaled on the shaft. The knob was made of white plastic, which over the 13 years had oxidized and developed hairline cracks. The man sued the company, claiming that the company had made the car with faulty materials, and won his suit. So did the woman who plugged a 115-volt vacuum cleaner into a 220-volt plug, causing the sweeper to "blow up." It is hard to see how a motor burning out could "blow up," but somehow the woman got hurt in the process.

In all three of these cases there seems to have been no negligence on the part of the manufacturers. These accidents did not occur because the manufacturers were remiss in their concern for consumer needs.

In another case, a man was injured when the steering wheel of the car he was driving came off in his hands in an accident. The car was so badly damaged that it was not clear whether the steering wheel had been faulty or not. Nonetheless the manufacturer was held liable. Today's consumerism seems almost always to hold manufacturers liable regardless of their culpability.

Hundreds of cases of extreme consumer protectionism can be quoted. In the vacuum cleaner case the court said the label should have warned that plugging it into a 220-volt line would be disastrous.

There are also cases (fortunately very few) where people contracted polio from polio vaccine. But in cases as serious as this, everyone would surely agree that the manufacturer of the vaccine should be liable. Clearly, consumer protectionism is sometimes of utmost importance.

Since manufacturers have only one source of income from which to pay for both greater safety and liability claims, these costs must be added to the costs of products for everyone.

What really should the answer be? How far should a manufacturer have to go to protect everybody against highly unlikely accidents? How much should *all* consumers be required to pay for such protection for the few who have trouble?

Recent references

Beattie, C. J., and R. D. Reader, *Quantitative Management in R & D*, Chapman & Hall, 1971

Coccia, Michel A., John W. Dondanville, and Thomas R. Nelson, *Product Liability*, New York: American Management Association, 1970

Galloway, E. C., "Evaluating R & D Performance—Keep It Simple," *Research Management,* March 1971

Ingersoll, Robert S., "What the Corporate Executive Expects of R & D," *Research Management,* March 1972

Jose, Frank C., Jr., *R & D's Role in Production Liability*, New York: American Management Association, 1970

McLaughlin, William G., *Fundamentals of Research Management,* New York: American Management Association, 1970

Malim, T. H., "What Causes Products to Fail?" *Iron Age,* August 6, 1970

Moskowitz, Herbert, *An Experimental Investigation of Decision Making in a Simulated Research and Development Environment,* Lafayette, Ind.: The Institute for Research in the Behavioral, Economic, and Management Sciences, Purdue University, 1971

12

Product design

Form and functional design

PRODUCT DESIGN deals with form and function. Form design deals with the product's shape and appearance while functional design deals with how it works. The need for functional design is obvious—the product has to work. But form design is important too, even though it adds nothing to a product's performance. Automobile companies are always trying to make their cars as attractive looking to the public as they can. They have found out many times that if people don't like a car's looks they are not likely to buy it.

Looks, even the looks of the package, are very important in selling anything to customers. Often customers can't really tell whether one product is better than another, so they buy the good-looking one, or the one in the most attractive package.

Sometimes, too, competing products have different substantive advantages and so are hard to compare. One vacuum cleaner, for example, may be the best for cleaning carpets but another is best for upholstery. Or one car may climb a mountain better than another which gives high gasoline mileage on the level. Which product does a consumer choose when he expects to use it under varied conditions? Probably the product with the most eye appeal.

FIGURE 12–1. Stages in transferring design into production

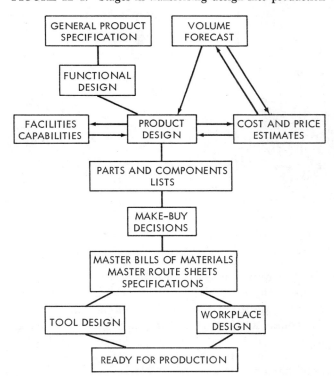

Design and fashion

Almost always, designers try to design the best-quality product possible for the price. A product's quality is in its characteristics, which the designers have to decide and which the factory has to impart to the product.

Yet "best quality" is an ambiguous term; it implies that quality is a matter of performance characteristics. But in the case of consumer products this is not always the whole story, or even the most important thing.

Style, fashion, design, pattern, looks, and taste are all, as consumers see it, part of quality. Not only are all of these very hard for a manufacturer to nail down or even to define, but "acceptable" or "high quality" is a concept in the *consumer's* mind. It differs between groups and it keeps changing. Today, hardly any man under 30 will buy the traditional suit of clothes made from regular cloth; it has to be double knit and bright in color. A fine French meal includes wine, fish, and rare meat, but many American don't like wine or half-cooked meat. In many parts of the world octopus is regarded as a delicacy, but by no means everywhere.

Design questions having to do with consumer taste plague manufacturers of clothing, textiles, furniture, automobiles, and even bicycles (see Figure 12–2). Which bicycle, for example, is the "better" one? Most

FIGURE 12–2

adults would probably choose the bicycle on the right, but the younger generation wants the one on the left. Customer desires become even more important in the prepared food, beverage, and tobacco industries. Beers, wines, coffee, and tobaccos taste different, yet which are best depends on who answers the question about which is best. High quality (or good design) to one user is low quality (or poor design) to another. Manufacturers have to define quality in the same way as their products' users. And they have to design products to suit customers. Furthermore, if consumer tastes change, manufactures have to change their designs and their definitions of quality accordingly or lose out. "Good" Scotch whiskey today is, for example, quite different from "good" Scotch whiskey a decade ago. It is lighter both in color and in taste.

There should be a constant dialog between manufacturers and their customers, who are paying for the quality they get, relating to *what is quality* and how much the customers are *willing to pay for it*.

Design and market segments

The market for many items extends all the way from outright poor quality to extremely good quality. Normally, too, there is a reasonable relationship between the quality level and the price. At any point along the quality scale there is a demand for a certain volume, but how big a demand depends on how many people are interested in that quality at the price asked for that quality.

Product designers have to try to balance out several interacting economic curves. Figure 12–3 shows the relationship of quality to cost, and Figure 12–4 might depict the demand curve of a man with limited means. Figure 12–5 might be the demand curve of a man of means.

FIGURE 12–3

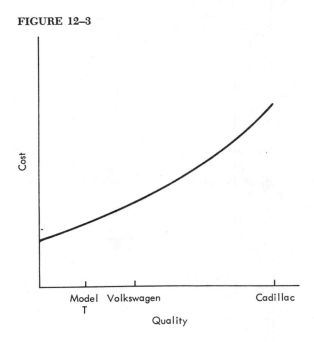

A sale can take place only if a man's demand curve is above the cost curve. Figure 12–4 shows the sales area for a man with limited means; he cannot buy a Cadillac because his willingness-to-pay line is below the Cadillac's cost. The more affluent man, however, can buy a Cadillac because his line exceeds the cost of a Cadillac. He might, on the other hand, forgo buying a Cadillac and buy a less costly car if he so chooses.

Top managers have to aim for some particular segment of the market. In doing this they have to guess how many people have demand curves like those in Figures 12–4 and 12–5. They also have to guess at what level in their sales area customers will exercise their options.

FIGURE 12–4

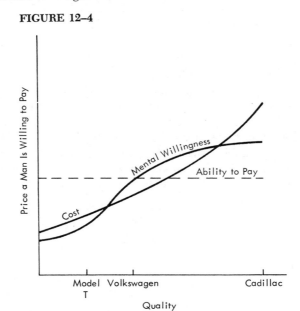

Once the strategy decision is made, it falls on the designers to make a product which aims for the market segment selected. This strategy decision will also affect the operations of other segments of the company.

FIGURE 12–5

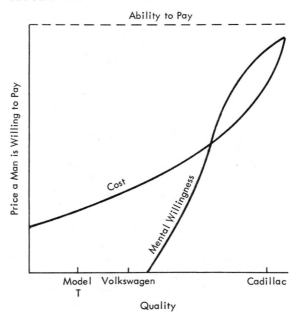

If the choice is Volkswagon, then cost control is very important. If it is Cadillac, then quality overrides all else.

Making the quality decision

Like so many things, quality is a continuum, usually even a multi-dimensional continuum. A product can be barely good enough, or it can be better, or it can be very good—and for each of its many characteristics.

An automobile may be economical on gasoline usage or not; it may be able to go 100 miles an hour or not; it may need frequent and early repairs or not, etc. An airplane can be fast or slow, it may land on a short runway or it may require a longer runway; it can climb fast or less fast, etc.

Probably a design committee should decide the performance and appearance a product should have, its general "configuration." Then the design engineer has to try to design the product to meet these specifications—*but within the cost limit allowed.* Designers should always do the best they can, but they should never forget costs. They need not actually produce the *best* design they can, but it needs to be "good enough"— good enough to meet the need but, if higher quality costs more, not any better. A $10 transistor radio can't have everything; it can't reproduce operatic or orchestral music with full quality. Nor does a light bulb need to be sturdy enough to withstand the impact of being dropped on a concrete floor.

Annual models

Paradoxically, in the intensely competitive American market it is often hard to tell one company's products from another's. Style designs often seem to be directed toward meeting competition with look-alike products.

Against this tendency, however, is the need to come out with something different all the time, so there are new, annual models in many industries. This is in spite of its being impossible to find a new and revolutionary design every year or so. It becomes "new look by gimmick"; and even the new gimmick better not look too different lest customers reject it.

Annual models are not wholly wasteful, though. First, there is the need to claim innovations (be they fact or fancy) and this need to claim innovations helps produce them as facts. New developments are pushed along faster so that new models will truly be better. Also, annual models provide an automatic "cutting in" or "zeroing in" point for improvements. Most improvements made within a model year are not put into the current products, thus saving the cost of making expensive changes during production runs. Putting all the improvements into effect at once saves the cost of changing during production and lets a company justly claim that next year's models are better.

Materials

In many cases designers can choose from among different materials for those they will use. Just as a carpet can be made of wool, cotton, flax, rayon, nylon, or other synthetics, so can industrial products be made from different materials. A gear can be made from steel, iron, brass, aluminum, nylon, Bakelite, or other plastics. Wrapping and covering materials can be made of cloth, leather, paper, or hard or soft plastic.

In making his choice from among the possibilities, the designer needs always to keep in mind (*a*) the need for the product or part to perform, (*b*) the relative material costs, and (*c*) the relative processing costs. Often, since each of the several possibilities will perform well, the real choice depends on the relative costs of the materials and their processing costs. And by no means does the low-cost material always win out. Many small metal parts, for example, are made out of copper or brass instead of steel—even though steel costs only $\frac{1}{20}$ as much—because copper and brass can be machined so quickly that processing costs are far less.

Zinc is often used for small, intricately molded parts instead of other metals because it works so well in die casting, which is a low-cost way of making high-volume intricate items. Yet zinc sometimes loses out to molded plastics because the latter can be die-cast even more readily.

When materials contribute to a product's final appearance, the designer can sometimes have the best of two worlds. A walnut cabinet makes an attractive television set, but walnut is quite costly and wood is not as durable as metal. But simulated wood-grain vinyl coatings can be put on metal cabinets and provide the attractive finish even though the cabinet is actually made of sheet steel and so is very durable.

The decision on what material to use is usually an enduring one. Yet sometimes the price of one material goes up and that of another comes down, thus making it economical to reverse the choice. In its early days, plastics cost too much for general use, but now they compete successfully with various metals.

Sometimes, too, the choice is related to volume. For low volume, costly but easily worked materials may be best since this economizes on processing costs. For high volumes, on the other hand, expensive machines can handle hard-to-work materials economically. A purchasing department should always be alert to price and volume changes which might justify changing materials.

Design by imitation

The greatest "newness" in any company's products comes not from innovation but imitation. This is only natural since a company cannot possibly be first with everything new in its industry. This means that part of every company's product development efforts should be directed at developing imitative equivalents of someone else's innovative products.

And the faster the rate at which new products are introduced in an industry, the more of this kind of development companies need to do.

Companies which adopt imitation as a policy can sometimes be the "second with the mostest." It is true that imitators start a step behind, but often they can move faster than the innovator since they have his designs and market success to look at. In the 1950s, Sperry Rand had the first computers, but IBM soon had most of the market. In the 1960s, 3M's Thermofax method unearthed the big paper-copying market, but then Xerox moved in and took it away.

The obvious gain from following instead of innovating is the saving of research and development money that the leaders spend on failures. Yet this saving is made at the risk that an early start will pay off well and quickly and generate a permanent lead.

The source decision

When an assembled product is designed, the engineers make a list of all its parts. This list, usually called a "bill of materials," should also show —for each part—whether a part will be bought or made.

For most parts there is no real question, because the company is in certain businesses and not in others. Where there is a question, it is usually decided by a make-or-buy committee which considers each part or component individually. Normally this does not preclude the decisions later being reversed if conditions change. Also, certain items would be "make" items when the plant is not busy but "buy" items when it is busy.

Value engineering and value analysis

Value engineering (usually done by design engineers) or value analysis (usually done in the purchasing department) means that everything that is made or bought is regarded as made or bought to serve a purpose. Before making or buying any equipment, parts, or materials, engineers and buyers study what purpose these things serve. Would other, lower cost designs work as well? Could another, less costly item fill the need? Would less expensive material do the job? And, on bought items, are the vendors' prices as low as they ought to be?

They should try to think of different ways of getting work done. If two parts have to be fastened together, the design engineer should not think first of how to design a low-cost bolt; he should think first about making the two pieces as one. If this can't be done economically, then he should consider riveting the pieces together, or welding or gluing them, or making the parts interlock like pieces of a jigsaw puzzle. If he still thinks that a screw or bolt will do the work best, then—and then only— should he go ahead and figure how to make or buy a screw or bolt at low cost.

Design engineers also need to be conscious of trade-offs. Silver, for example, conducts electricity better than copper; but silver should almost never be used instead of copper since it costs 50 times as much. Silver's extra conductivity is not sufficient to offset copper's lower price.

Sometimes, however, nonmonetary considerations must rule and more quality has to be put in even at a higher cost. In the early 1970s automobile designers had to reexamine their decisions on safety, whereas they had previously saved money by designing automobile bumpers as low-cost and not very substantial items. Pressure from the public for greater safety caused them to redesign the bumpers and build more protection into them, even though at higher cost.

Sometimes value analysis, particularly in purchasing, saves considerable money, as is shown in a few results of value engineering and analysis at General Electric. A screw of special design cost $.15, but value analysis turned up a way to make it for $.015. The annual savings were $20,000. A hand-made gasket, costing $4.15 each at GE, was found to cost $.15 from an outside gasket maker. A die-cast cover cost $.60 but, changed to a stamping, it proved better and cost only $.20. Annual savings were $39,000.

General Motors' Frigidaire Division points to these savings. For aluminum doors, bought for an evaporator, three vendor quotations ranged from $2.40 to $2.70. Frigidaire's estimate of what it should pay was $2.05. The final price was $2.10, for annual savings of $27,000. Food compartment door quotations ranged from $3.30 to $3.50. Frigidaire's estimate, $3.05. The final price was $3.05 and the savings $49,000. An escutcheon made from 0.032″ brass was changed to 0.025″ steel. Savings, $12,000.

Both engineers and purchasing men should try to avoid setting unnecessarily high specifications. In one plant the purchasing agent found that its engineers had specified that parts be made to close fits—although the parts were enameled (thus destroying any close fit) before they were used! Loosening the tolerance cut the purchase price. Before that the company had not been getting full value for its money. It had been paying for a close fit that it didn't need.

Value analysis as done by the purchasing department sometimes creates internal frictions because buyers are venturesome souls who are all too ready to set their ideas of quality against those of design engineers. Perhaps this should be expected if buyers are kept under pressure to cut costs, and perhaps this is good. Yet buyers and engineers should work together toward a common goal—lower costs.

In spite of what has just been said, there are times when value analysis should *not* be used. A man can use a paper clip to hold his necktie instead of a $5 tie clip, and it would do the job satisfactorily. So do buttons in place of cuff links. Where esthetics and price economy clash, designers and buyers need to decide which should rule. Value analysis focuses on function, not esthetics.

Modular design

With repair labor just about as costly in a factory as in a home and with breakdowns usually costly in both cases, designers are turning to modular construction, in which products are usually made of easily detachable subassemblies or sections. When an item fails, the whole module (of which the item is a part) is removed and a new module is put in. Later the removed unit can be repaired or thrown away. Electrical printed circuit boards (or "cards") and integrated circuits are usually components of this sort. Plug-in bases are made as integral parts of such boards, thus allowing for their easy removal. If a transistor or diode fails, the whole card on which it is mounted, along with several condensers, other diodes, etc., is removed and replaced by a replacement card.

The modular design idea is used extensively in computers, both in the microminiature and circuit board way, but also in a larger way. Standardized major components are made with their physical dimensions and electrical systems compatible so they can be hooked up in different combinations to make what are, essentially, different computers. In computers, for example, the units which store information, those which "read in" information to the calculating section, and the section which prints out results are available in several sizes and with varied capabilities. They can be connected with any combination of other major units. We also see this idea in automobiles, where cars can have six- or eight-cylinder motors or manual gear shifts or automatic shifts, etc. These features can be combined as the customer desires.

Design by computers

Computers are moving in on both the calculating operations required in design work and the actual making of engineering drawings. The movement is not rapid, however, because most automatic drafting machines cost $100,000 or more. But where companies have them, automatic drafting machines can take a computer's calculations describing the direction and curvature of lines and draw the lines at rates of 200 inches or more per minute.

General Electric uses computers to design electric motors. I-T-E Circuit Breaker uses them to design custom-built transformers. Allis Chalmers uses them to decide the best shapes for drying kilns. General Motors uses them in automobile design. And airplane companies use them to compute the contours of wings and to lay out integrated circuits.

When there are several ways to do something, a computer can quickly make all the comparisons and pick the best way whereas, without a computer, an engineer cannot make all the comparisons and would have to rely on his judgment. Once the computer has made its calculations, it can have the automatic drafting machine make the drawings while the computer itself proceeds to make all the instructions the factory workers will need for making the product. Or, before finally deciding, the designer can have several designs drawn up for his inspection; they can be put on paper or projected alongside each other on a viewing scope.

Computers can also project, on a scope, a drawing which it made from the design instructions put into its memory by the designer. Furthermore, if the designer wants to eliminate a line or draw in a new one, he can do it on the scope with an electric pencil and the computer will change its memory instructions so that it will thereafter project the revised drawing. The computer can also enlarge a picture, or turn it so that it can be seen from another angle, such as left front, rather than from the front. And it can pair up mating parts to see how they fit.

As if this were not enough, this process is now well enough developed so an engineer can even draw a preliminary design on the scope with his electric light pen and the computer will reproduce it whenever it's called upon. It will even straighten out lines, or smooth out curved lines, and reproduce the improved sketch on call. Computer manufacturers even point to direct voice communication with computers as not being far away.

The metric system

Some time in the next decade, Americans will probably adopt the metric system. It will take some getting used to. The milkman will leave a one-liter bottle of milk (.95 quart) and the husband may be asked to buy 450 grams of hamburger (1 pound) on his way home for supper. When the customer at the gasoline filling station says, "Fill 'er up," he may end up buying 60 liters of gasoline (15.8 gallons). And the air pressure in his tires ought perhaps to be kept up to 12.7 kilograms (28 pounds).

When a man steps on a scale he will find that he weighs 68 kilograms instead of 150 pounds. And instead of being 6 feet tall, he will be 1.83 meters tall. Pike's Peak in Colorado will be 4,301 meters high instead of 14,110 feet. On the small-sized end, an 8½ × 11 inch sheet of paper will be 21.6 × 27.9 centimeters.

A man in the city who owns a lot 60 × 150 feet will find that it is now 18.29 × 54.86 meters. A farmer who used to own 200 acres of land will have 81 hectares. Whereas it used to be 10 miles to town, it will become 16.1 kilometers. And the speed limit will be 120 kilometers an hour instead of 65 miles per hour. The distance from New York to Chicago will change from 840 miles to 1,351 kilometers.

Summers may seem cooler, though, when the thermometer gets up to only 35 degrees (centigrade) instead of 95 degrees (Fahrenheit). Winters too may seem colder. When a man looks at the thermometer he will see a reading of 10 degrees below zero instead of 14 degrees above.

It all sounds confusing to an American's ear, but it will probably come before very many years nonetheless. The increase in world trade makes the problem of differing systems of weights and measures a difficult one. And since most of the Western world uses the metric system, England and the United States will both probably have to change. England is already changing, and in the United States the U.S. Department of Commerce is already studying the problems involved in our changing too.

As far as manufacturing is concerned, the most satisfactory way, although cumbersome, is to put both measurements (millimeters and inches) on all drawings and machine calibrations. Then, in some 10 to 20 years, it will be relatively simple to drop the old measurements. Some American companies are already providing dual reading dials on their machines.

At some point, too, consumers will have to be introduced to, and get used to, metric measurements on food packages and a great many other things they buy.

Returning to the problem in manufacturing settings, another way to change would be to do it on a clean-break basis. On some selected weekend, inches and yards would be out and millimeters and meters would be in. Presumably, also, miles would become kilometers, pounds become kilograms, and gallons, liters.

A still different method of transition would be to leave the old system undisturbed, but to use only the new measurements on all new product designs. Ford Motor of England is doing it this way, as are most English manufacturers.

Educating people to the metric system may not prove to be the greatest problem so far as manufacturers are concerned. Rather, it might be their need to continue to supply repair parts on the basis of old measurements. Yet this, too, seems to be a problem which can be taken in stride since repair parts for old equipment could be made just as they now are.

Drawings and specifications

The last step in product design is the making of drawings and specifications. Drawings show the exact size and shape of a product, its parts, and subassemblies. Features other than physical dimensions are described in writing in the form of specifications. During the process of designing, product sketches and rough drawings are probably made, but before production can proceed, complete and exact drawings have to be made. And although, as was said, it is now possible to have drafting machines do a good bit of the actual making of drawings, they are expensive, and rarely can they do the whole job. Most drafting is still done by hand.

When similar items are drawn frequently, drafting time can be saved by using printed forms. The nut and bolt industry, for example, uses the same drawing for a long or a short bolt, or for a thick or a thin bolt, or for various numbers of threads per inch. Users of the drawings read a bolt's dimensions from its particular dimensions notations—they don't get them by measuring them off. The number of threads per inch also is read from the instructions.

Standardized shortcuts of other kinds are used. For example, screw threads are almost never actually shown on drawings; they are indicated by symbols. Standardized symbols are always used in drawings of electrical circuits, air conditioning and welding jobs, and pattern work. Drawing time is cut still more by using printed adhesive transparencies of standard parts or items such as switches or fuses.

Tolerances. Tolerances are the limits for deviations from perfection which are allowable. When setting them, engineers always try to balance off the need for close fits (so that a product will perform well) against the cost of making parts to such exact specifications. Tolerances should therefore be what the designer would like, modified by the ability of the company's machines to do the work at a reasonable cost. Not all tolerances deal with dimensions, but the problems are the same (balancing the value against the cost of near-perfect quality), whether the designer is dealing with the exactness of chemical composition, a material's strength, or whatever. In setting tolerances, engineers have to answer questions such as: How square is square enough? How round is round enough? How smooth is smooth enough?

Robert W. Pearson, when he was director of production of AMF Company, found that draftsmen, not design engineers, actually decided these matters in most cases and that they did it with very little appreciation of the costs of the tolerances they set. Furthermore, if a draftsman sets the tolerances and sets them closely, he determines the manufacturing process required by ruling out all but the most exact and costly methods of doing the work. Pearson says he found that his company's draftsmen were, in effect, specifying far more processes than anyone had any idea.

Pearson reported that overclose (and even unwritten) tolerances cost AMF more than half a million dollars on just two contracts. On one occasion a customer's unwritten practice of requiring a plus-or-minus tolerance of $5/1,000$ of an inch on sheet metal caused it to reject all the sheet metal work made by AMF to its $\pm\frac{1}{64}$ ($16/1,000$) of an inch tolerance. On another occasion AMF's standard on perpendicularity of ±1 degree wasn't close enough. After the work was done, the customer wanted $\frac{1}{4}$ of a degree! Why? Pearson says he has no idea—certainly the use of the product did not require *either* of these excessively tight tolerances.

Another company asked its foremen to point out the tolerance specifications with which they had the greatest trouble. Then the company took this matter up with the engineering department to see if the tolerances could be relaxed without hurting the product. In most instances no one knew who had set the tolerances, and no one cared whether they were relaxed or not. Moreover, the company discovered that the few persons in the engineering department who knew and cared about the specifications had no notion of what they cost in the way of extra work and rejections.

It would be a disservice to the engineering profession, however, to create the impression that engineers set tolerances capriciously and without regard to cost. Most tolerances are properly and intelligently set. It is, moreover, difficult to weed out every overly exact tolerance. However, a company should not let draftsmen decide tolerances unless they are well acquainted with costs.

Standardization and simplification

When a man buys an electric light bulb, he knows it will screw into the socket all right because light bulb bases are standardized (only a few kinds of bases are made). But an American light bulb will not fit into a socket in Europe, or vice versa. They won't fit because their bases are different.

Also, the ordinary person probably never even thinks about a light bulb's voltage, because in the United States 110 volts is standard in houses. But again, Europe is different; in fact, several different voltages are used there. Or suppose a man needs a new storage battery in his car. There is no problem here either; a few different sizes are made, but not many. Or if a man buys a new hose to sprinkle his lawn, he doesn't have to wonder if it will screw onto the water faucet. Of course it will; the size and screw threads are standard.

We have used the word "standard" as meaning that only certain specific sizes are made and sold. Some people prefer to call this process of cutting down on the number of sizes *simplification*. "Standardization," these people would say, is something else; it is the process of writing down the size, shape, performance, and other characteristics of the items chosen to concentrate on. The two concepts are so closely related, however, that we will use them here as being nearly the same.

Standardization (including simplification) usually means that non-standard items will not be made—except when a customer orders them specially (and pays extra for them). Sometimes standards have been enacted into law for safety or health reasons. Automobile windshields, for example, must be made of safety glass. Mostly, though, standardization is voluntary. Manufacturers of "style" goods, such as women's clothes, for example, do not standardize very much because women want "something different." But most industries, even those producing consumer goods, can and do standardize extensively, as in the setting of shoe sizes.

Industrywide standardization requires industrywide cooperation, and it is generally sponsored by industrywide professional associations or departments of the U.S. government. In the automobile industry, the Society of Automotive Engineers has developed many standards for materials and parts. Other societies have done similar work for other industries.

The American Standards Association, the American Society for Testing Metals, and the National Bureau of Standards are other important standard-setting organizations. Altogether, these organizations have set thousands of standards.

The sales department can contribute to standardization (of the simplification kind) within a company by analyzing the sales volume of products and cutting out slow-moving items. It can also work with the engineering department in helping to develop products which are not standardized in appearance (because they have different trims or finishes) but which can be made from standardized parts.

Specifications of outside agencies are used for the most part in buying and selling between companies because both parties will then understand exactly what is wanted. Within every manufacturing company the engineering department sets many standards, by far the greater part being the dimensions and characteristics of company-made products and parts and the standards for plant operations. The engineering department also sets standards for purchased materials where generally accepted standards do not exist, prescribes standard methods of testing products, and sets test scores which materials must pass.

Many standards concerned with the safety and health of workers and customers are incorporated into state and municipal laws and insurance company codes. The standards which boilers, elevators, and other potentially dangerous equipment must meet are covered by laws. The building codes of municipalities set standards for electrical wiring, plumbing, and so forth, as well as sanitation standards to protect employee and customer health.

Advantages of standardization and simplification

Standardization and simplification reduce the kinds, types, and sizes of raw materials which have to be bought. Standardization lets companies buy bigger quantities and so get lower prices per unit. Simplification also cuts manufacturing costs because manufacturers get longer runs on the fewer kinds of products they still make. This cuts down setup costs and allows more specialized machines to be used. Also, fewer patterns and tools are needed.

An example will illustrate the order of magnitude of such savings. Suppose a company makes 2,000 items of plumbing fittings. If it had 100 of each item in stock, it would have to carry a stock of 200,000 pieces. And if their average cost were as little as $.25 each, it would have $50,000 tied up in inventory. It would need 2,000 bins and 2,000 stock records. Besides, it would have to keep similar stocks and records in warehouses and in the hands of dealers all over the nation. But if, through simplification, 2,000 could be cut to 500, possibly the supply stocks could be cut to 100,000 pieces or 200 of each item. The inventory of each item would thus be twice as large, while at the same time the total inventory would be reduced by half. The company could thus give better service with only half as much inventory.

Disadvantages of standardization and simplification

Some manufacturers, especially those making assembled products, do not accept industrywide standardization because they find that using "the perfect part" is better than using a standard part that is not so well suited to their particular use. A company making power lawn mowers may not want the same motor which is used for chain saws, or motor-cycles, or outboard motors. Instead, it may be better to design an engine especially for power-driven lawn mowers.

Manufacturers using large volumes of nuts, bolts, wire, valves, bearings, electric motors, switches, and other parts also frequently find that "the perfect part" for a particular purpose is cheaper to use, even if it costs a little more to make, than a standard part. Sometimes nonstandard parts are used in such quantities that they can be mass produced and therefore cost no more than standard items. Sometimes, too, "the perfect part," originally nonstandard, becomes standard through usage.

There are other reasons why industrywide standardization programs often are only partially successful. Standardization tends to favor large, well-known companies whereas, small (or new) companies can rarely get much business by making and selling the same things and at the same prices as the big companies. They can't afford to go along with industry-wide standardization programs. They survive by offering something different at the same (or close to the same) price as standard products. These companies might be said to specialize in specialties, and by doing so they undercut standardization programs to some extent.

Furthermore, customers undercut standardization programs. Often they don't want the standard item unless it is priced lower. And the sales department sides with the customer in this. One of its strongest selling points usually is that "our product is different."

From the social point of view, there is a potential danger in standardization. If new products are standardized too soon, before they have become reasonably stable in design, standardization may become an obstacle to progress. Color television, for example, came to Europe later than to the United States. This permitted European television to incorporate more advanced technology and use 160 lines to the inch fineness instead of the American 120 lines to the inch; consequently their pictures are sharper. American television was standardized before some of the best technology was developed.

Typewriter keyboards, too (many years ago), were frozen too soon, and this has stood in the way of improvement. They have a poor arrangement of letters (60 percent of the work load falls on the left hand, whereas most people are right handed). We know how to arrange them better, but can't make the change because millions of typists are adept at using the present keyboard—to say nothing of our having millions of typewriters with the bad arrangement.

Improvements that call for different, nonstandard products must always be made if progress is to continue. A standard, as of any given time, is more the prevailing *style* than a permanent standard. Standards should not be permitted to "freeze," or be kept only for their own sake; they are of value only as they improve a company's product and service and lower its cost.

Review questions

1. How can product designers do a good job when customers want different things? How can a designer ever settle on a design?

2. How can a product designer resolve the cost/value problem?

3. It would seem that design by imitation would be a poor policy since all the followers allow the leader to get a head start. Is design by imitation ever a good policy? When?

4. Who is in the best position to weigh the pros and cons of make-buy situations? Would a committee help? Who should be on it?

5. Value engineering sounds like a device used by buyers in purchasing departments to put great pressure on vendors to sell at low prices. Is this the idea? Explain value analysis and value engineering.

6. How much trouble will be created in the United States if we adopt the metric system? How might such a changeover be accomplished in a reasonable fashion?

7. How are tolerances usually set? Is there a better way? What should a company do to try to have its tolerances set as reasonably as possible?

8. What are the dangers to society from standardizing too soon in the development of a new product?

Discussion questions

1. Should a product designer pay more attention to form or functional design? Why?

2. The ABC Company has made refrigerators for years but its market has been slipping. Its dealers say that the competitors' products look better, but ABC's managers don't think so. In fact they think that their refrigerators look better than any others, and besides they work better. What should be done? Why?

3. In automobiles, "soft" springs make for a smooth ride at low speeds. But at high speeds soft springs cause more swaying. And when heavily loaded, cars with soft springs ride very low. What kind of springs should be put into cars?

4. Design is always a compromise, a trade-off of quality versus cost. How can a designer know where to set the performance level?

   a) If a company makes carpets, should it make them to wear for 40 years of heavy traffic? Or to wear out in 5 years of light traffic? Or what?

   b) Should the company go for the $20-a-square-yard business or the $30-a-yard business?

5. Would you pay extra to get a hand-made product? Why? If you would, how has mass production failed?

6. Since the costs and risks of research are so great, why would it not be a good idea for a company to cut out research and let the other companies do it, and then either develop something similar very quickly or pay another company a royalty for using its idea?

7. How can a value analysis man do a very good job when he really doesn't know what it costs to do things in other companies? Besides, he doesn't know how "hungry" other companies are for business and what prices they might, under pressure, quote. Without such knowledge, isn't he limited in what he can accomplish?

8. Oscar Mayer is famous for wieners. How should a specifications writer for this company go about writing specifications for a wiener? What problems would be involved? Is a specification worthwhile here?

9. A government contracting office asked why a price was so high and the answer was "close tolerances." Upon the engineer's being asked the reason for the close tolerances, he said that he knew they couldn't be met but by setting them high he could get people to try harder. Comment on this situation.

10. Make a freehand sketch of the parts of the chair you are sitting on and show their dimensions and tolerances. Discuss the problems involved.

11. Do tight standards make for higher or lower manufacturing costs? Explain.

12. Should a manufacturer standardize his products? Why?

13. The designer for a nut and bolt manufacturer has been selected by his company to be a member of an industrywide committee on standardization. What should he want to know and how will he decide what is good for the industry, his company, and the consumer?

Problems

1. It is anticipated that a company will make 800,000 units of product A in a year and will have a factory cost of $2.50, of which $.95 will be spent for materials. The rest of the factory cost is for processing. Redesigning product A should save 2 percent of processing costs and 5 percent of materials costs. There is a question, however, about how much the redesigning will cost. The designers think that a $25,000 budget will do the job.

   a) If it is required that the $25,000 be recovered out of savings in 1 year, should this expenditure be approved?

   b) Suppose that the $25,000 is approved, and has been spent, but that the improvement is still far from finished. If it is cut off now, no gain at all would be realized, and the $25,000 would all be lost. The design engineer, however, is very enthusiastic and feels sure that for an additional $50,000 budget he can be certain of getting the savings originally expected. Should the top manager approve this additional $50,000? (Assume that he agrees with the designer's expectation of success.)

2. A part weighing 3 pounds can be made from steel or brass. In the case of steel, half of the original material is used up as cutting waste. For brass, a fourth of the original material becomes cutting waste. To machine the part from steel takes 25 minutes per unit, whereas brass takes 15 minutes. Steel costs $.60 a pound and brass $.90 a pound. Steel scrap is worth $.02 a pound and brass scrap is worth $.30 a pound. The machine and the operator together cost $10 an hour.

   a) From which metal should the part be made? How much will this choice save vis-à-vis the other method?

   b) What would the comparison be if brass went up in price to $1.10 a pound (and scrap went to $.40 a pound)?

   c) If the price of steel remains constant, what would be the price of brass at the break-even point between steel and brass? (Assume that brass scrap is still worth $.30 per pound.)

3. Two kinds of paint are being considered. A gallon of brand A costs $6 and will cover 300 square feet of surface. It will last about 3 years and can be applied at 75 square feet an hour. A gallon of brand B costs $10 a gallon and will cover 400 square feet of surface. It goes on at a rate of 90 square feet an hour. Painters cost $7 an hour.

   How long will brand B have to last to be competitive with A?

4. The ABC Company is bringing out a new product, the parts for which can be bought or made. If bought, they will cost $2 per unit for the 10,000 units expected to be made.

   a) Making these parts will cost $5,000 for tooling plus $1.30 per unit variable cost. Should ABC buy or make these items?

   b) ABC can go more automatic and spend $15,000 for machines, which would reduce variable costs per unit to $.60. Should ABC buy or make these items, and if it should make them, by which method?

5. Modular components are designed so that although each module contains several parts, a module can be put in or taken out as easily as if it were just one part. Almost always the modules are small, and their component parts are quite small—so much so that if one of the small parts fails it does not pay to repair the module. Instead it is removed, like a burned-out light bulb, and thrown away. This means that when one component fails, several good components are thrown out. It costs too much to disassemble the module in order to save the good parts.

   We are dealing with a module whose parts have the following probability of failure rates in 2,000 hours of operation. A: .003; B: .012; C: .004; D: .009; E: .020; F: .011; G: .006; and H: .012. Assume that these parts, separately, cost as follows: A: $.19; B: $.72; C: $.04; D: $.22; E: $.11; F: $.19; G: $.38; and H: $.30.

These parts have to operate sequentially, but they can be split into 2 modules between any 2 components; for example, between A and B, B and C, C and D, etc. Assembly work costs $.10 more if the parts are split into 2 modules. Should they be made as 1 or as 2 modules? And if the choice is 2 modules, which parts will go into each module?

6. The McAulliffe Company's engineers have developed a watertight, shockproof container for small, delicate instruments. The U.S. Navy has shown strong interest in this new product, which it believes will work well aboard ships and submarines. However, a competing firm has developed a similar product; it is only slightly inferior in shockproof qualities to that of McAulliffe's. The competitor's product has been offered to the Navy at $6.50 per unit. The waterproof casing on the competing unit is made of steel whereas McAulliffe's engineers want to make their outside waterproof casing of brass, thus giving better rust protection than the competitor.

The Navy is interested in McAulliffe's product, but its representative has said he can pay no more than $7.70 per unit, and might not be able to pay even that much.

McAulliffe's engineers have put together the following cost expectations:

	Steel	Brass
Material cost per pound	$.30	$.70
Gross weight per container (incl. scrap)	5 lb.	6 lb.
Amount of material scrap per container	2.5 lb.	3 lb.
Value of scrap per pound	$.02	$.25
Tooling cost	$2,000	$1,000
Direct labor cost per machine-hour	$5.00	$5.00
Overhead cost per machine-hour	$6.00	$4.50
Output per machine-hour	25 units	27 units

Can McAulliffe compete if it makes the container out of steel? If so, at what volume will its costs be below $6.50? At what volume can it manufacture the product from brass for less than $7.70 each? At what volume can it make the product from brass at a cost of $7.20? Should it take an order if it must bid as low as $7 to get the contract? If so, how big must the order be in order to net McAulliffe a profit of $.50 per container?

Recent references

American Standards Yearbook, New York: American Standards Association (annually)

Brichta, A. M. and Peter E. M. Shark, *From Project to Production,* New York: Pergamon Press, 1970

Fallon, Carlos, *Value Analysis,* New York: John Wiley, 1971

Gisser, Philip, *Launching the New Industrial Product,* New York: American Management Association, 1972

Principles and Applications of Value Engineering, Washington, D.C.: U.S. Department of Defense, 1970

Rutenberg, D. P., "Design Commonality to Reduce Multi-Item Inventory: Optimal Depth of a Product Line," *Operations Research*, March 1971

Smith, C. S., *Quality and Reliability*, New York: Pitman, 1969

Soltanoff, L., "Innovation Myth," *Industrial Research*, August 1971

Wakefield, Brian D., "Value Engineering: It's Come a Long Way," *Iron Age*, March 16, 1972

section five

Economizing on work inputs

SOCIETY looks to managers of production to produce goods and services in the most economical way possible. Our competitive system in the United States provides for the survival of effective producers and the ultimate elimination of organizations (at least in the private sector of our economy) which do not produce effectively.

Economical production is partly broadly conceptual and partly a matter of paying careful attention to minor details. Whether it is more economical to import products into France from the United States or to build a factory in France is a matter of broad concept. So are major make-buy decisions, such as whether General Motors should buy automobile tires from Goodyear or make them itself. These decisions can be very important, but they are of greatest concern only to top officials. Lower level managers may be affected by such decisions but rarely are they parties to making them.

There is, however, a great deal which can be done within an organization in the way of economizing on inputs. Chapters 13 and 14 deal with these possibilities.

Chapter 13 takes up ways to improve individual jobs. It shows how an analyst can go about trying to improve jobs. His working tools and how to use them are explained.

Chapter 14 offers a second approach to the general idea of how to conserve resource inputs. Cost-cutting drives and areas of cost savings opportunities are presented.

There are, however, several possible pitfalls to avoid. It is easy to embark on a program to economize on resource inputs, and then find that this has been done, but at the cost of unwise actions in other directions. The wanted gains are achieved at unwanted costs in other directions. Chapter 14 analyzes these dangers.

303

13

Job design

HOW TO MAKE PRODUCTS at less cost? How to make them with less human effort? How to make them from less costly materials? How to simplify work? All companies are always trying to solve these problems. They are always trying to figure out how to produce more economically—and if they improve their effectiveness today, they try to make further improvements tomorrow.

One might think that, after a while, few opportunities would be left to improve operations. And it *would* get harder, as time goes on, if products did not always keep changing. But products keep changing. New operations always keep coming on and early methods of performing new operations often can be improved.

Suppose, for example, that a company makes ordinary lawn mowers; then along come power lawn mowers. This means making motors, gears, mounts, and so on, and it means men doing new jobs—jobs not done before. Next come powered rotary mowers. Again it means making parts not made before, and most of the jobs for making them are new. Then it develops that some customers want power mowers they can ride, so the company makes that kind too. And again the company gets into making new parts and new jobs. And, as is usual, early methods are often not done in the most effective manner. So again there is a new opportunity to figure out how best to do the jobs.

The task of improving jobs never ends. It never gets down to where it is impossible to make any more improvements. The payoff from effort directed at improving jobs can be substantial since a great deal of unnecessary work is often eliminated.

Proper job design reduces human effort by figuring out how to do things the short way, yet, curiously, many people dislike the thought of saving human effort. Efficiency is a bad word. People seem to think that when anyone figures out how a man can do a job with less effort (maybe by getting him a machine), this somehow takes advantage of him because—using the new, short method—he turns out more products.

And the man on the job often thinks so too. But give a man a power mower and he will mow maybe twice as much grass as he did before, and without working as hard, but he is still likely to talk about it as if *he* were doing twice as much work (spending twice as much effort) as he did before. The same thing happens in factories. Men often oppose job improvement because they are sure they must be working harder when more output results. They are also opposed lest an improvement eliminate a job here or there. Curiously, the same man who objects to job improvement in the factory may buy a power saw for his basement workshop at home. He can see that the power saw saves his energy and lets him get more work done—and without his working any harder.

Negative attitudes can sometimes be turned into positive attitudes through suggestion systems. Men are encouraged to suggest improvements and are rewarded for suggestions which can be applied. They may be given money, or a certificate, and have their picture in the company paper.

Industrial engineers also find that they win support for improvements by getting other people involved. Participation and involvement often make people supporters for improved job design. Industrial engineers may have to "plant" ideas about improvements in foremen's minds and wait for the seeds to germinate. Foremen may then work hard to make "their" ideas work.

A few companies go even farther and make lists of places where they think better methods could be, but have not yet been, figured out. They give these lists to foremen. They also spend time showing foremen *how* to go about improving jobs. Often these men are willing but don't know how to figure out ways to improve jobs.

Job enlargement

Historically, industrial engineers have always felt that short, highly routinized jobs done by men specializing in single tasks was the most productive way to design jobs. Most such engineers probably still believe that this is the best way.

There is some evidence to the contrary, however. Psychologists have repeatedly reported greater productivity from *less* rather than *more* specialization. Job enlargement means including a greater variety of minor tasks in jobs. These extra duties are included for the purpose of breaking up boredom and job monotony.

The evidence is not clear on just how much less boring a 3-minute job is than a 2-minute job. Industry in general appears to be skeptical because although job enlargement programs appear to be gaining some favor, they are not yet highly popular.

Job improvement limitations

Jobs are not always improved as much as they could be, partly because there is so much change. There is always the need to start new jobs by performing them at first as best one can and then improving them as time goes along. Also, some jobs are not of much consequence, or they won't be performed very often. It costs less to let them be done inefficiently than to study them carefully and figure out how to improve them.

Nor does careful job study pay unless jobs are standardized. All of the relevant factors—products, processes, materials handling, working conditions, work-place arrangements, and methods and motions—need to be standardized. Of course the improvement and standardization of these factors is one main object of job improvement work, but if they vary continually and cannot be standardized, the improvement possibilities are limited.

It would seem to be unnecessary to add that top-level backing is needed in order for job improvement to be very successful. Yet such backing is sometimes not provided. When this is so, men find it easy not to put improvement suggestions into effect if doing so makes extra work even though the savings may be great.

Designing future jobs

Job design aims to improve jobs, yet how wasteful it is to start doing a job one way and then have to change. Also, with so many people opposed to changing, how much trouble it makes. It would be better to figure out the best way to do an operation before starting to do it at all.

This is where job design and methods study can really save money— and without getting anyone upset. Admittedly, it is hard to see ahead of time just how every operation might be done and then improve it before it is actually done. But this is just what mass producers of consumer products do. Before production lines are set up, industrial engineers try to visualize the bits and pieces of work to be done at successive work stations. They try to divide the work to be done evenly among the men, and arrange the work-places, and develop tools—all ahead of time. They even use work-place mockups. Then, when operations start, most of the changing has been done. Improvements developed this way avoid the costs of changing later (tooling changes, trial runs, etc.) and at the same time avoid almost all of the opposition to change.

Job design objectives

Just as product engineers design products, so should industrial engineers and foremen design jobs. They should study the needs of the operation and the capabilities of men and machines and develop jobs to strike the best possible balance which satisfies all of the constraining factors.

Almost always, one main objective is to save human effort and minimize labor costs. Yet job designers should not strive for ultimates. Frequently, if a person were to ask an industrial engineer what he is trying to do, the time-honored answer will come back: "I try to find the one best way to do every job." This is not really what he should be trying to do, though. He should be trying to find a *better* method. The difference is important. If he always tries to find the *best* way, he will spend all his time seeking ultimates on too few jobs. Job designers usually have to be satisfied with figuring out a *better* way at reasonable expense. It costs too much to be a perfectionist.

In trying to improve jobs and make them easier for workers, the analyst tries, on every job, to do three things: (1) to get rid of as many human movements as possible, (2) to shorten the movements he can't get rid of, and (3) to make the necessary movements less tiring.

But the job designer should not stick solely to human movements, lest he overlook other improvements. Often he can't simplify a man's movements unless he rearanges the work-place, or gives the man some special tools, or changes the machine or even the product itself. In fact, the analyst should not study a man's motions at all until after he has improved the job to the utmost in other ways.

Suppose, for example, the job is for a man to paint a part. The reason for the operation is to cover a surface—to protect it or to make it look attractive. The analyst ought *not* to start with the way the man handles his paint brush; he should start by asking: Does the job have to be done at all? Product engineers should be able to answer that question. Assuming that they say yes, the analyst should ask when, where, and how the paint should be put on. Maybe the paint ought to go on the part at no extra cost when the assembled product is painted. But if the part must be painted by itself, he should ask himself *how* the man should get the paint on. He can get it on with a spray gun or a brush, or by dipping the part in it or by smearing it on with a sponge. The analyst should pick the best method, and then—not before—get down to considering the man's movements and how he should make them. Job design work should not be confined to a study of the motions of workers.

Sometimes the first questions about a job must be answered by product design or tool or machine design engineers. If the job is to drill a hole in a steel casting, an early question might be: Why not make the part out of a steel stamping and punch the hole instead of drilling it? Or suppose that a man is putting pieces of material, one after the other, into a machine. The natural question to ask is: Could the tool engineers figure out an automatic feed? Again, the study of a man's movements comes as the *last* step in methods improvement.

Methods for improving jobs

The first tool a methods study man needs is an inquiring mind. He will not get far if he accepts such ideas as "We've always done it that way"; "The present method works, doesn't it? So it must be all right"; "What is, is right." Instead, he should assume that the usual way of doing a job is the wrong way. Or that if we are still doing it the same way we did it two years ago we are probably doing it the wrong way. Methods which "just grow" are almost never as good as those which can be figured out. The studied and taught way should always be a better way.

If wasted motions carried red flags it would be easy to improve jobs. But they don't. The analyst has to look at the job—and look at it part by part, not as a whole—to see what movements the worker makes. Then he, the analyst, must decide which are all or partly wasted. Then he has to try to get rid of them.

He has six working tools (beyond his inquiring mind) to help him in this:

1. Process charts
2. Motion study principles
3. Thought provoking questions
4. Micromotion study
5. Therblig analysis
6. Task-force groups

These tools can be used separately or together. Of the six, numbers 1 and 2 are most often used.

Process charts

There are any number of kinds of charts which the analyst can draw up to help him visualize a job and to see ways to improve it. Somewhat like a picture, a chart holds things still—so to speak—so they can be studied. And it lets the analyst see the overall picture, not just one little thing at a time. Often he can see things better on a chart than out on the factory floor. Or in the case of charts for new jobs, they let him see, ahead of time, how the jobs will work. If improvements seem possible, they can be made and a new chart drawn up—all before the new job is started.

Nonetheless, one cannot expect too much from charts. A chart, by itself, does not design a job nor does it improve a job; it takes a *man* to make improvements. All a chart can do is help him see the possibilities. Nor do charts need to be beautifully drawn in order to be useful. They should, however, go into considerable detail because some of the opportunities for improvement are in the details. The big things, the obvious things, that have needed fixing are probably already fixed. It is necessary to get down to *details* to improve most jobs.

Process charts of all kinds show the details of some action. They describe what is done. Besides this, nearly all charts have a symbol for each detail. The time it takes to do things and the distance things are moved are also commonly shown. Summaries of how often each kind of detail occurs are also common.

But why symbols? What good are little squares, circles, flat-sided circles, arrows, triangles, and so on? They are classifications of details. Big circles are usually operations; they show that something is being done to the product. Little circles or arrows mean that the product is moved. Triangles or flat-sided circles mean storage. Squares mean inspections. Classifying the details helps the analyst by telling him how often this kind of activity and that kind of activity happen. And it helps him see where these things are done. All of this helps him as he tries to rearrange details to combine some things and get rid of others.

When making charts, the analyst ought to make sure that his charts show what *is happening*—not what *is supposed* to happen. The only exception ought to be in charting future jobs, which should be charted to show how a job will be done—not how it might (but probably will not) be done.

The purpose of charting is to let the analyst see the job in detail so that he can search for ways to improve it. As part of the process, he will probably draw up one or more charts to depict improved methods and will finally adopt one as the proposed method to be used from here on.

It is too bad that names for the different kinds of charts are not standardized, but they are not, although those we will use are fairly common. Listed below are the kinds of charts most commonly used (all of which are illustrated in time and motion study books).

1. *Charts Which Show the Complete Processing of a Product*
   a) *Flow diagram.* A material flow diagram shows, on a floor plan, how a product moves through the plant. Symbols show where operations are done. This kind of chart is often used with another sheet of paper describing the operations and other details shown on the chart by symbols.

FIGURE 13–1. Flow process chart

		Present	Proposed	Saved
SUMMARY				
	Distance	50 ft.	40 ft.	10 ft.
○	Operation	13	11	2(17 min.)
⇨	Transportation	3	2	1
▢	Inspection	1	1	0
▽	Storage	0	0	0
D	Delay	1	0	1(10 min.)

ANALYZE PRESENT METHOD TO

1. Eliminate
2. Combine
3. Improve
4. Change—
   a. Sequence
   b. Person
   c. Place

ASK—Where, When, What, Who, Why, How

Fill in symbol	PROPOSED DETAIL DESCRIPTION	Time or distance	REASONS
1 ⇨	Deliver packed valves to stockroom on caster table	20 ft.	Delivers valves without carrying
2 ○	Clear up table for next order	1/2 min.	
3 ○	Pick up and arrange packing supplies ordered	1/2 min.	Ordering ahead saves delay time
4 ○	Requisition supplies for next order	3 min.	Helps stock man plan
5 ⇨	Push caster table back to packing room	20 ft.	Saves carrying valves
6 ○	Pick up tote box of valves	1/4 min.	
7 ○	Dump tote box on table	1/4 min.	
8 ○	Put prefolded cartons in jigs (2)		New cartons cost 4¢ more per 100
9 ●	Place flat instruction sheet over carton		Use instruction sheet as wrapper. Saves paper-9¢ per 100
10 ▢	Inspect 2 valves at a time	Total of	More complete visual inspection
11 ●	Place valves in cartons (2)	8 sec. per valve;	Use both hands
12 ○	Close cartons (2)	13 1/3 min. per	Handles 2 at a time
13 ○	Put on pressure - sensitive labels	100 valves	New labels 3¢ per 100 more
14 ●	Place cartons in shipping carton		Approval to Proceed: *James Carlson*

ACTION TAKEN AND RESULTANT SAVINGS—

Put casters on table, changed sequence, simplified packing, did 2 at a time, smoother motions, eliminated some packing supplies.
Better labels.
Saved 27 min. per order of 100, and 2¢ per 100 in supplies.

b) *Flow process chart* (see Figure 13–1). This kind of chart tells the same story as the material flow chart, but as a list without a floor plan. It also provides spaces for showing how much time it takes to do things and spaces for showing the distance materials are hauled. Figure 13–1 is actually the "after" chart of a "before and after" pair of charts. As a result of his study the analyst, in this case, reduced the number of operations from 13 to 11. The moves were cut from 3 to 2 and delays from 1 to 0. The 1 inspection and zero storages remains unchanged.

c) *Operation process chart.* This is similar to the first two charts, but it emphasizes how and where parts come together and what happens before and after they are assembled.

2. *Charts Showing Details of Single Operations*

   a) *Man-and-machine charts.*   These charts list the activities of a man (or more than one man) and the machine he operates. The vertical part is a time scale, and activities are listed at exactly the time they have to happen. Doing this makes sure that the man does not have to be in two places at once. Symbols are not often used in man-and-machine charts.

   b) *Operation chart.*   Figure 13–2 is a left- and right-hand chart without a time scale. Each hand's activities are listed op-

FIGURE 13–2.   Operation chart

OPERATOR ACTIVITY CHART

Operation:	Press insert into sleeve
Equipment:	#20 bliss press - 2 position
	Punch and die - holder for sleeve

Left Hand			Right Hand
Carry sleeve to holder	⦵		
Position sleeve in holder	⦵	⦵	Reach to insert
		⦵	Pick up one insert
		⦵	Move to sleeve in holder
		⦵	Position insert in sleeve
Idle	⦵	⦵	Release insert
Reach to sleeves	⦵	⦵	Reach to holder handle
Grasp one sleeve	⦵	⦵	Grasp handle
		⦵	Move holder under 1st punch
		⦵	Position holder under punch
		⦵	Press insert into sleeve
		⦵	Move holder under 2nd punch
		⦵	Position holder under punch
		⦵	Press assembly out of holder
		⦵	Move holder from under punch
Idle	⦵	⦵	Release holder

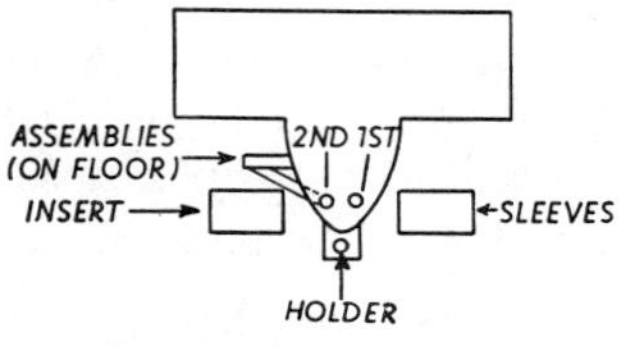

ASSEMBLIES (ON FLOOR)   2ND 1ST   INSERT   SLEEVES   HOLDER

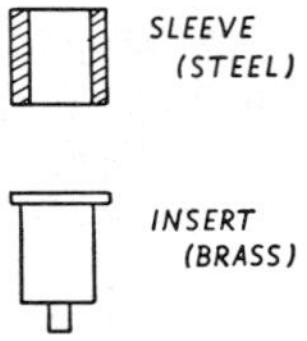

SLEEVE (STEEL)

INSERT (BRASS)

Source: H. B. Maynard & Company.

posite each other whenever they are done at the same time. Small circles are used for every activity, no matter what kind. (This is for counting and highlighting the lack of balance of work between the two hands.)

   c) *Simo charts.* Simultaneous motion charts are used in rare cases. They are extremely detailed and depict in detail what each hand does or even what each finger does.

3. *Office Procedure Charts*

Charts of the type described here can be used to analyze office work as well as factory jobs. Office procedures, however, introduce a problem not found in factory charts. Office forms are often made in several copies which go to different departments, so the chart maker has to devise charts which follow more than just one copy of a form. An office procedure chart is shown on page 542.

Motion study principles

Motion study principles, the second kind of job improvement tool, provide general rules to follow for improving jobs. Here is such a list:

  I. *Rules for minimizing human movements.* Never do a job the hard way if there is an easier way.

    1. Don't do jobs by hand if machines can do them. Transfer everything possible to machines. In particular, try to design machines which not only will do the operation but will first place the product in position and then eject it after the operation.

    2. Eliminate handling. Bring materials as close as possible to the point of work and remove them by gravity if possible; if this cannot be done, do it mechanically. If materials must be handled by a man, handle as many as possible at one time. Design machines to do two or more operations once the material has been put in position.

    3. Use the fewest motions possible. Move as little of the body as is necessary to do the job; in fact, move only the fingers if finger motion will do. Don't reach; put things where little reaching is necessary.

    4. Use fixed positions for all materials and tools. Put them close to and in front of the operator to reduce searching as well as reaching for them. Motions then become automatic.

  II. *Rules for making the best use of men.* A whole man produces more than part of a man.

    5. Use two hands but avoid using hands purely as holding devices. Idle hands do no work. If both are not busy, re-

distribute the work between them. On light assembly jobs mechanical holding devices can often make a job into a one-handed job, in which case an identical job can be done with the other hand. The man will not do twice as much work as with one hand but he is likely to do half as much more. Working with two hands may take practice, but it is quite possible. Typists do it all the time.

6. Use the feet as well as the hands if they can be used to push a pedal or do some useful movement. Hands and feet can both be used at the same time. Does it sound impossible? Fifty million of us do this every day when we drive our cars.

7. Study and analyze all hesitations and short delays within jobs and eliminate them when possible.

8. Where unavoidable delays occur, give men other work to keep working.

9. The time an expert takes is possible for everyone. Try to get all men to do as well.

III. *Rules for saving energy.*   Tiring movements waste energy.

10. Transfer all heavy lifting to mechanical lifting devices.

11. Use momentum where possible, rather than force. A man cannot, for example, *push* a nail into a board even with a hammer. But if he *swings* the hammer, its momentum does the job. Avoid momentum, however, if muscular effort has to be used to stop it.

12. Continuous, curved motions are easier and less tiring than motions involving sharp changes in direction.

13. Assign all work to the body member best suited for it; in typing, for example, don't do it all with the little finger.

14. Use the body to the best advantage mechanically. If force must be exerted, exert it at heights and in positions where the body can employ the most force.

15. Eliminate working conditions which add to fatigue. Use Use power-driven tools. Get rid of poor lighting, poor ventilation, fumes, dusty conditions, temperature extremes, and humidity. If possible, provide a comfortable chair and arrange work so the operator can stand or sit as he wishes.

16. On fatiguing jobs, allow rest periods. The heavier the task, the more necessary are frequent (but short) rest periods. Many short rest periods are better than a few long rest periods.

17. On monotonous jobs, provide an occasional break; monotony and fatigue are related. Consider job enlargement to lessen monotony.

IV. *Rules for placing men.*   Use manpower to its best advantage in view of the jobs to be filled and the men available.

18. Where several workers do the same job day after day, cut the job up into small tasks and let each worker specialize. Each will acquire greater proficiency, and the group will produce more.
19. Put workers on jobs well suited to them, and place only well-suited men on the jobs. Put women on jobs where they are better than men, usually light, fast jobs requiring finger dexterity. Put men on heavier jobs.
20. Avoid using high-price labor on low-price work even if this work is but a small part of a high-price man's job. Divide the job and assign work to the grade of worker required.

Thought provoking questions

Thought provoking questions are the next job improvement tool. They are much like principles, but they are more numerous and detailed. Merely asking some of the following questions about almost any job is likely to make a man think of one or more ways to improve it.

First there are general questions which apply to all jobs. They include: By whom, where, when, why, and how is the job done? Is this movement necessary? What does it do? What would happen if it were eliminated? Can it be shortened? Can it be transferred to the machine? Can it better be done at another time? Can it better be combined with another movement?

These questions should start almost anyone thinking, but they are not really what we mean by thought provoking questions, which are more specific. Here are a few (which apply mostly to metal products):

If the operation is performed to improve appearance, is the added cost justified by added salability?

If the operation is to correct a subsequent difficulty, is the corrective operation less costly than the difficulty?

Is this operation made necessary because of the poor design of tools that are used in a previous or a following operation?

Is the machining of a surface done merely to improve appearance, and, if so, can a suitable appearance be obtained in some less costly way?

If design requires special tooling, can it be altered so that standard cutters, multiple drilling heads, jigs, etc., can be used?

Is the job inspected at the critical point instead of after the job is done?

Is the supplier furnishing material on which he has performed an operation that is not necessary for its use?

Could molded or cast parts be substituted to eliminate machining or other operations?

Are closer tolerances specified than are necessary?

Micromotion study

This way of improving jobs (though rarely used) means taking moving pictures of jobs and then running the film slowly through a projector (even stopping the film to look at each picture separately). Since moving picture cameras take 16 pictures a second, counting the pictures will reveal how long its movements take.

It is possible to cut picture taking and analysis costs by using time-lapse photography. This means taking perhaps 1 picture a second instead of 16 per second. An even lower ratio of pictures may also suffice. (This is what is done in pictures of flowers blooming—a 3-day growth can be condensed into a 1-minute movie segment.)

Or the analyst can go in the reverse direction and get greater detail by using "memomotion" study—taking, say, 50 to 100 picture frames a second. This lets him study the movements in slow motion when they are run at normal rates.

Taking good indoor movies is not an amateur's job. Usually it is necessary to put up floodlights, string wires around, and generally disrupt a factory department in order to take the movies. It also costs money to do all of this, and most of the people concerned—foremen and men on jobs—don't like the idea. Unions nearly always oppose it. It is small wonder that micromotion study is rare in industry.

Moving pictures of jobs can also be useful in other ways. They furnish an enduring record of how a job is done and they can be used to help train new men.

Actually, micromotion study, using simo charts, can be used to advantage in large companies for short-cycle jobs that are done millions of times a year.

Therblig analysis

Therblig analysis, like micromotion study, is rarely used. It is just too detailed and costly except for very short cyclic jobs that are done thousands of times. A therblig is a small part of a job—a very small part. It is much too short to time with a stopwatch.

When a time study man sets production standards, he analyzes jobs part by part, but his parts of a job (he calls them "elements") would stop at, say, "tighten bolt." "Tighten bolt," however, is made up of several very short therbligs: Move hand, get ready to pick up wrench, grasp wrench, move hand with wrench, position wrench, and turn wrench. Other therbligs are: Search, select, grasp, move hands empty, move hands holding something, hold, release load, position something, preposition something, inspect, assemble, take apart, use, unavoidable delay, avoidable delay, plan, and rest.

Therblig analysis helps the analyst because it forces him to look at minor parts of a job. True, sometimes it is possible to cut out big parts of jobs, or even whole jobs, but sometimes still more time can be saved by looking at the therbligs, one by one. It is also sometimes possible to work out job improvements quite effectively with therblig analysis if such analyses are combined with predetermined times for fundamental movements such as methods time measurement povides (see p. 377). With this type of analysis the analyst can evaluate alternative methods *before* production is started and so adopt the best methods.

But let us return to the "tighten bolt" part of a job. The man reaches for the wrench and he reaches for the bolt; then he reaches again in putting the wrench out of the way. If the wrench and the bolt are put closer to him, the operator will save reaching time. Next, if wrench and bolts were always put in the same places, the man can pick them up more quickly. He doesn't have to grope for them or look each time to find them. Putting the wrench in a slot or holder so that it sticks up lets the man get hold of it quicker.

And it is the same with every therblig. Each needs to be looked at separately because different things are needed to improve each one.

After the analyst has done all this, the "tighten bolt" element will probably take less time than it did before. But the improvement will be the result of looking at the details, not the overall job.

Task forces

Another way to improve jobs is by using task forces. Usually they are set up as part of a special cost-cutting drive. Two or three industrial engineers and two or three foremen are appointed as a task force to study each foreman's department to see what improvements they can think of. Often they see opportunities for improvements which were missed before. Also, if changes in the layout, in tools or machines, in materials used, or whatever, are beyond a foreman's authority to make, the task force can bring greater authority to bear and so help implement the improvement suggestion.

Review questions

1. How widespread is the reluctance to try to improve jobs? How can a job analyst who is supposed to improve jobs win people to a cooperative viewpoint?
2. Jobs are not always improved as much as they could be. Why not?
3. "I try to find the one best way to do every job," says a methods study man. Discuss this statement.
4. How can an analyst do motion study work for jobs which have not yet been done? Why would he want to do that?
5. Which of the job analyst's tools for improving jobs are the most commonly used? Why are the others less commonly used?

6. How can a process chart be of any help to a job analyst?

7. What good are symbols on charts? Give reasons for their use. Are there any reasons for not using them? Explain.

8. Are charts or thought provoking questions more helpful in improving jobs? Discuss.

9. Can micromotion study ever be justified? Justify your answer.

10. What is the difference between micromotion study and therblig analysis? Are they more or less competing methods or do they serve different purposes?

Discussion questions

1. Are not the possible gains from improving manual jobs really quite limited? Aren't the truly large gains the ones which can come from mechanization? Discuss.

2. The ABC Company makes typewriters which it sells for $72 and which sell at retail for $100. Foreign imports of lower price, lower quality typewriters have been cutting into the company's sales, so the president tells his job analyst to "knock $10 out of the cost per typewriter so we can produce a model which will compete." How should the analyst go about doing this?

3. In the purchasing department the introduction of preassembled sets of purchase order forms reduced the order preparation time of the typists by one third. Yet after two months there was no visible evidence of any cost reduction. What problems may be present here?

4. The use of task forces, which are more or less job improvement committees, is supposed to make foremen more receptive to suggestions by "outsiders" about how to improve the work in their departments. Will it really work this way? Discuss.

Problems

1. Place five piles of paper before you, then assemble sets of five in order and staple them. Make a chart of the method you used. If you had to do this by the thousands, what improvements in method can you suggest? Develop an improved method and estimate the percent savings.

2. Observe a man lighting a cigarette and make a chart of his movements. Assume that this is a factory job to be done thousands of times, develop an improved procedure, and estimate the percent of savings.

3. The Champion Company's advertising department sends out thousands of direct mail pieces annually. A big item is a 5-page booklet which is hand assembled, stapled, and inserted into a mailing carton. Last year this job took 2,000 hours of clerical time. Next year the volume will be 2½ times as much.

Harry Trolley, the methods man, is asked to see what he can do to improve the job. Here are his times for the present method:

Element	Minutes per 100 booklets
Assemble 5 sheets	5.46
Stack 5 sheets	4.92
Inspect assembled sheets	6.67
Staple	7.21
Shape carton	6.04
Insert into carton and aside	4.32
Replenish pages	1.47
Replenish cartons	2.39
Total	38.48

Trolley estimates that by installing a fixture costing $400 he will save .02 minute per booklet of the assembling element and another .02 minute of the stacking element. He also expects to save half of the replenishing time by having a materials handler preposition the pages and cartons in a special rack costing $50. The handler's time is not important in solving this problem since he is on the job anyway. Clerical time costs $3.50 an hour.

Disregarding coffee breaks and other time out, what is the yearly output using the present method? How much will the proposed method save (if it will save anything) during the coming year? If the new method saves money, how long will it take to get back from savings the money spent for fixtures? Does it appear that Trolley has exhausted the savings possibilities?

4. The cost of a proposed improvement of a sequence of several operations is estimated at $20,000. The improvement will be useful for 4 years.

a) What annual savings must be achieved to yield 12 percent on this expenditure?

b) Assuming that all of the savings will come out of labor savings (labor now costs $100,000 a year on the operations concerned) and that wages will go up 3½ percent a year, what is the answer?

5. On machine M it takes .32 minute to unload a product from the machine and to load in the next part to be processed and .95 minute to machine the product. On machine N it takes .24 minute to unload and load and .85 minute for the machine to do the same work. Machine operating costs are $5 and $4 per hour respectively. The operators of both machines earn $4.50 an hour.

a) Make up a plan with 1 man running both machines. Each machine is automatic, once it is started. But the machines do not stop automatically when they finish their operations; the man must be there to stop them. A man can, however, stop and unload a machine and then attend to the other machine before he loads the first one. Machine unloading time is one fourth of the unload and load time.

b) As opposed to having 2 operators, 1 running each machine, how much will the company save (or lose) by the plan in (*a*)? How much operator idle time is there under each plan? How much machine idle time?

6. It costs $7.20 an hour to operate a retort to impregnate wood with a fire resistant chemical. The impregnating time (during which the retort is closed) is 38 minutes. It is possible to use 1, 2, 3, or 4 men working as a crew to change loads. The changing time is 33, 22, 17, and 15 minutes

respectively, depending on the size of the crew. The men have other work to do while the retort is closed, so there is no need to be concerned with them except during load changing times.

a) What is the optimum size crew if the men are paid $4.50 an hour?

b) How much bonus could the company afford to give the men if they reduced the changing time by 10 percent?

7. The ABC Company is building a parking lot and has to cut away a hill and use the dirt to fill a lower spot. It will be necessary to use a power shovel to scoop up the dirt and dump trucks to haul it. Here are the figures on how long this operation takes:

	Minutes
Load truck...........................	6
Travel to dump area..................	5
Dump load...........................	1
Return..............................	4

a) This is a big job, and the power shovel costs money, so it is desirable to keep it busy. To do this, how many dump trucks will be needed?

b) What is the most economical combination if the shovel costs $40 an hour and the trucks $22 an hour? Use a chart if it would be helpful.

8. On a large-volume item, the following figures show the time it takes for one of the operations needed to make the item:

	Minutes
Unload machine.....................	.2
Load...............................	1.7
Machine time......................	7.0

Several machines are doing this operation, and since the machines are automatic an operator can operate several machines. They are so close together that the time it takes him to go from one machine to the other can be neglected. The machines do not, however, stop after they have finished their operations; the man must be there to take out the finished pieces.

a) How many machines can a man operate? Draw up a man-machine chart showing how your plan works, or make a tabulation of consecutive times showing what the man is doing all the time.

b) Suppose that in answer (*a*) you have to concern yourself with costs and suppose that a man costs $.08 a minute and machine idle time costs $.10 a minute. The object is to minimize costs. Is the answer still the same? Show your figures.

c) Is the answer any different if the machines stop automatically after completing their operation, thus freeing the man from having to be there the moment the operation is finished?

d) If there were a large number of machines, is there any way to eliminate the idle time of both machines and men?

Case 13–1

The time study man has had a request to set a production standard on a new job done on milling machines. In line with his usual practice, he observed the operator perform the operation several times before starting to write down the times.

On similar jobs it is normal for the operator to fasten several pieces into the machine together and machine them all at the same time, much as a person might cut several pieces of paper at the same time on a paper cutter.

This was not the way the operator did it, however. He placed one piece carefully and then did the cutting operation on it, and then continued to the next pieces, but one at a time. The analyst asked the operator to put them in six at a time, but the latter refused, saying that this was the way he did the operation and this should be the way to be covered by the standard. The analyst called the foreman and told him that he could not set the standard unless the job was done as it should be done.

The foreman smiled and said: "Come on, Stan, give us a real study. You know you should mill six at a time." Whereupon the operator replied rather heatedly: "Look here, who is being time studied? You or me?"

What should be done? Who should decide work methods?

Recent references

Barnes, Ralph M., *Motion and Time Study*, 6th ed., New York: John Wiley, 1968

Gifford, J. B., "Job Enlargement," *Personnel Administration*, January 1972

Nadler, Gerald, *Work Design: A Systems Concept*, Homewood, Ill.: Richard D. Irwin, 1970

Neibel, Benjamin W., *Motion and Time Study*, 5th ed., Homewood, Ill.: Richard D. Irwin, 1972

Quick, J. H., "Management of Human Productivity," *Advanced Management Journal*, October 1971

Rathe, Alex, and Frank M. Gryna, *Applying Industrial Engineering to Management Problems*, New York: American Management Association, 1969

Rush, H. M. F., "Motivation through Job Design," *Conference Board Record*, January 1971

Susman, G. I., "Process Design, Automation, and Worker Alienation," *Industrial Relations*, February 1972

14

Economizing on resource inputs

WHERE does all the money go? How many times most of us have to ask ourselves that! Finding out where it goes won't bring it back, but knowing where it went helps us plan our future expenses and see where we can cut future outgo.

Not every resource input is money, but most inputs reduce ultimately to money. A man's labor is not directly a money input, but indirectly it is. And it is the same with materials and other input resources. All too often the inputs are made but too little resulting output flows out. It is almost always necessary to economize on the use of inputs and to hold costs down.

A manufacturing company's input control problems are a lot like our personal problems. If managers don't always keep watching costs and trying to control them, they grow and grow until they use up all the money that comes in (and more). The resources are used up without their having produced any reverse-image income inflows.

To combat this, managers need to reject the idea that costs are incurred because they satisfy some useful function and that resources are being well used. Indeed, it would be better if they assume that some inputs are being uneconomically used. Also, it is important for managers to keep in mind that very few people in most organizations can bring in more sales dollars but nearly everyone can help use resources more economically.

Cost *reduction* and cost *control* ought to mean about the same thing; both try to use resources to best advantage. Cost control that doesn't try to keep whittling costs down is mere record keeping. Yet cost reduction drives that go on forever get to be old hat. Many companies have found that an occasional special cost reduction drive pays big dividends, even though what they amount to is asking everyone to do better job at what he is (or ought to be) already trying to do well.

Input conservation leverage

So much attention is usually paid to selling that cost reduction sometimes does not get the attention it deserves. If it were equally difficult to increase sales 10 percent and to reduce costs 10 percent, this might appear to be a stand-off. But this is rarely so. If, for example, an item costs $50 to make and costs $30 to sell and sells for $100, it returns a pretax net of $20. Selling 10 percent more products would increase net returns by $2. But a 10 percent reduction in costs would net $5. A 10 percent change in the form of lower costs is worth 2½ times a similar change in sales.

Possibly, however, this comparison is unrealistic—it *is* quite possible to sell 10 percent more whereas it is probably almost impossible to cut costs 10 percent. Nonetheless, it remains an important point that the value of reductions in costs is much greater than proportional changes in sales. The value of savings in inputs justifies paying considerable attention to efforts to conserve inputs.

Labor contracts and productivity

Factory managers are not wholly free to use the company's resources as they think best because there are restrictions in the labor contract. They may, for example, give up some of their rights to make methods improvements which would result in the more economical use of input resources. Usually such restrictions on management's right to act are not agreed to voluntarily by managers but are concessions resulting from collective bargaining or even from a strike. Economically, such restrictions are unfortunate in that they often force the wasteful use of resources.

Worse, however, are situations where managers, by failing to exercise their rights to manage, lose their power to do certain things. Dana Corporation lost an arbitration case when it tried to install a permanent production standard for an assembly line because it had used a temporary (and too loose) standard too long. Because Dana had let this inefficient operation go on for a while, the arbitrator denied it the chance to improve the situation.

Dana also had trouble in another case. First it agreed to show the shop steward new production standards before they became effective. Out of this came the practice of the steward's initialing all standards as evidence that he had seen them. Standards did not go into effect without his initials. From here on the company found it couldn't set a job standard without union approval because of the steward's refusal to initial those he didn't like. The labor board upheld the union and agreed that the right to initial meant the right to approve or disapprove a standard. Later, at the bargaining table, the company had to win back its right to set standards.

Any kind of job control by a union stands in the way of possible job improvement. No company can make the best use of its resources, and have low operating costs, if its bargainers give away the managers' rights to set standards or to change methods, or if, by their practices, the latter abdicate their right to make improvements.

The affluent life and cost control

As top officials get on in years, they usually "have it made" financially. Their homes are paid for and their children are educated, so their expenses go down. Yet their salaries are higher than ever, and they may well have a growing income from investments. There is no need for them to pinch pennies—to drink beer instead of highballs or eat hamburger instead of steak. They can afford to live the affluent life, the comfortable life.

It is small wonder that such men often run their companies the same way, particularly when the company is affluent too. Suppose, with affluent managing, a company earns $50 million in a year whereas, with penurious managing, the figure could have been $60 million. Why should an affluent manager care?

Often the answer is he doesn't care. The fact that the stockholders pay him to serve them well and that he should do his best is beside the point. The point is that affluent managing may well happen, and it is dangerous. A company which is not always working at staying efficient becomes flabby. Companies which are well off are often that way only because they always try to use resources to best advantage. But if they let up and condone inefficiencies, their managers soon don't recognize inefficient operations when they see them, or what to do about them if they recognize them. The road back may be difficult. Top men always

FIGURE 14–1. Schematic display of cost-saving opportunities

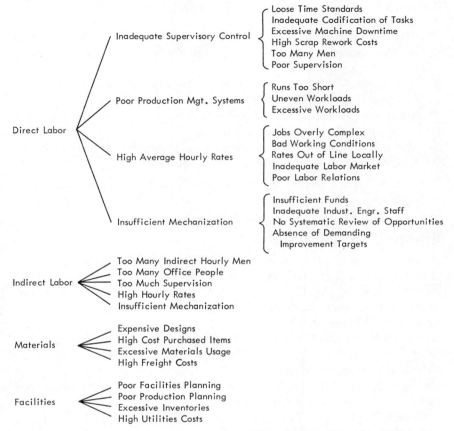

Source: Adapted from "Zeroing in on Cost Savings," *Manufacturing* (November 1970).

need to be vitally interested in cost control and economical operations.

A corollary to this point relates to the "good enough" idea discussed in other chapters. One aspect of affluence is doing things too well, which can relate to product designs, manufacturing policies, and the thoroughness with which work, particularly staff work, is done. Too much staff work, and too-well-done staff work, is common in well-off companies. Resources are used wastefully. These wastes are held down in cost-conscious companies.

Caditz's laws

Clement Caditz, president of Northern Metal Products Company, developed four rules covering cost control activities, and we have added two others (numbers 1 and 5):

1. It is easier to *keep* costs down than it is to *bring* them down.
2. Costs tend to increase in inverse proportion to the amount of effort put into cost control.
3. There is more profit in cost control when business is good than when business is bad. There is a strong tendency to let "fat" creep in when conditions are good.
4. The amount of effort put into cost control tends to increase when business is bad and decrease when business is good.
5. Many costs which are variable when business goes up suddenly become fixed when business goes down.
6. When business is good, companies tend to proliferate their activities and thus disproportionately increase their costs.

Perhaps this is a good place to add Northcote Parkinson's view as rule 7: Expenses rise to meet the amount of money available.

Resource conservation attitudes

Economizing on the use of resources is essentially cost control, which in turn is as much an attitude of mind as an activity. But, unfortunately, it seems not to be a natural state of mind. This makes the process of controlling cost become partly an educational process, which takes time because attitudes change slowly.

The attitudes which need changing might be called laissez-faire attitudes: "Leave well enough alone," "Wait and see," "You're messing up my operation," "It can't be done," "We've tried it before," "We can't cut costs any lower," "We are aware of this and we plan to do something about it (but we never get it done)."

Unfortunately, the whole matter of economizing on resource use is unpopular. None of us wants to be pushed nor to have to push other people; instead, we want to be liked. We would rather relax and choose the lines of least resistance. Cutting costs sometimes has unpleasant aspects, and we do unpleasant things only if we are actually forced to do them. We would rather do other things—almost anything else—first.

We might use the typical foreman's attitude to illustrate the problem. So many costs are incurred at the bottom level that (at least in a factory) the foreman is a key man in controlling resource inputs, and Phil Carroll does a fine job showing us the foreman's attitude in his book *How Foremen Can Control Costs*.[1] Here are his chapter headings:

Why should I worry about costs? Our company makes lots of money.
Costs are not my problem. That's the cost man's job.
What's the big hurry? We got plenty of time.

---

[1] Phil Carroll, *How Foremen Can Control Costs* (New York: McGraw-Hill).

All my men are working. What're they hollerin' about?
Stock chasers drive me crazy. Every day they want something else.
See the timestudy men. They're running the plant.
I get all the headaches. Nobody helps me get things right.
All I do is change setups. Why don't they get some long runs?
Can't they find any good men? All they have are punks.
How come my scrap is up? Cost men don't know how to figure.
Tools don't cost much. And they last a long time.
Material cost is my problem. But I can't do anything about it.
Maintenance won't fix 'em. How can I keep my machines running?
Why can't they let us alone? They're always makin' changes.
We always do 'em that way. Then we know they'll come out all right.
They think they're inventors. But their suggestions won't work.
Why do they gripe so much? Isn't anything right around here?
It's only a little change. Why stir up trouble?
Engineers can't understand. They never come in the shop.
You can't timestudy indirect. No two jobs are alike.
Why bother with budgets? They're just a lot of numbers.
Overhead is a mystery to me. We just listen and grin.
Why so many reports? I sure hate paper work.
Who cares about competition? We've been successful for years.

This picture of foremen is typical—not rare—and it typifies many others as well: Some higher-ups are the same way. It is hard to imagine such a foreman being concerned with controlling either inputs or costs. Carroll's foreman has to be instilled with a desire to conserve resources and provided with some know-how so that he can do it. Of course, it wil probably be necessary to keep prodding him.

Almost surely, at the start, he will be opposed to changing his ways in order to operate more economically. If he is won over to where he cooperates reluctantly, this is a gain. Finally, the top manager would hope to get him to be favorable. He will be won over more readily if he is "brought in on the act" and allowed to suggest improvements.

Naturally, too, top men will be more likely to get support for their improvement programs if they praise good work when they find it and are not just negative about poor performance. This helps build acceptance, without which little will be accomplished. If subordinates are negative, they can be quite ingenious with their foot dragging. Top men should try to avoid having subordinates feel threatened.

Some companies use foreman bonus plans to give foremen a direct financial incentive to operate their departments efficiently. Reductions in operating costs boost their bonuses. Curiously, incentive plans for foremen are uncommon, yet they seem to help foremen develop a greater interest in reducing costs.

Suggestion systems, too, seem to be a somewhat overlooked tool. Although may companies have suggestion systems, a great many do not.

Some of them once had such plans but abandoned them. Almost always, a well-administered suggestion system will pay for its costs several times over.

Cost reduction programs

In order to minimize inputs and to keep costs down, most companies find that they need an occasional shot in the arm—a special cost reduction program. Of course such a program will itself cost some money, but here a top manager has to resign himself to the need to spend a *little* money to save *more* money. Also, the program may not produce big results right away (it may take months to get into high gear), but the gains from having trained men become cost conscious and think of saving resources ought to persist for a long time. The program should end up by becoming a new and continuing way of life.

Some companies go at cost cutting by using edicts: The president tells his vice presidents to cut 10 percent off their costs. He may also tell them: "If things don't get better soon, there will be some new faces around here." The vice presidents tell their works managers, the works managers tell the superintendents, and the superintendents tell the general foremen, who tell the foremen: "Cut 10 percent." Cut, CUT, *CUT* comes the order to everybody at every level. No one cares very much how it is done, and no one shows his subordinates how to do it. They are just told to cut costs and still get their work done as usual.

Edict methods are ruthless but they don't always work out badly. Expenses *do* get cut. And probably they stop a certain amount of wasteful use of resources. Edict methods, however, can be unwise because worthwhile productive activities may also be cut in the process. Some years ago, Beckman Instruments cut 7 percent everywhere, including its sales force, but 7 percent fewer salesmen sold fewer products, so it was a poor economy strategy. Resource saving programs should pay attention to the essentiality of activities before cutting them off.

Some companies carry on cost cutting with a velvet-glove technique. They try to get the whole managerial team to pitch in and work together, willingly and enthusiastically, at cost cutting. They try to pinpoint weak spots which can be improved. There should be no mistake, however, about velvet-glove cost cutting programs; beneath the surface they are hard hitting. Subordinates are still expected to cut hard-to-cut items and to get along with a minimum of resources.

There are several requirements for a successful resource-economizing program of the velvet-glove type. First, the program needs top-management interest—and active interest. Everybody thinks that he has been doing a good job, that he has been working hard, and that he has done all he can. But in spite of this he almost certainly can, and will, do better if the high brass works with him and if he knows they are looking over his shoulder. And he will try especially hard if the top men make it clear that resource economy is part of the basis for judging promotions and pay raises.

The program really ought to start with the top managers' calling a meeting in the board of directors' meeting room to impress people. The general idea "We must cut costs" is put before everybody, and all are asked for their ideas as to how to go about it. If the crisis is serious enough, it helps for the executive to take a salary cut. Then everyone is *really* impressed.

Probably this original high-level committee will decide to set up several subcommittees to handle different areas (product design, materials, manufacturing methods, office costs, and so on). One or more of the near-top men will be on each committee, but some men who are lower down will also be put on these committees. Committee membership will cut across departmental lines. It adds push to the program if some high officials sit in with men who are further down when committees meet. That adds greatly to the chance of success of a program. Also, it is important not to leave out any area; every department should be included.

One might ask what is expected of such committees. First, higher level men need their help in setting cost cutting goals. Top men expect the lower men to look over their areas and to set resource saving goals to shoot for—short-term goals and long-term goals. The committees can look into all trouble spots and put a dollar value on each cost saving opportunity. The committees might also set up recording and reporting procedures to show the kinds and causes of excess costs. The battle to reduce costs is half won when opportunities have been unearthed.

Second, the committee members will, in the end, have to do the things which will result in conserving resources. They will not do this as committee members but as heads of departments. As individual men, some of them will hesitate to do anything about costs, some will defend the present practices, some will want to go ahead but will not know how. Being on the committee lets them see the need for saving resources. This makes everyone more willing to find cost cutting opportunities and to try to make the cuts.

Third, no program keeps going by itself after it is started. After goals are set, and as time goes along, reports are made of what is done and comparisons are made against the goals. The committees make the comparisons. And they pay particular attention to all spots where someone did not reach his goal. Where did he fail? Why? What else can he do to reach it? And so on. The committees go over all of these matters and so help make the cost cutting program work.

Fourth, committee meetings help develop a climate in which people will learn to appreciate that resource inputs either are money or they cost money. They will learn how to reduce costs. The committee meetings should be educational. Department heads who don't know how to go about cutting costs get ideas from their fellow committee members about how to do it. They also come to identify themselves more with the company and to think and work toward overall company goals. Then they are more willing to work out solutions which are best for the company, not just best for their own department.

Fifth, committees work in an ambience of social pressure. No supervisor looks good if he says that he can't cut costs when everyone else has agreed to do his bit. Nor does any supervisor look good if he doesn't cut the costs he told his fellow committee members he thought he could cut. Every supervisor knows that his fellow committee members are watching his results.

A few near-top committees don't do all this by themselves; each committee accepts the responsibility for overseeing a whole resource expenditure area. Each man on these committees gets a job of setting up one or more committees below him with the same kinds of assignments but in a lower, smaller part of the organization. Later, he reports his own committees' cost cutting successes back to the higher committee.

Members of these lower committees agree to set goals for cutting expenses under their jurisdictions and to get their men to do the same. The program ends up with everyone, including foremen, participating: everyone tries to save resources. Some companies even discuss programs with union officials before they proceed. Union men often appreciate the problem and are willing to "go along," but they cannot be expected to give any visible support. If they did, they probably would not get reelected.

Having everyone go to committee meetings would seem to be a costly offset to the gains produced by cost reduction programs. Hopefully, however, it would not work out this way. Everyone always finds the time to do the things he thinks are important. And cost reduction programs always get this top priority. Men find the time to work at cost reduction by themselves, cutting down on things that they have wasted their time on. Subordinates, themselves, also become more efficient.

Goals versus budgets

Cost cutting goals sound as if they are essentially budgets, yet they ought not be quite the same as budgets. A budget is one kind of goal, but a cost cutting goal, a resource economizing goal, ought to be different. A regular budget sets the amount that a departmental head can spend; he tries to stay *within* it, but he doesn't try very hard to *beat* it. In fact, he probably does not want to surpass it by very much lest future budgets be too tight. Besides, with regular budgets there are no meetings, daily or weekly, where men sit down (several of them) in committees and try to help each other reach their goals.

Cost cutting goals ought to be real challenges. Subordinates help set them, and usually they try hard to accomplish them. Also, special cost cutting programs get more high-brass attention than do regular budgets. Progress reports are issued and special attention and help are given to any who need it.

Yet goals may still *look* like budgets—and they ought to in spite of what we have just said, because this is just what the best-managed companies do all the time—with budgets. This is what an ongoing resource economizing program should do, and this is what budgets aim to do.

The difference ought to be in the shot-in-the-arm idea. We all go out to improve, and almost always do improve. Then, after we reach a new, high plateau of efficiency, we would like just to stay there—or better yet, keep on getting still better. Here is where the difference between cost cutting goals and regular budgets should fade away.

Making a program work

Some experts say that top managers should start by assuring everyone that no one will lose his job. They point out that a program will not work well if men are afraid of losing their jobs. Fortunately, many resource savings will be on materials and in other nonlabor categories, but some cost cuts will have to be savings in labor costs. This means fewer men on some jobs, but normal turnover helps here. A company can nearly always avoid layoffs simply by not hiring new men to replace those who quit. Displaced men can be put on the jobs left open when others quit. Yet perhaps the top man should not make outright promises that no one will lose his job; it might be necessary to lay off a man here or there.

Setting goals is the first step in the actual program to cut costs, but it is only the first step. Department heads, big and little, have to know what their goals are—and in detail, not just in total. But of course they helped set the goals, so this will not come as news to them. It is well, however, to get a specific commitment from each department head to accept and execute a program in terms of the things he plans to do and when he will do them. Then a detailed program of the goals he has agreed to reach in reducing resource inputs in his own department should be put into writing.

Second, in order to carry out the program each department head will need to get up-to-the-minute reports of how well he is doing—reports which also highlight places where he is not doing well. Probably this means some changes in the accounting and reporting system. It means that separate accounts will need to be kept for each department as much as is reasonably possible. Very likely it will also mean more reports and more detailed reports. This is where some money has to be spent in order to save more money—on better reports. The reports should also be hard hitting and relevant. Bottleneck areas or places where goals are not reached should be highlighted and emphasized, perhaps by means of charts.

Above all, it is desirable to make *each department head* responsible. *He* needs to get up-to-the-minute reports on how *his* department is doing. They should show clearly the places where *he* is not doing so well so *he* can fix things right away. In these reports, however, there is no need to worry about fourth decimal point accuracy. Not only do short-interval reports let the man get after bad things sooner but, when things go well, they reinforce his feeling of accomplishment sooner.

Also, top men should not depend on department heads to determine how the necessary reports should be made out. This should be done *for* them, and the reports should be designed to tell them what they need to know.

Department heads should also be shown how to use the reports. The reports should be kept simple, yet it is necessary that they *measure, compare, review, evaluate,* and give the man a chance to plan to do something. *He* can then appraise the work of *his* department—hourly, daily, weekly, and over longer periods.

Third, top managers need to stand ready to help and to show department heads how to go about making improvements. Most of them have little idea how to go about making improvements. Overhead may need to be explained to foremen. They may also need to be shown how using machines effectively economizes inputs. It will usually pay to have each foreman spend an hour each week in one or two other departments looking for suggestions to help other foremen. This way every foreman both gives and receives suggestions with no feelings hurt. Staff or other help should be given to department heads.

Maybe the cost cutting program can be dramatized. For example, Clark Equipment reduced tool breakage 20 percent by putting price tags on tools with a sign "Do not abuse." Some companies have put price tags on machines, materials, and even on scrap to help bring home to everyone that there is a money value to all of this. In its Long Island factory, Sperry Gyroscope has 6 full-time "cost coordinators" and 14 more men who sometimes also work as cost coordinators and help department heads develop economical methods. These men sometimes work with committees of the type described above and sometimes by themselves. Sperry's coordinators save more than $3 million a year.

The power to remedy trouble may be beyond a department head's authority, and if so, this is where a committee can help. Or if it is beyond the committee's authority, the committee can refer it upward. Special, temporary reports of bottleneck areas also help top men. They should stay close to problem areas until they get them fixed up.

It is a good idea to ask middle-level men, and foremen too, to write down any improvement ideas they have. Top managers are sometimes pleasantly surprised at the cache of ideas that some men have squirreled away. It is also good to emphasize the need for payout from improvements.

Fourth, there is need for frequent review (daily would be good) by every department head's boss. And occasional (weekly) review by the committee responsible for each area is also desirable. Each committee member can be chairman of the committee while his own department is being reviewed.

It is important to put some "brass" on the committee—the superintendent and the vice president of production, the manager of manufacturing, and maybe a budget officer and one or two staff men. These members keep the pressure on everyone to do his best. Finger pointing, however, should be avoided and review meetings should not be turned into punitive sessions. No one is on trial. The object is to find out why the goal was not accomplished so that the cause can be removed. The goal is to be corrective not punitive, although it is good to keep some pressure on everyone. Reviewing performance makes opportunities to help, and also praise good performance.

Fifth, everyone should try hard not to slip back. Charts of performance should be kept. Departmental efficiency ratings should be calculated. If anything slips back, it should be investigated right away and be gone over with the man responsible. The sooner a decline is spotted and looked into, the sooner it gets fixed.

Sixth, managers should try to force prospective gains to materialize. Ford Motor does not approve new equipment purchases unless the proposals are supported by estimates of their savings. When the equipment is in, the budget is immediately reduced by the expected savings. If things like this are not done, the gain may never be nailed down. Projects should be followed up until they are paying off as expected.

Seventh, the program should not be allowed to slacken off when business is good. Caditz's law, that it is easier to keep costs under control and to conserve on resources than it is to cut them back after operations have been lax, should be kept in mind.

Where to economize on resource inputs

Cost savings opportunities are everywhere—in every department and in every expense. Normally, foremen and other managers do a good job on the big costs, so the shot-in-the-arm program needs to be set up to find and stop middle-size and even little cost leaks. Caditz found, for example, that all the men in his company seemed to have six hands, judging from the rate at which they wore out gloves. Talking economy to the men did no good, nor did requiring them to turn in old gloves for new, but charging them half the cost of the gloves did. Usage dropped 60 percent. A little item, yes; yet the savings ran to several thousand dollars a year and it cost very little to make this gain.

"Getting fat" costs should come in for particular attention. When times are good, no one can figure how to get along without "assistants" or "secretaries." Yet once they are dismissed, no one can figure out what they did. Also, managers should look into "accepted costs," such as die maintenance. True, such costs are necessary, but are they too high?

Here are some ideas that could be followed up in just the production end. If production costs are too high because there are many new men, the foreman should try to train the new men well and quickly and also try to cut down on turnover so there won't be so many new men. Or if excessive absenteeism is making a foreman shift men around too much and do unfamiliar work, he should try to cut down absenteeism. Or it may be that his men sometimes have to wait for their next jobs, in which case losses can be reduced by better scheduling. Perhaps, too, when some men are better producers than others, the foreman should study how the good men do the work and then train the others to work the same way. If men on the assembly floor have to "fit and file" parts before they fit, the foreman should see that parts are properly made before they get to the assembly floor and thereby save this waste. Or maybe, if new and untrained men are put in with groups where they hold things up, the foreman should keep them out of the groups until he has trained them to hold up their end. Also, double work should be avoided: if one department inspects parts as they leave, the next department should not inspect them again as they arrive. Finally, buying from reliable vendors will reduce receiving inspection.

The foreman should not interrupt his men, or keep them waiting for instructions, tools, or orders. Similarly, he should cut the time wasted by men at starting and quitting times and see that they start promptly and don't quit until closing time. (A Battle Creek company changes the color of coffee cups every 15 minutes to keep coffee breaks from stretching out.) Nor should foremen let men waste time around the sandwich cart. He should hold down clean-up time, both of the work area and personal clean-up time. Nor should he allow union committee members to roam the shop to "investigate" grievances all the time. Nor should high-price machine operators have to go to a stock room for materials. Instead, the materials should be brought to them by lower-cost materials handlers or by conveyors.

Other savings opportunities. The above discussion illustrates how lower-level managers can conserve a company's resources. And even in the production areas there are many more possibilities of cost leaks than the few we have mentioned. There may be wage guarantees to piece workers while they are learning, extra pay as allowances to piece workers who are sometimes delayed, pay to men for attending grievance meetings, the cost of reworking products that need repairs, and the cost of lost production of machines that are not operating (for whatever reason).

There are savings opportunities in the maintenance area, as there are in the big area of materials, purchasing, store room operation, materials in process, finished goods, materials handling, etc. Other opportunities are related to scheduling, schedule changes, specifications, engineering changes, and supplies and tooling. Accident costs also offer savings opportunities.

Nor are all of the opportunities to conserve resource inputs confined to the production area. There are just as many places to save money in selling, warehousing, traffic, offices, paper work—in every part of the company. Sometimes, also, there are "leaks" in one department which are caused by another department. For example, the sales department causes extra costs in manufacturing when it asks for special products, or that nonstandard (and more costly) items be sold at regular prices, or for "gold plated" or "fur lined" free trimmings, free repairs, too easy a policy on returned goods, orders for one each of many things, rush deliveries, and free estimates for special items.

Office departments also offer opportunities, especially as all office workers are knee deep in paper. No physical activity is performed in our modern age without a piece of paper's going along to guide it. Someone has said that it takes two tons of paper to produce one ton of product, and although this may exaggerate, desk work and paper work go hand in hand. There is no escaping a huge flow of paper—so huge that it takes quite a staff of typists, stenographers, and clerks to make out reports and file them. Work directives are put out and reports of work done are received, letters and memorandums, are written, and forms are filed in duplicate, triplicate, and quadruplicate.

The worst thing about office work is that it grows and grows and grows. In a 1900 factory, only 1 out of every 40 employees worked in an office. By 1935 it was 1 out of 10. Now it is 1 out of 4! What will it be by 1980? Over the years, manufacturing has become more and more efficient but office work efficiency has not kept pace. Indeed, many consultants believe that office people work at only 50 percent of their capacity. Not only that, but they say that one third of what office people do is waste work anyway. And still worse, they say that even with big office staffs, managers don't get all the information they need.

Why does management put up with it all? Why doesn't it cut office work down to size? One reason, which cannot be escaped, is that the government requires a good many records and reports, and this makes more office people necessary. But this is not a *major* reason.

Another reason is the growth of staff departments. Fifty years ago companies had only a handful of them, but now there are all kinds of staff departments: sales promotion, public relations, education and training, and on and on. Why not cut them out? Because management feels they are worthwhile. Top management created them and approved setting them up as departments, so it must be that top management feels that they pay for themselves.

Many manufacturing companies today are so big and so complex that they just cannot be run without staff departments. In 1972 there were, in the United States, 60 industrial companies with more than 50,000 employees each. Such companies are too big to run without lots of staff departments. And there were 340 companies with more than 10,000 employees. Even these "small giant" companies are so big that they have to have a good many staff departments—and this means lots of office workers.

Yet we do not want to justify the growth of staffs uncritically. All that we are saying is that companies have to have more office workers. Nevertheless, staff departments probably grow as much from the operation of Parkinson's law as from real need.[2]

But regardless of how growth occurs, a company with 50,000 employees, of whom 10,000 to 15,000 are office people, *must* try to control their work and their cost. General Motors probably has 200,000 office workers, whose payroll cost is more than $2 billion a year. General Electric's office payroll probably exceeds $1 billion a year. Even a "little giant" company of 10,000 employees has 2,500 office workers, whose salaries come to well over $25 million a year. It is small wonder that office work is a new frontier for cost reduction.

Controlling office costs is harder than controlling factory costs because the work does not lend itself well to standards and budgeting. And since this is hard to do, most companies—in the past—have slighted it. But not today. It is still hard to do, but it is no longer overlooked. Standards, budgets, charts, reports, even mechanization—every device used in the factory to cut costs—are now being tried on office costs.

Living with hard times

When sales go down and stay down, resource conservation assumes even greater importance. Failure to prune may well bankrupt the company. Factory direct labor and material costs will go down almost automatically because they are closely tied in with production, but with other factors it is different.

In one such circumstance, Boeing, among many other actions, laid off 5 percent of all its indirect workers, cut inventories, and published the company magazine less often. Lockheed dropped its plans for an electronic computer because it would not pay off for 5 years. American Motors closed and sold an unused factory in Detroit, saving a half million dollars a year in heating costs alone. Glidden stopped making edible oils and sold its plant on Long Island. Buying the oils saved $300,000 the

---

[2] In the 1950s Northcote Parkinson, somewhat tongue in cheek, brought forward his "Parkinson's law": that over a period of years, office workers make extra work for each other. If the actual work that needs doing remains *constant,* the number of office workers will *increase* at an annual rate of about 5.5 percent per year.

first year. Besides this, all of the Glidden executives took a 22 percent salary cut. Shwayder Brothers (makers of Samsonite luggage and card tables) employees in Detroit took a $.50 an hour cut in order to lower costs to meet their competition rather than see their jobs move to Tennessee. (Mostly, though, blue-collar wage rates are exempt from reduction unless disaster threatens, although wage increases are firmly resisted in hard times.)

In general, economizing in hard times is like economizing at any other time, except that almost everyone tries to help. Even a wage cut doesn't hurt morale much because, when disaster threatens, it is gratifying to have a lower-paying job rather than no job at all.

Pitfalls in cost reduction

Cost reports comparing performance with goals are the heart of cost control, and resource inputs can be conserved only with the support of proper reports. But managers need to be very sure that they show what they seem to show and that reported improved conditions really mean improved conditions.

For example, maintenance costs go down (for a while) if everything is let go to rack and ruin. Or scrap is cut to zero if everything is passed as good. Production is grand (for a while) if the machines are run as fast as they will go (but it's better not to look at tool costs). Also, rework costs on rejects are low if the rejects are just scrapped (but don't look at the scrap costs). Absenteeism will be low if everyone, whether sick or well, is told to come to work every day. Inventories can also be cut to the bone (and the factory be out of stock half the time). A manager needs to look at *all* the figures, not just one or two, to see if things are better.

Even cutting out idle time can be wrong (but not often). Big, expensive machines, or series of machines, ought to be kept operating. Their idleness can cost hundreds of dollars a minute (as in a steel rolling mill). If one or two half-idle men have to be close all the time to keep big machines going, by all means this is better than having the big machines idle from time to time.

Managers need to be careful, too, about interpreting figures on reports. Is a department's indirect labor ratio up? (This shows that more labor dollars are being spent for indirect labor per direct labor dollar than formerly.) Normally this is bad; but it is not always good to have a low overhead ratio. The overhead ratio will go up every time there is a cut in direct labor costs unless indirect labor costs are reduced proportionally. Yet it is good to reduce direct labor costs even if indirect labor costs are not also reduced.

It is the same with overhead. When a department mechanizes, overhead goes up and direct labor cost comes down, so the ratio between them goes way up. Indeed, one General Motors' parts making plant has an overhead ratio of more than 1,500 percent! Overhead is over $15 for every $1 of direct labor payroll! This sounds bad but is not bad, because it results from automation, which, it is true, boosted overhead costs. At the same time, however, automation saved far more direct labor costs than the overhead increase.

Supervisors, inspectors, and service men are part of overhead costs. A department's indirect-direct ratio will look better if their costs were reduced, but if the number of supervisors is reduced the work may well suffer. If inspectors are cut, bad work may get by. And if service men are eliminated, the machine operators will have to go after their own materials and tools and sharpen their own tools, meanwhile leaving their machines idle. All of these potential economies must be evaluated in the light of the concomitant diseconomies.

It is possible, too, to keep the overhead ratio down by buying parts instead of making them. This substitutes material costs for machine and labor costs. It may result in cutting the overhead ratio, but at the expense of the more costly parts.

It is even possible to reduce the overhead ratio just by letting direct labor costs go up. Using direct workers inefficiently will make direct labor costs go up and so make the ratio of overhead to direct costs go down! No one would want that, yet if a manager were to look at just the overhead ratio, his worst foremen would look the best.

Nor should overhead be covered up under the classification direct costs. For example, if an allowance is put into a man's piece rate to pay for delays, his pay is partly for lost time, but it all shows as direct labor cost. By paying for it within the piece rate rather than as an extra outside allowance, too much is shown for direct labor and too little for wasteful overhead. The calculated overhead ratio gives a false picture. Also, foremen should not give idle men wasteful make-work jobs just so the costs will seem to be for productive day-work time and not for lost time.

Totals and averages should not be relied on if it is possible to get the details. Suppose that a foreman, in meeting his budget total, spends too much on one item and stays under the budget on another. The total is met but the facts show that there is a weak spot to be rectified.

Also, how are costs figured? On an average basis? Perhaps on a per pound basis? If so, a manager who looks at a department's reduced cost per pound may praise the foreman for reducing costs. But a heat treating department will have low costs per pound when it handles big, chunky items. So will a foundry. Next week, with smaller items, the costs go back up. For a while the record looked good, but it did not reflect more efficient operations.

Top managers should look searchingly, also, at the savings claimed for improvements—particularly savings in overhead. Often they are only illusions, or else they won't stay nailed down. Suppose, for example, that a machine is speeded up so it does its work in 7 hours instead of 8. Its overhead charge is $10 an hour. Has there been a savings of $10 of overhead? Are the taxes less? Is building depreciation less? Are research costs less? They are all overhead items, but there probably will still be $80 worth of overhead a day. It would therefore be better to increase the hourly overhead charge to $11 an hour because the shorter processing time probably did not save $10 in overhead costs.

Floor space is another example. Accountants say that floor space costs so much a square foot—for office space, perhaps up to $10 a foot per year. Cutting down job space by 30 square feet would seem to save $300 a year, but probably there is little or no real savings. Unless this space can be used profitably for something else, there is no savings at all.

Also, improvements in work methods—particularly for indirect people of all kinds, including office people—are often not worth making because they won't stay nailed down. Suppose the industrial engineers cut a one-hour task to half an hour. Is there any savings? Probably not. The employee just "soaks up" the time and does no more work. Or as soon as the industrial engineer leaves, the man goes back to his old hour-long method.

Pointing out pitfalls in interpreting figures (and there are many more than we have listed) warns of dangers but does not tell us how to avoid them. The truth is that there is no good solution. It just isn't possible to devise figures which tell the whole truth and nothing but the truth. Nevertheless, managers should not let their emphasis on a "good figure" cause the insubordinates to make a figure look good at the expense of the true situation.

Review questions

1. What danger should managers be aware of so far as labor contracts and their relationship productivity are concerned?

2. What are Caditz's laws? Knowing them, what might a manager do differently from what he would do if he had not heard of them?

3. How can a manager go about getting a foreman to cut costs? Why do foremen need special attention?

4. Can cost cutting drives really accomplish anything? If so, why not always try to do well enough so that there isn't much more that such a drive can accomplish?

5. How can a "velvet glove" approach to cutting costs accomplish anything? What other ways are there?

6. How should a good cost cutting drive be organized? What requirements must be met if it is to succeed?

7. How can committees help reduce costs? Explain.

8. In which areas are cost savings opportunities the greatest? In each case, what action might be taken?

9. Do employees have more respect for money than for materials, tools, and equipment? What can be done about this? Discuss.

10. The text warns of certain pitfalls in cost reduction; enumerate some of these and tell how to avoid them.

Discussion questions

1. You are the president of the company and you find this clause in the proposed labor contract:

    "The company shall have the right to change or eliminate any local working condition if, as the result of action taken by Management under Article Fifteen—Management—of this Agreement, the basis for the existence of the local working condition is changed or eliminated, thereby making it unnecessary to continue such local working condition; provided however, that when such a change or elimination is made by the Company, any adversely affected Employee may process a grievance on the ground that the changed condition did not warrant the change or elimination of such local condition."

    How would this clause affect your operations? Would you sign the contract? Give your reasons.

2. "Trying to get people to improve doesn't always get them to do it. There is a low compliance with management's requests for improvement. Foot draggers show considerable ingenuity to defeat the purposes of a cost control system." Discuss the validity of these statements. What can be done about them?

3. Why fight so hard to put in cost saving practices over the opposition of operators, and foremen as well? Why not just accumulate improvements and keep them, so to speak, in the desk? Then we would build a new plant somewhere else and incorporate all of the new ideas, meanwhile shrinking operations in the old, inefficient plant. Discuss.

4. After the meeting where the Agriculture Department expert told of new and better farming methods, one farmer said to the other: "It sounded pretty good. I think I'll give it a try. How about you?" "Nope," said his neighbor, "I ain't farmin' now half as good as I know how." How can business leaders get their subordinates to "farm as well as they know how"?

5. "It's the men near the bottom who have to make the cuts anyway, so why not just issue edicts from the top and let these men figure out where and how to make them." Discuss.

6. How can Pareto's principle of maldistribution be of help in keeping costs down?

7. Should a frequent need (or at least frequent requests for permission to work) for overtime be regarded as evidence that a department is understaffed? Discuss.

8. "Look, boss," said the foreman, "how can I ever satisfy you? You are always beefing about too much overhead, so I get my overhead ratio down, and now you yell because unit cost went up. I thought you'd be happy to see that lower overhead ratio." Discuss the foreman's position.

Problem

The purchasing agent wants to go outside to buy a product which costs $10 per unit to make. The $10 is made up of $3 materials, $3 labor, and $4 overhead. The purchasing agent can buy the item outside for $8 and save the company $2 and, 5,000 of these items will be used per year. Can the company afford to pass up these profits?

Case 14–1

"I represent the Work Simplification Associates organization," said the visitor. "As you probably know, we have been serving the Roper Company, across town, for three months, and they are well pleased with what we have done for them." "Yes," said the president, "I have heard of your work, but we just can't spend any money for consultants right now."

"I'm glad you mentioned that," said the visitor, "because our service is unique. Our charge comes only out of savings. Our men come in and try to improve your operations. If they don't do it, our service costs you nothing. If they save you money, you and we split the savings 50–50. You can't lose."

The proposition sounded fair to the president, who, with the approval of the board, signed a 5-year contract. The men sent in by Work Simplification were as good as had been promised and did indeed save money. In fact they saved $1 million the first year, another million from further improvements the second year, and still another million in years 3, 4, and 5. The company paid them $500,000 the first year, $1 million the second year, and so on, up to $2.5 million in the fifth year. Savings in the 5-year period totaled $15 million, of which half had gone to Work Simplification Associates.

Somehow, however, the savings did not seem to show up in profits. Profits were, in fact, going down. Discuss.

Recent references

Berg, C. J., Jr., "Cutting Overhead to Increase Profits," *Journal of Systems Management*, February 1972

Conners, M. M., and W. I. Zangwill, "Cost Minimization in Networks with Discrete Stochastic Requirements," *Operations Research*, May 1971

"Cost Cutting Moves Material Handling," *Industry Week*, May 10, 1971

Figler, H. R., "Goal-Setting Techniques," *Management Accounting*, November 1971

Gommersal, E. R., "Ten Percent Syndrome," *Management Review*, August 1971

Schley, N. E., "Cost Cutting in a Declining Economy," *Journal of Accountancy*, June 1971

section six

Standards for pay and production

WORK STANDARDS are needed in order for managers to manage well. They need to have some idea of what accomplishment may be expected both for planning and for controlling work. Yet production standards by themselves are not the essence of useful standards. The fundamental matter is how much it *should* cost to get work done and how much it *does* cost.

Bringing money into the picture calls attention to the need to be concerned with men's pay. Chapter 15 takes up the design of base pay rate structures and ways to establish equitable differences in pay for different work. Job evaluation is the most common technique for determining base-rate differences.

Many companies superimpose a piece rate method on the base-rate structure in order to reward good workers with extra pay. Men who do more than the standard amount of work receive extra pay. Standard output usually is decided by setting production standards individually for every operation. How to do this is the subject of Chapter 16. Such standards are used in many ways and not just for paying bonuses to productive workers. They are used for scheduling jobs, for cost determination, and in other ways.

Cost standards are fundamental to setting selling prices and for controlling internal operations. The systems used for calculating costs are explained in Chapter 17. Internally, one of the main uses of cost standards is in budgeting, which in turn is almost universally used in controlling production and operating costs. Budgeting systems are explained in Chapter 17.

15

Designing job price structures

PRODUCTIVITY on the job is heavily dependent on the workers' attitudes, and these attitudes in turn are heavily dependent on the men's feeling that they are being reasonably paid for their work. Most men who feel that they are being paid fairly will try to do a fair day's work.

In factories men are nearly always paid by the hour, although monthly salaries are not unknown. (Texas Instrument and International Business Machines pay some of their factory workers monthly salaries.) Ford Motor Company and Procter & Gamble guarantee almost a full month's work although they pay by the hour.

Some companies pay most of their *direct* production workers by incentive plans, usually on piecework. Incentive pay characterizes the shoe and the clothing industries and it is common in metal working and the basic steel industry, as well as in many parts of the electrical products industry. Such plans usually pay each direct worker his own, separate bonus based on his productivity.

Indirect workers, however, are almost never paid individual bonuses. Some plans, as in the steel industry, pay group bonuses instead of individual bonuses. Group bonuses are usually paid to all workers, both direct and indirect.

There are also other kinds of group plans, such as profit sharing and gain sharing plans. Of these, the Kaiser Steel and American Motors plans are the best known. Kaiser's plan shares cost reduction savings with workers. The American Motors plan shares profits.

No matter what method is used to pay workers, it is necessary to have a pay rate structure—some logical basis for deciding how much to pay for each job. It is therefore necessary to decide every job's base pay rate. And if piecework is used, it is also necessary to set production standards.

Job evaluation

The individual-job base rate part of a company's pay structure is usually determined by a job evaluation process. By far the most popular method for doing this is the point method, but a few companies use a factor comparison plan and a very few use grade descriptions. (Since almost no one in industry uses grade descriptions [this method, however, is common in the federal government], this method will not be described here.)

Point plans

There are many varieties of point plans, most of which are patterned after the National Metal Trades Association plan. This method regards all factory jobs as composed of varying amounts of 11 factors.[1] The amount of each factor in a job is determined and assigned a number of points, and the total of the points assigned for all factors becomes the rating of the job. After all jobs have been rated in this way, a scale showing the monetary value of the points is set up. Reference to the scale shows how much money should be paid on each job.

The manual or plan. When point plans are used, jobs are evaluated by comparing them to several preset definitions of degrees (usually 5 degrees are set apart) of each of the factors used. The definitions describe, in general terms, situations requiring the factor, graduated from

---

[1] In the NMTA plan these 11 factors are education, experience, initiative and ingenuity, physical demands, mental demands, responsibility for equipment and processes, responsibility for materials and products, responsibility for the work of others, responsibility for the safety of others, working conditions, and health hazards.

slight amounts up to considerable amounts.[2] The definition which most nearly describes the requirements of the job being evaluated is selected and its value (in points) is given to the job.

The job factors, degree definitions, and point equivalents used in the procedure all must be decided before job evaluation takes place. They are agreed upon and put into a small booklet called a manual or plan. Most companies do not develop their own manuals but, instead, use one of the well-known plans.

Specifications and evaluation of jobs.

When a job is evaluated it is compared with each factor in the manual. In making the comparison, the evaluators refer to the list of duties which make up the job. Such a list generally does not, however, furnish enough information for evaluation since it omits, for instance, a description of the working conditions which are necessary to make the evaluation. A specification or secondary type of description, therefore, is usually drawn up for each job.

The specification is, in part, a rewrite of the job description, listing the requirements of each of the factors rather than listing the duties. The specification is divided into sections paralleling the factors listed in the manual. In each section appears a statement of the job requirements of the job content of each factor. These are compared, by the evaluation committee, with the manual. The most appropriate degree of each factor is selected for the job; that is, the degree definition which most nearly covers the job content of the factor is determined.

Each degree of each factor carries a point value, so the selection of the appropriate definition automatically gives the job a certain number of points. After the selection of the proper degree has been made for each of the 11 factors, the points are added up to get the total points the job is worth.

The use of both a description and a specification may seem to be unnecessary, yet few companies try to evaluate jobs directly from job descriptions, and few try to write up specification sheets unless they

---

[2] For the physical demands factor the following are the definitions of the 5 degrees:

Degree 1 (10 points): Light work requiring little physical effort.

Degree 2 (20 points): Light physical effort in working regularly with light weight material or occasionally with average-weight material. Or operating machine tools where machine time exceeds the handling time.

Degree 3 (30 points): Sustained physical effort requiring continuity of effort and working with light- or average-weight material. Usually short-cycle work requiring continuous activity, such as the operation of several machines where the handling time is equivalent to the total machine time.

Degree 4 (40 points): Considerable physical effort working with average- or heavy-weight material, or continuous strain of a difficult work position,

Degree 5 (50 points): Continuous physical exertion working with heavy-weight material. Hard work with constant physical strain or intermittent severe strain.

have first written up separate job descriptions. There are too many un-answered questions concerning how much of each factor is required. On the other hand, the specifications, if written without a supporting descrip-tion, are merely lists of assertions relating to a job's factor content. The specification needs the support of the job description to justify the claims. Together, the descriptions and the specifications constitute a much better basis for job evaluation than either would be alone.

Job evaluation specifications are only indirectly "man" specifications, such as would help the personnel department in its selection process. A specification may say that a trucker must pull heavily loaded trucks, but it doesn't say that the proper man for the job should be a big strong man. It may say that an inspector must inspect small items carefully and that considerable visual effort is required, but it doesn't say that the inspector should have good eyesight. It is but a short step, however, from the specifications used for job evaluation to the making of a list of the characteristics that men on the job need.

Money value of points

When a job evaluation plan is first installed, it is necessary, after all the jobs have been evaluated in terms of points, to establish the jobs' monetary value. This procedure requires that the analyst know, for every job, its point rating and its existing base rate. The point ratings come from the job evaluation and the base rates come from the personnel de-partment records.

FIGURE 15–1. "Scatter plot" of job wage rates and their job-evaluation point totals (the diagonal [regression] line shows the average relationship between points and hourly rates)

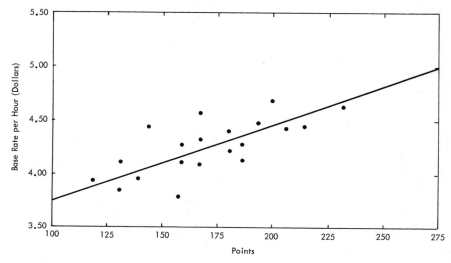

A dot for each job is then plotted on a chart, as in Figure 15–1, corresponding to its point total and its base rate. In general, these dots will fall along a line extending from the lower left to the upper right of the chart. The dots will tend to follow a line because it is probable that the old, informal job-base-rate structure was reasonable and, in general, paid small amounts for simple jobs and more money for more difficult jobs.

The next step is to calculate the exact location of the line, technically known as a regression line, which reflects the relationship between points and job base rates. Usually this is done by the "least squares" method. If the old, informal job evaluation produced base rates consistent with job content, the points will be close to the regression line, some a little below and some a little above. If not, many points will be farther from it.

Labor grades

The regression line showing the monetary value of all possible job ratings could be used directly for determining the base rate for every job (but probably never is) because there is a dollar-and-cents value for every possible point total. Were the line used to determine base rates, there would be a great many different job rates because only jobs with identical point ratings would have identical pay rates. Every difference in point totals among jobs, even a difference of 1 point, would produce different base rates. Such a base rate structure, though usable, would be unwieldy and awkward.

Furthermore, the fact that job evaluation is not a precise technique is a strong reason for grouping jobs in such a way that the same rate is paid for jobs with minor point differences. Every rating involves judgment to some extent and may, therefore, be challenged, even though it may be reasonably equitable and fair. If the exact monetary equivalent of every job point total were used as the job base rate, every rating would be a potential grievance. Even minor upward adjustments in any job's point total would mean that its base rate would go up. There would be no end of grievances, and these would be hard to settle because the job evaluation is partly subjective.

Considering jobs in groups is therefore customary. One group might comprise all jobs between 150 and 174 points; another, jobs between 175 and 199 points; and so on. All jobs falling between the group limits are treated alike and are paid the same base rate. The groups are called labor grades. The full range of point values for all jobs in a factory is usually divided into 10 or more labor grades. Labor grades may be of identical point ranges or may have wider ranges for jobs of higher point value. Having the same range of points for all grades is common, however.

The base rate for each grade is often treated as a range rather than a fixed rate. For example, instead of paying a $4 per hour base rate on all

FIGURE 15–2.   One arrangement of labor grades based on the regression line

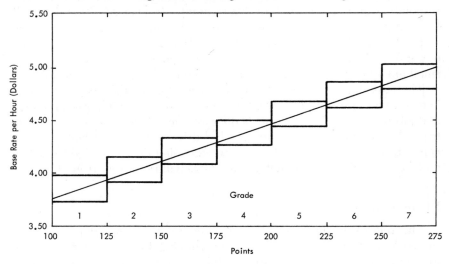

jobs within a grade, some companies apply a range of pay, say $3.90 to $4.10 per hour. The limits of pay for the range usually follow closely what the regression line indicates. If, for example, the direct monetary value of a job rated at 150 points is $3.90, this figure will probably be chosen as the minimum wage paid for all jobs rating between 150 and 174 points. If the line shows that 174 points should be paid $4.10, this will probably be the maximum rate. The full range of pay for the labor grade, however, is available for all jobs within the grade, whether they are at the bottom or the top of the point range of the grade.

Within the range of pay, the rate which is paid to individual employees may be based on the men's merit, which is usually determined by the fore-man's judgment. Different employees on a job may receive the minimum amount for the grade, or the maximum, or any figure between. In prac-tice, in many companies almost everyone gets the labor grade's top pay. In some companies, however, this is not permitted. A company might, for example, require that no more than one fourth of the men receive the top pay, with half at the middle range and one fourth at the low end.

Factor comparisons

The factor comparison method for evaluating jobs (used by perhaps 10 percent of manufacturing companies) considers the base rate paid for any job as a summation of the amounts paid for five separate factors: mental requirements, skill requirements, physical requirements, responsi-bility, and working conditions. The evaluation procedure decides how much to pay for each factor by comparing the jobs being evaluated with the amounts paid on "key" jobs.

The first step is to select a dozen or more key jobs to use as bench-mark jobs, to which other jobs will be compared. Key jobs should be those on which there are a good many employees and should, if possible, be well known to everyone. Then evaluators—and everybody else—can readily visualize their content when they compare the other jobs to them. Key jobs should also be jobs which are believed to be fairly paid, with the pay properly reflecting the difficulty of the work.

These key jobs are used to make up a series of five rating scales, or yardsticks, to which other jobs are compared. One rating is made for each of the five factors: mental requirements, skill requirements, etc. Several evaluators, who are well acquainted with all of the key jobs, apportion the pay rate for each key job among the five factors. Their several judgments are averaged and, after further review, are used to make up the scales.

After the base rates for all key jobs have been apportioned to the 5 factors, a vertical rating scale, marked off in cents per hour, is made for each factor. On each scale, next to its monetary value for that factor, the name of each key job is written in. To illustrate: the job title "pattern maker" is written opposite $2.10 in the mental requirements column. In the skill column, "pattern maker" appears opposite $2.22, and in the other 3 columns opposite $.72, $1.32, and $.36. These add up to $6.72, the pattern maker's hourly rate. After spotting the first key job on the 5 scales, the analyst goes on to the next key job, and so on, until all have been spotted in on all 5 scales.

Evaluation proper begins as soon as the scales are complete. The evaluation process for other jobs consists of making five comparisons: The job being evaluated is compared successively to each of the factor scales and a decision is made as to where the job being evaluated best fits. The title of the job being evaluated is not written in along the scale with the key-job titles but the monetary value of the point where it belongs is noted. The five values obtained from the scale comparisons, one from each scale, are added and their sum is the base rate for the job. With its determination, the evaluation of that job is complete except that factor comparison plans usually use labor grades (as is done in point plans). Jobs are grouped with other jobs of similar difficulty and a pay range is established for each labor grade.

Problems in job evaluation

Although job evaluation seems to be a reasonable procedure, there is a certain amount of subjective evaluation as evaluators decide the degrees of factors each job merits. This can make problems. There are also technical questions, such as what factors to consider, how much weight each should receive, what point values each degree of each factor should receive. Most of those questions are answered implicitly when a plan is selected.

Other problems concern the evaluation process. One is how finely to cut up jobs; for example, is unloading freight cars a laboring job in the same way as opening packages in the storeroom, and are these two kinds of job the same as that of a man who hauls materials to factory machine operators? Is there one kind of job here or three?

Another problem can arise when several men on the same kind of work earn different amounts of money. What rate should the analyst regard as the old pay rate? Another problem pertains to a man who does two jobs: on Monday he unloads freight cars and on Tuesday he opens packages in the stockroom. Is he more valuable than if he always did one thing? Does he have to have more skill? Should he be paid more? Is the answer the same for a man can do both carpentry and electrical work, and sometimes has to do each (although he is not really an expert in either)? Should he be paid more than another man who has only one skill?

All such questions will come up from time to time and need answering in some consistent and logical way.

Pay by the hour

Quite a few companies pay everyone on the basis of the time worked, either by the hour or on a monthly salary. A man's hourly pay (except for normal paycheck deductions) is his job's base rate as established by job evaluation. And even in companies where incentives are used for direct production workers, a good many men do work (this includes almost all indirect workers) which can't be satisfactorily measured, so they are paid by the hour; and again each man is paid the base rate as set by job evaluation.

Pay by the hour is easy to calculate and avoids the troublesome problem of trying to measure men's output. Paying men on a time basis has, however, one serious weakness: It overlooks what men do. A man's productivity plays almost no part in his wage. Once a man gets to the top of his pay bracket (and nearly all workers soon get there), the only reward left for him is satisfaction from doing his work well, praise from his foreman, or possibly promotion to a higher-paying job. Payment by the hour has very low incentive value. A good producer gets no more pay than a mediocre producer.

Measured daywork.   Measured daywork tries to couple high production with high hourly pay rates, but this is suitable only where productivity can be measured. A high daily quota is set and the man is given a high hourly pay rate for meeting it. Both the output expectations and the pay are higher than with regular pay by the hour. When a given quantity of output, and no more or less is wanted, measured daywork is often satisfactory. It has an advantage over regular hourly pay in that the company gets more production out of its machines, thus holding costs down, and at the same time the men earn higher pay rates.

Incentive pay systems

Incentive pay systems offer more money for more output. Most men, if given a chance to earn more by turning out more output, respond by producing more. Good producers earn more money than poor performers.

Consulting industrial engineers generally believe that incentive workers outproduce nonincentive workers by at least one third. On the other hand, possibly, monetary incentives no longer produce the drive that they did years ago. Workers are more affluent and may not care to work harder for more money. They are so well off *without* incentives that incentives may no longer be very important.

Typically, incentive workers earn bonuses amounting to perhaps 20 percent or more over their base pay. The starting points for incentive pay systems are job base rates and production standards. A man is paid his base hourly rate for standard production or less, and production in excess of standard gives the man extra pay. Many years ago there were many kinds of formulas for the calculation of bonuses, most of which paid less than proportional extra pay for extra output. Today, probably almost every plan pays proportionally extra for extra output.

It might seem that there would be little reason for a company to pay proportional extra pay for extra output since the company wouldn't gain anything. The unit cost of the product would stay the same. There is a gain, however, in lower machine and overhead costs per unit. So, since incentives normally result in greater productivity, they reduce total costs.

Incentive plans based on individual worker productivity are perhaps a little less common today than they were many years ago. Mechanization, automation, and assembly lines have changed jobs both by transferring skill and work to machines and by making men more into machine tenders and members of work crews or groups rather than independent workers. And today, because there are more service people, there are more jobs which are not suitable for incentives.

Nonetheless, individual incentive plans are still very much the rule in the men's and women's clothing industries and in the shoe industry. And by no means have incentive plans disappeared from metal working shops. In the steel industry, incentives of the group kind are the rule.

Curiously, many worker groups, such as the United Automobile Workers, are strongly opposed to incentives whereas the United Steel Workers will go on strike rather than give them up.

Over a period of time, unfortunately, incentives tend to become negative, and this is wrong psychologically. If a man is offered more money for extra productivity, and if he works hard and does something extra and is rewarded with more pay, this is positive. But time passes. The man keeps working hard and earning extra pay, until he gets used to it and no longer thinks of his pay as made up of two segments: the main part for doing his job and the extra portion for being very productive (or the bonus for extra accomplishment). Once he gets used to thinking of his total pay as the usual thing, the incentive becomes negative.

He cannot work harder and earn still greater pay. On the contrary, if he does not keep up his high level of productivity he will earn less. So, since he can do no better, although his production can decline (which would result in less extra pay), the incentive system is negative from that point on.

Problems with incentives

Incentive pay is for output above the standard; a first problem, therefore, concerns the standard itself. Normally, production standards are set by time study procedures (explained in Chapter 16), and even though this method is reasonably satisfactory, production standards are somewhat dependent on judgment. Men sometimes object to them and claim that they call for too much output.

Another problem is that standards get out of date. To be perfect, they should be reset every time a job changes, however little. And although industrial engineers should reset all standards when the jobs change, this is not always done right away, or even later. And since most changes reduce the time it takes to do jobs, it is not long before some of the standards do not ask for enough production.

Another problem is pay raises. If everyone gets a raise, all piece rates have to be recalculated. Furthermore, if pay raises are incorporated into the piece rates, men who have been earning large bonuses get a bigger pay raise than workers who have been earning small bonuses. The latter don't get the same pay raise that the good workers get. To avoid this problem, general pay raises have to be kept apart and not incorporated into the piece rates. A man's pay is then made up of his piece rate earnings plus the pay raise, which is added as an extra "override" or "overlay." This override is the same amount for good and poor workers alike.

Other problems are the following. (1) Piecework brings out dishonesty in men: Some men exaggerate the number of pieces when they report how much work they do. (2) There are problems of quality: Since men are paid for the *quantity* of work they turn out (that is, the quantity that passes inspection), quality will suffer unless quality standards are fully enforced. (3) Interferences to a man's work becomes a problem: If there are interferences and if they hold a man back, it seems reasonable to pay him an allowance to for the time he lost. The problem is whether there was indeed such interferences and, if there was, how much allowance to give. (4) Daywork done by a pieceworker becomes a problem: A man who normally does incentive work and earns a bonus but who is temporarily on nonincentive work wants to keep getting his regular incentive pay. Daywork pace, however, doesn't merit incentive pay bonuses.

(5) Men who are transferred to other work, which is new to them and for which at first they are not able to earn a bonus, want to be guaranteed their old earnings during their learning period. The problem is how much to guarantee, and for how long, when they are not producing at incentive pace. (6) Nonincentive workers constitute a problem. Skilled men on high-base-rate jobs (but without bonuses) don't like seeing incentive workers on relatively low-skill jobs making as much or more than they do (because of their bonuses). And men on low-base-rate jobs (without bonuses) feel they are denied the incentive workers' chance of working hard and earning higher pay.

Employee benefits

For every dollar paid in wages to American workers, an additional $.30 is spent for extra, fringe items. Fringes are of several kinds: (1) health benefits, (2) payment for time not worked, (3) payment for unusual work hours, (4) payment for job-related costs, and (5) company-paid life insurance.

Workers usually think of all these extras as above and beyond wages. They don't think that they are costing *them* any money. But to a company, the costs of fringe benefits are all just labor costs made in lieu of wage payments of comparable size. It is a matter of workers' choosing (although not always recognizing that they are making such choices) to take money in the form of fringe benefits instead of wages.

Actually, however, workers gain more from these benefits than they would gain from an equal pay raise. The costs of benefits are not regarded by the government as taxable income whereas the same money, if given to workers as wages, would be taxed. Besides this gain, the costs of such benefits as hospitalization and sickness and accident insurance are less when they are bought in group plans than they would be if bought by workers individually. And lastly, the benefits paid out to workers under the various protection plans are not regarded by the government as taxable income.

Health benefits include hospitalization and surgical expenses as well as sickness and accident insurance (including workmen's compensation for injuries, which is required by law). Dental costs are sometimes covered. Benefits sometimes amount to almost as much as a man's regular pay. Probably the benefits should never be quite this high because of the temptation to malinger. Men who are paid almost as much for not working as they get for working (and the benefits are tax free) get well very slowly.

Payments for time not worked include pensions, vacations, unemployment pay, paid holidays, rest periods within the workday, and wash-up time. In total, payments for these fringes cost much more than other fringes.

Pensions are usually the most costly of all fringe benefits. Most companies have their own pension plans, which are in addition to social security pensions. Between the two (company plans plus social security), retired employees often get total pensions of over half of their former pay. A bad feature of many private plans is that the employees don't have any claim to any pension benefits except by staying to retirement age. (Except that if they have paid any of their own money into the plan, they get back their own contribution, although they may have to wait until they retire to get it.) Employees who quit, or even those who are laid off, lose their equity in the plan. If they change employers late in their careers, they get only a small company pension from their last employer (although they also get full social security pensions). There is growing sentiment in favor of changing this so that employees who change jobs will still get full pensions.

Paradoxically, one of the best fringe benefits from the workers' point of view, extensive vacations for employees with many years' service, is bad from the company viewpoint. The employees with longest service are usually the best men in the department, yet they get the longest vacations and so are absent from work the longest (often 3 weeks every summer, and sometimes for 3 months every 3 years).

Payments for time not worked also include payments to former employees. Men who are laid off usually get severance pay of from one week's up to a year's pay, depending on their length of service. If they can't find a new job, they also get unemployment compensation for an extended period of time.

Besides this, they often get supplemental unemployment benefits (SUB benefits come out of a fund built up by employers) for several months. SUB benefits have made the payments to laid-off men so liberal that sometimes, if a layoff is expected to be short lived, the longest-service men ask to be laid off first instead of (the normal situation) having the newest men go first. The long-service men want to get paid for not working instead of having the new men get this benefit. Of course, they expect to return to their jobs soon; they wouldn't choose a permanent layoff.

Other fringes pay extra for unusual work hours. Time and a half pay for overtime hours is required by law, and even double time for Sunday is common. So is an extra payment of perhaps 5 percent for men working on the second and third shifts. Managers usually try to schedule their work so as to pay out as little as possible for these penalties. Payments for job-related costs, such as special work clothing, are also sometimes made. Company paid for life insurance amounting to more or less a year's wages is also a common fringe benefit.

Review questions

1. What part does job evaluation play in determining a man's pay? Explain.
2. What is the "manual" or "plan" in a job evaluation plan using points? How is it used?
3. How does a job specification differ from a job description? How is a job specification used in job evaluation?
4. Is a job specification also a man specification? Discuss the relationships between them.
5. How are job points made into job base rates in job evaluation procedures which use points? Explain.
6. What is the difference in the wage paid to a man on a job at the low end of a labor grade and to a man on a job at the higher end of the same labor grade? Why is this?
7. Explain the factor comparison method for setting job base rates. How does this method avoid using points?
8. "Positive incentives are good; negative incentives are bad." Discuss these statements.
9. Since pieceworkers usually earn more money than nonpieceworkers, why is piecework not used everywhere?
10. Describe measured daywork. What are its good and bad points? How common is it? What should a company do with a man who doesn't keep up?
11. What are some of the problems encountered in using piecework? How can they be handled?
12. Incentive plans for men who work on products are more common than for indirect workers. Why? What problems are there in putting indirect workers on incentives? What solutions are there to these problems?
13. Is it true that workers are better off because they receive fringe benefits? Or wouldn't they be better off to take the money cost of the fringes as an added wage instead?
14. In sickness and accident insurance the benefits are never intended to be higher than about two thirds of a man's wage. Why?

Discussion questions

1. What is the difference between a man's base rate, his day rate, and his earnings?
2. For job evaluation purposes, should job descriptions be written as jobs are *being* done or as they *should be* done?
3. "The girls in the billing department are in the same pay grade as us sales clerks, yet we work much harder." Discuss.
4. If a man feels that his job is not rated correctly by job evaluation, is this an appropriate grievance to carry to arbitration? How can an arbitrator— an outsider and usually a lawyer—be qualified to decide such a grievance?

5. At the Pennsylvania Steel Company the men doing chipping work on castings were told by the foreman to squirt oil on the castings so that they could see better what they were doing. The men said that squirting oil from a can was not in their list of job duties and they refused to do it. After a three-day layoff as a penalty for their refusal to do the work assigned, the men filed a grievance asking for pay for the time off, claiming that the layoff was improper. What should the arbitrator decide? Why?

6. There is one man who often shifts back and forth between two jobs, depending on which one becomes overloaded. Both jobs are rated in the same labor grade and so have the same pay rate. But the man thinks he should be paid more since he has the skills for both jobs and uses both skills. Neither job, however, requires skill of any high order. How should this be handled?

7. "I fill in for the boss whenever he isn't around." How should this situation be handled so far as job evaluation is concerned?

8. Some jobs of equal job content have different promotional opportunities: Some are dead-end, but others open doors. How should this be handled in job evaluation?

9. After a week's search, the personel department has been unable to fill a request by the line foreman for a skilled boring mill operator. The only apparently qualified applicant wants $5 an hour whereas the company's rate for this work is $4.50. Surveys have indicated that the company's rates are in line with other companies in the area. Should the man be hired and paid $5. What alternatives are there? What are the implications of this problem for personnel, production control, and line management?

10. Texas Instruments, Motorola, and a few other companies pay a good many of their employees on a straight salary basis (rather than on their former per hour basis). Why don't all companies do this? Is this something which other companies will soon be doing? Discuss.

11. The union has fined a company's employee for violating the production quantity ceiling the union set on a factory job. The man seems to have no alternative but to hold his production down and pay the fine or else quit or be fired. Is this reasonable? Is it legal? Discuss.

12. Why not get rid of across-the-board wage increases? How can they be incorporated into existing piece rates?

13. Would you work harder or less hard if you were a member of a group being paid on a group incentive plan? Why?

14. Rarely, and possibly never, does a company find an upward spurt in productivity as a result of giving more fringe benefits. So why give such benefits?

15. In most places of employment women are allowed six-month maternity leaves with pay. After the Civil Rights Act was passed several years ago, quite a few men complained that this discriminated against them. What should be done?

16. Women live longer than men (at least five years more on the average), which makes their pensions cost more. To be fair, shouldn't men get

larger monthly pensions so as to make their pension costs the same as those for women?

Problems

1. The ABC Company has completed the evaluation of its factory jobs and is ready to set up labor grades and pay ranges for each job. From the many job ratings, the following have been selected as typical:

Job	Point rating	Hourly base rates used in the past	Job	Point rating	Hourly base rates used in the past
Automatic screw machine operator	275	$5.00	Machine operator (tool room)	311	$5.46
Bench lathe operator	241	4.86	Punch press operator	271	4.98
Bench work (filing and assembly)	164	4.61	Soldering	216	4.73
			Stores clerk	205	4.73
Casting grinder and polisher	209	4.93	Tool crib attendant	246	4.86
Drill press operator	224	4.81	Tool maker	381	5.44
Milling machine operator	311	5.09	Turret lathe operator	331	5.26

Plot the ratings and base rates on a chart on coordinate paper. Using the least-squares method, compute the line of relationship between points and money. (The formula for the line is $Y = a + bX$. It can be plotted by solving the following two equations simultaneously: $\Sigma Y = na + b\Sigma X$ and $\Sigma XY = a\Sigma X + b\Sigma X^2$. The point ratings are the X values, the base rates are the Y values, n is the number of jobs. Note also that in algebraic notation ΣXY does not mean the sum of the Xs multiplied by the sum of the Ys. It means the respective Xs and Ys are multiplied by each other and then summed up. Similarly, ΣX^2 means to square the individual Xs and then add them up.)

Set up 10 labor grades based on the line, and in an accompanying table show the point limits for each grade; and using a $.05 per hour overlap, show the minimum and maximum wages to be paid for each grade.

Which jobs, if any, will have to have their base rates adjusted to bring them within the newly established limits?

2. When calculating a regression line for relating job points to wages for job evaluation purposes, how should the following situations be handled?

a) There is a job on which 1 man is paid $4.25 an hour. There is another job on which 10 men are paid $5 each. How many dots should go on the diagram?

b) On 1 job there are 5 men who receive $4.50, $4.60, $4.65, $4.70, and $4.80 per hour. How many dots should this job have and what money values should the dots carry?

c) On 1 job there are 2 men who are paid by the hour: $4.80. On another job, with a base rate of $4.50, there are 3 men on piecework who earn $4.55,

$4.70, and $4.75 repectively. How should this be handled in the calculation of the regression line?

3. According to the job evaluation plan, pattern makers should receive between $6.50 and $7 per hour. Men who drive the company's trucks on the road should get from $5.50 to $5.75. But the personnel department has not been able to hire pattern makers for less than $7.50 an hour or truck drivers for less than $6. What should be done? Before deciding, consider the repercussions on other jobs.

4. The company and the union are nearing the close of their negotiations and seem about to agree to a $.09 per hour wage increase. The union proposes that the increase be given as an override so that everyone gets the same amount, $.09. Yet the union does not seem strongly opposed to having the raise incorporated into the piece rate structure, provided only that everyone gets an increase of $.09 an hour.

You are given the job of working out a method of incorporating the increase into the piece rate structure. Try to do it so that Brown, White, and Black all get a $.09 raise. Brown works on daywork at $5 an hour. White's base rate is $4.80, but he is on an incentive job and earns $5.05. Black is on a $5.10 base rate incentive job, on which he earns $5.75 an hour. Show the figures to support your recommendation.

5. An employee will have a total pension retirement credit of $28,000 when he retires at age 65. His life expectancy is 13 years. What should his annual pension be if the fund is assumed to earn 6 percent interest compounded annually? (The man will get this pension until he dies, at whatever age, but the amount he will get annually is based on his life expectancy. He will also, of course, receive a social security pension, but it is excluded from this problem.)

Case 15–1

Todd Evers' father, Jim, had worked for the Heavy Duty Truck Company for 25 years. His job as stockroom clerk was not the highest-paid job in the department, but he liked the work, and the department head was glad to have so dependable a man and one who knew the stock so well.

After finishing high school, Todd and his parents thought it would be a good idea for him to work a year before he entered college. With his father's help, he got a job at the Heavy Duty Truck Company operating an external grinding machine. The work was piecework, and young Evers quickly became proficient. In less than three months his paycheck exceeded that of his father.

The father's feelings were a mixture of pride and chagrin. Todd's mother felt very differently, however. When Todd brought home a check larger than his father's for the second consecutive pay period, and it appeared that he would continue to do so, she berated her husband severely. What kind of a husband was he anyway? Through all the years she had lived on his meager earnings. Now she finds that in only three months her 18-year-old boy can make more than his father. Before long, Jim had to move out of his house in order to have any peace. Jim brought his problem to his foreman.

What is the basic problem? Is it job evaluation? Is it piecework? What should be done both in Jim's case and in the company to prevent similar problems in the future?

Case 15–2

The Transcountry Steel Company's business at its Elmsford plant has declined so that 5 employees are to be laid off. According to the labor contract, any worker facing demotion during a cutback can choose to be laid off instead if he thinks that the lower job is undesirable. Normally, however, recently hired men are laid off, and others take demotions if their jobs disappear.

Tony Scudo had 10 years of seniority and was to be demoted to his old job, which paid a little less than his present job. If Tony were laid off, he would get $70 a week unemployment compensation and $80 a week in supplemental unemployment benefits. This total was nearly the same as the after-tax pay for the lower job.

Tony asked to be laid off. He did not claim that the job to which he was to be demoted was undesirable. He just thought that UC + SUB = AST ("a soft touch"). The company said no. It did not want to lay off a skilled long-service man while keeping a new and unskilled man. Tony took the case to arbitration.

You be the arbitrator.

Recent references

Burgess, Leonard R., *Wage and Salary Administration in a Dynamic Economy,* New York: Harcourt Brace & World, 1968

Dunn, J. D., and Frank M. Rachel, *Wage and Salary Administration,* New York: McGraw-Hill, 1970

Fringe Benefits, Washington, D.C.: Chamber of Commerce of the United States (biennially)

Pasqualle, Anthony M., *A New Dimension to Job Evaluation,* New York: American Management Association, 1969

Von Kaas, H. K., *Making Wage Incentives Work,* New York: American Management Association, 1971

Walsh, W. J., "Writing Job Descriptions," *Supervisory Management,* February 1962

Winjum, P. R., "Negotiated Wage Rate Differentials," *Personnel Journal,* August 1971

16

Work measurement and production standards

IT IS quite desirable to measure work and to set production standards, be it in factories, offices, service establishments, or governments. Standards are needed so that the input of resources can be related to the production accomplished.

Yet saying that production standards are needed is not the same as saying that they are always used. Managers don't always use all of the managerial tools which are at their disposal. Furthermore, production can be accomplished without standards. Resource inputs (such as man-hours) will usually produce outputs, although not always as much output as there should be. And lastly, desirable though it is to have production standards, some kinds of work are not susceptible to measurement, so good standards cannot be set.

The discussion here concerns production standards as they are set and used in factory operating situations, but often these same techniques can be adapted and used for setting standards in other settings, such as offices.

In factories, production standards are most often set by a time study, using a stopwatch to time the work. In many companies the end product, the time standard, is used in setting piece rates for pieceworkers.[1]

There are other equally important reasons for wanting standards, so many companies which do not use incentives use time study and set up time standards. And, conversely, a few companies which use incentives set their time standards without using time study.

Aside from piecework, production standards are needed in order to find out what the current work ought to cost, to estimate the cost of new jobs, and to determine what it costs to do work in alternative ways. Standards are needed in order to know how much work machines will turn out, and for scheduling work as well as for setting quotas for machine-paced work. They are also needed for work along assembly lines so that men's work may be divided equally. And they are needed, too, for planning the number of machines and men needed for future production.

Concept of a production standard

A production standard embodies a concept of normality and reasonableness. Almost all jobs can be done fast, or slow, or in between. The idea of a standard implies choosing a particular rate as being reasonable and expected. Other performance is then regarded as better than standard or poorer than standard. The process of choosing and deciding is implicit in standard setting, as is the fact that choosing means judging. Standards always contain a subjective element of judgment. Standard setters cannot escape having to judge normality as they try to set fair and reasonable standards.

To illustrate how important this is, we might consider the simple task of walking a mile. If several men were to walk a mile, some of them would finish before the others. Perhaps the fastest man would finish in 15 minutes, the slowest man would take 30 minutes, and the others would be spread out in between, with most men taking 19 or 20 minutes. (A pace of 3 miles per hour is somewhat leisurely for most men.)

---

[1] *Production* standards and *time* standards are the same thing. One says that a man ought to do a job 20 times in an hour and the other says that the job is a 3-minute job. Occasionally, when a standard is stated as a *quota*, the latter usually represents the quantity of production needed in a given period of time in order to keep unit costs down to the figure used in setting selling prices.

Probably if it were cold weather or if rain were threatening, the average time would be less. The men would have an incentive not to dawdle. The same would be true if those who finished the mile in 20 minutes were to get a reward; probably almost everyone would make it and be rewarded. But if only those who finished in less than 16 minutes were to be rewarded, some of the men would not make it. A man has to hurry to walk a mile in 16 minutes, and to some of the men the incentive might not be enough to cause them to hurry this much.

FIGURE 16–1. How job study leads to greater production

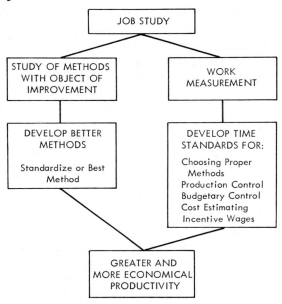

Several points are involved here which are pertinent to setting production standards. The casual workaday pace of men differs and their best performance capabilities also differ. So does their response to incentives. Furthermore, performances differ both because of chance variations (some of the men might have to wait for traffic or a traffic light) and the effort a man is willing to exert. A man can go faster or he can slow down, as he wishes. All of these variables exist in production jobs. The time it takes man to do jobs varies, and for similar reasons.

It might seem that the proper way to set production standards would be to see how long a job takes and use that time as the standard. But this would depend on whom was observed and his performance during the period of observation. It might be a 15-minute mile or it might be a 30-minute mile, but neither 15 nor 30 minutes would be a reasonable standard. More certainty of reasonableness is needed than just accepting the time observed as standard.

The next step in the way of improvement in standard setting would seem to be to see how long a job takes on the average—over several performances and with several men. This method is much better than using the time taken on one performance as the standard. Yet it is still not perfect as a standard setting procedure because the men observed might all be fast (or slow), and if this is so their average time would not be a reasonable standard. If the men observed were all very good, an average of their times would not allow enough time for the standard.

Using the average of the observed times is an imperfect solution because men can control their work pace. If the time a man takes is to become the standard, he would be working against his own best interest if he performed in his minimum time. It would only be human nature for him to slow down and stretch out the time. Furthermore, he would have few friends among his fellow workers if he did not try to do his part to get loose standards. The surprising thing is that men don't always slow down when standards are being set. There is enough slowing down, however, to make it unwise to accept observed times, even an average of several observed times, as reliable for standards setting purposes.

It becomes necessary, therefore, not only to gather data on how long it takes to perform jobs but also to judge the normalcy of the performances observed. If 10 men were observed walking 1 mile and they all did it between 15 and 17 minutes, their average would be 16 minutes; but this average should not be accepted as standard. This performance is better than normal and should be rated as such by the standards setter. His pace rating should indicate that this is, let us say, 125 percent of standard. Thus the standard, when it is set, will allow more time than the 16 minutes actually taken; in this case 25 percent more time, or 20 minutes in total.

Or, at the other extreme, the men observed could have walked very slowly and averaged, perhaps, 25 minutes. If this were so, the standard setter's pace rating should be below 100. This time, when he calculates the standard time, he should arrive at something less than the average of the times observed. If their performance was rated at 80, then .8 of the time observed will become the standard, and $.8 \times 25 = 20$ minutes. Again, a 20-minute mile would be regarded as the standard.

As we said, it is necessary for the standards setter to judge the normalcy of the pace observed, but the concept of normal is somewhat abstract. As applied to factory jobs, it should be the pace, or time, that it would take an ordinary, experienced worker to do a job while applying himself in a normally diligent fashion (but not his pace when he is really pressing himself).

This concept of normality is particularly important where wage incentives are used because the production standard is the basis on which a man's bonus is calculated. If a man's job is regarded as a 5-minute job, then he is expected to perform the job 12 times in an hour. For greater production, he will receive a bonus. Should 6 minutes be regarded as the standard time, however, the man would get a bonus for all production in excess of 10 an hour. The *reasonableness* of the standard is very important.

Number of cycles to time

Production standards are usually set by a standards setter (a time study man) who watches the operator doing his work and writes down how long it takes him to do each part of the job. When the operator finishes his job, however, he repeats it on another unit of product, and this goes on and on. If the analyst watches only a few work cycles, he gets a fairly good idea of how long the job takes, yet his findings are not as re-

FIGURE 16–2

| Cycle time | Number of cycles per year | | |
	10,000	1,000–10,000	1–1,000
	Number of cycles to study		
8 hr.	2	1	1
3.	3	2	1
2.	4	2	1
1.	5	3	2
48 min.	6	3	2
30.	8	4	3
20.	10	5	4
12.	12	6	5
8.	15	8	6
5 min.	20	10	8
3.	25	12	10
2.	30	15	12
1.	40	20	15
.7.	50	25	20
.5 min.	60	30	25
.3.	80	40	30
.2.	100	50	40
.1.	120	60	50

liable as they would be if he watched a larger number of cycles. One question, therefore, is how many cycles are enough to provide reliable figures rather than just happenstance averages which might differ from typical job averages.

For the moment we will overlook the possibility that the worker slows down while being studied. Most companies want the calculated time value to have a 95 percent probability or more—of being within 5 percent of the true average of observed times. So they set up tables for analysts to use, tables which specify how many work cycles to study in order to provide the desired reliability. Westinghouse uses the table shown in Figure 16–2.

It is, of course, very important to observe enough cycles so that enough times are recorded to provide reliable averages. Yet the standards setter should not mislead himself by thinking that many recordings will of necessity give him a more accurate average time for the job. If the man slows down, then the average of his times will be an average of poor performances. Thus there is little safety in large numbers of observations. The analyst will still have to rely on his pace rating adjustment in order to set a proper standard.

Need for timing jobs by elements

It might seem that the way to time a job would be to look at the clock when the job starts and again when it ends. The elapsed time is the time for the job. But even apart from the pace rating problem, this is too simple a method to give accurate results.

In order to get accurate results it is necessary to consider the separate parts of each job and to time each part, and this in spite of the fact that the parts add up to the whole. When the analyst considers the job part by part (he calls these parts "elements") and watches the man do the whole job several times, he finds two things. First, he finds that the time the man takes to do parts of the job vary and, second, that the list of subparts of the job is not always exactly the same every time the man does the operation.

If the analyst timed the job only on an overall basis, he would never know about either of these things. Or, if he noticed them, he wouldn't know what to do about them. So, in order to figure out a proper rate, he needs to write down a list of the job elements and to time them separately.

Writing down the times for each element's performance helps the analyst get a better idea of how long each regular job element takes. In successive work cycles the amount of time it takes to perform an element varies somewhat. The time study man needs to consider these differences when he makes his choice of the time to use as the element's time.

Writing down separate element times also helps the analyst arrive at the appropriate time to allow for irregular elements, those which occur only now and then. He needs to know how long they take as well as how often they occur. Furthermore, some of these irregular elements will prove to be necessary for the job but some are likely to be unnecessary. (Operators sometimes do extra things that are not part of the regular job in order to make it take more time during the period of observation.) In order to get a proper production standard, the analyst needs to exclude all extraneous elements, but he must be sure to include the time taken for all necessary but irregular elements (according to how often they occur).

Taking the study

The first thing the analyst does when he starts to collect data for a production standard is to decide the job's elements, the parts of the job he will time separately. Then he writes the element descriptions in sequence on his recording sheet preparatory to recording their times.

This can be seen in Figure 16–3, which is a time study of an operator assembling roller skates and packing them into cartons. This study was done in a college classroom as a demonstration and with only the skate

FIGURE 16–3

Element	Time in hundredths of a minute					
Preassemble toe clips..................	08	36	315	55	47	94
	8	*14*	*16*	*13*	*10*	*13*
Toe clips to frame and run on............	30	55	33	76	72	811
	22	*19*	*18*	*21*	*25*	*17*
Assemble front wheels to frame..........	47	70	47	506†	86	27
	17	*15*	*14*	*(30)*	*13*	*16*
Tighten axle nut and aside....:.........	56	80	62	16	95	37
	9	*10*	*15*	*10*	*9*	*10*
Assemble rear wheels to frame..........	71	93	88*	29	710	54
	15	*13*	*(26)*	*13*	*15*	*17*
Tighten axle nut and aside..............	82	205	99	42	35‡	63
	11	*12*	*11*	*13*	*(25)*	*9*
Attach frame halves, bolt and nut on......	100	28	418	64	55	79
	18	*23*	*19*	*22*	*20*	*16*
Tighten nut and skate, aside.............	22	53	42	87	81	900
	22	*25*	*23*	*23*	*26*	*21*
Skates, straps, and ankle cushion						
pads into carton liner......................		83		620		31
		30		*33*		*31*
Carton liner into and close						
carton, aside............................		99		37		53
		16		*17*		*22*

° Picked up wrong piece
† Received instructions from foreman
‡ Dropped nut off axle
Performance rating for whole job: 110

key for a tool. Obviously, this work would go much faster when done in a factory on a repetitive basis and with appropriate tools used at a properly designed work place by an experienced worker. For Figure 16–3 the elements are "Preassemble toe clips," "Toe clips on frame," and so on.

From here on the analyst writes in the time it takes to perform the elements. Usually he lets his stopwatch run continuously and records its reading at the end of each element. Later he subtracts the elements' ending times from their starting times to get the net time for each element (hence the two sets of times for each element in Figure 16–3).

In Figure 16–3 the elements succeed each other in vertical sequence. Thus, for the first work cycle, element 1 took $\frac{8}{100}$ of a minute, element 2 was finished at $\frac{30}{100}$, element 3 was finished at $\frac{47}{100}$, etc. When the operator finished the first roller skate, he went right on to the second one, and again the element times follow in vertical sequence. This time, however, the operator had a pair of skates, so he packed them into a carton, and he continued in this way after every second roller skate.

Before leaving the job, the analyst should also record his pace rating of the operator's performance so that he can later make the appropriate adjustment when he calculates the standard time. In our roller skate assembly study this rating was 110.

Setting the standard

The first step in setting the standard from the raw data is to subtract the elements' ending times from their starting times. This was done in Figure 16–3, producing the actual time that each element took. These times are in italics and are the figures used in the calculation from this point on.

FIGURE 16–4

| | | Hundredths of a minute | |
| | | *Element* | *Time per pair of* |
Element	*Frequency*	*time*	*skates*
Preassemble toe clips........................... 2		.123	.246
Toe clips on frame.............................. 2		.203	.406
Assemble 2 wheels.............................. 4		.148	.592
Tighten axle nut............................... 4		.108	.432
Attach frame halves............................ 2		.197	.394
Tighten frame nut and bolt..................... 2		.233	.466
Pack 2 skates into carton liner................. 1		.308	.308
Insert liner into carton and aside............... 1		.183	.183
Total average cycle time observed.................................			3.027
Add 12% for fatigue and personal time...........................			.363
			3.390
Adjust for performance rating of 110%...........................			.339
Time standard in minutes per pair...............................			3.729

Standard hourly output: 60 ÷ 3.729 = 16.1 pairs per hour
Piece rate at $4.50 an hour: $4.50 ÷ 16.1 = $.28 per pair

There are several readings for each element, and it can be seen that the individual times vary somewhat. In this analysis we used a simple arithmetic average of the element times observed, except that the times in parentheses were omitted as not typical.

These averages appear in Figure 16–4 as the *element time* figures. Next, these times were multiplied by how often the element occurs per unit of output. When our sample study was taken, the analyst timed putting on the skate's front wheels and tightening the axle bolt as different from assembling the back wheels, but these turned out to be identical activities; so, in the write up in Figure 16–4, putting wheels on appears as only 1 element but is said to occur 4 times per pair of skates.

After each element's time was multiplied by how often it occurred, the typical cycle time was totaled up as 3.027 minutes. To this was added a 12 percent allowance for fatigue and personal time. Next, the 110 percent performance rating was used, causing the addition of 10 percent more time and a total time standard of 3.729 minutes per pair of skates.

This method, as described here, is typical of how time standards are set. Personal and fatigue allowances are sometimes set a little lower, perhaps at 10 percent.

A good many factory jobs, of course, are more complicated than assembling roller skates. If they have quite a few miscellaneous elements that are done irregularly, this makes it difficult to find out how much time to allow for them. One way, however, is to take a much more extended time study and handle such elements on a proportional basis, just as we did with putting the skates into cartons.

This, however, may take a long time to do well because of the infrequency of many such elements. Sometimes, therefore, the analyst turns to "work sampling" (explained later in this chapter). If a man is observed performing miscellaneous tasks one fifth of his time and main elements four fifths of his time, it is assumed that miscellaneous elements take one fourth as much time as main elements and they are therefore given one fourth the time of main elements.

Machine time within work cycles

Many factory machines are semiautomatic; once they are set up and the material is inserted, the machines perform all the operations. All that the operator does is take out the product just finished and put in the next one. While the machine works, there is nothing for the man to do, so there is a question of how the element "wait for machine" should be handled in the production standard. If the wait is short or if the machine needs watching, "wait for machine" should be listed along with all of the other elements and incorporated into the standard. If a job takes 2 minutes to unload and load and then a ½ minute wait while the machine runs, this would be a 2½ minute production standard. But if unload and load time is 2 minutes and then the machine runs by itself for 10 minutes, this job probably should be considered a 2-minute, not a 12-minute, job. The man is given other work to do during his idle 10 minutes—possibly operating other machines.

Setup and change time

Machines nearly always have to be "set up" for each job or "changed over" from the previous job. The tools, tool holders, material holders, and so on all must be put in place and adjusted. But before that starts, the old setup from the last job has to be torn down and its tools and gadgetry put away. Besides this, the operator usually has to make a trip to the tool crib to return his last-used tooling and get the next tooling, and perhaps a drawing. Along the way he rings out on his old-job time card and rings in for his new job.

The work of setting up on many semiautomatic machines is often done by a setup man who does nothing else. He is usually paid by the hour, so there are no production standards for tearing down and setting up.

Many men on incentive pay plans, however, are on jobs where they set up their own machines and then run them themselves. There are three choices (none of which is perfect) of how to pay for setting up: (1) pay for it by the hour, (2) set standards for setting up and pay for it on an incentive plan, (3) put the setup time in with the running time on a pro rata basis and have one production standard cover both setting up and running the machine.

Number 1, paying for setup at an hourly rate, is a somewhat unsatisfactory choice, particularly if a pieceworker is to be paid his regular job's base rate for it. Since he is earning no bonus doing this work, he feels that his pay is cut while he is setting up. But if he is paid his average earnings, including his usual bonus, while setting up jobs without standards, he will take a rest while doing it. In fact, on his time card he may exaggerate the time the setting up takes and so boost his earnings.

Number 2, having standards for the setup jobs, is a better choice, and the best so far as incentives are concerned. But it is bad in that there must be hundreds of standards for hundreds of kinds of setups. These standards are slow and costly to make up because the same setups don't turn up very often and they take a long time when they do turn up. It may take weeks before the time study man can have an opportunity to watch even two or three setups of a given kind. Also, the operator can sometimes use part of the previous job's tooling, so that complete setups are not always required. (A similar problem arises in processing situations, as, for example, in paint mixing. It takes more time to go from black to white than from white to black because in the former case the equipment has to be cleaned more thoroughly.)

Number 3, allowing time for setup on a pro rata basis within the regular rate, is chosen sometimes, and is a fairly satisfactory method. It does not solve the difficulty of having to do considerable standards setting work, nor of having to set standards for setups based on very few observations, or of partial setups. It *does* avoid having hundreds of standards for setups on the records, but they have to be set anyway before they can be put into the standard for operating a machine on an average basis, so there is no saving of standard setting effort.

Putting setup time into the standard for operating a machine on a pro rata basis usually works reasonably well, but not if the average length of run changes a great deal. Running a duplicating machine will illustrate the trouble. To operate it, a man has to put on a new master copy for each new order, but the main job is running sheets of paper through the machine. From past experience the analyst knows about how many sheets are usually run off each time. If the average run is 200 sheets, perhaps the operating time for turning out 200 sheets is 4 minutes; and suppose that it takes 2 minutes to change masters. These two times can be added together to show that it will take 6 minutes to run off 200 sheets of paper, or 3 minutes per 100.

This works fine if the runs average 200. But if the operator gets numerous orders for 25 sheets, he has to run 8 such orders to turn out 200 sheets. He will spend 4 minutes running the machine and 16 minutes changing masters, a total of 20 minutes. Yet the standard gives him only 6 minutes' credit and 6 minutes' pay. On the other hand, he might get a run of 1,000. He takes 20 minutes to run them off plus 2 minutes' master change time, a total 22 minutes, but the standard allows 30 minutes.

Including anything—in this case setup time—on a pro rata basis makes standards tight or loose if the frequency of occurrence changes.

Problems in setting production standards

Most of the problems in setting production standards center on situations where the analyst has to use judgment. And of these, pace rating (also called leveling) is probably the most open to question. It is apparent that some particular pace ought to be thought of as reasonable and that this pace should not be either a man's best or poorest performance. Yet it is hard to convince everyone that the end result, the time standard, is exactly right.

No better way seems to be available than to have the standard setter make a leveling judgment. Some companies try to refine this by having him make several pace ratings, one for each element, and adjust each element's average time to "normal" before summing up the times to get the whole-job standard. A very few companies even try to have their analysts rate every occurrence of every element. Probably such extra effort on his part produces a better standard, yet the process is still one of judging.

It might seem that the need to judge pace could be reduced, or even eliminated, by studying all the members of a group and using their average time as the standard. But we have already noted that this is unfair to groups of good workers who turn out more work than a fair standard should call for. And we also noted that such a standard would be equally wrong if it were an average of slow performances. There is the added difficulty that there are only one or two men on a good many jobs. And there is the still greater difficulty that men who are being studied usually slow down somewhat, be they one or ten in number. There is no safety in numbers.

Judgment must also be exercised in the matter of how often certain things should be done. A man may have to gage the material, or sharpen a tool, or replace a worn or broken tool, but how often? It is a matter of judging. In rare cases there is even a question whether certain elements are really needed for the job. Again, judging plays a part in the setting of the standard.

Limitations to use of time study

Production standards can be and *are* used in many instances where the work itself cannot be timed. Most such production standards, however, are only approximations. Rarely are they as good as time study standards, yet approximate standards are usually better than none. The weaknesses of time study as a method for setting production standards can be enumerated as follows:

1. An analyst can time only what he can see. This eliminates the timing of the thinking parts of jobs and leaves only manual jobs.

2. If an analyst times a job, it has to be a specific job—with starting and stopping points and separable into units so that it is possible to count how many times it is done. This cannot be done with, say, the work of a janitor or plant guard, or with many other jobs.

3. It doesn't pay to set standards for some jobs because they are not repetitive enough. The gain from setting standards for a small job that will be done only once or twice in the future won't pay for the analytical work. Standards setting by time study is limited to repetitive jobs.

4. Nor does it pay to time jobs and set standards on them when men do a great many things. A maintenance department carpenter, for example, does too many things to have standards for all of them (his daily work report would sometimes be several pages long). Also, it is too costly to verify what he says he did. And when no one checks reports, many men on piecework will report that they have turned out more work than they did.

5. It usually doesn't pay to have standards for only part of a man's work. If it isn't possible to put all of their work on standards, some men will exaggerate the time they report spent on daywork (for which they get paid by the hour) and so keep their earnings up. A man may have spent 4 hours on piecework and 4 on daywork (not in single stretches of time but all mixed up during the day) but he may report that he did the piecework in 3 hours and the daywork in 5 hours, and no one can

prove that he didn't. It looks as if he did 9 hours' work in the day (4 hours of piecework [done in 3 hours] plus 5 hours of daywork) instead of 8. The foreman is put on the spot of having to give him 9 hours of pay or arbitrarily (although perhaps correctly) cutting his claim of 5 hours of daywork to 4.

6. If quality is hard to define (as in polishing a surface), standards and production incentives may cause quality to fall off. A man may say that he has done the job well enough when he hasn't.

The analyst should think twice before accepting this criticism of production standards, though. If a man is *not* on piecework but is on daywork instead, he might, and if he is allowed to maybe *will*, shine a polished surface all day and be proud of the fine job he does. Unfortunately, he cannot be allowed to spend so much time on an operation that it makes the cost go way up. Jobs where quality is hard to define are exactly the places where production standards, as well as quality standards, are needed.

7. Unions often oppose time study; and where a union is opposed and where it is very strong, it may be able to stop, or preclude time study work. Standards might be set by other methods, but not by time study.

Work sampling

Work sampling (occasionally called ratio-relay study) means observing, at irregular time intervals, what is going on. An analyst goes past a work place, say 500 times, over a period of weeks and notes what the operator is doing each time. Perhaps an office secretary might be observed typing 250 times, filing 150 times, telephoning 50 times, and doing personal things 50 times. Thus 50 percent of her time is spent on typing, 30 percent on filing, 10 percent on telephoning, and 10 percent on other things.

This method can be used to find out how often the minor job elements of factory jobs occur and so provide the information needed to incorporate time for them into factory production standards. Work sampling can also be used to set complete standards for factory jobs and not just the time for the miscellaneous parts of jobs. Work sampling is also useful for setting production standards for hard-to-set work, such as most office work.

Work sampling is often thought of as a low-cost way to set standards, and this may be true. Yet this is not always true because the job being observed may require a trip for each observation; also, the observations should be taken at various times of the day and not be concentrated in the hours when the observer may happen to be near the operation. Also, it takes a long time to get 500 observations. If, for example, 500 observations are wanted, it will take 50 a day for 2 weeks.

One advantage of work sampling is that it probably represents true-to-life situations. Operators don't get much chance to dress up their performance to try to mislead the analyst. Against this is the disadvantage that there is no pace rating.[2] In order to set a standard without pace rating, the analyst would have to know how many units were turned out in a day. Both a fast and a slow typist might very well be typing 50 percent of the time, but the fast typist types more pages in a day. Thus there would be a question of how many pages to expect in a day. Work sampling does not get at this and is therefore of limited value in standards setting.

Other ways to set production standards

Production standards for semiautomatic machines are sometimes set by starting with a machine's ultimate output possibilities. Something less than this, say 90 percent of perfect output, is then decided to be the best that can be hoped for. Then a decision is made that even 90 percent of perfect is very good and that this much output merits a bonus, perhaps 25 percent. So 90 percent of the best expected production is regarded as being 125 percent of standard, and so the standard is $100 \div 125 \times .90$, or 72 percent of perfect. Thus if a machine could, theoretically, turn out 500 pieces an hour, 450 units would be regarded as top production and the standard would be 360 units per hour. A pieceworker who turned out 450 would earn a 25 percent bonus.

Production standards for piecework purposes are sometimes set by direct negotiation between a company's industrial engineers and the union's standards committee. In the shoe and textile industries it is common for these men to sit down together, look over the new patterns, compare them to the old patterns and standards, and thereupon agree on the new standards. Such a practice, however, would be unusual in other industries.

Another method for setting standards, which is used commonly enough to merit mention, is simple estimation. The foreman or an experienced estimator looks at a drawing or product design and, based on his past experience, estimates how long the work should take. Contractors in the building trades have to do this all the time when they bid on contracts to build houses. And in factories, too, this may be about the best that can be done when it comes to setting a standard for making such a product as a dust collecting duct system for a construction project.

Production standards for office work

Most office work is different in nature from most factory work. Usually it is not possible to set office production standards by using stopwatches

---

[2] The analyst, however, could watch the activity a little longer each time and pace-rate the observations.

and timing jobs. In practice, office standards (except for budgets) are not used very often. They are sometimes used, however, when office jobs can be timed in the same way as factory jobs. In other cases work sampling is used.

Standard data

New jobs are often similar in many respects to old jobs. Often, certain parts of a new job are identical to parts of old jobs. In such cases, using the time values from old standards for the same activities would save considerable standards setting costs. This situation is common enough that time values for certain activities and sets of movements can be regarded as established data that are available for use in future standards.

Such standard data are of two main kinds. One uses job element times from past studies in what can be called a "macroscopic" method. The other regards all jobs as collections of very short or minute movements, which can be called a "microscopic" method. Once someone makes a catalog of their times, no one ever has to do it again—for any job. All anyone has to do is list every little movement an operator makes, get the time for each movement out of the catalog, and add the times up.

Macroscopic methods are like building a prefab house: the analyst works with the big parts (elements) of a job, just as a prefab house is made from preassembled sections of walls, floors, cabinets, windows, and roofs. Microscopic methods are like building an ordinary house—out of bricks, nails, boards, and glass. Such jobs are made up of little movements: reach, pick up, carry, insert, and so on.

Macroscopic methods are limited to particular operations, such as operating a turret lathe, and they apply to any and all jobs done on that size and kind of lathe. Microscopic methods are universal and can be used for all operations and all jobs.

Macroscopic Methods.   Macroscopic methods use standard data which are often put into formula form and so can be easily computerized. Sometimes they are put into precomputed tables, and sometimes they are presented in charts.

Macroscopic methods assume that, as between jobs done on the same machine or similar machines, certain elements are constant irrespective of the specific operation. Oiling a machine's bearings takes the same amount of time irrespective of the job a man is working on. So does blowing or brushing out chips. So does loosening or tightening tool holder jaws.

Certain other elements are variable. The time it takes to drill a hole, for example, or to plane or grind a surface depends on the depth and diameter of the hole or the size of the area to be planed or smoothed and how much metal is to be removed. The times for the job element varies, *but in a predictable way.* Other elements, such as making spot welds, are constant, but their total time depends on how many times they need doing.

In all of these cases the analyst, by looking at a drawing, can predict the time an element will take on a new job. Most elements are either clearly constant or they are variable. And in almost all cases where an element's time varies, the analyst can determine, by formula, how long it will take. He can then list the times for constant elements and the calculated times for variable elements. Adding these figures produces production standards for new jobs without waiting for them to be done.

Microscopic methods. In Chapter 13, therbligs—the basic, minute movements which make up all of a man's physical movements—were discussed. They provide the basis for the microscopic method for setting job standards.

Industrial engineers have developed lists of minute human movements (reach, grasp, move hands, etc.) and have also, by using high-speed moving pictures, studied these movements carefully and set a time value for each. Catalogs of times for these minute movements are available, and part of such a catalog is shown in Figure 16–5.

FIGURE 16–5. Time values for therblig "reach" in TMUs (.0006 minutes)

Distance moved (inches)	Kind of movement				Case and description
	A	B	C	D	
¾ or less......	2.0	2.0	2.0	2.0	A. Reach to object in fixed loca-
1.........	2.5	2.5	3.6	2.4	tion, or to object in other
2.........	4.0	4.0	5.9	3.8	hand or on which other hand
3.........	5.3	5.3	7.3	5.3	rests.
4.........	6.1	6.4	8.4	6.8	B. Reach to single object in loca-
5.........	6.5	7.8	9.4	7.4	tion which may vary slightly
6.........	7.0	8.6	10.1	8.8	from cycle to cycle.
8.........	7.9	10.1	11.5	9.3	C. Reach to object jumbled with
10.........	8.7	11.5	12.9	10.5	other objects in a group so
15.........	11.0	15.1	16.3	13.6	that search and select occur.
20.........	13.1	18.6	19.8	16.7	D. Reach to a very small object
25.........	15.4	22.2	23.2	19.8	or where accurate grasp is re-
30.........	17.5	25.8	26.7	22.9	quired.

Source: MTM Association for Standards and Research.

The time values shown in such a catalog are listed in very short intervals. Perhaps the best known type of these catalogs of times is called methods time measurement (MTM). MTM times are shown in TMUs (time measurement units), which are $\frac{1}{100,000}$ of an hour (30 TMUs = 1 second).

To use microscopic methods, the analyst lists the operator's movements in great detail and then looks at his catalog of times to see how long each movement will take. This work is not for the amateur since an operator sometimes is doing one thing with one hand and another with the other. The analyst has to pay attention to which time to use.

Proponents òf microscopic methods say that by using these methods an analyst can get very accurate time standards more quickly than by any other means. They also claim that the thorough investigation needed to write up the bits of a job causes the analyst to see so many places to improve the job that he is always able to make numerous improvements.

MTM standards are usually quite accurate but each one takes a good bit of time to set up, even with the catalog of times available. The time required and the cost entailed are serious handicaps in companies where the labor contract requires standards to be set within three days on all new jobs. And this is a common requirement.

To meet this problem, MSD (master standard data), GPD (general-purpose data), and MCD (master clerical data) have been developed—to shorten the standard setting time. These adaptations of MTM combine sets of therblig data into bigger "building blocks," not so big as time study elements but big enough to drastically reduce the MTM standard setting job. Using bigger building blocks reduces the cost of setting standards and thereby allows its use in more places, including offices.

In some companies MSD, GPD, and MCD are kept on computer tapes, which has further lessened the time and cost of setting standards. IBM, not unnaturally, is one of the companies which uses computer files for such basic data. The standard setter just lists the code for each basic data time and a computer calculates the standard.

Review questions

1. Why are production standards necessary even in companies not using piecework? What are they used for?
2. Discuss the need to time a large number of work cycles by way of adding to the reliability of the averages of the work time observed for standards setting purposes.
3. Why is it desirable to time jobs element by element, as against overall timing? How will this produce a better standard?
4. What is the "allowed time" for an element? How is it figured?
5. Some people don't like leveling. Why?
6. Where is judgment usually exercised in setting production standards? Discuss how julgment can be eliminated, reduced, or improved in standards setting.
7. Briefly explain how a time study man makes up a time standard after he gets back to his office with his data.
8. In practice, time study cannot be used everywhere. Why not?
9. What should be done with machine running time when time standards are set up? Discuss.
10. Should there be separate standards for setting up machines? In what other ways could setup time be handled? Compare them.

11. Could production standards be set by work sampling without using a stop-watch? How satisfactory is work sampling? Why?

12. When and how does a time study man use constant and variable elements?

13. Compare macroscopic and microscopic methods for setting production standards by using standard data instead of time study.

Discussion questions

1. When a time study man sets a time standard and has a choice of workers to study, should he study a good worker? Or whom? Why?

2. "A manufacturing standard is a description of repetitive work." Is it? If it is not, what *is* a standard? Discuss.

3. What should a foreman do when one of his men says that the piece rate is too low and that he thinks it should be adjusted upward?

4. A leading industrial consultant reports that management often permits a standard to be bargained instead of measured. Or it permits a man to do the job his own way instead of the best way. This consultant sees both practices as bad. What is wrong with these practices?

5. Both the United Automobile Workers and the International Ladies Garment Workers unions have time study engineers on their payrolls. Wouldn't this be a big help in deciding upon the reasonableness of disputed standards? The union's time study man and the company's time study man could, together, study the job and jointly arrive at a standard satisfactory to each. Discuss.

6. Why are unions forever grieving over standards? Why do companies get so excited when unions want the standards relaxed, or want larger fatigue allowances? Wouldn't incentive rates solve all of these problems? Discuss.

7. Compared to time study, when is work sampling better? When is it less good?

8. In the text it is said that ratio delay is not a good way to set production standards because it reports only what men do and contains no judgment factor concerning whether the observed performance is good or bad. How might this weakness of the ratio delay method be remedied?

Problems

1. A man took 8 hours to set up his machine and turn out 130 units of product. For this job the standard time for setting up is 50 minutes and 4 minutes per piece for doing the work.

   a) What was the man's "efficiency" for the day?

   b) If the man were working on piecework and the job has a base rate of $5 an hour, how much money would he earn?

2. What is the time standard for the following job? Add 15 percent for allowances and show the figures. The times shown are continuous watch readings in hundredths of minutes.

Element	Cycle							Performance rating
	1	2	3	4	5	6	7	
Get 2 cases..........	.11		.55		1.05		1.51	1.05
Put part into case.....	.22	.41	.65	.83	1.16	1.34	1.60	1.15
Fasten parts into position............	.29	.48	.73	.97	1.23	1.41	1.82	.95

3. The following data cover the assembly and packing into a container of wooden washboards. The washboards are made up of 2 side pieces, 1 top crosspiece, 1 middle crosspiece, 1 bottom crosspiece, and a wooden back piece for the upper section of the board and a corrugated glass scrubbing board. The pieces are fitted together and held in place by 6 nails. Six washboards are packed in a container. The following is a copy of the observation sheet. The times recorded are continuous watch readings in hundredths of minutes. The number of full minutes is shown only when it changes.

Element	Operation cycle						
	1	2	3	4	5	6	7
Assemble top to first side................	.12	.58	.43	.36	.25	.15	6.01
Assemble back piece and middle crosspiece..	.29	.82	.60	.55	.41	.32	.19
Assemble scrubbing board and bottom piece.	.44	.94	.76	.70	.55	.48	.32
Assemble second side piece..............	.64	2.00	3.02	.89	.78	.63	.50
Nail 6 nails and lay aside...............	.89	.33	.24	4.12	5.04	.91	.75
Get and form container.................	1.08	...	...	...	...	..	.95
Place 6 boards in container and set aside....	.51	...	...	...	...	..	7.31

Discard the extremely long and extremely short elemental readings and determine the selected elemental time for each element by averaging the remaining time values. Assume that the time study man rated the man's performance at 110 percent of normal.

Determine the cycle time for the job before allowances are added. Assume that the allowances for miscellaneous necessary duties, fatigue, and personal time come to an additional 30 percent. Determine the time standard for the job. Express the production standard in terms of washboards to be assembled per hour.

4. Martin Wilkie and Norman Hutchinson both operate punch presses of the same kind and both work on piecework. Their base rates are $4.50 an hour (this is guaranteed). The production standards for the 4 products which they spend all their time on are: product A, 5 per minute; B, 10 per minute; C, 15 per minute; and D, 20 per minute. In 1 specific week when they worked 8 hours every day, their production records were as follows:

Product	Wilkie					Hutchinson				
	M	T	W	T	F	M	T	W	T	F
A..........	1,200		1.500		900	600			1,500	300
B..........	3,000	3,000			900		900	1,200	1,800	3,600
C..........			900	8,100	900	5,400	5,400	3,600		
D..........		5,400	3,600	3,600	2,400	4,800	2,400			2,400

a) Calculate the wages, day by day, of these 2 men.

b) If both men work consistently hard, which (if any) of the standards would appear to be out of line? Which are the tight standards and which are the loose standards?

5. A and B do the same operation on 2 similar machines. The machine cost in each case is $5 an hour. A turns out 120 pieces per hour and is paid $4.50 an hour. B turns out 115 pieces per hour.

a) What is A's cost per piece?

b) What would B's hourly rate be if his unit cost is equal to that of A?

6. Workers A and B each produce 100 pieces per hour, but A's rejects are 2 percent as against ½ percent for B. Rejects are repairable at $.18 each.

a) Each man is paid a straight hourly pay rate of $4.50 an hour. What is the cost per unit of this item for each man?

b) If you paid each man so that both men would have A's cost per unit, what would each one's hourly rate be?

7. Jim Farley, the shop steward of the union local, returned after finishing the union's course in time study and promptly filed a grievance over a proposed standard for a boxing operation. Below is a copy of the data furnished to him by Bill Kerr, who had set the standard. Although Kerr rated each element as is shown on his computing sheet, he also made an overall rating of 105 for the whole job. In his work-up of the rate he used the element ratings, not this overall rating.

Farley came up with the calculation shown below.

Kerr explained that the difference between the actual average time and his selected average time lay in the fact that wherever his notes (made during the study) showed that something extraneous had caused an element to take too long or too little time, he had eliminated that time value before averaging to get his selected average.

See if you can resolve this dispute.

Kerr's calculation

Element	Number of readings	Arithmetic average	Selected average	Element rating	Leveled time	Occurrence per unit	Standard time (minutes)
Pick up blank, form box.........	50	.085	.083	110	.091	1/1	.091
Insert belt..........	50	.071	.069	105	.073	1/1	.073
Close, seal, box into carton........	48	.155	.154	90	.139	1/1	.139
Replenish boxes.....	1	.200	.200	50	.100	1/50	.002
Replenish belts......	4	.500	.500	100	.500	1/25	.020
Carton aside to conveyor.........	7	.258	.250	110	.275	1/5	.055
Total.....							.380
Personal and fatigue time (10%).....							.038
Standard time per unit.....							.418
Standard production per hr.....							143.5 units
Piece rate per 100 (job base rate is $5).....							$3.484

Farley's calculation

Element	Arithmetic average	Occur-rence	Time
Pick up blank, form box	.085	1/1	.085
Insert belt	.071	1/1	.071
Close, seal, box into carton	.155	1/1	.155
Replenish boxes	.200	1/33	.006
Replenish belts	.500	1/12.5	.040
Carton aside to conveyor	.258	1/5	.052
Total			.409
Leveled time (105 rating)			.429
10% for personal and fatigue time = 6 min. per hr.			
Work time in each hr.: 54 min.			
Standard production in 54 min			125.9 units
Piece rate per 100 (job base rate is $5)			$3.971

8. A part is made on a 4-spindle multiple drilling machine. Present volume (200 pieces per day) keeps 5 such machines busy for 2 shifts (at 87.5 percent utilization). The element breakdown and times are:

Element	Minutes
Clear and load jig	3.0
Drill 4 large holes (first spindle)	4.0
Spotface 4 large holes (second spindle)	2.5
Drill 6 small holes (third spindle)	4.0
Remove from jig	0.5
Tap 6 small holes (fourth spindle)	4.8
Deburr 6 tapped holes (first spindle)	1.8
Put piece away and get another	0.4
Total cycle time	21.0

The company wants to step production up to 240 pieces a day yet it does not want to operate the machines any more hours because the plant is completely closed down on the third shift and Saturday and Sunday work costs overtime. It is possible to use other, less well-suited machines to get extra production.

One possibility is to use 5 small single-spindle bench drill presses. They drill, spotface, tap, or deburr only 1 hole at a time. Loading and unloading these drills takes 1 minute less than on the 4-spindle drill. Will these machines add enough capacity to allow for the production of 240 units a day?

9. For purposes of determining the allowance for miscellaneous elements for setting a job standard, the analyst has collected 500 ratio-delay figures. These show that the operator was performing the operation 392 times. He was away from his machine 32 times, and 76 times his machine was not running while he adjusted it, gaged the work, and did other miscellaneous work associated with making products. From time study data the analyst had previously established that just doing the main parts of the operation takes 4.2 minutes. What should the job standard be?

10. If every stroke were used to turn out products so that a semiautomatic machine could produce 600 units per hour, what would the production standard be if 85 percent of top possibilities were regarded as worth a 20 percent bonus?

11. The following data have been collected to provide a basis for setting up standard data for winding coils in a coil winding department. The winding times have been leveled to make them comparable (otherwise they would sometimes reflect either fast or slow performances).

Study no.	Core diameter	Core length	Length of wire wound	Wire gage	Winding time
1.	1½″	5″	3,200′	30	2.10 min.
2.	½	4	1,500	10	1.60
3.	1	4	1,800	20	1.25
4.	1¼	5	2,600	15	2.30
5.	½	3	1,200	40	.55
6.	1	3	1,525	30	.89
7.	¾	4	1,475	15	1.27
8.	1	5	2,000	25	1.30
9.	½	4	1,600	35	.78
10.	1¼	5	2,400	10	2.60
11.	¾	3	1,500	25	.99
12.	½	2	600	40	.42
13.	1	4	2,200	15	1.80
14.	1¼	5	2,800	20	2.10
15.	½	2	1,500	40	.70
16.	¼	1	200	15	.50

a) Set up curves so that time values for new sizes of coils can be read off.

b) Using the curves, read off the time for the element "wind coil" for coils which will have a ⅜ inch core diameter and a core length of 2 inches and will contain 3,800 feet of 37 gage wire.

c) Do the same for a 1-inch core diameter and a core length of 4-inch coils containing 2,200 feet of 12 gage wire.

Recent references

Aronson, A., "Benefits of Work Measurement," *Office,* January 1972

Jackson, B. L., "Determining Efficiency through Work Sampling," *Management Review,* January 1972

Nadler, Gerald, *Work Design: A Systems Concept,* Homewood, Ill.: Richard D. Irwin, 1970

Nance, Harold W., and Robert W. Nolan, *Office Work Measurement,* New York: McGraw-Hill, 1971

Niebel, Benjamin W., *Motion and Time Study,* 5th ed., Homewood, Ill.: Richard D. Irwin, 1972

Reider, H., "Work Simplification Simplified," *Office,* October 1971

Reuter, V. G., "Work Measurement Practices," *California Management Review,* Fall 1971

Witt, W. E., "Work Measurement of Indirect Labor," *Management Accounting,* November 1971

17

Cost calculations and budgets

INTELLIGENT managerial decisions must always rest on a basis of knowl-edge—knowledge concerning organizational capabilities, market oppor-tunities, competition, products, prices, costs, and many other things.

Of these factors, *cost* is one of the most important because all actions and all activities cost money, so costs pervade everything. The determi-nation of costs is therefore an important activity. Yet *cost determination* is only the *basis* for managerial decision. The objective is to *control* costs, to get work done at reasonable costs.

Budgets play an important part here. And although they don't reduce costs directly, successful budgeting reduces costs because budgets are holding devices or restraining mechanisms which help hold costs down and help keep them from growing larger. Budgets may be said to reduce costs indirectly.

Calculating costs

Successful operation of a manufacturing company rests on operations resulting in a situation like that depicted in Figure 17–1, where the sum-

FIGURE 17–1. **Composition of manufacturing costs and their relationship to sales income**

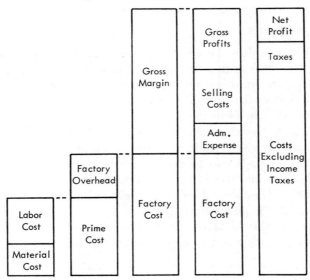

mation of costs is less than the total income. Yet, as Figure 17–1 shows, total costs are made up of several components. In actual operation, these components need individual calculation and control in order to keep them at reasonable levels.

Finding out what it costs to make individual products is not easy, however, because many costs are not incurred just for one kind of product. Products have to be assessed with their share of the general costs of doing business. And because such assessments have to be fairly arbitrary, any individual product cost figure is always an approximation.

It is like figuring out what a meal at home costs. Should part of the house rent be counted? Should part of the cost of owning a car for going to the store for groceries be counted? How about the cost of the silverware used on the dining room table? How about the housewife's time? The cost figure arrived at would depend on how these and other costs are valued and apportioned.

The problem in a factory is no easier; it is just as hard to figure out what it costs to make a product. And it is just as crude a figure when it is obtained. There is really no need to figure labor and material costs to the fourth decimal place of accuracy when large amounts of overhead are allocated on some rather arbitrary basis. The implied accuracy of such detailed product cost figures is specious.

But it is still necessary to have cost figures, crude though they are, in order to set selling prices and to calculate profits. And inside a factory, cost figures are needed for budgets and controls. Besides, the government requires the keeping of certain cost records for tax calculation purposes.

Charts of accounts

In order to calculate the costs of products or departments it is necessary to classify costs as they are incurred according to the purpose of the expense. Separate accounts need to be kept in the accounting department for each product or department so that the costs incurred for their benefit can be charged directly to them.

In order to do this there needs to be a "chart of accounts," which sets accounts apart on a systematic basis so that all of the reports which will later need to be made can be made without using many arbitrary allocations. The accounts should reflect transactions by accountabilities and responsibilities. They should reflect the responsibilities of individual people wherever this is possible.

Each account should have its own account number, which fits into the overall pattern. Such a system might start with this general pattern:

		Account number series
Balance sheet items:	Assets..............	100 to 199
	Liabilities...........	200 to 299
	Equity..............	300 to 399
Profit and loss items:	Income.............	400 to 499
	Expenses...........	500 to 599
	Taxes..............	600 to 699
	Etc.	

Within each number group, subgroups might be assigned as follows:

Assets: Current assets............ 100 to 129
Investments.............. 130 to 139
Fixed assets............. 140 to 159
Intangible assets.......... 160 to 169
Deferred charges.......... 170 to 179
Other assets............. 180 to 199

These numbers would cover the main accounts and would be the first three digits for subsidiary accounts, which would show a greater breakdown. Account number 100 might, for example, be cash: 100–200 would be cash in the payroll account; 100–234 would be cash in the payroll account in the ABC Bank in St. Louis. Or account 560 might be repairs, 560–400 would be repairs in the foundry, and 560–420 would be floor repairs in the foundry.

Each company needs to develop its own chart of accounts appropriate to its operations and appropriate to the analyses which will later be needed.

Past and future costs

Cost accounting is nearly always two-sided—it shows how much things *have been* costing. This is historical. And nearly always, too, cost accounting shows how much future products are *likely* to cost. Most cost accounting work is the record keeping needed in order to report past costs. But its more valuable part helps predict future costs and so helps managers set budgets and plan for the future.

This is not, however, to dismiss the record keeping part of cost accounting as just record keeping. Records of what happened yesterday furnish managers with the figures they need to *control* their organization. Yesterday's actual costs can be compared with the plan to see where they are different. This leads to finding out why and to correcting bad spots. Improvements in the future are built on records of past performance.

Job-lot costs

Job-lot costs are used in companies that do varied work and every job is given a number to identify it. Then an account for it is set up in the cost accounting department. (Production control uses the same job number when scheduling the lot's production.)

As a job moves through manufacturing, all of its costs are listed in its account. Materials requisitions supply the value of the materials used. Factory workers' job tickets supply the cost of labor on the job. Then overhead is allocated. When all of these costs are added up, plus any other costs incurred for the job, the total shows the cost of making the lot. Dividing by the number of units yields the unit cost.

The same thing is done when it is necessary to quote a price on a future job that the sales department wants to bid on. The estimating department lists all of the materials that are *expected* to be used, the

FIGURE 17–2. Information flow system to generate standard costs for job lots

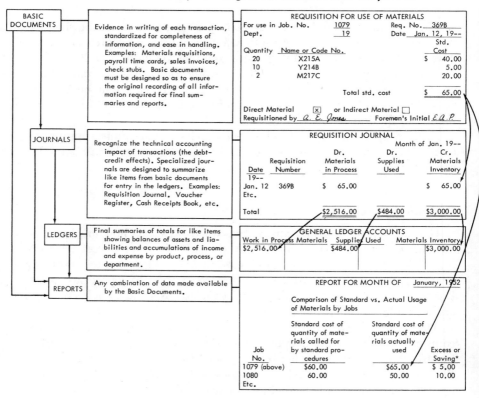

labor it will *probably* take, and overhead assessed at the usual rate. When these are added, a reasonably accurate cost projection is obtained.

Process costs

Continuous production has to use process costs. Process costs are always average costs because it isn't possible to separate the cost of making one gallon of gasoline from another, or one television set from another of the same model, or of one bolt of cloth from another bolt of the same cloth. Nearly all products follow the same path through production.

To find the process average cost it is necessary to keep a record of how much it costs to carry on an operation for a period of time, perhaps a week. Dividing this total by the number of units produced shows the operation's average cost. Where there are several operations in a process, the cost of each one is added in to get the total cost per unit for the whole process.

Direct and indirect costs

Direct costs are those which can be traced directly to a product—the cost of materials used and the cost of labor put into it. All other costs are indirect—costs not incurred for any one product. Indirect costs include the wages of men who do not work on the product and the cost of supplies, office expenses, insurance, depreciation, and taxes. In total, indirect costs often amount to double the direct costs.

Unless a company uses direct costing (described on p. 394 and not to be confused with direct costs), every product should be charged with a share of the overhead costs. Every item's cost should include its own direct costs plus its share of indirect costs.

Direct costs are sometimes called "variable costs," meaning that the *total amount* spent for them in a month or year goes up or down along with production. The more a company produces the more it spends, in *total,* for these items. Indirect costs are called "fixed costs," meaning their total is not affected much by volume changes. Neither of these terms should be taken as a hard-and-fast term, however. Not all variable costs would be cut in half if production were cut in half. Nor would every fixed cost stay unchanged if production were halved.

Cost elements and cost units

When getting a product's cost, accountants have to deal with (*a*) the items for which money is spent: materials, labor, services, depreciation, insurance, taxes, and (*b*) the things for which cost information is wanted: products, operations, and areas of responsibility. What money is spent for, accountants call "cost elements." What information is wanted about, they call "cost units."

Cost accounting *collects* information about what money is spent for. With that information, it then *computes* the cost of products, operations, programs, and areas of responsibility.

In general, the larger the cost unit, the more cost elements can be charged directly to it. If the cost unit is a manufacturing department, the foreman's salary, as well as depreciation on all equipment in his department, become direct costs of that department. But if the cost unit is a large department occupying a whole building, even depreciation on the building itself becomes a direct charge to that area of responsibility.

The *cost collecting procedures* need to pay attention to *cost units*. If a manager wants to find out the costs of small areas—a single department, for example—he needs to set up the chart of accounts so the accounts show this single department's costs apart from others wherever this is possible. It will be necessary to set up separate departmental accounts paralleling most of the plant-wide accounts.

There is, for example, probably a plant-wide account for floor repairs. This account can be subdivided by departments so that each department can be charged with its own floor repair costs. The same can be done with supplies, tools, and many other things. If this is not done, it will be necessary to apportion the plant-wide costs of these expenses to departments without knowing just where the money was spent. It is better to keep each department's expenses apart than to make such apportionments.

The same things should be done with *product* costs. Everything possible should be charged directly to individual products. This means less apportioning later, and it produces better cost data.

Load centers. A load center (or "production" or "machine" center) is just a part of a department. Often it is a very big and expensive machine or group of similar machines. So far as cost accounting is concerned, a load center is one kind of costing unit—it is a distinct part of a plant. Its costs are collected separately, just as if it were a department. Collecting costs for load centers helps pinpoint costs of operating the load center so the right amounts can be charged for its use to the products using it.

Allocating cost elements to cost units

The end product of cost accounting is the cost of the cost unit. Departments are one kind of cost unit. Department costs are often end results in themselves but they are also steps on the way to getting product costs. It is not possible to get good product costs without having previously got department costs.

We have said that only people can do anything about costs, and department operating costs are needed so that responsibility can be traced to individuals. The man in charge of every department is supposed to keep his department's costs down. Department operating cost figures, therefore, are useful in themselves.

To get department costs the accountant starts by keeping, in *each* department's account, all of its own costs. To its costs are added a share of overhead costs incurred outside the department. But allocating the outside costs requires several steps. First, *plant-wide* overhead costs are assessed to *all* departments. Then the costs of all *indirect* departments are assessed to the *operating* departments (those that work on the product). This is necessary because costs cannot be allocated to *products* except by charging them with the costs of the departments that worked on them. So it is necessary to charge operating departments with the costs of all nonoperating departments. After this has been done, the department's own overhead, its assessments, and its direct labor and material costs are summed up, producing the cost of running the department.

If only department costs were wanted, the cost accounting job would be done. But since product costs are wanted too, it is necessary to allocate each operating department's costs to the products it turned out. This starts by comparing the direct labor cost in a department to the rest of the department's costs (the department's own overhead plus its overhead assessments). Suppose that last year the direct workers in a department put in 1 million hours of work and were paid $4.5 million in wages, which comes to an average of $4.50 per hour. And suppose that the department's overhead costs came to $4.5 million, which is equal to 100 percent of direct labor costs. (Materials costs are left out of this example because they are usually charged directly to the product and do not have to be allocated.)

Now the record of direct work done in the year comes into play—how many labor hours or dollars were spent on products A, B, and so on. Suppose the record shows that the men put in 20,000 hours working on product A and turned out 30,000 units of product A. Direct labor costs for product A came to $90,000. The overhead assessment, at the rate of 100 percent of direct labor, would also be $90,000. Total costs (omitting materials) come to $180,000, or $6 per unit for product A.

Now we have the cost of making product A in this department. But product A also required work in other departments. The costs of working on product A in other departments are figured the same way and then added together to get product A's total cost. Materials costs are also added in. The total is divided by the number of product A made to get its individual unit cost.

Product A's cost in each department needs to be figured separately. This way it is possible to make heavy charges for overhead to products which are made on big, expensive machines. Departments with expensive machines sometimes have overhead charge rates of 400 to 500 percent instead of the 100 percent used in our example.

Allocating overhead

Allocating overhead costs to departments on the basis of the direct labor hours of work done in each department is not suitable for some overhead costs. For example, labor hours would not be a good basis for allocating real estate and property taxes, or depreciation. Departments without many machines but with large numbers of men would get big assessments. Heavily mechanized departments with fewer men would get off lightly. This just reverses the cause of the expense because the heavily mechanized departments boost a company's taxes and depreciation. Mechanized departments should be charged with heavy tax and depreciation charges.

Accountants solve this problem by looking at each overhead item by itself and allocating it in the most logical way they can think of. Real estate and property taxes and depreciation on buildings might be allocated to departments, according to the amount of their floor space. Depreciation on machines ought to go to departments according to the machines they have, based on each machine's depreciation schedule. Electric power ought to go to departments according to the power they use.

Absorption of overhead

In our product A example we found that overhead amounted to 100 percent of direct labor costs. That was last year's experience figure. Barring changes, this is what should be expected for the year ahead. But if volume goes up or down (and no one knows whether it will change or not), this ratio will be different for the coming year.

If a company forecasts that there will be no change in volume, it will start out the year saying that the cost of this year's products will include overhead charges figured at 100 percent of direct labor. And if the volume does not change, this will be about right. But if the company has a good year and sells one fifth more products than it expected, direct labor costs will come to $5.4 million instead of the expected $4.5 million.

During the whole year the company will be charging overhead at 100 percent of labor, so it assesses products with $5.4 million of overhead costs. But the overhead might actually stay at last year's $4.5 million since most of it is fixed cost. If it stays the same, the company ends up overcharging its products to the tune of $900,000. If overhead in fact goes up to $4.8 million, the company would end the year assessing $560,-000 too much. It "overabsorbs" its overhead, overstates its costs, and understates its profits.

If business goes down, the reverse happens. The company ends up passing on too little overhead (underabsorbing it), understating costs, and overstating profits.

What can be done about this? It doesn't seem very smart for managers to quote wrong costs all year and then, all at once, wake up at the end of the year to find that they have made more or less money than they had thought. This is not exactly how it works. The managers know full well, all year long, what is going on. They don't wake up and discover it at the year's end.

Then why should they quote wrong costs all year? This is not exactly the way they look at it, either. They want to know what their costs are, including a normal overhead assessment, if they can get their usual sales volume. They try to set selling prices to yield some profit at this volume level. They know that greater volume will *reduce* the proper overhead assessment per unit of product. They know full well that they will end up making *more* per unit than their first calculation (for the expected normal volume) showed. And they are just as aware of what happens on the downside.

The real point is that they do not cut prices when business is good in order to hold profits down, nor can they raise prices when business is bad. They let prices pretty well alone, so they may as well let their calculated unit costs alone too and recognize that, because of overhead, high volume results in extra profits while low volume makes losses.

Cost accounting problems

We said earlier that what accountants say an item costs depends in part on how they assess overhead costs, which is one of cost accounting's big problems. But there are other problems besides this. Several other questions must also be answered by management. And, as with overhead, different cost figures result, depending on how these questions are answered.

Standard costs. One question is: Should "standard" costs or "job-lot" costs be used? The problem here is that successive lots of materials usually end up costing different amounts of money per unit of product. In part this is because some lots are bigger than others, thereby making the setup cost per unit different. And in part this is because—from one order to the next—men work at different paces, the amount of scrap varies, the price of purchased materials changes, and so on.

What should be done about it? Should it be said that the items made in the lot finished on January 15 cost a different amount from those in a lot finished on February 15? The items look alike and are alike, and they will probably be sold for the same price. Or, if they are parts, they will be put into finished products whose costs will be figured as if the parts had cost the same each time.

Most companies use some kind of standard cost. Usually this standard cost is the average unit cost of several recent lots.

Some companies, however, use quite a different kind of standard cost. They figure out every product's *ideal* cost—what it ought to cost if everything goes perfectly. They do this even though they know that actual costs never get so low, and they certainly would not use this kind of cost as the basis for setting selling prices. Companies using standard costs of the ideal kind use them in factory budgets. But they are not just trying to delude themselves. What the managers of these companies are after is to keep the cost of inefficiencies forever before them.

Standard costs of the ideal kind are based on the least costly way to make products. Suppose that an automatic screw machine is best for a job but that these machines are busy, that the foreman has to put the job on a turret lathe, and that he beats turret lathes' standard costs. Is this a good variance? No—because costs on automatics are much less and it is wasteful to do the job on a turret lathe, no matter how efficiently.

At the moment it matters not that the automatics were tied up. All differences from the best should be shown as bad variances, and then managers will see the costs of poor methods as well as the costs of poor performance on the method used. All excess costs over the ideal are costs of some kind of inefficiency.

The method of *collecting* cost figures depends on whether job-lot costs or standard costs are used. Job-lot costing requires collecting each lot's costs and figuring the cost of each unit. The items in each lot are charged into finished parts stock of finished products inventory at that unit price.

But if standard costs are used, the costs of successive lots are not kept apart. As we said, the combined cost of making several lots, as a total, is figured and the average unit cost is calculated and used as the standard cost for the next accounting period.

Direct costing.   A second question is: Is it realistic to follow the time-honored practice of assessing *products* with *all* the costs of doing business? Should the accountants of a company making electric light bulbs say that the cost of a bulb includes the cost of labor plus material plus *overhead?* How realistic is it to say that a light bulb's share of the real estate property taxes is $0.0002 per bulb? Some people would say that costs or expenses that are not directly connected with a product's manufacture should not be added into its cost.

In this method, called direct costing,[1] an item's reported cost is confined to its own direct costs (largely labor and material). All overhead costs, such as building depreciation and taxes, are regarded as costs of doing business and not as part of the cost of making, say, a light bulb.

But if *products* do not bear *all* of a factory's costs, who or what does? The products end up carrying the costs, but they do it collectively—not individually. Direct costing shows very low costs to manufacture. When calculating profits, a company subtracts from income all of its direct costs, leaving a large gross margin. Then it subtracts all overhead and finds the profits.

The end result is the same calculated profit that would be obtained by doing it the conventional way, so why make any change? One reason is simplicity: direct costing is simpler than conventional costing (overheads are not allocated). A second reason is that an item's computed cost does not go up and down as a company's total volume changes. This seems

---

[1] Sometimes this method is called variable costing because products are assessed only with their own variable costs. This term is supposed to remind managers that they are charging only the variable costs to the product but that there are also other costs.

to be a very worthwhile advantage because it remedies a weakness of ordinary methods.

With ordinary costing the units produced when a factory is operating at half time have to stand their own direct costs plus *all* of the overhead. Low volume makes them seem to cost a great deal—but it is not their fault that there is not more volume over which to spread the overhead. The reverse happens in high periods, when high volume cuts the overhead assessments to each product so that they seem to cost less. But do they? Direct costing is not the rule, but it is used by many companies.

Direct costing also helps a company develop pricing and marketing strategies by emphasizing the profit contribution of products. The profit contribution for some products, as was brought out in Chapter 2, is greater than that of others. Managers should emphasize and push the sales of high contribution ratio products.

Joint costs.   A third problem is joint costs. Money is spent, for example, buying one raw material, but the buyer gets two or more kinds of raw materials. When a meat packer buys a cow he gets meat, leather, and other things. How, then, should he allocate the cost of the cow to its products? How much did he pay for sirloin? For hamburger? For leather? A workable answer is "Look to the income." If sirloin brings in 5 percent of the sales income, sirloin should be charged with 5 percent of the cow's cost.

Most companies working on nature's products in early stages of manufacture find that when they buy one material they get two or more. Usually only one is valuable and the other(s) has to be thrown away. But not always. Copper ore sometimes contains silver, both of which are valuable, so a company would divide the ore's cost between copper and silver.

Sometimes waste materials can be made into something worth money. If so, they are called *by-products*. But unless they are worth a good bit, they are never charged any material costs. Instead, the materials are considered to be free of materials cost. They are said to cost only the cost of the work that is done on them to make them salable. Meat packers used to do this with medicines obtained from animal waste. These medicines were claimed to be very profitable, but this was partly because the companies figured that their raw materials were free.

Machine setups.   A fourth problem is machine setups. Because machines must be made ready for jobs, this usually means taking off the special tooling for the last job and fastening on the tooling for the new job. Some setups are simple, taking only a few minutes. Some take hours. Some take several men.

It is possible to charge setups to specific orders. Or they can be charged to an overhead account for setups. It is necessary to do one or the other, and neither suits perfectly. If the order is charged, then the setup part of the cost per unit of products made in different lots will vary inversely with the size of the lot. The bigger the lot, the less the unit cost, and the smaller the lot, the greater the unit cost. The bad part is the way unit costs jump around.

But if setups are charged to an overhead account, this is bad too. Then the high cost of frequent small orders may never be noticed because the wasteful part—the cost of extra setups—is not charged directly to the orders. The costs for extra setups go into the costs, of course, when overhead is allocated to products. But their getting into costs this way does not indicate the cause. A manager might delude himself about how much is saved by keeping inventories very low and reordering little dribbles frequently.

Timing of costs and benefits. A fifth question is: How closely should costs be tied to the products which get the benefit of the expense? Should today's research costs be assessed as costs of making today's products? Should today's foreman training program costs be charged to today's products? Logic says to charge the products which will get the benefits. Practically, however, it gets to be too involved, so companies end up charging most such costs to today's products.

Budgets

A budget is the main element of a planning and control system. It can be expressed as a plan for money income, or outgo, or both. In a factory, budgets are always spending plans. Yet one can ask: What good is a spending plan? Will it help to cut spending? Viewed just as a plan, a budget will not cut spending, but it is *more* than a plan.

A budget should also be a goal—department heads should have to work hard to keep down to the planned amount. A budget ought to motivate them. A budget is also a yardstick. Actual costs will be compared to it to see where, and by how much, subordinate managers did better or worse. These comparisons will lead on to "why," and to what can be done to keep bad variances from happening again in the future. So managers arrive at their real goal: controlled, and lower, costs.

Budgets do not, however, solve all problems. A budget to increase the sales or to cut costs does not, by itself, do either. With or without budgets, managers ought already to be doing their best to boost sales and cut costs. A company can't exactly budget itself into a profit, but budgets help it get there. Most people do a better job with budgets than when they don't have them, so, in a sense, managers can budget their companies into a profit.

Budgets need to be used with discretion because it is possible to save money unwisely. Indeed, on page 337 we list several "pitfalls of cost reduction." Suppose, for example, the budget allows a foreman only a small amount of money to spend for repairs. If he spends less than the budgeted amount, this is good—or is it? True, the company has saved money, but was this wise? Possibly the foreman spent less merely by postponing needed repairs. Or suppose that the budget sets a low ratio of rejects as the goal for the foundry foreman. He meets it, but partly by sending to the machine shop some castings which should have been rejected in the foundry—castings which will probably make trouble and extra costs in the machine shop.

Also, budget makers tend to tighten up budgets every time a new one is made out. Usually this is good, because everyone should always try to do a little better, but it would be bad if *several* improvements could be made *today*. A foreman might hold back and put in only *one* improvement in each budget period lest a real good showing would only bring on new and tighter budgets. Holding back on improvements is not what top men want and is not what they get from their good men. But the temptation is there.

A review of the past is an important part of the procedure of using budgets. But it is easy to get off the track here. The past is frozen; only the future is fluid. A manager can do nothing about the past and he should look at it only to help him see how he might improve the future. So budgets should be almost wholly forward looking. They are for things that are to happen in the future.

Furthermore, only *people* can make things happen. If a *product's* costs goes over its budget, it will stay there unless some *person* cuts it in the future. If a product's cost goes over this budget, is is necessary to find out why and to trace the cause back to a department. Then the supervisor can go over the matter with the *man* in charge. It is the job of the man in charge to get the cost back in line.

Budgets, therefore, need to be plans for things which are to happen with reference to the *people* who will make them happen. This means that budgets need to cover the responsibilities of people. There should be a budget for the works manager, which should include all items over which he has charge. There should also be a budget for the plant superintendent, and there should be other budgets for each foreman and supervisor. Each man's budget should cover *his* and *only his* area of responsibility. Then the results of *his* work will be apparent when his superior reviews his performance at the end of the budget period.

But all this may still seem to be emphasizing the wrong thing. In a factory, supervisors make *products,* and they run their departments wholly for this purpose. Would it not be better, then, to set up budgets for product costs instead of for department costs? Top men can and do set up product budgets, and these budgets help subordinate department heads control the costs of the products. Yet they are *not* the real control. The real control is department budgets, not product budgets.

FIGURE 17–3. Budgetary information flow system

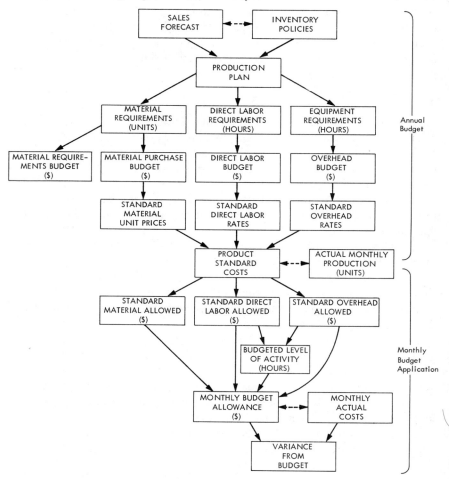

Budgets as spending limits

Budgets are sometimes only *plans* for spending but they can also be used as *authorizations*. As authorizations, they let a department head spend the budgeted amount for each item without asking permission. Actually, if work *has* to be done, a supervisor can spend more, although he will have to explain it later. But if he is spending *very much* more, he should report it right away so the man at the top will know what is going on.

Budgets that *limit expenditures* are commonly used on construction or repair jobs, research projects, and for special nonrecurring expenses. Budgets even for special projects do not, however, provide perfect control over the amount of expenditure because the costs of work, once started, cannot always be held down to the amounts originally planned. When a project uses up its budget before it is completed, it is usually better to go ahead and finish it rather than drop it and lose the money already spent. But with budgets and progress reports, managers get to decide whether or not to continue.

Sometimes managers must choose between meeting their schedule or meeting their budget. Usually, when a plant is very busy, any job that gets behind schedule can be got back on schedule only by working overtime. If the delivery date is important to the customer, it is usually better to deliver on time, even if the overtime makes the costs go over the estimate.

Budgets sometimes work in reverse as spending limits. If a department head is near the end of a period and has not used all the money available, he spends it lest he get a smaller budget next time. Otherwise, he thinks (and probably correctly) that he will have to fight to get it back. Budgets should not work this way, but sometimes they do.

Controllable and noncontrollable costs

Some of the costs of running a department are in no way controllable by its supervisor. A foreman, for example, has no control over his department's assessment of general factory overhead costs, nor is he expected (in his budget) to hold that cost down.

A foreman's controllable costs are those over which he can exercise *some control.* They include direct and indirect labor in his department, materials and supplies used, repair costs, losses from poor workmanship, accident costs, and so on. Calling these things controllable doesn't mean that his superior thinks that the foreman can get rid of them altogether but just that he can, by trying, keep them down.

The savings which are expected from using budgets come altogether from keeping controllable costs down. Budgets usually set the amount for controllable cost elements at low enough figures to require the department head to do a good job if he keeps within the budgeted figures.

Controllable costs are set apart in considerable detail—*item by item*—in each department's budget. During the budget period the records of each department's costs of operating are also kept item by item so that comparisons can be made between budgeted and actual expenditures: individually for direct labor, indirect labor, and each of the other items. Reports are made showing these comparisons, and the department heads are asked to explain all cases where actual costs exceed budgeted amounts.

Most noncontrollable costs are noncontrollable *only for minor departments.* The share of the general factory overhead assessed against a foreman's department is noncontrollable so far as he is concerned. But in the factory manager's budget, some general factory overhead items

FIGURE 17–4. Diagram of the responsibility path

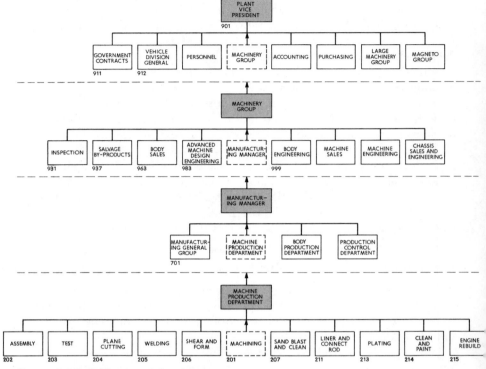

Source: American Management Association.

are controllable so far as he is concerned. The cost of the factory time-keeping department, for example, is a controllable item in the factory manager's budget. On the other hand, the charge for property taxes on the factory building is noncontrollable, even in the manager's budget. The distinction between a controllable and a noncontrollable cost hinges on whether the head of the department covered by the budget can, in any way, hold it down.

Making up budgets

Budgets or spending plans start with a look at the past. Most of the things for which money will be spent tomorrow are things for which money was also spent yesterday. So the budget setter needs to know, for yesterday, how much was spent for each item, where (in what departments) it was spent, what for, and how many products were turned out.

Next the budget setter turns to the future. What products are going to be made, so far as can be figured out, in the coming period: what products, how many of each, when, in what months? This forecast is then broken down into more detail. How many man-hours of work will be needed in each department, month by month?

The job sounds easy—the budget setter just decides how much it will cost to do this and that. But anyone who has tried to make a personal budget for a vacation knows that it is one thing to say "Make a budget," another thing to make it, and still another to live up to it.

The accounting department gets the job of making up budgets, although it alone does not decide all the figures which are set as goals. The company's overall forecast of sales is gone over by the top men of the company. After they approve it, it becomes the basis for all of the manu-

FIGURE 17-5. Monthly report of performance compared to budget and showing variances for one man's area of responsibility

RESPONSIBILITY OF
MR. FOREMAN OCTOBER AREA 201 MACHINING

	CURRENT MONTHS		AREA OR ACCT.	DESCRIPTION	YEAR TO DATE		
BUDGET	ACTUAL	UNDER OR OVER (-) BUDGET			UNDER OR OVER(-) BUDGET	ACTUAL	BUDGET
$ 3,568	$ 4,553	$ 985-	100 MANAGEMENT		$ 2,165-	$ 45,331	$ 43,166
286	285	1	110 CLERICAL		52-	1,750	1,698
3,184	3,709	525-	120 MATL HANDLING		1,691-	33,842	32,151
152	122	30	140 LOST TIME		80	955	1,035
1,943	2,023	80-	150 PROPY ATTEND		411-	19,691	19,280
	603	603-	170 SALABLE LABOR		867-	867	
1,985	2,059	74-	180 SUNDRY LABOR		420-	16,930	16,510
$ 11,118 *	$ 13,354 *	$ 2,236-*	TOTAL INDIRECT LABR		$ 5,526-*	$ 119,366	$ 113,840 *
2,815	3,729	914-	200 VACATION PAY		9,140-	37,290	28,150
2,476	2,004	472	210 HOLIDAY PAY		4,720	20,040	24,760
1,738	2,316	578-	220 FICA		5,780-	23,160	17,380
934	2,222	1,288-	230 UNEMPLOY TAX		12,880-	22,220	9,340
410	473	63-	240 WORK COMP INS		430-	4,530	4,100
1,157	1,661	504-	250 SOCIAL INSUR		4,815-	16,517	11,702
1,661	2,362	701-	260 PENSIONS		7,010-	23,620	16,610
	37	37-	270 OVERTIME PREM		85-	85	
929	1,044	115-	280 SHIFT PREMIUM		1,150-	10,440	9,290
$ 12,120 *	$ 15,848 *	$ 3,728-*	TOTAL PAYROLL COSTS		$ 36,570-*	$ 157,902 *	$ 121,332 *
1,579	805	774	300 DURABLE TOOLS		5,651	6,218	11,869
7,355	5,939	1,416	800 UTILITIES CO		14,160	59,390	73,550
200	434	234-	810 INTRAPLT TRNS		2,340-	4,340	2,000
19,705	18,372	1,333	820 MFG SERVICES		13,330	183,720	197,050
4,241	4,625	384-	830 MANPOWR SERV		3,840-	46,250	42,410
864		864	840 ENG SERVICES		5,650	3,050	8,700
7,544	6,489	1,055	850 SPECIAL SERV		10,550	64,890	75,440
$ 39,909 *	$ 35,859 *	$ 4,050 *	SERVICE CHARGES		$ 37,510 *	$ 361,640 *	$ 399,150 *
$ 9,079 *	$ 7,061 *	$ 2,018 *	UNCONTROLLABLE EXP		$ 15,175 *	$ 75,615 *	$ 90,790 *
$ 82,256 *	$ 84,192 *	$ 1,936-*	TOTAL OVERHEAD COST		$ 17,150-*	$ 835,862 *	$ 818,712 *
45,405	51,512	6,107-	10 DIRECT LABOR		49,918-	509,819	459,901
$ 127,661 *	$ 135,704 *	$ 8,043-*	TOTAL AREA COSTS		$ 67,068-*	$1,345,681 *	$1,278,613 *
20,920-		20,920-	EARN VARIANCE		171,090-		171,090-
$ 106,741 *	$ 135,704 *	$ 28,963-*	TOTAL EARNINGS		$ 238,158-*	$1,345,681 *	$1,107,523 *

(to Exh.82)

CURRENT MONTH VARIANCE ANALYSIS

LABOR				OVERHEAD		EARNINGS	
CAUSE	STANDARD	ACTUAL	VARIANCE	CAUSE	VARIANCES	CAUSE	VARIANCE
HOURS	19,321	21,735	2,414-	LABOR EFFICIENCY	$ 5,214-	PRODUCT MIX	$ 13,391-
EFFICIENCY	100 %	88.9 %	$ 5,673-	SPENDING	$ 1,260	VOLUME	$ 7,529-
RATE	$ 2.35	$ 2.37	$ 434-	UNCONTROLLABLE BUDGET	$ 2,018		

Source: American Management Association.

facturing budgets. First, there is one overall manufacturing budget showing how many of each product are expected to be turned out each period and how much is expected to be spent.

The overall budget itself, however, is a total of all the budgets for every subsidiary department's operation. Details of exactly how much to allow each department for its every expense are usually decided only after talking to its head. He is told how much production he is expected to get out and is asked, item by item, how much he will need to spend to get the work out.

One should not be misled, however. The department head is not going to set his own budget. He knows that the budget is one yardstick by which his work will be judged. If he keeps costs below the budget, his superior will say that he has done a good job. Naturally, if he set his own budget he would probably set a comfortable goal—one he can easily beat.

But why should a superior ask him if he is not going to pay any attention to what he says? Actually, the superior and the budget setter do pay some attention. The department head gets a chance to explain how volume changes will change certain costs. The amount of supervision the operators will require might, for example, stay the same for a minor volume change but would jump up if volume rose to where another supervisor would be needed. Asking a foreman about these things lets him have his say and makes him more agreeable to the budget he gets, even if it not just the way he would set it.

Budgets are usually set up for a year or more ahead and are kept that far ahead by being extended every quarter. There are also quarterly, monthly, and weekly budgets for near-future periods. It is these near-future-period budgets which are of most use in controlling costs. Longer range budgets are for longer range planning, particularly financial planning.

Flexible budgets

Changes in production volume and product mix upset budgets because schedules end up asking for (and getting) different quantities of products than those first planned for. The old budget is not likely to be a fair statement of cost expectations.

Accountants have tried to take care of this by setting up flexible budgets—budgets which vary with volume and product mix changes so that they are always fair statements of cost expectations. Actually, however, the possible combinations of changes are too great for any kind of flexible budget to cover everything.

One thing which accountants do (they call it using flexible budgets) is to set up budgets for several different levels of production (see Figure 17–6). The idea is that if the level of production changes, this automatically provides a new budget that authorizes a different amount of ex-

FIGURE 17–6. **Finishing department budget, Watson Manufacturing Company, month ————, 19——**

	Standard hours of direct labor		
	70,000	80,000	90,000
Labor cost @ $4.50 per hr...........	$315,000	$360,000	$405,000
Other variable costs...............	40,000	47,000	52,000
Semivariable costs................	21,000	22,500	24,000
Fixed costs......................	125,000	125,000	125,000
Total........................	$501,000	$554,500	$606,000

penditure. Figure 17–6 shows three budgets, one each for 70,000, 80,000, and 90,000 standard hours of work. In a real situation, of course, there could be 50 or more cost items in the budget, not just 4.

After a period is over, accountants use—when comparing actual costs with those budgeted—the budget for the level which is nearest to the actual level of production (see Figure 17–7). At the close of the period in our example, it was found that 90,000 standard hours of work were done. This means that the third column of figures in Figure 17–6 becomes the budget figures. In our example, direct labor ran $8,000 over the budget. Other variable and semivariable costs ran $2,500 under, so the total was $5,500 over the budget.

But what if the department turned out 91,000 standard hours of work, not 90,000? There is no budget prepared for that. Then what? A new budget just for that level of production could be made up (in fact it would be easy for a computer to do this), but normally this is not done. Instead, the budget for 90,000 hours is used. Obviously, the extra 1,000 standard hours of work would run up the direct labor and the variable and semivariable costs a little.

These would show on the analysis as variances (the "over" and "under" columns in Figure 17–7). Then, when the top manager looks over the variances item by item, he can, in his mind, allow a little. He knows that a little extra expense is justified. It is better to handle minor production differences this way than to go to the expense of making up whole new budgets to cover the exact quantities made.

FIGURE 17–7. **Review of finishing department operations, Watson Manufacturing Company, month ————, 19——**

	Budget	Actual	Over	Under
Direct labor, 90,000 standard hrs. @ $4.50.............	$405,000	$413,000	$8,000	...
Other variable costs.........	52,000	51,000	...	$1,000
Semivariable costs..........	24,000	22,500	...	1,500
Fixed costs................	125,000	125,000	...	...
Total.................	$606,000	$611,500	Over $5,500	

Flexible budgets are *not*, however, hazy or vague budgets. They are not freewheeling budgets. They do not allow supervisors to spend money any way they want to. Also, flexible budgets do *not* mean making new budgets every week or month. Nor do flexible budgets automatically adjust upward if a machine breaks down. That is exactly the kind of variation that *all* budgets, flexible budgets included, are intended to show up.

Budget variances

Budget variances should never go unnoticed—particularly the bad ones. Someone spent too much—why? Department heads should always have to explain—because a foreman who knows that he will have to explain variances tries not to let them happen. Variances which are justifiable will, he knows, be accepted. But other variances, such as for labor inefficiency, are often not wholly justifiable. He will have to explain these, too. He has to try to keep within the budget and so keep costs down—which is just what budgets try to get him to do.

Naturally, management's response to budget variances must be judicious. Good reasons for bad variances should be accepted, and help, rather than punitive action, should be offered.

Review questions

1. How accurately can the cost of making a product be calculated? What makes it hard to do?
2. What is a chart of accounts? How is it used in the calculations of costs?
3. Why bother with past costs? Aren't we just wasting our money on something we can't do anything about? Discuss.
4. When are job-lot costs used? What costs are included in job-lot costs?
5. Contrast job-lot costs and process costs. When would each be used? How are product costs obtained in each case?
6. Contrast standard costs and job-lot costs. When would each be used?
7. What is direct costing? Is it gaining acceptance? Why?
8. What is the difference between direct *costs* and direct *costing?*
9. What are cost elements and cost units? How are they related to each other?
10. Assume a department with a high degree of automation and not very many workers. Should such a department be charged with depreciation, interest, and taxes on the basis of labor cost?
11. Can overhead be overabsorbed? How? Is this good? Discuss.
12. A budget is a plan for spending money and getting work done, but sometimes the money gets spent although the work is only partly done. Should this happen with budgets? If it does, how does, or how can, a budget help?

13. What is a flexible budget? Why do flexible budgets exist? What good are they if they are flexible?

14. Why are budgets for people (as distinguished from budgets for products) so important?

15. List some of a foreman's controllable costs. What good does it do to classify some costs as controllable?

16. Should a department head be asked to help set his own budget? What kind of a budget would he probably set? Give reasons for your answer.

Discussion questions

1. Do variable costs actually vary with production volume? What effect does overtime pay have? How about quantity discounts?

2. The Solvay Company computes each production department's direct labor excess-cost ratio by dividing the actual cost by the standard cost of the work done. Is this a good way? Explain. Suppose that some men beat their standards and others do not; is the answer the same?

3. In a store's sales departments should overhead be allocated on the basis of sales dollars or not? Why?

4. If operations can be performed on products on any of several machines, should the cost of each operation be budgeted as if it were always to be performed on the best machine for it? If yes, is the proper answer still yes if the best machine is busy so that the work has to be done on a less well-suited machine? If the work is done in less than standard time on this machine yet still at a higher cost than that of the best machine, how should this be handled?

5. What base for allocating overhead would be appropriate for allocating:
   a) Workmen's compensation taxes?
   b) Building depreciation?
   c) Electricity?
   d) The works manager's salary?
   e) Real estate taxes?
   Give reasons for the choices made.

6. The company accountant thought that it would be simpler to lump all overheads with direct labor so far as maintenance was concerned. This produced a $30 an hour charge for maintenance work. Soon, each department began to acquire all kinds of minor repair equipment. It was cheaper to buy a new stepladder and to do one's own minor maintenance than to call in the maintenance department. Comment on this matter.

7. "Budgets," said the president, "are a waste of time. We stopped using them five years ago and have saved $20,000 a year since. We fired those pencil pushers—their budgets weren't any good anyway." You notice, as you glance out of the window, that a big addition to the plant is being built. What questions do you want to ask the president?

8. "Budgets? Cost accounting? We don't need budgets or cost accounting. We just sell products, collect bills, and pay bills. We set prices where we

have to meet competition. If we have more money at the end of the year than we started with, we know that we made money." Comment.

9. How are cost cutting programs different from budgets? Discuss.

10. To what extent might budgets cause supervisors to be too department minded at the expense of the company as a whole?

11. Trying to improve the budget every year may have disadvantages. What might they be and when would they occur?

12. Budgets are usually expected to limit expenditures. Do they ever cause money to be wasted? Explain.

13. Is it true that budgets almost always should be a little too tight because it is easier to loosen them than to tighten them?

14. Why is it thought to be a good idea to let department heads help develop budgets for their departments?

Problems

1. The following figures show certain information about products A, B, and C:

	A	B	C
Sales price per unit...............	$120	$100	$75
Raw material cost per unit.........	35	30	20
Production hours per unit..........	4	3	2

These products are all made on the same production facility and so are, in fact, alternative uses of that facility. Direct labor costs $7 per hour. All overheads, including depreciation, come to $14,000 per year.

Which product should the sales department push? How much will the best choice gain for the company as against each of the two less profitable choices?

2. Assume that the overhead cost ratio in a department is 150 percent of the labor cost based on last year's costs, when the labor bill in the department came to $1 million. Business this year is much better and labor costs for the higher business volume have come to $1.5 million. Overheads also went up to $1.8 million. Were the overheads overabsorbed or underabsorbed? By how much?

3. Company A applies overhead as 100 percent of direct labor costs; company B applies overhead at 100 percent of material cost; and company C applies overhead at 50 percent of the sum of direct labor and material.

The companies make the same products. In setting its prices, each company adds 50 percent to factory costs to cover selling and administration costs and to provide a profit.

What will the prices of each company be if direct labor costs $2 a unit and material $8 a unit? What will they be if labor is $8 a unit and material $2 a unit?

Would you expect there to be an industry problem here? How can you resolve it?

Case 17–1

"We can't make any money on that job, it has too much labor in it," says Joe Guzik, the foundry foreman, to Harry Taylor, the cost estimator for the ABC Iron Foundry. The foundry, *like its competition,* always estimated costs (on which prices for jobs were based when quoting prices on prospective orders) on a per pound basis.

Complex castings were regarded as class A castings and were quoted at a higher price per pound than more simple castings. Somewhat complex castings were class B and were quoted at a lower price per pound. Still simpler castings, class C castings, were quoted at the minimum per pound price.

In the case of the order at hand, Guzik felt that the class A price would not be high enough. It would almost surely cover all variable costs but would contribute little to carrying overheads.

Should ABC start quoting higher prices for castings requiring extra labor? What will happen if it quotes prices that fully cover all costs? Should the estimates be based on the cost of the man-hours required plus materials costs?

Recent references

Berquist, R. E., "Direct Labor vs. Machine Hour Casting," *Accounting,* May 1971

Dunbar, L. M., "Budgeting for Control," *Administrative Science Quarterly,* March 1971

Fremgen, James M., *Accounting for Managerial Analysis,* Homewood, Ill.: Richard D. Irwin, 1972

Frye, D. J., "Combined Costing Method, Absorption and Direct," *Management Accounting,* February 1971

Jones, Reginald L., and George Trentin, *Budgeting: Key to Planning and Control,* rev. ed., New York: American Management Association, 1971

Martino, R. L., *Dynamic Costing,* New York: McGraw-Hill, 1970

Shillinglaw, Gordon, *Cost Accounting,* 3d ed., Homewood, Ill.: Richard D. Irwin, 1972

Wagner, J., and L. J. Pryor, "Simulation and the Budget, an Integrated Model," *Sloan Management Review,* Winter 1971

Weiss, A., "Supervisor and the Budget," *Supervisory Management,* May-June-July 1971

section seven

Production control systems

WITHIN all operating systems it is necessary to decide what to make and who should do things in order to bring about production. Work hours must be set for departments. Allocations of machine time to orders must be made. And many directives must be prepared telling people what to do.

All of these must be coordinated if resource inputs are to be utilized economically and if the capacity of the production facilities is to be used to best advantage in turning out products or services.

There are many managerial considerations to be taken into account in controlling production. The capacities of individual machines and the work loads they can handle, the required sequencing of operations and the timing requirements, and the problems which arise in the shop from things never going quite right are examples.

Chapter 18 takes up production control from an overall viewpoint. It considers the development of master production schedules as bridges between the demand from the sales department for productive capacity and the allocation of this capacity to products. This chapter also considers how the information flow telling what is needed is translated into factory instructions so that the desired products may be produced in the desired quantity and at the desired time.

Directions to make products, however, need to be translated into terms of items to be made and operations to be performed in the factory. Chapter 19 considers the systems available for carrying out this translation and the generation of the necessary work orders for the factory. And since the production control system should be a closed loop system, the feedback flows of accomplishment information are provided for. These provide the bases for making corrections wherever necessary.

In some cases operations research techniques are helpful in assigning work to machines or men. How the simplex method and the assignment method can be used are explained in Chapter 20.

Mass production, characterized by assembly lines, allows for the elimination of certain parts of the usual production control systems. Because of the repetitive nature of the work, it is possible to cut out a great deal of the paper work required in order control systems. Chapter 21 analyzes the flow control system which applies here.

Network analyses using such systems as PERT have proved to be of great value in the production of extremely complex products and of large projects whose production takes many months. The whole productive activity is viewed as many subsystems of component activities, all of which must, in the end, tie in together as the final product is made or as the project is finished. PERT and similar network analysis systems are taken up in Chapter 22.

18

Production control concepts

PRODUCTION CONTROL is the factory's nervous system. In a very real sense, very little of a factory's work is making *products* because most products are made of *parts* and most of a factory's activities have to do with making *parts*. Until the parts are assembled there is no product, just parts. Production control tells the factory what kinds of parts to make, and how many, and when. And it tells the factory what assembled products to make, and when, and out of what parts.

But parts are not made complete in single operations. To make a chair leg, for example, it is necessary to saw, plane, sandpaper, drill holes, and

411

FIGURE 18–1. Information flows in a production planning and control system

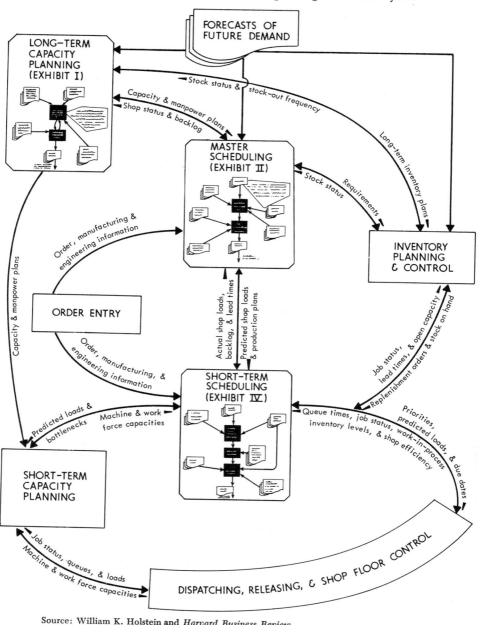

Source: William K. Holstein and *Harvard Business Review.*

do other things to a piece of wood. It ends up the right size, shape, and finish to be a chair leg but the whole change is not accomplished all at once. It is accomplished bit by bit, operation by operation. So it is in a factory. Production control does not just tell the factory to make chair legs. It gives the factory detailed directions telling the men to do certain operations to certain lots of materials. Making parts is a directed process with production control giving the directions.

Manufacturing is just as varied as the products we buy—only more so because many products are made and used that we consumers never see. (They are component parts which are hidden away, like the inside of a television set. Or else they are equipment or supply items used up in manufacturing processes.)

Production control is also very different in different companies and different industries. It takes different kinds of directions to tell the men what to make in a shoe factory, a nut and bolt factory, and an airplane factory.

The hardest production control job is in factories making assembled products out of metal parts, and the most difficult production control of all is in the airplane and spaceship industries. In no other industry is it necessary to make a quarter of a million parts, all on schedule, so that they can be put together into one product.

Production control is difficult, though, even with products simpler than airplanes. An automobile has 16,000 parts. Even a typewriter has 2,000 parts. A metal part which can be made in as few as 10 operations is a simple part. When making assembled products from metal parts, production control must direct thousands and thousands of operations.

In talking about production control we will spend most of our time on assembled metal products. No can of beans, or glass jar, or pair of shoes is as hard to make as almost any assembled metal product.

Production control functions

Although production control work is different in every situation, there are nevertheless certain activities that are common in all production control work. These include:

1. Help make master production schedules. Tell sales what promise dates are feasible for prospective customers' orders.
2. Help make plans for the men needed to meet schedules.
3. Receive orders to manufacture products.
4. "Explode" the orders for assembled products, thus determining the parts and operations needed. Issue purchase requisitions for parts to be bought.
5. Determine the raw materials requirements.
6. Determine the tools necessary for production. Issue purchase requisitions for tools to be bought.

7. Operate the raw materials stockroom and maintain the stocks. Issue purchase requisitions for the necessary materials.
8. Do original routing (determine, the first time a product is made, the operations and machines required to make products and parts).
9. Make production orders directing the performance of the operations necessary to make parts and products.
10. Make schedules for the performance of operations and the use of machines.
11. Make sure that everything needed for production will be ready.
12. Decide and assign jobs to particular men and machines.
13. Direct the transportation of materials in process.
14. Receive reports of work done and compare them with that scheduled. Keep up-to-date records of progress of jobs through the plant.
15. Help remove reasons for delays in production.
16. Remake plans when original plans are not carried out and when there are changes in the size of an order or its wanted completion date.
17. Operate the finished parts stockroom and control the stock of parts.
18. Operate the finished products stockroom and control the stock of finished products.
19. Answer inquiries concerning the progress of orders in process.
20. Help make cost estimates for prospective new orders.

Most of these basic functions are assigned to the production control department in most companies but, sometimes a few of them are assigned to other departments. Sometimes also, one or more nonproduction control duties, such as operating the plant's mail service or the tool storeroom, or setting time standards for incentive purposes, are assigned to the production control department.

There might appear to be one important omission in this list: Only numbers 2 and 12 mention men. Production control has very little to do with manning the factory. In some companies production control figures out how many men the factory will need, and in some companies it assigns work to men, but it is the foreman's and the personnel department's job to provide men. Except during extremely high levels of production, production control does most of its work just as if it could count on there being men to do the jobs.

Terms

If only industry would settle on words and definitions, it would be easier to talk about production control. But industry is not consistent in its use of terms, so we have to do with terms as custom has set them and this means that we cannot set exact definitions.

For example, the name of the main department doing most of the production control work may be the "production department," "produc-duction control department," "production planning department," "production planning and control department," or some similar title. In metal working industries, more companies probably use "production department" than any other term. This means that the "production" department is *not* a factory department working on the product. It is the department which makes and issues directives to the factory and controls production.

Various parts of production control work also have different names in different companies. A list of parts for an assembled product may be called a "bill of materials," a "materals list," a "parts list," or a "requirements list." A list of operations for making a part may be a "route sheet," a "process sheet," a "layout," or an "operation list." "Scheduling" may mean: (1) setting wanted dates for the completion of *orders,* (2) setting wanted dates for the completion of individual *operations,* (3) setting specific *starting* and *stopping* times for operation performances, or (4) making up lists of jobs needing certain machines. There is no part of production control where words mean the same everywhere. The student should know that this is so and not be confused when, out on the job, he runs into usages that are different from what he has learned.

The production control department

Production control is usually headed by a production control manager who reports to the plant manager.

In middle-size companies the production control department may be told to do all the things in our list of functions (above). In small companies some jobs, such as forecasting manpower needs, are not done at all. At the other extreme, giant companies separate some of the work, particularly raw materials control, and take it away from production control. Original routing, or deciding how things are to be made, also is often done by production engineering, not production control.

Also, production control's work in continuous production differs from its work in job-lot manufacturing. In continuous manufacture, production control's work is to keep production inside the plant flowing, to see that the *rates* of *making* and *using* items match up, and that is about all it does. Its work is still very important, but there is only a fraction as much paper work and plant directives as in job-lot work.

The point is that *how* the department is set up depends on the work it is given to do. And although the things given to a production control department to administer depend in part on the kind of manufacture, they also depend on the managers' views. Some companies say: "Engineering *designs* the products; production control (with the help of the factory) decides how to make them." Others say: "The engineers design the product and also specify how to make it."

Also, there is the matter of who tells the man in the shop what job to work on next. Production control does this in some companies, but in others it just sets the dates by which jobs are to be done and the foreman assigns jobs to his men.

Inside the production control department there is a fairly common pattern: Almost always there are two main divisions. One, often called the planning department, handles all the way-ahead details. It takes schedules for weeks and months ahead and figures out the parts, materials, and even the tools needed. Then it checks to see what is already on hand or on order and makes out orders for whatever will be needed.

The other main division of production control deals with the near future and the here and now. Often called the scheduling department, it makes up the factory orders to do work and it sets the time by which things are to be done. It also keeps track of what is done and, whenever things do not go right, keeps after them and tries to see that production comes out on schedule.

FIGURE 18–2. Relationship of planning and scheduling subdepartments of the production control department

Production control department	
Planning department	*Scheduling department*
Capacity calculations	Shop order making
Overall manning require-	Shop loads
ments	Order release to factory
Distant-future schedule	departments
construction	Order priorities
Procurement of tooling	Progress reports
Procurement of long lead-	Expediters
time raw materials	Shortages and delays
Drawings, specifications	Rework and makeup
and inspection instruc-	orders
tions, and equipment	Internal transportation
	Order closing

Curiously, this scheduling section of production control is sometimes called the production control department. This does not happen, of course, if the whole department is called by that name. This terminology is common, however, in companies which call the main department the "production department."

Original authority to make products

Among the objectives of production control is never to have the factory make anything which *can't* be sold, yet to make as many of everything as *can* be sold. This means that *all* production needs to be authorized. The factory should not make anything without an authorization.

Production control gives the factory its authorizations, but almost never does production control itself decide what the factory should make. Production control, in turn, has to get authorizations.

But from whom? Someone, somewhere, has to start things. Generally, production control gets its orders in the form of a master schedule covering the next several months. Sometimes master schedules are made by a master scheduling department. But both production control and sales participate in the schedule making.

Master schedules: Manufacture to order. When products are made to customers' orders, the job of master schedule making is largely one of looking at the factory's future work load of orders already on hand and seeing when the customers want their orders and when new order deliveries can be promised. This means that the schedulers must know approximately how many man-hours (or tons) of work the orders already on hand will amount to in each major department. This reveals how soon there will be some open capacity in each department. Then, for the orders that the sales department is bidding on, estimates need to be made concerning how much capacity they will need department by department.

It is necessary to pay attention to the sequence of work loads in different departments. If an item has first to be designed, then the engineering work load will have to come early. Capacity will be needed in the foundry or forge or sheet metal shop later on, and still later in the machine shop, and so on. Unless the work loads needed in the early-stage departments can be handled early, work in later-stage departments will be delayed even if they have open time earlier. After all of this checking, a promise date can be given. If the order is obtained, its work load is added in for the appropriate departments and times.

Production control's authority to tell the factory to go ahead comes from *sales orders,* not from the master schedule itself. The master schedule, in this case, is only a summation, at the end of each month, of the booked but unfinished jobs for future months. It extends as far ahead as the last delivery date on the last order already on hand. And it shows, month by month, the orders that will be finished and shipped.

In this kind of master schedule making the production control department takes an active part in setting the schedule. Often, when manufacture is to order, there is no other master scheduling department.

Making to order is not without its headaches so far as schedules are concerned. Sometimes, as in job bidding, tentative promise dates are made on several possible contracts, although only one contract is expected. All of these promises are predicated on using the same open time, but this makes trouble if several of the orders are obtained. Another problem arises when a promise date is offered and the customer places the order but wants delivery sooner. Also, there are cancellations, or the factory may not get things done on time, or customers may dally overlong about signing the contract and then still want the factory to make good on the original promises about delivery.

When sales are tied directly to customers' orders, a copy of the sales order (or an abstract of it) is production control's authority to prepare the factory directives and see that the products are made. One important exception occurs where the sales order is a blanket order (usually from another manufacturer or a chain store or mail order company) for a large quantity of a product to be delivered in frequent small shipments as directed by the customer's production control department. Such orders constitute a large part of many manufacturers' business. In this situation new releases of authority to make more products come from the various customers and not from anyone inside the company. Separate releases will come from each customer, and they will come at different times.

The production control department in these companies gets many authorizations from many sources and at different times, instead of a long list of products every week or month. Similarly, in manufacturing directly to sales orders the orders probably come to production control day by day as they are received rather than all at one time, but in this case they come to production control from the sales department and not directly from the customer.

Master schedules: Making to stock. Makers of almost all consumers' products—the things you and I buy—manufacture to stock. Products are made and put into finished goods inventory. Then, as they are sold, they are withdrawn from stock. But when they are being made they have not been sold and no one knows who will buy them. Companies making to stock must try to forecast what and how many of everything their custom-

FIGURE 18–3. Proposed allocation of factory capacity to varying quantities of several main products

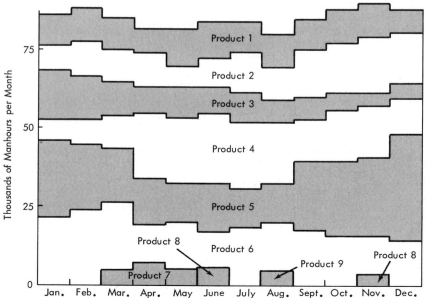

ers are going to buy and then make those things in those quantities. This kind of forecasting will be discussed on page 605 along with inventory control.

The schedule making starts with a sales forecast, but, as we said in Chapter 6 when discussing capacity, the sales forecast will nearly always have too many ups and downs to allow its use directly as a production schedule. The peaks and valleys need some leveling out. This can be done by building up inventories sometimes and cutting them down at other times. Also, there is need, as in the case of automobile tires, to forecast the product mix pretty closely because some of the factory's equipment is special for certain tire sizes. After some juggling, a master schedule is developed.

Production control takes part in the juggling before the schedule is made, and it has to figure out whether the factory can handle the tentative schedule and how the ups and downs will work. Will there be enough machines? How about factory men—will more be needed? Or will some have to be laid off? These and other questions production control must answer.

After getting the answers it shifts the schedule around and gets one that suits both sales and the factory as well as possible. In this process the production control department helps set the master schedule, which becomes its authority to produce.

Production programs.   Many companies make things which can be made complete in a very short time (hours or days), but these are made out of materials which take more time to get. Such companies work from production programs, or lists of general classes of products to make. And because of the high volume (as in automobile upholstery fabrics and automobile tires), they use so much material that they have to plan for and order materials months ahead of time.

Production programs differ from other master schedules, though, in that an approved program does *not* give production control authority to do anything. It gets its authority to go ahead in the form of weekly "releases" against the program. The releases are decided by the finished products inventory control group, which is closely associated with the sales department.

The factory's production control department gets the releases only two or three weeks before the products are wanted. This method, therefore, can work only when the manufacturing cycle is short. However, it gives the factory considerable flexibility to shift from one product to another (as from one tire size to another, or, in a shoe factory, from one size or style of shoe to another) and to follow market trends. It requires only that the total volume forecast be reasonably accurate and that the factory's machines be flexible enough to handle normal variations in the product mix.

The total volume forecast has to be reasonably accurate because raw materials come in on a schedule to meet this volume. With production program releases, production control has *nothing* to do with getting raw materials. Materials control, a separate department, controls the raw materials stockroom. Materials control orders materials on the authority of the *program,* not from the weekly releases. Production control has no concern about there being raw materials when it gets a weekly production release. The materials are supposed to be there.

Master schedules: The time period.   Master schedules may cover production for a year ahead, and they need to if it takes a long time to make products. Not many things, though, need a year's lead time for manufacturing.

But *forecasts,* on which master schedules are based, need to extend a year or more ahead most of the time—particularly when a company makes annual models. Forecasting a long way ahead is necessary so that decisions can be made about how much mechanization (the "depth" of tooling) to go in for. Big volume will make heavy mechanization pay off well. But all of the new machines have to be determined and installed at the start of the model year.

Companies making annual models forecast the whole year's sales to help them decide on mechanization. But they do not make actual production schedules nearly so far ahead. Mostly, they use production programs and releases. Only the releases authorize production.

Some companies (makers of machinery, locomotives, etc.) make long lead-time items and take months to make their products. Companies in such businesses have to have master schedules that actually authorize production months ahead. They need to be far ahead, not only because the products take a long time to make but because raw materials control is likely to be production control's job too. The production control department has to know what products are going to be made at least six months ahead in order to figure what materials to get. Then it has to order the materials and, when they arrive, start making the parts.

There are two different kinds of way-ahead master schedules. One kind always covers the next five or six months. When one month ends, the sixth month ahead is added. That is the way General Motors does it in its Electro-Motive Division, which makes diesel locomotives.

The other way goes more in jumps: Six months at a time are added. In February a schedule is set up clear through December, but it is not extended any farther in March or April. Then, in August, a schedule is isued for a whole six months, January to June, of the next year. Then nothing more until February, and so on. The Cincinnati Milicron Company does it this way and so do many other machinery makers.

Why the difference? It is a matter of volume and standardization. The first method (where one future month is added every month) should be used wherever there are not many kinds of products and where at least a few of them are on every schedule. They are being made all the time. But when the products are more varied, the second method (six months at a time) is likely to be better.

The second method is better because it is desirable to make some products in lots. Suppose that one kind of machine sells 12 units a year. Making them at a rate of 1 per month sounds good until we think of making the parts. How will they be made? It would be possible to make enough parts in January for all 12 units and keep them in bins, some until December. It is also possible to set up machinery to make the parts for 1 product in January, and then do it again in February, and so on every month, or 12 times.

It would almost certainly be wasteful to make parts for 1 machine at a time. Surely it would be less costly to make parts for, say, 6 machines at a time and then 1 lot of 6 could be assembled in March and another lot of 6 in September. This would allow for manufacturing at a reasonable cost and would also allow customers to be given good service. A customer who orders in January or February can be told to wait until March, but a March customer gets his machine right away. Then the other 3 machines can go into stock, but they won't stay there long. They will be gone before July.

But, one may ask, why can't this be done just by adding 1 month at a time to the schedule? Why is it better to move the schedule forward several months at a time? It is because some products will be made (assembled) over a 2- or 3-month period rather than over 1 month.

Here is the trouble. Suppose that at the end of February the schedulers "firm up" July's assembly schedule and add it to March–June. In July, let us say, 10 units of product X appear on the schedule (having been off the schedule for a while). It is necessary to order the material right away and start making long lead-time parts.

At the end of March, August is added. August's schedule has 10 more product Xs on it. And later, when September is added, 10 more product Xs turn up on that schedule. The difficulty with this kind of schedule is that the factory's production controllers find out about the parts requirements a little at a time. And in March, on the long lead-time items, they ordered parts in lots with quantities to suit July's assemblies. Had they known about August and September, they could have made some of the parts orders in big enough quantities to take care of them all—and at much lower costs. In April and May it is too late to boost the lot sizes of the parts orders for July's products because they are halfway through production.

But what if the parts can be made in a short time? It does not take months to make *every* part. What has just been said does not apply to short lead-time items. For them, July's parts won't be started until June anyway. By that time the schedulers know all about August and September and can increase the lot quantities to cover them all if they want to. This whole matter of scheduling far ahead is to take care of *long lead-time items.*

Master schedules: Classes of products.   Some companies make thousands of kinds of products, very few of which (by themselves) amount to much in dollars. Companies making plumbing fittings, pipe connections, tees, ells, and so on, or nuts and bolts, or even medicines of hundreds of kinds and in all sizes of packages, are like this.

Some companies that make thousands of items use approved master schedules only for whole classes or groups of products. Their quantities are shown in dollars, tons, pounds, gallons, or some other unit common to all items in the class. Their planned inventories are shown only in terms of classes of products.

It is up to production control to decide when to make the individual items and how many to make. Production control has to try to meet the planned overall inventory size and keep the factory working as planned, and it must try not to run out of any items. Production control sets its own finished products schedule. To do this, of course, it must have charge of the finished goods inventory and the records, item by item, of past manufacture and sales.

Master schedules: Basic components.   Complex products are often made in considerable variety for example, factory machines such as lathes, grinders, and drill presses. Yet this variety is often in the form of accessories or sets of components. The components themselves are (or can be) the same for nearly all kinds of finished products.

In Chapter 25 these standardized components are called "basics" and it is noted that they can be made on schedules of their own which are not directly tied in with the schedules of any particular kind of finished product. Storage batteries and automobile carburetors are examples of basics. And 8-cylinder motors for automobiles can be made without regard for the product mix between convertibles, station wagons, and 2- or 4-door cars. As they are finished they are assigned to specific finished products.

This idea can be carried even further because basics do not even have to be assembled components. They can be sets of parts which attach individually to finished products. Using the basics idea uncouples the manufacture of such items from assembly schedules and allows for more economical production.

Parts

Production control's authority to make things almost always comes as orders or schedules for whole products. In highly repetitive manufacture, production control does not have to concern itself with bought items, whether they are raw materials or bought finished parts or components.

But production control has to see to the making of all made parts. Authority to make parts is always covered by the authorization to make finished products. Production control has to figure out what parts will have to be made, how many, and when. In fact, for some general-use parts (like nuts and bolt) production control does not even have to pay much attention to assembly orders. When such parts (the B and C items referred to in Chapter 24) get low, production control just orders more of them. It doesn't bother calculating how many of them the schedule will call for. Nor does it need any direct authorization to order more.

But with more varied end products with varied parts, it is different. Here the production control department figures the parts needed for the assembled products already scheduled and orders just the right number. ("Just the right number," of course, means ordering enough extra to allow for the normal number of rejects during production.)

Service parts or spares

Customers sometimes need repair parts. For wearing parts, such as bearings or cutting tools, the sale of extra parts for repair purposes is big business. Even nonwearing parts (automobile fenders) also get banged up and need replacement.

The need for service parts means that more parts should be made than will be needed for the end products being assembled. Past experience will show about how many extra parts of each kind to make. Sales and production control together work out the numbers. There is even need to make a few extra parts right away so service can be given to customers with new products which for some reason need a new part or who want a spare part or two in reserve.

It is also necessary to keep on making some parts long after the main product is out of production. Someone, somewhere, is still using a 50-year-old product and now and then wants a repair part. Hunting up the old blueprints and the old tooling and making one or two of a part is a real headache to production control, but it has to be done sometimes. Computers can usually find the old blueprints and drawings rather quickly, but old tooling often makes problems. It is lost, or rusty, or has been partially dismantled, or it fits machines no longer in existence. It may be necessary to make repair parts for long since discontinued products on a custom basis, possibly in the maintenance department's machine shop.

Capacity in schedule making

We said (p. 419) that master schedules and production programs try to level out sales peaks and valleys. Actually, however, not very much of this is done because it costs so much to carry inventories. Also, seasonal peaks and valleys are all mixed up with business getting better or worse, with one company getting more or less of the market, and with some products selling well (better than expected) and others lagging behind.

Production controllers end up having to be fast on their feet and doing a lot of adjusting up and down as they go along. They may adjust the capacity by changing work hours, or the number of work shifts, or the number of work days, or the number of men.

Often, too, more permanent changes are made, particularly on the expansion side. If business picks up and can't be handled with the present machines, more machines are bought or else more items are bought outside. An addition to the present factory can be built or a new plant can be built somewhere else. Production control's part in such decisions is to tell management whether or not the factory can handle a proposed schedule and to tell the top men how many ups and downs there will be in work hours. Then the top managers can decide if they want to get more equipment or just how they want the final schedule to be set up.

Regardless of the method by which production control gets the authority to make products, as schedules are being made some kind of check on the overall quantities should be set up. The factory's normal capacity is usually relatively fixed. It can be expressed, for control purposes, in terms of the number of tons, the dollar value of products, or other appropriate measures that can be produced in a period of time. The capacity requirements of the orders sent to the production control department should be in accord with the plant's capacity to produce.

In the last analysis, however, the orders sent to production control depend upon sales, and sales are not wholly related to the company's capacity nor to its desire to operate steadily. If the orders require less than the plant's capacity, it will be necessary to go on short hours. If orders exceed present capacity, some orders must be delayed or the capacity expanded, or else more things will have to be bought outside.

Within reasonable limits, however, steady operations override other considerations. If the backlog of orders begins to build up a little, the sales department gives new customers more distant promise dates. But if backlogs build up *very* much, most companies would choose to expand capacity because they don't want to lose customers. And, conversely, if the backlog shrinks, capacity is not cut at first. Instead, new customers get earlier promise dates on their orders. If it shrinks some more, operations will be curtailed.

Producing authority

The factory gets its authority to make products from the production control department. Nearly always, production control tells the factory four things: (1) what to make, (2) how many, (3) when, and (4) how.

The first three give the factory "producing" authority to go ahead and make products. The fourth gives the factory "processing" authority.

Producing authority tells the factory (1) to assemble parts into finished products, (2) to make individual piece products (as a casting sold as such), (3) to make individual piece parts, or (4) to process bulk materials (liquids, powders) and pack them into big and little packages.

Assembly orders tell the factory's assembly department what finished products to make, and how many, and give a list of the subassemblies and parts needed for each assembly order. The manufacture of parts and individual-piece products, however, requires more detailed producing directives. In most companies *every operation* done on parts and integral products must be separately planned for and *individually authorized.*

Producing authority is one-time authority. When the factory finishes what it has been authorized to do, it needs more directions. New producing authorizations have to be issued all the time. And although we call it "authority," the factory has no discretion. Production control's directions are also *orders.* This "authority," then, tells the factory to make the products the schedules call for, and not something else. And the factory must try to "hit" the quantity ordered (not go very far over or under) and it must try to get things done on schedule.

Processing authority

Processing authority is the *how* in making products, which little companies leave to the foreman. They let the engineers figure out the product's shape, size, and materials but let the factory figure out how to make it. There is no visible evidence of processing authority in small companies because the foreman has it.

But, in big companies, leaving it up to the foreman leaves too many things to chance. Engineers design parts and products, then other engineers decide how to make them. Some of these men are called product engineers, and sometimes they work in the production control department. Industrial engineers and methods men also help decide how workers are to perform operations—not only in parts making but also in assembly.

Production control is much concerned with processing authority in the big in-between area—things made neither in ones and twos nor in millions. But even in this in-between area production control is more likely to be a forwarding agent than an originator of producing authority.

Engineering puts out "master bills of material" (lists of subassemblies and parts) for assembled products. And it puts out, for each part, a "master route sheet" showing the operations needed to make it. Production control gets both of these masters, both "bills" and route sheets.

When production control gets an order to make a certain number of products it makes out individual bills and, for the parts, individual route sheets. Both are actually orders for the factory to go to work. Both tell the factory what to make and so constitute producing authority. We call the orders to assemble "order bills" and the orders to make parts "shop orders."

Order bills differ from master bills by showing what is wanted *this time*. If the order is for 50 products, the quantities of all the items on the master bill are multiplied by 50 (it shows how many of every part is needed for 1 product). Also, the order number is put on (its identification) and the schedule (dates by which the products are to be made). Copies of order bills go to the assembly department, the finished-parts stockroom, and wherever else they are needed.

An order bill is therefore both a producing as well as one kind of processing authority. If it were only a list of parts, it would be only producing authority. But the listing of parts can be so arranged as to indicate the order in which the parts are to be assembled. Arranged this way, it would be a kind of processing instruction. If other assembling instructions are needed, they would come from the engineering department.

The order bill also shows which items go together first into subassemblies rather than directly into the product as piece parts. Engineering usually decides this, but in some companies production control can switch things around. It is not always possible to tell, on a drawing board, which way is best. Should, for example, an automobile door lock be assembled first and then put into the car door, after which the door goes into the body, and finally the body be put onto the chassis? Or should the door be put on the body and then the lock assembled to the door? Sometimes such questions can be decided better after people see how things go in the shop.

Shop orders are more directly processing authority. Their list of operations tells the factory just how to make an item. Figure 18–4, a

FIGURE 18–4. A shop order (all the information, except the order number, quantity, processing times, and start dates, comes from the master route sheet)

ROUTING SHEET

| PART NAME | | PART NO. 8 6 3 8 P | | NO. OF SHEETS 1 | |
| DATE 1 0/2 0 | DATE DUE 1/2 0 | ORDER NO. 1 6 2 4 | | ORDER QUANTITY 2 0 0 | |

OPER.	OPERATION DESCRIPTION	MACH. CENTER	TOOL NUMBER	ITGENT	PROCESSING TIME	START DATE	DEPT.
	CR STEEL SAFE 1020						
10	CLEAN	1		1	320	572	25
20	PAINT	2		3	100	581	25
30	FACE SHORT HUB SWEEP 1 IN DIA FORM HAND GRIP	30	3687	2	334	584	34
40	FACE FIN TURN AND RAD HUB FORM RAD ON GRIP CTR DR AND REAM	30	6211	7	306	594	34
50	DR AND REAM	21		5	86	587	31
80	BROACH	53	6329	8	180	603	33
90	BURR	3		9	160	608	33
110	POLISH	47		4	60	610	33
120	INSPECT	4					44

Source: Sperry Rand Corporation.

shop order, shows such a list of operations. Shop orders tell operators what to do, but their descriptions of operations are so brief (the words "clean," "paint," "broach," and so on are operations) that the factory does not get very much instruction. Of course an engineering drawing goes along with the shop order, so there *are* more instructions.

The right-hand columns in Figure 18–4 show how much time each operation will take in turning out the full order of 200 items. Cleaning will take 32 hours, painting 10 hours, and so on. The *start date* column may be confusing because this company is using a "1,000-day calendar" and cleaning is to start on day 572, painting on day 581. With 1,000-day calendars, every workday (for four years ahead) is given a consecutive number. These numbers are used on all work schedules instead of regular dates. Everyone in the company also has a regular calendar with the equivalent day-number printed in. Outside purchase orders use regular calendar dates.

Master bills of materials and master route sheets confer *continuing* processing authority on the production control department. They can be used again and again for repeat orders for the same product.

Shop instructions

In some companies the engineering department designs the product and the shop decides how to make it. This is not only small-company practice but also the way some giant companies do it. The manufacturing department's production engineers figure out how to make products. They can even redesign parts in minor ways to suit manufacturing needs. They can also change the way parts are put into subassemblies. The production engineers also can decide whether to make or buy some items.

But no matter who decides how to do the work, engineering makes up drawings and master bills of materials (parts lists). Master bills show subassembly arrangements, parts names, identification numbers, how many of each part is needed to make one assembled product, and whether the item normally is made or bought.

A master bill of materials for an entire product lists subassemblies as if they were individual parts. Each subassembly, in turn, has its own master bill of materials. If the subassembly is composed, in part, of lesser subassemblies, each of them has its own master bill.

The production control department, as we said, uses these master bills in making up production orders. Items on the bill may be listed in order of part number, in order of assembly, or in order of the arrangement of the finished-goods stockroom. Ordinarily, the master bills sent out by the engineering department are arranged in tentative order of assembly. Engineering also issues master route sheets for individual parts. Master route sheets (also known as process layouts or operation lists) list the operations necessary to make a part, the sequence of operations, the kind of machine required for each operation, the special tools called for (if any), and the amount of time each operation takes on one unit of product. They may even show the operation's piece rate and the worker's labor classification. They also show the kind of raw material needed and, usually, how much of it is required to make one part.

In some companies everything having to do with getting production started is turned over to a product engineer. He will have the final say on how things are made. He may even have to choose the machines, order their purchase, decide the layout, supervise machine installation, and stay with the job until production is going smoothly. The product engineer will, of course, have had to decide on all of the tools needed and order them. He also has the last word on materials to use, but production control probably places the orders for materials.

Manufacturing instructions are incomplete without instructions concerning the tests the items need to pass. Engineering must write up instructions about how tests are to be carried out and how the inspectors can tell good and bad parts apart. Often, special testing equipment has to be bought (or developed) for particular tests. Inspectors need to be trained in their use. Also, procedures need to be set up for reporting test results back to engineering so that it can keep informed about the quality of work done by manufacturing.

Engineering also has to provide sales with information about the product, how to use it, and how to service it so that sales can make up manuals and parts catalogs for customers. Engineering also furnishes information, and sometimes pictures, for advertising.

Most factory workers do about the same thing every day, so that there is no problem of shop instructions. Drawings are normally quite sufficient. Sometimes, though, particularly on tricky assembly jobs and jobs with many wires to fasten, more is needed. Sometimes a man's assignment covers a half hour or more of work and includes a hundred or more little things that he has to do.

Here he needs very careful instructions on the whole set of things he has to do when he first does the job. And he may need occasional instruction later, too, if he forgets or if something goes wrong. Tape recordings and colored slides help in such cases. Hughes Aircraft has used such an arrangement for a long time. Hughes reports production gains of more than 50 percent, and inspection and supervision costs were reduced 75 percent when this kind of instruction was first put in.

The assembler can also be supplied with a tape telling him what to do step by step. He can turn it on any time he forgets. Collins Radio has developed a sound-track moving picture projector with a 6-inch screen to serve this same purpose. The operator can turn it on and see and hear how to do his job. General Electric uses closed-circuit TV to flash pictures or drawings to the drafting, assembly planning, and assembly areas. Users can even control a zoom lens from their viewing station if they want a close-up.

All of these methods for passing out instructions are big improvements over less thorough methods used in the past, but they are costly and so will not pay off everywhere.

Cost estimating

Before any product is made it is highly important to estimate its cost. Production control does not make cost estimates very often but it works with engineering, accounting, and sales as they make estimates.

In job-lot manufacturing, where most manufacturing is to customer's order, cost estimating is very important because the prices quoted to customers are based on the expected cost of producing the orders. Competition for orders is generally keen enough that a company will not get very much business if it quotes prices much above its costs. At the same time, no one wants to quote such low prices that he gets the business but loses money on it.

In cost estimating the attempt is to do cost accounting in advance, so it is necessary to figure the expected costs of materials, labor, overhead, and extras. Calculating these ahead of time is considerable work—almost as much, in fact, as would have to be done if a company already had the order and was planing its production. For assembled products this work needs, first, a parts list; second, decisions on the kind and quality of raw material required for each part; third, figuring out, for each part, the operations needed and the special tooling required (if any) for every operation; and fourth, the cost estimates of all these materials, operations, tools, and extras. Assembly costs, too, need to be estimated. All of these costs are then added up and the overhead added in to get the cost estimate.

Job-lot shops have to bid for many orders that they don't get, which makes it necessary to hold down the cost of making estimates. Customers often ask several companies to submit bids, but only one gets the job. Some job-lot shops have to bid on five to ten or more jobs for every one they get. Often they can't afford to go through all this work in making their estimates. They just have to use short-cut estimating methods even though this sacrifices some accuracy.

Here are some short cuts. From past jobs they get the cost per pound or per ton of the job and use that figure on new jobs. How much will a new job weigh? Multiply by the old cost per pound and the estimators have a rough cost estimate. Or, on sheet metal jobs, how much per square foot of metal used have past jobs cost? How many square feet will the new job take? Multiply and get a cost estimate. House builders figure the cost per square foot of floor space, or even per cubic foot, in houses they build. With these figures in mind they can look at plans for a new house and guess rather closely what it will cost to build.

Rough estimates do not necessarily lose money. Some will be a little low and the company may lose money on them, but others will be a little high and it will make extra on them. But will it average out? It is not certain that it will. Smart customers will give a company all the jobs where it is low and give its competitor all the jobs where the competitor is low. Companies typically do not get many of the jobs when they are high. They need to make their estimates as carefully and accurately as they can afford to.

Cost estimates on big jobs, even if carefully worked out, are often just starting points for more talks. The customer may want lower figures, so he will let the bidder cut a corner here and there. Maybe this will produce a lower figure. Customers are sometimes quite demanding, however, and insist upon "value analysis." Buyers often tell vendors what *their* estimators say the vendor's costs ought to be and so insist on getting their price near that figure—but without any further design changes.

FIGURE 18–5.   Cost estimate summary

COST ESTIMATE SUMMARY

DIVISION _____

Date Completed

Customer's Name _____

Customer's Part No. _____ Part Name _____
Date Required _____ Delivery Promised _____

Customer Quantity Requirements _____
Total Quantity this Order _____ Tool Design Flow Time _____ Tool Design $ _____
Quantity for Tool Recovery _____ Tool Mfg. Flow Time _____ Tool Mfg. $ _____
Quantity per Set-Up _____ Production Flow Time _____ Tool Purch's. $ _____
Material - Purchased ( ) Furnished ( )   TOTAL FLOW TIME _____ TOTAL $ _____
MATERIAL _____ Add ____% _____
_____ TOTAL TOOL $ _____

No.	DEPARTMENT NAME	STD. D.P.L. Hrs. PER 100	STD. D.P.L. $ PER 100	DEPT. COST PER 100 PCS.	SET-UP HRS.	SET-UP COST	SET-UP CHARGE SUMMARY
301	Automatics						Set-Up Cost (without Scrap) _____
302	Turret Lathes						____ Pcs. Set-Up Scrap - Mat'l. _____
303	Milling Etc.						____ Pcs. Set-Up Scrap - ½ Labor _____
304	Drill Presses						SUB - TOTAL _____
305	Surface Grinding						Add ____% G and A, Div. Adm. _____
306	Cylinder Grinding						
307	Bench Work						TOTAL _____
308	Punch Presses						
309	Comp. Machining						
310	Assembly						
311	Flex. Rotor Pump						COST ESTIMATE SUMMARY
312							Manufacturing Cost /100 _____
313	Nene Machining						Add ____% G and A, Div. Adm. _____
314	Inspection						SUB - TOTAL _____
315	Packaging						Royalties _____
316	Pre-Production						_____
319	Hydraulic Coupling						_____
320	Comp. Mach'g. Exp.						_____
321	Tumbling						SUB - TOTAL _____
122	Rubber Lab.						Profit ____% _____
323	Repairs						
324	Heat Treat-Plating						
	TOTALS						SALES PRICE _____

Add ____% Variance _____   QUOTATIONS TO CUSTOMER:
Add Material Cost per 100 _____   Date _____ _____
Add ____% Scrap Allowance _____   Price per ____ Pieces $ _____ $ _____
         SUB - TOTAL _____   Separate Tooling Charge _____ _____
Add Tooling Recovery per 100 _____   Set - Up Charge _____ _____
Manufacturing Cost (without Set-up _____
Notes on Quotation _____

Source: TRW, Inc.

Vendors, of course, try to whittle costs all they can to meet the figure. But if business is bad or if the contract is big, a vendor may just cut his price and take the contract even at a slight loss. If he gets the contract he may recover his overhead, or most of it. Besides, as he keeps making products to fill the contract his people will probably figure out ways to save a little here and there. Also, a vendor can ask the customer to send his estimators to his plant to tell his men how they figure he can make the product at such a low cost.

Cost estimates should always be tied in with volume. Volume lets a company use greater depth of tooling (more mechanization). But for little orders a company can afford to sink only small amounts in special tooling, so its costs will never be very low. The point is that costs and bid prices depend on how many products the customer wants to buy. A bidder needs to know this before he can quote a price.

Sometimes, however, companies make products to stock and not to customers' orders. It would seem, therefore, that such companies would not need to estimate costs. And sometimes it is true: they can avoid making estimates. If a company makes thousands of items and is thinking about making another item whch requires no new machines, it is almost as simple just to make some of the new items and see what they cost.

Seldom, however, can make-to-stock companies escape estimating so easily. In fact, cost estimating for stock items is *very* important on high-volume products. It ties in with good market forecasting of prices and sales volumes and with depth of tooling. A company which knows its future volume and its selling price can choose the right depth of tooling and so get the lowest possible cost for that volume.

The production control department plays only a minor part in all this. And then only in job shops and only on rush jobs. Quick deliveries are sometimes possible only if some of the work is done on overtime or on poorly suited machines (because the best-suited machines are busy). These things affect costs, so production control is sometimes in on cost estimating.

Review questions

1. When manufacturing to order, and when business is good, the master schedule allocates the plant's capacity to existing orders for some time ahead. Under what circumstances would still more orders be added to current loads rather than as further extensions of capacity allocations into the more distant future?

2. When the company manufacturers to sales orders, how does the production control department get authority to make parts?

3. When using production programs, how does the production control department get its authority to issue orders to the factory to go ahead and produce?

4. Contrast the use of master schedules in production control work when manufacture is to order and the use of master schedules when manufacture is to stock.

5. Why are some master schedules extended another month ahead, continually, as months go by whereas in other companies future schedules are pushed ahead six months at a time?

6. When should master schedules be stated in terms of classes of products instead of in terms on numbers of specific products?

7. How does the idea of using "basics" and scheduling their production independently from final assembly help in schedule making?

8. Is a shop order for a certain lot of parts an example of producing authority or processing authority? Where does it come from? Explain.

9. What is processing authority? Where does it come from?

10. How accurately should a company try to estimate costs before it makes products? Why not more accuracy or less accuracy?

Discussion questions

1. The factory needs to keep operating in order to keep costs down. Is it therefore so bad for it, sometimes, to go ahead and produce unauthorized production? Presumably this excess production would be for products known to be reordered frequently. Discuss.

2. In the women's clothing industry dress manufacturers cut cloth for exactly the number of dresses ordered. Then any faulty dresses which can't be repaired become shortages on the order to the customer (and are not replaced).

   Isn't this a good practice for all companies to use? What problems would it make in the dress industry? In other industries?

3. Is production control or time study a better place for a young man to learn how a factory operates? Why?

4. Where does the production control department get all of the information it needs, and what kinds of information does it need? To what departments does production control issue orders, and how does it go about getting goods produced? How does it get everything to come out on time at the shipping dock?

5. The lead times for special orders are one month. Yet, under pressure, the factory has from time to time got "hot" jobs out in a week. Why not let the sales department really treat its customers well by using one-week lead times for all jobs?

6. "Engineers design products, but they should let the factory decide how to make them." Discuss.

7. A member of the American Production and Inventory Control Society asked for ideas about how to set up a short-cut method for estimating labor for the machine shop, mechanical assembly, and electric assembly work. His company is seeking "ball park" figures and a nomograph, chart, or slide-rule-type method. What suggestions might be given him?

8. What part does estimating play in companies manufacturing to stock? If the cost estimators have to stay within certain cost limits because of inflexible sales price, what does this limitation do to the estimating procedures?

9. The text says that cost estimates should always be tied in with volume and that, nearly always, the cost per unit will be less for large volumes. It would seem that the text should also say that cost estimates should be tied in with quality. Why might the text have omitted this? Discuss.

Problems

1. The proposed schedule calls for considerable variation in production levels. It is possible to level out production by building up inventories during slack periods. And because this would not require such a big factory, steady production would save $20,000 a year in depreciation, interest, etc. And by avoiding overtime, steady production would also save $22,000 in direct labor costs. Average inventory investment would, however, go up $225,000. And the company would have to build more storage space: a $90,000 addition with a 10-year life and $25,000 salvage value. Other costs caused by the inventory would add another $15,000 a year. At an interest rate of 15 percent, which alternative should be chosen?

2. The sales department expects the sales of model A record players to go up this year (from last year's total of 10,000) to 15,000. Past experience shows the following probable seasonal sales pattern and next year's calendar shows the number of work days:

Month	Percent of average month	Number of possible regular work days
January	60	23
February	50	20
March	60	23
April	120	20
May	200	22
June	180	22
July	90	11*
August	70	23
September	90	20
October	120	22
November	100	21
December	60	19

* Plant closed first half of July.

Make up a schedule of expected sales, month by month, for model A record players for the year. Be sure to pay attention to the fact that sales are trending upward. This means that the trend is upward within the years and not just between the years.

To solve this problem, first calculate the monthly average for each year. Then find the difference between the two averages and divide this difference by 12 to get the increment by which the trend increases each month.

The average for the first year is regarded as the trend figure for the middle 30 days of the year, or June 15 to July 15. Adding one monthly increment gives the trend value for the next 30 days, July 15 to August 15. Next, these two months' trend figures are averaged together to get the trend for the calendar month of July, the 30-day period centered on July 15. (The different number of days in months is neglected in calculations of trend values.)

After the figure for July is arrived at, trend values for other months can be obtained by adding the appropriate number of monthly increments until the trend is extrapolated for each month in the year ahead.

Finally, each month's sales estimate is obtained by multiplying each month's trend value by the month's seasonal percent. The January trend would be multiplied by .60, February's by .50, etc. Once the sales estimates are calculated for each month, production and inventory planning can proceed.

If these products are all made in the month of sale, what will be the daily average rate of production each month? If production is leveled out, what will be the daily rate each month? Show, month by month, what the month-end inventory will be. If it costs $2 a month to carry a finished record player in stock, what will the inventory carrying cost come to?

3. The customer has, in the last 6 months, ordered a total of 30,000 closure covers at $10 per unit and has just now sent in an order for 10,000 more. He has always ordered 10,000 at a time, each time saying that he does not know whether he will want any more of this design.

It costs $4,000 to set up for a run of these covers and $4 per unit for labor and materials. The production control manager points out that the company could save money by making 20,000 or 30,000 and storing the excess until the next order. It costs $.10 a month to store these covers. And if it should turn out that the customer no longer wants this design and the inventory has to be scrapped, they have a salvage value of $1 each.

How many, if any, should the company make ahead if there is a 90 percent chance that the customer will take them? Seventy-five percent? Fifty percent?

4. The new scheduler has found that the production operators, being on piecework, turn out work in less than standard time. Here are last month's records of five workers:

Worker	Hours spent on jobs without standards	Hours spent on jobs with standards	Standard hours of work turned out
A.	23	145	172
B.	5	163	203
C.	16	152	169
D.	8	120	152
E.	11	149	167

a) How much work should the scheduler expect week by week from these men in the future?

b) What problems will he have to contend with?

5. Part number 127B requires the following operations and has, from past experience, produced the following information:

Operation	Setup time (hours)	Standard operation time per piece (minutes)	Piecework operator efficiency	Scrap percentage
1	.5	4	133	25
2	1.3	9	120	none
3	.6	2	100	30
4	.3	4	115	10

For an order of 200:

a) How many pieces should be started in each operation?

b) Using overlapped scheduling (where the following operation starts on the first units before the whole order is finished in the preceding operation), how many hours after you start to set up operation 1 should you start to set up operations 2, 3, and 4? (Do not start fast operations until a big enough bank has been built up to let them complete the order in 1 uninterrupted run.)

c) When will the order be finished?

Case 18–1

The ABC Company has had trouble with parts not arriving at the assembly floor. The difficulty has not often been serious but has caused minor delays. Parts intended for particular assembly orders have been made up and put into the finished-parts stock instead of being taken to an accumulation bin in the assembly department. When assembly starts, their absence causes delays because they must be brought from finished stores.

Parts are manufactured on individual manufacturing orders and show the part identification and the indentification number of the product they go into. The fact that some or all of the parts on the parts order are to be used for a particular assembly order is not shown on the parts order.

Should the assembly order number be put on all manufacturing orders for parts to be used for that assembly order? What if more parts are called for on the order than this particular assembly order requires? Would it be a good idea to deliver all parts directly to an accumulation bin at the assembly floor? How will the accounting department find out about parts orders finished and delivered to the assembly floor instead of to finished stock first? Will it matter if the parts are for two or more different assembly orders? Or will it matter if some of the parts being made are for stock whereas the others are for a particular assembly order?

Case 18–2

In a situation similar to that of the ABC Company, the DEF Company delivers parts directly to accumulation stalls in the assembly area. The assemblers help themselves to parts from these accumulation stalls as they need them. Parts which don't fit are tossed aside or back into the supply bin and other parts are used. By the time the assemblers near the end of an order, they are short of parts or have only parts which don't fit. How can production control handle this situation?

This problem has also extended into the finished parts stockroom. The assemblers, needing more of a part, go to the stockroom and help themselves. How should this be handled?

Recent references

Buffa, Elwood S., *Production-Inventory Systems: Planning and Control,* rev. ed., Homewood, Ill.: Richard D. Irwin, 1972

Greene, James H., *Production and Inventory Control Handbook,* New York: McGraw-Hill, 1970

Journal of the American Production and Inventory Control Society (bimonthly)

Kunreuther, H., "Production-Planning Algorithm for the Inventory-Overtime Trade-Off," *Operations Research,* November 1971

Moore, Franklin G., and Ronald Jablonski, *Production Control,* 3d ed., New York: McGraw-Hill, 1969

Niland, Powell, *Production Planning, Scheduling and Inventory Control,* New York: Macmillan, 1970

19

Order control systems

PRODUCTION control systems differ so much that we cannot describe them all. But we can describe some commonly used types even while admitting that few companies fit the picture perfectly. A good many companies fit the patterns fairly well.

We start with job-lot shops. Everything they make, they make to order. Sometimes they get repeat orders for the same thing; but they make very few things, or even nothing, to stock. Manufacture is in lots; nothing is made continuously.

Job-lot shops use "order control." Every lot or order is given a number and its production is planned individually. Separate directives are made to cover every lot's production, and usually a separate cost record is kept for every lot.

Order control is expensive because all of the production control work has to be done over again for every order. Paper work costs are high. Sometimes some paper work can be eliminated by controlling operations only loosely. But loose control means that things will go wrong (orders will get lost or not be finished on time) more often. And even with loose control, most of the paper work will still have to be done; not very much of it can be cut out.

Planning

All way-ahead production control work is called planning. For assembled products it starts with an order to assemble certain quantities of each product. Planning has to "explode" the order for each kind of assembled product into the hundreds of orders to do the individual activities that the factory needs to carry on in order to produce the products.

Exploding an order starts with the master bill of materials (the parts list), which shows how many of each part are needed in order to make one unit of the product. When the quantities needed per unit are multiplied by the quantities of finished products wanted, this yields a "parts requirements" list.

This list becomes an assembly order when the order number and the assembly period (the week or month) are put on. One copy of this assembly order goes to the foreman of the assembly department to tell him what his men are to make. Another copy goes to the stock room foreman to tell him that he has to gather the parts by a certain date and deliver them to the assembly floor. Today, computers usually make up all of these orders.

Parts orders. While assembly itself is still in the future, this requirements list is checked by the production control staff against the supplies of parts on hand and on order. Wherever there are not enough, production control orders more of the items that are made inside and asks purchasing to get more of the things which are bought. Again, computers will do the comparing and make up the lists.

Computers can also make up schedules and set dates. The planners may, for example, plan in March for products which the factory will assemble in August. Some of the parts will not be needed until August, but others will need to be ready by the middle of June so they can be put into assemblies, which later go into bigger subassemblies, which go into the final product. The computer will calculate all the necessary schedule dates.

Materials orders.   Before parts can be made, it is necessary to get raw materials. So the computer calculates, item by item, the raw materials needed. This produces another requirements list, this time a raw materials requirement list. And again, for each item, what is needed is checked against what there is on hand and on order. And, still again, purchasing is asked to get more wherever more is needed.

Lead time is important here too. The parts that have to be ready by June 15 take time to process. Maybe it will be necessary to start processing some of them by May 1. And if it takes a month to get raw materials, the order for the supplier has to go out by April 1, which is tomorrow.

Manufacturing facilities.   Planners must also check to see if the necessary tools and machines are available to make the products and parts. Normally these are available, but sometimes new products which require new machines come along. Or perhaps parts are to be made a new way and so need new tools or jigs. Planning people have to keep checking on such accessories because, unless they prod, some tools will surely not be ready on time. In some companies the planning department itself orders all new tools and jigs. And this, of course, has to be done still further ahead. Some companies call this preplanning.

Order scheduling

Assembled products schedules show certain quantities to be made (assembled) in a month or week. Some are actually assembled early in the month, others late. In job-lot work, normally *all* the parts and subassemblies are finished and complete *before* the first finished product in the lot is assembled. This makes for some big piles of parts on the first day of a month. To keep the piles within reason, parts lots are sometimes cut up into several smaller lots and scheduled to be finished one after the other during the month.

But whether a month's supply is processed as one lot or not, and whether the assembled products are to customers' orders or to master schedules and as yet unsold, schedule setting for subassemblies and for parts starts with the assembly schedule. The scheduler works back from the final-assembly completion dates to final-assembly start dates, then to subassembly completion dates and to subassembly start dates.

This provides the dates by which parts need to be finished. And again the scheduler works back from the finishing date for the last operation to its necessary starting time, then a between-operations time allowance to the end of the preceding operation, back to its starting time, etc., and finally back to establishing times to start first operations. All of this, of course, has to be done separately for each different part. Usually this is all done on a computer.

FIGURE 19–1. Processing cycle of a shop order

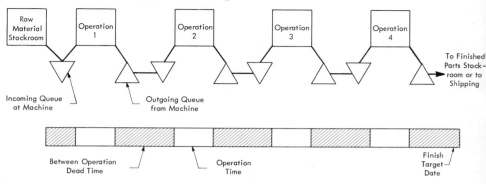

This process produces a desired start date for each parts order and is the date that goes on the shop order. Nearly always the wanted completion date for every operation is put on the order also. Then it will always be easy for foremen to tell which jobs to do first and which, if any, are behind schedule.

When an order falls behind, it is usually not too hard to get it back on schedule if the cause for its delay is fixed quickly. The total time allowed to make the order usually has a good bit of "fat" in it. More time is allowed between operations than is really needed. Also, operations are almost never overlapped (meaning that operation 2 does not start on some products before all of them get through operation 1). Jobs behind schedule can often be pushed along by "squeezing out" some of the between-operation time allowed for in the normal scheduling procedure. Or else operations can be overlapped or work can be done on overtime.

The method described here of calculating job start and finish schedules would seem to take care of getting first jobs done first. But it does not always work out this way. Men don't always look at dates, or they work on the easy jobs first, or maybe the tools are not ready and a job gets laid aside (and there it stays). Or rejects run a little high so a whole order is laid aside until the rejects are reworked. Or there are just too many orders to get out in the time available. The operation schedule times discussed above were set according to each order's needs but without any check on whether the specific capacity needed was available.

The one problem which is almost impossible to solve well is having too many orders. Overall schedules do not contemplate overloading the work centers, but variations in the product mix sometimes cause some departments to end up with unplanned overloads.

Overloads are also sometimes caused by customers who send in their orders today and want them tomorrow. So sales pushes the factory to add a few more orders, all in addition to the regular schedule. These

FIGURE 19–2. **Time compression possibilities for shortening processing time by overlapping operations**

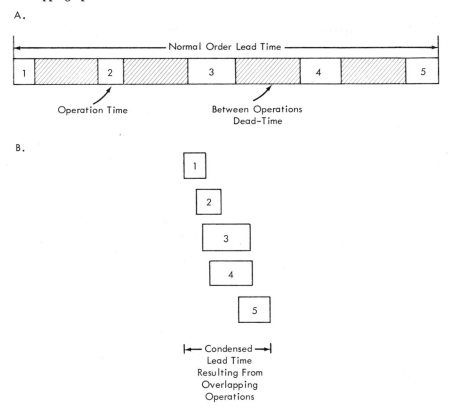

extra orders can easily be added if the original schedule was a little light. They can also be handled easily if the department is working on some orders for stock as well as other direct orders for customers. The orders for stock items can be pushed aside and finished later. So long as they are finished before they run out of stock, no harm will be done.

But why should the factory always be in a jam when rush orders come in? Could not the schedules allow a little space in the schedule for them? This is just what is often done. In the original plans, dates for finishing orders are set as if the plant were only 90 to 95 percent as big as it is. The other 5 to 10 percent of the capacity is thus available for last-minute rush jobs. Often this works out reasonably well.

Loads

The factory's load is its work ahead. It can be expressed in tons, dollar value, time, or in other ways. Mostly, for production control use, it is expressed in time. A plant, department, or machine has so many hours', days', weeks', or months' work ahead—that has already been authorized and scheduled.

Master schedules should not be approved until their load requirements are compared to the factory's capacity. Generally this is done only in the overall terms mentioned above, or, if the company makes only a few kinds of products, in product units. If the company manufactures to stock, the approved master schedule gives the factory its load (a full load when business is good) for a given period into the future.

But if a company manufactures to order, the load of new orders is just added to the present load, not as an increase in today's load but as an extension of the load into future months. Orders are accepted for early-delivery promised dates up to normal capacity. Then additional orders are also accepted, but they are given more distant promise dates and their load is added to the loads for more distant months.

A plant with a load that matches its overall capacity usually has all departments loaded about equally. But not wholly so. Product-mix variations sometimes throw unequal loads onto departments. Also, *within* departments individual machine loads vary. When it appears that the approved schedule will provide for a nice, smooth operation, it does not always work out quite so smoothly at the machine.

The point is that orders can be scheduled the way we described on page 439 (working back from assembly dates to get start dates for shop orders) and to expect that there is enough time on machines to carry out all the operations, and then to find that some machines are over-scheduled while others are underscheduled.

Some companies keep an individual machine load record for every likely bottleneck machine. Every time a new order comes out they calculate how many hours of machine time it will take on such a machine and add these hours to the machine's load. Every time a job is finished, they subtract its time. This gives them an up-to-the-minute record of work scheduled but not yet done on the machine.

One minor point: the load record probably should be kept in terms of *standard* hours of work ahead of the machine. And when a job is done, its standard hour time—not the actual time it took—should be subtracted from the load record. Doing this gets rid of the total's being affected by how fast a man works. On the other hand, if men work at 125 percent efficiency they will do 10 hours' work in 8. A work load of 200 standard hours for a machine would be about 160 hours (4 weeks of actual work). If all men always worked at a given efficiency rate, the load could well be expressed in terms of actual expected hours. Since they vary, it is probably better to use standard hours.

Load records give advance warning of trouble spots. Suppose that a new order comes out with a due date of April 15 for work on a machine which is already loaded till May 1. Using load records, this is discovered right away—today—a month or so ahead of April 15. Possibly something can be done about it in time so that there will be no holdup for later operations. Maybe the machine can be worked overtime, or possibly the job can be sent outside, or this particular order's schedule can be changed.

Machine scheduling

Rarely are schedules made for individual machines—except for big, important machines. It is always possible, though, with any machine, for the scheduler to go through the orders ahead and find out not only its total load of work but also decide *when* each order should start and *when* it ought to finish. This, then, would be a *machine* schedule.

Normally this is not done because it serves no useful purpose. It is simple to stack the orders in sequence and let this pile of orders be the machine's schedule. Then, if one order is held up and is not ready for the machine when it is supposed to be, this order can be laid aside. Operators go on to the next order in the pile (provided that that job has arrived in the department and is ready). It is unnecessary to redo a whole plan for the machine's use. And when the held-up order is ready to go, it can be put on top of the pile ahead of the remaining orders. Again, no change in a plan is needed.

The same is true if the machine gets behind. If orders are running several hours behind schedule, no records need changing. Even if, in order to catch up, foremen have to go to overtime, the record changes still are few.

It is different, however, on the big machines and on bottleneck operations. For them it may be very desirable, as a regular practice, to plan each machine's use.

The discussion up to here has, however, been too idealistic. Often a company has several large contracts or finished-product lines each generating its own work loads for the common parts-making department. The loads of work thrown onto the parts department frequently goes beyond its capacity. Then there is a problem of choosing which orders to process first and which to let wait. Dispatching policies need to be set up which try to get the most needed orders processed first. (We will discuss these on p. 446.)

How much centralization?

The production control department makes out the factory's assembly orders and shop orders for parts; it orders materials; and it tells each foreman what jobs are coming to him, what work to do, when it ought to be finished, and where next to send the job.

These directions finally have to go to the man on the job; he has to be told what to do. Here, at the firing line, there is a choice. Production control can put in its own men in all departments to pass out orders to the men, or the foreman can do it. If the foreman does it, it is called *decentralized* control. He, the foreman, decides *who* works on each job, and if there is a choice among machines he decides which machine to use, and he decides *when* to do the job (so long as he meets the due date).

Centralized control. In the centralized method, by contrast, the production control department has its own dispatch offices in every department. The foreman usually gets copies of all the shop orders which his men are, or will be, working on; but they are only to tell him what his men are doing or will be doing. With tightly centralized control, all directives (including materials requisitions, individual job tickets for every operation, and move orders to tell truckers where to take jobs) are made up in the central office. These are sent to dispatch offices in the various departments, where they are held until the jobs come along. Then the dispatch clerk issues them directly to the men when each job's turn comes.

Usually, with tight centralization, copies of the man's job ticket (showing when he finished the job), inspector's reports, and move tickets are turned in after the work is done. These keep the production control department informed. The central department almost always knows where everything is all the time. Job progress reports come through the dispatch offices to the central office, where the computer keeps the record up to date on the progress of every order.

Decentralized control. Decentralized control does two things. First, it transfers part of the work from the production control department to the foremen and, second, it cuts out part of the paper work. Production control still makes up assembly orders and parts orders. And parts orders still list all operations and their wanted or finish dates. Copies of these work orders go to all foremen of departments that will have anything to do on the order.

From here on it is up to the foremen. The foreman decides when to do the job and who does it. After the operation is done, he sends the job to the next department, where the next foreman takes over. Each job has a "traveler" copy of the shop order, which stays right with it. That identifies it and tells truckers where it goes next. There are no written move orders for truckers.

Cutting out paper work. One of the gains from using decentralized control used to be the savings in paper work. It reduced the need for written move orders for truckers and written reports of completed work that men in the central office used to hand-post as records of job progress. Today, with computers and electrical reporting on an almost on-line basis of work done, the paper work has been largely cut out whether centralized or decentralized control is used.

Actually, even before computers, there was not necessarily much loss in control if some of this paper work was cut out. Unless the factory is swamped with work, most jobs will come through production on time. They *have* to come through because the factory is working and turning out jobs hour by hour and day by day. There is a "pull" that pulls work through the plant. It is not necessary to "push" jobs through. So long as the factory is not given more orders than it can handle, and so long as the foremen pass out first jobs first, most orders will come through, and on time too.

The trouble is, and computers have not stopped this, that troubles, big and little, interfere. Men are absent, a machine gets out of order for a day or two, more materials are spoiled halfway through than was expected, an order gets lost, and so on. Usually none of these things happens, and most orders come through on time, but a refrigerator can't be assembled without its door hinges. *All* the parts are needed. If a few items get held up, there is trouble.

If the reporting system were cut out, the production control department would not find out about delays until the finished item was wanted. By then the item would be needed badly, but computers have made a double improvement here. They have gotten rid of most of the paper work, yet, by being on line, they keep right up to the minute on the status of jobs. They immediately call attention to all orders that fall behind.

The system also needs to keep production control supplied with a physical count of items as individual operations are finished because it needs to know the "attrition" rate (how many items are spoiled or rejected and thrown out after each operation). The number of such items in a lot goes down a little after most operations, but good reporting is vitally important if very many pieces are scrapped. If an order ends up with too few pieces, it may be necessary to send through a rush order for enough pieces to bring the lot up to size—and such orders are very expensive. A report only of jobs on time or behind does not show enough if the attrition rate is getting too high.

False counts and "disappearing" orders also make trouble. Piece-workers sometimes report that they turned out more than they did. Or sometimes men spoil items and throw them away without reporting them. If the controllers believe the job card reports, they may not know about a shortage until several operations later. It might therefore be better to have inspectors count production when they inspect the products.

Orders get lost, too. There are so many trays, racks, or tote pans of materials for jobs ahead, jobs done, or jobs held up and lying around that jobs just get lost now and then. Sometimes traveler copies of the shop order get lost, so no one knows what the half-made parts are. Or a lot is held up until some of its rejects are reworked, or because it is rejected, or because the next operation's tools aren't ready.

Every company and department has its nooks and corners where such things pile up, with no one interested in them, until some day when a wild-eyed expediter comes desperately looking for them.

Expediters. Expediters ("stock chasers") are a necessary evil in order control. They move fussy or rush jobs through the plant, find lost orders, circumvent reasons for holdups, and push orders through in a hurry. They work from a "hot list" of orders behind schedule. They are necessary because things go wrong, and they help get them straightened out. They are an evil because the only way they can rush things through is to get foremen to disregard regular schedules, and even tear down machine setups to do the rush job. This is most unfortunate because it wastes machine production time, reduces total output, and makes more expediting necessary.

It is all very costly and irritating, but there seems to be no other way to do the work they do. Hopefully, only a small fraction of jobs should ever need expediting. Probably there is a little less expediting today than there used to be since computerized production control keeps better track of things.

Dispatching

Dispatching means handing out work orders to the men. Not much is heard about dispatching in decentralized control, where the foreman passes out the jobs. Instead, the term is used when production control's "branch office" (the dispatch office) in each department tells men what jobs to work on. And there are such branch offices only with centralized control. Dispatching also includes getting reports back from the men when they finish jobs.

Earlier in this chapter (p. 442) we said that departmental loads sometimes get to be too big. The orders for work to be done in a period are more than can be handled. When this is so, some kind of order priority system has to be developed, and the wanted dates on the orders won't fill this need because they call for more work than can be done. So it will be necessary to neglect the wanted dates, at least to some extent, and set up some other rule or set of rules to decide which orders go first and which won't be done on time.

Operations researchers have studied this problem and have tried by simulation to see which dispatching policy is best. Among the rules they have tested are: first come, first served; first come, first served, but with dollar classes; shortest time for present operation; longest time for present operation; least slack time in department; least slack in all remaining departments; least average slack time between remaining operations; longest wait up to now; greatest cost penalty if due date is missed; most remaining operations; fewest remaining operations; later passage through overloaded work centers; later passage through presently idle work centers; importance of customer; and profitability of the item. We have intentionally left out "hot jobs first" because if the customer or the assembly floor needs an order quickly, any good set of priority rules will push such orders through first.

Unfortunately, computer simulation has shown that no one policy is always the best. Doing short jobs first causes the fewest holdups. Hughes Tool Company has finally settled on "hot jobs first." Then, after the hot jobs, priority goes to jobs with the least average slack time between the following operations. By following these rules Hughes has been able to let the computer set schedules for factory departments, and has at the same time reduced the number and seriousness of behind-time orders, at the same time reducing expediting costs. New schedules for each department are run off every few days.

The Hamilton Standard Division of United Aircraft uses this formula to establish priority, by which lower-priority numbers go first:

$$\frac{\left(\begin{array}{c}\text{Work hours available} \\ \text{until due date}\end{array}\right) - \left(\begin{array}{c}\text{Standard hours} \\ \text{remaining in job}\end{array}\right)}{\text{Number of operations remaining}} = \text{Priority}$$

At Hamilton Standard, priority numbers are not absolute, superseding the dispatcher's knowledge of shop conditions. Rather, they are guides which are nearly always followed.

Replanning and rescheduling

It is never possible to get all of the output out of a plant that ideally it should put out. The schedulers and managers know this and allow for it in master scheduling. Managers approve only the total load they really expect to get.

But individual orders must always be planned and scheduled as if nothing ever goes wrong, because nothing does go wrong on most orders most of the time. It is known, for example, that tools sometimes will not be on hand and that men will be absent. Sometimes an inspector throws out many more than the usual number of rejects (or even much less than was allowed for). Now there are not enough pieces in the lot (or too many). Or some pieces just disappear. Or a whole order gets lost. Or engineering (or the customer) changes the design so that some operations have to be done over. Or the customer wants to raise the quantity—or cut it. Or he decides that he has to have his order now instead of next month.

Occasionally there are even mistakes in the order. It may not list every operation, or it may list a wrong operation or ask for the wrong quantity. Neither master bills of materials nor master route sheets are always perfect. And once in a while there are errors in the calculations of quantities needed.

All of these changes upset production control's plans and schedules. And none of them can be anticipated as probably going to delay specific orders. Because of this, individual orders must all be planned and scheduled as if no delay would occur to them. Then when delays come up they have to be replanned. Men doing production control work probably spend more of their time remaking plans and schedules than they spend making them up the first time. Here again, however, computers can update everything so fast that they have made a big problem into a little one.

Graphic systems

Over the years people have tried to picture machine schedules on charts. Henry Gantt did it 60 years ago, and occasionally Gantt-type charts are used today. They can be used to show planned machine use before a period starts. As pictures of plans they are not bad, but charts are poor as control devices. After production starts and some jobs get behind schedule, and perhaps other orders get ahead, charts get all mixed up. They are not at all suitable for showing changes and replans and reschedules.

Today it is possible to buy any one of many kinds of commercial variations of Gantt charts. Productrol boards, Schedugraphs, and Boardmasters have been used for years. All of these, like many of the other commercial devices, use a time scale across the top. Along the left side are lists of machines, orders, or inventories, whichever are being pictured. Bars extend from the left to the right according to the activity being depicted. Control boards are most often kept in the central production control office and not out in the shop.

There are other commercial devices, such as magnetic boards and roll charts. With magnetic boards it is only necessary to place metal bars on the board and they will stay wherever they are put. With roll charts, the chart is rolled from right to left, one day's space each day, and the bars are extended on the chart to the right.

The best thing about all control charts is that they highlight trouble spots, and often will show prospective trouble before it occurs. The worst thing is that all the work of keeping them up is extra. They replace no records. Also, unless they are posted right up to the minute, they are always out of date, and many may actually be misleading. Furthermore, as days pass they run off the right side of the board and it is necessary to keep redoing them and moving them back to the left. During slack times visual controls are of little value to most companies because there is no problem in getting orders out. But when a company is swamped with orders, visual aids can help.

Actually, graphic controls are uncommon because computers can print out new up-to-the-minute lists so easily whenever anyone wants them. They will list the jobs ahead of each machine and show when each one ought to start on the machine and when it ought to finish. And they are just as good with inventories. They will show how many of everything are on hand, how many are likely to be needed, when more should be reordered, etc. There just is not much need for charts anymore.

Electrical production reporting

Electrical reporting of production is now common and is replacing older methods. Big, important machines can be wired directly into a central computer so that their output is reported as it occurs. More often, however, electrical reporting is less directly on line. When a worker finishes a job he puts the job ticket (a prepunched tabulating card) into a nearby reporting box, which transmits a report of the job's completion to the computer. The computer then updates all its records and flashes warning lights whenever something is out of control.

Sometimes, though, it is too expensive to have a computer even this much on line. Many companies do the electrical *reporting* as work gets done, but the computer updates its records only once a day. It holds all reports until the end of the day. Then it updates all records and puts out a report of how things stand for managers' use the first thing the next morning.

Reproducing shop directives

Two or more copies are needed of most shop directives used in controlling production. Xerox and other copying methods are widely used. Most such directives, however, are now made by the printing units attached to computers. In most companies the production control department must also prepare hundreds or thousands of identification tags for orders in production. Special tag-printing machines are available for this work.

Review questions

1. Trace the steps involved in the "explosion" process from the list of finished *products* needed back to the parts and raw materials required.
2. If master schedules are in line with the factory's capacity, how does it happen that individual machine centers sometimes end up with more work than they can take care of?
3. What is the difference between order scheduling and machine scheduling? Is either one necessary? Both? When could either one be done without?
4. Are machine loads and schedules the same thing? If they are different, where should each be used?
5. It would seem to be unnecessary to keep records of work loads ahead of any machines at all since work loads for machine centers are reasonably in balance and the operation's wanted start and stop dates are on shop orders, thus establishing job priorities. Why might work center work load records be needed?
6. When might the production control department eliminate making schedules for machines?

7. What is the difference between centralized and decentralized control? In general, what are the advantages and disadvantages of each?

8. What is the "pull" of the factory? What has it to do with production control?

9. Graphic systems for controlling production are somewhat uncommon. Why?

Discussion questions

1. What might the production control department do to help solve the "contractor's dilemma"? (When the men see the end of a contract or job approaching with no other job in sight, they slow down to perpetuate their jobs, or even create overtime possibilities in order to get the contract out on time.)

2. It is nearly always possible to push one more order of parts through the plant quickly if the individual operations are "lap phased" instead of "gap phased." Lap phasing means to overlap operations and to start operation 2 on the first units finished by operation 1 before operation 1 is finished with all items in a lot. Lap phasing is not used very often in job-lot production. Why not?

3. Why not simplify the matter of dispatching and just adopt a policy of "do the shortest job first"? Would this result in the fewest number of delayed orders? What would happen to long-production-time orders? Is this a good policy to adopt?

4. Discuss the pros and cons of permitting changes to be made after production has been started in a schedule period.

5. An air rifle company, after its Christmas sales peak, has to repair thousands of misused and out-of-order rifles in the early months of each new year. What problems does this make for production planning and control?

6. The customer has just sent a design change notice. The company is already halfway through making the parts affected so it doesn't want to change. The manager of production control calls the customer and then hands you the telephone so that you, the production scheduler, can explain your problems to him. What do you tell him?

Problems

1. An order for an item which requires 3 operations is to be scheduled. The setup times for the 3 operations are 25, 45, and 15 minutes respectively. Machine operation times are 10, 12, and 6 minutes respectively. Scrap losses on each operation are 1, 4, and 2 percent respectively. For a lot of 200 pieces:

   a) How many items should be started into production?

   b) What is the least time (using gapped scheduling) to finish the order? (Allow 1 hour between operations for moving materials to the next operation.)

   c) In order to start operations 2 and 3 as soon as the order arrives, how many minutes after the setup on operation 1 is started will it be necessary to start setting up for operations 2 and 3?

d) Using overlapped scheduling, what is the answer to question *b?* (Do not, however, start operation 3 until it can operate steadily; do not have it wait 6 minutes each for items from operation 2.) The transportation delay can also be cut by 20 minutes when overlapped scheduling is used.

e) At $.50 per trip for carrying products from machine to machine, how much extra in transportation costs will overlapping cost as against gapped operations (where only 2 trips are required)?

2. The ABC Company has an order to make 50 units of a large part. Its costs are $100 per unit plus $1,000 setup costs. Extras over 50 units are all loss, yet shortages under 50 have to be made up. The rejects which cannot be repaired normally come to 10 percent. (In this calculation, for simplicity's sake, it is possible to neglect the possibility that a replacement unit would itself be a reject.) Losses are on a Poisson distribution, however, and not on a normal curve. (The fewest possible number of rejects, if 55 were started through production, would be zero, or 5 less than the average. Yet, in the other direction, the number of rejects could be more than 5.) Here are the Poisson probabilities of defectives if the starting quantity were 55, 56, 57, 58, 59, or 60.

| Number of rejects | Number started | | | | | |
| | 55 | 56 | 57 | 58 | 59 | 60 |
	Probability					
0	.0041	.0037	.0033	.0030	.0027	.0025
1	.0225	.0207	.0191	.0176	.0161	.0149
2	.0618	.0580	.0543	.0509	.0477	.0446
3	.1133	.1082	.1033	.0985	.0938	.0892
4	.1558	.1515	.1472	.1428	.1383	.1339
5	.1714	.1697	.1678	.1656	.1632	.1606
6	.1571	.1584	.1594	.1601	.1605	.1606
7	.1234	.1267	.1298	.1326	.1353	.1377
8	.0849	.0887	.0925	.0962	.0998	.1033
9	.0519	.0552	.0586	.0620	.0654	.0688
10	.0285	.0309	.0334	.0359	.0386	.0413
11	.0143	.0157	.0173	.0190	.0207	.0225
12	.0065	.0073	.0082	.0092	.0102	.0113
13	.0028	.0032	.0036	.0041	.0046	.0052
14	.0011	.0013	.0015	.0017	.0019	.0022
15	.0004	.0005	.0006	.0007	.0008	.0009

How many products should be started into production? What will be the most probable cost of starting this quantity? Show the figures.

3. The order is for 100 aerial rotaters, a product requiring several parts which are different from anything the company has ever made before. The customer makes it clear that he wants 100, no more and no less.

How many of part A, which goes into the rotaters, should be started into production? The finished product requires 4 units of part A for each rotater, and extras are waste.

On somewhat similar items made in the past, the following has been the rate of spoiled parts.

Spoilage percent	Number of jobs
0	0
1	0
2	1
3	1
4	4
5	7
6	12
7	4
8	1
9 and over	0

The setup cost is $100 and the material and processing cost per unit is $30. Rejected parts have zero value. Keeping in mind that if there is a shortage it is always possible to set the machines up again and produce enough more items to meet the requirements, how many parts should be started into production?

4. There is an order for 2,000 units of product X, which requires the following sequence of 4 operations. Their operating data are:

Operation	Machine service time daily (minutes)	Percent loss after operation	Operation time/unit (minutes)	Operator lost time/8-hour day (hours)
1	40	1	2.41	.5
2	28	2.5	6.20	.5
3	17	1.5	0.76	.6
4	44	3	1.37	.4

How many clock hours will it take to process this order if 4 hours are allowed between operations? How many parts will have to be started into production?

5. The following 10 work orders must have the same pair of operations performed on them, and always on machine 1 before machine 2:

Machine					Time in hours						
	A	B	C	D	E	F	G	H	I	J	Total
1	3.5	2.8	4.6	4.1	7.2	5.8	3.1	1.8	5.9	5.6	44.4
2	2.2	2.4	6.0	1.7	10.0	3.4	2.4	4.7	3.3	4.5	40.6

Determine the sequence for sending these jobs out to get the least amount of machine idle time. In no case may operation 2 start on any order until operation 1 is finished, but it is not necessary to allow for any transportation time from machine 1 to machine 2. How many hours does the ideal schedule take on machine 1? On machine 2? How much machine idle time is there for each?

6. Here are figures for a new part which will take 5 operations:

Operation number	Setup time (minutes)	Standard operation time per unit (minutes)	Operator efficiency	Percentage of time operator works on standard work	Scrap percentage
1	10	6	110	100	10
2	20	12	140	90	none
3	50	20	130	100	15
4	40	15	115	80	5
5	20	10	105	90	none

The time between operations is 40 minutes after an operation is completed until the next one starts, but setup can start before the lot arrives. How many hours will it take to get out a lot of 1,000 pieces?

7. The scheduler at the ABC Company is to work out a schedule assigning work to 5 turret lathes, keeping in mind the wanted dates for orders as well as minimizing setups.

He is to make a schedule for March, which has 23 work days. March 1 is Wednesday. The 5 turret lathes work 3 shifts daily but not on Saturdays or Sundays. Of the 7 orders to be scheduled, 5 have definite wanted dates but the other 2 are stock orders not in urgent need. In this schedule it is not necessary to consider setup time as such. The orders are:

Order number	Number of shifts required	Wanted finishing date
1	50	Mar. 8
2	40	Mar. 13
3	15	Mar. 16
4	65	Mar. 23
5	100	Mar. 31
6	100	No hurry
7	47	No hurry

How will this work out? Are there any problems?

8. Setup time is .3, .7, and .2 hours respectively on machines A, B, and C. In order to save a little capacity for rush orders, ½ hour of each machine's time each day is not considered in the regular schedule making. Machine operators on these 3 machines are 110, 125, and 105 percent efficient respectively. Scrap losses are 1, 3, and 2 percent of production on each machine.

a) How many clock hours would it take to get out a job with a standard time of 21.4 hours on any one of these machines?

b) How many 8-hour workdays will it take to get out an order which requires 3 such operations in sequence, 1 operation on each machine? (Allow 1 hour between operations for moving the job to the next machine.)

9. The ABC Company has just received a rush order for 50 units of part A73. This part is made complete in 2 operations done on 2 adjacent machines. Instead of processing them all through operation 1 as a lot and then through operation 2, it is possible to pass each piece directly from operation 1 to operation 2. Operation times vary as follows:

Minutes	Operation (percentage of cases) 1	2
6	5	0
7	20	5
8	50	10
9	20	20
10	5	30
11	0	20
12	0	10
13	0	5

Using Monte Carlo, find out how long it will take to get this order out. What percentage of the worker's time on operation 2 will be wasted? What percentage on operation 1?

10. How fast can the following rush job be turned out? The order calls for 1,000 pieces and each operation has to be completed on the whole lot before the next operation can start. Furthermore, there is need to allow 1 hour between jobs. Setting up, however, can be started before the lot arrives.

Operation	Setup time (minutes)	Standard time/unit (minutes)	Operator efficiency on both setup and machine operations	Scrap loss after the operation
1	20	6	90	8%
2	4	12	115	0
3	15	15	130	16
4	10	17	118	4
5	9	9	107	0

a) How many items should be started into production?
b) When should each operation be started?
c) When will all 5 operations be finished?

Case 19–1

In order not to run out of stock, the Headington Engine Company tries to have all parts in parts stock one month before starting final assembly. Headington makes large diesel engines requiring several thousand parts, some of which are first subassembled into components which later go into engines as units. Assembly goes on more or less steadily from month to month, but there is some change in the product mix between sizes and types, and most engines sold are special in minor ways.

Assembly orders are passed out to the production control department five months before assembly is to start (assembly usually takes two months). The production controller calculates the parts required and orders them all four months before the month assembly is to start. The parts are all expected to arrive in finished parts stock during the next 90 days. This gives the production control department 30 days for expediting any items not on hand a month before assembly starts.

As a consultant, you are asked for suggestions. What do you say?

Case 19–2

The Waynesboro Furniture factory called the Wheeling Stamping Company to check on its order for 1,000 hinge and catch combinations for card tables. The call was made on the 25th of the month and shipment had been promised on the 4th of the month following. A check on the progress of the order showed it to be nearly complete with no expediting required.

On the 8th of the following month the Waynesboro company called again, stating that the hinges had not arrived. It asked that they be sent on immediately. A search was made, and it was found that the production control department dispatcher had transferred the hinges from the Waynesboro order to an order for the Pensacola Furniture Company. Shipment to the Pensacola company had been made on the 2d of the month. The hinges originally on the Pensacola order were still in process and would be complete and ready for shipment on the Waynesboro order on the 15th. When asked why he had made this change, the dispatcher explained that the Pensacola order had farther to go, and since it would take several days longer in transit he had arranged to get it finished first.

Under what conditions should material for one order be used for another? What authority should be necessary? Who should be notified? What records should be changed if a transfer is made?

Case 19–3

Every order for special items is assigned to an expediter who sees it through production. The expediters are somewhat demanding at times. If orders ahead of a special order would tie up all the available machines for several days, they insist on their specials being put ahead of the other orders, even rush orders for regular items temporarily out of stock. They also insist, at times, that machine setups be torn down and production halted on other orders to get the specials out faster. The plant superintendent has finally told his foremen never to tear down a setup to put a special order on the machines and to let the specials wait their turn after regular-stock rush orders.

What lines of authority should be set up to cover production situations like the above? Who should decide priority among orders? What authority should expediters have? Or should there *be* any expediters? What kind of procedure would take care of the company's problem?

Recent references

Berry, William L., *Priority Scheduling and Inventory Control in Job Lot Manufacturing Systems,* Lafayette, Ind.: Institute for Research in the Behavioral, Economic, and Management Sciences, Purdue University, 1971

Conway, Richard W., William L. Maxwell, and Louis W. Miller, *Theory of Scheduling,* Reading, Mass., Addison-Wesley, 1967

Doll, C. Loren, *An Integer Constrained Economic-Order-Quantity-Based Single-Machine Scheduling Heuristic,* Lafayette, Ind.: Institute for Research in the Behavioral, Economic, and Management Sciences, Purdue University, 1971

Schussel, George, "Job-Shop Lot Release Sizes," *Management Science,* April 1968

"Visual Controls Tell Where It's At," *Administrative Management,* September 1971

20

Operations research type scheduling techniques

Linear programming

LINEAR PROGRAMMING is one of the most commonly used operations research methods. It is particularly helpful in situations where there are several or many calls on certain scarce resources and where it is difficult to see how best to allocate these limited resources.

Before we explain linear programming, however, a word of warning about it. The relationships between factors must be *linear* or the answer will not be valid. Linear relationships means that when one factor changes, so does another, and in a given amount. An hourly paid employee's working hours and his wages are linear: the more hours, the more money. Setup time, on the other hand, is nonlinear. The setup time does not increase along with the quantity produced. Getting a machine ready to perform an operation is independent of the quantities produced. Technically, therefore, linear programming cannot be used if setup time is a factor. (Actually, it is possible to get approximate answers in spite of a nonlinear factor by assuming that it is linear over small spreads. It could be said that setup costs are $1 per unit for orders of 11 to 20 units, $.50 a unit for orders of 21 to 50, $.20 for 51 to 100, etc.)

Linearity can be negative without affecting its validity: If a man starts with a $20 bill, the more he spends, the less he has left. This is negative linearity. We have negative linearity in our sample problem on page 465 when we cut products A and B in order to get metal for product C.

We will use three simple examples. First, a "graphic" example; next, an example of the simplex method, so simple that it can be solved by algebra; and third, a simplex example using tableaus.

A "graphic" example. Using a hypothetical automobile factory and making the problem simple enough to explain in a few pages, we will assume that the factory makes only two models: a 2-door 6-cylinder car and an 8-cylinder station wagon. We will deal with three manufacturing departments: metal stamping, engine assembly, and final assembly, in which there are two assembly lines: one for 2-door cars and one for station wagons. Both can operate at the same time.

The stamping department can, in a week, turn out enough parts for 7,000 2-door cars or 12,000 station wagons. But it can't do both at the same time. It is possible to do one *or* the other, or it is possible to have parts for *some* 2-door cars and *some* station wagons. It is the same with engines. It is possible to get 9,000 6-cylinder engines for 2-door cars or 6,000 eights for station wagons, or combinations of the two.

The 2-door-car assembly line can turn out 6,000 cars as a maximum. The station wagon line's top is 4,000. Here, however, both lines can operate at the same time. Boosting the output of one line does not mean cutting the other.

These facts provide several "parameters" (limits beyond which we cannot go). But no *one* limitation sets limits for all possible combinations. It is possible to make 9,000 6-cylinder engines, but only 6,000 2-door cars can be assembled. Assembly is the limiting factor. Or it is possible, so far as assembly is concerned, to assemble 6,000 2-door cars and 4,000 station wagons. But actually this can't be done because it is not possible to make enough stamped parts or engines. The stamping capacity will allow making parts for 5,000 2-door cars and 3,430 station wagons—but this can't be done either. This time engine manufacture is the limiting factor. If 5,000 6-cylinder engines are made, then there is remaining capacity to make only 2,670 8-cylinder engines.

Figure 20–1 shows the area of feasibility for engine production. The enclosed area encompasses all possible combinations of 2-door cars and station wagons. The diagonal line is the limiting parameter. Any combination of numbers of 2-doors and station wagons which falls on the diagonal line will keep the engine department fully occupied. Combinations within the enclosed areas are also feasible but will not keep the department busy. It would be possible, for example, to produce 3,000 8-cylinder engines and, at the same time, 3,000 6-cylinder engines, even though this will not keep the engine making department busy.

FIGURE 20–1. Engine making feasibility area

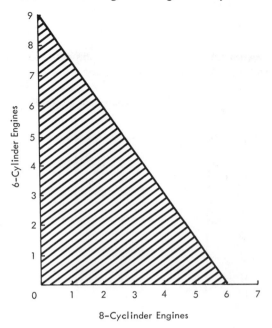

FIGURE 20–2. Stamping department feasibility area

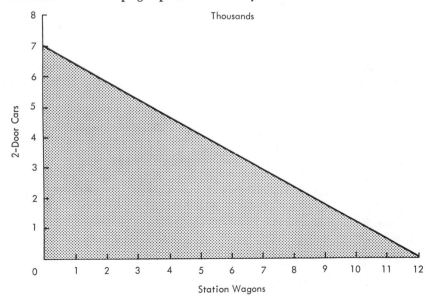

Figure 20–2 shows the solution feasibilities for stampings. Again, the diagonal line sets off the maximum production. And again, lesser combinations are feasible even though they would not keep the stamping department busy.

The two other parameters, the assembly capacity for each kind of car, are shown in Figure 20–3. These parameter lines are not mutually de-

FIGURE 20–3.   Assembly department feasibility area

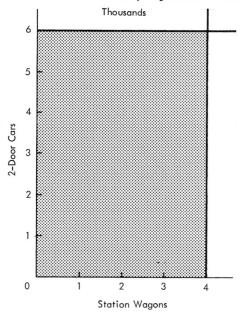

pendent on each other and so do not make a diagonal line. Again, the enclosed area encompasses the feasible combinations so far as these two parameters are concerned.

Figure 20–4 brings in the profit objective and shows the profit results of different mixes of products and different volumes of business. A whole set of such profit lines could be constructed (they could be called a family of "isoprofit" lines) to show how much volume and product-mix combinations would be needed to produce $1 million, $1.5 million, $2 million, etc., in profits. Figure 20–4 shows the $1 million and $2 million isoprofit lines.

Figure 20–5 combines the first four charts into one. The enclosed area *A–B–C–D–E* encompasses all possible feasible solutions to the problem. The isoprofit line for $2.6 million touches the feasible solution area at its maximum point, *C*.

It is possible to make 2-door cars and station wagons in any combination in the shaded area. We can make 6,000 2-door cars and no station

FIGURE 20-4.   "Isoprofit" lines

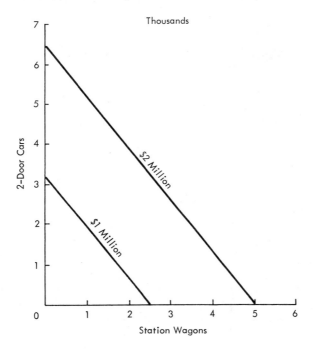

wagons (point *A*), or 6,000 2-door cars and anywhere up to 1,715 station wagons (point *B*). But from there on, in order to get any more station wagons, it will be necessary to cut down on 2-door cars because the stamping department is up to its limit. By the time we get down to 5,727 2-door cars and up to 2,183 station wagons (point *C*), we run into engine limitations. From this point on, as 2-doors are cut in order to increase station wagons, engines limit us until we get up to 4,000 station wagons (point *D*). By this time we are down to 3,000 2-door cars. From here on station wagons can be increased no more because we are up to the capacity of the station wagon assembly line. We can cut 2-door cars below 3,000, but that will not help station wagon production.

So far we have found out how the limiting factors set off the number of 2-doors and station wagons against each other. The plant is operating at its full capacity in at least one department at any point on the parameter line, the line connecting the vertex points *A*, *B*, *C*, *D*, and *E*. At points *B*, *C*, and *D* the plant is operating at full capacity in two departments.

The real goal, however, is not just to keep departments busy but to earn the most. Thus the goal is to find out at what point the earnings will be maximized. If we assume that $300 is earned on every 2-door car and $400 on every station wagon, here is how this works out profitwise:

Point	Number of		Total profit		
	2-doors	Station wagons	2-doors ($300 each)	Station wagons ($400 each)	Both
A..........	6,000	0	$1,800,000	0	$1,800,000
B..........	6,000	1,715	1,800,000	$ 686,000	2,486,000
C..........	5,727	2,183	1,718,000	873,200	2,591,300
D..........	3,000	4,000	900,000	1,600,000	2,500,000
E..........	0	4,000	0	1,600,000	1,600,000

The shaded area in Figure 20–5 shows the limitations of the several manufacturing departments. The $2.6 million isoprofit line touches the shaded area only at point *C*, so that is the profit which will be realized at this maximum point.

The simplex method

Algebraic solution. Many business problems have dozens of factors, and when they do it is necessary to turn to a different linear programming technique, the simplex method. This method allows for solving algebraic equations that have more unknowns than there are equations. This process is a little different from that of ordinary algebra.

We will present, first, a simple example of apportioning two scarce metals to three products. Suppose that because of government regulations we are allowed to use only limited amounts of nickel and copper. The goal is to divide the supply among three products in such a way as to make the most profit.

The first step is to list the materials requirements for the products:

Metal	Amount needed			Daily allotment
	Product A	Product B	Product C	
Nickel..............	2 lbs.	4 lbs.	6 lbs.	160 lbs.
Copper..............	3 lbs.	2 lbs.	4 lbs.	120 lbs.
Profit per unit.........	$50	$60	$120	

We start by saying: An unknown number of product A times 2 pounds of nickel, plus an unknown number of product B, times 4 pounds of nickel, plus an unknown number of product C, times 6 pounds of nickel will use up 160 pounds or less of nickel. We call the unknown numbers x, y, and z. We can make a similar statement for copper. We cannot as yet make algebraic equations to help us get answers, though, because the best solution may mean having a little nickel or copper left over. So it is neces-

FIGURE 20–5. The simplex algorithm system

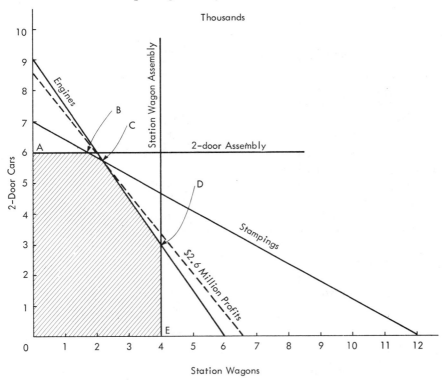

sary to add two more letters: n for leftover nickel and c for leftover copper. Now two equations can be set up:

Equation I for nickel: $2x + 4y + 6z + n = 160$
Equation II for copper: $3x + 2y + 4z + c = 120$

These two equations, I and II, contain five unknown values: x, y, z, n, and c. When there are only two equations and five unknown numbers, there are many sets of five numbers that will fit the equations.

Using the linear programming method, it is not necessary to find all the possible numbers which might fit. Instead we find one set and then look for other sets which will improve the result. The improved result we are looking for is greater profit. In order to calculate it, a third equation, equation III is needed. P in this equation means the profit. It is the "function" we are trying to maximize.

Equation III: $50x + 60y + 120z = P$

The solution starts by using equation I and assuming that only product A will be made and none of either B or C. In that case y and z are zero, and the three equations become:

$$\text{I: } 2x + n = 160$$
$$\text{II: } 3x + c = 120$$
$$\text{III: } \quad 50x = P$$

Now another assumption: that we will use up all of the nickel in making product A. This makes $n = 0$, so equation I becomes $2x = 160$, or $x = 80$. The amount of nickel available will allow the making of 80 units of product A. But when we try equation II with $x = 80$, it becomes $3(80) + c = 120$, or $240 + c = 120$, $c = -120$. We are 120 pounds short of enough copper to make 80 units of product A.

So we try equation II first. If we use up all the copper, c will be zero and equation II becomes $3x = 120$ and $x = 40$. We have enough copper to make 40 units of product A. Using $x = 40$ in equation I shows that there is enough nickel to make 40 units of product A and have 80 pounds of nickel left over. Now we go to equation III to see how good a solution this is. This shows that making 40 units of product A at a profit of $50 each will produce earnings of $2,000.

The second step in the simplex method is to see if some combinations of products A and B would be more profitable than making only product A. (We will omit product C, which will come in the third step.) The equations now become:

$$\text{I: } 2x + 4y + n = 160$$
$$\text{II: } 3x + 2y + c = 120$$
$$\text{III: } \quad 50x + 60y = P$$

We suspect that the most profitable combination of products A and B will use up all of both metals, so we start by setting n and c at zero. This leaves equation I as $2x + 4y = 160$ and equation II as $3x + 2y = 120$. These are simple algebraic simultaneous equations. Solving them, we get (using I first):

$$2x = 160 - 4y$$
$$x = \frac{160 - 4y}{2}$$
$$x = 80 - 2y$$

Substituting in II, we get:

$$3(80 - 2y) + 2y = 120$$
$$240 - 6y + 2y = 120$$
$$-4y = -120$$
$$y = 30$$

Returning to equation I:

$$2x + 4(30) = 160$$
$$2x + 120 = 160$$
$$2x = 40$$
$$x = 20$$

It is possible, therefore, to make 20 units of product A and 30 units of product B. This will use up all the metal available.

Now we must see how this affects earnings. According to equation III:

$$\$50(20) + \$60(30) = P$$
$$\$1,000 + \$1,800 = P$$
$$P = \$2,800$$

So this is a better solution than making 40 product As and nothing else.

We still do not know about product C. Earnings might be still higher if some C items were made in place of so many of A and B. The proposal above uses all of the nickel and copper, so the only way to make any Cs is to forgo making some products A and B. How many products A and B will need to be given up to make 1 unit of product C?

Algebra will provide the answer. Let a stand for the amount that product A would have to be cut to get enough material to make a contribution of metal to 1 unit of product C. Then, if b stands for the cut in product B, a and b together will produce enough nickel and copper to make 1 unit of product C.

We now have two new equations. For nickel, the new equation is $2a + 4b = 6$; for copper it is $3a + 2b = 4$. These simulation equations are solved as above, starting with the equation for nickel:

$$a = \frac{6 - 4b}{2}$$
$$a = 3 - 2b$$

Substituting in the equation for copper: $3(3 - 2b) + 2b = 4$, $9 - 6b + 2b = 4$, $-4b = -5$, $b = \frac{5}{4}$. Returning to the equation for nickel: $2a + 4(\frac{5}{4}) = 6$, $2a + 5 = 6$, $2a = 1$, $a = \frac{1}{2}$. In order to produce 1 unit of product C, it will be necessary to give up $\frac{1}{2}$ unit of product A *and* $\frac{5}{4}$ units of product B.

Will we be better off if we do this? Looking again at the earnings figures, we see that giving up $\frac{1}{2}$ of product A means forgoing $25 of profits and giving up $\frac{5}{4}$ of product B means giving up $75 in profits, making the total decrease in profits $100. But 1 unit of product C brings a profit of $120; so certainly at least 1 unit of product C should be made. We are $20 better off.

Would it be still better to make more than 1 unit of product C? Yes, the relationship of profitability stays the same. It paid to drop some products A and B to make 1 unit of C, and it will pay just as well to keep on dropping A and B to make C. We should keep cutting A and B until one of them is eliminated completely. Which will go out first and how many product Cs will the "saved" metal allow to be made?

The first program called for making 20 product As. Every time $\frac{1}{2}$ of an A product is cut out, it contributes to making 1 product C: $20 \div \frac{1}{2} = 40$. Cutting A completely would contribute metal for 40 units of C. The first program called for making 30 of product B. Every time $5/4$ units of B are cut, metal is contributed to making 1 C: $30 \div 5/4 = 24$. Cutting product B completely will contribute toward making 24 units of product C.

These 24 units, then, are the number of product C to make. Product B is cut out completely. Product A has to be cut from the starting number, 20, at the rate of $1/2$ for every product C: $24 \times 1/2 = 12$; $20 - 12 = 8$. Eight units of product A can still be produced.

Now let's check the earnings. This time they total $3,280, arrived at as follows: 24 units of product C at $120 each = $2,880, plus 8 units of product A at $50 each = $400, or a total of $3,280.

This is the end of this example. The earnings have been maximized and all of both kinds of metal have been used in the most profitable combination. The maximum earnings product mix might, in some cases, leave some of one material over, but this did not happen in our example.

Linear programming not only shows which is the best action among alternatives but also how much it costs to follow other actions. In our problem, for example, maybe it would be best to keep on making a few product Bs to round out the product line with customers. This will cost us money, though, because for every product B we make we will lose $16. Of course we do not actually *lose* $16 by selling a product at a $60 profit; instead, we could have earned $76 by using the same materials for making other products. Maybe, even knowing this, the choice will still be to make some product Bs, but it will be done with open eyes. We will know how much that decision costs.

Tableaus and matrices. Business problems are never so simple as in our example above. For more complex problems it is still possible to use the simplex method, but it has to be a different form: the simplex "algorithm" set up in tabular form with rows and columns of figures. Unfortunately, the process is not simple. Several steps and several tables of numbers, called "tableaus," "matrices," or "iterations," are needed.

The problem we will use to illustrate the simplex method by using tableaus is deciding how many products to buy outside. We are concerned with 4 parts which are needed in large quantity—more than we can make ourselves—but we have some open machine time available. The following machine hours are available: lathes 300, drills 500, and broaches 500.

The first part, *bearing race*, takes 6 hours of lathe time, 2 hours of drill time, and 1 hour of broach time per 100 units. The next part, *spring holder*, takes 2, 5, and 2 hours per 100 respectively. *Carriage clips* take 0, 4, and 3 hours and *ferrules* takes 8, 2, and 4 hours per 100 units. Excess parts, bought outside, cost extra: $10, $4, $7, and $2 per 100.

The first step is to put all this information in tabular form, as is done below. (From this point on we are going to speak of 1 unit or 1 product as meaning 100 actual units.)

Machine	Hours available	Hours per unit (of 100)			
		Bearing race	Spring holder	Carriage clip	Ferrule
Lathes.................	300	6	2	0	8
Drills..................	500	2	5	4	2
Broaches..............	500	1	2	3	4
Outside extra cost........		$10	$4	$7	$2

As a next step, we substitute P_1, P_2, P_3, and P_4 for the product names. We must also provide for possible leftover hours on each kind of machine. This is done by saying that in each idle hour we make an imaginary product which takes an hour on one machine and on which we make no money. Those products are P_5, P_6, and P_7.

Next we set up equations covering the use of each machine's time. In these equations we change from capital P to small p, with the small ps representing unknown quantities.

The equations, then, are:

$$\text{(Lathes)} \quad \text{I: } 300 = 6p_1 + 2p_2 + 0p_3 + 8p_4 + 1p_5$$
$$\text{(Drills)} \quad \text{II: } 500 = 2p_1 + 5p_2 + 4p_3 + 2p_4 \qquad + 1p_6$$
$$\text{(Broaches)} \quad \text{III: } 500 = 1p_1 + 2p_2 + 3p_3 + 4p_4 \qquad\qquad + 1p_7$$

Equation I means that 300 hours of lathe time will be used to make 6 times an unknown number of units of P_1 plus 2 times an unknown number of P_2 plus zero times P_3 plus 8 times the number of P_4 plus an unknown number of idle hours.

Besides these three equations for machine-time use we need one for savings since we are trying to maximize savings.

$$\text{(Savings)} \quad \text{IV: } = 10p_1 + 4p_2 + 7p_3 + 2p_4 + 0p_5 + 0p_6 + 0p_7$$

Now we recast these four equations into tableau form:

Tableau 1 — Key number

Program	Saving	Quantity	P_1 $10	P_2 $4	P_3 $7	P_4 $2	P_5 0	P_6 0	P_7 0	
P_5	0	300	6	2	0	8	1	0	0	←Key row
P_6	0	500	2	5	4	2	0	1	0	
P_7	0	500	1	2	3	4	0	0	1	
Base row I	0		0	0	0	0	0	0	0	
Base row II			$10	$4	$7	$2	0	0	0	

Key column

Tableau 1 differs in several ways from the four equations. In the first place, we took out the ps, returned to capital P, and put them at the column heads, leaving only numerals (the coefficients) in the body of the tableau. As column captions, they now represent products.

Next, at the left we added *program* and *saving* columns. The *program* column at the start of the simplex method is a list of the imaginary products, and the *saving* column shows the savings per unit which we will realize by making the product, in this case, zero.[1]

Base row I is easier to explain later. We can say now, though, that it starts off all zeros. *Base row II* is the figure at the top of the column minus the *base row I* figure.

We are now ready to try to improve our first program. In *base row II* the largest number is $10. This tells us that making P_1 items will contribute the most profit per unit. The P_1 column is the "key" or optimum column.

So we now set about making all of the P_1 items that we can. And how do we tell how many? The 300 idle hours of lathe time divided by the 6 hours needed per unit tells us that, so far as the lathes are concerned, we can make 50 units. The drills would permit us to make 250 units and the broaches 500 units, so the lathe limit sets our figure. The most P_1 items we can make is therefore 50.

This first decision, therefore, is to make 50 P_1 items. To effectuate this decision we will substitute a new P_1 row in place of the old P_5 row. And in order to do this it is necessary to divide every number in the old P_5 row by 6, the number of lathe hours required to make 1 unit of P_1. This 6 is the limiting value and is sometimes called the "key number." We also insert $10 into the *saving* column in the matrix since we will save $10 on every unit of P_1 we make. Thus the new P_1 row to be inserted becomes:

| Old row: | P_5 | 0 | 300 | 6 | 2 | 0 | 8 | 1 | 0 | 0 |
| New row: | P_1 | $10 | 50 | 1 | .33 | 0 | 1.33 | .17 | 0 | 0 |

P_1 items also take time on drills and broaches, so there will be less free time on them. It is necessary to scale down all the figures in the old P_6 and P_7 rows. The initial P_6 row (for drills) read:

$$P_6 \quad 0 \quad 500 \quad 2 \quad 5 \quad 4 \quad 2 \quad 0 \quad 1 \quad 0$$

The P_6 itself does not change, nor does the 0 in the *saving* column, because there is still idle drill time in the program, and it continues to save no money. But some of the 500 hours available on the drills will be used up making the 50 bearing races, so this 500 has to be reduced. So, also, do all the other numbers in the original P_6 row.

Drilling time per unit is 2 hours, as against 6 for lathes, so making 50

---

[1] The simplex method is a step-by-step procedure which leads from one feasible solution to a better one until the best is found. It is necessary, however, to start with a feasible solution, and the only one known at first to be feasible (which allows all of the equations to be valid) is the zero program. We know that if we make no products, there will be no profits, and we know that this is an action which can be taken. The step-by-step improvement procedure can then take over.

units of P_1 will use up 100 of the 500 P_6 idle hours, leaving 400 hours. All the other numbers in old row P_6 are also reduced but the calculation is different. The ratio between the key number, 6, in the key column to the number 2, in the P_1 row in the key column is determined. It is $\frac{2}{6}$, or $\frac{1}{3}$. The two old rows, P_5 and P_6, are set next to each other, as follows:

Old row P_6: 0 500 2 5 4 2 0 1 0
Old row P_5: 0 300 6 2 0 8 1 0 0

The new P_6 row is calculated by subtracting $\frac{1}{3}$ of the old P_5 number from its paired P_6 number. The calculation thus becomes:

Old	Old	New
500 − (300 × $\frac{1}{3}$) = 500 − 100 =		400
2 − (6 × $\frac{1}{3}$) = 2 − 2 =		0
5 − (2 × $\frac{1}{3}$) = 5 − .67 =		4.33
4 − (0 × $\frac{1}{3}$) = 4 − 0 =		4.00
2 − (8 × $\frac{1}{3}$) = 2 − 2.67 =		−.67
0 − (1 × $\frac{1}{3}$) = 0 − .33 =		−.33
1 − (0 × $\frac{1}{3}$) = 1 − 0 =		1.00
0 − (0 × $\frac{1}{3}$) = 0 − 0 =		0

The new P_6 row is now:

P_6 0 400 0 4.33 4.00 −.67 −.33 1.00 0

Products P_1 also take time on the broaches, so old P_7 must be similarly scaled down:

Old	Old	New
500 − (300 × $\frac{1}{6}$) = 500 − 50 =		450
1 − (6 × $\frac{1}{6}$) = 1 − 1 =		0
2 − (2 × $\frac{1}{6}$) = 2 − .33 =		1.67
3 − (0 × $\frac{1}{6}$) = 3 − 0 =		3.00
4 − (8 × $\frac{1}{6}$) = 4 − 1.33 =		2.67
0 − (1 × $\frac{1}{6}$) = 0 − .17 =		−.17
0 − (0 × $\frac{1}{6}$) = 0 − 0 =		0
1 − (0 × $\frac{1}{6}$) = 1 − 0 =		1.00

The new P_7 row is:

P_7 0 450 0 1.67 3.00 2.67 −.17 0 1.00

We are now ready to make up a partial Tableau 2:

Program	Saving	Quantity	P_1 $10	P_2 $4	P_3 $7	P_4 $2	P_5 0	P_6 0	P_7 0
P_1	$10	50	1.00	.33	0	1.33	.17	0	0
P_6	0	400	0	4.33	4.00	−.67	−.33	1.00	0
P_7	0	450	0	1.67	3.00	2.67	−.17	0	1.00

At this point *base row I* should be put in. To do this we multiply every figure in each row against this row's savings. For row P_1 this is:

$$
\begin{array}{rrl}
\$10 \times & 50 & = \$500.00 \\
10 \times & 1.00 & = 10.00 \\
10 \times & .33 & = 3.30 \\
10 \times & 0 & = 0 \\
10 \times & 1.33 & = 13.30 \\
10 \times & .17 & = 1.70 \\
10 \times & 0 & = 0 \\
10 \times & 0 & = 0 \\
\end{array}
$$

Since there are no savings in any other row, this set of figures becomes *base row I* in Tableau 2. We have also calculated *base row II*, by subtracting the dollar figure in *base row I* from the figure at the top of each column. If there is a negative balance, this balance shows in *base row II* with a minus before it. Here is the complete Tableau 2:

Tableau 2

Program	Saving	Quantity	P_1 $10	P_2 $4	P_3 $7	P_4 $2	P_5 0	P_6 0	P_7 0
P_1	$10	50	1.00	.33	0	1.33	.17	0	0
P_6	0	400	0	4.33	4.00	−.67	−.33	1.00	0
P_7	0	450	0	1.67	3.00	2.67	−.17	0	1.00
BR I	$500.00		10.00	3.30	0	13.30	1.70	0	0
BR II			0	.70	7.00	−11.30	−1.70	0	0

We now go on to Tableau 3, using the same procedure used to get Tableau 2. P_3 is the key column and P_6 is the key row.

Since there are now two real products in the program there are savings on two products. *Base row I* requires more calculating than before. It is the saving on P_1 products times each number in the P_1 to P_7 columns. The $10 is multiplied by 1, .33, 0, 1.33, .17, 0, and 0 to get 10, 3.30, 0, 13.30, 1.70, 0, and 0. The same process is carried through for product P_3: $7 times 0, 1.08, 1, −.17, −.08, .25, and 0. This gives 0, 7.56, 7, −1.19, −.56, 1.75, and 0. These numbers for columns P_1 to P_7 are then added to get *base row I*:

	P_1	P_2	P_3	P_4	P_5	P_6	P_7
	10.00	3.30	0	13.30	1.70	0	0
	0	7.50	7.00	−1.19	−.56	1.75	0
Base row I	10.00	10.86	7.00	12.11	1.14	1.75	0

Tableau 3

Program	Saving	Quantity	P_1 $10	P_2 $4	P_3 $7	P_4 $2	P_5 0	P_6 0	P_7 0
P_1	$10	50	1.00	.33	0	1.33	.17	0	0
P_3	7	100	0	1.08	1.00	−.17	−.08	.25	0
P_7	0	150	0	−1.58	0	2.17	.08	−.75	1.00
BR I	$1,200.00		10.00	10.86	7.00	12.11	1.14	1.75	0
BR II			0	−6.86	0	−10.11	−1.14	−1.75	0

The problem is now solved, as is shown by the fact that there are no plus numbers in *base row II* in Tableau 3. There are no products which we should be making which would add to the profits.

The answer is the program at the left in Tableau 3. We should make 50 units (5,000) of bearing races and 100 units (10,000) of carriage clips. This will save us $1,200, as against buying these items outside. P_7 is, however, still in the program. This tells us that the most profitable program, although it uses up all the lathe and drill time, leaves us with 150 hours of unused broach time.

Tableau 3 also produces "shadow prices." It tells us that if we choose to make some of our spring holders or ferrules (perhaps in order to have a double source of supply), this protection will cost a shadow price of $6.86 per 100 for all the spring holders we make and a shadow price of $10.11 per 100 for ferrules. This is in spite of our saving money by making these things inside. But in order to make them inside we would have to make fewer bearing races and carriage clips, on which the "inside making" profit is even greater.

Actual simplex applications are, of course, far more complex than this little example, and even this example might have required another tableau or two to get an answer.[2] It *would* have if the greatest loss *per unit* of product had not been a reliable guide to the best program. It sometimes happens that items on which less is saved *per unit* take so little machine time that they are actually the most profitable to make. If this were the case, the simplex method would find it out, but it would take another tableau or so to discover it. This is because the simplex method always pays first attention to where the greatest *per unit* savings are in prospect. Later the *total gains* come into play.

Simplex analyses are also helpful to managers on a "what if?" basis. Once the procedure is computerized, it is easy for a manager to get answers to such questions as: What would the situation be if we bought another lathe? or What if the vendor reduces his price by $3 per 100 on carriage clips while at the same time raising his price $2 per 100 on ferrules? In each case this would require a new calculation, but the computer could run through it quickly.

Computers are a big help in all simplex method problems because they can handle so many calculations so fast. Simplex problems, however, sometimes become so complex that they are real jobs even for a com-

---

[2] There is also a rare difficulty called "degeneracy." This would happen if two choices were equal. Suppose that, in our example on page 467, product P_1 required 10 hours per unit on broaching machines. Dividing the 500 hours available on broaches by 10 gives 50, the same as we got for lathes by dividing 300 by 6. Which would be the key row? That for lathes? Or that for broaches?

Look for the *1* in the first of the two rows concerned. It is in the P_5 column. Divide this *1* by the key number, 6 in our case, and get ⅙. Next, divide the other key number, *10*, into the number in its row in the P_5 column. This number is *0*, and $0 \div 10 = 0$. The smaller answer is the choice. Now go on with the simplex method, clearing out the P_7 row and putting P_1 products in their place

FIGURE 20–6

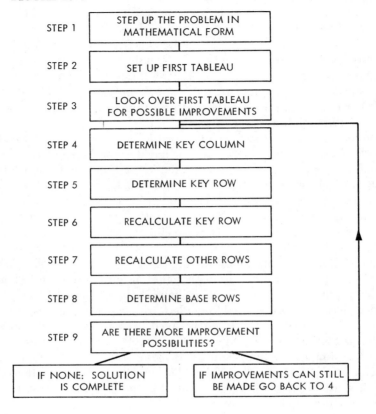

STEP 1	STEP UP THE PROBLEM IN MATHEMATICAL FORM
STEP 2	SET UP FIRST TABLEAU
STEP 3	LOOK OVER FIRST TABLEAU FOR POSSIBLE IMPROVEMENTS
STEP 4	DETERMINE KEY COLUMN
STEP 5	DETERMINE KEY ROW
STEP 6	RECALCULATE KEY ROW
STEP 7	RECALCULATE OTHER ROWS
STEP 8	DETERMINE BASE ROWS
STEP 9	ARE THERE MORE IMPROVEMENT POSSIBILITIES?

IF NONE: SOLUTION IS COMPLETE	IF IMPROVEMENTS CAN STILL BE MADE GO BACK TO 4

puter. Operating an oil refinery, for example, may require matrices as big as 200 rows and 1,000 columns, requiring perhaps 100 million separate calculations. The calculating time can be lengthy even for a computer.

The assignment method

Sometimes it happens that one or two machines are ideal for certain work and others are less well suited. Yet the perfect machines are few in number, so some jobs will have to be put on machines where costs are higher. (Or in the case of assigning jobs to men, the best man may be very good, and even the best for any of several jobs, but he can do only so much work, so some jobs have to be assigned to less capable men.)

The operations research assignment method can help here since it selects the best (or rather the least bad) way to make assignments of jobs to machines.

An example will illustrate the method. We will assume that there are four machines to which four jobs must be assigned. The machines are of unequal capability, however, and the goal is to assign each job to the best machine, all things considered. The problem is complicated by the fact that one machine is very good on most of the jobs but it can do only one job, so the other jobs must go on less well-suited machines.

Matrix A shows, for a hypothetical situation, the relationships of machines, jobs, and relative efficiency. The numbers in the body of Matrix A are the machines' relative efficiency, high numbers representing high efficiency and low numbers representing low efficiency. They could be viewed as the quantities of products each machine would produce on each job in return for $100 of cost.

Matrix A

Machine	Job			
	1	*2*	*3*	*4*
A	60	20	30	10
B	70	40	30	20
C	80	100	70	30
D	70	70	50	40

The first step is to find the highest number in the body of the table, which proves to be *100*. Then Partial Matrix B is made up by subtracting every number from 100 and putting in the difference. This provides the numbers for Partial Matrix B.

Partial matrix B

Machine	Job			
	1	*2*	*3*	*4*
A	40	80	70	90
B	30	60	70	80
C	20	0	30	70
D	30	30	50	60

Partial Matrix B is then changed to Matrix B by adding one more column on the right and one more line on the bottom. The extra column is merely a listing of the smallest number in each row. In a similar way, the newly added extra row is a list of the lowest number in each column. With the addition of this new row and the new column, Matrix B is complete.

At this point the assignment method requires that a choice be made between the newly added column and row. This choice is necessary in order to provide a basis for the next step. To make this choice, the numbers are added. The total of the numbers in the "small number" *column* is *100*. The "small number" *row* total is *110*.

Matrix B

Machine	Job 1	Job 2	Job 3	Job 4	Small number
A	40	80	70	90	40
B	30	60	70	80	30
C	20	0	30	70	0
D	30	30	50	60	30
Small number	20	0	30	60	100 / 110

The larger total (the *row* total at the bottom of Matrix B) is the choice and it indicates which numbers to use for the next step, which will lead to Matrix C. To get Matrix C, each number across this bottom row in Matrix B is subtracted from every number in the same column above.

The next step is to draw in vertical and horizontal lines to cross out all zeros, *using as few lines as possible*. These lines have been drawn in on Matrix C, but there are two such lines. Yet the instruction to draw as few lines as possible is ambiguous. For example, should the zero in block *D4* be crossed out by a horizontal or a vertical line? Another rule covers this: the line that is drawn in should be the one which leaves the lowest number open. A horizontal line would leave a *20* open; a vertical line would leave a *10* open. So the vertical line is the choice.

Matrix C

Machine	Job 1	Job 2	Job 3	Job 4
A	20	80	40	30
B	10	60	40	20
C	0	0	0	10
D	10	30	20	0

There is no answer to the problem yet because all the zeros are crossed out with only two lines. There will be an answer only when it takes four lines (because there are four machines) to mark out all of the zeros.

It is therefore necessary to go on to Matrix D, which is made from Matrix C. The first step is to find, in Matrix C, the smallest number that is not lined through, which is *10*. This number is *subtracted* from all open numbers and is *added* to all numbers where lines intersect. All other numbers remain unchanged.

The process used in Matrix C, of drawing lines through the zeros, is carried through again in Matrix D. In Matrix D it takes three lines to mark out all the zeros, so there is still no answer and it is necessary to go on to Matrix E. To get E from D, the steps used to make Matrix D from C are repeated.

Matrix D

Machine	Job 1	2	3	4
A	10	70	30	30
B	0	50	30	20
C	0	0	0	20
D	0	20	10	0

Ten is again the lowest open number, so it is subtracted from all open numbers and added to all intersecting numbers. And again, all other lined-out numbers are left the same.

Matrix E

Machine	Job 1	2	3	4
A	10	60	20	30
B	0	40	20	20
C	10	0	0	30
D	0	10	0	0

Again there is no solution, because all the zeros can be marked through with only three lines, not four, so it is necessary to go on to Matrix F.

Matrix F

Machine	Job 1	2	3	4
A	10	40	⓪	10
B	⓪	20	0	0
C	30	⓪	0	30
D	20	10	0	⓪

This time there is an answer because it requires four lines to mark out all zeros in this matrix. (The lines have not been drawn in on Matrix F but it can be seen that four lines are required.) And what is the answer? The machines should be assigned to jobs where zeros show. The circled zeros are the assignments. There is only one zero for *job 1*, so *B* must do *job 1*. There is only one zero for *job 2*, so *C* must do *job 2*. And since *B* is doing *job 2*, it cannot do *job 4*, so *D* must do *job 4*. And *A* must do the job left over, *job 3*.

This operation research method requires a square matrix. If the machines and jobs are not equal in number, a square matrix can be constructed by adding imaginary machines or jobs. All that is necessary is to add jobs or machines with extremely low efficiency numbers, say zero, to the original matrix. The process will rule them out and will not include them in the choices.

Review questions

1. What is meant when it is said that linear programming requires linear relationships between factors? What other kinds of relationships are there? Give examples and show how it may be possible to use linear programming in spite of this difficulty.
2. What part do constraining parameters play in linear programming? If they could be changed, what effect would this have on problem solutions?
3. Briefly outline how the algebraic application of the simplex method can operate with more unknowns than there are equations.
4. Do linear programming problems that are solved by the simplex method have to start with the poorest solution possible? Why or why not?
5. In the assignment method is it necessary to have a square matrix? Why? If a problem does not happen to be a square matrix, does this preclude using the assignment method? Explain.

Discussion questions

1. If the basic figures in a linear programming problem change, how much can be salvaged from an earlier solution? Discuss.
2. "The simplex method seems to be so precise that it can easily mislead a person." When could this happen? Discuss.
3. Suppose, in the text's example of making automobiles, that any one of the three departments could be expanded by 20 percent. Which one should it be? Assuming that all the cars made can be sold, what would be the new production program? How much better would this choice be than the next best choice?

Problems

1. Present production is 800 of product A and it is proposed to produce 1,100 of product B. The two products each require operations on the same three machines, whose capacities for operation 1 are: A, 1,200, and B, 0; or B, 2,400, and A, 0; or proportional combinations of A and B. For operation 2 the capacities are: A, 1,500, and B, 0; or B, 1,000, and A, 0; or combinations. For operation 3 the capacities are: A, 2,400, and B, 0; or B, 1,200, and A, 0.

Can the present equipment continue to produce the 800 units of A and also 1,100 of product B? If not, which operation's capacity will need to be increased and by how much? (Solve this problem graphically.)

2. A company making typewriters and adding machines has three major departments: stamped parts, machined parts, and assembly. The capacity of each department depends on what they make. The departmental capacities are given below:

	Typewriters	Adding machines
Stamped parts...............	2,000	6,500
Machined parts..............	1,500	10,000
Assembly....................	2,500	5,500

Assuming that the typewriters contribute $50 each and adding machines $40, what is the optimal combination of output? (Solve graphically.)

3. Solve problem 2 algebraically and assume that the quantities in problem 2 are the output capacities for a 40-hour week. This makes the time requirements for each product become:

	Typewriters	Adding machines
	hours per 100 units	
Stamped parts....................	2.00	.62
Machined parts..................	2.67	.40
Assembly.......................	1.60	.73

4. Suppose that, in the example on page 462, product B required 5 pounds of nickel instead of 4 and that product C yielded a profit of $100 instead of $120. Solve this new problem algebraically and find out how best to utilize the limited supplies of the two metals.

5. A company makes four products, A, B, C, and D, which go through four departments: drill, mill, lathe, and assembly. The hours of department time required by each product, per unit, are:

	Drill	Mill	Lathe	Assembly	Amount saved by making instead of buying
A........................	4	0	2	3	$ 9
B........................	8	3	5	5	18
C........................	5	7	1	6	14
D........................	1	8	6	3	11
Hours available...........	60	90	80	110	

How many of each product should be made?

6. Suppose that, in the example on page 467, it would be possible to free 100 additional hours of lathe time, but at a cost of $200. Should this be done or not? If it is done, how much money will the company make or lose from this change?

7. Suppose that a supplier quotes a new and lower price of $6 on bearing races but that the price for spring holders goes up $1. What changes in the program should be made?

8. Five jobs are waiting to be assigned, but since there are only four machines available, one job will have to wait. Any of the four machines can do any of the jobs but at different costs. The following table shows how many

units each machine will produce for an expenditure of $25. Using the assignment method, assign these jobs to machines in the most economical way.

| | *Machine* | | | |
Job	A	B	C	D
1....................	10	7	9	6
2....................	5	5	6	4
3....................	10	9	10	8
4....................	2	3	4	5
5....................	8	7	6	5

9. The company has some spare machine hours available during which it can make more of products A, B, C, and D. At the present time the company buys most of its requirements of these products, but if capacity were available it would pay to make them.

These products require time on milling machines, drill presses, and grinders. Available are 450 hours of milling machine time, 200 hours of drill press time, and 300 hours of grinder time. Product A takes 10 hours per 100 units on milling machines, 3 hours per 100 on drill presses, and 5 hours per 100 on grinders. B's requirements per 100 units are 2, 4, and 2 hours on each kind of machine. C's requirements are 2, 2, and 2. D needs 3, 0, and 1. By making instead of buying, the company saves $10 per 100 on product A, $15 on product B, $2 on C, and $5 on D.

What products should be made during these machine hours? How much will this program save as against buying? How many idle hours will still be left on any of the machines?

Recent references

An Application of the Work Flow Structure Information, Lafayette, Ind.: Institute for Research in the Behavioral, Economic, and Management Sciences, Purdue University, 1970

Holstein, William K., and William L. Berry, "The Labor Assignment Decision," *Management Science*, March 1972

Levhari, D., "Property of a Closed Linear Model of Production," *American Economic Review*, June 1971

Levin, R. I., and R. P. Lamone, *Linear Programming for Management Decisions*, Homewood, Ill.: Richard D. Irwin, 1969

Plane, Donald R., and Gary A. Kockenberger, *Operations Research for Managerial Decisions*, Homewood, Ill.: Richard D. Irwin, 1972

Sadleir, C. D., "Use of the Transportation Method of Linear Programming in Production Planning," *Operations Research Quarterly*, December 1970

Searle, Shayle R., *Linear Models*, New York: John Wiley, 1971

Thierauf, Robert J., *Decision Making through Operations Research*, New York: John Wiley, 1970

Wagner, Harvey M., *Principles of Operations Research*, Englewood Cliffs, N.J.: Prentice-Hall, 1969

21

Other production control systems

ALMOST ALL companies use order control systems somewhere in their operations, but very few companies use *only* order control. Whenever a company begins to get repeat orders for anything or to get long runs, its managers should begin to think of using simpler procedures and cutting out part of the repetitive instructions. Most of the short cuts that volume permits don't have names, but one system is called "flow control." Other less common systems include "load" and "block" control.

Line-assembled products

Big manufacturings' bread-and-butter items are all made on production lines—stoves, washing machines, automobiles, farm tractors, television sets, and many more. This is where flow control is used.

A product is put together one part at a time as it moves down the line. The men stay put at separate work stations (perhaps only 5 or 6 feet apart). As soon as a man puts on his part, the product moves on and another product comes to him for its part.

Products *flow* down the line, past the men and off the end of the line, minute by minute, all day, all week, and all month long. *Parts and subassemblies* must *flow* to the men along the line at a rate *equal to their use.* Flow production control has to match up the rates of flow of parts, subassemblies, and final assemblies.

Yet within this flow there is need to control a certain amount of *variety,* and in finished products as well. Autos, for example, come in different models, colors, number of cylinders, with (or without) power brakes and power steering, and with all kinds of different trims and accessories. Ford and Chevrolet each have so many possible combinations of different things that they could run all year and never make two cars exactly alike. Cars still need to *flow* off the assembly lines, but there is need to be sure that red cars get red wheels and that 4-door cars end up with 4 doors, not 2. Also, if 50 cars are to have 8-cylinder engines, not only are 50 8-cylinder engines needed but 50 6-cylinder engines are *not* needed. Not every manufacturer has as much variety as auto makers, but most line production companies have some variety.

Getting the flow of parts to match their use is also a problem. Perhaps automobile wheels are used at the rate of 5 per car, and each assembly

FIGURE 21–1. Assembly of electrical products along a horseshoe-shaped line. Operators push the units by hand between work stations. Each assembly is mounted on a carriage which can be rotated. Parts are brought in next to operators on mobile carts.

line makes 1 car every minute. Forgetting for the moment that there may be several lines, wheels are needed at the rate of 1 every 12 seconds.

Making 1 wheel every 12 seconds may not be the most economical rate for making wheels. Maybe the wheel making line works best when it turns out 1 wheel every 5 seconds, or 12 a minute, instead of the 5 a minute that the final assembly line needs. This makes a problem. The wheel line could, of course, be slowed down. Almost never, however, would this be economical because the men along the line would be idle five twelfths of their time, which would be a costly waste. Almost always it would be more economical to turn out 12 wheels a minute and pile up the excess. Before noon each day there would be enough extra wheels to keep the final assembly line busy during the rest of the day. If there were only 1 final assembly line, the wheel line could be closed down and the men could be put on other work. Often, however, there are 2 or more assembly lines in the company's several factories, so the extra wheels can be shipped to them.

Sometimes it is the other way around. The wheel assembly line can make only 2 wheels a minute when 5 are needed. Then it is necessary to work 2 or 3 shifts on the wheel line to 1 shift for final assembly, or to put in a second wheel assembly line, or to buy some wheels from outside.

Lack of perfect balance between production rates of parts and subassemblies and final assembly use is the rule, not the exception, *yet production per day or per week must balance,* and without carrying big inventories. Flow production control must cope with this.

The problem of matching parts production and use without carrying big inventories, and without running out of anything (if anything runs out, this stops the assembly line, which in turn stops everything else), is even greater for most individual piece parts. Many parts are made in lots; and if they were made continuously a year's supply would pile up in a week or two. These items are usually made in an unending series of successive lots a week or a month apart. It is unnecessary, however, to use order control for them because new lots are made so often that everyone knows what the items are and what operations to perform. (There is no need to make new operation lists each time, nor to collect the costs of making each lot, nor to tell truckers where to haul materials, etc.)

Items bought outside also come in as successive lots. Kelsey-Hayes makes auto wheels, but Kelsey-Hayes can't deliver them to Ford or General Motors 1 every 30 seconds. The best it can do is to send truckloads or freight-car loads at the rate of so many a day or a week.

To sum up: Flow control has to keep products flowing off the assembly line; it has to keep subassemblies and parts flowing to the assembly line; it has to control variety; it has to cope with lack of balance in production rates of parts and their use; and it has to deal with parts coming in in lots instead of in a steady stream.

Finished assembly line control

Controlling finished assembly is almost altogether a matter of controlling the *variety*—seeing that each separate product gets the combination of parts and accessories which is wanted. We omit the work of telling men *what* to do because industrial engineers figure out everyone's work assignment when the line is originally set up. After the first few days the men don't have to be told what to do. And we omit almost all instructions about *moving* materials. At the start it might be necessary to send a few instructions telling men how to do their jobs or telling truckers where to move things, but again, instructions are needed only at first. And along the line itself, day by day (except for instructions concerning variety), no instructions at all need be given. Products being assembled move right along the conveyor.

Instructions covering *variety* are probably more complicated for making automobiles than for making anything else because there are so many possible combinations of options. For auto assembly, an "order of run" or a "building sequence" list is needed for the assembly line. It lists every car to be made in a day and its sequence. For each one, it lists the kind of car, motor, steering, brakes, tires, accessories, trim, and all other details.

Copies of this list go to several points along the line to tell assemblers what items to put on and to tell parts supply men what parts to line up for cars that will be coming along. Some companies don't send such lists to the shop at all because they would have to change it sometimes. Instead, they use Tele-Typewriters, Tel-Autographs, and computer printers to send written directions to key points just before the cars come along the line. Of course, more instructions keep coming all day long. Also, by way of a check, every car carries a tag listing the parts and accessories it is to have. This is not very helpful, however, in controlling the parts because the men along the line don't get to see the list until the car comes along. Often this would be too late for them to get different parts from stock. Normally, too, they don't have time to read tags.

Most line-assembled products are easier to schedule than automobiles. Much of the work in making clothing, shoes, radios, television sets, typewriters, cash registers, and telephones is bench work. Except in the cases of clothing and shoes, all that is needed are simple tools—bolt tighteners, soldering irons, and so on. Most of the people along the line do almost the same kind of work. They put parts in place, or sew them together, or screw them down, or bolt, rivet, or solder them.

This gives production control considerable freedom to raise or lower schedules without changing shift hours, provided there are a few extra men available. It is often possible to put in a few more men at extra work spaces along the line and send more work down the line. Normally, production control does not have to concern itself with the effects of minor production ups and downs on manpower. The burden of getting more men (or cutting some off) falls on the foreman, and so does the job of redividing the bits and pieces of the total work so everyone will be busy. The foreman needs to be warned, though, of coming ups and downs in schedules so he can plan his work force.

Central production control

Most companies that are big enough to use flow control are also multiplant companies. Some of the production control work is done in the company's central production control department. Some is done in each plant's production control department. The company's central production control department starts from sales forecasts and such customer orders as are already on hand for specific products. It, the central production control department, makes up weekly and daily final assembly schedules for each factory. It also makes up, for each factory, lists of the subassemblies and parts each factory will need. Central production control also sets up schedules for subassemblies and parts production or purchase.

It would seem unwise to try to make up in, say, Chicago production schedules for Atlanta, Dallas, Seattle, and elsewhere. It would seem better to let each factory's production control department make up its own lists of subassemblies and parts. And it is, of course, better to let each plant make up its own schedules wherever this is feasible. Also, individual plants can be allowed to make their own schedules for items which they make for themselves. But it is different where components come in from outside, whether from sister plants or outside suppliers.

Supplier plants have to ship to a dozen or more of a customer company's plants. They, the suppliers, have to know the customer's *total* requirements so they can plan their production. A maker of fabric for automobile seats, for example, has to plan his runs of each fabric. He can work out his production and shipping schedule much better if he gets one list from a central production control department rather than separate releases from a dozen of a customer's factories.

The central production control department makes all of these schedules and lists (and there are thousands of them) every week or month. Every month the Ford Division of Ford Motor Company sends out schedules to 800 suppliers, giving them schedules for sending 11,000 parts to 16 plants.

Lists from the central production control department always show delivery schedules day by day or week by week, and they also show cumulative figures—how many in total have been released (ordered) since the start of the year. That lets everyone see how the order stands. If *total deliveries* are below *total releases,* the supplier has to catch up. Underruns in any period have to be made up in the next. When deliveries have not kept up with releases, this means that the customer's supply banks are running low. Or, still worse, it means that he runs completely out of an item now and then and so loses production in final assembly.

Besides, all of these schedules have to be redone when there are changes. The company's forecasters can never guess the future market perfectly, so there are changes in the quantities wanted. Sometimes it becomes necessary to make an urgent design change, and again old schedules have to be changed. Such changes mean that all of the lists already out in various plants and supplier companies have to be adjusted and new lists given to them. Change, change, change. Schedules have to be made and remade all the time.

Factory production control

Each plant has its own production control department. It takes the weekly schedules sent from central production control and makes order-of-run lists for final assembly. It also makes specific "loading sheets" to tell loading men in stock rooms, what to put on the supply conveyors which bring subassemblies and parts to the assemblers along the line. A loading sheet tells the supply men to load a blue dashboard onto the supply conveyor for car number 20, a red one for car 21, and so on.

Back in the supply area, the plant's production control staff watches the size of the banks all the time. Materials supply men tell production control men when the banks build up or shrink. To production control men, either one means trouble somewhere. If a bank goes up, final assembly is behind schedule. If it goes down, something is wrong in subassembly production. Production control also gets hourly reports, or even on-line, up-to-the-minute reports of final assembly's production, so it knows the final line's use. But with the thousands of things it must watch, watching the banks (instead of relying wholly on production reports) is a quick way to detect trouble.

Subassemblies

Final products should always be made out of subassemblies whenever possible. It would be hard to imagine, for example, putting, one by one, the separate pieces of an automobile speedometer onto a car going down the assembly line. The assembly line is no place to handle $\frac{1}{8}$ inch parts. The speedometer should be put together as a unit and be fastened onto the assembly as a unit. In fact, and better yet, the speedometer should be put into the dashboard first, and then the whole dashboard should be fastened onto the body of the car.

Most subassemblies are made continuously along assembly lines of their own at rates which match the final assembly line's needs. Production control's work with assembly lines is like controlling final assembly. There is some variety, and it is still necessary to match up the rates of parts production and their use. But controlling any one subassembly line is simpler than controlling the final assembly line because there are fewer parts and less variety.

Three things about subassemblies are different. First, the quantities made are always greater than the final line uses because some extras have to be made to allow for a few rejects and for customers' repair service. Second, the main user is final assembly. If the subassembly production rate per hour doesn't match final assembly's needs (as well as take care of the extras), the subassembly line will have to operate different hours—longer hours if its rate is slower, shorter hours if its rate is faster. Third, the main factory makes some subassemblies for all of the company's other plants. In these cases the subassembly quantities are related to the company's total needs and not at all to the main factory's assembly needs.

FIGURE 21–2. Use of Lazy Susan turntables for making subassemblies. The simple assembling fixtures are quickly changeable for many models. A setup man prepares empty tables for the next job.

Because of different production rates between final assembly and subassemblies, because of the extras for customer repairs, and because of the needs of sister plants, managers have to reconcile themselves to having inventories. Subassembly production and final assembly needs can't be matched perfectly. Subassembly lines usually feed their output into temporary storage areas, from which final assembly is supplied. But the supply or "bank" of items ought to be small, even though this risks stopping final assembly. At the same time, should final assembly stop, subassembling will also have to stop from lack of space to store its output.

Bought items or items shipped in from sister plants are a little different. If they come from nearby, maybe the assembling plant can get by with only a few hours' supply in the bank. But if they come from farther away, it becomes necessary to try to schedule freight cars on the days when the new supplies will be needed. However, rail service from distant points is not too dependable. The using plant cannot count on getting its items exactly when it wants them, so it will have to carry more on hand to be sure of not running out if a freight car is delayed. On the other hand, giant companies have to watch their freight-car schedules very closely. General Motors receives more than 2,000 freight cars of materials every day.

Parts control

Assembly lines are the "showy" parts of manufacturing, where the product takes form. All of the parts are ready—they are the right shape, size, color—and they are ready on time. But behind all the smooth flow of final assembly lines lies a still bigger job: making subassemblies, and making parts for subassemblies. All of their production schedules must mesh with assembly line use.

Controlling parts production is much like controlling subassembly production except that there are thousands of parts to make or buy and only dozens of subassemblies. All their production schedules, again, must tie in with the assembly line needs.

FIGURE 21–3.   Release against purchase order, Economy Motor Division, Standard Motors Corporation

Release No.: 16
Date: 3–14

Source:
XASCO PRODUCTS CO.
1500 Roag Road
Detroit, Mich. 48140

Purchase Order No.: 112579
Description: Cigar Lighter
Part No.:   1318534

Date to ship	Ship to				All-plant total
	Flint	*South Gate*	*Linden*	*Kansas City*	
Prev. Cum.	109137	34878	38805	39923	222743
Week 3–14	5321	2631	2600	2573	13125
Cum.	114458	37509	41405	42496	235868
Week 3–21	5322	2631	2600	2573	13126
Cum.	119780	40140	44005	45069	248994
Week 3–28	5321	2630	2600	2573	13124
Cum.	125101	42770	46605	47642	262118
Week 4–4	5321	2567	2599	2572	13059
Cum.	130422	45337	49204	50214	275177

Most parts differ from subassemblies, too, in that they are made in lots and not continuously. Only big parts are made continuously. But, as we said earlier, making parts in lots does not mean using order control. These lots are repetitive lots. With repetitive lots the lot quantities are set to suit the lines' needs and sent through, say, a new lot every week. Repetitive lots have no lot numbers and use no move orders, route sheets, or drawings. Individual job tickets and job-lot cost collecting are also cut out since standard costs are used.

If it takes a week to process a "lot" of a part, a lot is started into production on, say, Monday. By some time Tuesday the whole lot will be past operation 1, and some of the items will be past operation 2. Some may be even past operation 3. By the second Monday the first of the lot will be

FIGURE 21–4

Economy Motor Division
Status of assembly plant parts shipped

Page: 17
Date: 3–14

Part number	Part name	Assembly plant	Shortage 2d. prev. week	Shortage prev. wk.	Required to ship cur. wk.	Shipped	Schedule through current week
1167494	Pointer	FL	1286	3692	6981	39758	46739
1167494	Pointer	SG	1126	3720	6795	45787	52582
1167494	Pointer	LI	704	3129	6144	47042	53186
1167494	Pointer	KC	402	1888	4515	29540	34055
1167497	Pad	FL				52496	52148
1167497	Pad	SG				51437	51052
1167497	Pad	LI				52221	51844
1167494	Pad	KC				35996	35743
1167516	Ring Horn	FL			5499	42322	47821
1167516	Ring Horn	SG				48525	48091
1167516	Ring Horn	LI			4691	29317	34008
1167516	Ring Horn	KC			4027	19503	21598

coming off the last operation and the whole lot of that part will be finished by, say, the second Tuesday evening. Suppose that this lot was for enough pieces to last two weeks. If so, it will not be necessary to start the next lot through until the third Monday. Then everything will be gone through all over again. By the fourth Tuesday there will be a new supply on hand. Production control decides how big the lots are to be. And it figures out ahead of time when it will be necessary to have a new lot finished and when it must start into production. It also watches the banks of parts being used up as new supplies near completion and makes sure that the supply never runs out.

Production control has to watch, too, to see that it does not overload machines. The machines are used all the time, but for successive lots of *different* parts. If a "lot" of one part is planned to start on a machine on Monday morning, that machine should be free on Monday morning. It cannot still be working on some other part that should have been finished last Friday.

Making repetitive lots in this way is sometimes called cycling. Cycling allows most of the shop papers that go with order control to be cut out. Directions are unnecessary because everyone knows what operations to perform, what tools to use, where to move products, and so on.

Cycling, however, causes many machine setups, and these will be costly unless the engineers design tooling so that it can be put on and taken off machines quickly. Cycling allows machines to be used for several parts and so keeps the machines busy.

Some companies don't go quite this far in cutting out shop paper. Identification tags may still be needed, for example, when different parts look a great deal alike.

GM's Electro-Motive Division (it makes diesel-electric railroad engines) assigns a sequence number to each repetitive, cycled lot. First it makes out a raw materials requisition for enough materials for the lot. This requisition goes to the foreman whose department will do the first operation. The foreman, when his man is ready to work on the job, withdraws the material from the stock room. Sequence numbers are a little like job order numbers in order control in that they identify the job. But they are also job priority numbers. Foremen must process low numbers first.

There is no regular shop order, however, so the foreman has to be otherwise told what operations to perform. Usually he knows, without any new instructions, because he has made many lots of the same item before. Actually, he has in his office a list of every part regularly coming through his department. And for every part he has an operation list covering the operations to be done in his department. He can turn to his book of operation lists if he is in doubt. If an item is not a regular item, he will get a regular shop order, as in order control; it will tell him what to do.

Electro-Motive's method also tells the factory's central production control office how the lot is moving through production—but only as it moves from one department to the next, not as it moves within a department. Products going out of a department pass a final inspector who not only inspects what goes out but reports to production control which lots and how many units have gone on to the next department. Foremen always tell production control, though, when any lots are held up in their departments, so production control knows right away about holdups. Should there be any problem of frequent holdups, this whole reporting system could be tightened up by having operation completions reported to the computer on an on-line basis.

Service conveyors

Except for small parts, only small amounts of supplies can be stored at work stations along the assembly line because of lack of space. Almost always it will be necessary to put in conveyors to bring a steady stream of parts from stock supply areas to the assembly line. These service conveyors are usually closed-circuit loops that travel continually. Men in the supply areas put parts on the pans or trays or hooks, from which the assemblers help themselves.

Loop-service conveyors should have many pans, and they should all (or nearly all) be filled as they leave the stock supply area so assemblers ready for parts will almost never have to wait. Whenever they need a part they should be able to reach out and get it from the pan moving by. When there are several assemblers doing the same work, say assembling electric motors, they all use the same parts. Even if the pans are all full to start with, the last man served by the conveyor may have to wait while several empties go by before he finds one still carrying parts.

To keep this from happening often, there should be more pans per minute going past the assemblers than they will ever empty at one pass. Whatever they do not use just stays on the conveyor and goes around again. Since service conveyors often come from distant points and move slowly for ease of unloading and loading, it may take an hour for them to move from the supply point to the assemblers. And since a good many parts go around more than once, there may be several hours' supply of parts on the service conveyor all the time. In the automobile industry, all of the inventories on service conveyors, and also on assembly lines, are called "float."

Lead time

As we said in earlier chapters, lead time is the time between ordering an item and getting it. Production control has to know the usual lead times on all items, and particularly on all items made in lots or items shipped in. Lead times make trouble because they are irregular, especially for the shipped-in items. Rail freight from distant suppliers is something like the mail. Sometimes it comes through fast and other times not so fast.

Production control sets all start dates for making parts and assemblies with the usual lead times in mind. It is the same with vendors; the schedules of shipments that production control sends them allow for the usual lead times.

It is so easy to say "allow for the usual lead times" that it makes it sound simple. General Motors Assembly Division's production control department has to make up several thousand schedules every month just for assembly work alone. How many more schedules its separate factory production control departments make for piece parts GMAD has never counted.

Lead times vary from 0 to 10 days for items coming in to the typical GMAD plant. *How* long depends mostly on where they come from, but part of the time allowed is to take care of irregularities in shipping. It takes from 0 to 30 days to make parts and subassemblies. It takes 5 to 8 days to ship home-plant-supplied parts to the other plants. Then it takes from 0 to 10 days in the other plants. These lead times follow one another, chain fashion. First it is necessary to allow lead time to get bought materials or parts, then time to make parts and subassemblies, then time to ship to other plants, then time for final assembly. Finally, it adds up to anywhere from 5 to 58 days. Production control has to know what the reasonable lead time is for every item.

Besides this are such matters as scheduling things to arrive on different days of the week so whole freight trains will not be waiting to be unloaded on Monday morning and then have nothing coming in on Thursday. It is apparent that schedulers in continuous manufacturing can keep busy. Furthermore, every time the forecasters miss the market a little, all of these schedules have to be changed hurriedly in order to try to bring production back into line with sales. There are also strikes in supplier plants, or a snowstorm or flood along a railroad. These also upset production schedules and make it necessary to do them all over again.

Load control

Back on page 442 we considered how a factory doing job-lot work set schedules and paid attention to the load of work ahead. If, however, a man says that his company uses "load control," this is a little different from what we talked about on page 442. Anyone talking about load control is usually referring to making schedules for one or more big, important machines.

A big or key machine is used for many sizes and varieties of products, and the load control idea is to apportion its time to jobs. Usually the key machine is a fast producer, such as a printing press that prints magazines, telephone books, Sears, Roebuck catalogs, books, and so on. Some of these printing presses turn out as many as 10,000 magazines an hour.

But, in one sense, even such a fast machine is a bottleneck. It is a bottleneck compared with the minor operations before it and after it. The point is that the minor jobs do not need to be scheduled at all. There is plenty of capacity to handle all the big machine turns out. Its schedule is everything.

Load control requires order numbers so that quantities can be controlled. It is necessary, for example, to get the right pages into the right magazines or books.

The rubber industry has a different situation with its calenders (large machines for rolling rubber mixtures into sheets of exact thicknesses). They are kept busy all the time on certain material. The only schedule they need is the amount of each size of the product to run each day. Small increases or decreases in the quantity can be cared for by varying the number of hours worked daily. And if they run a little over or under in one day, they even it out the next. (This cannot be done, however, in printing. Extra pages for one book do not make up for a shortage of pages of another book.)

Process manufacturing

Processing industries change the physical or chemical form of large quantities of materials. Included are companies making gasoline, chemicals, paint, flour, glass, rayon, nylon, cement, asphalt tile, plaster, and even paper. "Production" takes place inside tanks, retorts, vessels, and furnaces as materials are mixed or heated and as changes go on. Equipment is connected by pipes and ducts which move the material around. The production is not visible.

Normally such equipment runs at full capacity or not at all. Changing quantities means changing work hours. Normally, however, big companies have several processing lines, so they can vary production by changing either work hours or the number of lines in operation.

Production is usually to stock or to large sales orders, but even if it is to stock, not much stock is carried. Volume is so great that a few days' production would fill all the storage tanks or warehouses.

Process companies use flow production control, but it is a little different from the automobile kind. The factory gets weekly lists of products, quantities, and sequences for running different products. These lists are sent out to only a few places—just to men in charge at key points, where the equipment has to be reset to make different products. When there are duplicate lines, production control makes up schedules for each one.

Production control gives out no processing instructions telling the factory *how* to make products. All processing instructions are in the foreman's specification books. Nor are there any move orders or cost collection reports since standard costs are used. Production control, however, does get reports, perhaps hourly, of production, and at the end of each day it gets reports of the exact quantities run. And it gets a telephone report right away if anything goes wrong during the day. On-line reporting is common.

As in automobile flow control, production control in processing companies has to send out vendor release schedules. And the tremendous volume (one or more whole freight trains a day) necessitates carefully worked out incoming materials schedules.

It is the same thing on the going-out side. It takes just as many freight cars to haul products away as it did to get raw materials in. Production control, however, is usually not concerned with the going-out freight cars—only with having the material *ready* to go out.

Production control in processing companies has two problems that differ from other flow control. One occurs early in production, the other late in production.

Processing industries usually start with products of nature, which are never quite consistent; sulfur, iron, sand for glass, and wood for pulp are not homogeneous. The laboratory has to be ever watchful in inspecting the materials for chemical or physical variations. Nearly always there is some variation and this has to be compensated for. Sometimes all that is necessary is to mix and blend materials from different shipments. This helps make the material which goes into processing more homogeneous. Or it may be possible to adjust mixing formulas, processing temperatures, processing times, or other factors to compensate for nature's variations. The production control department is concerned with the last of these—the processing times—because they will affect the rate of output.

Production control in processing industries also often has special work to do for the last stages of production, particularly with packaging and labeling. It has to issue specific directions for the packaging operations so that the right number of each size of package, or brand name, or the right cuts to size are made.

Batch manufacturing

In early stages of manufacture it is often necessary to mix and process batches of materials. Batch processing occurs in many branches of the food processing and canning industry where materials are mixed and then cooked. In the paint industry, paints and coloring materials are made in batches. It is the same with rubber, which is mixed with its ingredients in batches. Drugs and pharmaceuticals are processed in batches. Glass is often made by melting fixed quantities of sand at a time. Iron, steel, and other metals are usually made in "heats."

The size of the batch is usually dependent on the size of the equipment. Several hundred pounds of ingredients are brought together into batches and put into masticators or mixers. Sometimes, as in extracting metal from ore, the process is heating rather than mixing. Sometimes chemical reactions are involved.

In batch manufacturing the production control department has to schedule the mixing or heating equipment in accord with the time cycle for each batch as specified by the laboratory. Also, production control has to set finished-product quantities to use up whole batches. Batch sizes are usually fixed, and only full batches are made. Then the whole quantity, produced by full batches, is made into finished products. (Often, as in the case of foods and rubber, this must be done to save loss because mixed but unfinished material is perishable. If it is mixed, it has to be made into finished products immediately.) The quantity of finished products made at a given time is more dependent on batch sizes than it is on the need for exactly so many finished products.

The control system most often used in batch manufacturing is load control. Order numbers, operation job tickets, and move orders are not needed.

Block control

Block control, a variation of order control, is used in the men's clothing industry. Before men's suits are manufactured, styles and cloth patterns are decided upon and pictures and samples are sent out to the retailers. Retailers make their selections and order the suits they want, distributed as they see fit among sizes, styles, and patterns.

The factory's ability to turn out suits is relatively fixed at so many suits per day. Production control groups the orders by cloth pattern and by style. Then it adds groups together into "blocks." A block is the number of suits the factory can turn out in half a day.

All orders in the block will be issued to the plant at once. A new block is issued each half day. Within a block, *every suit has its own individual suit number* so that the sleeves, pockets, etc., for the suit will be brought together into the right coat. All suits belonging to the same order carry the order number also, and all suits in the block carry the block number.

Each suit is inspected several times during its manufacture, and its individual suit number is checked off as it passes the inspection station. Any suit in process can be located readily from the records at the inspection stations. Departments are required to finish a whole block before clearing the block. If any suit gets behind, production control knows it right away or that suit is replaced in the block by one from the next block.

Block control is both a method of releasing identical amounts of work to the factory at half-day intervals and a method of pushing orders through. It does not cause any more suits to be produced, but it makes sure that no suit gets pushed aside and forgotten.

The ladies' shoe industry uses a method quite similar to block control except that no block numbers are used and individual pairs of shoes are not given individual numbers.

Ladies' shoes are not so standard as men's suits, so it is not feasible to assume that the plant can turn out the same number of pairs of shoes every day or half day. Instead, production control looks at the piecework cost of cutting the leather upper part of the shoes on each order. The records show how much money the cutters in the cutting department earn every day, and this is a relatively fixed amount of money. So in order to release orders to the factory in an even flow, it is only necessary to add up, order by order, the cutting cost for each pair of shoes until the total equals what the cutters earn in a day. This many orders, and no more, are then issued to the factory for the day.

Once started into production, the shoes go through checking points where the progress of each order is recorded. A report is also made to the production control department, where the date the operation is completed is noted in a book showing the progress of all orders.

In both men's clothing and the ladies' shoe industries, shop orders are made out showing the number and kind of products to make. Operations are so standard, however, that printed operation lists are used. The list is printed on lightweight cardboard, on which each operation is represented by a detachable stub. When an operation is performed, the piece worker (nearly all work in both of these industries is done on piecework) detaches the stub for the operation he has completed, puts it with the others he has accumulated, and turns them in as his report of the work he has done.

Block control uses no schedules in the usual sense of the term. What starts in at one end of the factory has to come out the other end, and in about the usual time. If it slows down, this will show up when it fails to pass the checking stations.

Nor is there any concern over the ability of all departments to get out the work. There could be bottlenecks sometimes, but not often, because the size of successive departments is in balance. The sewing department is just the right size to handle all that the cutting department turns out, and so on with other departments. Fortunately, normal differences in product mix have little effect on the work loads of different departments.

Review questions

1. How can the production control department reconcile the steady use of parts with their being produced or received in lots without carrying large inventories?

2. What problems are there in scheduling work along an assembly line? Explain.

3. What problems differ in controlling subassembly and parts production lines and final assembly lines? How does this affect production control?

4. In a multiplant company, what work should the company's central production control staff do and which work should be left to be done by each plant's own production control staff?

5. How does cycling operate in the manufacture of parts for assembly lines? How is cycling like, and how is it different from, order control?

6. What is the difference between load control and the subject of machine loads as discussed in Chapter 20?

7. How are block and load control alike? How are they different? Under what conditions would each be best to use?

8. How do the variations in raw materials as nature provides them affect the work of controlling production in mass-production industries?

9. In companies using block control little attention is paid to the capacities of departments other than the key department whose load is used as the control. How do such companies keep from sometimes ending up with substantially unequal work loads in other departments?

10. How does manufacture by batches affect production control? Explain.

Discussion questions

1. Suppose that a product has several generations of subassemblies (a part goes into a minor subassembly, which goes into a bigger assembly, which goes into a major assembly, which goes into the final product). And suppose that final assembly is continuous. What are the pros and cons of making the earlier generations of subassemblies continuously as against making them in lots? What happens to inventories? To production costs?

2. Are lead times more important in flow control than in order control? Explain.

3. When changing models, is it better to close down the plant during the changeover or to phase new models in gradually? Discuss the problems involved.

4. How does parts manufacture for volume production differ from final assembly so far as production is concerned? What problems are peculiar to parts production? What should be done about them?

5. Assembled product manufacturers using assembly lines often go ahead and assemble a product discovered early along the line to be defective in some way. At first this does not sound very smart. Under what conditions might it be smart? What should be done at the end of the line with the faulty product? What should be done with the parts if they are not attached?

6. At the close of its model year, one of Detroit's big three car companies had 160,000 door handles left over. How can very large-scale production "balance out" and finish with just the right number of parts to complete the final products coming off the line yet not have, say, 160,000 door handles left over? In discussing this problem one should keep in mind the lead times listed in the text as applying at GMAD.

7. In batch or semicontinuous processing operations, how do the materials handling operations differ from those where order control is used? Would one be more likely to find centralized or decentralized materials handling control procedures? Would highly automated handling systems likely be found in these operations?

8. In terms of the required information flow, how do block and load control compare with order control? For operations of comparable size, would the work load on the production control staff be less or greater with block or load control as opposed to order control?

Case 21–1

The ABC Company wanted to make the most effective possible use of its machines used in making parts. Accordingly it adopted a "cycling" arrangement whereby certain equipment was used on several jobs during the course of each two days. A set sequence of jobs and regular quantities of parts were turned out each two days. In all, the machines in the cycled group were each used for seven operations.

The objectives of the management (getting a steady flow of parts and full machine utilization) were realized. The management's satisfaction in this accomplishment was somewhat deflated, however, when the records showed that one quarter of the pay of the men on the cycled machines was paid to them for changing machine setups and that the machines were idle one quarter of the time while being set up.

What are the values of short cycles? Are the benefits great enough to justify higher setup costs and machine idle time? Is there any way to work on short cycles and not lose considerable money and capacity because of setups?

Case 21–2

The ABC Spark Plug Company was somewhat chagrined to learn that its spark plugs were being marketed in the city where the factory was located at a retail price below its factory selling price. A check of dealer records disclosed that Joe's Handy Shop, where the spark plugs were being sold, was not listed as a purchaser. The spark plugs were genuine ABC plugs and were of first quality. It appeared certain that they were being stolen by workers in the factory. A careful watch was kept of all finished stock, but the leak was not discovered.

Production records disclosed no disappearance of materials in process, yet Joe's Handy Shop continued to sell ABC plugs at prices under factory costs. All the checking was done without fanfare and was carried on for a whole year. One day an unannounced inspection of empty lunch boxes of workers leaving at the end of the first shift was made. One lunch box was found to contain a substantial number of porcelain parts for spark plugs. Upon being confronted with this evidence, the employee explained the leak. Three employees were involved. Each took home an occasional handful of the completed parts made in his department. The spark plugs were assembled at their homes and sold to Joe's Handy Shop. Spark plug parts were made in very large numbers and no exact counts were made during processing. Production records were all kept in terms of pounds instead of pieces, and tote boxes of parts were filled reasonably full and then sent on to the next operation. The few scrap pieces produced were thrown into scrap cans at the site of the operation. Generally no check was made on the volume of scrap except for an occasional check to see that it remained within the limits permitted. It was easy for workers to remove a few pieces at a time at any point in the operations without detection.

How might a system be devised to control such a situation? Is petty thievery a problem in very many companies? Should a company institute regular lunch box inspection?

Case 21–3

Richard Hamer, newly appointed head of the production control department of the Rigney Foundry and Machine Company, was 28 years old. He came to the company after two years of college and had been with the Rigney company ever since. In a factory management magazine he read an article describing the operation of "block" control in the textile industry. It pointed out how scheduling was greatly simplified by assigning orders to "blocks" which moved through successive departments more or less as units. The idea seemed good, and Hamer decided to try it out.

He decided that the logical way of grouping orders was to use the molding department as the basis. A block was set as an amount of work which would keep the molding department busy for a half day. Various jobs were to be assigned to each block. Their total molding time requirements would equal that available in a half day. Individual orders would show the block number in addition to the order number. The foremen of all departments were to be required to complete all orders in a block before another block would be cleared out of their departments.

What difficulties would probably arise in using this system in the foundry? What would happen in the machine shop (still assuming that block numbers were set to equate molding requirements of orders)? Can any part of the block idea be used in the case above? A requirement of block control is that the production capacities of successive departments be equal. How can that be accomplished in the above case?

Recent references

Gopta, J. N. D., "Improved Combinatorial Algorithm for Flowshop Scheduling Problems," *Operations Research,* November 1971

Pai, Ashok R., and Keith L. McRoberts, "Simulation Research in Interchangeable Part Manufacturing," *Management Science,* August 1971

Sass, C. J., "Cost Control on the Production Line," *Business Automation,* July 1971

Schrier, Elliot, "Production Planning in a Multiplant System," *California Management Review,* Summer 1969

22

Information systems and network analyses

THE SYSTEMS CONCEPT has come into common use in the study of production and operations management. In this context, it deals with all of the activities which take inputs and, using them, create values, and result in outputs. And although production systems vary with different industries and companies, there is a common thread in these different applications. This is the viewing of organizations as functioning totalities composed of somewhat unlike components or subsystems which must function both within themselves and as parts of the total system.

A man is a totality which functions as a total system, yet he has subsystems for breathing, eating, blood flow, and other functions. Each system receives stimuli and reacts and operates as a system, yet its operations are compatible with the other subsystems which make up the total system. Each subsystem operates within itself, yet it receives information from and sends information to other subsystems. The combined effects of everything operating together constitute a man in action.

In production organizations the systems idea has to do with both the flow of information and the subsets of activities which must be carried on and coordinated in order for the organization to be productive. Information flows into subsystems and causes certain actions. This generates results, or production, and so resulting information flows out. Each subsystem operates in a logical way, both internally and as a part of the whole. Both the actual work done and the related information flow system need to function as coordinated parts of a single management flow system.

In a man, nature designs both the subsets of operating systems and the subsets of information flow. And nature makes the information flows compatible so that when a man's nervous system reports that his finger is on a hot iron, his muscular system uses that information and instantly jerks his hand away.

But in production organizations the information system which ties the subset operating systems together has to be man made. Managers have to figure out what information they need and how to generate it. The goal is to get information to the right people, who then should do whatever they *should* do. And the information which goes from department to department needs to be compatible so that each person receives the information he needs in the form he can use.

Almost always, in a business organization, the management information system includes the analysis of accounting, payroll records, inventory records, the making of manufacturing orders, purchase orders, and the handling of customer orders and accounts. It includes all reports about them and changes in any of them. These different parts of the total activity used to be handled in a disjointed way, as many little separate systems and procedures, but computers can now handle them all as parts of a single unified system.

Systems are not always concerned with the continued operation of an ongoing enterprise. "Systems" can be a methodic way of planning and coordinating the work needed to produce a single complex project, such as a 5-mile-long bridge, or a nuclear powered ship, or building a new factory or shopping center. Everything has to be coordinated and planned with an eye to the successful completion of the whole project by a certain time and within the budget. The PERT system (taken up later in this chapter) typifies this kind of system.

Systems designers must often be concerned with the *reliability* of a system (one application of this idea was discussed on p. 264). A system's reliability is of utmost importance in such a product as a moon space ship. And it is just as important in an airplane, and only slightly less important in an automobile.

The reliability of a moon-ship system relates to the certainty that the spacecraft will operate well under the extreme conditions of outer space. The whole spacecraft is a "system" made up of electronic, physical, and chemical subsystems. If the spacecraft fails to perform, it is because one of its subsystems fails.

A system can also be a mathematical model, a formula. Particularly, it is a system if it has information feedback and a time dimension. Certain factors (all of which can be simulated quantitatively in a formula) interact and produce a certain result. This result then becomes the starting point for a second generation set of interactions which produce a new result. This in turn sets off another round of interaction and result, etc. Such mathematical models can also show the results of extreme or unusual combinations of factors. All that is necessary is to put the appropriate values for the extreme or unusual conditions into the formula and calculate the answers.

To some people, systems are nonmathematical simulation models. A model builder decides how several factors will interact and sets up a model which incorporates these interactions. Then he pretends that certain events occur and sees what the results would have been had those events really occurred. (Simulation was discussed in Chapter 2.)

There are also other ideas of what systems are, but there is not space here to go into them all. Our discussion will be confined largely to systems as the integrated flow of information.

The systems department

Since integrated systems cover the flow of information throughout the organization, it is desirable to have a staff department develop them and oversee their operations. In many companies this department is called the management information systems (MIS) department. In General Motors it is called the Corporate Information Service (CIS) department. One of CIS's most important areas of work is production control and procurement because all of GM's automobile divisions need a central clearing house for identifying and grouping orders for car options and accessories.

When a company does not have a central department, order forms, reports, and records grow up piecemeal in separate departments and are designed with only one department's needs in mind. Not often is the next department's need for some of the same information thought of. This is uneconomical because it means a great deal of copying whatever facts the next department needs from the reports and putting them into a different form.

A central systems department can integrate the information flow. When a sales order arrives, it can be immediately recorded with the customer's name, the items he wants, when he wants them, where he wants them sent, and all other such data onto tabulating cards or magnetic tapes. Then the computer can start to handle the order. It can check to see which items can be shipped immediately and which will have to be manufactured or bought. And the computer can make out all of the various papers connected with the order. It gives information and orders to many departments and gets reports back from them. But in every case the design and amount of detail on the instructions and reports consider both the department directly concerned and the needs of other departments.

Some companies have tried, when they put in a computer, to put individual procedures, one after the other, onto the computer and to integrate them as they are computerized. This does not seem to work out very well because they sometimes have to change their first computerized procedures when they hook in other procedures. Companies which have started from scratch, paying little attention to existing procedures, seem to have had better experiences. They have often developed new procedures from the ground up.

This thorough study of systems and procedures streamlines the paper work so much that savings come as much from streamlining the systems as from letting the computer do the work.

Systems and procedures. Systems and procedures are not quite the same thing. "Systems" covers more ground. Making out a customer's bill (an invoice) is an example of a *procedure*, not a system. It is restricted, being concerned only with the invoice, and usually with only one or two departments. Studies of how an invoice ought to be designed and who should get copies containing what information will help an analyst see where he can cut some corners. But if he studies only the way to handle an invoice, he is likely to miss seeing how it fits into the big picture, the whole system.

Developing an integrated system

It is highly desirable that a wholly integrated system be developed if this is possible. Then all of the subsidiary information flows will be compatible and will supplant and reinforce each other.

This idealistic goal may, however, be unrealistic. Giant organizations are just too complex. Possibly the best that can be expected is to have compatible integrated systems within major subunits of the whole enterprise. It might be likened to the need for a federal government, and for separate state governments, and city and county units, each with its own system that is largely set up for its own use and only loosely integrated into the larger units.

John Dearden says that it is impossible for giant organizations to have wholly integrated management information systems. And, he says, companies which try to set up such systems are trying to do something which cannot be done.[1] In fact, Dearden sees harm in the idea that there can be a completely integrated system because it leads to resources being wasted trying to do an impossible job. He would settle for such systems covering whole areas, such as financial accounting, marketing, or production, but would not hope for a single system covering the whole. He would leave subject interface relationships to be handled more on an individual basis. Within this limitation—that an MIS can cover only a large segment of the organization—it is probable that it can contribute significantly to effective operations.

Usually the development of an MIS needs to be done by a central systems department. When such a department is first set up, there may be some resistance to its work because it will change the status quo. Every department head already has an MIS of his own, which may not be well developed or fit in very well with anyone else's MIS. And it may or may not furnish him with the information he needs. It may, in fact, *mis*inform him sometimes. But he likes his system and does not want to turn any part of his power over to a central staff group.

The job of the systems men is made doubly difficult because they need the help of these reluctant department heads in order to develop an integrated system. The analyst developing an integrated system has to find out from the various department heads what information they need, and where it comes from, and what information they send on to someone else. All too often the various department heads tell him how necessary their reports are and that they need every bit of information there is on them (and more).

In his investigation the analyst should always try to focus on the work to be done and the information necessary to do the work. He should try to find out what details of information each man now gets (and also what he sends on to someone else). And he should try to see if each item of information is needed in order for him to perform his function.

He should try to answer such questions as: How is the item used? Is it an instruction? Does anyone take action based on it? Or is it just for background? What would the man do if he did not get this report? Does the item need to be reported daily? Weekly? Does it change often? Would periodic summaries do or are details necessary? If it is an instruction, can it do double duty and serve also as a report of work done? Does anyone ever copy any information from one form onto another?

Does the man need absolute numbers? Or ratios to the plan or to the budget? Or does he need reports of variations? Will reporting only the exceptions do? Or, as in inventory control, will it suffice to report only

---

[1] See "MIS Is a Mirage," by John Dearden, in *Harvard Business Review* (January–February 1972), pp. 90–99.

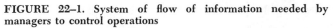

FIGURE 22–1. System of flow of information needed by managers to control operations

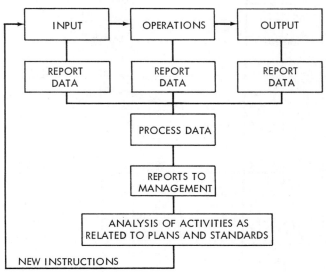

items nearing or past the critical point? Are there any legal requirements about record keeping?

Where is the best place to make out this report? In a central office? In a separate department? Out on the shop floor? Can the computer prepare it? When should instruction forms be made out? How should they travel about?

Process charts of the kind described in Chapter 13 (on job design) can be employed to advantage in analyzing office procedures for improvement purposes. Each step in the procedure—entering the information, transferring it to other departments, transcribing it to other records, etc. —can be indicated on process charts.

Systems analysis usually shows that too many kinds of reports are made and too much unused information is put on them. Copies are sent to too many places and to too many persons who don't need them. Sometimes a whole report can be cut out; if not, certain steps in its preparation can be omitted. One report, perhaps with slight modifications, can be made to serve two purposes.

The analyst may have to resort to a form of trickery to cut down on copies of reports. If he asks each man on the list if he needs to get a copy of the report, the man will always say yes. (Being on all the lists to get all the reports is partly a matter of prestige.) The analyst, however, should try not sending him the report a few times. Companies which have tried this report that some of the men who just had to have copies never missed them.

FIGURE 22–2.   Integrated purchasing and inventory control system

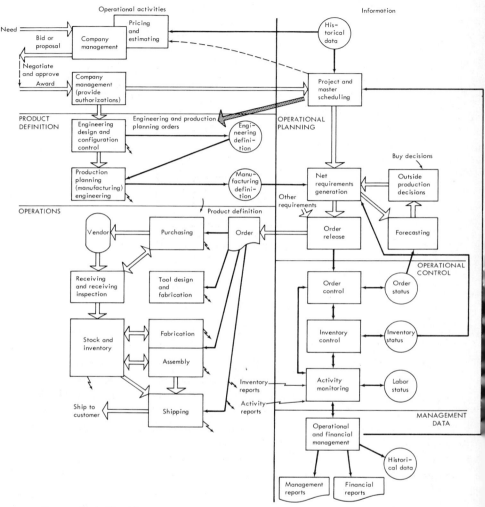

Source: A. A. Kusnick.

Reports

One of the main end products of information flow is reports—reports which tell managers what is going on so they can take action when it is needed. Every manager has, in large part, to direct and control his organization by indirect means; that is, by what he learns from reports. Reports serve as his eyes. They tell him what has happened, how what has happened compares to plans, and what new action is being taken. Figure 22–3 lists some of the reports that managers need.

FIGURE 22–3. **Periodical reports**

WEEKLY REPORT

Type of Report	*Who Gets It*
Production: major items	Plant managers, top management, foremen
Order backlogs	President, sales management, plant managers
Inventories: raw materials, finished goods	Top management, sales management
Budget comparisons: overhead, sales, direct and indirect labor, etc.	President, top management
Manufacturing efficiency	Plant manager
Payroll: hourly, incentive, overtime	Controller, personnel
Employment: numbers employed	Personnel management, plant foremen

MONTHLY REPORT

Type of Report	*Who Gets It*
Shipments per man-hour	Controller, plant foremen
Orders booked	President, sales management, plant management
Production: comparative and cumulative, against budget	All top management
Inventories: finished, in process, raw materials	President, sales management, manufacturing management, plant foremen
Costs by functions: purchasing, accounting, etc.	Top management, middle management
Profit margins by product	Top management
Product profit and loss	All executives, directors
Cost trends	President, controller, manufacturing management
Budget comparisons: budget and variance, purchases to budget, sales to budget, purchases to gross sales, etc.	All top management, board of directors, middle management, plant foremen, plant supervisors
Interpretive comment (graphs, oral briefings, etc.) by controller	Top and middle management

SPECIAL REPORTS

Type of Report	*Who Gets It*
Break-even points	President, directors, all top managers, middle managers
Capital equipment on order	President, directors
Appraisals of employees	Personnel management
Tax effects	President, controller
Industry comparisons	President, sales, and plant management
Overhead	President, controller, top management
Price and cost trends	President, controller, top management

Computers and reports.   Computers, with their enormous capacities and speeds, have made the problems of reports both simpler and more difficult at the same time. They have made them simpler in that managers can now get better, quicker, and less costly reports. But computers have made the problems more difficult because they can easily turn out a flood of reports. Managers can get so many reports, and they are so complete, that they will swamp the managers unless the latter exercise restraint in requesting them.

Production units.   In Chapter 6, when talking about capacity, we noted that it is not possible to talk very intelligently about capacity in many companies because there is no one product. Instead of a single kind of output there are many kinds of outputs—but no one "unit of output." The product mix destroys the reliability of any one production unit as being representative of capacity.

This difficulty undermines the usefulness of reports because the unit of reporting is a shifting base. If, for example, a steel foundry makes more big castings one week than it did the week before, its tonnage of castings made will probably go up. Possibly the number of small castings went down, so the efficiency of the foundry was about the same both weeks. But the report of tons produced would make one week's output look better. Depending on the mix of big and little castings, the tonnage can go up or down when in reality there is no change in the operating effectiveness of the department.

The product mix difficulty does not keep managers from being able to make any comparisons at all. But it does necessitate more detail in reports. This difficulty also puts a bigger burden on management to interpret the figures furnished them in reports. When the foundry's tonnage goes up or down, the top manager has to try to find out if it was because of product mix changes or if it came from better or poorer work by the foundry organization.

Information retrieval

Yesterday it was filing, today it is information retrieval. The change, however, is more than a change in names.

It is still necessary to file correspondence, reports, receipts, time cards, personnel records, and other records. And contracts and drawings also have to be filed. All of these items need to be put away in some logical order so they can be found when someone wants them. And, of course, papers no longer needed should be thrown out.

Retrieval has to do with finding what is wanted; and we would still call it filing if it were only putting away and getting letters or drawings out of files. But, with microfilm, hundreds of times as many documents (or rather pictures of documents) can be stored in small storage spaces. Original documents can be photographed and reduced to inch- or half inch-square size. (Information already on a computer tape, such as a payroll register, can go directly onto microfilm without photographing.) And later, if a document is wanted, it can be blown back up to size on a viewer, or a big positive print can be made. Microfilming lets a company get rid of the originals—unless they are legal contracts, in which case the actual documents have to be retained. Sometimes, too, government regulations require that original records be saved.

It is hard enough to find letters and drawings just filed regularly, but their being on subminiature film makes their retrieval a much bigger job. In microfilming's early days, a document's picture was hunted up by passing a roll of film past a scanner until the wanted picture turned up, but now this is too slow. Today's systems are infinitely faster.

There are several systems now in use. One is the aperture card, which is simply a tabulating card which has a hole in it to hold a 35 mm. film picture of a document. The other part of the card contains punch-coded information about the document which lets a machine find the card. When it is located, it goes into an enlarging viewer. Aperture cards are particularly useful for engineering drawings.

A second system uses "chips" about ½ inch by 1 inch in size. Each chip contains a small film of one or two documents. The chip also contains a system of coded dots that the machine uses to identify the chip. One variant of the chip idea is called microfiche. Microfiche cards are larger, however, usually 4 by 6 inches. Each microfiche card contains many filmed miniatures, perhaps as many as 200.

A third system puts the pictures on a roll of film tape with an identification code between every four documents. This lets the machine locate a picture quickly. This method makes it possible to locate the document from a condensed film file of a million pages and make a photo facsimile of it in less than half a minute.

Microfilms have also entered a submicro stage. National Cash Register has a filming arrangement it calls Microforms by which it can reduce 3,200 8½ by 11-inch pages and put them on a 4 by 6 plastic sheet. (Enlarged copies of whatever is wanted cost about $1 each.) It is hard to visualize the Sears, Roebuck catalog or the New York City telephone book being put on a postcard-size sheet of pastic, yet it can be done. This method seems to have great possibilities for catalogs, encyclopedias, and libraries. Like all miniature systems, Microforms requires a good cataloging system which lets things be found quickly.

Records retention

It is bad enough that someone wants to keep every letter and report, yet the possible future need for most items is so little that they should be retained for only a short time (if at all). There is, however, good reason to keep copies of patents, property titles, contracts, and other legal documents. And files of drawings for old products need to be kept so that repair parts can continue to be made.

Besides these, many records that are otherwise of little value must be kept to meet legal requirements. Records related to income taxes need to be kept for many years if a charge of fraud might be made, since the statute of limitations does not apply to possible future questions by the government on income tax matters. The law also requires that employees' time cards be kept for two years. Social security and unemployment compensation laws require that records of employee pay be kept for four years.

The important point here is not the need to keep records for from two to four years but the need to keep a records disposal calendar and to throw out old records as soon as the law allows.

Network models

Network models can be of several kinds, but the principal one is PERT. PERT is a kind of assembly chart showing how the separate parts of a big job tie together. "Milestone" charts, another variety of assembly-type charts, are often used in conjunction with PERT. Line-of-balance (LOB) charts, a third type of network model, are also often used in conjunction with PERT. DART is a fourth type of network model. All of these models also have certain similarities to Gantt-type charts (which have a long history).

PERT

PERT ("program evaluation review technique") is a precedence matrix method that is used to plan and control large, complex projects that require many activities which must all finally come together to produce the completed project.[2] PERT is of most help where there are many subparts of work, some of which have to follow one another whereas other activities can go on at the same time. The chart shows which activities have to be done before others, which can go on concurrently, and which are more or less unrelated.

Figure 22–4 is a schematic PERT network and is made up of little circles connected by lines. The lettered circles, or nodes, are called "events" although they are not really events. Sometimes they are called "milestones." They represent the completion of certain work. The con-

---

[2] Many other terms are used besides PERT. CPM is the critical path method. LOB is line of balance. RAMPS means resource allocation and multipurpose scheduling. MAP means multiple allocation procedure. Other terms are PRISM, or program reliability information system for management; PEP, or program evaluation procedure; IMPACT, or integrated management planning and control technique; SCANS, scheduling and control by automated network systems; MPM, or metra potential method; BBN, or building block networks, and PPS, or project planning system.

FIGURE 22–4. A simple PERT diagram

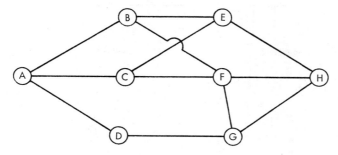

necting lines, called "activities," depict work being done. All of the work which goes on goes on along the lines and not in the circles. The length of the activity lines in a PERT diagram has no meaning at all, and they are short or long according to chart making convenience.

The next step, once the activity sequence has been established, is to make time estimates of how long activities will take. Since the activities are often somewhat unstructured, no one really knows just how long they will take. Consequently, the PERT process sometimes uses three time estimates for each activity. The main figure of these three estimates is the

FIGURE 22–5. PERT diagram with expected activity performance times

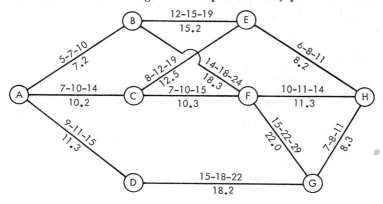

one for the most probable time. An optimistic estimate for the shortest reasonable probable time is also estimated, as is a pessimistic time for the longest reasonable probable time.

All three of these time values are shown in Figure 22–5 along the activity lines. They are then averaged together on a weighted basis, with the most likely time given a weight of 4 and the optimistic and pessimistic times a weight of 1 each. Thus the calculation for activity A–B is (the optimistic time + 4 × the expected time + the pessimistic time) ÷ 6, or $5 + 4 \times 7 + 10 = 43 \div 6 = 7.2$. The 7.2 is, from this point forward, used

FIGURE 22–6

Activity		Time estimates			Weighted-average t_e
Beginning event	Ending event	Optimistic	Most likely	Pessimistic	
A	B	5	7	10	7.2
A	C	7	10	14	10.2
A	D	9	11	15	11.3
B	E	12	15	19	15.2
B	F	14	18	24	18.3
C	E	8	12	19	12.5
C	F	7	10	15	10.3
D	F	15	18	22	18.2
E	H	6	8	11	8.2
F	H	10	11	14	11.3
F	G	15	22	29	22.0
G	H	7	8	11	8.3

as the expected time for the activity and is referred to as the t_e for the activity. Figure 22–6 shows the t_es for all of the activities (the numbers are weeks of time).

These t_e times have been written in on Figure 22–5 along their respective activity lines. In this example it is possible, by inspection, to see what all of the various pathways are. Their activities can then be listed and their t_e times added up to get a total time for each path. (In real life on big projects, this would all be done on a computer.) The paths and the sums of the activity times are:

	Path	Expected time in weeks	Total
I	A-B-E-H	7.2 + 15.2 + 8.2	30.6
II	A-B-F-H	7.2 + 18.3 + 11.3	36.8
III	A-B-F-G-H	7.2 + 18.3 + 22.0 + 8.3	55.8
IV	A-C-E-H	10.2 + 12.5 + 8.2	30.9
V	A-C-F-H	10.2 + 10.3 + 11.3	31.8
VI	A-C-F-G-H	10.2 + 10.3 + 22.0 + 8.3	50.8
VII	A-D-G-H	11.3 + 18.2 + 8.3	37.8

This listing shows that pathway A-B-F-G-H, the "critical path," requires 55.8 weeks. Its time sets the minimum possible time for completing the project. From a scheduling point of view, this critical path is the most important of all the paths. If activities in this path are not done on time, the project cannot finish on time.

Since the other pathways take less total time, extra or slack time is available somewhere along them. The total slack in each path can be found by subtracting its time from the critical path time. It is usually desirable to find out where the slack is because activities relevant to two or more chains have to be done at times suitable to all the chains. The slack in a whole pathway may not be available all in one lump sum at any one place in the path.

FIGURE 22–7

Path	Event	Estimated time (t_e)	Earliest possible time (T_E)	Latest possible time (T_L)	Slack time
		1	*2*	*3*	*4*	*5*
I	A	0	0	25.2	0
	B	7.2	7.2	32.4	0
	E	15.2	22.4	(47.6)	25.2
	H	8.2	30.6	55.8	0
II	A	0	0	19.0	0
	B	7.2	7.2	26.2	0
	F	18.3	25.5	44.5	0
	H	11.3	36.8	55.8	0
III	A	0	0	(0)	0
	B	7.2	7.2	(7.2)	0
	F	18.3	25.5	(25.5)	0
	G	22.0	47.5	(47.5)	0
	H	8.3	55.8	(55.8)	0
IV	A	0	0	24.9	0
	C	10.2	10.2	35.1	0
	E	12.5	22.7	47.6	0
	H	8.2	30.9	55.8	0
V	A	0	0	24.0	0
	C	10.2	10.2	34.2	0
	F	10.3	20.5	44.5	0
	H	11.3	31.8	55.8	0
VI	A	0	0	5.0	0
	C	10.2	10.2	(15.2)	5.0
	F	10.3	20.5	25.5	0
	G	22.0	42.5	47.5	0
	H	8.3	50.8	55.8	0
VII	A	0	0	18.0	0
	D	11.3	11.3	(29.3)	18.0
	G	18.2	29.5	47.5	0
	H	8.3	37.8	55.8	0

Figure 22–7 sums up the t_e times cumulatively from the start of each path. This calculation provides the basis for finding out where the slack exists. The cumulated sums of the individual t_e times for each path are shown in column 3 of Figure 22–7. The time sums are labeled T_E, which represents the earliest time an event can be reached considering the need to do first activities before second activities.

As we know, pathway III is the critical path because it takes 55.8 weeks, which is more time than any other path. This shows in Figure 22–7, where the T_E for event H in pathway III is 55.8.

The next step is to add to Figure 22–7 a new column, column 4, which shows the T_L, the latest possible time for each activity. These numbers start by our listing the 55.8-week total as the latest date for every pathway. All paths have to be finished by 55.8 weeks or else the project's completion will be delayed. From this number, 55.8, the individual t_e

activity times in each pathway are subtracted, going up the column toward the start of the pathway. For path I this is $55.8 - 8.2 = 47.6 - 15.2 = 32.4 - 7.2 = 25.2$. There is a total of 25.2 weeks of slack in pathway I. So far as pathway I is concerned, the activity between A and B can start 25.2 weeks after the critical-path activities start. Actually, since the activity between events A and B is also in the critical path, the slack in pathway I occurs later in the chain. Activity A–B has to start early or the critical path itself will be delayed.

The next step is to consider where, in the noncritical paths, slack exists. For this we need to put parentheses around some numbers in Figure 22–7. For every event, its T_L number is bracketed, *but only once. If an event occurs in two or more paths, only the smallest* T_L *is bracketed.* If the two smallest T_Ls for an event are the same, and one of them is in the critical path, only the one in the critical path is bracketed. This will produce one T_L number, and only one such number bracketed for every event.

Next, the slack-time column can be filled in. To do this we pay attention first only to the bracketed T_L figure for each event. The difference between the bracketed T_L figure for an event and its T_E figure is its slack. There should be some slack time for every bracketed event except those in the critical path, where all slack figures are zero.

Now zeros can be filled in for all remaining events whose T_Ls were not bracketed. There is no slack for them even though it may appear that there is. This is because such events are in two or more paths and must be done at certain times to suit other paths. Even though, in one path, they could be delayed, they really cannot be delayed or that would hold up other paths.

At this point a schedule for the whole project and for each part of it can be set up, paying attention to both the T_E and the T_L requirements. Schedules can be set by working forward from point A and finding the dates for all activities and events up to H, which will be 55.8 weeks from the start date. Events without slack have fixed schedules, while those with slack can be done at any time between the permissible T_E date and the required T_L date.

One needs to be careful, however, if two or three activities which follow each other have a common amount of slack. When this happens, they can't each use it all.

Probability of meeting PERT schedules. One of PERT's unique contributions is that it allows the calculation of the probability that the schedule will be met.[3] Only the critical path is concerned here. For each activity in the critical path, it is necessary to find the difference between the optimistic time and the pessimistic time. These differences are squared and divided by 36 (because 6 standard deviations encompass virtually the whole universe and the standard deviation is the square root of the

---

[3] This is true only if 3 time values are used for each activity. Many companies use only 1 time value for each activity, and so cannot carry forward this kind of calculation.

variances). This gives the variance for each activity. These variances are then summed up cumulatively for every activity in the critical path. Then the square root of the cumulated variances is calculated to get the standard deviation. Figure 22–8 shows this calculation. (This is the same standard deviation which was explained in Chapter 11 in discussing stress and strength analysis.)

FIGURE 22–8

Activi- ties	Time estimates			Difference squared	Variances (t_e^2)	Cumulated variance (earliest T_e^2)	Standard devia- tion (T_e)
	Opti- mistic	Pessi- mistic	Differ- ence				
A-B........	5	10	5	25	.69	.69	.8
B-F........	14	24	10	100	2.78	3.47	1.9
F-G........	15	29	14	196	5.44	8.91	3.0
G-H........	7	11	4	16	.44	9.35	3.1

It is now possible to see how likely it is that the scheduled completion dates for the whole project, or for the successive stages in the critical path, will be met. The entire project is expected to take 55.8 weeks, but the calculation we just finished tells us that the standard deviation is 3.1 weeks.

This standard deviation shows that there is a 68 percent probability that the actual time for the project will prove to be between 55.8 ± 3.1 weeks, or between 52.7 and 58.9 weeks. And there is a 95 percent probability that it will be done in 55.8 ± 6.2 weeks, or between 49.6 and 62 weeks. And it is almost certain that it will be finished in 55.8 ± 9.3 weeks, or between 46.5 and 65.1 weeks.

All of these relationships can be put into chart form so that a person can read off the chances that, if operations go ahead as usual, the project will be finished earlier or later.

Figure 22–9 shows these possibilities. At the bottom, two scales are shown; the first one is in terms of standard deviations and the second one in weeks. If a manager asks what the chances are of finishing in 50 weeks, he can read across to 50 weeks and go up to the curve. His vertical line coming up from 50 weeks intersects the curve at 5 percent. So there is only a 5 percent chance that, if nothing extra is done to hurry the project along, it will be finished in 50 weeks. If the question is 60 weeks, the probability is 92 percent.

The value in finding out about these probabilities is that managers may want to increase the chances of finishing early and so decide to put more resources into moving activities along faster. Conversely, if the project is highly likely to finish comfortably earlier than is needed, resources can be diverted to other work without putting the finishing date for this project in jeopardy.

FIGURE 22–9. Probability of finishing a project in more or less than the expected time if no changes are made in input resources

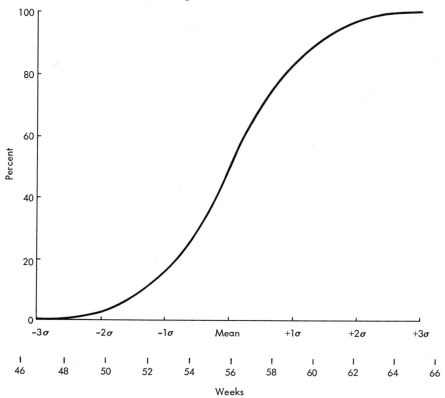

PERT/cost. Although PERT is usually thought of as a means of scheduling the activities required by complex projects, it also provides a framework for cost planning and cost control. All activities cost money; so PERT/time and PERT/cost go hand in hand. When a company plans for and schedules an activity, it also estimates its cost, and it automatically gets cost estimates for each part of the work, which are shown separately in the PERT analysis.

PERT/cost has become increasingly important over the years as people become more aware of its value. Actually, in many cases managers are more interested in the cost of a project than in exactly when it will be finished. And, as in the case of PERT/time, PERT/cost provides a good control mechanism while projects are under way. Reports of work done tell managers when they reach each event point. This gives them frequent opportunities to compare the costs incurred with the expected costs for the work done to date. If the project is running behind on either the time or the money schedule, the managers learn about it early, perhaps in time to do something to make up the lost ground.

FIGURE 22–10.   Event milestones, shaded to show the kind of resources needed

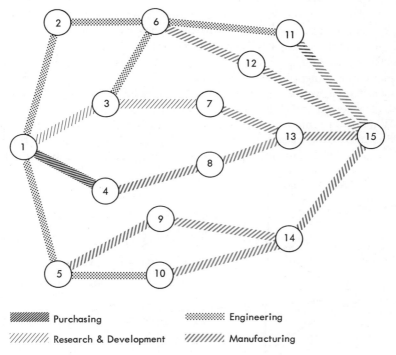

Time and resource trade-offs. PERT activities are actually work load assignments and are not directly calendar time assignments. Yet they are usually shown as work which will take a certain amount of calendar time. These times are based on the expected commitment of normally used resources to the activity.

There is a problem here, however. One hundred man-hours of work will take 100 hours of clock time if 1 man is assigned to do the work. But if 100 men were assigned, this same activity would become a 1 clock-hour job. There is often, therefore, a possibility of trade-offs between resource allocation and calendar time. Engineers on noncritical path work, for example, could be transferred to critical path activities and thus shorten the calendar time required, and possibly at no additional total resource cost. Slowing down the noncritical activity won't hurt because of the slack in the noncritical path.

In many cases, unfortunately, the resources are not wholly transferable. If the activity could use more machines and machine operators, neither may be available of the kind wanted. Furthermore, sometimes both the expected time and money are spent but the activity is not complete. The work is taking longer and is costing more than was planned.

This poses a question of what to do. Time slippages can usually be made up if extra money can be spent. Ordinarily, almost any activity can be speeded up by putting more men on it, by working overtime, by using air express to get needed parts, or otherwise using more resources. An activity could be speeded up even by relaxing some of the technical specifications. And, once in a while, work that was planned to be done in sequence can, in part, be done concurrently.

Cost slippages, on the other hand, usually can be made up only at the cost of a certain sacrifice in quality in other activities.

When the problem is purely one of trading off the costs of extra inputs against the value of saving time, it may be possible to find out the best thing to do by balancing out the costs. Figure 22–11 is a simple PERT

FIGURE 22–11

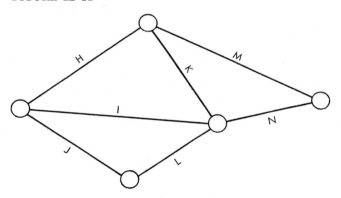

diagram which illustrates how time and costs might be related. All but one of the activities can be speeded up, although at a penalty cost. Activity sequence *H-K-N* is the critical path and requires $3 + 5 + 4 = 12$ days. The analyst estimates that *K*'s time can be cut (Figure 22–12) at a cost of $40 for each day saved. Cutting *K* by 1 day will allow the project to be finished in 11 days at an extra cost of $40. Still another day can be cut off *K* for another $40 in cost. This would reduce the critical path to 10 days.

But at 10 days, *I-J* and *H-M* also take 10 days, as well as *H-K-N*. All 3 paths are now critical to any further time reduction. To get down to 9 days it will be necessary to cut both *H* and *N* because *K* can't be reduced any more. Cutting both *H* and *N* 1 day would cost $120, but *K* could then be extended 1 day, so there would be a savings of $40 here, making the net added cost $80. To get to 8 days it would be necessary to cut *M* and

FIGURE 22–12

Activity	Normal		Crash basis		Cost per day to save days
	Days	*Dollars*	*Days*	*Dollars*	
H.................	3	50	2	100	50
I.................	6	140	4	260	60
J.................	2	25	1	50	25
K.................	5	100	3	180	40
L.................	2	80	2	80	..
M.................	7	115	5	175	30
N.................	4	100	2	240	70
Total		610		1,085	

N another day, each at a cost of $100. To get to 7 days it would be necessary to cut *I*, *K*, and *M*, at a cost of $350.

Should the managers make the time cuts proposed at the costs in prospect? This would depend on the value of the time saved. Suppose we are talking about repairing a machine which is out of production, costing $60 a day every day it does not operate. Here is how the costs line up:

	Days					
	7	*8*	*9*	*10*	*11*	*12*
Cost of repairs..............	$1,000	$ 870	$ 770	$ 690	$ 650	$ 510
Cost of production loss.......	420	480	540	600	660	720
Total...................	$1,420	$1,350	$1,310	$1,290	$1,310	$1,330

This critical path analysis shows that activity *K* should be put on a crash program aiming for a 10-day completion. This will hold costs down to $1,290, less than the cost of any other program.

PERT advantages

More than any other technique, PERT gives managers some degree of control over difficult-to-estimate projects and over projects which are surrounded by considerable technological uncertainty. By forcing them to think of the parts of the whole and how they link together, PERT forces managers into making time and cost estimates for individual parts of the whole. Doing this seems to produce greater overall accuracy.

PERT also helps stop the "crash everything" attitude. It answers questions such as: If there is a delay in an activity, will the whole project be delayed? And if so, how much? PERT also avoids the frequent and lengthy meetings needed for coordination. And it cuts down on cross-checking unrelated activities.

PERT helps detect trouble while things are still in the planning stage.

It shows, ahead of time, which activities need the most attention so they will not hold up other activities. It also points to bottleneck activities which may have to be speeded up even on a crash basis. PERT also reveals the existence of near-critical paths. They too need watching because a minor holdup in one of their activities will make *them* become the critical path instead of the original critical path. And in the case of holdups in noncritical path activities, PERT shows whether the slack in those paths is enough to absorb the delay or whether costly speeding-up action needs to be taken.

Critical path analyses sometimes surprise managers. On one construction project, Du Pont's engineers thought that manpower and overtime would be the factors critical to its completion date. Critical path analysis showed that these factors were unimportant and that the tight factors were the electrical design time and the delivery dates of certain equipment. As a result, they juggled the sequence of electrical equipment installation and saved 21 days, thus getting into production 3 weeks sooner.

Aerojet-General found, when developing one of the early Polaris missiles, that its new fiber glass motor casing was taking longer to develop than was planned. PERT showed that this would probably delay the project for three months. The warning came early enough to give time to switch back to an earlier type of steel casing and avert the delay.

PERT also sets up progress checkpoints. As reports of work done come in they are fed into a computer, which compares the progress of each activity with its planned progress. If any chain of activities is falling behind (if there is any "slippage"), PERT shows it up. Managers find out about slippages right away, before very much harm to the program has been done.

Still another advantage of PERT is that it can be used to simulate certain conditions so that one can see how a whole network will be affected if less or more time were spent on certain activities.

PERT has the peculiar characteristic (which can be bad as well as good) of being self-validating to some extent. Because it provides dates for subsidiary events, everybody works toward them and so meets them.

PERT often can be abandoned in the last stages of a project. By then there are only a few things left to do and they can be watched without the aid of PERT. PERT is most useful in the early stages, when hundreds or thousands of activities, almost all of which lie in the future, have to be coordinated with each other.

Pert disadvantages

By no means everyone is "sold" on PERT. Most building contractors seem not to like it because they say it doesn't help them. They know how long it takes to build a building. They say that PERT only makes duplicate planning.

There are also critics at the other end of the line, out where projects are near technical frontiers—where PERT is supposed to be at its best. Yet Joseph Freitag of Hughes Aircraft says that it is not possible to use PERT to control or coordinate changes in the configuration of complex electronic projects because this work "is just not networkable." Nor do time estimates for uncertain activities become any more certain from statistical manipulation.

Some managers resist PERT because they see it as taking away part of their jobs. Construction superintendents like to be fountainheads of all knowledge about how long work will take and how the delay of one activity might affect the whole activity. And it is true that when a job is made the subject of a PERT analysis and put on a computer, this takes away part of a man's work. When PERT is first introduced, the resistance it sometimes meets (which may amount almost to sabotage) makes it almost useless. Most companies report that such opposition soon disappears, but there may be losses at first from using PERT.

Some people find fault with PERT's use of three time values. Indeed, some companies do not use three time values at all.[4] They use the "most likely" time only. They say that the most likely time ought to be just that. With only one time, men aim toward it and try hard to meet it. Men feel that they have a real deadline.

An International Telephone & Telegraph official says that asking people for pessimistic estimates only gives them a built-in excuse for failure. IT&T built a post office building in Providence, Rhode Island, and when part of the work fell behind, the men responsible said: "I told you that it might take that long."

Another objection to PERT is that, almost always, pessimistic times vary more from the most likely times than do the optimistic times. The weighted average, therefore, is always biased toward a longer time than the most likely time, and this puts unintended and unwanted slack into all calculations.

Some critics of PERT don't like it because it forces men to estimate times for activities. They say that when an official presses men to make estimates, they will put in a "fudge" factor and that all time estimates will be too liberal. If this happens, none of the ensuing calculations rectify the inaccuracies. Worse yet, liberal estimates may make people work toward minimum performance (since that is all the program calls for) and not anything better. Perhaps this objection has more validity for PERT/time than for PERT/cost because overliberal cost estimates boost bid prices and lose contracts.

---

[4] Twenty years ago, when PERT networking was first developed by the Navy, an almost identical idea, the critical path method (CPM), was being developed by Du Pont. Today the terms PERT and CPM are used almost interchangeably. One difference, however, was that CPM did not use three time estimates, only the most probable time.

Still another objection to PERT is the cost of reviewing all the figures every week or so to see where things stand. PERT can help only when it is up to date, and this means frequent computer reviews of the data at considerable cost.

There are still other objections to PERT, but a good many of them are really more complaints that it is not perfect than that it is bad. PERT does not, for example, show if the company has the resources the project will need. Nor does it reveal whether the project will need the same resources for different activities at the same time. Nor does PERT reveal if resources are interchangeable.

PERT makes it look like things have to be done in sequence when, in fact, they can sometimes be overlapped or done in parallel. It is not always necessary to complete one activity before starting the next one. And after projects get under way, PERT shows up delays but doesn't reveal anything about causes. Nor does it show up delays until after the activities are supposed to have been completed.

PERT does not provide a level work schedule because it pays no attention to the work load it creates in relationship to departmental capacities and work loads caused by other jobs. PERT doesn't work well if the priorities of different projects are changed very much. Nor does it solve the problem of low-priority jobs getting pushed back forever.

PERT is limited in the detail it is practical to show. Rarely should minor details, which take only hours or days, be charted. So PERT does not show everything. Nor are charts updated all the time. It is too costly to make up big new charts frequently.

Yet in spite of the list of objections just given, PERT has "arrived" and is widely used. The Department of Defense used to require all of its major contractors to use it on all new projects (this is no longer required of companies which plan well). Industry in general has also taken to PERT. Merck, Sharp, and Dohme uses it for new project planning. Ford Motor uses it when tooling up for new models. Chrysler uses it at every stage in the planning and building of all new plants. PERT has also been used by builders of apartment buildings, office buildings, bridges, and roads. Small contractors as well as large are among today's PERT users.

Milestone charts

Milestone charts are a variety of Gantt chart. They are horizontal bar charts set on a time scale. Each bar starts when an activity is scheduled to start and finishes at its scheduled completion date. Its scheduled completion is a "milestone." This is the same as an "event" in PERT diagrams.

Milestone charts are sometimes used as PERT projects near completion and cover fewer activities, although they can also be used apart from PERT. Milestone charts, having a time scale attached, are more useful for *control* than PERT, which is more useful in *planning*.

As used for control, milestone charts are both a planning device and a progress recording vehicle. As each day passes, accomplishment is reported and plotted on the bars on the milestone chart.

At the start of a planning period, milestone bars are in outline form only. They are the plan. As time passes and work is done, the bars are filled in solid up to the point of accomplishment. If that accomplishment is up to schedule, the bar will be solid up to the current day. If the bar

FIGURE 22–13

Gantt-Type Assembly Chart

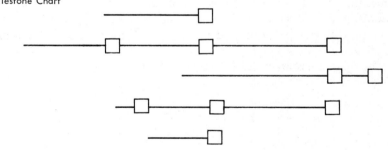

Milestone Chart

is open to the left, the work is behind schedule. If the bar is filled in solid to the right, the activity is ahead of schedule. Figure 22–13 is a milestone chart.

Line of balance (LOB)

Line of balance (LOB) is another variant of a Gantt chart. It differs from PERT in that it is not single project-oriented. Rather, it concerns production and delivery schedules for finished products, their major component parts, and for items made in quantity. And like milestone charts, LOB is more a tool for control than for planning. It is most useful in the transition stage, where one-time activities change to the production of limited quantities.

A program, for example, may call for the delivery of end products on the following schedule:

Month	Each month	Cumulation
April	0	0
May	0	0
June	0	0
July	0	0
August	4	4
September	7	11
October	12	23
November	22	45
December	40	85
January	60	145
February	100	245
March	100	345

Subassemblies and parts to support this end-product delivery schedule will obviously have to be started into production considerably in advance of the end-product need dates. How far ahead will depend on each item's cumulative lead time.

Suppose that the following lead times are required: subassembly A, 1 month; parts 1 and 2 for subassembly A, 2 months; subassembly B, 2 months; parts 3 and 4 for B, 2 and 3 months respectively; sub-subassembly C (a part of B), 1 month; and parts 5 and 6 for C, 1 and 3 months respectively.

The lead times ahead of final assembly, in this case, are:

Item	Months	Total
Subassembly A	1	1
Part 1	1 + 2	3
Part 2	1 + 2	3
Subassembly B	2	2
Part 3	2 + 2	4
Part 4	2 + 3	5
Sub-subassembly C	2 + 1	3
Part 5	2 + 1 + 1	4
Part 6	2 + 1 + 3	6

This tabulation of lead times prepares the way for the next step, which is calculating the number of parts which should be in the pipeline and how far along they should be at any given date. Here is a listing of the quantities which will be needed at the end of each month in order to support the final assembly schedule:

| Month | | | | | Item | | | | |
	A	1	2	B	3	4	C	5	6
April........	0	0	0	0	4	11	0	4	23
May.........	0	4	4	0	11	23	4	11	45
June........	0	11	11	4	23	45	11	23	85
July........	4	23	23	11	45	85	23	45	145
August.......	11	45	45	23	85	145	45	85	245
September....	23	85	85	45	145	245	85	145	345
October......	45	145	145	85	245	345	145	245	
November....	85	245	245	145	345		245	345	
December....	145	345	345	245			345		
January......	245			345					
February.....	345								
March.......									

An LOB chart is a picture, at some given point of time, of the plan versus accomplishment. Suppose that it is the end of July; at this point we find the following:

Item	Quantities scheduled to be finished	Quantities actually finished
6..................	145	160
4..................	85	75
3..................	45	50
5..................	45	35
1..................	23	28
2..................	23	24
C..................	23	20
B..................	11	10
A..................	4	5

Figure 22–14 is a chart that shows these figures. The line of balance is the solid line which shows the quantities of each item which should already be finished if future end-product schedules are to be met. The vertical bars are the actual production. These show that items 6, 3, 1, 2, and A are ahead of schedule. But 4, 5, C, and B are behind. Extra effort will have to go into getting them up to schedule or the end-product schedule cannot be met.

DART

DART means daily automatic rescheduling technique.[5] It is a variation of PERT which has been developed by the Air Force for use in airplane repair work. It can also be used for scheduling work on other complex yet somewhat individually unique products.

---

[5] A good description of the DART procedure appears in "DART—Description and Implementation Consideration," by Bob Gessner, in *Production & Inventory Management* (1st quarter 1969), pp. 51–56.

FIGURE 22–14

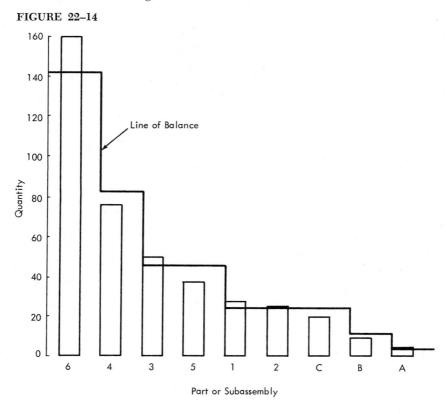

For repair purposes, each airplane is considered to be unique. The work to be done on each airplane depends on the hours it has flown, the number of engineering changes to be made, unpredictable damage, and the modifications necessary to remodel the airplane to adapt it for specific missions.

The purpose of DART is to control the allocation of the three kinds of resources to be used: (1) time-consumed resources (job sequence, labor, and work areas), (2) use-consumed resources (parts, supplies, and kit materials), and (3) nonconsumed resources (facilities, tools, and data).

The DART system starts with a PERT-type master network which covers all of the work which an aircraft could possibly require. This master network is then remade and tailored in scope for each airplane so that it becomes that particular airplane's individual and unique PERT network.

The DART plan also embodies a summation of the resource requirements of the several or many individual PERT networks for the several airplanes being repaired. Whenever too much of any resource is called for, the individual airplane's PERT networks are redone and stretched out over more time so that they reflect the time when the master resource allocation schedule will allow the work to be done.

Such rescheduling is done in accord with a priority list which assigns critical work early priority code numbers. Reports of work done are made daily to the central scheduling office. There each aircraft's progress record is updated daily. If any are falling behind, the reasons are promptly investigated and the causes removed as soon as possible.

Both the individual networks and the overall DART work load summary are updated daily. This allows for a constant review and for changing priorities according to current situations. Thus DART is a working tool which continually monitors the use of resources and redirects them wherever they are needed the most.

Review questions

1. A systems department is often told to develop an integrated system to handle the flow of information so that the information is reported in a form compatible with the needs of several departments. But systems analysts can't know who needs what information. How do they find out? And how can they tell if a man really needs all of the information he says he needs?

2. What is the difference between an office procedure and a system? Of what importance is this distinction?

3. Have computers helped as far as report making is concerned? Or have they hindered? Explain.

4. How far down into detail and subdetails should PERT analyses be carried?

5. Can an analyst calculate the probable time for completing a project covered by a PERT plan if the plan is used only one time for activities? Can the analyst tell how probable it will be that the project might get finished one week earlier even if no effort to speed up is made? Or does the analyst need three time estimates for each activity in order to answer either of these questions?

6. If PERT activities are truly *work load* assignments, why are they so universally spoken of in terms of the calendar time they will take? Isn't the time a direct function of the resource inputs? Discuss.

7. If PERT reports show that cost slippages are occurring, how can managers pick up this slippage and so end up doing the whole project within the planned cost limits?

8. It is sometimes possible to shorten a project's completion time but at a cost trade-off for the time gained. Explain how this works and show how far it can be carried.

9. Why do many people not like PERT?

10. Is line of balance a management-by-exception technique? Explain.

Discussion questions

1. How does the question of charging cost elements (the cost of labor, materials, etc.) to cost units (products and departments) relate to the matter of systems design?

2. The president has been impressed with the accomplishments of a computer in another company's work. He calls in his analyst and tells him to develop an integrated system for his company. How should the analyst go about carrying out this assignment?

3. How can a system like PERT help in setting time schedules for hard-to-plan activities, such as designing? It is just not possible to tell how long such things will take? Or is this possible?

4. PERT does not unearth the critical resources needed to accomplish the work along the critical path (or does it?). So it really cannot help get the work done on time. Is this so? Discuss.

5. How can a manager tell, during the *assembly* part of the work on big projects, whether the work is up to schedule or not? Also, how can he tell whether it is running ahead or behind the cost budget? Furthermore, if it is behind either timewise or costwise, what can he do about it?

6. Valuable though PERT is on giant projects, it is still costly to rerun it on the computer every few days. Yet it would have to be rerun often if it were to be a very helpful managerial tool.
   a) How can a manager judge the cost value of reruns of PERT?
   b) Suppose that the manager is not concerned with the costliness of rerunning PERT; in this case how often should it be rerun? Why?

7. Conceivably, every path could become the critical path. And near-critical paths may need just about as much attention as the critical path. How does PERT handle the possibility of other paths becoming critical paths?

Problems

1. The following information covers part of a large PERT diagram:

Starting event	Following event	Expected time (weeks)	Starting event	Following event	Expected time (weeks)
A	C	11	D	H	12
A	D	6	E	F	2
B	D	5	F	H	8
C	E	7	F	I	12
C	F	5	G	H	4
D	F	9	H	I	8
D	G	10			

What is the critical path and how many weeks will it take to complete this work?

2. What is the critical path in the following set of related jobs? How long will it take to get the work done? If we could cut 3 days off the longest job in

the critical path how would this affect the solution? If there is a new critical path, what is it?

Event sequence	Time in days	Event sequence	Time in days
1–2	6	5–8	7
1–3	4	5–10	8
1–4	5	6–7	7
2–5	7	6–9	3
2–7	6	7–10	9
3–5	8	7–8	3
3–7	10	8–11	8
4–6	4	9–10	6
		10–11	5

3. Suppose that in problem 1 there were the following variances:

Activity	Variance (weeks)	Activity	Variance (weeks)
A–C	4	D–H	5
A–D	3	E–F	1
B–D	3	F–H	3
C–E	2	F–I	6
C–F	1	G–H	1
D–F	3	H–I	1
D–G	4		

What are the time limits within which there is a 95 percent chance of the work being completed? What are the extreme times that might possibly occur according to the figures in our problem?

4. Suppose, in problem 1, that it would be possible to shorten A–C to 6, C–E to 5, D–F to 6, D–H to 10, and G–H to 3. Which of these changes, if any, would affect the critical path? How long will the new critical path take?

5. Suppose, in problem 1, that it would be possible, by putting on extra workers, to shorten the times for the activities at the following extra costs:

Activity	Possible time reduction	Cost per week gained	Activity	Possible time reduction	Cost per week gained
A–C	2	$100	D–H	2	$500
A–D	2	400	E–F	0	—
B–D	1	300	F–H	1	200
C–E	3	200	F–I	3	100
C–F	1	100	G–H	0	—
D–F	1	300	H–I	1	300
D–G	3	300			

a) If it were highly important to save all the time possible, regardless of cost, which activities should be shortened? What would the new critical path be? How long would it take? How much would it cost to make the necessary reductions?

b)   If there were a $1,000 limit on the amount that could be spent to move things along faster, what would the answers be to the questions in (a)?

6. The following data are from a large PERT diagram:

Immediately preceding	Event	Immediately following
	0	1, 2
0	1	3
0	2	3
1, 2	3	4, 5, 6
3, 5, 6	4	8, 9, 10
3	5	4
3	6	4, 7
6	7	9
4, 12	8	13
4, 7	9	11, 12
4	10	11, 12
9, 10	11	15
9, 10	12	8, 13
8, 12	13	14
13	14	15
11, 14	15	

Here are the expected times (in weeks) to complete each activity and the expected times.

Event sequence	Time	Event sequence	Time	Event sequence	Time
0–1	4–6–8	4–9	1–3–4	9–12	1–2–3
0–2	6–7–10	4–10	2–2–3	10–11	4–6–9
1–3	1–1–2	5–4	1–1–2	10–12	1–2–4
2–3	1–2–3	6–4	1–1–1	11–15	2–3–4
3–4	3–4–6	6–7	1–3–6	12–8	5–7–10
3–5	1–3–5	7–9	3–4–6	12–13	1–3–5
3–6	2–3–5	8–13	1–2–3	13–14	1–2–3
4–8	5–6–8	9–11	3–4–5	14–15	4–6–9

Draw up a PERT diagram showing these relationships.

What is the critical path? How many weeks will it take? What are the maximum and minimum probable limits? If this path could be shortened by 4 weeks, what path would then become critical? How long should it take and what is its probable maximum?

What are the chances that the project will finish 2 weeks early without any extra effort having been put forth?

Recent references

Anthony, Robert N., John Dearden, and Richard F. Vancil, *Management Control Systems,* Homewood, Ill.: Richard D. Irwin, 1972

Dearden, John, "MIS Is a Mirage," *Harvard Business Review,* January–February 1971

Gorry, G. A., and M. S. S. Morton, "Framework for Management Information Systems," *Sloan Management Review,* Fall 1971

Kaiser, Julius B., *Forms Design and Control,* New York: American Management Association, 1969

Martino, R. L., *Critical Path Networks,* New York: McGraw-Hill, 1970

Nenzel, G. J., "Critical Activities Network," *Journal of Systems Management,* August 1971

Neufville, Richard de, and Joseph H. Stafford, *Systems Analysis for Engineers and Managers,* New York: McGraw-Hill, 1971

Ringer, L. J., "Statistical Theory for PERT in Which Completion Times of Activities Are Inter-Dependent," *Management Science,* July 1971

Shell, R. L., and D. F. Stelzer, "Systems Analysis: Aid to Decision Making," *Business Horizons,* December 1971

Swanson, Lloyd A., and Harold L. Pazer, "Implications of the Underlying Assumptions of PERT," *Decision Sciences,* October 1971

Systems and Procedures Journal (bimonthly)

section eight

Materials inputs

THE production process adds value to materials by changing their form into a more individual form well suited for particular uses. In this new, individualized form the materials have far greater value than they had as raw materials.

In this section of the book we are concerned with the input of materials, with the system which determines what materials will be needed, and with providing these materials. Although the original source of demand for outputs—and therefore, indirectly, for inputs of materials—is the sales department, the purchasing department does not get its directives to procure materials from the sales department. Instead, in large-scale production and for the main items, it finds out what and how much to buy from production programs or from long-term schedules. In contrast, for nearly all items bought in somewhat lesser quantities, the procurement system provides that specific requirements for buying materials shall come from the stores department or the factory's production control department. Chapter 23 tells how materials procurement systems operate.

Once materials are on hand, they have to be stored, kept track of, and issued on demand. Chapter 24 takes up handling, storing, keeping the records, and issuing materials.

Controlling inventories, the subject of Chapter 25, is a most important job. Here is where inventory controllers try to balance out the conflicting goals of keeping inventories very low while incurring only a minimum of penalty costs from being out of stock very often or from high unit costs from frequent reorders for small quantities. The several systems for controlling inventories are presented, together with their merits and discussions of the conditions where each is at its best.

Economic order quantities are usually regarded as just a facet of inventory control. And they are. But EOQs actually constitute a vehicle or method for helping many managerial decisions which go beyond ordinary inventory control. These applications are taken up in Chapter 25.

23

Purchasing

MOST manufacturing companies spend more than half of the money they take in for materials or for component parts that are already made up. Chrysler spent $4.4 billion for materials in 1970—or $18 million a day. Ford spends $34 million daily, and General Motors pays out $54 million for materials every 24 hours.

But it is easy to *spend* money; that is, it is easier to pay out the dollars than to bring them in. And it is easier to buy cleverly than to make things economically. When buying, a company can get the benefit of effective management just by placing orders with the lowest cost suppliers. But when a company makes its own components, its costs depend on its own operating effectiveness. It is easier to *choose* an effective source than to *be* an effective source.

Purchasing is more, though, than just spending money. A man who spends wisely pays less for what he buys. If a company sells $1 billion worth of products (in 1971, 127 manufacturing companies in the United States sold more than $1 billion worth of products of which 52 percent was spent for bought items), it is selling products which probably contain purchased materials that cost some $520 million. The difference between a good and a bad job of buying could well be more than 5 percent. But even at 5 percent, the possible savings on purchased materials would come to $26 million for a company with $1 billion of sales. So even though purchasing is easier than selling, purchasing is still very important.

In some cases the money which can be made (or lost) on inventory can outweigh the earnings-or-loss possibilities from regular operations. The price of cotton and wool varies so much that textile companies can lose heavily by poor buying. Meat packers and flour millers have the same headaches.

Purchasing's main job is to get the things the factory needs when it needs them, and to pay as little as possible considering the quality needed. But this looks at the job too narrowly. Today many companies say that the purchasing department is responsible for "outside manufacture." This puts a different slant—a managerial slant—on the job. Vendor companies are thought of almost as if they were departments of the customer company.

With this view, purchasing becomes less passive. The purchasing agent views his job as more than just placing orders. He becomes interested in the supplier's costs and his quality control procedures. Should the vendor need it, the buyer even arranges to send his own company's specialists to the vendor's plant to help it become a more effective source of supply.

Materials managers

Some companies which buy quite large quantities of materials have set up a materials manager job in order to coordinate everything having to do with materials. The container industry, for example, spends 70 percent of its sales income for bought materials. It would seem logical to have such a materials manager in such a case.

Purchasing is one of the big activities. And so is the operation of the stores department and the inventory control work. These activities are closely associated with purchasing but they are usually not under the direction of the purchasing agent. They would become part of the assignment of a materials manager. The traffic department, too, would probably become part of his domain.

FIGURE 23–1. Place of a materials manager in companies using this arrangement

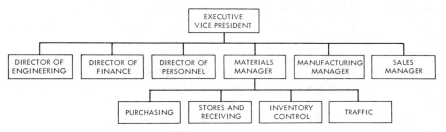

On the other hand, the factory's production control department probably should remain outside his jurisdiction even though it has much to do with materials used and with controlling inventories in process. Production control's closest ties are with the factory's producing departments, not with purchasing.

Purchasing department organization

The purchasing department is headed by a purchasing agent or director of purchases. He may be a vice president, but more often he is not, in which case he usually reports to the executive vice president, or even to the manager of manufacturing.

No two purchasing departments are alike, but all of them buy thousands of different things, and usually from thousands of suppliers. U.S. Steel buys 40,000 items from 50,000 vendors. General Electric buys from 40,000 suppliers. Having to buy so much material and from so many sources means that buyers get a chance to specialize.

Besides buying materials and manufactured parts for the company's products, the purchasing department also buys supplies, containers for products, power (or coal), equipment, and repair parts. In most companies the purchasing department also operates the salvage department and sells or disposes of scrap and low-value by-products.

Here are the men whom General Electric's Apparatus Division purchasing agent (he is a vice president) has reporting to him, together with their specialties:

Buyer and assistant buyer—Fabricated copper, brass, bronze, nickel, silver (except ingot), lumber (including poles, ties, etc.), packages and packing materials (wood, cleated, corrugated, bobbins, reels, etc.), woodwork patterns.

Buyer—Refrigerator hardware and accessories, asbestos, rubber and rubber parts, molded parts, glass (including globes and lenses), hose, pipe covering, name plates, nonferrous metals except copper.

Buyer—Mica, mercury, polishing and grinding supplies, textiles, rope and twine, springs, leather and leather products (including all kinds of belting).

Assistant buyer—Paper and paper products (except carbon and abrasive papers), transmission appliances (including bearings, gears, etc.), hardware (except refrigerator items), refrigerator insulation gaskets, packing, and fiber.

Buyer—Large tools and machinery, automobiles, jewels, coal.

Assistant buyer—Steam, gas and water supplies (except hose, gaskets, packing, and pipe covering), oilers and lubricators, small tools, brushes and brooms.

Assistant buyer—Oils, greases, and petroleum products, furniture (including typewriters, desk calculators, etc.), roofing materials (except paper), steel shelving and racks, partitions.

Assistant buyer—Electrical supplies (including clocks and meters), instruments, carbon brushes, and painters' supplies.

Assistant buyer—Screw machine products, stampings, bolts, nuts, washers, rivets and screws, hospital supplies, stationery and printing, and office supplies.

Buyer—Steel (sheet, strip, and stainless), aluminum (including wire and all forms except ingot), alloys, and nickel.

Buyer—Pig iron, castings, ferro alloys, chemicals, foundry supplies, factory supplies (except coal, oils, greases, and petroleum products), sand, gravel, and clay.

Buyer—Iron and steel (except sheet, strip, stainless, pig iron, and castings), nails, forgings, railway supplies, iron and steel wire, packages and packing (except wood and corrugated material), and tanks.[1]

Purchasing departments are not large, rarely going as high as one half of 1 percent of the employees. But small numbers only highlight the importance of buyers, who spend from $2 million to $4 million each in a year—or from $1,000 to $2,000 an hour! It costs anywhere from one half a cent up to more than one cent to spend $1. And it costs $10 or more to handle an order.

Buyers should know and abide by all laws about purchasing and shipping products. Besides, they should keep up on new materials and tell engineering about them. Engineering will probably already know about new materials but not about their prices. Sometimes both the engineering

---

[1] Stuart F. Heinritz, *Purchasing Principles and Practices* (2d ed.; Englewood Cliffs: Prentice-Hall), pp. 65–66.

and manufacturing departments are too busy to keep up with information about new materials. Purchasing men are in a better position to do this.

Buyers should always be on the lookout to see if less costly materials can be used. Naturally, they can't tell whether the less costly materials will do the job (engineering has to decide this), but they ought to tell the others about the prices.

FIGURE 23–2. The usual organizational arrangement for materials management

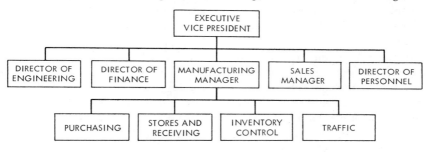

They should listen to suggestions from salesmen, who may have something new to offer. And if something sounds good, they should not keep salesmen from seeing people in other departments who are qualified to judge new things. Some buyers act like little tin gods who won't let a salesman (or a suggestion) get into the plant.

Make or buy

Make-or-buy decisions are junior-size vertical integration decisions. But make or buy is specific: this item, this order—does a company make or buy it? As a rule, the more it buys the less a company's investment in machines, and the smaller the company need be. But it also earns less money because it does a smaller fraction of the total manufacturing job. In general, the pros and cons of making versus buying are the same as they are for large vertical integration matters. And, as before, it does not always pay for a company to "do it yourself."

Purchasing departments are always concerned in make-buy decisions because they always have to supply the cost figure for buying. And if the decision is to buy, they have to do the buying.

Normally every company is in a certain business and not in others, so there is no major make-buy question. For most items this sourcing decision is made by a committee when each product's original bill of materials is made up by design engineers. For most items, a company—clearly—makes certain parts or components or else it does not make them.

Yet a radio manufacturing company which assembles transistorized radios could make the transistors. It could also make the integrated circuits and plastic cases it uses. Possibly it will make them all, but more likely it will buy them all because companies specializing in these items can make them at less cost than most buying companies can make them. Such make-buy decisions are more or less permanent and normally a company does not change back and forth from buying to making.

Sometimes a company makes a portion of its needs of certain items in its own plant and buys the balance outside. In other cases a company concentrates on making particular items inside while buying other items outside. In some cases which items to make and which to buy is almost immaterial: a company has the machines and know-how and could make or buy the items.

Since a company usually earns more money on what it makes than on what it buys, there is a real question of why it should buy anything which it can make. One reason for buying, in such a case, is that the company is so busy doing its main work that it can't make everything it uses. A second reason is that two sources of supply (making and buying at the same time) provide insurance. On difficult-to-make items that is important. A machine breakdown, stopping a company's internal source, will not close the operation down. Third, outside price competition helps keep inside departments sharp on costs.

Making and buying at the same time has some disadvantages. It cuts the volume both for the inside department and for the outside maker. Cutting each one's volume may raise unit costs a little. Besides, a company needs two sets of tooling, gages, and so on. And it may be hard to get both sources to make the products exactly alike.

Sometimes a company buys what it could make because the seller does it better and cheaper than it can. Ford Motor once tried making automobile tires but went back to buying. Goodyear and the other tire makers can make tires at less cost than Ford.

Make-buy decisions are influenced by the amount of money involved. Most metalworking companies could make the paper clips they use in their offices, but for $10 to $20 a year making them is not worth the bother. But add a few zeros and the answer is different. Daisy Company, maker of air rifles, over the years changed from wooden gun stocks (which it made) to plastic stocks (which it bought) for almost all of its models of guns. The day came when it was buying $1 million worth of plastic gun stocks a year, and Daisy then went into the plastics business itself. At IBM, making or buying magnetic tape is a top-level decision. Firestone Tire used to buy all its nylon cord for tires; now it makes its own.

Make-buy decisions on specific items sometimes depend on work loads. When a company is very busy, it sends many orders out, but when work is slack, it brings them back. This lets it operate more evenly, and since it already owns the necessary machines, no new machines have to be bought. As a company goes from boom to slack and back again, make-buy decisions become matters of priority. Which work goes out first? Which last? Which comes back first? Which last?

FIGURE 23–3. Relationships of value of bought part of products to the value added by making

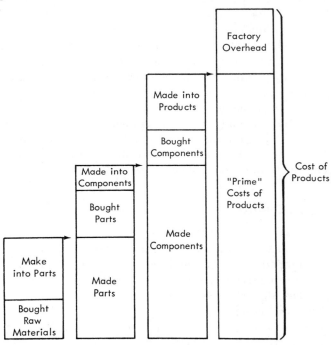

Perhaps a company should send out the easy jobs first because vendors will not have trouble with them. But if it has had trouble making certain items and can find a really capable vendor, or if its costs are high, it might do the reverse and send the troublesome items out first.

Up to here the discussion about make-buy has been in terms of products, parts, and materials. But it is sometimes a decision about a process instead of a product. Should a company do its own heat treating? Electroplating? Painting? Sometimes it is a matter of services. Should a company buy or do its own research? How about maintenance? And minor construction? The pros and cons are like those for making or buying products.

There is probably a bias in most make-buy calculations that favors a make decision. Particularly is this true when the question comes up during slack periods. Various overheads are not put into the calculation because they are already provided. Making would be a matter of using idle capacity and underused staff and therefore would seem to cost only varible costs. This is true so long as the slack continues. But when normal operations resume, the full costs of making will creep up. Before long, making will be causing its full complement of overhead costs, something the calculation did not cover. At full costs, making may be uneconomical.

Make-buy in multiplant companies. In multiplant companies, sister plants sometimes make items which come up as make–buy choices for a particular plant. Somewhat different considerations apply here.

If, for example, one division of a company wants to make an item which it has been buying from a sister plant, it will probably be allowed to do so unless this decision would idle a substantial output capacity in the division which formerly made the item. In such a case the buying plant may have to continue buying, or take over the formerly used production facility and operate it itself. (This would be highly improbable.)

Similarly, on items bought outside the plant, sister plants are usually given a preference. Usually items are transferred at a price lower than outside prices. And again, the buying plant is usually free to buy where it wants to except when large amounts of money are concerned. Then it may be required to buy from a sister plant.

Purchasing procedures

No one procedure is satisfactory for buying all of the 50,000 items or so that big companies buy. Some items (like sheet steel for a can maker) are shipped in steadily and, over a period of time, cost millions of dollars. Other items (like the equipment to make automobile motor blocks automatically in a new factory) are one-shot orders that cost millions. Between these extremes—steady, high demand or giant one-shot contracts—there is every combination of volume, repetition, and variety —clear down to 10-cent items bought once a year.

Besides variety in kind and quantity, purchasing deals with bulk items (liquids, powders), packaged items, standard items, special items, items always bought, and items sometimes bought and sometimes made (or both).

Big and steady-use items. For big, important items that are used all the time, the purchasing department gets its authority to make purchase commitments directly from the approval production schedules for the months ahead. It does not need requisitions from either production control or the stores department. Purchasing has, in its files, lists of all the things to buy, and it knows how much to buy in order to make a single unit of each of the company's major products. All it has to do is look at the scheduled quantities and multiply to get the amount of material needed.

Most big and steady items are bought on "blanket" or "open end" contracts which cover a whole year's supply. Blanket contracts leave quantities and times of delivery (and sometimes price) to be set as the materials are needed. The buying company sends out monthly (or even weekly) new release orders telling the vendor how many or how much to deliver and when and where. These releases usually go to the supplier directly from the factory's planning department. Purchasing is not active in this part of the contract's operation.

Contracts for these steady-use, high-volume items are not really open to competition in the wide-open sense, except that a company may buy from *two* sources instead of one just for safety. The buyer-seller relationship is much like that of a company department with a sister department. Supplying companies often keep certain contracts for years. ELTRA, for example, made most of Chrysler's auto ignition systems for 30 years. Goodyear has never failed to get a good share of General Motors' tire business since World War I.

Mostly, big contracts do not "travel around" because the seller takes as good care (price-, quality-, and servicewise) of the customers as anyone else could. Also, these contracts are so big that no competitor could take one on and deliver overnight. He would have to build whole new factories, then tool up, and line up whole new work forces.

One exception is basic raw materials (materials of nature: cotton, wool, rubber, lumber, wheat, and so on). There are a good many suppliers of such items, and their prices go up and down. Here buyers do not always stick to one vendor but go where they can get the best deal each time they let a new contract. Buyers should not forget, however, that dependable service is important in such items. It is best not to switch a company's whole volume to unknowns, though an unknown might well be given a trial order now and then.

Big one-shot jobs. Big one-shot propositions are different. They usually are machinery for a newly built factory, or equipment for an electric-power dam, or some other construction, or even for a warship. On these projects, months go into planning. Discussions are held with several machinery makers. Alternative designs are considered. Sometimes the advance work takes so many man-hours that the customer pays an engineering fee to prospective bidders. Otherwise a prospective vendor may be unwilling to spend $50,000 on engineering work planning for a job he might not get. Vendors have to bid separately for every one of these big jobs.

Middle-sized orders. Here the buyer in the purchasing department is nearly always buying only after someone else inside the organization has asked him to. He gets a purchase requisition from the production control department or from the stores department. Quite a little of the work done in purchasing departments is for such orders. Figure 23–4 shows how they are handled. Production control sends in purchase requisitions for items needed for making the products on the factory's production schedule (except for the heavy and steadily used items discussed above).

FIGURE 23–4. Office procedure chart of a purchasing procedure

Step	Activity	Using Dept.	Purch. Dept.	Inventory Control Dept.	Inspect. Dept.	Receiving Dept.	Acctg. Dept.	Vendor
1	Using (or control) department issues P.R., T.R., or B/M.	P.R. #1 / P.R. #2 (1)	P.R. #1					
1a	Check to see if material is in stock	File	(1a) P.R. #1 (1a)					
2	Investigate potential sources, negotiate, determine price, and select supplier. Then issue P.O.	File ← P.O. #5 (2) / P.O. #7 & P.R. #1	P.O. #1 and Acknowledgment form #2 / P.O. #6 / P.O. #4 / P.O. #3					
3	Vendor acknowledges order.		Working file	Follow-up file				
4	Follow up activity (as needed).	(4)	Acknowledgment form (3)					
5	Vendor ships material.	File ←	Follow-up inquiry / Follow-up response (4)					
6	Receiving dept. checks material against packing slip and P.O., and issues R.R.		R.R. #1, #2, #3 (6)	material	Material & packing slip (5) / R.R. #4 P.O. #4 Packing slip File			
7	Inspection dept. inspects material and issues I.R.	Use ← / File ← R.R. #3 and I.R. #3 to using or control dept.	Material (7) R.R. #1 & I.R. #1	R.R. #2 & I.R. #2 File / I.R. #4 / I.R. #4 File				
8	Purch. dept. closes order.		(8)				Invoice (9)	
9	Vendor issues invoice in multiple copies		P.R. #1 P.O. #6, #7 Acknowledgment R.R. #1 & I.R. #1 Other correspondence Closed, order file				(10) Check / Invoice P.O. #3 R.R. #2 I.R. #2 File Voucher	
10	Acctg. dept. checks invoice against P.O., R.R., and I.R., and issues voucher and/or check							

P.R. = purchase requisition; T.R. = traveling requisition; B.M. = bill of materials; P.O. = purchase order; R.R. = receiving report; I.R. = inspection report.

Source: Lamar Lee, Jr., and Donald W. Dobler, *Purchasing and Materials Management*, McGraw-Hill, 1971.

The raw materials stores department is often under production control's direction, in which case production control's requests to purchasing also cover new supplies or raw materials needed. Otherwise production control tells the raw materials stores department what it will need in the weeks ahead, and stores writes the purchase requisitions.

Middle-size repeat orders are usually placed with the same vendors. But they don't work like releases against blanket orders. Vendors get specific purchase orders from purchasing for every order. Every new order

FIGURE 23–5. A purchase order

ALUMINUM COMPANY OF AMERICA
PITTSBURGH 19, PA.

**PURCHASE
ORDER**

A-B-C Box Company
2345 Main Street
Pittsburgh 5, Pa.

REQ'N NO.	P.O. DATE	P.O. NO.
510444		657508
AUTH. NO.	DEL'Y REQ'D	SHIPM'T PROMISE
		As Req'd

SHIP VIA
Motor Freight

Aluminum Company of America
Building 242
New Kensington, Pa.

F.O.B.
New Kensington, Pa.

TERMS OF PAYMENT
1% 10 days - Net 30 days

Please ship the following items as instructed above.

ITEM NO.	QUANTITY	DESCRIPTION AND SPECIFICATIONS	PRICE
1	50,000 -	No. 3383-24 Alcoa Wrap Cartons, size 12-3/8 inch x 8-3/8 inch x 12-1/2 inch, 175 lb. test, R.S.C., printed 1C - 4 P.	$91.50 per M
2		Set-Up Charge for Each Release	9.75
NOTES			
A		Cartons must be manufactured with extreme care since they will be filled and sealed by automatic equipment.	
B		Cartons must be palletized 400 per pallet, with protective cover on corners to prevent top layers of cartons from becoming distorted.	
C		Each pallet to be marked with quantity and item number.	

KRG:mrw

NOTE: In accepting this order it is understood the Seller agrees to the terms and conditions shown above and printed on the back hereof. The Buyer hereby objects to any conflicting or additional terms or conditions.

ALUMINUM COMPANY OF AMERICA

BY _____

Source: Aluminum Company of America.

again describes the product and orders a certain quantity to be delivered by a certain date.

But whether middle-size orders are for old or new items, it is common to ask two or three vendors to bid. Generally the contract goes to the low bidder if he is dependable. Sometimes, if middle-size orders are for standard catalog items (and particularly on rush orders), the buyer may not shop around to try to get the best price but just order the material wherever he can get a good price with an agreement to deliver soon.

Small orders. Small orders are one of the headaches of purchasing. It cost $10 or more in clerical costs to handle a purchase requisition and to place a purchase order, so it would help to be able to cut out all the little orders for one or two items or for fifty cents or $1 worth of materials. Unfortunately, such items are needed and, worse yet, they may be as badly needed as big items. They, too, can be rush orders.

Most companies let these orders go through the regular procedure, cost what they may. Some, however, try to cut the cost down. American Can uses the following policies to reduce small order cost. (1) Don't reorder little things often; order two or three years' supply. It doesn't matter that some day part of the supply of some item may not be needed and may be thrown out. It is still less costly than buying little dribbles all the time. (2) Let departments buy directly all things costing less than $25. Don't bother the purchasing department about them. (3) Place blanket orders with suppliers; then just order by telephone what is wanted now and then, without making out a purchase order every time. Cut out the paper work. Kaiser Aluminum sends a blank check along with its order and lets the vendor fill it in.

Follow-up. Keeping large supplies of materials on hand is so costly that no one wants to do it. This means things are not bought, or at least are not delivered, until shortly before they are needed. But this also means that if anything goes wrong and the vendor doesn't deliver on time, the customer is in trouble. So buyers "follow-up" orders for things that are on a tight schedule. (The factory production control department should keep the buyer informed about which items they are most anxious to get.)

The buyer might call the vendor on the telephone or write him a letter and ask him whether the order is coming along all right. He might even "hound" and annoy him and repeatedly remind him that he is counting on getting his order on time. All this helps. The vendor will get the order out just to get the buyer off his back.

Most purchasing departments have a few expediters who do most of the follow-up, even going to vendor plants to see if the vendor needs any help. Not only does follow-up of this sort get more orders delivered on time, but if an order is going to be delayed the customer finds out about it sooner. This gives the customer company more time in which to change its plans.

It might seem that it would be cheaper just to carry a few more items in stock and then not every delay would catch the company short. Actually, however, this often does not pay because it takes too much extra inventory to provide much protection. Besides, even with the bigger inventory, vendors will still let customers down sometimes and not deliver on time. So it would be necessary to do some follow-up anyway, and the customer would still be out of some material now and then.

Whenever anything is bought from overseas, follow-up becomes doubly important. Not only are the suppliers a long way off but the whole world, sometimes even including western Europe, seems to have a *mañana* complex when it comes to meeting delivery promises.

Receiving inspection. Purchasing is not complete until the material is in hand. Because receiving usually is not under the purchasing department, purchasing has to be told (it gets a copy of the receiving report) when materials come in as ordered so that it can clear the orders out of its file and tell accounting to pay the bill. The bill (or invoice) has by this time come in by mail to the accounting department. So has the freight bill covering shipping costs. If the material is not right in any way, purchasing has to handle all dealings with the vendor concerning what to do about it.

Yet sometimes it isn't possible for receiving inspectors to tell if incoming products pass inspection unless they make special tests—chemical, electronic, or other. Normally, for example, a receiving clerk can't tell if a shipment of thermostats for stoves is all right. Or picture tubes for television sets. Sometimes he will need to call on engineering or the laboratory to pass final judgment.

How much centralization?

When a company has several (or many) plants scattered around the country it is possible to have one central office do all of the buying or only part of it. There is no pat answer as to which is better. Nearly all companies end up doing some of it centrally and some of it locally. General Motors decentralizes its buying to 52 divisions, which in turn decentralize the actual buying to more than 100 purchasing offices. To aid prospective vendors, GM puts out a directory booklet listing all its purchasing offices and something about what each one buys.

Buying centrally means dealing in larger volumes, and this sometimes means better prices, possibly up to 10 percent better. The total volume of any item is not, of course, increased by central buying. But the volume dealt with on a single contract will be the whole company's volume, not just one plant's volume, so this will probably mean a better price.

More specialized men will be doing the buying when it is done centrally. Buyers don't have to be so all purpose as buyers in small divisions of a company. Also, central buying cuts out duplication of orders and so saves clerical costs. It gives top management tighter control over the whole company's inventory policies and it forces more standardization in designs.

On the bad side, centralization is often slow and too cumbersome for minor items. The thousands of little things can be bought better by separate purchasing departments at the plant level. Also, plant inventories cannot be controlled very well from a central office. The controls are quite likely to become too rigid. Central people just cannot know local needs.

Also, even with central buying it is risky to buy *all* of any important item from only one supplier. It is well, just as insurance against strikes and other holdups, to divide the orders for most important items and place orders with at least two suppliers. But, of course, if this is done, part of the possible quantity discount expected from centralized purchasing is lost because each supplier gets smaller orders.

Freight is another item. If high-volume orders are placed with only one or two suppliers, and if they ship to all of the customer's plants, long freight hauls may cancel out any quantity discount obtained from volume buying. This does not apply, however, if the vendor is also a multiplant company and can ship to a customer's Midwest plant from its Midwest plant, to the customer's Pacific Northwest plant from its Pacific Northwest plant, and so on. But if the vendor of any item does not have plants close by, it will probably pay to give up central buying of that item and let each plant order its needs from a nearby plant just to save freight.

Materials which don't pass inspection and "short" shipments also turn up at times. These can be handled much better locally than centrally. Local buying also gives plant managers more responsibility, and it creates community goodwill.

Big companies usually end up centralizing all buying where big amounts of money are involved or where highly technical knowledge is required. They also centralize most capital expenditure buying because of the enduring nature of the commitment. Buying is also centrally done where reciprocity enters the picture. All other things are bought *decentrally* in the separate divisions. Often some dollar limit is set for local purchasing and all contracts for more money must clear through central purchasing. The central purchasing department also sets up policies and procedures for the decentralized groups to use.

Value analysis

Value analysis tries to reduce the costs of purchased materials by studying the purpose to be served by a part or component being bought and by seeing if there are other, less costly ways of accomplishing this purpose. Although the purchasing department is almost always active in this work, value analysis is encompassed in the somewhat large subject of value engineering (which we took up in connection with product design on p. 289).

Known cost

The known-cost idea is very similar to value analysis, and usually includes some value analysis work. "Known cost" is a term sometimes used to describe a policy of large retail buyers, such as Sears, Roebuck or Kresge.

The customer company's buyer decides, for complete finished products or for parts, what he can afford to pay for an item, considering his resale price. Then he buys them on a set-price basis. He hopes to get good, or even fine, quality; yet the price is often set so low (because of the low end-product sale price) that there is strong pressure to reduce the item's production costs. Sometimes the supplier can't get his costs this low without sacrificing quality. If so, a compromise is reached and the price is raised or the quality lowered, or both.

The term "known cost" comes from the idea that the customer company knows the price it will pay before negotiations start. The negotiations are concerned more with the quality it can get for the price than with the price which will be paid for a given quality. If either price or quality has to yield, quality—not price—becomes the variable factor.

Manufacturer buyers as well as retailing company buyers also practice the known-cost idea.

Mass production purchasing

General Motors spends more than $1 billion a month for materials. It takes some 200,000 tons of steel, costing more than $5 million for bumpers and springs alone for Chevrolet cars in one year. But a company does not have to be General Motors to find itself buying many items in million-dollar quantities in a year.

Almost always these contracts are so big that neither buyer nor seller wants to take any chances on price, yet each wants to be sure of the contract. So the contracts are often written with the price left open, to be settled every now and then during the year. Quantities are also left open, to be set as the customer orders week by week. Or the price, if the item is a manufactured product, is often set at cost plus a fee. If steel prices go up, General Motors pays more for its bumper steel, or the reverse if steel goes down. That way no one gets hurt too much when prices change. Often there are penalty charges if the vendor does not deliver or if the buyer cancels.

Quantities in mass production are so big that neither buyer nor seller wants to carry enough inventory to last more than a few days, so both try to mesh their schedules exactly. Supplier dependability is even more important than price. In busy times Chevrolet cars eat up steel for bumpers and springs at the rate of 1,000 tons a day, and at 50 tons to a freight-car load that means 20 freight-car loads a day! Yet the factory rarely carries more than a day or two's supply on hand. In fact, it would want the freight cars of steel to come in at regular intervals all day long rather than all at once. Both the vendor and the railroad know this and try to deliver on this kind of schedule.

On the other hand, lead time is very important. To get steel in July, it needs to be rolled in the steel mills in June. Steel mills, then, plan June's production in May, so General Motors has to place its order in April. But in *April*, Chevrolet's July car-making schedule has not yet been firmed up. Of course everybody knows that cars will be made in July, but not how many or exactly what kinds. Purchasing has to go ahead anyway and place the order, and then, in May or even June, ask the vendor to change the quantities to correct for any misguesses. All of this schedule changing makes young men grow old fast in the purchasing department, and in the vendor plant's production control department.

How many to buy at one time

Very few purchases are one-shot items. Nearly everything bought is bought again and again, so there is a question of whether to buy few and often or more at a time and less often. For big day-to-day, bread-and-butter items the answer has already been given: use blanket contracts covering perhaps a year's needs and then get frequent shipment as needed. For the bulk of other items—those bought repetitively but not on blanket contracts—the purchasing department usually buys things only in response to specific requests from someone else. (These matters were discussed on p. 541.)

Purchasing should not be too passive, though, in following other people's requests because they may ask for small quantities to be bought often. And it is expensive to order small items in little dribbles. Yet buying more at one time increases inventory carrying costs, so someone should try to balance out these costs. Inventory control and purchasing men should work together on problems of how many items to order at a time.

Companies sometimes speculate when buying big-volume, regular-use raw materials. If they think prices will go up, they buy big supplies—even enough for a year or more's future needs. (Rarely would they take delivery so far ahead, but they would place the contracts.) Taking such risks would be only with the board of directors' approval because of the large financial commitment. Contracting for a year or more's needs is generally called speculation, for 3 months to a year is called forward buying, and for 1 month to 3 months ahead is called buying to requirements. Contracting for less than 1 month is called hand-to-mouth buying, and is done only when companies are short of money or when they think prices will go down. Of course, such short-term contracting usually results in higher unit costs because of the small quantities bought on each order.

Setting the quality

Setting the quality would seem to be an engineering and not a purchasing job. It is, however, also a purchasing job because engineers are not so well acquainted with prices and price changes as is purchasing. Besides, engineers do not always know how much money is spent for this or that item *in total*.

Engineers don't talk to visiting salesmen nearly so often as do the buyers, who can ask salesmen to point out places where little design changes will lower prices. These and other suggestions from salesmen can be passed on by the buyer to engineering. Actually, important quality decisions should be made by a committee in which both purchasing and engineering are represented.

Maybe the engineers are unknowingly asking for off-standard materials, which cost extra. Or maybe they are asking for features they don't realize cost extra. Or maybe they ask for something they know costs extra but they don't realize how much. Or maybe their drawings specify many dimensions and tolerances but only a few of them are really important; perhaps the others can be relaxed and money can be saved. Purchasing can save money if it works with engineering, finds out which tolerances are critical and which are not, and then tells the vendor the places where he does not have to be so fussy.

Product descriptions

Purchasing is a matter of buying what the factory needs, but when a vendor is 500 miles away from his customer he has to figure out from a piece of paper (the customer's purchase order) what the buyer wants. And if the vendor has several things which are almost alike, the customer doesn't get to choose except as he chooses from the vendor's catalog, where the differences are described.

This isn't like a man going into a paint store for a paint brush, where he can see and feel the brushes. He can ask about them; he can tell the clerk what he wants the brush for and ask for his recommendation; and he can come away with a brush which suits him. Compare buying a brush this way with telling someone else to buy you a brush of the kind you need. Anyone who has tried to help someone else out by buying something for him knows all too well that his friend often doesn't like what is bought.

Actually, describing products is not easy. Sometimes, though, it is unnecessary to write lengthy specifications. Often standards that are generally understood by the trade can be used. Or the customer can specify an item's catalog number, or a trademark name, or maybe he can furnish a drawing or sample.

Written descriptions of materials are called specifications and they must be used for many items which can't be described any other way. Specifications describe an item in considerable detail and list certain requirements, such as chemical content, surface hardness, tensile strength, moisture content, heat content, etc. Usually the requirements are stated as test scores which will have to be met when the material is given certain tests.

Sometimes specifications have to describe characteristics that are not

FIGURE 23–6

PURCHASING SPECIFICATION   2010996

RADIO CORPORATION OF AMERICA
PRODUCT ENGINEERING CORPORATE STANDARDIZING CAMDEN, N.J.

PAGE-1 OF 3
DATE- MARCH 15

SUBJECT	LAMINATED SHEET, EPOXY, GLASS-CLOTH BASE, FLAME-RETARDANT, COPPER-CLAD (MILITARY TYPE GF, NEMA GRADE FR-4)	CODE IDENT NO. 49671	REV
		COMM CODE 1602	5

1. Scope - This specification applies to flame-retardant, glass-cloth, epoxy-resin laminated sheet with copper foil bonded to one or both sides.

The material is intended for use in the manufacture of printed circuits with fine etched lines when moisture resistance and high mechanical strength are required.

2. Reference Specifications - The following RCA Purchasing Specifications form part of this specification:

2010995 Laminate, Glass Epoxy, Flame Retardant (NEMA Grade FR-4)

2015200 Test for Solderability (Solder Dip Method)

2015218 Flame Retardance of Plastic Laminates,Test Procedures and Requirements

3. Material - The copper-clad laminate shall meet all the requirements for Type GF in Military Specification MIL-P-13949C and any additional requirements of this specification.

3.1 Laminate - The glass-cloth base, epoxy laminate shall conform to the requirements of RCA Purchasing Specification 2010995, except that the color, finish, and punching quality shall be as prescribed in this specification.

3.2 Copper Foil - The copper foil shall be at least 99.5 percent pure and shall be uniform in quality and condition. It shall be clean, sound, smooth and free from internal and external defects detrimental to fabrication and uniform etching.

Pits and dents shall not exceed those allowed by Class A

The thickness tolerances for sheet material as given in Table 1 are in accordance with Class I tolerances of Military Specification MIL-P-13949C for thicknesses of .031 inch and greater. At least 90 percent of the area of a sheet shall be within the tolerances given, and at no point shall the thickness vary from the nominal by more than 125 percent of the specified tolerance. Cut sheets less than eighteen inches by eighteen inches shall meet the applicable thickness tolerances in 100 percent of the area of the sheet.

The tolerances for thickness of the copper foil shall be as follows:

Nominal Thickness, Inch	Tolerance, Inch
.0014	+.0004, -.0002
.0028	+.0007, -.0003

4. Properties and Methods of Test - The material shall conform to the following requirements:

4.1 Composite Sheet -

4.1.1 Squareness - The sheets as received from the vendor shall have the edges straight and the corners square within the limits of ninety degrees plus or minus 0.25 degree.

4.1.2 Warp or Twist - The warp or twist of the sheet as received from the vendor shall be measured within one hour after the shipping package is opened and shall not exceed 0.5 inch on sheets 18.25 inches square to 18.25 inches by 21.25 inches. The measurement shall be made at the highest point on the sheet

Source: RCA Corporation.

easy to describe. A surface may be required to be "reasonably free from surface defects"; a finish may be a "smooth satin finish"; a specially made product may have to be "of good and workmanlike quality." These seem to be rather vague instructions, but sometimes it is hard to do any better.

Materials specifications are usually written either by the engineering or the purchasing department. Or the customer uses standards published by some recognized agency, such as the American Standards Association, the Society of Automotive Engineers, or the United States Bureau of Standards.

Sometimes, in purchasing, the customer has a choice of using a brand-name item or of ordering practically its equivalent by specification. Which to do is a moot question. Such choices are available with wire, chemicals, cement, flour, tool steel, cutting oils, grinding wheels, cleaning compounds, paints, etc. All of these can be bought by using the vendor's trademark or catalog numbers. Or the customer company can ignore these and write his own specifications, stating what he wants in the way of chemical composition, size, performance requirements, and so on.

When a customer company buys all of its large quantities by specification, it will usually save money. It gets exactly what it wants. Trademark items may not be just right for a given job—maybe they are too good, or not good enough. Also, trademarked items are advertised and people who buy those items pay for the advertising.

On small orders, on the other hand, specification buying will probably cost more than buying trademarked materials. If the vendor has to make a special run of materials for an order, the cost of the special item may be more than the price of trademarked items. In general, for small quantities of anything, the customer should buy trademarked items.

Choosing vendors

The purchasing department nearly always decides which company to buy from. Equipment buying is an exception; so are some trademarked items that engineering or someone else insists on; and so are reciprocity deals, where top management tells the purchasing department whom to buy from.

To choose vendors intelligently the purchasing department's buyers need to know which things are sold by which companies. This they learn from salesmen who call on them and from advertisements in technical and trade directories and buyers' guides. Also, they have a file of catalogs of vendor companies and their price and discount lists.

When deciding who gets an order, buyers should consider the overall. Price, important though it is, is not the only thing. Reliability usually is more important than small price differences. Can and will the vendor company deliver the order on time? Will the materials pass inspection after they arrive? If they don't, will this vendor fix things up right away without argument? Schedule changes may also be a factor. Will this vendor take care of schedule changes and rush orders? How about service if something goes wrong? Or will he extend credit? Any of these matters might be important.

In recent years many companies have found that they could often buy materials and parts overseas at much less than domestic cost. The price differential is often great enough to offset the headaches of variable quality, long lead times, transportation costs, and uncertain delivery schedules. Wherever the labor content products is large, it is probable that they can be bought cheaper abroad.

Assuming that all other factors are equal, often it is still not altogether clear which vendor's price is the lowest. In the following case, for example, from which vendor should the company buy? Each of the companies has submitted a bid in which a separate charge is listed for the special tooling which will be required plus an additional charge per unit.

			Discount for volume	
Supplier	Tool charge	Cost per unit	Price	Volume over
A................	$220	$.80	$.70	1,000
B................	320	.72	.60	3,000
C................	180	.96	.85	500

This problem can be solved by the break-even comparison method described in Chapter 2. The choice is, in all cases, the source with the lower tool cost for all volumes below the equal-cost point and the source with the lower unit cost for volumes above the equal-cost point.

1. To compare A and B at regular prices:

$$220 + .80x = 320 + .72x$$
$$x = 1,250$$

This is an irrelevant answer since, at a volume of 1,250 units, A's discount price applies.

2. To compare A and C at regular prices:

$$220 + .80x = 180 + .96x$$
$$x = 250$$

Buy from C for quantities up to 250 units, from A for greater quantities.

3. To compare B and C at regular prices:

$$320 + .72x = 180 + .96x$$
$$x = 583$$

This is an irrelevant answer since C's discount price would apply before this point. (See comparison 5.)

4. To compare A's regular price with B's discount price:

$$220 + .80x = 320 + .60x$$
$$x = 500$$

This is an irrelevant answer since B's discount does not apply to volumes of 500 units.

5. To compare A's regular price with C's discount price:

$$220 + .80x = 180 + .85x$$
$$x = 800$$

In this case we found (in comparison 2) that C should get contracts for quantities up to 250 units and A should get the contracts for greater quantities. Here we find that once the quantity passes 500 units, because of the quantity discount C should get all orders for from 500 to 800, where again a change should be made back to A.

6. To compare B's regular price with C's discount price:

$$320 + .72x = 180 + .85x$$
$$x = 1,077$$

This is an irrelevant answer since A is a better buy than either B or C at this volume.

7. To compare A's discount price with B's regular price:

$$220 + .70x = 320 + .72x$$
$$x = -5,000$$

This is a theoretical, negative quantity. There is no positive quantity where the costs of these two methods are equal. A's cost is less at all volumes.

8. To compare A's discount price with C's regular price:

$$220 + .70x = 180 + .96x$$
$$x = 154$$

This is an irrelevant answer since A's discount price does not apply to orders for 154 units.

9. To compare B's discount price with C's regular price:

$$320 + .60x = 180 + .96x$$
$$x = 389$$

This is an irrelevant answer since B's discount price does not apply to orders for 389 units.

10. To compare A's discount price with B's discount price:

$$220 + .70x = 320 + .60x$$
$$x = 1,000$$

This is an irrelevant answer since B's discount price does not apply to orders for only 1,000 units.

11. To compare A's discount price with C's discount price:

$$220 + .70x = 180 + .85x$$
$$x = 267$$

This is an irrelevant answer since C's discount price does not apply to orders for 267 units.

12. To compare B's discount price with C's discount price:

$$320 + .60x = 180 + .85x$$
$$x = 560$$

This is an irrelevant answer since B's discount price does not apply to orders for 560 units.

To summarize: As far as small quantities are concerned (this is where regular prices prevail), comparison 2 shows that it will be most economical to order from C for up to 250 units. Above 250, A should get the orders. Comparison 5 brings C's discount into the picture and shows that at the 500 point, and up to 800 units, the orders should be switched back to C. Above 800, A should get the orders. There is no point where B should get the orders. Figure 23–7 shows these crossover points graphically.

Reciprocity

"Dear Red," wrote FMC Corporation's board chairman to a Ford Motor Company vice president. "This is just a note to express appreciation for the good news we had, that your company had decided to purchase part of your Nashville requirements for soda ash from our company.

FIGURE 23–7

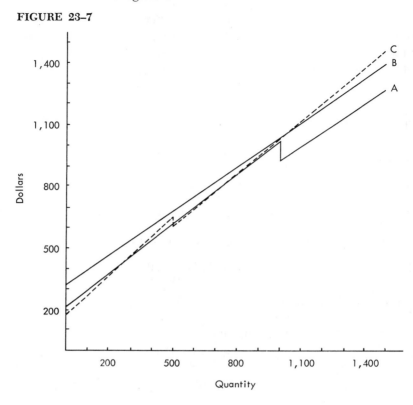

"Effective as of now, wherever possible, our people are to purchase Ford products. I believe that our salesmen and service fleet now amounts to 600 to 700 cars. As you know, our two company chauffeured cars are Lincolns which we buy new each year and our family has only Lincolns."

It took a court order to unearth this letter in a Federal Trade Commission investigation of reciprocity practices. Thus reciprocity is industry's version of "You scratch my back and I'll scratch yours"—or you buy from me and I'll buy from you. Back in the old days, when Henry Ford and Harvey Firestone were alive, they were friends; so Henry put Firestone tires on most new Fords and Harvey used Ford cars and trucks in his tire company.

Buying from each other sounds reasonable, although most people—particularly purchasing agents—condemn it. Most companies even deny they practice it; but, on the other hand, they don't give customers a cold shoulder when they place purchase contracts. That would be a fine way to lose customers. Customers are not at all above asking "If we buy from you, are you going to buy from us?

The FMC board chairman, for example, also sent a "Dear Roger" letter to the head of U.S. Steel in which he pointed out that FMC had bought

$3,446,000 worth of U.S. Steel products whereas U.S. Steel had bought only $453,000 worth of products from FMC. Then he wrote: "I wish you would send my letter to whomever is in charge of reciprocity for your company and would see that they are alerted to our relationship with your company. There are a number of chemicals which we are in a position to sell your company." He suggested that an FMC vice president meet with the proper U.S. Steel executive. In many companies the reciprocity man is called the "trade relations man."

Actually, every company has to buy from someone, so it is not surprising that reciprocity is a common practice. Purchasing agents regard it as a necesary evil. But one might ask what is bad about it? Does it matter what make of steel filing case is used in the office? Or whether salesmen drive Chevrolets or Fords? Why shouldn't purchasing agents face up to the fact that the company has customers?

Purchasing agents don't like reciprocity because they have to buy some items where they are told to and don't get to shop around. They are afraid they might have to take inferior materials, or pay higher prices and get poorer service. This would not be particularly important for supply items which are consumed, but it could be quite important for materials and components that go into finished products.

It is true that all of these things *may* occur—and some of them *will* occur once in a while. But purchasing agents look at only one side of the coin. Just as sure as a company sometimes loses a little on buying, it gains on the selling end. Surely a company gets some sales where its products are not the very best or least costly. Probably reciprocity balances out.

If reciprocity hurts anyone, it is small companies. They don't buy enough to command much attention. Big companies have to buy from their *big* customers to keep them. Their big customers demand it. Small customers, demanding a share of what a big company buys, do not always get far with their threat to buy elsewhere. Actually, though, even small customers often get a share of a big company's purchases. Big companies try to satisfy *all* their customers by dividing their ordering at least a little.

The Federal Trade Commission has been instigating action against reciprocity. But although its effort started a decade or more ago, it has not been pushed very hard—not hard enough to curtail the practice very much.

Bidding versus negotiated contracts

When the government lets contracts, normally it is supposed to ask for bids and take the lowest price, provided the lowest bidder is deemed capable of fulfilling the contract. Private industry has no such required rules. Sometimes private companies don't even ask for bids but just dicker with their main supplier and agree on a contract, price and all.

At first this doesn't sound very smart. How can a company tell if it is getting a good buy? Usually the purchasing agent knows because either the company makes some of the same things itself and he knows the company's costs or he occasionally asks for bids from other companies. Or possibly he will have his company's engineers go over the vendor's expected cost figures to be sure that he is reasonably efficient and that his price is reasonable. In the end, some of the biggest buying contracts are negotiated and not bid.

On the other hand, most middle-size orders and most large one-shot contracts are bid for. And if the purchasing agent does not give the contract to the lowest bidder, at least the one who gets it has to be near the low bid. Buyers, supposedly, should always choose the lowest bid from among those from vendors who probably can do the job well.

But thousands of little things that are bought are neither negotiated nor bid. They are just ordered from a catalog at list price less the usual discount. About all the buyer does is look in two or three vendors' catalogs and order from the one who quotes the lowest price. The money involved doesn't justify much effort in trying to save a few pennies.

Government contracts

More than $20 billion a year of government contracts go to companies making defense products and space products. Most of this goes to airplane, missile, and electronics companies.

Often single contracts total hundreds of millions of dollars, and often, too, each individual product (an airplane, for example) costs many millions of dollars. As a rule the government places a contract for a complete contract with one company and it becomes the "prime" contractor. Prime contractors then buy whatever components they themselves don't make. In a few cases the government will buy and furnish major components, such as jet engines for airplanes. Boeing, Lockheed, and the others do not make these components, nor do they themselves buy them. The government buys them from General Electric or other firms and supplies them. But for the thousands of other items bought, the prime contractor places the order.

Prime contracts are usually (but not always) let on a competitive basis. Sometimes, when they are essentially continuation contracts, the terms are set by negotiation. Prices are usually set expecting the contractor to earn 7 percent of the sales price as a profit (10 percent of research contracts). The government's pricing policies, however, shift from time to time.

As of 1972, most of the largest contracts were not at fixed prices but were "incentive" contracts. Such contracts specify a price that is based upon expected costs, performance, and delivery schedules. But if costs overrun and go higher, the company and the government share the excess. Or if there are cost savings, these too are shared. Similarly, bonuses are given for performance above expectations and for delivery ahead of schedule. And, in a parallel way, subspecification performance and late deliveries are penalized.

Government contracts differ from most others in that they rule out assessments of overhead not related to the contract. The government also expects the learning curve (see pp. 146–50) to operate. Prices on large contracts contemplate that final products will cost less to make than initial products.

The prime contractor, if it were an airplane maker, probably has to buy such items as aluminum sheets, landing gear, and radar because it doesn't make these items. It is free to buy these items wherever it wants, except that the government requires it to buy American-made items and that a stated portion of subcontract business be given to small companies.

Besides having to subcontract, the prime contractor is responsible for seeing that the subcontractor is capable of doing the work, that the prices paid to subcontractors meet all regulations, that the sub can finance the contract, and that it does not make too much money on the contract. The prime contractor is responsible for seeing that all subcontractors obey all work-hour, nondiscrimination, and wage regulations, and also that the quality and reliability of their products meet government requirements and that they meet their promised delivery schedule. Sometimes subcontractors are so anxious to get contracts that they promise anything the prime contractor asks and then can't make good. The prime contractor's purchasing department may have to send in various specialists, particularly inspectors and quality control engineers, to help out.

Purchase contracts

Purchase orders, after acceptance by the vendor, become legal contracts which bind both parties. If either one doesn't live up to the contract, the other can sue. Almost never is there any trouble, though, because both parties do what they agree to. And if one side violates a small part of the contract (as when delivery of the materials is a few days late), the matter is rarely of enough importance to make much difference. Or if a small part of a shipment is rejected, the customer accepts the balance and pays accordingly. Or if it is all rejected, either the vendor replaces it or the contract is dropped and the order is placed elsewhere. Even if a customer cancels an order or wants to return materials, the vendor is usually willing to do what the customer wants just to keep him satisfied.

It is easy for each side to be agreeable in most minor contract violations because no one is going to lose much. But if someone has to take a big loss, the contracting parties are not always quite so agreeable. If the prospective loss is great, the two parties sometimes submit their differences to arbitration, or even go to court. In court the *contract as written* is the basis for the decison as to whether an actual breach of contract has occurred. Whichever party is judged to have breached the contract will be liable for damages.

Standard printed contracts are used as the order form when the amount of money is small, but on large orders special contracts are written almost every time. Such things as the possible return of goods, contract cancellation, price adjustments, and provision for the arbitration of disputes between buyer and seller are all written into the contract. If there is any doubt about a contract's wording or interpretation, the purchasing department should consult the legal department before contracts are signed.

Discounts

In the United States, at the retail level, we are used to a one-price system. The seller sets a price and we either pay it or don't buy. Discount houses flourish, though, in all of our big cities, proving that most of us shop around to get the best buy. We don't argue with a vendor about price, but in effect we bargain on prices by going elsewhere when we think a price is too high.

Company purchasing agents almost never buy at retail prices, nor does the one-price system work very well in industrial buying. As we have seen, purchasing agents ask for bids or negotiate prices on all big and middle-size contracts, and on all small contracts for special items. On smaller orders for catalog items, they expect, and get, discounts from list prices.

Sometimes they get two or three discounts in series (such as 20 percent off, then 10 percent off the balance, and maybe another 5 percent off that) on the same order. Catalog items' list prices are supposed to be retail prices, and they are the prices a manufacturer almost never pays.

Regular discounts are of three kinds: trade, quantity, and cash. Trade discounts are supposed to be a certain percent for retailers and a bigger percent for wholesalers, jobbers, or other manufacturers. Manufacturers of items that are sold finally at retail sometimes get only as little as one third of the retail list price. Trade discounts are supposed (even required by the Robinson-Patman Act, a federal law) to be the same for all buyers in the same class (as, for example, wholesalers). The law is not too effective in the case of manufacturers' buying from other manufacturers because they ask for slightly different items—items not sold to others at all. So there can be no direct comparison between what they pay and what someone else pays.

Quantity discounts, which are generally offered to customers who buy big quantities, are usually quite small compared with trade discounts. Quantity discounts are in addition to trade discounts and are supposed to be equally available to all customers. Large buyers are sometimes able to coax still bigger discounts (for themselves only) out of vendors by threatening them with buying elsewhere. Under present laws, vendors are allowed to pass on, in the form of lower prices, the savings in cost that large orders make possible, but *no more* than that. The difficulty of figuring the exact savings keeps this law from being very effective.

Cash discounts are often offered as inducements to pay fast. Most bills are due in 30 days, but vendors don't want to wait that long for their money. Cash discounts of 2 percent if the bill is paid in 10 days (instead of 30) bring in most of the money sooner. Besides, they also cut bad-debt losses. Two percent off for paying sooner is a fine windfall for the customer; it is equivalent to 36 percent a year on his money. Most customers will pay up fast even if they have to borrow money from a bank to do so. Yet why would a vendor rather have ninety-eight cents in 10 days than one dollar in 30 days? Probably he would rather wait and get more, but he has to meet industry customs.

Competition has brought other kinds of concessions that amount to discounts. Freight equalization is common when competing vendors are not located the same distance from the customer. A faraway vendor offers to pay the difference between the freight cost from his plant to the customer's plant and the freight cost from a competitor's plant that is nearer to the company's plant. Other practices, amounting in effect to discounts, include postdating the bill, thus extending credit for longer times; offering to pay part of the customer's advertising costs on the assumption that he will advertise the vendor's product; and offering free engineering or other help.

Purchasing problems

How much price pressure? Although the same prices are supposed to be quoted to all customers in each class (manufacturer, jobber, wholesaler, retailer), it doesn't always work that way. A very big customer in any class can chisel down the price he pays until it is not far above an item's cost to manufacture. All he has to do is threaten to place his order somewhere else or to make his own items. Little customers can play at this game, too, although not quite so effectively.

Gifts. Should an appreciative vendor show his appreciation for getting a contract? That is, should he show it by giving the man who sent him the order (another company's buyer) a gift? It is so easy to answer no that we seem to have disposed of the problem. Any other answer opens the door to kickbacks, rebates, and outright bribery—to the detriment of the buying company—because bribed buyers will place orders where *they* get the most out of it, not where the company benefits the most.

But the problem won't be put down so easily. Vendors are appreciative, and most of us like to be appreciated. We corrupt easily on the receiving end, when we receive gifts. Spending money just seems to breed graft, at least small-scale graft. Most companies have hard and fast rules against their buyers' accepting expensive gifts, but most of them don't object to, say, free meals, a box of cigars, a cigarette lighter, or a few bottles of liquor at Christmas time. But a TV set or an automobile—no. Mink coats and lavish entertainment during big-city visits also are out.

Curiously, the ethics of gifts seems to be all one-sided—we always hear about the man who *receives* a gift and whether this is proper. But someone has to *give* gifts. Can a company logically forbid its buyer to receive a gift and at the same time pay the bills for the gifts given by its own sales department?

Conflicts of interest. A decade ago William C. Newberg, president of Chrysler for eight weeks, resigned because of a conflict of interests. Specifications to buy certain parts for Plymouth cars were written so that only one supplying company (a company owned largely by Newberg) could get the contract.

American companies, most people believe, are quite free from this kind of conflict of interest. Certainly everyone concerned with placing large purchase contracts should avoid substantial investments in supplier companies.

Miscellaneous functions of the purchasing department

The purchasing department should always be on the lookout for less costly materials. Sometimes this means that they need to try out new materials. This means sample runs in the factory and performance tests to see how the new materials work. Purchasing should follow all such trials, reporting on their success or failure. Purchasing should also keep informed about the quality of what it buys. Whenever the factory has trouble with bought items, purchasing should take it up with the vendor and try to stop the trouble.

Another duty of purchasing is to handle all matters relating to rejected purchased materials—whether they are rejected right away in receiving or later in processing. All correspondence having to do with disposing, reworking, or returning anything is handled by the purchasing department. Purchasing also sells all of a company's salvage and waste materials. It gets this job, rather than the sales department, because these are materials, not finished products. The purchasing department knows materials markets better than does the sales department.

Years ago many industrial purchasing departments bought products for company employees (this is now against the law in some states). These items were ordered by the company's purchasing department, so that it got the company's usual discount, and the products were passed on to the employees at cost. Officially, not much of this goes on today, but the problem nevertheless persists. A study by *Purchasing* magazine found that one third of the companies studied bought for employees as a regular thing, and more than one third did it occasionally. But probably most of it is done only for officials.

Most companies require the purchasing department to make various statistical reports periodically. The idea is to get some notion of how efficiently the department is running. Such reports analyze the dollar value of purchases by divisions or locations; summarize cash and other discounts; summarize waste, scrap, and salvage operations; show relationships of purchases to sales; and report on the number of purchase orders handled and the size of the purchasing department. From the comparisons, management gets an idea of whether purchasing is being efficiently done.

Review questions

1. How important is purchasing? If wages make up 20 percent of a company's total costs, how important is it to get greater productivity from workers as against doing a more effective job of purchasing?
2. Suppose that purchasing is regarded as "outside manufacture." In what way does this viewpoint affect purchasing?
3. What part should the purchasing department play in make-buy decisions? When, if ever, should the purchasing department instigate a change from one policy to the other? How would the purchasing department come to realize that such a change should be made?
4. The text says that big, steady-use items are often bought on a more or less continuing basis for years from the same supplier and that contracts for such items are not really open to competition. Is this wise? Discuss.
5. What is the "known-cost" idea? This idea brings purchasing closer to quality determination problems. Should this be? After all, the purchasing department is not highly qualified in the quality area. Or is it? Discuss.
6. Most large companies buy their big items by specification rather than by brand name or trademark. How far down the volume scale should this practice be carried? Why?
7. The Federal Trade Commission does not like reciprocity. Why, then, does it not order it stopped? Discuss.
8. Purchasing agents usually object to reciprocity as a practice. Why? What might the company president's views be? Why?
9. How does the typical American one-price system operate so far as industrial buying is concerned? What part do discounts play in actual pricing?

Discussions questions

1. The president wants to know if his purchasing department is doing a good job, so he calls in a consultant and asks him to investigate and tell him. How should the consultant go about his work?
2. Purchasing and sales are two sides of the same coin. Is there any occasion for having men with different training in these two departments?
3. A large company with government contracts finds from its past experience that small suppliers are so often unreliable that it would be better off in every way to cut way down on subcontracting. Should it do so? Why?
4. When a company buys instead of making parts, it would seem that it would incur extra transportation and packing costs and that it would

have to carry more inventory and be out of stock more often than if it made the items itself. How, therefore, can it ever be wise to buy instead of make?

5. Should one division of a company be allowed to buy from the outside when the same items are made by a sister division of the same company? (The buying division thinks it can save a little money by doing this.) Discuss.

6. A San Francisco plant manager wants to buy his printed forms locally and not have them printed by the central print shop in the Chicago office. Should he be allowed to do this? Discuss.

7. When a company buys by specifications, it writes its own specifications. Isn't there a danger that these may not be rewritten and updated enough to incorporate new developments? How can a company protect itself against obsolescence in the design of purchased parts?

8. Assume that you are the buyer who places orders for all of the blackboard erasers in your school. How do you decide what kind to buy? How do you decide when to buy them? Would you buy them by specification? Write out the item description you would use.

9. In order to convince the vendor of the urgency of the company's need, the expediter wants to go to the vendor plants involved. Should the company send him? What can he do? To whom will he talk? When should outside-of-the-plant expediters be used?

10. The expediter is happy. He got the order through even though it took air express to get some of the parts. Should this please the president? Why?

11. What should the president tell the purchasing agent about how much price pressure to put on vendors?

12. It is found that the purchasing agent owns 100 shares of Du Pont stock, a company with which he places orders for paint for the company. What should be done about this situation?

Problems

1. Should the company buy or make steel stampings in the following example? They can be bought for $44,000. The company figures that it will cost $50,000 to make these same stampings, with its costs being as follows: materials, $15,000; direct and indirect labor, $7,500; machine costs, supervising, tool design, handling, labor fringe benefits, etc., $20,000. These total $42,500. General overhead of $7,500 brings the inside costs up to $50,000. The plant is not operating at capacity and could make these stampings if this were the decision. Discuss.

2. Should the company make or buy the following three items?

	Product		
	A	B	C
Quantity needed	40,000	15,000	24,000
Material costs/unit	$ .046	$.0185	$.0275
Direct labor hours required	360	300	100
Purchase price/unit	$ .141	$ .172	$ .090

The direct labor cost rate is $4.40 per hour. There are also variable overheads, which go up and down with labor, which cost $4 per labor hour. Fixed overhead is $2.20 per direct labor hour (based on 2,000 hours a year).

If the decision is to make these items, would the fact that the plant is heavily loaded, or is working far below capacity, change the decision in any way?

3. The steel supplier quotes the following prices for rolls of strip steel:

Number of rolls ordered at a time	Price per roll
0–24	$24.00
25–74	23.85
75–199	23.75
199 and over	23.70

The company uses 400 rolls of this steel a year. It costs $50 to place an order and 20 percent to carry inventory. How many rolls should be bought at a time? Note: The economic lot size idea explained in Chapter 25 would help here, but it is not necessary for getting an approximate answer.

4. Two suppliers have sent in bids for supplying component part X. These parts will be needed at the rate of 1,000 a month for a year but not thereafter.

Supplier A is 1,000 miles away and has been known not to deliver on time every time. His quality control is also a little less than perfect, and once in a while a shipment will have to be rejected. His proposal:

Cost of tooling (to be paid by you)	$1,000
Up to 1,000 units	.28 ea.
1,000 to 5,000	.27 ea.
5,000 and over	.26 ea.

Supplier A will ship as many or as few as are wanted, according to the customer's delivery schedule, but he needs 10 weeks' lead time.

Supplier B is 100 miles away and is very dependable. His proposal:

Cost of tooling (to be paid by you)	$1,000
Up to 1,000 units	.32 ea.
1,000 to 2,000	.31 ea.
2,000 to 4,000	.30 ea.
4,000 and over	.29 ea.

B will also ship according to the customer's delivery schedule and needs 2 weeks' lead time. Buying from B saves $.01 per unit in freight costs.

It costs ¼ cent a week to carry product X in stock.

What purchasing and stocking policy should the company follow if it expects B never to let it down but A to let it down 4 times in a year, each time costing $200 for the delay?

5. The company is considering making versus buying a heavily used part. This part goes into a new finished product whose total volume is very much a question. The market forecasters estimate that there is a 90 percent proba-

bility of selling at least 5,000 units. They estimate that there is a 75 percent chance of selling at least 15,000 and a 40 percent chance of selling as many as 30,000.

To make the items, it would be possible to choose between 2 alternative methods. The first would require an investment of $5,000 in tooling and $1.30 per unit in variable costs. The second would require $15,000 for tooling and $.50 per unit in variable costs.

These items can be bought in quantities up to 5,000 for $3 per unit. For orders of more than 5,000, the price is $2 each. For orders of over 10,000 units, $1.50, and for orders above 15,000, $1.25.

What should the company do? Show the figures.

Case 23–1

The plant manager is on the telephone calling you, the purchasing agent, about production holdups. He says that several jobs are being held up in the factory from the failure of purchased parts to arrive. He has just called the supplier, who has told him that there is no reason for the delay. The supplier could easily have got the parts delivered if he had only known that you wanted them.

What happened was that, because of production trouble with materials, an unusual number of items were spoiled in process and more were needed. The factory's production control department, being forbidden to call suppliers direct, had called the buyer in the purchasing department asking for a rush shipment. But the buyer was out sick with a cold for two days and didn't get the call and missed learning about it when he came back.

Should the factory's production control department ever call suppliers direct? What reasons are there for and against their doing this?

Case 23–2

The Mississippi Company found that it could buy the wiring systems used in the machines it made for considerably less than its past cost for making them. Since the savings came to $25,000 a year, the company decided to buy instead of make, even though this meant laying off 10 workers and putting others in the wiring department on short hours.

The union said that the company had no right to do this and asked for an arbitrator to decide. The company refused but the union carried it to court; it lost in the district court but was upheld by the appeals court, which ordered the company to arbitrate. The labor contract said nothing about making or buying.

You are the arbitrator. You decide. Does the company have the right to subcontract work outside in this case?

Case 23–3

The manager of the ABC textile mill looked forward glumly to the next three months. They were the low months of the year, months when there would be only four days of work a week for only one quarter of the usual work force.

Then his phone rang. It was a buyer from a large chain store with a proposition. He offered to buy enough material from ABC to keep the mill operating normally through the whole slow period. Furthermore, he hinted at repeating the offer next year if this year's arrangement worked out well.

There was a catch in the deal, however. The chain store buyer quoted a price which was not very much over the cost of materials and labor. If ABC accepted the order it would get back only a small amount of the overhead costs it stood to lose if it refused the order. So if ABC accepted, it would be selling below total costs.

The offer was not easy to refuse, however. If it were accepted, the work force would be kept busy and ABC would be less bad off than if it turned the offer down. In the short run, ABC would be better off to accept the offer. But in the long run the low-price items offered for sale by the chain store would cut the throats of ABC's regular customers. To make the choice even more difficult, ABC's manager couldn't prevent his customers' getting hurt just by holding his head high and turning the offer down. There were too many other textile mills. Someone, somewhere, would accept the offer.

What should be done in this case?

Recent references

Ballot, Robert B., *Materials Management,* New York: American Management Association, 1971

"Basics for Buyers: What's the Right Price?" *Purchasing,* October 28, 1971

"The Business of Business Gifts," *Industrial Marketing,* October 1969

Finnegan, T., "Purchasing/Engineering Team Sparks Product Improvement," *Purchasing,* July 22, 1971

Grano, R. J., "How Much Does It Cost to Buy?" *Purchasing,* October 28, 1971

Hollingshead, A. W., Jr., "Linear Pricing Approach to Purchasing," *Management Review,* September 1971

Lee, Lamar, Jr., and Donald W. Dobler, *Purchasing and Materials Management,* 2d ed., New York: McGraw-Hill, 1971

Peckham, Herbert H., *Effective Materials Management,* Englewood, Cliffs, N.J.: Prentice-Hall, 1972

Ravnick, D. A., and A. G. Fisher, "Probablistic Make-Buy Model," *Journal of Purchasing,* February 1972

24

Inventories

DURING 1970 General Electric sold $8.7 billion worth of products; at the end of the year it owned $1.6 billion worth of inventories—stocks of materials and products. General Foods sold $2.2 billion worth of products and ended the year owning $380 million worth of inventories. RCA sold $3.3 billion worth of products and services and finished the year owning an inventory of $410 million. In these three companies (and they are typical) inventories tied up more than one fourth of all the money invested in them.

Some inventories are in the form of *raw materials and purchased items,* to be used in making products. Some inventories are *supplies,* to be used up. Some are *half-manufactured items* in factory departments. Some are *finished parts,* ready to be put into assembled products. Some are *finished products* in shipping rooms and warehouses.

Inventory is *money* that is temporarily in the form of a bar of brass, a sheet of steel, an iron casting, a bag of chemicals, a bolt of cloth, or a spare grinding wheel. But it isn't at all like money in the bank. It is money on which the company *pays* interest rather than earning interest. After a year, $100 in the bank may be worth $105. After a year on the shelf, $100 of inventory is worth nearer $90, and it has *cost* an additional $10 in expenses to carry it.

Most companies figure that it costs 20 percent or more of the value of inventories to carry them for a year. This is not because any one cost is so big but because inventories cost money several ways. They take up space; they have to be put into storage and got out again; they tie up money, so that in a sense they cause an interest charge; and usually they are insured, and insurance costs money. So do property taxes on inventories. They need to be kept track of (they even have to be counted now and then), so it is necessary to keep records. They need to be protected from the weather and from pilferage, but, even so, some things will deteriorate or disappear. Some items (rubber products, for example) have only a limited shelf life, and some obsolescence goes on all the time. All of these costs, added together, may easily exceed 20 percent.

Inventory control keeps track of inventories; but there is more to it than record keeping. Inventory control aims at (1) never running out of anything while (2) never having much of anything on hand and (3) never paying high prices because of buying in small quantities. This is the problem that managers face: What is the proper inventory level to maintain in the face of the two conflicting goals of giving good service while holding down the costs?

It is not easy to make and sell big volumes of products while owning almost nothing in transit, and at the same time never run out of anything or pay high prices because of hand-to-mouth buying or making. Yet big money is involved. If GE, through poor control, let its inventories go up 10 percent, it would have to put $160 million more into the inventories it owns. But if good control were able to cut 10 percent off its present investment, it would have $160 million in extra money. Besides that, GE would save some more millions from not having to store all the extra inventory. Ten percent means $38 million to General Foods and $41 million to RCA. Ten percent of its inventory investment means a whopping $410 million to General Motors.

FIGURE 24–1. The inventory control system

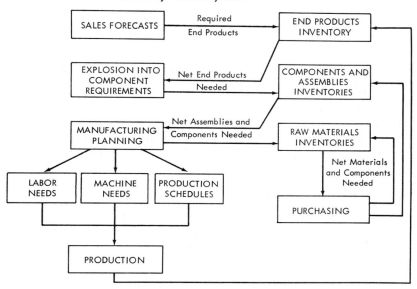

An uncontrolled inventory is usually *too much* inventory. It is particularly bad because it is painless—even pleasant. No harm is done if new supplies do not come in on time. The production department never runs out of anything. Nor does a customer ever have to wait for a finished product. Everyone is happy; but the money tied up in inventory is enormous, as are all the costs that big inventories entail.

It would not be quite so bad if everything finally got used up. But uncontrolled inventories always seem to contain a good many buggy whip items which finally have to be thrown away. Their investment is lost, as are the expenses of carrying them for several years before they are thrown away.

Now we need to back up a little. Inventory control which looks *only* at holding down the inventory is suboptimizing and is poor control. A manager runs a whole company and must consider the whole picture. As we said in an earlier chapter, it is sometimes desirable to build up inventories in order to allow the factory to operate economically. Our attention here is directed wholly at holding down inventory costs, yet sometimes this should *not* be done in the interest of overall effective operations.

Raw materials

Heavily used raw materials are usually bought on blanket contracts with deliveries scheduled to match the factory's need. Almost no reserve supply is carried—incoming shipments are scheduled to arrive daily or even at specific times during the day. This usually works well if the items are made locally. But for shipped-in items it is necessary to allow more leeway. Rarely is it safe to carry less than two or three days' supply. Release orders to suppliers, telling them exactly how much and when to ship, are given to the vendors by production control. This amounts to the production control department's (not the materials control department's) controlling the little inventories of heavily used raw materials which are carried.

Less heavily used raw materials are controlled by dollar limits, time limits, or other methods discussed later in this chapter.

One minor problem in raw materials control is shrinkage, but not the petty thieving kind, although it is often a minor annoyance. Shrinkage comes from buying in one unit and issuing in another. For example, sheet steel is bought by the ton and issued by the sheet. If the sheets are a little thicker than usual, there are not as many sheets in a ton as would be expected and the sheets will run out sooner than if the sheets were thinner.

Also, some things are measured out as they are issued: wire (bought by the pound, issued by length), liquids, pipe, lumber, and so on. Issuers nearly always give liberal measure, so the supply ends up short. Or, as in sheet metal, pipe, lumber, or glass, the lengths or sizes bought are standard but there is wastage in cutting to size. Experience will reveal what shrinkage to expect, but inventory controllers must be sure to expect it.

In-process inventories

Materials on the go make up most (at Westinghouse they are 80 percent) of all the inventories in companies that have manufacturing cycles of weeks or months. Controlling inventory in process is largely a matter of moving products through production as fast as possible, but it is also concerned with getting first orders out first. This is a scheduling problem and is production control's responsibility. But even companies which count their manufacturing cycle in days instead of weeks have substantial amounts of money tied up in inventory in process. They, too, need to keep production moving.

Supplies

Supplies are materials that are used up in running the plant or in making the company's products but which do not themselves go into the product. (Sometimes these are called MRO items—for maintenance, repair, and operating supplies.) Normally the cost of MRO items, over a year, is low compared to that of materials going into products, but it is still too high to neglect. They need control. In many companies, unfortunately, particularly small ones, supplies are handled carelessly and wastefully. They are handed out without requisitions, and no check is made on their use. Since all supplies are expendable, except perhaps complicated tooling, it is difficult to check on their proper issuance and use.

To control supplies it is necesary to have several separate supplies stockrooms: one for maintenance department supplies and materials, another for tools and tooling, another for cutting oils and lubricants, another for stationery supplies, and so on. Materials (except for very little things) should be issued from them only upon presentation of written requisitions, properly authorized and showing the account to be charged. Budgets can be established limiting departments in their use of supplies in order to discourage numerous little "private inventories" besides those of the stockrooms.

Obsolete items

At home, old things clutter up the attic. In a factory they clutter up stockroom bins and odd corners. The annual physical inventory is a fine time to review the need for keeping things that were not used during the year. Every six months would be better. It would be a good idea to have the computer print up a list of all items in stock which have not been used for six months. Then managers can look them over, one by one, to see which to keep and which to scrap. Usually not much money will be realized from the sale of the scrapped products, but at least selling them will stop the 20 percent a year cost of continuing to keep them.

Obsolete items are not always just overstocks of items that once were used in volume. They include production overruns on past orders where fewer items than expected were scrapped in process; repair parts on old long-gone machines; old supplies and old tooling, patterns, etc., kept in case more old items are needed for repair purposes; extra copies of old tooling where several sets used to be needed; and old, worn, but not worn-out parts taken out of machines when they were rebuilt, etc. Mostly the company is better off without all this junk.

Enclosed stockrooms

Most materials, particularly infrequently used items, are kept in enclosed stockrooms, from which they are issued only when a man presents a requisition. Materials in enclosed stockrooms are generally better cared for than things left out in the open. Also, enclosed stockrooms usually provide good records of the stock and what comes in and goes out. Separate stockrooms are needed for raw materials, semifinished items, finished parts (including finished subassemblies), finished products, and supplies. Often, more than one stockroom is needed for each kind of material so each will be near the point of use.

Having small sub-stockrooms is, however, a mixed blessing. Even if one-day replenishment service is given from central stores, substores tend to accumulate supplies as if they were the sole source. Each sub-stockroom manager remembers that "Central stores was out of stock last time"; or he says "It's too much trouble to reorder so often."

Timken Roller Bearing found that 3 substores were each using 20 U belts a month, and each one averaged 50 on hand. Besides this, central stores used 40 a month and carried 200. In total, a stock of 350 belts was carried to support a usage of 100 a month. Timken then changed its procedure and saved over half of the inventory by not allowing the substories to reorder until they ran out, and then confining their reorders to only one month's needs.

Individual stockrooms often stock several thousand items so often there are some real problems with receiving materials, identifying them, knowing where they are kept, and putting them away. Besides that, there are record-keeping problems as well as problems of stockroom arrangements, and indexes to where things are stored.

Open stockrooms

A great deal of paper work and handling of materials can be saved by point-of-use storage (storing materials right next to the operation where they are needed). This can be done where the same kinds of material are used day after day and where the materials are not likely to be stolen. It can also be done with parts along assembly lines. As parts are made, or as bought parts arrive (particularly if they arrive in small quantities in frequent repeat shipments), they are checked in and taken directly to their point of use and left there rather than in stockrooms. The operators just help themselves to whatever they need. In the accounts of the company, the value of the materials used is charged to the products made on a standard cost basis. Neither reports of materials used nor requisitions are necessary.

When open stores are used, the supply (or "bank") of materials stored at the operation is usually relatively small. Rarely (for big items) is it more than enough to carry on an hour or so. New supplies must be continually added from larger "backup" storerooms.

When parts are made in lots instead of continually, they go first into finished-parts stores (enclosed stores), from which the assemblers' supply bins are kept filled. Assemblers work from open bins which are replenished continually from these enclosed stores.

Open stores don't work quite so well, though, where assembly is by lot. Before even one finished product can be assembled, it is necessary to accumulate *all* the different parts needed and in the right quantity for the lot. Then the total supply of all the parts can be issued, and the products are put together one after the other. It is best to keep such lots in enclosed stores until all the parts have arrived, thus permitting assembly to start. It is probably best, however, to take only a day or so's parts needs to the assembly area at any one time, lest they take up too much room, or get damaged, or disappear.

There is also a second, very different kind of open stores. In this case "open stores" refers to the arrangement of the stockroom itself, and it really means random stacking of metal storage containers mounted on pallets. Sometimes a stockroom stores several hundred such portable storage bins containing component parts. The stock of one single kind of part may fill up one or even several of these storage containers. These containers have rigid corner posts some 3 feet high, thus permitting loads to be stacked and tiered a half dozen or more tiers high. Maybe, also, the stocks will need to be stacked 3 or 4 rows deep. In any case, many kinds of parts will be stored in a given stores section and the loads will be quite mixed in a random arrangement.

This is all right. It is only necessary to keep a card file of all locations of loads in the storeroom office next to the storage area. Permanent spaces are not assigned to any products. When new supplies arrive they are put wherever there is room. Then the trucker reports the location of where he puts each load. Whenever withdrawals are to be made he finds the location from the storeroom office. It doesn't matter if supplies of a single item are stored in several locations, nor does it matter if the trucker has to move several loads to get to the one he wants. With tiering fork lift trucks, he can put in or take out loads quickly and be on his way.

This kind of random access storage is a tremendous space saver. Such storage areas are usually "open" in the sense that they are not in an enclosed area. Loads don't disappear since each one consists of a half ton of largely unsalable parts (unsalable to a thief) which cannot be reached without a tiering lift fork truck. So there is little need to worry about thievery.

Physical inventories

Records never stay wholly accurate, so an actual count needs to be made (a "physical inventory") of what there is on hand from time to time. Companies used to close down for a week at the end of the year to count everything. This is still done sometimes, but now it is more common to count all the time. The stores clerk counts what is on hand in the bins in one section this week, another section next week, and so on. This periodic checking usually costs very little because regular stockroom clerks do it in their spare time. Maybe they get all the way around two or three times a year.

Counting at least once a year is usually desirable. The government insists that a company's inventory records be accurate because income taxes depend on profits. And profits are the difference between sales income and the cost of sales. And the cost of sales equals the January 1 inventory value plus the cost of things bought and made in the year, minus the December 31 inventory. It is kind of a long way around, but the amount a company claims its inventory is worth affects its profits, and that affects Uncle Sam's taxes, and so he says: Be sure it's right—count.

Besides federal taxes, local property taxes on inventories have to be paid. So local authorities, too, are interested in there being a proper value put on inventories.

Actually, it is not legally required to count everything at the end of the fiscal year. A company's auditors are allowed to certify the accuracy of the counts if their small sample counts verify the card records or the computer tape records on the items they sample.

Identification systems

It is hard to imagine a supermarket where the cans are without labels. No one would ever know what he was getting. Factory stores items are more varied in looks than tin cans, but without identification they are just about as hard to identify. Figure 24–2 is a picture of springs, but they are all different. A person cannot tell what they are for just by looking at them. An assembler asking a stock clerk for a certain kind of spring might be hard put to describe it rightly.

An identification system is mandatory. First, word descriptions of each item are needed—descriptions which tell what every item is and descriptions which set every item apart from other items. But word descriptions which clearly set every item apart from every other item are too long and cumbersome for most uses, so, second, a number system is needed. Numbers are shorter and easier to tell apart. Coded number systems (or number-and-letter systems) are used to give similar numbers to similar items. This helps people who have to work with the records to recognize the items more readily.

For raw materials, the code usually shows the kind of material. Groups of numbers are reserved for sheet steel, steel bars, tool steel, steel wire, steel castings, malleable iron castings, and so on. Other groups of numbers stand for brass items. Paints and varnishes have a totally different number set.

The coded part of coded numbers is on the left. If an item's whole number has six or eight digits, the first two or three show its general

FIGURE 24–2. Word descriptions alone will hardly do the job of identifying items such as these springs

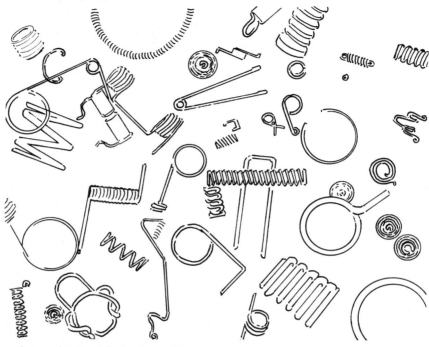

Source: Associated Spring Corporation.

class. The next one or two show its subclass. Only the last three digits are probably uncoded. An index is then used to find out exactly what the item is. The index would also provide the full word description.

The base used for coding raw materials (the *kind* of material) cannot be used with finished parts and components because finished items are often whole, assembled products. They might be pumps, electric motors, compressors, or such items. None of these can be classified according to what it is made of. Besides, trying to classify finished parts by what they are made of doesn't help people tie the product and its number together in their minds.

Using kinds of materials would give different numbers to steel, brass, nylon, and fiber gears. But since all are gears and serve the same purposes, it would seem better to have groups of similar numbers for the *kinds* of items. Then gears of all kinds would have similar numbers. Some companies do this. But this is not a perfect arrangement, either, because it gives the parts of any finished product unlike numbers.

For finished parts, it seems best to class things on a basis of use. Separate groups of numbers are set aside for parts for each finished product or each kind of finished product. This is the way most number codes for finished parts are set up, although there will always be many exceptions.

Using related use, electric motors, pumps, roller bearings, and oil cups would be numbered in the number system of the product they go in. But that would cause unlike numbers for electric motors. Pumps, bearings, and oil cups, too, would bear unlike numbers.

Common parts also upset all orderly numbering schemes. Such parts are used in several products, and so their number is always out of series in all lists for a product's parts except one. Some companies give common parts a separate series of numbers; but then, of course, the number tells nothing about the item except that it has several uses.

There are also problems, in all numbering systems, because design changes cancel some old parts and their numbers and add others. Old part numbers should not be reassigned to new parts (at least not for years) or there will be confusion.

Airplane companies use a double numbering system. Every part on an airplane has a regular number, but—besides—it has an "indent" number. The indent number tells at what point the part enters the airplane. This information is needed to schedule its manufacture at the right time. A part may, for example, go into the left wing flap, which goes into the left wing, which goes into the airplane. Some items go into one subassembly, which goes into another subassembly, which goes into another, and so on for seven or eight "generations."

It gets to be quite complex, but there is no other way to get the quarter of a million parts of a big airplane together at the right time and in the right order. Indent numbers help get the parts and subassemblies ready at the right time.

The government may also upset a company's numbering system. Companies selling products to the government may be required to use the government's parts numbers. Sometimes the government furnishes some parts that are identical to parts the contracting company uses regularly in other products, but with the government numbers attached. Thus these companies have to use two numbering systems.

Engineering drawings both help and confuse identification problems. Most parts for assembled products have drawings showing their size, dimensions, and other information. In the engineering department, the drawings must be numbered. So many companies just use the drawing number as all or part of a part's identification number. But some parts, such as pieces of wire in a radio set, and such materials as welding rods and paint need identification numbers, but have no drawing numbers. Their numbers are usually part of the raw materials series.

So drawing numbers do not solve all problems. In fact they make a new one. Drawings come big and little, and they are filed in the engineering department by the size of the sheet of paper they are on. Each

size has its own number series (A-722 or B-1461 and so on), which is fine
for filing, and finding drawings. But using a drawing's number as an
item's number gives no clue to what the item is.

Identifying materials

An identification system which suits the records is fine, but it is also
necessary to identify the items themselves. There are two easy ways to do
this so far as items in stock are concerned. For packaged items, the items'
descriptions can go on the package. And for all items, packaged and un-
packaged, a tag on the storage bin can identify its contents. For materials
in process, the material or its container can be tagged. This is important
because the material is changed in form a little after every operation,
making it hard to tell what an item is by looking at it.

Tags and labels take care of most of the problem. But tags get lost
and materials get separated. And tags can't be run through heat treating
furnaces or degreasing tanks. They have to be removed from the containers and later be reattached. Thus errors can easily occur. Also, some
items—steel sheets, castings, and others—are often not suitable for tag-
ging, nor are they kept in bins. In these cases it is better to stamp, mold,
paint, or etch some kind of identification on every item. Castings nearly
always have their numbers molded on. Bars and sheets of metal are
stacked and are painted with coded colors on the end.

A few companies have a curious identification problem. To prevent
employees' stealing of parts they can sell, the companies intentionally
put wrong numbers on them. TV and radio manufacturers sometimes put
false numbers on popular kinds of parts so they won't be stolen.

Materials requisitions

A materials requisition is a request to the stockroom to issue materials.
It shows the kind and quantity of materials wanted, the use to be made of
them (or the account number to be charged), and the signature of the
authorizing person. When the stock clerk hands out the material, he writes
down the material identification number on the requisition and sends it to
the stock record clerk. The record clerk subtracts the quantity issued from
his record card, writes in the amount he has left, puts the price per unit on
the requisition, and sends it to the accounting department. There the unit
price is multiplied by the quantity to get the value of the material issued.
The record clerk subtracts that amount of money from the materials account and adds it to the account for which the material was withdrawn.
All of this detailed work is, of course, almost always done today by computers rather than by hand.

Requisitions for *supplies* are generally made out by foremen for quantities which will last the department for some time. Requisitions for

materials to make into *products* may be made out by the foreman of the department doing the first operation. More often this is done ahead by production control, using a computer. The requisitions are either given to the foreman of the first department for him to use when he wants the material or they are held in production control's dispatch office until shortly before the first operation is to start. Then they are sent to the stockrooms, from which the materials are delivered to the first operation just before they are needed.

Requisitions for parts for *assembled* products are often copies of the assembly manufacturing order. This order lists the parts and quantities of each part needed. A copy goes to the finished-goods stockroom and serves as the stockroom clerk's authority to issue all the parts listed.

Materials requisitions are just so much extra paper work, and sometimes they can be eliminated. The use of regular day-to-day items is easy to figure because every product takes its required items and amounts of material. If 1,000 electric irons are to be made, the stock clerk knows that 1,000 handles, 1,000 heating units, and so on will be used. Assemblers don't need to use requisitions or get heating elements out of enclosed stockrooms. The men pick handles and heating units out of bins at their workplaces without paper records of every part issued.

This is a little dangerous, and once in a while things will disappear but not often, because most parts are not worth much to a thief. And if men don't steal parts, not many disappear. It is true, however, that in order to avoid criticism, men occasionally throw rejects into the trash can and don't report them. And it is also true that small, valuable, salable items (like gold in a jewelry factory or even clocks for stoves) need to be kept in enclosed stockrooms.

Some companies make workers who install valuable small items responsible for them by giving the men "meal ticket" requisitions. Standard quantities are issued from time to time to such a man, and a hole is punched in his requisition card. Then he must see that those items go into the products.

Except for the possibility of theft, requisitionless issuing of materials is best for regular-use items.

Pricing the materials issued

When materials are made into products, their money value is taken out of the raw materials account and added into the account showing the value of materials in process. Later, their investment is taken out of the materials-in-process account and added into the finished products account.

This sounds simple, but there is a troublesome problem. There is, say, a bin full of an item—say 125 in all. Suppose that they were acquired (whether by purchase or manufacture is immaterial) as follows: 25 units at $5 each, 50 units at $6 each, and 50 units at $7 each. These differences are extreme, but they will illustrate the point. The actual investment is $775 (although buying them all at today's price would cost $875). Now suppose that 100 pieces are issued. What price should be put on the requisition—$5, $6, $7, or some combination thereof?

There are five choices or methods for answering this question: FIFO, LIFO, average cost, last cost, and standard cost.

FIFO. FIFO means "first in, first out." Using FIFO, the first 25 items issued would be priced at $5, then 50 items at $6, and 25 of the last 50 items at $7, giving a total of 100 items issued and reported as costing $600. The 25 items left in stock would be shown to be worth $175.

LIFO. LIFO means "last in, first out." Using LIFO, the first 50 items issued would be priced at $7, the next 50 items at $6 for a total of 100 items costing $650. The 25 items left would be shown to be worth $125.

Average cost. The 125 items cost $775, or $6.20 each on the average. So, using average cost, the 100 items issued would be priced at $6.20 each, or a total of $620. The 25 items left would be shown to be worth $155.

Last cost. The last price was $7 each, so, using last cost, the 100 items issued would be priced at $7, or a total of $700. The 25 items left would be shown to be worth $75. Accountants like this method least of all because it permits inventories to cause hidden profits or hidden losses, which never show up as such.

Standard cost. Here some standard figure that items *ought* to cost is determined. This method is commonly used for items a company makes itself because no two lots ever cost exactly the same. Suppose the standard cost in our example is $5.75. All items going into inventory would be priced at $5.75 each, with all *actual* cost differences being carried to a variance account. If 100 items were issued, they would all be charged out at $5.75—a total of $575. The remaining 25 items left in the bin would also be valued at $5.75 each, or a total of $143.75.

This may all sound picayunish—just a play on numbers because the actual costs are the same and so are the selling prices, no matter how the matter is handled. Actually, it is not picayunish, because the problem goes on forever (prices and manufacturing costs are always changing), and it affects nearly every item used in making products.

Each method produces somewhat different product cost figures. This means the calculated profits are different, and this affects the company's income taxes. Also, if prices are set based on manufacturing costs, the method of charging for material used affects the income, and maybe the sales volume too. It is just not certain that the different methods will work out the same in the long run.

FIFO gives lower cost figures during periods of price increases. In such a case, FIFO would show more apparent profit and would result in higher income taxes. Also, inventories will be shown as worth today's higher prices.

LIFO is the reverse. As prices go up, the calculations say that the last bought, and most costly materials, are used first. LIFO boosts apparent costs, and holds down profits and taxes, but it values inventories too low. The other three methods usually fall between LIFO and FIFO.

On price downswings, everything is reversed. Here FIFO shows high costs and lower profits, and cuts taxes. LIFO shows lower costs and high profits, and results in higher income taxes.

Inventory levels and buying to market prices

As we saw at the beginning of this chapter, the cost of materials is a very big item in most manufacturing companies. And, as we will see in the next few pages, the biggest part of this cost is for a relatively small portion of all of the items bought.

Automobiles, for example, use millions of tons of sheet steel every year. So do can makers. Automobile tire makers use many millions of tons of rubber. And shoe companies use millions of cowhides. Chocolate companies and coffee distributors use millions of pounds of just a few kinds of raw materials. And bakeries use enormous quantities of flour.

The usual inventory control techniques, as described in this and the next chapter, often do not really apply to the inventories of these big items. Often these materials are bought on organized commodity exchanges where prices fluctuate daily. Sometimes they are bought on large, blanket contracts from basic materials suppliers.

In any case, the prices of these raw materials fluctuate in response to worldwide conditions of supply and demand. And the amount used in big companies is so great that these fluctuations need careful watching. Not only do they need careful *watching*, but they should generate appropriate *actions*.

If a steel strike is in prospect or if Brazil has a poor coffee growing season, higher prices are in prospect. And when higher prices appear to be quite likely, the buying of such raw materials is done farther ahead. The quantities bought are increased to cover more than the near future needs. Similarly, if lower prices are in prospect, a hand-to-mouth buying policy is adopted and only enough is purchased at one time to last for a short while.

As a consequence, inventory levels are much more the result of a company's forecast of future materials-market conditions than they are of any inventory control policy as such. Inventory levels of these materials are *results* of raw material price expectations rather than the levels planned to be economic in support of near future finished product sales expectations.

The stockkeeping unit (SKU)

When a company has factory warehouses and regional warehouses as well, and when single factories have a central stockroom and sub-stockrooms at several locations around the plant, there are several inventories of each item to control. Each stock of each item is a "stockkeeping unit" in that each one has to meet the demands made on it while its inventories are held down. In order to control inventories, each stockkeeping unit needs to be treated separately and should be controlled separately from other SKUs.

Inventory turnover

Inventory turnover is the cycle of using and replacing materials. It is a ratio—the number of "turns" of the investment a year. If a company sells $100,000 worth of products a year and has an average inventory of $50,000, it has two turnovers a year. But if this company could get by with an inventory worth $25,000, it would have four turns a year. More turns reduce the investment, and save carrying costs as well.

Some companies use the turnover ratio as an inventory control method. They insist on a certain number of turns a year. This idea should not be carried very far, however. A high turnover rate means very low inventories, but very low inventories mean being out of stock more often. Low inventories also force frequent, uneconomical, small reorders and higher unit costs.

Volume and reasonable turnover ratios are also related. It is not hard to get more turns when volume is high. But if volume falls off to half, and inventories are also cut in half in order to keep the turnover ratio up, there will surely be too many cases of running out of stock. And too many reorders will be of the costly, frequent, small-quantity kind.

Inventory ABCs

Big companies have to stock and keep track of 50,000 or more different items. Controlling these inventories takes hundreds of clerks, whose salaries run into hundreds of thousands of dollars.

Yet one purpose of inventory control is control at the least clerical cost. Some factory items are like paper clips and rubber bands in the office: They aren't worth keeping records of. It is better just to keep a supply of such items on hand and let people help themselves. It doesn't matter if these little things are used wastefully because it is cheaper to pay the waste than to keep the records.

On the other hand, *loose* controls should be limited to little things. This means that a decision has to be made as to which items are little things and which need more careful control. Pareto's "vital few" and "trivial many" idea, the "20-80 principle" mentioned earlier, helps here. The inventory controller should look over the stock records, item by item, and classify them into A, B, and C groups.

Back in Chapter 9 we worked out an example of how to construct a

Pareto curve. Such a curve would show clearly which items are A, B, and C. Figure 24–3 is actually the same chart as the one in Chapter 9, as are its numbers and calculations. Here, however, we assume that the numbers are for the usage of materials and parts. And again the conclusion is the same: A few of the items are responsible for most of the cost of all materials and parts used.

FIGURE 24–3.   Typical ABC inventory distribution

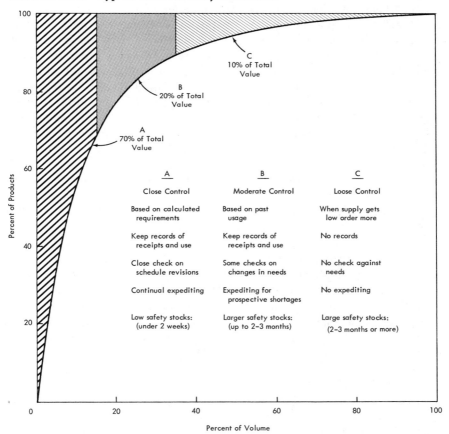

A items are the big investment items: the vital few. General Electric, in one division, found that 8 percent of the items used up 75 percent of the money. Ten percent of the items commonly account for 70 percent of the investment. A items should get the full record keeping treatment. Their needs should be calculated ahead of time according to the period of use. Then their manufacture or purchase should be scheduled so that they arrive just before they are needed. They should be ordered a few at a time and often. This will help hold their inventories very low. These items should be issued to the men according to their use needs but without requisitions. And inventory levels should be watched very carefully.

At the same time, there will be occasions when the inventory of particular A items should not be controlled (in the usual sense) at all. This will be true for basic materials (bought in enormous quantities) when buying to market prices is so important as to make their inventories subordinate to forward buying policies based on future price expectations. (These problems were discussed on page 579.)

B items should get "middle" treatment. They are the next 15 to 20 percent of the items, which account for some 15 percent of the investment. They are less important than A items but are worth keeping careful record of their use. Here minimum-maximum controls should be used. Past usage, rather than future schedule requirements, should be the basis for reordering. Minimum stock limits and standard reorder quantities can be set and used. "Economic order quantities" can be used to advantage here. Replenishment reorders should occur automatically whenever the stock of an item gets down to its reorder point. B items should be issued from stockrooms in exchange for written requisitions.

C items are the wasters: the trivial many. GE found that 67 percent of the items cost only 5 percent of the value of materials used. Seventy-five percent of the items commonly account for only 10 percent of the investment. C items should get short shrift on planning and records. It is only necessary to order plenty of paper clips, cotter pins, washers, solder, etc. It is a good idea to use some kind of a bin minimum or "last container" arrangement. The reorder point quantity can be tied up in a sack, or a cardboard can be put on top of the reorder quantity in the bin. When the sack has to be opened or the cardboard removed, this should trigger a reorder for a quantity large enough to last for a good while. C items can be put at the operatives' workplaces, where they can help themselves without using requisitions. Future needs of C items should not be calculated. Nor should they be priced to products individually. They can be charged to an overhead account.

Loose controls of C items will boost their investment and their costs from shelf wear, obsolescence, and wasteful use, but not nearly so much as to offset the savings in record keeping costs. The organization will end up ahead with loose controls on C items.

Dollar limits

Most companies set dollar limits or budgets on the amount which they will allow to be invested in each class of materials. Each class has its account in the accounting department showing its investments. The inventory control manager is responsible for seeing that the amounts stay within the allowed budgets.

Because they would have to be set individually for every item, dollar limits are not used for specific items very often (except for the big items). Nor do dollar limits tell the inventory controller when or how much to reorder. All they do is tell him not to go too high in total. He has to figure out how much of each individual item he can have, while keeping the investment within the limit.

Dollar limits need to be used with discretion when price or business levels change; otherwise they automatically tighten or loosen the amount allowed to be carried. There is need to recognize what the method does to inventory control policies. If, for example, prices go up and the dollar limits are not changed, the inventory control manager has to cut the quantities he carries.

Time limits

Time limits are the common way to put dollar limits into effect. To make time limits out of dollar limits it is only necessary to divide the dollar limit by the dollar usage per month. A $20,000 limit is a two-month limit for an item used at a rate of $10,000 per month.

Dollar limits can be used directly to control only a few big-use items, but time limits can easily be applied to every item. In fact, one time limit can apply to any number of items at the same time.

Time limits don't exactly say when to reorder or how much. They merely say: Don't, at any time, have more than (say) 30 days' supply on hand. Indirectly, this sets top limits on how much can be ordered at one time. To hold the average investment for a class of items down to a month's usage, the inventory controller can never order much more than a month's supply of any item on a single order.

For long lead-time items, time limits control *when* reorders go out as well as *how much* is ordered. If it takes three months to get an item, and orders are limited to one month's supply at one time, it will be necessary to place a new order every month for one month's needs, but each order will always be for the third month ahead. There will always be several orders out at the same time. Items on order don't count in the inventory so far as investment is concerned. But in a very real sense the inventory "coverage" (the quantity on hand plus the amount on order) is the true inventory which is available.

Time limits are easy to set, easy to change, and easy to operate. And they can be different for different items. If an item's *use* changes, the time limit can stay put because the reordering quantity will change itself.

A bad feature of time limits is that they are not often the very best for whole groups of products, although they are usually applied to whole groups. A 30-day limit is probably too much for some items in a group and too little for others.

Fixed review time reordering

Many, perhaps most, companies do not send requests to buy more materials to purchasing every day. Instead they do it once a month, or possibly once a week, for everything that is running low. Warehouses commonly order stock this way. The first week of the month they order all the steel items, the second week all nonferrous items, the third week all bought components, etc. Ordering whole classes of products all together saves clerical work because the whole order is just one long list.

This method has one bad feature: Most of the time it probably will result in inventories' being slightly higher. At the end of any review period the inventory controller has to look ahead to see if the stock might get down to the reorder point *at any time before the next review period.* If it might run short, he has to reorder more right now because (except for emergencies) he cannot order more in between. So he orders now, and the new supply comes in before it is really needed. This does not have to happen, however. An order can be placed and the vendor can be told not to deliver it right away.

Another disadvantage to ordering at regular intervals is that the quantity ordered is usually enough to bring the inventory back to some predecided maximum total. The reorder quantities are always different, and

FIGURE 24–4.   Reordering on a periodic basis results in reorders occurring regardless of the exact quantity on hand at the date for reordering

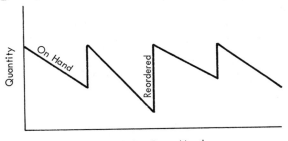

Reordering Every Month

are really set at quantities to replace recent usage. Probably it would be more economical to reorder in economic lot quantities (explained in the next chapter). Figure 24–4 shows how the reorder quantities might vary.

Standard quantities

With purchased items it is necessary to pay attention to standard packages, full barrels, and whole bundles. Nearly always, if an order is for part of a package, the price per unit is higher. So the quantities actually ordered should be adjusted where necessary to come out to full, standard packages.

On small items, it is often possible to set a fixed quantity (which recognizes standard packages) to reorder every time. Supplies are often ordered that way. So are minor "free issue" items, such as nuts and bolts. Ordering fixed quantities saves clerical time and costs.

This type of savings also applies elsewhere. It often applies where freight or truck rates are consequential. Perhaps the full railroad-car freight rate for steel applies to orders of 30,000 pounds or more, but the inventory controller wants only 25,000 pounds right now. The shipping rate per pound is higher on all shipments of less than 30,000 pounds. It might even result that the total freight cost on 25,000 pounds at the less-than-carload rate would be *more* than the cost for 30,000 pounds at the full-carload rate.

Unless the controller just does not want the extra 5,000 pounds *at all*, or not for a long time, he may be better off to order 30,000 pounds. The freight-cost savings will outweigh the costs of carrying the extra 5,000 pounds a little longer than usual.

Review questions

1. The text says that holding inventories down may be unwise suboptimization. How is it that this might be unwise?

2. Compare enclosed and open stockrooms. When should each be used?

3. How often should actual physical counts of inventories be made? Why?

4. What kind of an identification system seems best for raw materials? Why? What kind is best for finished parts? Why?

5. Why are materials requisitions used? Can they ever be done without? Why?

6. Should actual purchase costs or actual production costs be used for pricing requisitions? Why or why not? What problems are involved? If neither of these cost figures should be used, what price should be used?

7. What methods for pricing materials out of stock are available? Which is best? Why?

8. Should each separate subinventory of items stocked at several points in the same large factory be controlled separately? What problems are involved?

9. Inventory turnover is commonly used as part of the method for controlling inventories. What dangers might appear if this idea is pursued too far?

10. How do inventory ABCs work? How does a company, which recognizes this concept, benefit as compared to one which does not? Discuss.

11. Describe the differences in inventory control techniques which should be used for A, B, and C items in inventory.

12. If a company uses dollar-limit control and the limits stay fixed, what hap-

pens to the inventories when business volume increases? When prices decrease?

13. What kinds of items should be controlled by fixed quantities? Dollar limits? Time limits? Economic lot sizes (discussed in Chapter 25)?

Discussion questions

1. Who should the inventory controller listen to as he tries to do his job? The purchasing agent does not want to have to expedite orders. The treasurer wants him to hold down the average inventory investment. The sales manager wants him never to run out of anything. The plant manager doesn't want to have production held up by not having materials, and he also wants long runs on production jobs. Try to reconcile these conflicting desires.

2. A question from the inventory controller: "How can I get the the information I need to analyze and to prove that I am doing a good job?" How can this question be answered?

3. If a company is to end up with a certain number of obsolete items in stock, where is it worst for this to occur? In raw materials? In in-process materials? In finished parts? Or in finished products? Why?

4. Do inventories contribute to reducing overall company costs or do they increase total costs? Discuss.

5. Do large inventories have any effect on worker productivity? If so, what effect?

6. Should a company ever engage in speculation? Discuss.

7. Isn't it more or less fruitless to try to hold inventories to the barest minimums when railroad companies sometimes hold freight cars for several days in order to make up long trains? Discuss.

8. How hard should a company try to keep inventories down on parts it makes itself when the machine setup costs in some departments run as high as 25 percent of all labor costs? Is this bad? Discuss.

9. How can a company count heavy material, such as bins partly full of 100-pound castings?

10. In the 1960s many companies changed from FIFO to LIFO inventory charging practices. Why?

11. Will fixed reorder cycles result in higher inventories than fixed reorder systems? How would this work?

Problems

1. Item 294's record shows the following:

Received January 24	300 @ $.42 each
Received February 15	200 @ .46 each
Received March 27	400 @ .51 each
Received April 15	200 @ .47 each
Received May 25	350 @ .54 each

Issues were as follows:

From January   24 to February   14............................... 176
From February 15 to March   26............................... 145
From March   27 to April   14............................... 502
From April   15 to May   25............................... 120
From May   25 to June   1............................... 47

If the company uses FIFO, what price was put on the withdrawal requisitions for the stock withdrawn in each period? What would the prices have been if the company had used LIFO? What would be the calculated remaining inventory value each time a new stock came in?

2. Suppose that the following 15 items are representative of the 40,000 items kept in stock. Construct a maldistribution curve and find out what proportion of the items are A, B, and C items. What fraction of all items probably is responsible for the greatest 80 percent of the value of all items used?

Thousands of dollars of value use in 1 year

Item	Dollars	Item	Dollars	Item	Dollars
1	6	6	32	11	12
2	45	7	2	12	5
3	17	8	1	13	60
4	4	9	40	14	3
5	13	10	9	15	26

Case 24–1

The ABC Company has analyzed its stockroom investment turnover and found it to be considerably below what the management thinks it should be. A quick review of the stock cards showed that a six months' supply of many items was on hand. Very few items had less than two months' supply on hand. The purchasing agent of the company bought the major materials used in the company's products. They were bought on the basis of price forecasts, and it was felt that that practice should be continued. The stocks of items ordered from the cards by the stock card clerk were regarded as excessive. The record clerk ordered replenishment supplies of these items as he saw fit, although he was supposed to order no more than three months' supply on any one reorder. He could, however, use his own judgment as to when to reorder, and if he thought that the demand might increase, he ordered a new supply sooner than he normally would, even when the current stock was ample for the time being. Before he took the job, the shop had been held up frequently for lack of stock. He was quite proud of having solved that difficulty.

Is there a problem here? Since it will all be used in due time, is there any harm in having plenty of stock on hand? Set up a procedure to reduce the inventory without running out of stock.

Recent references

Apte, S. S., "Predicting Spare Parts Needs," *Plant Engineering*, November 13, 1969

Buffa, Elwood S., and William H. Taubert, *Production-Inventory Systems Planning and Control*, rev. ed., Homewood, Ill.: Richard D. Irwin, 1972

Eilon, S., and J. Elmaleh, "Adaptive Limits in Inventory Control," *Management Science,* April 1970

Killeen, Louis M., *Techniques of Inventory Management,* New York: American Management Association, 1969

Landel, R. D., "Managing the Inventory Investment," *Systems Management,* July 1971

Plossl, G. W., and O. W. Wright, *Material Requirements Planning by Computer,* Chicago: American Production and Inventory Control Society, 1971

Thomas, A. B., *Inventory Control in Production and Manufacturing,* Boston: Cahners Books, 1969

Inventory control systems

WE HAVE SEEN that inventories require big investments which need to be controlled. Several systems of control are available, each one having its individual good and bad points. Some are particularly well suited for certain situations but not for others. Managers need to know about the alternative methods, and their strengths and weaknesses, in order best to control the thousands of items their companies carry.

Reordering for known future demand

The inventory control man in a job-lot shop has to contend with ups and downs and shifts back and forth in the use of his items. But he still has to try to avoid running out of anything and do it without carrying big inventories.

He can do a fairly good job of doing both at once if he is willing to do a little extra recording work by paying attention to future needs insofar as they are already known. As soon as the production control man gets an order to make a product, he can figure the materials needed. He can also look at the schedule to find out when they will be needed. He can then check with the inventory control manager, who in turn can check his stock record for each item. The inventory controller can then allocate enough of the available material to take care of the order. If there is not enough available, he can order more right away so it will be on hand when needed.

In order to make such allocations, two extra columns for figures are needed on the stock record card or in the computer's file. The first added column, called "allocated," "apportioned," or "reserved," shows the order numbers and quantities needed for all future orders for which material has been reserved. (This allocation is purely a record. The "reserved" materials are not actually set aside.)

The second extra column is the "available" column. It shows the sum of the present stock, plus the quantities on order, minus the quantities reserved. Reserving stock does not always secure new supplies as soon as they are needed, but the inventory controller is warned ahead of time if a shortage is in sight, and he has more time in which to get more stock.

A procedure quite similar to this is sometimes used for finished components, or "basics." Basics (which were mentioned briefly in Chapter 18) are components, such as electric motors, which are actually finished products that are used in several styles or sizes of products and which may even be sold separately. In companies which make their own components of this sort and then use them as parts of bigger products, these items are often made to meet a general forecasted demand total without the specific use demands having been totaled up. Then, as these products go through production, they are allocated or assigned to specific end product uses.

Ordinarily, all are so assigned by the time they are completed, but if not, they could become shelf items and be available for allocation to orders as they come in. When the demand is heavy, perhaps all of the basics in process might already be assigned. As more are started into production, they are assigned immediately to certain end uses. In fact, even those not yet started can also be allocated. "Available" items could therefore be those already on hand, or they could be those already in process, or they could be future items not yet started into production.

Ordering for assembly needs

Ordering for assembly needs (one textbook author calls this "time-phased requirements planning") might be called a separate method of inventory control, although it is just one kind of time-limit control. It starts with the schedules for assembled finished products. Such schedules are issued months ahead to allow time to buy materials and to make parts.

When ordering parts (and materials for parts made in the company), the first thing is to calculate the kinds and quantities needed for one month's assembled products—say August's. (This is done several months ahead, perhaps in March.) To assemble in August means that most of the parts should be finished in July. Some of the parts, however, will go into subassemblies which will be put together in July, so these parts need to be finished in June.

Having set completion dates for parts, the next thing is to look at how long it takes to make them. This provides a starting date for making each one. Different parts will have different starting dates, depending on their time to make.

The date to start to make a part is the date by which it is necessary to get raw materials for it. So the next calculation is to work back through the time it takes to get raw materials to get a date for ordering.

So far this sounds like a scheduling matter, and so belongs in our production control chapters rather than in a discussion of inventory control. It *is* a scheduling matter, but it is *also* an inventory control matter. August's assembly needs determine the *quantities* of some items which have to be ordered in June, or May, or April, or even earlier.

Mostly, the only quantity figure paid any attention in this process is August's requirements. Whatever quantities are needed to take care of August's finished products are ordered. Then, a month later, enough is ordered to meet September's requirements. When and how much to order depends on assembly requirements—and not much else. Ordering is as late as can be done while yet getting materials in time. Rarely do orders provide for quantities in excess of one month's need of anything. Sometimes the month's requirements are even cut into parts and sent through as several small orders.

This matter of ordering quantities in line with the needs of the assembly floor for successive time periods applies both to internal inventory control and to purchase orders for bought items. The quantities bought and the delivery schedules are tied in with assembly floor needs.

Calculating parts requirements. Different end products often require many of the same component parts, so it is highly desirable to bring together these separate requirements into totals for each part. Then the part can be made in one lot—in a quantity adequate to take care of all the assembly floor needs.

Figures 25–1 to 25–3 show how these calculations could be made.

FIGURE 25–1

	End product				
Month	*1*	*2*	*3*	*4*	*5*
April................	20	20	10	10	30
May................	5	10	15	20	30
June................	40	20	20	30	20
July................	10	0	5	15	5

Figure 25–1 is a listing of end-products to be assembled in a four-month period. Figure 25–2 shows how many common parts A, B, and C are

FIGURE 25–2

End product	Common parts		
	A	*B*	*C*
1.....................	2	5	4
2.....................	0	10	10
3.....................	5	8	4
4.....................	1	1	2
5.....................	6	2	4

needed for each end product. Figure 25–3 shows the calculation of the total quantities of each part which will be needed in order to allow the assembly of the scheduled numbers of end products 1 to 5.

In an actual case, all of this would be further complicated by differing lead times for making each part, as well as by the possible downward adjustment of the quantities needed if any of these parts were already in stock or coming through on earlier orders.

Materials short lists. At each stage of the calculation of parts and components needed, a comparison should be made with stocks which may already be on hand or which may be coming through as unassigned basics. Often such stocks will fill a portion of the needs. In such a case only the unfilled quantities need to be ordered.

Sometimes this remaining list of needed parts is called a "parts short" list, meaning that these parts still need to be made in order to meet the assembly floor's requirements.

Production attrition. Order quantities almost always need to be

FIGURE 25-3

Part	End product 1		End product 2		End product 3		End product 4		End product 5		Total
	Per unit	total	Per unit	total	Per unit	total	Per unit	total	Per unit	total	
April		*20*		*20*		*10*		*10*		*30*	
A	2	40	0	0	5	50	1	10	6	180	280
B	5	100	10	200	8	80	1	10	2	60	450
C	4	80	10	200	4	40	2	20	4	120	460
May		*5*		*10*		*15*		*20*		*30*	
A	2	10	0	0	5	75	1	20	6	180	285
B	5	25	10	100	8	120	1	20	2	60	325
C	4	20	10	100	4	60	2	40	4	120	340
June		*40*		*20*		*20*		*30*		*20*	
A	2	80	0	0	5	100	1	30	6	120	330
B	5	200	10	200	8	160	1	30	2	40	630
C	4	160	10	200	4	80	2	60	4	80	580
July		*10*		*0*		*5*		*15*		*5*	
A	2	20	0	0	5	25	1	15	6	30	90
B	5	50	10	0	8	40	1	15	2	10	115
C	4	40	10	0	4	20	2	30	4	20	110

greater than end needs because of production attrition. Almost every operation will produce its occasional defective product which will not pass inspection and will have to be discarded, thus shrinking the quantity moving on to the next operation. Rarely are rejects numerous enough to make serious trouble, and sometimes they can be repaired quickly enough to rejoin the good ones as the lot moves on to the next operation.

In order to have the final quantity equal to quantity really wanted, it is necessary to start a greater number in at the beginning to cover the normal rejects. If 100 are wanted and they will go through 3 successive operations whose loss ratios are 10, 15, and 5 percent respectively, the starting quantity has to be $100 \div .95 \div .85 \div .90 = 138$. Ninety percent of the 138, or 124, will survive the first operation. Eighty-five percent of these, or 105, will survive the second operation. And 95 percent of these, or 100, will survive all 3 operations.

Almost never would the loss ratio be so great as this. Yet if it were, production control would have to pay attention, in scheduling machines, to the greater quantities going through early operations.

Minimum-maximum controls

B items and perhaps some A items should get minimum-maximum control. These lie in "computer country." In order to use minimum-maximum control it is necessary to figure out, for each item, its typical usage and its typical replenishment time. To this is added a small quantity, as a safety factor, and the reorder point will have been determined. Whenever the stock gets down to this point, an order is placed for more. How many more? Economic order quantities (EOQs), or quantities based on one of the other control methods already discussed. Operating together, these relationships constitute minimum-maximum controls. All of this can be done well by computers. *How* they do it is explained later in this chapter.

Reordering points (ROP)

When and how many regularly stocked items to reorder are the perennial inventory control questions. Reordering points are the "when." It is easy to lay down a rule but hard to apply it. The rule is to reorder far enough ahead so that the new supply comes in just as the last of the old stock is used. The reorder point is a number; it is the sum of the quantity of an item expected to be used during the reorder cycle time plus a small additional "safety" quantity which serves as protection against variations.

The trouble is that, in many cases, no one knows exactly how many items will be used during the replacement lead time, nor does anyone know exactly how long it will take to get a new supply. And this problem

FIGURE 25–4. Relationships between reorder points and usage when usage is regular

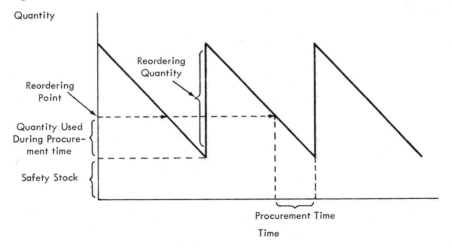

is the same for raw materials, bought finished parts, parts a company makes itself, and finished products.

The inventory controller can look to the past, and he does. If, on a particular item, the use has been 50 per month lately, this will be his guess for the near future (unless he has some good reason to think that it will be different). It is the same with how long it takes to get more. How long did it take in the past? Usually six weeks? Then this is the lead time he will use.

The ROP operates as a "trigger" point which triggers the reorder. If a company uses reorder points, each item has to have its own figure. The quantity might be as little as the number of units expected to be used in

FIGURE 25–5. Figure 25–4 is a simplified diagram of an item's use and replenishment cycle as if use were steady. In fact, however, the use of most items is more likely to be in irregular steps, as is shown here

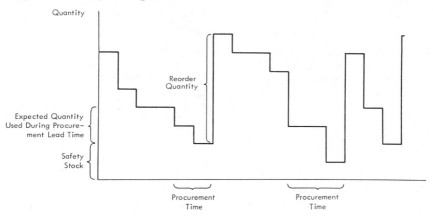

the replenishment lead time. In our example below, it could be as little as 75—the number normally used in the six weeks that it usually takes to get more.

Safety stocks with cost penalties for being out of stock. Using the expected usage during the replenishment lead time as the ROP would almost always be too risky. Sometimes (although this is not included in the example below) more than 50 a month are used and sometimes it takes more than 6 weeks to get more. Either way, the company would be out of stock too often. It would be better to boost the reorder point, perhaps to 100, in the example. The 25 units added as a safety stock are not, however, actually held back or set aside. Normally it is the quantity which will still be on hand when a new order comes in.

The need to have a safety stock boosts the inventory and so costs money. But so does being out of stock. Managers sometimes make an estimate of the costs and the chances of running out of stock. Then they try to set the safety stock at a level where the combined costs are the least. They find that for some items it pays to carry very little and to run out now and then, rather than carry a large safety stock. In other cases, carrying a little extra safety stock is cheap insurance against irregular lead time and variable use.

An example will show how these costs might be balanced off against each other:

Use: 50 per week
Cost of running out: $200
Cost to carry 1 unit in stock for 1 week: $.75

Past reorder experience:

Weeks between ordering and receiving new supply...... 3   4   5   6   7
Number of instances in last 25 reorders................ 2   6   10   4   3

The problem is to find the proper reorder point. If orders are placed 3 weeks ahead, the reorder point will have to be for at least 150 units because 150 units will be used during the 3 weeks. At the end of 3 weeks the inventory will be down to zero: then it will jump up to 150 and begin to work down again. The average inventory will be 75 units.

On a weekly basis, the cost to carry 75 units is $75 \times \$.75 = \$56.25$. But because most orders will not be received in 3 weeks, this item will almost always be out of stock (in 92 percent of the cases) before the new lot comes in. So the out-of-stock cost will be $.92 \times \$200 = \$184$ every 3 weeks, or $61.33 per week. The total cost per week of this program is $117.58.

Next, the same calculation can be made using a reorder point of 200 units, the normal 4-week usage. Other calculations can be made for the other possibilities, and the results are shown in Figure 25–6. In this example it is easy to tell by inspection that the proper reorder point is a little less than 5 weeks' usage, say 240.

FIGURE 25–6

Lead time (weeks)	Num- ber of in- stances	Per- cent of in- stances	Usage during lead time	Weekly average inventory during lead time	Weekly cost of carrying average inventory	Per- cent of time out of stock	Cost per order of outage	Cost per week of outage	Total cost per week
3	2	8	150	75	$ 56.25	92	$184	$61.33	$117.58
4	6	24	200	100	75.00	68	136	34.00	109.00
5	10	40	250	125	93.75	28	56	11.20	104.95
6	4	16	300	150	112.50	12	24	4.00	116.50
7	3	12	350	175	131.25	0	0	0	131.25

Calculating reorder points this way pays no attention to economic lots as reordering quantities. Nor does it indicate what fraction of the inventory is regarded as the safety stock. The safety stock is implicit in the calculation. If 240 units are ordered each time, they will be received in 3 weeks 8 percent of the time. Ninety units would still be on hand. They will arrive in 4 weeks 24 percent of the time. Forty units would still be on hand. The rest of the time the stock will have run out before the new supply comes in, so there would be no stock on hand. Having 90 units 8 percent of the time and 40 units 24 percent of the time averages out to 17 units all of the time ($90 \times .08 + 40 \times .24 = 16.8$ units). In this instance a safety stock of 17 units is implicit in the reorder calculation.

Actually, this method of determining reorder points and safety stocks is much less commonly used than calculations based on "service levels," which are discussed later in this chapter.

Economic lots or economic order quantities (EOQ)

The optimum number to order at a time is called the "economic lot" or the "economic order quantity" (or sometimes the ELS, the "economic lot size"). The optimum production-lot size is the quantity which yields the lowest cost per unit. The EOQ idea works for both purchased and manufactured items. In theory, this decision model is simple. It costs money for all the paper work needed to place a purchase order. And in the factory it costs even more money to make up all of the necessary shop papers for an order. Besides this, it usually costs a good bit of money to set up machines and get ready to run the order. These are "acquisition" costs, and are the same for big or little orders. So the more of an item made or ordered at a time, the less they cost *per unit*.

But the bigger the lot, the higher the "costs of possession." These in-

FIGURE 25-7. Although the economic lot can be computed as a specific quantity, the unit cost is relatively flat over a range of 25 percent above or below the economic lot

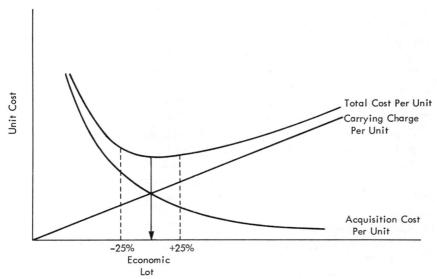

clude inventory carrying costs, shelf wear, handling costs, record keeping, bin cost, interest on investment, and the risk of obsolescence. At some point—some quantity—the two will balance. This is the economic lot size. Any larger lot runs up the costs of possession more than the decline in the per unit cost of acquisition. Any smaller lot does not spread acquisition costs enough.

Figure 25–7 shows these relationships in graphic form. It is interesting to see that the total cost curve is almost flat for some distance. This means that it is not necessary to hit the economic lot exactly right in order to get low costs. In fact, costs are usually almost as low for reorders up to 25 percent more (or less) than the economic lot.

Since it is unnecessary to hit the EOQ exactly in order to get low costs, most companies that calculate economic lots use simple formulas which leave out such minor factors as the likelihood of obsolescence. Here is the most commonly used formula:

$$\text{EOQ, in units} = \sqrt{\frac{2 \times \text{the number of pieces per year} \times \text{the setup cost for an order}}{\text{Labor, material, and overhead cost per piece} \times \text{carrying charge rate}}}$$

Economic order quantities can also be expressed in terms of months' supply. The formula is just expressed differently:

$$\text{EOQ, in months' supply} = \sqrt{\frac{24 \times \text{the cost to place an order}}{\text{Monthly usage in dollars} \times \text{carrying charge rate}}}$$

Economic lots in purchasing decisions. Whenever the purchasing department can get quantity discounts, this makes a different EOQ for each price offered. But sometimes the economic lot cannot be bought at the price quoted because the vendor does not offer his lower price unless more than the economic quantity is bought. Yet his price cut for larger quantities may save enough to justify buying more than an economic lot.

Suppose, for example, that it costs $10 to place a purchase order and 25 percent a year for carrying costs, and that 2,000 units a year are needed. The vendor quotes a price of $2 per unit for all orders under 500 units and $1.95 for 500 or more. How many should be ordered?

To answer this question it is first necessary to calculate the EOQ for each offer. So far as the buyer's needs are concerned, at $2 the EOQ is 283 units and at $1.95 it is 286 units. The price difference is so small that it doesn't change the EOQ much. But, actually, the buyer does not get to choose between these two EOQ quantities because he cannot get the $1.95 price unless he buys 500. Will it pay to go up to 500 to get the benefit of the $1.95 price?

If the customer buys 283 units at a time, he will spend, in a year, $71

FIGURE 25–8. Quantity discounts for purchased items complicate reorder problems because the price reduction often makes it economical to reorder considerably more than the economic lot

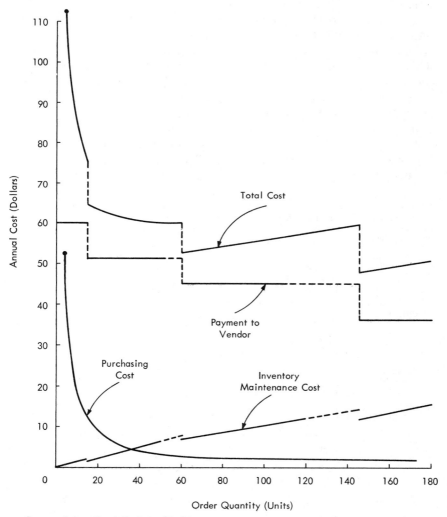

Source: International Business Machines.

for 7.1 orders and another $71 to carry an average inventory of 142 pieces valued at $2 each. The total annual cost of this practice will be $142.

The alternative is to buy 500 units at a time for $1.95. With this policy the costs will be $40 for 4 orders and $122 to carry the average inventory of 250 units valued at $1.95 each. This policy will cost $162 a year, or $20 extra. But at the $1.95 price there will also be a savings of $100 in price.

This is an offset to the $162, leaving a net annual cost of $62 for buying 500 units. The manager's decision should therefore be to buy 500 at a time and save $80 a year.

Economic lots with delivery over a period of time. Sometimes the ordered items do not all arrive at once. Particularly is this true with high-volume steady-use items which the company makes itself. When the whole lot does not arrive all at one time, the formulas just given will produce too small an answer. They assume that the peak inventory will always include a complete new lot. But actually, since some of the items are being used as they are delivered, the peak inventory may never be that high. The carrying charges are overstated.

When a new supply comes in over several days, part of it is used up before the last of the order comes in. The saw-tooth diagram in Figure 25–4 becomes slanted, as in Figure 25–9.

FIGURE 25–9. Delivery of an order over a period of time allows it to be used to hold down maximum inventories

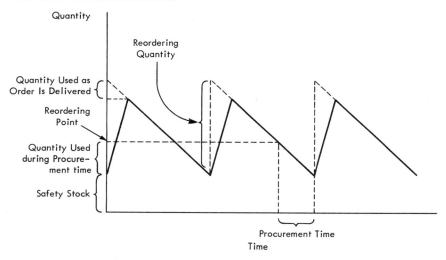

To correct for this in the calculation of the EOQ, it is necessary to adjust the denominator under the square root sign in the EOQ formula by multiplying it by:

$$1 - \frac{\text{the use rate}}{\text{the production rate}}.$$

Here is how this works:

Use per year............................... 100,000 (400 per workday)
Setup cost per order....................... $30
Labor, material, and overhead cost per piece... $15
Carrying charge rate....................... 20%
Maximum production rate per year........... 300,000 (1,200 per workday)

First we will solve this problem with the whole lot arriving at one time:

$$\text{Economic lot} = \sqrt{\frac{2 \times 100{,}000 \times \$30}{\$15 \times .20}}$$

$$= \sqrt{\frac{6{,}000{,}000}{3}}$$

$$= \sqrt{2{,}000{,}000}$$

$$= 1{,}414, \text{ which is about } 3\frac{1}{2} \text{ days' usage.}$$

Now, allowing for usage during the delivery of each order:

$$\text{Economic lot} = \sqrt{\frac{2 \times 100{,}000 \times 30}{15 \times .20 \times (1 - 100{,}000 \div 300{,}000)}}$$

$$= \sqrt{\frac{6{,}000{,}000}{3 \times \frac{2}{3}}}$$

$$= \sqrt{\frac{6{,}000{,}000}{2}}$$

$$= \sqrt{3{,}000{,}000}$$

$$= 1{,}732, \text{ or about } 4\frac{1}{3} \text{ days' usage.}$$

It is also possible to express all economic lots on a daily use, a daily supply, and a carrying cost per day basis. Doing this does not, however, affect the answer.

Economic lots with unknown demand. When the inventory controller does not know what the future call for an item will be, he has to rely on past use. He can either use the actual use during the last year or he can estimate 12 months' usage by using the last 2 or 3 months' use as starting points. Then he can go on calculating economic lot quantities.

Reasons for not using EOQs. Some companies don't use economic lots because they require such figures as the cost of reordering, or factory setup costs, or realistic carrying cost rates—which they don't normally have and which would cost money to get. Besides, the figures (rates of use and materials costs in particular) keep changing, and this makes the economic lot keep changing. The problem can get somewhat mixed up, and it could cost more to get answers than can be saved.

Furthermore, the formula assumes that items are used steadily throughout the year. Often such use is not the case, particularly if there is a strong seasonal pattern in an item's demand. The EOQ formula can be adapted to handle seasonal variation, but the mathematics is more complicated.[1]

Another reason for not using EOQs is that they suboptimize, which is

---

[1] For a method for handling seasonal variations, see "A Simple Modification of the EOQ for the Case of a Varying Demand Rate," by Edward A. Silver and Harlan C. Meal, in *Production and Inventory Management* (4th quarter 1969), pp. 52–65.

not always advantageous to the whole company's operation. Particularly is this true in their overuse of capital. Ordering a little less than the EOQ will almost always release a certain amount of capital at the equivalent of a very low interest rate.

Probably, however, the two main reasons for not using economic lots are, first, that they are not applicable to the biggest A items or to most C items. The big A items need even more careful attention, and most C items need very little attention. The second reason is the common use of dollar limits, time limits, making parts against known future demands, and making parts directly to assembly's needs as methods of control. These methods provide their own reorder quantities, so EOQs are not used.

EOQs in managerial decision making

So far we have discussed EOQs only with respect to setting the size of manufactured or purchased lots. They can, however, be used to help managers choose the best course of action when there are alternatives.

Releasing capital.   Suppose, for example, that money is tight and management would like to reduce inventories in order to release capital. This means that order quantities would be reduced and reorders would be placed more often. The managers know that placing extra orders for smaller quantities is somewhat uneconomical, but this is the price they will have to pay in order to reduce the inventory investment.

The question is: How much will it cost to release the capital? We will use our earlier problem as an example. It cost $10 to place an order, 25 percent a year for carrying costs, and $2 per unit for the 2,000 units needed in a year. The EOQ was 283 units. If we omit the safety stock, the average inventory would be $283 \div 2 = 141.5$ units, which would have a value of $283.

Management asks: How much will it cost to cut the inventory investment by one fourth, thus releasing $71? The new ordering quantity would be 212 units. The average inventory would be 106 units, valued at $212. Ordering 212 units will necessitate 9.43 reorders a year ($2,000 \div 212 = 9.43$), which will cost $94.30. The carrying charge will be $.25 \times \$212 = \$53$. So the total of the two comes to $147.30, which is $5.30 more than the $142 cost if reorders are at the EOQ. The inventory reduction of $71 can be obtained at a cost of $5.30, the equivalent of paying 7.5 percent for the money. This rate seems reasonable, so management might well go ahead and order the inventory reductions.

Actually, order quantities might almost always be set at something less, possibly as much as 25 percent less, than the EOQ. This is because of the relatively flat curve in the area near this ideal quantity. Quantities below the EOQ *do* cost a little more but they release capital, as in the example above, and at reasonably small equivalent interest rates.

A manager should be careful, however, when using this kind of analysis. The answer we have just got is quite wrong if the unit price is for different order quantities. If, for example, the vendor charges $2.05 per unit for orders of 212 units (as against $2 when ordering in lots of 283), then in a year the buyer would have to pay $2.05 per unit and not $2. So the extra unit cost would push the total cost up $100. This would make it cost $105.30 to release $71 of capital from inventory investments. The calculations should always include everything, or the manager may be misled by the answer.

Enlarging reorder quantities to make work during slack periods. Another instance where EOQ analysis can help may arise during slack periods. The question in this case is whether to make more parts or products than are needed in the immediate future in order to keep the men busy. We will continue to use the same example, except to consider the $10 ordering cost as the cost of making out a shop order and setting up machines.

Again the EOQ is 283 units and the average inventory is 141.5 units. But in order to keep the men busy, management wants to know what it will cost to double the ordering quantities. This means making lots of 566, or 3.5 orders, a year, costing $35. The average inventory would be $566, which would cost $141.50 to carry. Total costs would be $176.50, or $34.50 more than the lowest cost using EOQs. Actually, management would not, of course, plan to do this all year long but only over a short period of 1 to 3 months. The actual cost, therefore, for the part year involved would probably be less than one quarter of $34.50, or $8 more or less. Knowing this cost, management can decide what to do more intelligently than without this analysis.

EOQs as tests of rule-of-thumb practices. Managers can also test rule-of-thumb practices. One company, for example, which does not use EOQs, uses the following practices in determining reorder quantities for parts it makes. If setup costs are less than $10, it orders 4 months' supply. On up to $25 setup costs, it orders 6 months' supply. At $25 and over, it orders 8 months' supply.

This policy may be costing the company money as against using EOQs. To test it, examples can be worked out. One example could be a usage of 7,500 units a year, setup costs of $20, and inventory carrying charges of 25 percent; material and labor costs are $3 per unit.

In line with company policy, the inventory controller orders 6 months' supply of this item each time. Thus he reorders 3,750 units twice a year. The average inventory is 1,875 units, having a value of $5,635. Inventory carrying costs are $5,635 × .25, or $1,408.75. Ordering costs are 2 × $20 = $40. So the total annual cost for handling this inventory this way is $1,488.75.

To use EOQs, the EOQ must first be calculated:

$$EOQ = \sqrt{\frac{2 \times 7,500 \times \$20}{\$3 \times .25}}$$

$$= \sqrt{\frac{300,000}{.75}}$$

$$= \sqrt{500,000}$$

$$= 632$$

If 632 units are ordered each time, the ordering cost per year is 7,500 ÷ 632 = 11.9 orders per year × \$20 = \$238. Carrying costs would be 632 ÷ 2 = 316 units average inventory × 3 = \$964 average investment × .25 percent = \$241. The total cost would be \$479.

The company's rule-of-thumb is, therefore, in this example, costing \$970 extra to handle the inventory of this one item in a year (\$1,449 − \$479 = \$970). Similar tests could be made for other examples. If other items are anywhere near comparable to this example, the failure of the company to use EOQs is costing it a great deal of money.

Imputed interest rates inherent in rule-of-thumb policies. The EOQ idea can also be reversed to show what the imputed interest rate inherent in a policy is. In the example above, for example, the calculation would be:

$$\text{Imputed rate} = \frac{2 \times \text{annual usage} \times \text{setup cost per setup}}{\text{Cost per unit} \times (\text{ordering quantity})^2}$$

$$= \frac{2 \times 7,500 \times \$20}{\$3 \times 3,750^2}$$

$$= \frac{300,000}{3 \times 14,062,500}$$

$$= \frac{300,000}{42,187,500}$$

$$= .0071$$

The company's reorder policy would produce an economic lot size of 3,750 if carrying charges were only .7 of 1 percent. But for any higher rate the economic lot is less than 3,750.

Relative importance of factors. Managers can also use EOQ calculations to see how sensitive the answer is to changes in any of the factors that go into its calculation. They can change the carrying charges, for example, to see how sensitive the answer is to the operation of this factor. (It will usually be found that the formula is not very sensitive to minor changes in any single factor but is quite sensitive to large changes. The change in the EOQ varies according to the square root of changes in individual factors.)

Curiously, this kind of analysis, using EOQs to help in decision making, seems to be rare. All of the several possible applications given here seem to have greater merit than is recognized. Admittedly, however, EOQs and this kind of analysis is usually applicable only to B items and perhaps a few A items.

Computerized inventory control

Inventory control is one of the most common computer applications. Quite a few books on inventory management explain how to use computers to control inventories. Computers have replaced many clerks, and saved their salaries, but they have done even more. They have actually improved upon the way the work is done and so have reduced inventory investments.

Before taking up how they do this, it should be said that these savings have come more from reducing inventories of "on the shelf" items than from reducing inventories in process. Often they have resulted in big cuts in the inventories of finished goods, particularly in companies which make thousands of items of minor value, such as scissors, wrenches, switches, sockets, nails, grinding wheels, adhesive tape, medicines, and on and on. Mostly these are B items in ABC inventory control procedures.

Computerized inventory control assumes that all day-to-day inventory transactions are handled on the computer. The computer has, in its memory, a record of every item carried in inventory. It knows stock numbers, unit prices, and quantities on hand. It keeps records of how often and how many of each item is withdrawn from stock. It also keeps a record of reorders: when they are placed, for how many units, and how long it has taken to get new supplies.

But before a computer can actually control inventories it needs certain additional information. For each item, the computer needs to be told the cost of placing an order, or, if it is an item the company makes itself, both the internal paper work cost and the job setup cost. The computer also needs to know the carrying charge rate and, for each item, a cost figure for running out of stock, or else the "service level" goal.

Next, the computer needs rules telling it how to balance the costs of producing small lots often versus large lots less often, and the costs of carrying big stocks at high carrying costs versus smaller stocks but at the risk of running out.

The rules tell the computer to look to the past and see how many items have been sold month by month or week by week. The computer calculates what the average has been and how variable the demand has been. It also looks for trends and seasonal patterns. After looking at all of these possible patterns in the past demand, the computer projects them forward to find the expected use of the item in the next two months or so.

The computer notes how long it took in the past to get new supplies and how variable the "lead times" were. Finally, the computer prints out that, on a certain date, an order for a certain quantity of each item should be placed.

Actually, of course, no inventory controller could give such careful consideration (as we have been describing) to every one of the 5,000 to 10,000 items he has charge of. This is why a computer can do it better. But the computer needs to have very detailed instruction which it can follow woodenly.

Forecasting by computers

Forecasting in inventory control, as done by computers, is one and two months' ahead of not-distant-future forecasting. And it forecasts the demand for the thousands of small items, such as 6-inch nickel plated scissors, which are not individually important enough to justify costly forecasting item by item.

The simplest forecast of next month's demand is this month's usage, but rarely is this very reliable. The usage of most items jumps around too much. Furthermore, the inventory controller does not even know what this month's usage of an item has been until the end of the month, and by this time the order for *next* month's supply has already been placed. Yet these two objections are quibbles and not fundamental objections. When the inventory controller does not know what the future will be like, he can do no better than look to the recent past and decide that the future will be like that. And this is true even if past usage has jumped around, and even if it is necessary to forecast farther ahead than he would like to.

So-called statistical inventory control starts here, with the look backward. Then, using what the past shows, forecasts are developed. As an example to show how this works on computers, Figure 25–10 is a working table which might be set up for the purpose.

In practice, an inventory controller would never have a table like Figure 25–10 because once the procedure is set up, every month would add a new line of figures at the bottom of the table and the computer would drop off a line at the top. As our example is set up, the computer would retain in its memory only the last three months. And it needs two of these three months only because it has to check up on the forecasts to see how reliable they were.

Figure 25–10 includes a method for smoothing out some of the irregularities so that forecasts will be improved. This procedure, which is known as exponential smoothing, is quite mechanical and is one that a computer can follow.

Column 2 shows the actual monthly use of an item over a 12-month period. As can be seen, this item's use jumps around a good bit in rather unpredictable fashion.

The purpose of all the calculations in Figure 25–10 is to provide the figures in columns 6, 7, and 11. Column 6 is a forecast of how many units are likely to be used in the next month while column 7 is a forecast of

FIGURE 25–10

Date	Use in month	Moving average	Change in col. 3	Trend	Expected use	Forecast of use in lead time	Actual use in lead time	Error in predicted use in lead time	Average of deviations squared	Standard deviation in units
1	*2*	*3*	*4*	*5*	*6*	*7*	*8*	*9*	*10*	*11*
Start		201.0		0				30	901	30.0
Jan.	194	200.3	−0.7	−0.07	199.7	399	373	26	879	29.7
Feb.	211	201.4	+1.1	+0.05	201.9	404	393	11	803	28.3
Mar.	162	197.5	−3.9	−0.34	194.4	389	428	39	875	29.6
Apr.	231	200.9	+3.4	+0.03	201.2	402	371	31	884	29.7
May	197	200.5	−0.5	−0.02	200.3	401	393	8	802	28.3
June	174	197.9	−2.6	−0.28	195.4	391	466	75	1285	35.9
July	219	200.0	+2.1	−0.04	199.6	399	492	93	2021	45.0
Aug.	247	204.7	+4.7	+0.43	208.6	417	468	51	2079	45.6
Sept.	245	208.7	+4.0	+0.79	215.8	432	432	0	1871	43.2
Oct.	223	210.1	+1.4	+0.85	217.8	436	398	38	1828	42.7
Nov.	209	210.0	−0.1	+0.76	216.8	434				
Dec.	187	207.7	−2.3	+0.45	211.8	424				

how many units are likely to be used during the time it takes to get a new supply (assumed to be 2 months in this example). Column 11 is a measure of the reliability of recent forecasts.

Column 3 is the first step in getting to columns 6, 7, and 11. Column 3 is made up of successive, weighted moving average figures. The calculation starts by taking the average use of the item during the 3 months before the figures in our table start. Or the inventory controller could just pick some reasonable number in order to get started. We started with an average of 201 units. At the end of every month this average is revised, giving the old average considerably more weight than the new month. We used .9; that is, each new average is $\frac{9}{10}$ of the old average plus $\frac{1}{10}$ of the new month's actual use.[2] The effect is to calculate a moving average.

The calculation for the figures in column 3 goes .9(201.0) + .1(194) = 200.3; .9(200.3) + .1(211) = 201.4; etc. As time goes along, the original starting average soon washes out. This is why it is possible to be a little arbitrary in choosing the starting average.

If it is desirable to make the average more sensitive to recent figures, it is necessary only to change the weights (.9 and .1 are, however, commonly used). Using .8 and .2 would give more weight to the latest demand experience.

Adjustment for trend. Both columns 4 and 5 are for trend analysis. They are refinements that usually add somewhat to the accuracy of the

[2] Statistical inventory control books often refer to the weight given to the new month as alpha, or α. The weight for the old average then becomes $1 - \alpha$. The formula for the new average thus becomes: New average = $\alpha \times$ (new demand) + $(1 - \alpha) \times$ (old average).

forecast, albeit at the expense of more lengthy calculations. Column 4 is merely the change, month by month, in the column 3 moving average figures. Column 5 is a refinement of column 4. Just as column 3 carried on from column 2, column 5 carries on from column 4. And again the old figure is weighted at .9 and the new at .1. The calculation goes $.9(0) + .1(-0.7) = -0.07; .9(-0.07) + .1(+1.1) = +0.05$; etc. If weights other than .9 and .1 were used for calculating column 3, those same weights should be used for calculating column 5.

Column 6 comes next. It is simply column 3 plus an adjustment for the trend. To calculate the adjustment it is necessary to find the relationship between the weights. In our case it is 9. The old averages are weighted at 9 times the weight of the current period. If we had used .8 and .2, the old averages would be 4 times as important as the current figures and 4 would be the number we would need there.

The column 5 figure is multiplied by this number to get the adjustment for the trend. Then it is added to the column 3 figure to get column 6. Here is the calculation: $9(-0.07) + 200.3 = 199.7; 9(+0.05) + 201.4 = 201.9$; etc.

Expected use during lead times. The figures in column 6 are the forecast figures. They are our best guesses about the near future usage of our sample item. The column 6 figure for January is 199.7. This means that our best guess, made at the end of January, for the demand for February and March is 199.7 units each month. Or, moving down toward the bottom of Figure 25–10, we find that, at the end of October, our best guess for November and December is 217.8 units each month. By the end of November, and having the actual November figures before us, we revise the column 6 expected figure to 216.8 for December and January. Since the demand for this item continued to fall off in December, the revised expectations for January and the projection for February, made at the end of December, came out as 211.8 for each month.

Column 7 shows how the "expected" figures are used—the quantities expected to be used during our assumed replenishment lead time of 2 months. So column 7 is twice the figure in column 6. This is why, in column 7 for January, the forecasted use during the lead time is given as 399 (twice 199.7), etc. In October, the expected use in November and December is 436 (twice 217.8), etc.

Errors in expected use during lead times. Column 8 compares actual use in the lead time to the projected use. It is filled in after the lead time has gone by. Our item's use in February and March actually was 373 units. This contrasts with the expectation of 399 units. March and April's actual use totaled 393 units as compared to 404 expected.

Column 9 continues the comparison of forecasted use with actual demand. It shows how far wrong the forecasts of use during the procurement lead times were.

Column 10 is based on column 9, and is similar to columns 3 and 6 in that it is a moving average number, updated monthly. To get column 10, we need a starting figure. We assumed that the column 9 figures for the 3 months before our table started were 29, 30, 31 in each month. So we square the 29 (multiplying it by itself) for the October before our table starts and get 841; we square the 30 for November and get 900; and we square December's 31 and get 961. These squares are added, to get 2,702. This is divided by 3, giving us the 901 figure at the top of column 10— a starting figure. From here on the calculation of new column 10 figures goes on just as for columns 3 and 5, except that we square the figures in column 9 before we add them in. The calculation for the January figure goes $.9(901) + .1(26^2) = 811 + 68 = 879$. February's is $.9(879) + .1(11^2) = 791 + 12 = 803$.

Column 10 exists only for the purpose of getting column 11, which is the square root of column 10. The square root of January's 879 is 29.7; the square root of February's 803 is 28.3; etc. This square root is the standard deviation (sometimes called sigma or indicated as σ) of the errors in the forecasts. This is the measure of the reliability of the forecasts, which is helpful in order to know how big an item's safety stock ought to be. (We will take up column 11's use later.)

All of these calculations have been for the purpose of providing two figures, those in column 7, which furnish a reasonable estimate of the use of the item after a replenishment order is placed and before the new supply arrives, and those in column 11, which show the standard deviation of the forecast errors.

Everything has been reduced to rules. A computer can do all of the calculating we have done and do it for 50,000 items. This method can also be individualized for different products; it does not require that all items be treated alike. If it seems desirable to use weights other than .9 and .1 for weighting old and new figures into new averages, this can be done. Different weights can also be used for different items.

Service levels. The purpose of calculating standard deviations of expected usage is to provide a basis for having the computer calculate the safety stock. Managers decide the "service level" they want. If this is 95 percent, it means that 95 percent of all reorders will arrive before the old stock runs out. In 5 percent of the cases the stock will run out before the new supplies arrive.

In order to implement this decision it is necessary, first, to know the expected use of an item during its normal replenishment lead time. In Figure 25–10 a 2-month lead time was assumed. In October, the November and December's expected use was 436 and the standard deviation of forecast errors was 45.6 (at any given time, the column 11 figures are always 2 months behind the column 7 figures).

Next we have to refer to Figure 25–11, which shows how far out on a cumulated normal curve it is necessary to go to arrive at a point which includes 95 percent of the area under the curve and excludes 5 percent.

This proves to be 1.67 standard deviations above the arithmetic mean—or, in our example—from the forecasted use. Figure 25–11 shows this point. In our example the mean plus 1.67 standard deviations is 77 units ($46 \times 1.67 = .77$). So the safety stock is 77. The ordering point is 513 units (the safety stock, 77, plus the expected usage during the lead time, 436).

FIGURE 25–11

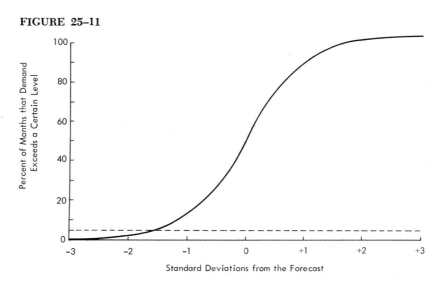

It might seem that companies should want more protection against being out of stock than a 95 percent level will give. Probably managers would *like* more protection, but more protection costs disproportionately more money. Safety stocks may need to be twice as big to give 97 or 98 percent protection than they were for 95 percent protection.

Further refinements. Space does not permit us to pursue the matter of statistical inventory control further, but there are many more facets to it. Some of them are quite complex.

We have not, for example, pursued the possibility of lead times varying just as usage does. If lead times vary by much, then the safety stock will need to be increased a little. Just how much to raise it to allow for variable lead times, as well as variable usage, gets into complicated calculations.

Nor have we gone into the overall service level, considering that 95 percent protection against reorders' not arriving on time is only part of the story. Sometimes, for example, the stockroom is out of stock but the factory is not. The 50 items the factory just withdrew depleted the stockroom's stock, but they will keep the factory going for a week. The factory is not out of stock.

How long an out-of-stock situation continues also is often very important, but this is not in the calculations. So, also, is the question of *how many* items is the stock short, which is not in the calculations. Nor did we really get into how costly it is to run out. Sometimes, too, a little money spent on expediting would bring the new supply in quickly, thus holding down the out-of-stock costs.

Nor did we say anything about substitutions. If there is need for a 75-watt light bulb and it is out of stock, sometimes a 100-watt bulb will do very well instead. But this upsets the statistics for both items. Sometimes, too, people wait for an out-of-stock item, and when it comes in its use is unnaturally high. This distorts the usage figures for the month when the new supply arrives. We also mentioned seasonal patterns in demand, but did not go into what to do about them. Also, earlier in this chapter we said that sometimes it is better to forgo low inventories and build up stocks in order to give the factory reasonable operating schedules. Or, if money is short, it may pay to cut not only reorder quantities but safety stocks as well.

Some of these complicating conditions can be handled well by computers, but some of them remain problems that baffle even computers. Monte Carlo simulation can help in such cases. In general, however, computers can do most of the work we discussed in this chapter and do it economically.

Review questions

1. Explain the difference between reordering for known future demand and ordering for assembly's needs.
2. Explain how to calculate the size of the safety stock by the method which uses a dollar penalty figure for being out of stock.
3. How are minimum-maximum controls related to (*a*) reorder points and (*b*) economic ordering quantities?
4. Does the reorder point depend on the reorder quantity? Why or why not?
5. What is the relationship between the reorder quantity, the average inventory, and order frequency? Would ABC analysis help in analyzing policy alternatives arising from these relationships?
6. Is it true that in all EOQ diagrams, such as that shown in Figure 25–7, the EOQ is at the point where the declining and sloping curved line crosses the rising straight line? Explain.
7. The text says that it is not necessary, for economical operation, to reorder exactly in economic lots. Why is this?
8. Would it ever be true that the EOQ curve is *not* relatively flat for volumes of, say, 25 percent above and below the EOQ? If yes, explain how it could be.
9. Is the economic order quantity ever a part of the safety stock? When?
10. In practice, EOQs are by no means always used. Why not?
11. Explain the procedure which could be used to find out how much it would

cost to release capital from investment in inventory by ordering less than economic lot quantities.

12. The company is considering using mathematical decision rules to set the size of safety stocks. The analyst is told to gather the necessary data. What data does he need and why?

13. In computerized inventory control, why does the computer calculate the expected error in a product's usage during the reorder lead time?

14. On page 596 in the calculation table, the following figures appear on the first line: 8, 150, 75, $56.25, 92, and $184. How were these calculated?

15. If a company aims for a 95 percent level in reordering, does this mean that 95 percent of the time when stock is needed it will be on hand but it will be out of stock 5 percent of the time? Explain.

Discussion questions

1. What relationships, if any, are there between materials short lists and economic lot sizes?

2. "We don't use reorder points because our turnover is so high that we are often out of stock before the replenishment order arrives." Is this a reasonable statement? Discuss.

3. "Most mathematical treatments of stockouts exaggerate the problem a little because when the stockroom issues 50 units to the factory, thereby running out of stock, no one is yet being held up. The 50 just issued will take care of the factory's needs for several days. There is stock on the assembly floor even if there is none in the stockroom." Discuss this statement.

4. Is it possible to put a figure for being out of stock into EOQ formulas? How? Should a company want to do this? Why?

5. In a company using direct costing, will its calculations of economic order quantities be like everyone else's? Why? If no, whose kind of calculations gives the right answer?

6. If the new labor contract gives everyone a pay raise, is it necessary to recalculate all EOQs? Discuss.

7. The company's stock of storage batteries has a loss of life of 3 percent a month from shelf wear. How can this be handled in EOQ calculations?

8. "One reason why it appears to cost little to reduce ordering quantities is that the cost of greater exposure to running out of stock (from ordering more often) is not included in the calculations. EOQ formulas put no penalty charges into the formula for this. Consequently, the gain from releasing capital at minimal costs is slightly specious because it overlooks these occasional costs." Comment on this situation.

9. In EOQ formulas, a carrying charge of 20 percent or more is common. Yet the calculations in the text claimed that, by ordering less than the EOQ, capital could be released at an implicit interest charge of a much lower rate, perhaps 7 percent. If this is so, isn't there something wrong in the calculation which bases the EOQ on a claimed cost of 20 percent? Discuss.

10. "As a forecasting technique, exponential smoothing is nothing more than a form of weighted average, and it suffers from the same deficiency as all other weighting techniques. It cannot distinguish between random variations and significant changes; therefore it responds equally to both. Forecasting requires forward-looking information as well as past history. Without adequate forward-looking data, exponential smoothing could prove to be an exercise in futility." Comment on this view. Is there any way to take care of the difficulty posed?

Problems

1. The inventory record card for item G–2357 reads as follows:

Date	Quantity ordered	Received	Used	On hand
1–15	—	300	—	300
1–16	—	—	75	225
2–16	—	—	75	150
3–16	—	—	75	75
3–17	300	—	—	—
4–16	—	—	75	0
7–19	—	300	—	300
8–25	—	—	75	225

These items are worth $7 each and cost $.10 a month to carry in stock. Assuming that standard package limitations can be neglected, set up a reordering policy. When should they be reordered and how many?

2. Calculate the reorder point for the following item:

Use	2,000 per week
Cost of running out	$1,200
Value of 1 unit	$20.80
Carrying cost	25%

The past record of time elapsed between ordering and getting new supplies is:

Weeks	Number of instances
3	1
4	2
5	6
6	6
7	7
8	3

3. Vendor A is located 500 miles away from the Davis Company. Shipment of part M–62, an item bought in quantity by Davis, is by rail. From ½ to 1 week must be allowed for shipment. Vendor A's plant needs another 2 weeks to process orders.

The smallest quantity of M–62s which can be produced economically is 5,000, or ½ week's usage of the Davis Company. Davis's usage, however, fluctuates between 8,000 and 12,000 per week.

How far ahead should Davis release orders? How big an inventory of item M–62 should Davis carry? If more data are necessary in order to answer, what data? With such data, how should one go about calculating the answers to these questions?

Annual usage has been 7,500 units. Setup cost is $20, carrying charges 25 percent against a worth of $3 per item. Policy has been to order 1,000 units at a time, placing 750 items into a first barrel and the rest into a second barrel. When the first runs out, a reorder takes place. What would you estimate as the longest delivery period ever encountered? Disregarding safety stocks, is this policy saving or losing money?

5. Given: an item whose value is $3 per unit, reordering cost $25, and inventory carrying cost 20 percent. This item's stock record card shows the following:

	Withdrawal quantity	Days until next withdrawal	Reorder lead times (days)
	69	12	20
	58	19	30
	93	8	15
	76	12	20
	81	17	20
	59	10	10
	64	7	30
	51	7	20
	49	19	25
	60	14	30
Total	660	125 Average	22

Find

a) The reorder quantity

b) The reorder point

6. Given the following:
   A safety level of 75 units
   Replenishment lead time of 15 days
   Maximum inventory of 810 units
   Usage of EOQ in 35 days
Calculate the reorder point in units and days.

7. What is the economic lot size for the following item?

Setup and order writing costs.............. $12
Cost of holding 1 unit 1 year............... $1.07
Production cost per unit.................... $8
Weekly use rate........................... 150 units
Weekly production rate.................... 250 units

8. Calculate the economic lot quantity for the following products:

Product	Cost per unit (excluding setup)	Cost of 1 setup	Carrying charge	Annual usage
A........................	$ .50	$ 100	20%	10,000
B........................	.20	60	15	25,000
C........................	2.00	300	25	100,000
D........................	.75	1,000	25	500,000
E........................	5.00	1,000	20	40,000

9. In problem 8, what change occurs in the EOQ if product A's carrying costs are 10 percent instead of 20 percent? 30 percent? From these answers, what should be concluded about the sensitivity of EOQs to variations in the carrying charge rate?

10. In problem 8, what change occurs in the EOQ if usage of product A is cut in half? If it doubles? From these answers, what should be concluded about the sensitivity of EOQ to variations in the usage rate?

11. In problem 8, how much capital will be released from inventory by an edict to cut the overall investment by 25 percent? What will be the cost effects of such an edict? What will be the effective interest cost rate to the company for the released capital?

12. After the cut required in problem 11, what will be the implicit interest rate if the new ordering quantities are regarded as the EOQs but at a higher rate?

13. The Equipment Manufacturing Company has decided to purchase a certain type of rheostat required in the operation of a machine which it manufactures. The company uses 2,000 rheostats per year; the average use is 8 per working day; the minimum use is 5 per working day and the maximum is 10 per working day. It takes 30 working days to receive delivery on the rheostats after the ordering point is reached. The cost of putting through each order is $10. The inventory carrying charges are 20 percent of the average inventory investment. The purchase prices are as follows:

$4.60 each on orders of 200 or less
4.50 each on orders of 201 to 400
4.40 each on orders of 401 to 600
4.35 each on orders of 601 to 800
4.30 each on orders of 801 to 2,000

Determine the safety reserve, the ordering point, the ordering quantity, and the normal maximum inventory.

14. A company uses 100 bars of 1-inch-diameter steel bars a month (20 workdays). Management wants the inventory controller to keep a minimum of 10 days' supply on hand since there are some irregularities in both usage and the normal 8-day lead time required to get more bars. If 125 bars are reordered at a time, what will be (a) the expected minimum quantity on hand,

(*b*) the order point, (*c*) the average inventory, (*d*) the number of reorders per year, and (*e*) what will be the answers to (*a*), (*b*), and (*c*) if slow deliveries double the replenishment lead time?

15. In the past a company has followed this general rule and has not calculated economic quantities:

Setup cost	*Order*
Under $10	4 months' supply
$10–25	6 months' supply
Over $25	8 months' supply

Following this policy, item 319, with a setup cost of $20 and an annual usage of 6,800 units, was ordered in lots of 3,400. Labor and material for item 319 cost $.75.

If it costs 25 percent to carry inventory, how good is the company's general rule? How much does following the rule on item 319 cost the company in a year? If item 319 constitutes 2 percent of all inventories, and if this finding applies to all other items proportionally, what is the approximate cost to the company of following these general rules?

16. A company uses 500 units in a year and pays $3.10 each for them. They have been ordered 100 at a time and ordering costs are $25. What is the implicit interest rate?

17. An item's use record has been, month by month, 57, 43, 62, 51, 63, 72, 77, 69, 62, 43, 67, and 70. Using the method described in the text, what is this item's expected use in the reorder period of 3 months following the last month of those given here in this example? Also, what is the standard deviation of the errors in reorder quantities?

If the policy is to reorder so that new supplies arrive before present stocks run out in at least 90 percent of the cases, what is the reordering point?

Recent references

Berry, William L., *Lot Sizing for Requirements Planning Systems*, Lafayette, Ind.: Institute for Research in the Behavioral, Economic, and Management Sciences, Purdue University, 1971

Gleason, J. M., "A Computational Variation of the Wagner-Whitin Algorithm: An Alternative to the EOQ," *Production and Inventory Management*, First Quarter 1971

Kelly, Joseph F., *Computerized Management Information Systems*, New York: Macmillan, 1970

Lanford, H. W., *Technological Forecasting Methodologies*, New York: American Management Association, 1972

Miller, B. L., "Multi-Item Inventory Model with Joint Back-Order Criterion," *Operations Research*, October 1971

Roberts, S. D., and R. Reed, "The Development of a Self-Adaptive Forecasting Technique," *AIIE Transactions*, December 1969

Schneeweiss, C. A., "Smoothing Production by Inventory—An Application of the Wiener Filtering Theory," *Management Science,* March 1971

Tsao, C. S., "Bayesian Approach to Estimating Decision Parameters in Replacement Inventory Systems," *Operations Research Quarterly,* December 1971

Whybark, D. Clay, "Information Quality and Inventory Replacement," *Journal of Purchasing,* February 1971

section nine

Quality control systems

QUALITY PERMEATES most of total production and operations management system. The image of the company and its position in the economy is closely related to the quality decisions the company's managers have made and to the way in which these decisions have been carried into effect.

The need to design products to reach and appeal to certain segments of the market has been discussed in earlier chapters. So has the relationship of quality to costs. Here, too, the company's managers have to relate their quality desires to the factory's ability to produce the desired quality at a cost which can be supported in the market place by appropriate prices.

Whatever the quality-cost relationship goals may be, they become—once decided—parameters for the factory. The established standards are then put into effect by the company's quality control system.

Chapter 26 considers quality control from a conceptual viewpoint and as a totality. It gives an overview of the whole problem of product quality enforcement as it is carried on in the shop. Chapter 27 then takes up statistical quality control. Each of the common uses of statistical quality control is considered, both from a technical viewpoint and as they operate in the shop. Concluding Chapter 27 is a discussion of "zero defects," an approach which complements and supports statistical quality control.

26

Quality standards

"Quality," to most people, seems to mean "high quality." And it is a little like mother, God, Queen, and country—everyone is for it, and the more quality the better. But do people really want the *highest possible* quality of everything? The answer has to be no, because costs are always a part of the picture.

Supermarkets sell millions of pounds of candy, millions of water glasses and dishes, and millions of other things—practically all of which are admittedly of medium or low quality. Not *all* people buy their candy and glassware and dishes from supermarkets, but a *good many* do. People don't all want the very best of these things—at least not to the extent of

621

being willing to pay the cost of high quality. What most of us usually want is the best quality we can get for the money we are willing to spend. Our quality-cost calculus is sometimes even more cost sensitive than it is quality sensitive.

This is why Sears, Roebuck is the world's biggest merchandiser, even though it never carries the highest quality of anything. And this is what *quality* means to a manufacturer. He tries to make the best product he can for the price he can get. Hormel doesn't put top-grade pork loin into Spam because Spam users wouldn't pay the price.

A manufacturer does not object to high quality as such. He is as much in favor of it as everyone else, but he has to contend with cost. As a rule, the higher the quality, the higher the cost. Worse, even, costs usually go up faster than quality. A *little* more quality usually costs a *good bit* more money.

Year by year the quality of most products improves. An automobile or a television set which was a best seller in 1960 was no longer acceptable in 1970. It wasn't good enough. And 1970 cars and TV sets will not be acceptable in 1980. *They* won't be good enough. Quality improves because of technology advances and because both customers and competitors force everyone to incorporate these advances into their products.

Sometimes, however, consumers don't see quality improvement because they take the gain in lower prices rather than still more quality for the old prices. Today's color television sets, for example, are both better and cheaper than they were at first. But they could be *even better* today if customers were willing to pay more.

Quality control men wince at the idea that most manufacturers try only to make the best for the money instead of simply the best. And even production managers don't like to agree with this view because they like to think that they are making the best. Yet neither quality control men nor production managers can afford to forget costs. Men making Volkswagens are not making Cadillacs, nor are they going to sell them for Cadillac prices.

Quality control people are likely, too, to wince at our discussion of tolerance setting (p. 294), where we noted that tolerances are sometimes too tight. They like to feel that the standards they so zealously enforce rest on solid ground and not on some draftsman's protect-himself-safe specification. Actually, designers of military products sometimes put in a "military fear factor"; they make the product three times as good as will probably be needed. Designers of consumer products also sometimes overdesign products. When they do this, it is literally true that the quality specifications ask for too much.

The factory is often accused of being quantity—not quality—minded. Foremen don't see why the engineers ask for such exact measurements. Partly their objection is just lack of understanding of the real need for exactly fitting parts. But partly, also, it is knowledge (knowledge that engineers share) that every specification is a little arbitrary.

Everyone knows that products slightly beyond the pale are acceptable for most purposes. Suppose, for example, that a Lennox china dish has a speck of ingrained dirt on the underside. Or suppose the cord on an electric iron is 6 inches too long. Each of these products is not according to specifications. Possibly they should be rejected. But these items are perfectly all right for practically every use. Of course it is necessary to draw the line somewhere and say that this goes but that doesn't go. Yet this decision, of necessity, has to be somewhat arbitrary.

Besides, as consumers, we often can't detect differences. The competing products are frequently, in fact, all very good products. Is, for example, a Ford, a Plymouth, or a Chevrolet the best car? Which has more quality? Is a Black & Decker drill better than a Craftsman (Sears, Roebuck) drill? Also, which are better buys when price is considered? Is a Chevrolet a better buy than a Cadillac? Quality is a hard concept to pin down, or even detect. Mixing in price differentials complicates it still more.

A product's quality is determined by its characteristics. It is necessary for the manufacturer to decide what the characteristics of his products should be, and then have his engineers design products which embody these characteristics. Then the engineers have to describe the products' design (characteristics) in language which can be understood in the factory. And the engineers have to set the tolerances, the limits of acceptability for deviations from perfection. In some companies they also set up inspection methods, although quality control engineers do this in many large companies. These steps are all necessary to insure the manufacture of a product of its desired and consistent quality.

Purposes of inspection

Obviously, products should be inspected in order to weed out inferior units. Inspecting products while they are being made also saves wasting further work on already defective units. But if these savings are all that the inspector accomplishes, then bigger gains are being overlooked.

The big reason for inspection should be preventive—not remedial. The object is to stop making bad items. This makes the inspection job a little different. Inspection tells managers not only that a product is a reject but also why: it reports what is the matter with it. Then the managers can concentrate on fixing the situation so there won't be so many rejects in the future. Statistical quality control is helpful here because it goes on right at the operation and helps prevent more bad production right now.

Bad-work reports sometimes show that there are problems beyond a foreman's ability to solve. Possibly, for example, rejects could be reduced by using better materials. If so, top managers will have to decide whether it will pay to buy better (and more costly) materials. Or maybe the machines are too old and worn to do as close work as is demanded. Managers will have to choose between suffering high scrap, or rebuilding the present machines, or relaxing the standards.

Responsibility for quality

The much greater emphasis in the 1970s on manufacturers' responsibilities to consumers is more a matter of product design than anything else. Yet design is only the starting point. Manufacturing has to incorporate the design into products and the quality control staff has to monitor product quality.

This sounds as if it is in no way new or different. But today quality control is more important than it used to be since responsibilities to consumers are so important. In the factory, the effect is to expand the responsibilities of the quality control and assurance departments.

It takes everyone working together to make good products at reasonable costs. An example from General Electric will illustrate how everyone is responsible. One of GE's plants had trouble with one kind of the magnets it made out of powdered metal. Too many of the magnets were not magnetic enough. GE tried to find out why, and so analyzed all five of the major steps in making the magnets: material mixing, processing, sintering (heating until the compacted powdered metal fuses together), grinding, and testing.

At first it seemed that the sintering operation was not controlled closely enough. Yet improving the sintering did not make the magnets much better; so GE had to look further. It finally turned out that there were three major causes for the excessive number of rejects. The magnets were not shaped in the best way to let the laws of magnetism work to advantage; so the magnets were redesigned. The sintering furnace temperatures needed even more exact control; so GE took care of this. And, lastly, the receiving inspectors had not been able to inspect incoming materials closely enough because they didn't have the right kind of testing equipment. So GE bought them better testing equipment to check incoming materials. After these changes, the magnets came through all right. But it took quality control men and engineers working together to solve the problem.

Historically, in most companies engineers designed products and set quality standards while inspectors enforced these standards in the factory. Although this sounds like a reasonable arrangement, it left no one directly responsible for preventing poor work before it was done. Hence today most companies have assigned quality control to one department, a department with more far-reaching responsibilities than the old inspection departments had.

Figure 26–1 shows the Honeywell Corporation's inspection organization

FIGURE 26–1. Honeywell's inspection organization before change

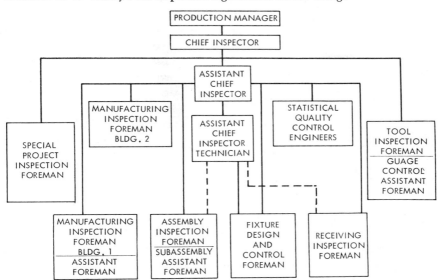

as it was ten years ago. With this arrangement the number of defective products was too high to satisfy Honeywell's top managers. And it didn't seem possible to do any better. Honeywell then changed and adopted the structure shown in Figure 26–2. The main change was to put in a "director of quality" who reports to the general manager. Under this new arrangement, with a quality engineering section, Honeywell realized steady gains in quality. In due time it reduced the costs of poor quality one third.

Testing and inspection

Testing is one kind of inspection. "Inspection," a broader term than "testing," includes all activities, among them testing to see if the products are up to standard. If, to inspect an item, a man has to do more than just look at it or measure it, it is usually called "testing" rather than "inspecting."

Tests may be performance or operating tests, or they may be "destructive" tests that end up ruining the particular product being tested. The question may be: How much will products stand before breaking? or How long will it be before they wear out? In tensile strength testing, for example, the products are broken in the test. A test may also be a chemical analysis of a sample of the product. It, too, destroys the sample. Not all tests, however, destroy the product. Some—X-ray pictures, for example—are nondestructive. Hardness tests too are nondestructive, since

FIGURE 26–2. Honeywell's revised inspection organization chart

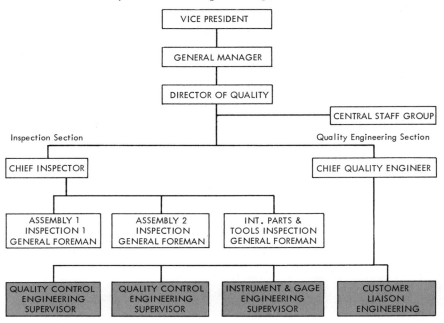

they merely make a slight dent on the surface of the product. Performance and operating tests of finished products are also typically nondestructive.

Inspecting purchased goods

As a rule, all bought items should be inspected to see that they are of the right kind and quantity and so that damaged or unsatisfactory items can be returned to the supplier and new ones obtained right away. It is also necessary for the records, so the accounting department will know what has come in and so can pay the bill.

Most materials and bought parts create no problems in this kind of inspection. But bought *components* often make trouble. Such things as a specially designed instrument, a hydraulic pump, or an electrical control item are hard to inspect or test. Receiving inspectors can't tell whether they are good or not, so they need special checking instructions from engineering. Possibly the engineers themselves may need to inspect highly technical items.

The receiving department is usually under the direction of the stores department, although it may be administered by the purchasing department. It used to be that the receiving inspection department had little or no direct connection with the factory inspection department, but today receiving often uses sampling inspection techniques in its inspection of incoming materials. Here it may be necessary for the factory's quality control department to help in setting up the proper methods.

Above it was said that, "as a rule," everything bought should be inspected, but this rule can be relaxed for materials from vendors whose final inspection has proved reliable. A company doesn't need to spend money looking again at materials which have already passed a rigid inspection in the vendor's plant. Automobile's "big three" have cut out *all* receiving inspection on many incoming items. They put one of their own men in the vendor's plant to oversee the vendor's inspection of these items before they are shipped. This "source inspection" or "surveillance at the source" improves the certainty that only good lots are shipped, and it saves double inspection and the wasted freight costs of faulty lots being shipped out and then returned.

Inspecting materials in process

Inspectors actually do very little of all the inspecting that goes on. Every worker inspects his own work enough to see if he is doing the job right. And if things go wrong, he and maybe the setup man, assistant foreman, or foreman try to straighten things out so that he turns out good products again. Also, on jobs that are running along all right, the man keeps checking now and then to see that products are still all right. Workers also catch a good bit of the bad work that comes their way from earlier jobs and throw it aside for the inspector to look over. Easily seen defects are usually caught this way.

Regular inspection does not usually come under the foreman. The inspectors in a foreman's department nearly always work for a chief inspector, who reports to the works manager or a director of quality control.

This separate chain of command exists because it is almost always a good idea to separate checking from doing. As a rule, managers ought not let anyone pass final judgment on the quality of his own work lest the man begin to emphasize quantity and not quality. In a sense, a foreman would be passing judgment on his own work if both operators and inspectors worked for him.

A few companies (International Business Machines is one) believe that it is possible to make a foreman responsible for both quantity and quality, so they put the inspectors under the foremen. Also, in many companies the inspectors who are located along assembly lines work for the foremen. Letting the foremen have charge helps make their jobs more important, and is worth something on that score.

Regardless of the method used to inspect work in process, the *final inspection* of the product ought to be done by an independent inspection department which does *not* report to factory foremen. Final inspection, unlike most in-process inspection, often includes a performance test.

FIGURE 26–3. Performance testing of two meshing gears. The inspection jig duplicates operating conditions and shows whether the gears actually mesh.

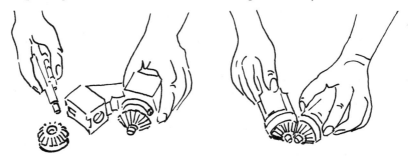

(Performance testing can rarely be used to test partly fabricated products.)

The engineering department sometimes eliminates large amounts of inspection of products during their manufacture by building automatic inspection devices into the machines. The machine (or its tool) may even be automatically reset to correct any deviation from standard. The engineering department also helps with inspecting work in process by developing special devices, so the workers on the job and the inspectors can inspect well and quickly.

How often to inspect

Because of its cost, it is best to inspect as little as possible, while still insuring the product's quality. In one sense, passing judgment or reporting on a product's quality is largely waste: the products which pass inspection are in no way changed or improved by the inspection process.

But since it is probably never wise to cut out inspection altogether, there is always a question of when and how often to inspect. This comes down to a matter of costs. What does it cost to inspect versus not to inspect? This is often, however, more a philosophical question rather than a practical question because in many cases one can never know the costs of not inspecting. In actual practice, companies usually spend 5 percent (or a little more) of their labor cost for inspection. Here are several general rules about when to inspect.

1. Inspect after operations which are likely to produce faulty items so that no more work will be done on bad items.

2. Inspect before costly operations so that these operations will not be performed on already spoiled items.

3. Inspect before operations where faulty products might break or jam the machines.

4. Inspect before operations which cover up defects (such as electroplating, painting, or assembly).

5. Inspect before assembly operations which can't be undone (such as welding parts or mixing paint).

6. On automatic and semiautomatic machines, inspect first and last pieces, but only occasionally in-between pieces.

7. Inspect finished parts.

8. Inspect before storage (including purchased items).

9. Inspect and test finished products. Be sure that nothing is shipped out without inspection. From here on the customer is the inspector, and he will give a company only one chance. If the product fails, he goes elsewhere. Worse yet, he tells everybody that this company's products are no good.

How many to inspect

Should some, most, or all of the products be inspected? Ideally, the products should be made so well as not to need inspection at all. Practically, however, it is necessary to inspect some. One of General Electric's plants inspects 5 percent of production during runs of machined parts, but goes up to 10 percent for hand-produced items. For extrusions and stampings, it cuts inspection down to 2 percent.

How many to inspect is again a matter of trying to weigh the cost of inspecting many items against the cost of inspecting only a few. But here the element of probability is more important than it is in deciding *when* to inspect.

Probability is important because in many cases inspection can be done only by samples. One hundred percent inspection—looking at every item—can't be used in tests which destroy the items tested.

Bulk materials must also be sample inspected. It isn't possible to test a whole coal pile or burn up a tank car of gasoline to find out their heat content or to look at every grain of wheat in a freight car to see if it is moldy. Because of inspection costs, samples are nearly aways used for many items which otherwise could be 100 percent inspected. How big these samples should be is taken up in Chapter 27.

Where to inspect

Inspection by an inspector can take place either at the job or in a central inspection crib. If it is done at the job it is called "floor" inspection. Both floor inspection and central inspection have advantages and disadvantages. Floor inspectors, sometimes called "patrolling" or "roving" or "first piece" inspectors, go from machine to machine to catch bad work before a large quantity has been produced. They also check the products of semiautomatic machines from time to time and record the measurements on control charts. Defective operations are caught and remedied before serious loss has occurred.

As a rule, floor inspectors have authority to stop an operation if it is out of adjustment. On the other hand, if the item is badly needed by assembly or the customer, or if the defect can be remedied by rework, engineering may let the operation continue temporarily, even though unusual numbers of off-standard items are coming through. In some companies, though, only the foreman can stop an operation. The inspector can require 100 percent inspection, but he is not allowed to order the operation stopped.

Floor inspection saves extra handling of materials and lets materials move faster through the plant. They don't have to be hauled to and from central inspection, nor do they lie around waiting their turn to be inspected. And, of course, floor inspection is the only possible way to inspect big, unwieldy items.

One bad thing about floor inspection is that men and machines sometimes have to wait for the inspector. He may be busy somewhere else when a man gets his machine all ready to go, but the operator can't go ahead with the job until the inspector approves his setup.

Another bad thing about floor inspection is that the inspector has to carry around his inspection tools. Yet it is impossible for him to carry around delicate testing or measuring equipment, so inspection that requires this has to be central—if not in a central department at least at the inspector's work bench. Most roving inspectors have a "home" inspection work bench somewhere in the area where they check things that take special gages or are too tricky to check right at the job.

Central inspection is almost the reverse of floor inspection. Materials to be inspected are trucked to a central inspection crib, where they are left to be inspected. Central inspection has several advantages. First, it saves inspectors' time because they never have to wait for jobs to inspect. Second, the work can be done by less costly inspectors, who work under close supervision and are away from the pressure of the men whose work they inspect. Third, special equipment can be used to good advantage at a central inspection location.

But there are some bad features to central inspection. Materials handling and transportation costs are higher because of all the trips materials make to and from central inspection cribs. And there are more delays, so materials move more slowly through the plant. Scrap and rework losses are higher because of the time lag between production and inspection. If anything is found to be bad, probably a good bit of bad work has been turned out before this was found.

Assembly line inspection of mass produced products is really another type of floor inspection in which inspection becomes just another operation along the line. The inspector, instead of going from job to job, inspects each unit as it comes along. Occasionally, inspection on a sample basis is done. This method is a form of central inspection and is used, for example, for inspecting automobile body tops made of single sheets of steel stamped into the proper form. The contour of the stamped sheet of steel can be checked only by taking a body top from the line occasionally and inspecting it at a center, where it can be carefully checked against a master.

The final inspection of a product is usually done centrally. If the product is an operating mechanism, it is put through a performance test.

On-line quality control

More than ever before, quality control today is being directed toward the quick detection of faulty work so that its cause can be eliminated. Often computers are used, and often they are "on line."

Being "on line" means that an operation is electrically connected at all times to a computer in the central office. The machine's output is constantly monitored and defects are reported immediately. The computer keeps track of the defects as well as of the good units turned out. Should the ratio of defectives go up, the computer reports this (usually by flashing lights) to the man whose job it is to fix the trouble.

Some companies call their procedure on line when it really isn't— because operations are not connected to the computer. Instead, there are a number of reporting stations in operating departments from which inspectors make frequent reports. Each reporting station serves as a report center for several operations. They are often at "buy off" points, where the products go from one department to another, such as weld, paint, electrical, and final assembly line.

It might seem that such a system would not be of much help since the only new thing about it seems to be the quick reporting. But in large factories quick reporting, and the quick recognition by the computer that the ratio of defects is going up, can be very helpful.

Picture, for example, how helpful it must be in Chrysler's plants, where they use the method we have described. Chrysler's typical automobile assembly line is 2 miles long and has 1,200 people spread along it. Some 1,500 cars are in the system at any time. Each car has 6,400 parts and 4,500 welds. There are some 4,000 points where defects can occur. Even when things go well, there will be some 30 defects per car, or 15,000 defects in an 8-hour day. Most of these details are minor, and almost all of them are discovered and remedied.

The point to on-line reporting is, however, that the computer watches *trends*. Inspectors are busy watching for defects, as such, and they are not likely to notice *trends* in defects. This is where the computer helps. It keeps track of every kind of defect reported and calls immediate attention to every instance where the *ratio* is going up. Chrysler reports that its on-line quality control has paid big dividends.

Inspection shortcomings

Judgment is involved in almost all inspection, even when mechanical devices such as micrometers, gages, or comparators are used, because there are always borderline cases. Often an inspector has to judge whether a product passes or not. In the case of micrometers, for example, a tight fit—as against a loose fit—probably changes the measurement indicated by at least .0005 of an inch. Plug gages and thread gages can fit snugly or loosely. An inspector discovering a slight blemish on a surface must decide whether it is bad enough to justify rejection.

The inspector must decide whether the item passes or not, and his decision is important because he enforces quality standards. If he passes products which should be rejected or rejects products which should pass, he is really making a new and unofficial set of standards for the company. Care should be taken to be sure that inspectors do not substitute their own standards for those set by engineering.

Inspectors are human beings; all of them make errors once in a while. Particularly in central inspection, the work is often repetitious and monotonous. Fatigue may cause the inspector to miss some of the bad products. And even if he is not tired, he will, at best, surely miss *some* of the bad ones.

In one study of how much bad work inspectors actually miss, 100 defective items were mixed in with a large lot of good ones. The inspectors were not told about the experiment. Then the whole lot was 100 percent inspected by regular inspectors, who found only 68 of the defectives. Still without telling the inspectors, the lot (with the remaining 32 bad ones still mixed in) was sent through inspection again as if it were another lot. This time the inspectors found most, but not all, of the defective items. The process was repeated a third and a fourth time, after which 98 bad ones had been found; but 2 of them were still in with the good products.

The results of this little experiment may be surprising. What kind of inspectors do such poor work? Well, they *are* just human; they *do* miss things now and then. Also, they do have to pass judgment. Maybe they saw the two defectives all right but decided that they were not bad enough to reject. Suppose a man has to look at 100 pieces of toast in a restaurant and decide which are too burned to serve to customers. Factory inspectors don't pass judgment on toast, but some of their deciding is just about that hard to do. We just have to recognize that inspection is partly subjective.

Managers should also be very careful about letting inspectors think they are using their own judgment. The inspection procedure ought to try to cut out as much of the judging as possible. Still, inspectors like to judge and to think that they have superior judgment. Some think that just passing things that are like the specifications is only a girl's job—anyone can do that. They prefer the kind of judging which allows them to pass things not in accord with the drawings. If the specifications say "Cadmium plate .003 inch thick" and the plating is .0025 inch, the inspector would like to "judge" that it should pass. (After all, the engineers have sometimes accepted such items before.) Managers should be careful that inspectors do not set and follow their own standards.

Reducing inspection work

Most inspection requires handling the product being inspected: the piece is picked up, turned over, and put down. This is repeated every time a product is inspected during its manufacture. It all adds up to quite a few inspectors doing a great deal of manual work. Repetitive manual jobs, including inspection, can often be mechanized. Of course the visual part of inspection often cannot be mechanized, but the manual part usually can be. And even the visual part of inspection can sometimes be transferred to the machine. In the automobile industry, for example, mechanical selectors sort oversize valves from undersize valves and put each in with other valves of the same size. In the bearing industry, ball bearings are sorted mechanically by size. Such mechanical devices eliminate, or transfer to the machine, even the "visual" part of the inspection job.

A different approach to the problem of mechanizing inspection is to build machines which check their own work. Some of today's machines do this; some will stop the machine if it is out of adjustment. Others will even correct their settings so they are put back into adjustment. Thickness gages on calenders in the paper, rubber, and linoleum industries are examples. They give continuous readings of the thickness of the material being produced, although usually they don't automatically reset the machine if it gets out of adjustment. The inspection of some of these machines is actually done by computers which analyze hundreds of performance checks every minute and then adjust the machine if it needs it.

Still another approach to the problem of cutting inspection costs is to improve the machine so that it does not get out of adjustment. Such machines (for example, the presses and dies that make automobile fenders) can turn out only good pieces when they are set properly. All that is necessary is to inspect the first few pieces, and then another piece occasionally just to be sure the machine is still in adjustment and there has not been too much wear.

Sometimes it is unnecessary to know a part's exact size but only that it is between two limits and not beyond. This lets inspection time be reduced by using go–no-go gages, which incorporate the two dimensions but show no measurements. They have two slots, one for the product's smallest and one for its largest acceptable dimension. A part which can slide into the small slot is too small; a part which will not slide into the large slot is too big. If an item does not fit the first slot but does fit the second, it is within limits. Go–no-go gages are so simple that inspection can be done by unskilled men.

Selective inspection

Selective inspection is sorting inspected parts by size so that over- and undersize parts can be matched. This is important where parts have to fit together and work as mating parts. Selective inspection cuts the losses which would otherwise be suffered where close fits of mating parts are necessary. Instead of rejecting or reworking parts just over or just under the tolerance limits, they are put into piles by size for use with matching parts having offsetting discrepancies in size.

Automobile motor blocks are an example—they have holes for the pistons. If inspection shows that one or more of the holes is either too large or too small, the block does not need to be reworked or thrown away. Instead, each hole is matched with a piston that fits. This is not hard to do because some of the pistons come out a little too large and some a little too small.

Obviously, this process should not be carried too far. Products which vary too much from the standard should be reworked or scrapped. Also, assembly work is a little more complicated with selective inspection because the parts are not completely interchangeable. But, properly operated, selective inspection is not only economical but actually makes a good product since, in spite of the fact that the parts are imperfect individually, they are matched to compensate so that the assembled product operates with well-fitting parts. This will not even mean making trouble for future repairs because, after the product has been used long enough to need repairs, the repair parts are not going to fit perfectly—no matter whether the original block and pistons fit perfectly or not.

Inspection and testing equipment

Quality standards are often so high that the inspector cannot, by looking at a product, tell whether or not it is acceptable. He has to have special gages.

The inspector has to check many characteristics, including dimensions, smoothness of surface, contours, hardness, strength, ductility, resistance to abrasion, ability to withstand flexing, resistance to rust or wear, internal strain, shrinkage, chemical analysis, plasticity, viscosity, color, fastness of color, solubility, life of the product in use, efficiency and speed of operation, electrical connections, and other things.

Sometimes the test simulates the product's use (or even abuse) to see how long it lasts before giving out. In other cases the item is used in its normal way until it wears out. Light bulbs are burned until they burn out. Auto tires are put on cars and driven day and night till they wear out. Paints are put on trial pieces and put out on the roof to see if they will fade in the sunlight and how they weather. Most tests give answers about a product's acceptability right away; but with "wearout" tests it is necessary to wait for answers.

For close measuring (such as detecting variations of less than $\frac{1}{1000}$ of an inch), inspectors need some kind of magnifier or electronic inspection gage. There are also many kinds of magnifiers which throw an enlarged shadow of the product's outline on a screen, where its contour or size can be compared with the specified contour already marked on the screen. And today there are surface smoothness gages which are accurate to a millionth of an inch. There are even devices to gage the thickness of a coat of paint. Automatic electronic sorters, which sort items by size, have already been mentioned in connection with selective inspection.

In inspection, infra-red rays can detect minute separations in bonded or laminated materials. X-rays (beta rays) are used to take pictures through opaque materials, just as a dentist takes pictures of teeth. Internal flaws show up as dark spots, or as being different from the surrounding material. X-rays are not very powerful, however. To take a picture of a casting or forging, or a welded joint, by directing rays through it, it is necessary to go to gamma rays, which are many times more powerful.

Both beta and gamma rays are also useful for measuring the thickness of paper, steel, plastic sheet, etc., or even an electroplated coating. The accuracy of the measurements can range down to millionths of an inch. Radioactive materials are also sometimes mixed in, in minute quantities, with other materials (perhaps metal for making into castings), or into fluids. Later, by detecting the strength of the emissions in various spots, it is possible to study the flow of the metal or fluid.

In another application of science to inspection, the steel industry uses pictures of the spectrum of light to show the chemical makeup of steel in the making. A photograph is taken of the spectrum of light coming from a "heat" of molten steel. The lines that appear in the spectrum show the chemical elements present, and their width shows the amount of each element. The pictures can be taken and developed quickly, thus permitting corrections to be made in the chemical composition of the heat before it is poured. TV cameras also are used to show operations which are otherwise impossible to watch—as inside a furnace or vat or machine. TV tapes are sometimes used, so the scene can be played over again and studied if anything went wrong.

Disposition of rejected material

Rejected parts and material are rarely thrown out. Sometimes they can be made right by rework operations. If this can't be done, or if it is too expensive, maybe they can be made into other items, perhaps smaller sized ones. Or maybe the rejected material can be sold as "seconds," as is done with dishes or nylon stockings.

Illogical though it may seem to be, there is still another way to get rid of rejected parts and material: to use them up just as if they had passed to start with! And do it with the engineering department's approval! Some companies have material review boards to pass on rejected material. These boards include everyone who will be affected by the fact that the items may be rejected: the superintendent, the chief engineer, and, in the case of airplanes, the customer (the government). This often happens where parts are not quite so perfect as they should be but where the product's operation will be affected little if at all.

This sounds as if standards are set up and then disregarded. But, actually, the standards are not disregarded. The point is that sometimes no harm is done if a borderline lot is passed. Yet passing borderline products should not be a regular practice. If an automobile tire tread is supposed to be a half inch thick and it comes out nearer to five eighths, this does not hurt the tire if it is still in balance; the customer just gets more rubber than he is paying for. Or if the gasoline gage in an automobile is supposed to be 3 inches from the speedometer but the hole for it in the dashboard is $2\frac{7}{8}$ inches away, it can be passed. Or if electroplating is supposed to be a certain thickness and it is more, this does no harm. There are cases where the specification can be relaxed without harm being done. Yet such "relaxations" should be individual decisions, not the general practice.

Another important reason for relaxing standards temporarily comes from the common practice of carrying practically no inventory of parts. This gets a company into a jam every time there is any holdup in parts supply. If very many parts get held up, the assembly department will soon have to close down (and then all other parts departments). This is the case where a top-management policy (to hold inventories down) has an effect (loosening up on quality) that it probably does not want, and in fact hardly recognizes as a consequence of the inventory policy.

If a lot is rejected, which would close down the final assembly department, engineering—rather than close down the plant—gives in and says OK—pass them just this once but don't do it again. The same thing happens with purchased parts. The assembly department is almost out of the parts which the inspector wants to reject (and on purchased items it may take weeks to get a new supply); so the question becomes: Are the defectives bad enough to justify closing down operations, or can they be passed? Again, there is a strong temptation to say OK—pass them this time but don't let it happen again. But of course it *does* happen again. Actually, these temporary relaxations rarely seem to cause much trouble —the products still work, and work well. It makes one wonder if the standards were not too high in the first place.

Of course vendors were not born yesterday, and they know all about hand-to-mouth inventories. So when a customer returns a lot of parts, the returned goods inspector in the vendor's plant may just put the lot to one side. Sooner or later the customer will be very anxious for an extra shipment, which he can get only if he accepts the rejected lot. They are the only extras available. The vendor gets rid of the substandard lots and helps the customer out of his tight spot. Customers will eat burned toast when they are hungry and there is nothing else to eat.

Quality standards are, therefore, in fact, somewhat flexible. If a factory is to operate effectively, quality standards must yield at times to pressures which conflict with their strict enforcement.

Reworking rejects. Generally, rejects are either clearly scrap or reworkable. To rework them, additional—and often different—operations are needed, depending on the nature of the defects. Defective items are sorted according to the kind of defect, and the rework operations for each group are decided upon.

All rework is extra cost which should be charged to the department responsible for it. But this is not always easy to determine. Suppose that a coat of paint tends to flake off. Is it the purchasing department's fault for buying the wrong kind of paint for the job? Or did engineering fail to specify the right kind of paint? Or is the material under the paint the right kind? Or did the shop fail to get the right surface finish on the piece? Or did the cleaning department fail to get every bit of oil off the surface?

Work away. In some industries it is possible to "work away" unacceptable materials by mixing them, a little at a time, into future mixtures. Off-color material, for example, can be put into mixtures of dark materials in the rubber, glass, paint, and chemical industries, thus saving the full value of the raw materials. If chemical mixtures contain too much of certain chemicals, they can be mixed into new batches that are intentionally made up with too little of those chemicals.

"Work away," as a way of getting rid of rejects, is sometimes used by vendors in a somewhat questionable manner. A customer rejects a certain lot of materials—say it is nuts and bolts—because he find it contains 3 percent defectives whereas the contract said no more than 2 percent. The customer sends the lot back, and the vendor merely mixes it with the next lot, and back they all come as part of the next shipment. But this is not always as bad as it sounds. If the next lot started with only 1 percent bad, the new mixture will be 2 percent bad, which is the quality specified.

Review questions

1. The text says that "quality" is a hard concept to pin down. Yet a factory has to make products of specified quality. Why not always try to make the best?

2. Students were visiting a factory which makes ready-made dresses for sale by Sears, K-Mart, and other chain stores. A student asked how they determined the quality of the cloth, belts, zippers, etc. The answer was: "We start with the price, subtract a profit and cost for making, and use the best materials that we can afford to buy with what is left." Comment on this practice. Is this a good way to set selling prices? How would the buyer know what he was going to get? (How could a piece of cloth be defined?)

3. "Quality control starts when the product is still on the drawing boards." Discuss this statement. Shouldn't it both start and finish here?

4. Why do foremen often think that engineering sets tolerances too tightly? Is there any merit to their position?

5. Discuss the matter of foremen being responsible both for turning out work and also being in charge of the inspectors.

6. "You can be sure if it's Westinghouse"; so why should a company buying parts from Westinghouse spend money to inspect incoming products which are almost always perfect? After all, Westinghouse gave them a thorough check before shipping them.

7. How should a company go about deciding how often and how many items to inspect? What kinds of rules or guidelines should be issued to the factory?

8. If maintaining quality is so important, why not always use 100 percent inspection?

9. Compare floor inspection and central inspection, giving the advantages and disadvantages of each.

10. How reliable are inspectors? If they carry out 100 percent inspection, how sure is it that the outgoing quality is all that it should be? Discuss.

11. What happens to rejected materials? Is this bad? Discuss.

12. "Selective inspection represents a compromise and weakens the enforcement of quality standards." Comment on this statement.

Discussion questions

1. There is always someone who can make it cheaper—but weaker or poorer. And there is always a customer who wants it that way. What should be done about this?

2. Which is the better buy, a deck of Bicycle playing cards bought at a variety store for $.75 or a deck of Congress playing cards bought at a gift shop for $2.50? What makes your choice the better buy?

3. The Firstline Company makes the "best electric iron you can buy." But one of its competitors makes the cheapest. Which is the right policy? Why?

4. What does a high-quality bicycle look like? Does it have small wheels and a "banana seat" set high over the rear-wheel axle? How can a manufacturer of high-quality bicycles maintain his leadership in the bicycle market?

5. Pick some commonplace minor item, such as a pair of scissors, a paper stapler, or a ball-point pen. Decide on and define its quality. What are the critical characteristics which you think should be inspected for?

6. In the text it is suggested that customers might have trouble deciding whether a Ford, Plymouth, or Chevrolet is the best car. Which is actually the best? What makes it so?

7. Assume that you have been appointed general manager of the division making the car you put at the bottom of the list in question 6. You are told to make it the best of the three, but you must still operate at a profit. What will you do?

8. A college student got a summer job in an automobile factory loading seat cushions onto the supply conveyor which took them to the men on the final assembly line. He came to a cushion with a badly frayed spot, which obviously made it defective, so he reported it to his foreman and asked what to do. "Load it on," said the foreman, "maybe no one will complain." Discuss.

9. The text says that "how often to inspect" depends on the cost of doing it versus the cost of not doing it. How can a company find out what it costs *not* to inspect?

10. In an airplane factory it is necessary to test the fuel lines and develop a test which will insure that the lines which pass will operate 150,000 hours without a failure.
   a) How can 75 years of use be simulated?
   b) Suppose that after a simulation of 60,000 hours, the line being tested fails. What has the company learned? What should be done?
   c) Suppose that the sample unit does not fail. What does this tell the company? (The question is how much a sample of one can reveal about the other items not tested.)

11. Free service during guarantee periods on new cars costs over $50 a car. Why not spend more on inspection at the factory and cut down on this expense? Discuss.

12. A company has decided to use incentive pay for its inspectors who look for defects in instrument "clusters" that go on the dashboard of the automobiles it makes. What should be done about defects? Should an inspector be paid less for clusters found with defects? Or should he be paid more? And if the decision is to pay more, may it not cause the inspector to pull a wire loose once in a while in order to raise his pay? Discuss.

Problems

1. A machine is starting on a run of 500 parts. This will keep the machine busy for 4 hours at a cost of $10 per hour. The machine has been set up by its operator, a relatively unskilled man, at a $5 cost; so it may not be set up just right. Rejects may therefore be 5 percent—decidedly more than the probable 1 percent rejects if a regular setup man had prepared the machine.

The concern here is not with making up the lost quantities but with whether or not a regular setup man should check the setup before starting the job. If he does check, the total cost of added machine deadtime, plus the idle operator, plus the setup man's own cost comes to $7. Forty percent of all rejected products have to be scrapped, at a loss of $.38 each. The other 60 percent of rejects can be repaired at $.20 each.

    a)   Should the setup man check the setup?

    b)   Will it pay to check the setup if defects would otherwise be 4 percent? Five percent? Six percent? What is the break-even ratio, where it doesn't matter whether the setup is checked or not?

2. If a part A is not inspected carefully, the 3 percent defectives which are produced will all go through. If they are inspected carefully, one third of the rejects would be caught, thus raising the quality of the parts passed along to the customer to 2 percent bad. Should careful inspection be done if the cost of inspecting is $.01 per unit and the cost of each defective is $4? What would the answer be if inspection cost $.05 per unit? At what point would it be a toss-up?

3. Supplier A charges $15 per 100 and sends products which are 3 percent defective. It costs $2 to inspect 100 units and to catch 90 percent of the defectives, which are scrapped. Defectives which get through and into assembled products have a 50 percent chance of causing a $25 damage. Supplier B charges $14.50 per 100 and sends 5 percent defectives. From which vendor should these items be bought?

4. In problem 3, vendor A suggests a sliding price scale, depending on how high a quality is desired. He proposes this scale:

Price per 100	Percent defective
$14.00	10.0
14.25	7.5
14.50	4.0
14.75	3.0
15.00	2.5

Using the other figures from problem 3, which price-quality offer should be accepted?

5. A machine has been developed to produce a special product. It costs $9,000 and will probably have a 5-year life and no salvage value. Interest is at 15 percent. This machine produces 5 units an hour, and can easily produce the 8,000 units needed in a year. The total cost of operating this machine (excluding depreciation but including the operator's wage) is $8.80 per hour.

The machine produces 6 percent scrap. Scrap products lose all of the $7.30 per unit cost of the materials used.

    a)   What is the cost of each nondefective unit?

    b)   How much could the company afford to spend to rebuild the machine so that it would produce only 2 percent defectives?

6. The normal scrap loss for 4 successive operations is 2, 6, 10, and 20 percent respectively. How many units should be started through in order to finish with 1,000 pieces? How much machine time will be needed if the operation times are 4, 2, 7, and 4 minutes respectively?

7. If the normal scrap loss on the milling operation is 5 percent, on the following slotting operation it is 6 percent, and on the follownig drilling operation it is 4 percent, how many pieces should be started into production in order to get 180 finished pieces? Suppose that the operator actually spoils 11 percent on the milling operation; how many pieces short is the order likely to be after the last operation? If the order needs 180 pieces and it is held up until a replacement lot can be brought up through milling, how many pieces should the replacement lot contain?

8. A product can be made from grade B material, which costs $1 a pound (each unit requires 1 pound of material) and takes $2 in labor to make 1 unit. The supplier suggests to the customer company that it buy grade A material, which costs $1.25 a pound but probably would save 5 percent of the labor.

Products made from grade B material are 4 percent defective, but half of them can be repaired at a cost of $.75 each. The other half are scrapped, resulting in the loss of both the original material cost and the labor cost. Grade A material is claimed to reduce rejects from 4 percent to 2.5 percent, half of which can be repaired, also at $.75 each.

The customer company thinks that there is perhaps a 50-50 chance: if it changes to material A, the supplier will be proven correct in his claims. But there is a 50-50 chance that nothing will improve at all, even if it changes. Since certain processing adjustments will have to be made if material A is used, the company wants to feel fairly sure that changing is the better thing to do. Should the company change to material A?

Case 26–1

Consider that in the following paragraph all letter *f*s are defects. Inspect the whole paragraph once and count the defects. Mark down your count. (You can check the count later for accuracy.)

"Effective quality control in manufacturing enterprises, in office operations, in service functions, and in job shops has undergone many innovations of late. From early times it has been presumed that if you had few inspectors and they were on the ball, your quality of product would be okay. If your firm still adheres to this outmoded concept, you may be missing an immense potential for quality improvement and defect elimination for your operation. If this test demonstrates anything, it should show the difficulty of finding all defects, even if you have 100 percent inspection. Far better to never build defects into the product in the first place. How can this be done? Many firms have found the total approach to quality control called *zero defects* is the only systematic way to achieve perfection in quality, but it does mean that from first to last you'll have covered most of the possible loopholes in purchasing, receiving, material control, process design, and shipping and packing, at which key points in final product quality are checked out. Above all, ZD is a team effort, which should energize the entire organization toward a common goal. If you'd like to discover how this method has worked, and test its possible application to your quality problems, why not enroll one or more of your supervisory management team in the seminar offered by the University of Michigan's Bureau of Industrial Relations. The time will be well spent."

How many *f*s did you find? Have three other people count the *f*s. What do the results of this experiment tell you about the reliability of 100 percent inspection?

Case 26–2

Many years ago Japanese-made products were always the cheapest and the flimsiest of all. Now their reputation in such areas as cameras is very high.

One of the reasons for this change is the development in Japan of the "QC circle" concept.[1] A QC circle is a small group of workers, sometimes led by the foreman, who volunteer to find ways and means for improving the quality and reducing the costs of the products on which they work. There are many thousands of such groups in Japan. These groups meet, often on their own time, and try to make improvements.

Like the American "zero defects" idea (explained in Chapter 27), QC circles try to find causes of defects and remove the causes. These programs, however, are unlike zero defects programs in that they are initiated from the bottom, by the workers themselves, instead of being instigated by executive decree. QC circles are, in fact, only loosely connected with management. Management does, however, cooperate by furnishing statistics, charts, and help on control charts, sampling, and testing.

Wouldn't this be a good idea for American industry to adopt?

Recent references

Adam, E. E., Jr., and W. E. Scott, Jr., "Application of Behavioral Conditioning Procedures to the Problems of Quality Control," *Academy of Management Journal*, June 1971

Eshelman, R. H., and J. B. Pond, "Gaging and Testing," *Automotive Industries*, March 1, 1972

Gedye, Rupert, *A Manager's Guide to Quality and Reliability*, New York: John Wiley, 1969

Harris, Douglas H., and F. B. Chaney, *Human Factors in Quality Assurance*, New York: John Wiley, 1969

Juran, Joseph M., and Frank M. Gryna, *Quality Planning and Analysis*, New York: McGraw-Hill, 1970

Kirkpatrick, Elmwood G., *Quality Control for Managers and Engineers*, New York: John Wiley, 1970

Peterson, Cecil, "Selecting a Product Quality Level," *Industrial Engineering*, August 1970

Proceedings of the American Society for Testing Materials (annually)

Quality Assurance (monthly)

---

[1] This method is described at length in *Modern Manufacturing* (March 1970), pp. 66–68.

27

Statistical quality control

STATISTICAL QUALITY CONTROL (SQC) applies the theory of probability to sample testing, or inspection. A great deal of inspection work has always been done by sampling; a small part of a certain lot of products is inspected and its quality is assumed to be the quality of the lot. Doing this is a little risky because it is always possible that a sample will not have exactly the same characteristics as the lot. Years ago, before statistical quality control, no one knew how much risk was involved. Sometimes larger samples than necessary were inspected. These entailed wasted inspection costs. Other times, more risks were taken of bad work getting through than anyone realized. This allowed the costs for bad work to be much too high. With statistical quality control, inspection is more reliable, and it allows for balancing off of these costs at their least costly combination.

Statistical quality control deals with *samples* and their reliability as indicators of lot characteristics. Sampling inspection, where it can be used satisfactorily, eliminates most of the cost of 100 percent inspection, and it is the only possible method for products which must be tested until they fail or break (as in tests of length of life or tensile strength). Sampling is also the only way to test the chemical or physical characteristics of liquids and powdered or granulated material, or the thickness gage of sheet metal, paper, and cloth. Sampling is therefore desirable in many cases because it saves money. And in other cases there is no other way to inspect.

Statistical quality control doesn't *make risks*, nor does it *get rid of risks*. With or without statistical quality control, there is a chance that any sample will not be exactly like the rest of a lot. What statistical quality control does is show how reliable the sample is and how to control the risks. It lets a manager decide the risks he is willing to take (that bad products will slip by or that good products will be rejected). He can then decide whether it will cost more to catch the possible bad products or to let them go and save inspection costs. He can make a conscious decision about how much risk he wants to assume. SQC also helps during processing by warning managers if machines are getting out of adjustment so that they can be reset before many bad products are made.

When SQC deals with checking products already made, it is called "acceptance" sampling. This is where most of the idea of controlling risks applies. But SQC (still using samples and still dealing in risks) can also be used to *control* processes *while things are being made*. Not only does SQC show when a process is out of adjustment and turning out bad work, but it warns the operator if his machine is getting out of adjustment. It catches and shows any drift toward defectives. This helps prevent making defectives, and so cuts scrap losses.

Curiously, control charts seem to improve nonautomatic jobs—the kind where quality depends on the operator more than on the machine. There is no mathematical reason for this happening at all, because the fact that a man makes one good product gives no mathematical assurance that the next one will also be acceptable. This is in contrast with machine operations, where, if the machine is set correctly and so turns out one good product, it is highly probable that the next one will also be acceptable.

Keeping the charts right at the operations and letting the workers do their own measuring and plotting of points gets them interested. They become more quality conscious and are more careful.

Areas of use

Statistical quality control has three general uses: (1) to control the quality of work done on individual factory operations while the work is being done, (2) to decide whether to accept or reject lots of products already produced (whether bought or made within the company), and (3) to furnish management a quality audit of the company's products. A fourth result—checking the reasonableness of the quality standards and specifications setup—is generally accomplished, more or less, as a by-product of SQC in operation.

When statistical quality control is used to control operations, control charts are kept right at the job. Samples of products are checked from time to time, and their *measurements* are plotted on the control charts. Since it is impossible to make two absolutely identical products, some minor variations in measurement always occur, even when the machines are in adjustment. A machine will even produce an unacceptable item, once in a long time, even when it is in adjustment. Control charts show when operations are making too many unacceptable products, and so tell operators when they need to reset their machines.

Statistical quality control for accepting or rejecting whole lots of products ("acceptance" sampling) usually deals with the *proportion* of rejects found in a sample. When a lot contains considerably more or considerably less than the allowable proportion of rejects, this will almost surely be revealed by even a small sample. Additional samples need be taken only when the small initial sample provides borderline (or near borderline) results.

Statistical quality control as a quality audit also operates on a sample basis. Faults in samples of completed products are classified according to their seriousness, and demerits are assigned. Major defects—those which will interfere with the product's salability or its operation, or which might be dangerous—may be assigned, say, 25 to 50 demerits, depending on the seriousness of the defects. Minor defects, which might shorten the life of the product or increase its maintenance costs, may be assigned 10 demerits. Incidental defects, such as appearance blemishes, may be given 5 (or even only 1) demerit, depending on their seriousness. Ratios of the number of demerits found, per unit of product inspected, can be compared for products made at different periods of time. Ratios can also be combined to get department—or even plantwide—averages to use in further comparisons.

An SQC by-product is the check they give on the reasonableness of tolerances and specifications. SQC may reveal that the standards cannot be met satisfactorily with the men and machines the company now has. If so, the men may need to be trained to do better work. If that won't do the job, the company may have to buy some better machines. Or, finally, if

FIGURE 27-1. Portion of a demerit list for quality defects

DEMERIT LIST—STEP-BY-STEP SWITCH MECHANISMS

Item	Dem.	Defect description	Item	Dem.	Defect description
		1. ELECTRICAL			Rotary pawl springs:
			2010C	10	opening in loop exceeds
101B	50	Breakdown between (*parts*)			specified limit
		on (*specified*) voltage			Rotary pawl play:
		Cross or ground between	2011C	10	rotary pawl binds
		(*parts*):			Vertical position of rotary
102A	100	affecting circuit, not			armature:
		readily corrected	2012B	50	no overlap
102B	50	affecting circuit, readily	2012C	10	overlap not as specified
		corrected	2013C	10	Rotary pawl position not as
102C	10	may affect circuit			specified
103C	10	Clearance between insulated			Rotary magnet position:
		parts insufficient	2014C	10	rotary dog and ratchet
		Open circuit:			tooth clearance not as
104A	100	not readily corrected			specified
104B	50	readily corrected	2015C	10	armature does not strike
		Current flow; release magnet			both magnet cores
		coil:			Rotary pawl front stop posi-
105B	50	more than 10% outside			tion:
		of specified value	2016C	10	clearance between rotary
105C	10	10% or less outside of			pawl and front stop
		specified value			not as specified
106C	10	armature does not release			Rotary pawl guide position:
		after operation on	2017C	10	rotary pawl tip does not
		specified current			strike tooth as speci-
107B	50	Contacts dirty; breaking con-			fied
		tinuity			Normal pin position:
			2018C	10	rotary pawl does not
		2. MECHANICAL			strike first tooth in
2001C	10	Bank or wiper contacts not			same relative position
		cleaned or treated			as other teeth

Source: *Western Electric Company.*

the rejects are still high, the managers may have to relax the standards or simply "live with" high reject rates.

SQC may also show that the design itself is faulty. If individual parts meet all the quality standards but the finished product still does not perform well, then the fault is in the design and not in the manufacturing processes.

Attributes and variables

When an inspector looks at a product and says "It passes" or "It is a reject," he is dealing with "attributes." But if he measures "how much," "how big," "how thick," "how round," and so on, he is dealing with "variables."

A distinction needs to be made between attributes and variables because they require different statistical procedures. Attributes deal with *percentages* of products rejected. Variables deal with *averages of measure-*

FIGURE 27–2. The quality-production interaction system

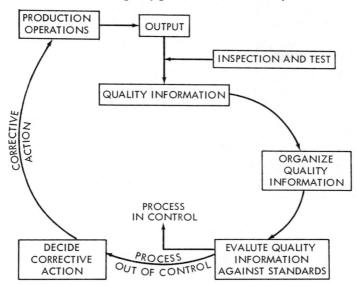

ments and the *extents of the deviations*. Attribute inspection is most important in acceptance sampling—inspecting products away from the operation and after considerable quantities have been made—as in the case of purchased items. Variable inspection is more important in controlling operations as they are being performed because most of it is done at the job.

Attribute inspection is used (1) when items are obviously good or bad (an alarm clock rings or it doesn't); or (2) when the characteristics can't be measured, thus forcing an inspector to judge them (as in the degree of shine on a polished surface or deciding whether a soldered connection is good enough); or (3) when a characteristic can be measured but the exact measurement is not needed (as when go–no-go gages are used to inspect for size). Most inspection of metal, glass, cloth, or painted surfaces for cracks, scratches, or surface irregularities, and most inspection of color finish, are attribute inspections.

Most measurements of dimensions, however, as well as all types of length-of-life tests, are inspection of variables. The tested items always differ somewhat, and it is necessary to tabulate and analyze the frequency of each measurement.

Representative samples

In statistical quality control, the whole lot from which a sample is taken is called the "inspection lot," the "total population," the "parent population," or the "universe."

If statistical quality control is to operate successfully, samples *must* be "representative," meaning that they *must* have the same characteristics as the whole lots from which they are taken. A sample which does not have such characteristics is not a representative sample. In SQC, the word "sample" always refers to a representative sample. It does *not* mean a nonrepresentative, nontypical, or poor sample. When samples are referred to as "random" samples, the intent has been to get a *representative* sample. A random sample from a barrel of material would include materials taken from the top, middle, bottom, outside, and inside of the barrel. A random sample of automatic machine products should include a few items taken from the start of the run, a few periodically during the run, and a few at the end.

Products being sampled ought to be, and usually are, homogeneous (the same throughout). If they are not—if some tote pans of parts have more bad items in them than other pans—the inspector must be very careful to see that he gets a representative sample. He should, for example, take a few items from every tote box. In fact, the inspector should always do this, whether he suspects that the various boxfuls are of unequal quality or not.

In factory inspection, ordinarily only one universe, such as a shipment of products received from one vendor or one run of products from an automatic machine, needs to be considered at a time. It is desirable, however, to consider each day's output of automatic machines as separate lots. A random sample of each day's, or each hour's, output should be inspected separately in order to catch gradual changes in the products which might be caused by tool wear or by the machine's gradually getting out of adjustment.

Size of sample

It seems logical for big samples to be more reliable than small samples. One might even suspect that if one sample is twice as big as another it would be twice as reliable. Big samples are better, but not at all proportionally better. We can't say exactly *how much* better a big sample is because, whereas a sample of 20 is considerably more reliable than 10, there is almost no gain in reliability if a sample of 1,000 is increased to 2,000—yet in each case the sample size is doubled. In fact, in the inspection of variables the gain in reliability from inspecting a sample of 300 instead of 200 is rarely worth the added inspection costs. Samples up in the hundreds are all quite reliable. From there on, little reliability is added by inspecting more pieces. For attribute inspection, the numbers are a little higher, but they too become quite reliable at the 300 or 400 level.

Even small samples are almost completely reliable for lots which are quite good or quite bad. When inspecting variables, a 25-piece sample will produce virtually conclusive results if it is found to be *much better* or *much worse* than the limit of acceptability because it is very unlikely that a sample will be very good or very bad when the whole lot is not correspondingly good or bad. A sample of 100 pieces, in such a case, would add little to the reliability of the results found in the smaller sample. But if the 25-piece sample turns out to be of borderline quality, it is not so certain whether the whole lot should pass. Inspecting a 100-piece sample adds a great deal of certainty that the lot is borderline good or borderline bad.

Another matter is the size of the sample as it relates to the universe. The reliability of a sample does not depend on its *proportion* of the universe; its reliability is almost entirely dependent on its *numerical* size. The size of the whole *lot* has little effect on the *sample's* reliability. A sample of 200 taken from a lot of 5,000 is almost as reliable an indicator of the whole 5,000 as a sample of 200 taken from a lot of 1,000. Yet in the first case it is a 4 percent sample as against 20 percent in the second case. This fact, used in sampling inspection, permits considerable inspection cost savings by confining the sample to the smallest practicable quantity. Only very small samples, proportionately, need be inspected from large lots.

Eastman Kodak sets the sample size for much of its inspection by using the following formula (in which n is the sample size and N is the whole lot):

$$n = \sqrt{2N}$$

Using this formula, a sample of 200 would suffice for a lot of 20,000. Eastman inspects larger samples for products it thinks might be of uneven quality. But the biggest samples, even if Eastman suspects that a lot is of uneven quality, are limited to 2.5 times the usual sample size, or 500 in the case of a 20,000 lot.

The normal curve and standard deviations

Statistical quality control is based on the idea that no two things are exactly alike, but that when either man or nature tries to make indentical products, their actual sizes will vary from small to large but most items will be close to the middle. The most frequent size will be the middle size; the least frequent sizes will be at the two extremes—larger and smaller than the middle size.

A large number of such items can be measured and tallied according to size. The count of items by size, when plotted on a chart, nearly always approximates a "normal" or "bell-shape" curve. Most items, when measured closely, show this normal distribution. Occasionally the curve is pulled off to one side ("skewed"), showing there are more extreme deviations above the norm or more extreme deviations smaller than the norm.

If there is a pronounced variation from the normal distribution, different statistical procedures need to be used and the usual kind of statistical quality control should *not* be used.

In a normal distribution there is a progressive tapering off of the number of items above and below the point of greatest frequency, which itself is the highest point on the curve and is in the middle of the curve. This highest point is the average measurement (the "arithmetic mean") of the series. Expected variations in measurement of individual items from the mean can be figured on the basis of this normal curve.

But SQC deals with samples, not whole lots. Each item of a sample is measured. Then a tabulation of the frequency of each measurement is made. Next the tabulation could be plotted on a chart. (It is not actually necessary to plot such a chart.) Almost always, such a chart would turn out to be a miniature bell-shape curve (miniature in the sense that it is based on 50 to 100 cases rather than 10,000). The spread of measurements between big and little in the sample will be about the same as in the parent population. (This can be proved mathematically but there isn't space here for the proof.) If the sample is of reasonable size and is representative, it will show how the whole population measures up.

In statistical quality control it is necessary to figure the "standard deviation."[1] (The standard deviation is usually indicated by the Greek letter sigma, σ.) This is a measure of the variation of individual-item measurements from the sample's average. In all normal distributions, the mean plus-and-minus-1 standard deviation gives values between which 68.3 percent of the measures of the sampled products fall. The mean plus-and-minus-2 standard deviations gives limits between which 95.5 percent of the cases fall. Three standard deviations, each way, set limits which include 99.7 percent of the cases. These mathematical relationships are the bases on which statistical quality control rests.

An example will show how it works. If a part 4 inches long is being manufactured, close measurement will show that the parts vary in size, most of them being close to but not *exactly* 4 inches long. The *average* size of the pieces in our sample, however, ought to be almost exactly 4 inches. We will say that the average length of the parts in our sample is actually 4 inches and the standard deviation is .002 inches. Therefore 4 inches + and − 1 standard deviation is 4.002 and 3.998 inches respectively; so 68.3 percent of the sample measurements (or very close to it) are between these limits. Measuring out 2 standard deviations produces

---

[1] This was explained earlier (on p. 268) but is repeated here for convenience. To compute the standard deviation, it is necessary to find the amount of difference (or deviation) between the value or measure of each item and the value of the arithmetic mean. These deviations are expressed as numerical quantities. The procedure for arriving at the standard deviation is as follows: square each deviation (that is, multiply it by itself), add the squared numbers, divide the sum by the number of items, and take the square root of the quotient. The square root, so obtained, is the standard deviation. It is expressed in the same measure as the value of the individual items and the mean. If the value is inches, the arithmetic mean and the standard deviation are both expressed in inches.

FIGURE 27–3. The normal curve distribution pattern which lies behind statistical quality control

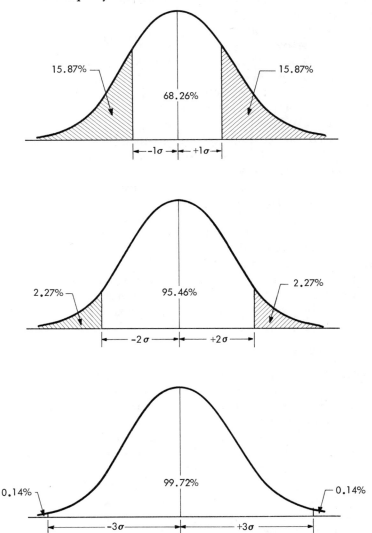

measurements at 4.004 and 3.996 inches. These measurements will include 95.5 percent of the cases. Three standard deviations out each way, or 4.006 and 3.994 inches, will include 99.7 percent of the cases.

Mathematicians have developed short-cut methods for doing all of this calculating. On page 654 we give an example showing how to use a short cut for setting control limits for control charts.

SQC is also helpful in the few cases where extremes are important, as for example with the weakest link in a chain. It is all very good for the average strength of each link to be well above the minimum, but if even *one* link is too weak the chain breaks. Charts can be set up so that attention is focused on such extremes.

In other cases consistency is the important thing. Suppose a company buys 2 lots of $\frac{1}{8}$-inch diameter ball bearings. And suppose lot A averages .1248 inches but lot B averages a perfect .1250 inches. But *within* lot A the individual balls range between .1247 and .1251 inches, while in lot B, with the perfect *average*, the individual sizes range from .1240 to .1260 inches. Which lot would probably work out best? Probably lot A, because no ball bearing varies more than $\frac{3}{10,000}$ of an inch from perfect, while in lot B some are off $\frac{10}{10,000}$ of an inch. Many SQC applications deal with this matter of consistency.

Whether the interest is in averages, extremes, standard deviations, or percentages, statistical quality control is directed, first, at getting the measurements, test scores, or percent defectives for the items in the sample; second, at computing the combined measures for the sample; and, third, at comparing the combined sample measures to preset scales showing the limits of acceptability. Lastly, if the measures exceed the limits of acceptability, some action must be taken to remedy the situation. The statistical procedures used for these purposes are all based on the idea of the normal curve and the standard deviation.

Control charts for operations

Books on statistical quality control do not furnish control charts already computed and set up for general use. Instead, they explain how to set up and use control charts. This is because every control chart has to be unique for the operation it serves.

Figure 27–4 shows the steps to go through for setting up control charts—the end product of a process that starts with collecting and analyzing certain figures about an operation. This has to be done separately for *every* job where control charts are to be used.

To make a control chart it is first necessary to measure a number of items made by the operation. Suppose that 40 such measurements are made of parts intended to be 4 inches long. The average of the 40 prove to be 4 inches and the standard deviation .002 inches, as in our earlier example. The 3-standard-deviation control limits (3.994 and 4.006 inches respectively) are then spotted in along a vertical measurement scale (as in Figure 27–4). Horizontal lines are drawn across to the right to "fence in" the area of acceptable measurements. The horizontal scale is a time scale for plotting the measurements taken periodically throughout the day.

Before using a control chart, however, it should be checked against the job's specified tolerance limits. The 3σ limits are 3.994 and 4.006

FIGURE 27–4. Steps in setting up a control chart

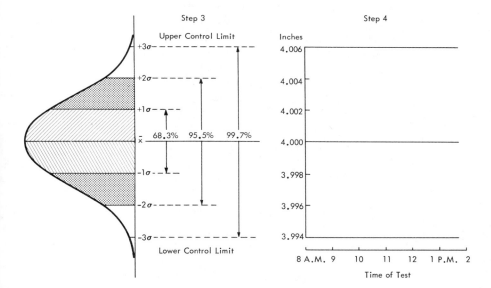

Step 1
Actual Measurements (Inches)

4.002
3.999
3.996
4.000
4.001
4.001
3.998
4.003
ETC.

Step 2
Frequency Distribution (Inches)

3.994
3.995 I
3.996 JHT II
3.997 JHT IIII
3.998 JHT JHT II
3.999 JHT JHT III
4.000 JHT JHT IIII I
4.001 JHT JHT IIII
4.002 JHT JHT
4.003 JHT IIII
4.004 JHT II
4.005 II
4.006

Step 3

Upper Control Limit

+3σ

+2σ

+1σ

x̄   68.3%   95.5%   99.7%

−1σ

−2σ

−3σ

Lower Control Limit

Step 4

Inches

4.006

4.004

4.002

4.000

3.998

3.996

3.994

8 A.M. 9   10   11   12   1 P.M. 2

Time of Test

inches respectively. If the specification says 4 inches ± .010, then the operation can proceed because all of the production is well within the 4.010 and 3.990 limits. But if the specification says 4 inches ± .004, then only 95 percent of the products will pass. The operation will probably have to be improved.

Now that the control chart is set up, it is used by having the inspector out at the job in the factory measure a very small sample of products (maybe as few as 3 or 5 every half hour or so and plot the average measurement on the chart, as is done in Figure 27–6. If one of these averages falls outside the control limits, something is the matter with the job. The chart has done its work: it has flashed the signal and the inspector and the operator are warned to stop the machine and get it back into adjustment. (Some companies also show, on the chart, lines for ± 2 standard deviations. When the averages being plotted get beyond these limits, this serves as a warning that the machine is getting out of adjustment.)

As we said, however, statisticians have figured out a short-cut method for setting up control limits for making control charts. It is still necessary to get a starting set of measurements to start with. Suppose we plan to inspect a sample of 4 every half hour after the chart is set up. It is necessary, first, to take a sample of a good many items, say as many as 40, and separate this big sample into 10 subsamples of 4 each. These measurements should *not* be sorted into any order (as from large to small). *They should be used just as they come.*

For *each* set of 4, its average measurement is figured, and also its range (the difference between the largest and smallest item in the set). This produces 10 averages and 10 ranges. Next, the grand average should be figured (by adding the 10 averages together and dividing by 10) and the average range (by adding the 10 ranges together and dividing by 10).

Reference can now be made to Figure 27–5. We read down to *4,* the number in our subsamples, and find the factor: *.73.*

FIGURE 27–5

Number in each small sample	Factor
2	1.88
3	1.02
4	.73
5	.58
6	.48
7	.42
8	.37
9	.34
10	.31

The upper control limit is obtained by multiplying the average range by .73 and adding the result to the grand mean. The same amount is subtracted from the grand mean to get the lower control limit. Let us assume that the pieces are supposed to average 4 inches long and we find that the grand average is 4 inches and the average range of the 10 samples is .009 inches. Multiplying .009 by .73 gives .006. Adding this to—and subtracting it from—4 inches establishes control limits of 4.006 and 3.994 inches. We can now draw in these lines as the control limits on the control chart.

We have been talking about controlling the *average*, but nearly always there is need to control variability as well. Two pieces, one 3 inches and one 5 inches long, average 4 inches long. But this is not much comfort to an assembler who wants two pieces each 4 inches long.

Variability is controlled by paying attention to the *range* (the difference between the largest and smallest items in the samples). Control charts to keep track of the range are made up in almost exactly the same way as charts to control averages. And here, too, a short-cut method (explained in statistic books) is available to allow such limits to be set up in a matter of minutes.

Control charts for variables

The example we just used to show how to set up a control chart dealt with a dimension. It required *measuring* the sample items, so it dealt with a *variable*. It also dealt with the *average* size. Sometimes the interest

FIGURE 27–6.   A control chart in use. Samples are taken periodically during the day and the averages and ranges are plotted.

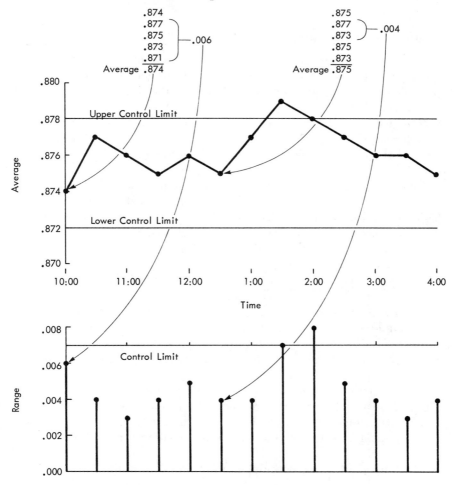

is in the extremes, the largest or the smallest; and sometimes there is much more concern about the product's *consistency*—the usual variation between extremes. Charts can be made up to control any or all of these.

Sometimes there is need to watch two or more variables at once. If so, it helps to combine their charts and put them one below the other on the same chart, as in Figure 27–6. This makes charting simpler and it ties together all the results from each sample because they are all charted on the same vertical line. In Figure 27–6 the 10:30 A.M. sample of five items averaged 0.877 inches in diameter, and the largest item in that lot was 0.004 inches larger than the smallest.

Control charts are usually kept right at the machine. A worker or an inspector checks a small sample of the product periodically and plots its average size on the chart. If any of the measures is beyond the permissible limit, the products are unacceptable and the operation should be stopped.

Control charts for attributes

Attributes are the "yes or no" characteristics; products pass or they don't pass. These things are not measured. Sometimes it is either impossible or very difficult to measure them (as the shininess of a polished surface or the excess solder on an electrical connection), so the inspector just decides. Sometimes there is no need to measure them (a glass tumbler has a crack in it or it doesn't), so there is no problem deciding. Instead of *measuring* every item in a sample, the inspector just looks at it and decides.

Control charts for attribute inspection (sometimes called P charts) are based on the *percentages* of products rejected by the inspector. Making control charts for attributes usually costs less than charts for variables because the inspection itself is generally less expensive and the information required is available whether charts are made or not.

To make a control chart for attributes, the past performance record will usually supply the information needed. Figures for a dozen or so samples are needed. Here the samples need to be big—up in the hundreds of items in each sample. (Because rejects are integers, it isn't possible, for example, to have ½ percent rejects until at least 200 have been inspected.) Each sample is 100 percent inspected and the percentage of rejects for each sample is figured. These percentages are required for making the control charts.

These figures are used just as were the measurement figures on which Figure 27–4 was based. After getting quite a few percentage figures for successive samples, the next thing is to calculate the grand average percentage of rejects and the standard deviation, and set up control limits.

Attribute charts show both upper and lower control limits. If 2 percent rejects are normal for an operation, the control limits might be 1 and 3 percent. But why have a lower limit? Isn't it good to get rejects down to as near zero as possible? Yes. But if rejects actually go below 1 percent, the job is not being run the way it used to be. Going below the low limit reveals that.

If a manager could be sure that the good record came about from good reasons, he would look no further into the matter and would set new control limits to cover the new performance. This should be done if rejects are down because the worker is doing a better job. But the record could be improving because of bad reasons, so going below the lower control limit justifies investigating. Maybe inspectors are passing too many bad items. Maybe the men are producing better but fewer products. If the men are now working slowly and carefully, this would raise costs. If either of these things is happening, it may be better to return to the old situation. In such cases it may be better to have a few rejects than none.

Not all attribute control charts deal with percentages. Some deal with *ratios*—often the number of defects per 100 items. Defect ratio charts are set up the same way as other attribute control charts. Defect ratio control charts are helpful in controlling surface defects in metal, wood, or paper, insulation defects on wire, air bubbles in glass, and imperfections in a bolt of cloth or in rolls of film. In most of these cases the defects are not repaired; they are just accepted as facts. But a decision is made that a certain ratio is enough and that all products having more are rejects. The attempt is also made, of course, to try to improve so that there will be fewer rejects in the future.

In the case of defect-per-unit-ratios, it is possible to have ratios way above 100. One kind of "black box" part of a radar set made by Lear Siegler has 1,800 possible trouble points. An inspector has a most difficult job checking an assembly of transistors, diodes, resistors, printed circuits, integrated circuits, wires, and so on for possible defects. Here is Lear's list of defects that its inspectors look for when inspecting this particular black box:

Improper solder	Riveting
Burnt wires	Missing part
Wrong component	Defective part
Improper installation	Improperly sleeved
Probable shorts	Broken wires or strands

It isn't necesary to go so far afield as radar to picture the inspectors' problem and the possibility of having more defects than products. In an automobile dashboard, with its gages and meters, hundreds of kinds of defects could turn up.

Either of these examples is a good place to use ratio charts of defects per unit. Also, either situation is ideal for the auditing kind of quality control. Back on page 646 we described how Western Electric classified different kinds of defects and set up a demerit point scale: serious defects mean 50 demerits, lesser defects mean fewer demerits, and so on. New demerit ratios (the average number of demerits per unit of product) are figured every day, so before long the manager could set up a control chart of demerit ratios. This kind of chart is useful when checking finished products or assemblies. These are so many things which can be wrong, and there is no other way to get an overall picture of quality changes.

Acceptance sampling

Acceptance sampling means accepting or rejecting whole lots of completed products on the basis of what the sample shows. Inspectors are told how many pieces to inspect and how many bad items to allow: so many, or less, and the lot passes; more than that, and the lot is rejected.

Most often acceptance sampling is found in the receiving inspection department, where receiving inspectors look over the things that the company buys. Acceptance sampling is used less in one's own plant because control charts are used right at the operations in so many places. Large lots of products are never completed and *then* inspected.

Acceptance sampling is nearly always attribute inspection rather than variable inspection. And even more than in the case of operation control charts, acceptance sampling is a matter of calculated risks because it deals with large quantities of already finished products. There is always a slight chance that bad lots will be passed or that good lots will be rejected.

Always, when there are large quantities of products, there are going to be at least a few defective pieces in every lot. Both buyer and seller understand this and contracts are drawn accordingly.[2] In fact, the allowable number of defects will be reflected in the price. If the buyer wants the items he buys to have a very low percentage of defectives, he pays more than if he is less demanding.

When the products arrive at the buyer's plant, he inspects them and either accepts or rejects them, depending on whether the number of bad items in the sample he looks at are above or below the ratio allowed. Both buyer and seller (SQC calls them the "consumer" and the "producer") take some risks. The consumer runs the risk that now and then he will accept a lot with too many defectives (the sample might not have the proportional share of defectives). The producer runs the risk that now and then a good lot will not pass inspection (if the sample happens to contain more than its share of defectives). In both of these cases the sample is, in fact, not representative, although this is not known.

Acceptance sampling does not get rid of these risks, but it *does* let

---

[2] Actually, the buyer and seller relationship is unimportant. The problem of accepting or rejecting complete products exists regardless of whether a company buys or makes the items.

managers decide how much risk they are willing to accept and to inspect accordingly. The more certain they want to be, the bigger samples they must inspect (and pay more for inspection costs).

With acceptance sampling—and unlike control charts—users of statistical quality control do not have to make up their own tables of sample sizes and rejection numbers for their inspectors. Statisticians have whole sets of them all figured out and published in books.

The published inspection tables also provide figures for several levels of inspection. A company's receiving inspectors normally inspect until a vendor has sent several satisfactory lots; then the customer company cuts out part of this inspecting and inspects only now and then. But if a lot is rejected, the procedure reverts and the receiving inspectors go to more frequent inspecting for a while.

Operating characteristic curves

Every acceptance sampling plan has an "operating characteristic" (OC) curve which shows how it works. It is, however, a "result" curve in that it does not determine the plan. The plan comes first and the curve depicts how it works.

The starting point of an acceptance plan is what we will call an "objective" defective percent. As the plan is developed, this objective percent disappears and is not seen in the final numbers which constitute the plan.

The objective percent is some particular percent of bad items which the buyer expects to accept. The buyer does not want to accept lots with more defectives, nor does he expect lots to be much better. (If they are much better, the supplier will probably have to put so much extra effort into making them better that they will cost more than the buyer is willing to pay.)

Both buyers and sellers appreciate these points. They also know that a "plan" is one which will average out. The seller is going to deliver, over a period of time, many lots of parts. Some will surely be very good and contain fewer than the allowable fraction of defectives. Others will be poorer and will contain more than the allowable fraction bad.

An acceptance sampling plan is one which, based on inspecting a small sample, accepts nearly all lots which are better than the objective percent and rejects most lots which are worse. If the lots submitted are of quite varied quality, some good, some bad, the average fraction of defectives contained in all accepted lots will be close to the objective percent. In the example we will work out, this objective percent is set at 2 percent defective.

Having first decided the objective percent, the next step is to choose four other numbers. The first is called the "acceptable quality level" (AQL). In our example we set this at 1 percent defectives. The AQL is always a better quality level than the objective percent. In fact, "acceptable quality level" is a misnomer in the sense that the term is a considerable better quality level than the objective percent. It is *so much better* that the inspection plan is set so as to accept the AQL percent defectives in almost every case where such good lots are submitted.

Usually the plan is designed to incorporate a 5 percent risk at the AQL. This is called the producer's risk, or the α (alpha) risk. It means that lots with so few defectives as the AQL will be accepted 95 percent of the time.

Interestingly, the producer usually does not determine either the AQL fraction defective nor the percent of the time that lots that are good will pass. Instead, the buyer sets the numbers. The vendor then reacts and sets his price accordingly. If his very good lots have much chance of being rejected, he sets his price higher.

The third figure to be set is the "lot tolerance percent defective" (LTPD). This is sometimes also called the "lot tolerance fraction defective" (LTFD). In our example this was set at 3 percent defectives. This is the consumer's risk.

The customer (the consumer) wants the inspection plan to catch and reject almost all lots with, in this case, 3 percent defectives. The consumer's risk, also called the β (beta) risk, is usually set at 10 percent. This 10 percent is the fourth of the four numbers needing a decision. This means that lots with as many as 3 percent defectives will be rejected 90 percent of the time. Still poorer lots have less chance of passing.

These four decisions, the AQL (1 percent), the alpha risk (5 percent), the LTPD (3 percent), and the beta risk (10 percent), are the constraints to the inspection plan. The objective percent is not a factor in the calculation except that it was behind the setting of the 1 and 3 percent limits.

From this point on, setting up the inspection plan is mathematical and is based on complicated formulas. The end product is a set of instructions to inspectors. These instructions tell inspectors, for all possible sizes of lots, how many to inspect as a sample. And they will tell them how many bad items in the sample are acceptable and how many constitute too many bad ones.

In our example, it turns out that, for a lot of 10,000 or more, the inspector should inspect a sample of 400 and reject all lots whose sample contains 8 or more rejects. (The plan would be expressed as $N = 10,000$, $n = 400$, $c = 7$). With 7 or fewer defectives, the inspector accepts the lot. But if the lot is only 1,000, we get the same quality assurance by having the inspector inspect a sample of 275 and accepting the lot if he finds no more than 5 defects. If the whole lot is 200, he should inspect 125, and accept it if he finds 2 or fewer rejects. The plan therefore tells the inspector, for each size lot, how big a sample to take and how good it has to be.

Figure 27–7 is this particular plan's operating characteristic curve. On this chart, the horizontal line at the bottom is an "if" line. *If* a lot submitted has 1, 2, 3, 4, etc., percent defectives, then we can read up to the curve and across to the left to see what the chances are that such a lot will be accepted. Lots which actually contain 1 percent defectives will pass about 95 percent of the time. Lots with 2 percent bad will pass 40 percent of the time. Lots containing 3 percent defectives will get by only 10 percent of the time. And poorer lots have very little chance of getting by.

The real meaning of OC curves is more apparent when there are many successive lots of products. OC curves have to do with *average*

FIGURE 27–7.   An operating characteristic curve

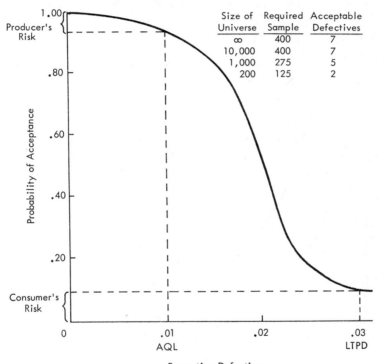

Size of Universe	Required Sample	Acceptable Defectives
∞	400	7
10,000	400	7
1,000	275	5
200	125	2

results covering many lots. If over a period of time, in our example, several hundred lots of a product were submitted, and if some of these lots were very good, some very bad, and some in between, then the OC curve tells us what would happen.

This plan will accept lots with 1 percent bad, 95 percent of the time, but although there is no intention to do so, it will accidentally reject 5 percent of the lots submitted which are this good. It will also reject lots with 3 percent bad 90 percent of the time. And again, although it is unintentional, it will accept lots this bad 10 percent of the time.

Lots of in-between quality will be accepted or rejected as the curve shows. If the lots vary all the way up and down, from very good to very bad, the average quality of those accepted will be a little more than 2 percent bad.

Every acceptance inspection plan has its own operating characteristic curve. The shape of the line depends on the quality wanted and the degree of certainty that this quality will be assured. The slope of the curve reflects the plan. If managers want more or less assurance, they can change any of the four original decisions. If they want more certainty,

FIGURE 27–8. Family of operating characteristic curves. These curves are for four different inspection plans and show how much the change in the acceptable number of defects changes the plans.

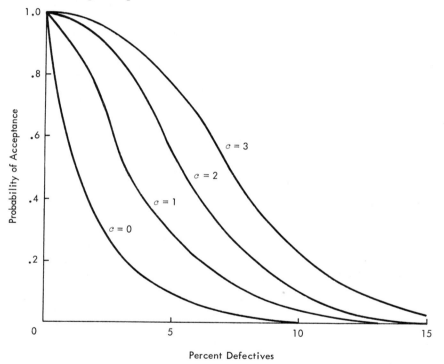

for example, they could increase the sample size and hold the acceptable number constant. Doing this, however, changes the whole plan, including the AQL and the LTPD. This new plan would have its own OC curve.

Single, double, and sequential sampling

For very good lots or very poor lots, relatively small samples are all that are needed because the samples will be so good or bad that there is little doubt whether the whole lots are good enough to pass. This can be taken advantage of in SQC by first inspecting only a very small sample to see whether it is clearly good or bad. This may leave a good many in-between, borderline cases where it is not clear what to do. When this happens, it is necessary to inspect another sample and add it to the first. Having a larger sample allows the inspector to decide more certainly whether a borderline lot is just good enough to pass or not quite good enough.

Some people, though, prefer to use just one sample and no more. This is "single sampling." Here one and only one fairly large sample is used. After inspection, the lot is accepted or rejected. There are no more samples.

"Double sampling" means using a smaller sample first. With it alone, the inspector accepts or rejects all but borderline lots. With borderline lots, he inspects a second sample, adds it to the first one, and then decides. Figure 27–9 shows how this works.

FIGURE 27–9. Single, double, and sequential sampling alternatives. These three diagrams are for essentially the same inspection objective. If numerous lots are submitted and some are inspected one way and the others a different way, the same number of acceptances and rejections would result.

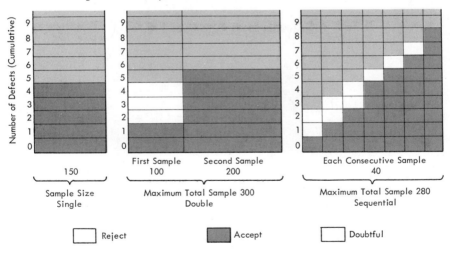

"Sequential sampling" means starting out with quite small samples. Even these very small samples are conclusive for very good or very bad lots, so they can be accepted or rejected right away. But there will be more doubtful cases because the very small first sample is conclusive for only very good or very bad lots. If the first sample is inconclusive, another small sample is inspected and added to the first. Putting the two samples together makes a larger-size sample, and this provides more certainty, so more of the borderline lots can be passed or rejected. But a few will still be very close to borderline lots—not yet passed or rejected. So a third sample is inspected and added to the first two. This provides more certainty and disposes of more cases. If there are still close-to-borderline lots where the sample is inconclusive, the inspector goes on to a fourth sample (or more). Figure 27–9 shows how the successive samples work.

Average outgoing quality level (AOQL)

If rejected lots were always scrapped, the average quality of products would probably be about halfway between the AQL and the LTPD, although this would also depend upon the average quality of the lots submitted. But when bad lots of *parts* can be 100 percent inspected, the lot's quality can be improved just by taking out the bad items. This means that the quality of the lots which pass end up being quite good—and the *worse* the quality of lots first submitted, the *better* the ending quality. Figure 27–10 shows how the average outgoing quality level, the AOQL, relates to the quality of the lots submitted. If most lots are rather bad, SQC will catch nearly all of them, and after 100 percent inspection, they will end up nearly perfect. Averaging these in with the other lots which passed, including the few bad lots that got through, produces an outgoing quality level which will be better than if most lots were just good enough to pass.

Figure 27–10 probably claims a little too much, however. The true

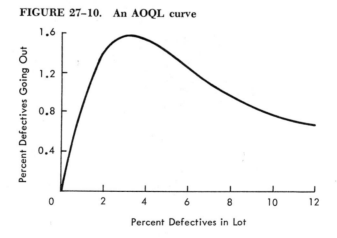

FIGURE 27–10.   An AOQL curve

AOQL will probably not be quite this good because 100 percent inspection is not 100 percent perfect. It won't catch quite all of the defects. The true AOQL will contain a few more defectives than, theoretically, it should.

Degrees of defects in acceptance sampling

Many products can have major or minor defects, or both, and at the same time. If so, the receiving inspectors may need to use two or three inspection plans at the same time and on the same sample. It may be necessary, for example, to allow no defects at all in the sample for critical or major defects. The curvature of a spring for an automobile door latch might be critical. If it curves too much it might exert too much pressure and break and let the door swing open. If a sample contains even one major defective, probably it would be well to reject the lot.

It might also be highly important to have very few or no major defects even where danger is not involved. If an automatic seat adjuster in an automobile does not have enough pull, the seat will be hard to adjust, and although this is not a critical defect, the customer won't like it.

Sometimes it may be desirable to watch for defects because they will jam machinery. The diameter of the head of a rivet installed by an automatic assembly machine must not be too big or it will jam the machine. The defect is unimportant functionally, yet it is important in keeping production moving. Again, it might be necessary to use an inspection plan which allows for no defects in the sample.

But minor defects which will not affect the product's operation are not so serious. It would be all right to accept lots with a few minor defects. Possibly a plan should be used which would accept the lot even if the sample had 10 percent minor defectives. The inspectors could be applying two or three inspection plans when they inspect a sample. The rejection number would be low for serious defects and high for minor or trivial defects.

SQC in operation

SQC may not work out in practice quite the way it is supposed to. On the good side, there is an extra degree of reliability from samples' being inspected thoroughly. Because they are only samples, they are usually checked carefully, whereas inspectors on 100 percent inspection jobs get careless. Western Electric says that sampling provides more reliable information about how many bad electrical connections there are on a switchboard with 10,000 soldered connections than does 100 percent inspection.

Also, some 100 percent inspectors get to thinking that they have to throw out a few products or the boss won't think that they are doing a good job. They get to be hypercritical and adopt a "They shall not pass" attitude. SQC seems to correct this.

On the bad side, particularly with acceptance sampling, SQC may end up *not* being as reliable as it is supposed to be. Tables for acceptance sampling are set up to give certain average qualities—but with knowledge that an occasional good lot gets rejected and an occasional bad lot gets through.

This should end up producing an average result. But what really happens when a lot which is actually good enough to pass is rejected? It goes back to the vendor, who checks a sample and finds it good enough to pass; so back the lot comes as the next regular shipment, and it probably passes this time. The result is that no good lot ever stays rejected. The vendor cannot be criticized for doing this because he is sending lots that are of acceptable quality. Having this happen does not invalidate SQC.

The harmful part concerns poor lots. A few of these slip through the first time; the others go back to the vendor. Some vendors are not above sending them back for a second try. Maybe there is only one chance in four that they will pass. But one fourth of such lots got by the first time. Another one fourth of the remaining bad lots will get by if the vendor tries again. If he tries two or three times, he will get quite a bit of bad work accepted. Of course, good vendors don't do this.

Another thing (and this may happen with control charts, too, but it is more common in acceptance sampling) is the tendency for inspectors not to follow the rules. An inspector dips into a lot and finds just enough rejects in his sample to make him reject the lot. But he doesn't always *reject* the lot. As likely as not, he throws his sample back and takes another sample, and maybe this time he gets a sample that passes; so he accepts the lot. Inspectors sometimes do things like this, so the result is likely to be a poorer quality than SQC should ensure.

Zero defects

"Zero defects" means rejecting a lot if *any* defects are found in the sample inspected. It tries to get men to "make them right the first time" and to instill in them a pride of workmanship. And it tries to minimize such ideas as "To err is human" and "How little can we get by with?" The zero defects idea, started in the early 1960s, became overly popular, but has since bedded down and continues to be useful in a limited way.

Obviously, taken at face value, it would be wasteful to reject 99 good items if 1 bad one were found in a lot of 100. And this is why the zero defects idea has backslid. It *is* uneconomical to reject such lots. It is even illogical from a statistical quality control point of view. SQC assumes that products will vary and that an occasional bad item will be produced even when a process or an operation is fully in control.

In its early application in any company, zero defects is often quite effective. Workers and foremen are quite shaken up to find that their almost perfect work is not accepted. As a consequence, the early response to a zero defects program is to try harder to make products right. Quality goes up.

But, in the long run, quality depends upon the machine, the operator, and the standards. None of these is a new factor; so if zero defects does not change one or more of them, and change them permanently, the program will not remain effective. In practice, most of the attention on ZD programs goes into getting the workers to be more careful. Programs have often been started with mass meetings, posters, and pledge cards, and these have been followed with awards, badges, and daily ZD reports. All this effort improves quality for a while, but the effects usually diminish with time.

Perhaps ZD's greatest contribution has come out of everyone's trying harder and out of the added attention given to causes of rejections and removal of the causes. Interestingly, sometimes the cause has been found to be faulty design. When an item is made to exact tolerance and it still doesn't work well, this shows that there is a design fault to correct and not a factory operation to improve. Gains from trying harder may not endure, but those that come from removal of the causes of bad work *do* endure.

Review questions

1. If statistical quality control neither makes risks nor gets rid of risks, what *does* it do? Discuss.
2. If SQC is to be used as a quality audit system, does this mean that a certain amount of faulty work is expected to pass? Explain.
3. Compare random and representative samples.
4. How are the normal curve and the standard deviation made use of in statistical quality control?
5. Why is it that books on SQC do not supply precalculated data for control charts that can be used "right now" in factory operations? Such books *do* supply precomputed numbers for acceptance sampling, so why don't they do the same for control charts?
6. Distinguish between attribute and variable inspection. Show why the distinction is important.
7. Should there be a lower control limit on a control chart for percent defectives? Why? Could such a limit ever be a minus number? Explain.
8. What is meant by "consumer's risk" and "producer's risk"?
9. A quality control plan in operation has an AQL of 5 percent. Just what does this mean to the supplier? To the purchaser?
10. When should sequential sampling be favored over single sampling? Why?
11. When a zero defects program is successful, where do the gains come from? Will these gains endure? Discuss.
12. How can it be that the AOQL gets better as the quality produced gets worse? Explain.

13.   SQC sometimes doesn't work out in practice quite the way it is supposed
to. How does it work? Is what happens good? Explain.

Discussion questions

1.   How could statistical quality control be used to help control the quality
of roof repairing jobs?

2.   How can a person tell, in statistical quality control, if there has been a
change in "population"? What difference would it make if there had
been?

3.   A specification says 4 inches ±.002 inch. The control chart shows .398
inch as the average with a standard deviation of .009 inch. Do these
figures call for any action by anyone? Who? What action?

4.   A specification calls for the dimension to be 5 inches ±.005. The control
chart shows a mean of 4.998 inches and a standard deviation of .001 inch.
What should be done about this? Suppose that the control chart showed
a mean of 5 inches and a standard deviation of .002 inch. Should anything different be done? Why?

5.   What should be done about the individual pieces outside the control
limits?

6.   A company had promised to ship 1,000 pieces to an important customer
on the very day when something went wrong and most of the pieces had
a defect which the foreman felt sure would not pass the customer's inspection. The boss "blew his top" and then ordered: "Ship them anyway!
I promised to deliver today and we'll do it even if the whole shipment
comes back." Discuss.

7.   Does a zero defects program mean that a company puts quality above
money? If yes, should this be so? Discuss.

8.   To what type of process would the zero defect concept appear to be most
applicable? How should a quality control man go about "selling" this
idea to workers? Does it have application in maintenance work?

Problems

1. The quality control analyst is setting up a control chart for part A, which
is to be 1 inch in length. The plan is to inspect a sample of 4 every half hour.
Here are the actual measurements obtained from 10 sets of 4 parts that were
made to provide the data for the control chart:

Group	Measurement in inches			
1.	1.011	1.008	.995	.991
2.	.991	.988	.986	.989
3.	.987	.996	1.007	1.013
4.	.999	.990	1.002	.991
5.	1.001	1.008	.991	.998
6.	1.009	.990	1.008	.993
7.	1.013	.988	.996	.993
8.	.987	.994	.999	.990
9.	.995	1.001	.988	1.012
10.	1.001	.999	1.010	1.007

a) Set up control limits for this operation.

b) Suppose that we already had set up this control chart with the limits just obtained and that the above measurements were obtained by measuring a sample of 4 every half hour during the day. Was the operation ever out of control? When?

2. In order to set up a control chart, the following 10 samples of 4 items were measured. These measurements are:

Sample		Measurement		
1.	6	15	13	6
2.	11	12	7	12
3.	9	14	7	8
4.	5	9	10	10
5.	14	13	16	14
6.	6	13	12	16
7.	9	18	8	12
8.	11	8	13	9
9.	13	15	9	5
10.	8	10	10	9

a) Set up a control chart for this operation.

b) After this chart was constructed, measurements of production were made every half hour. Here are the first 4 sets:

Time		Measurements		
8:30.	7	10	10	7
9:00.	10	11	10	8
9:30.	10	8	9	11
10:00.	16	12	15	8

Is the operation in control? Is there any tendency toward bad work? Show the figures.

3. According to the control plan, 8 bolts will be measured every half hour and the machine will be stopped if it is out of adjustment. Ninety-five percent of the bolts should be within 4 inches ±.004 inches. The last set of 8 showed these measurements:

4.001	3.990
3.998	4.002
4.009	3.998
3.997	4.000

Should the machine be stopped and reset? About what percent of the bolts is likely to be beyond the limits the way the machine is now running?

4. Using the short cut figures given in the text for setting up control limits, calculate the upper and lower control limits for charts for the mean, the

range, and the percent defectives from the following figures. The mean is 30 and the standard deviation is 4. The average range is 5 and the standard deviation of the ranges of the small samples is 2. The average percent defective is 5 and the standard deviation is 2.

5. Construct a control chart for percent defectives based on these data (percent defectives found in samples of 400):

Sample number	Number of defects	Sample number	Number of defects
1	2	11	3
2	0	12	0
3	8	13	5
4	5	14	6
5	8	15	7
6	4	16	1
7	4	17	5
8	2	18	8
9	9	19	2
10	2	20	1

6. What will be the average percent defectives which will be received and passed if the quality of 20 lots is the same as those listed in problem 5? In this case, use the OC curve on page 681.

Recent references

Burnstein, Herman, *Attribute Sampling*, New York: McGraw-Hill, 1971

Cathey, P. J., "Is Zero Defects Still Alive and Well?" *Iron Age*, February 25, 1971

Grant, Eugene L., and Richard S. Leavenworth, *Statistical Quality Control*, 4th ed. New York: McGraw-Hill, 1972

"Quality Control Says Go or No-Go" *Iron Age*, May 20, 1971

Wethermill, G. B., *Sampling Inspection and Quality Control*, London: Methuen, 1969

Wolff, P., "Quality Control: Survival of the Fittest," *Purchasing*, November 1, 1971

section ten

Management tomorrow

MANAGERS of production organizations in the future will surely find their jobs as challenging and interesting as were their predecessors' jobs. If the changes now going on were to be described in a few words, it would be proper to say that tomorrow's managers cannot be so self-centered. Nor will they be able to operate with the profit objective overriding all other considerations. Instead, the atmosphere will be even more one of society requiring that managers operate with a blend of several objectives in mind.

This may not require tomorrow's managers' doing an about face either in objectives or methods. As every year passes, an additional class of new young men move into the lower echelons of organizations. Already, these men have built-in awareness and appreciation of these social demands. Moreover, nearly all of these young people are also fully in agreement. As they move into the higher managerial ranks they will find these constraints more comfortable to live with than do most older managers.

Indeed, there may be a new danger that they will excessively downgrade the need to operate economically. A few years ago Boise Cascade Company put $40 million into backing minority-group real estate operations in New York City, partly because of its social desirability. Unfortunately, however, all the money was lost and Boise Cascade had to give up on this effort. Tomorrow's managers will still need to operate their organizations effectively while at the same time meeting social obligations as best as they reasonably can.

28

Production management in the future

JUST AS production management today is different from what it used to be, so tomorrow it will be different from today. Perhaps the changes now over the horizon can be summarized briefly by saying that most organizations will be larger, their activities will be somewhat more diverse, and their managers will use more sophisticated techniques. And because the service sector of our economy is growing faster than the physical goods sector, more of tomorrow's managers will have to produce services instead of physical goods. Tomorrow's managers will also have to operate within the framework of a more confining set of socially determined constraints.

Production in the service areas

Our economy's fastest growth is occurring in the areas of services, particularly *social services*—the kind of work which can best be done by governments—and in areas associated with the general good and which need doing by agencies established to serve us all.

673

This means that managers of production, with services being considered as production, will have to deal more and more with directing activities which are hard to define, hard to direct, and hard to control. For example, it is hard to judge the effectiveness of the work of a housing commission, or a federal loan-assistance program.

Managers of services of all kinds, including airlines, hotels, communications, as well as police and fire departments, have always had to try to operate effectively in areas where productivity is hard to define. Often it is hard to judge whether the service rendered is good or bad, and it is even harder to judge whether it is worth the cost resources used. Frequently, too, if performance is judged to be poor, it is hard to know what to do to try to improve it.

This situation is not new, but in the future an even larger segment of our economy will be in these difficult service areas. More managerial work will have to be done where it is difficult to do.

Well-educated employees

Over 60 percent of today's high school graduates in the United States go to college. Most of them pursue general courses of study, such as history, literature, or economics, which are not directly career oriented. Others take programs more directly career oriented.

As a result of all of this training and study, young people coming into the labor market are better informed on matters of social interest and more mentally alert.

So far as their working to earn a living is concerned, this is a mixed blessing. The individual jobs needing doing in this world are not all of them all that interesting all of the time. And there are not nearly enough interesting jobs to challenge the intellect of such a large fraction of the population. So far as job needs are concerned, the younger generation is overeducated. They are not necessarily overtrained in the specific knowledge needed for the jobs—but it is hard to get excited by the challenges of a day-to-day job after studying world conditions and how national governments operate.

Managers of all organizations—service, government, manufacturing—all will have to contend with their staffs' being made up of well-educated men and women. Thus managers everywhere will have to try to do as much as they can to make the jobs interesting.

Affluent employees

Not only will tomorrow's employees be better educated than today's workers, but they will be more affluent. Our standard of living goes up from 2 to 4 percent a year. Average factory worker wages are working up toward $10,000 a year, and many families have two wage earners.

This means that a great many families are affluent and live at a comfortable level. The family's main bread winner does not have to put in every day possible working on his job. So far as he is concerned, he can afford more days off even though he is paid for only the days he works. As a consequence, absentee rates everywhere have increased a great deal. In the early 1970s they were double what they had been a decade earlier (perhaps 8 percent as against 4 percent).

High absentee rates make the managerial jobs more difficult because work which needs to move ahead has to be reassigned when the men who should do it are absent. High absences also require an organization to be continually overstaffed just in order to get the regular amount of work done. All of these things make managerial work more difficult.

Innovations

It is so easy to be impressed with the innovations of a lifetime that it is tempting to conclude that equally impressive innovations will occur in the future. And undoubtedly many such changes lie ahead.

Against this, however, is an already apparent trend to reduced payoffs from research. So much research has gone on in the last twenty years, as against so little which was done before, that startling innovations are less frequent than they were in the first rush to research. It may well be that the pace of innovation will slow down a little. The easy, fundamental discoveries have been made. From here on the pace will be slower.

Nonetheless, there will surely be enough new and different things to reward the innovators. Tomorrow's managers must be alert to innovation possibilities in every area: production, distribution, finance, whatever.

Management tools

The whole array of operations research techniques for solving the problems which managers face has come of age and will surely be used increasingly as these techniques are further refined and adapted to particular problems. With the advent of computers, the matter of solving operations research problems has been simplified. Operations research techniques will therefore have greater impact.

This may not occur overnight, however, in spite of the availability of both the techniques and computers which can solve the problems. Many of today's older managers are not familiar with these tools and so do not make use of them. As time passes, new and younger men, who are familiar with operations research techniques, will be moving into responsible administrative positions and will use these techniques more and more.

Not only will the next generation of managers be better equipped to use management-science tools but there will be even greater need for their use because of the growth of worldwide markets. The greater volume of products and the diversity of markets for such varied products will make it more desirable to be able to respond quickly to market needs.

Decision making

Not only will computers make further applications of operations research feasible, their operations will be extended in the direction of making minor, repetitive decisions in the production control, scheduling, and inventory control areas.

Most of the procedures for doing this are described in this book. But, in fact, not many companies are presently using these procedures in the various aspects of production control. The programming work is quite complex, and anyone who has got a wrong bill from a credit-card charge knows how hard it is to straighten out a computer mistake. Time will, however, see more and more of these problems solved and more and more of this large area of low-grade decision making taken over by computers.

The social element

Until recent years there was a slowly evolving trend toward business managers' becoming more socially responsible. Then, rather quickly, the pace quickened, until now these responsibilities are held to be of utmost importance. This change has had little effect on government services except to expand those concerned with the regulation of the activity of other organizations. But other organizations, particularly business organizations, now find that they must operate under a new set of rules. The social good must be considered in all major decision making.

Effective operations are no longer defined solely in terms of the profits earned. Rather, managers have to define their missions more broadly. For many years there has been a growing recognition that socially oriented objectives need to be considered. But in the past, only lip service was paid to this recognition in most cases. Business managers often acted as if the profit objective was the only objective. It was to be maximized even if all other objectives were put into second place.

It remains true that only profitable companies can meet social objectives, so tomorrow's managers will still have to keep sight of the profit objective. But, more and more, social objectives will become restraints on profits. Quite a few activities will have to be carried forward because they are in the public interest, even though they cost money without generating any counterpart profit.

Consumerism

The wave of consumer consciousness which came on a flood tide in the early 1970s poses an interesting problem. Production managers will undoubtedly have to be more responsive to consumer wants and protection. These managers must be most careful to produce products which are as safe and reliable as possible.

It may be, however, that this movement will soon crest and not go much further, because consumers are in some cases being deprived by law from being allowed to make choices. Although studies show that very few people wear seat belts in cars, everyone has to pay for having them in his car. There is also a question of how comfortable a car can be which is built to take 50 mile-an-hour crashes, and whether people should be required to sacrifice comfort for a little added safety in crashes. There is also the question whether people should be denied the right to buy low-quality products at low prices.

Pharmaceutical, medicine, and food processors also sometimes get into a dilemma. A medicine or food which helps 10,000 people may prove allergic to 1 person. It seems illogical to prohibit the 10,000 people from being able to benefit from such products, yet there is need to give the exception as much protection as possible. Such legal restrictions need to be carefully drawn.

Whatever the long-range implications of consumerism, the older, free-wheeling days of "let the buyer beware" appear to be gone. Producers must do the best they can for consumers.

Constraints

Probably the greatest change in tomorrow's managers will come from the increased social responsibilities which necessitate the reevaluation of the supremacy of the profit objective.

This takes several forms: antipollution of air and water, antinoise, more consumer protection, and greater attention to safety. Carrying out these obligations will require managers to be broader-gage men than those of yesterday. Equal employment opportunities, regardless of race or sex, also requires greater managerial capability. Managers must do a better job of being fair in their hiring, training, and promotion practices. Indeed, they must go out of their way to hire a good share of hard-core unemployed. And in general, in every area of human relations, managers will have to be more alert to worker reactions and views.

On a worldwide basis, all of this means that multinational companies have to serve each of the various economies in which they operate with that economy's good in mind. They will have to—even more than they have in the past—train each country's nationals and upgrade them into managers. At the same time, they will have to operate in the face of more local restrictions than was formerly the case. In summary, they will have to manage better than today's managers.

Appendixes

A

Answers to problems[*]

THE ARRIVAL RATE or number of calls per hour is shown by the Greek letter lambda, λ. The service rate, the number of calls the man can handle in an hour, is shown by the Greek letter mu, μ. The average number of machines waiting to be served is then equal to:

$$\frac{\lambda^2}{\mu(\mu - \lambda)} \text{ or } \frac{(1.5)^2}{2(2 - 1.5)} = \frac{2.25}{1} = 2.25 \text{ machines}$$

The average numbers of machines being served and waiting is equal to:

$$\frac{\lambda}{\mu - \lambda} \text{ or } \frac{1.5}{2 - 1.5} = \frac{1.5}{.5} = 3.00 \text{ machines}$$

Average time per machine waiting for service is:

$$\frac{\lambda}{\mu(\mu - \lambda)} \text{ or } \frac{1.5}{2(2 - 1.5)} = \frac{1.5}{1} = 1.5 \text{ hours.}$$

Average time machines spend waiting and being serviced is equal to:

$$\frac{1}{\mu - \lambda} = \frac{1}{2 - 1.5} \text{ or } \frac{1}{.5} = 2 \text{ hours.}$$

The second problem on page 35 dealt with two service men—a "multichannel" problem. These two men service 50 machines which generate 24 calls per day. The service time still averages 30 minutes. There are five questions to be answered

1. What will be the average number of machines idle while waiting for service?
2. How many machines, on the average, will be idle either because they are being serviced or are waiting for service?
3. What will be the average idle time of machines waiting for service?
4. What will be the average idle time of machines, including waiting time and service time?
5. How much time will the service men be idle?

---

[*] On pages 34 and 35.

The first thing that queuing formulas for multichannel systems require is the calculation of the likelihood of there being no machines "in the system," meaning that no machines are either being serviced or waiting for service. Here are the symbols in the formula:

P_0 is the probability of there being no machines being serviced at any one time and none waiting to be serviced

M is the number of service men, 2 in our example

n is the least number of service men you could have, 0 in our example

λ is the average number of service calls per hour, 3 in our example

μ is the average number of calls a man can handle in an hour, 2 in our example

! means "factorial" (3! is $3 \times 2 \times 1$, or 6; 4 factorial would be $4 \times 3 \times 2 \times 1$, or 24; etc.)

Solving, first to find a value for P_0.

$$P_0 = \cfrac{1}{\left[\sum_{n=0}^{M-1} \cfrac{\left(\frac{\lambda}{\mu}\right)^n}{n!} \right] + \cfrac{\left(\frac{\lambda}{\mu}\right)^M}{M!\left(1 - \frac{\lambda}{\mu M}\right)}}$$

$\sum_{n=0}^{M-1}$ tells us to get the sum of a series of answers to the other part of the expression inside the brackets. It also tells us that the series we are to add up starts with 0 and ends at M minus 1. $M - 1$ becomes $2 - 1$, or 1.

In our problem the part of the formula inside the bracket then becomes:

$$\left[\frac{\left(\frac{\lambda}{\mu}\right)^0}{0!} + \frac{\left(\frac{\lambda}{\mu}\right)^1}{1} \right]$$

$$\frac{\left(\frac{\lambda}{\mu}\right)}{0} \text{ becomes } \frac{\left(\frac{3}{2}\right)^0}{0!} = \frac{1}{1} = 1$$

(Any number raised to a zero power is 1; hence $(\frac{3}{2})^0 = 1$. Also, zero factorial is 1; hence $0! = 1$.)

The right-hand part inside the brackets becomes

$$\frac{\left(\frac{3}{2}\right)^1}{1!} = \frac{\frac{3}{2}}{1} = \frac{1.5}{1} = 1.5$$

And the value of the whole bracket is $1 + 1.5 = 2.5$. We are now at this point:

$$P_0 = \cfrac{1}{2.5 + \cfrac{\left(\dfrac{\lambda}{\mu}\right)^M}{M!\left(1 - \dfrac{\lambda}{\mu M}\right)}}$$

$$\left(\frac{\lambda}{\mu}\right)^M \text{ becomes } \left(\frac{3}{2}\right)^2 = 1.5^2 = 2.25$$

$$M! \text{ is } 2 \times 1 = 2$$

$$\left(1 - \frac{\lambda}{\mu M}\right) \text{ becomes } 1 - \frac{3}{2 \times 2} = 1 - \frac{3}{4} = \frac{1}{4}$$

$$\text{and } M!\left(1 - \frac{\lambda}{\mu M}\right) \text{ becomes } 2 \times \frac{1}{4} = \frac{1}{2}$$

Our example has now come down to

$$P_0 = \frac{1}{2.5 + \dfrac{2.25}{.5}} = \frac{1}{2.5 + 4.5} = \frac{1}{7} = .144$$

The probability of there being no machine being serviced or waiting for service at any given time therefore is $\frac{1}{7}$, or .14.

Now we can go back to the five original questions:

1. What will be the average of machines idle while waiting for service? Let A be the number we are after:

$$A = \frac{\left(\dfrac{\lambda}{\mu}\right)^{M+1}}{(M-1)!\left(M - \dfrac{\lambda}{\mu}\right)^2} \times P_0$$

$$= \frac{(\frac{2}{3})^{2+1}}{(2-1)\ (2 - \frac{3}{2})^2} \times .144$$

$$= \frac{(1.5)^3}{2(.5)^2} \times .144$$

$$= \frac{3.375}{.5} \times .144$$

$$= 6.75 \times .144$$

$$= .97 \text{ machines}$$

2. How many machines on the average will be idle either because they are being serviced or are waiting for service? Let B be the number:

$$B = A + \frac{\lambda}{\mu} = .97 + \frac{3}{2} = .97 + 1.5$$

$$= 2.47 \text{ machines}$$

3. What will be the average idle time of machines waiting for service? Let C be the number:

$$C = \frac{A}{\lambda} = \frac{.97}{3}$$

$$= .32 \text{ hours}$$

4. What will be the average idle time of machines, including waiting time and service time? This is merely the average idle waiting time, .32 hours, plus the service time, .5 hours, or .82 hours.

5. How much time will the service men be idle? The 2 men are available for 2 man-hours per clock and in each clock hour the machines require 3 calls of a half hour duration each, or 1.5 hours. The men are therefore idle one fourth of their time.

The third problem posed on page 35 dealt with 3 service men. The solution becomes:

$$P_0 = \cfrac{1}{\left[\displaystyle\sum_{n=j}^{M-1} \frac{\left(\frac{\lambda}{\mu}\right)^n}{n!}\right] + \cfrac{\left(\frac{\lambda}{\mu}\right)^M}{3!\left(1 - \frac{\lambda}{\mu M}\right)}}$$

$$= \cfrac{1}{\left[\dfrac{\left(\frac{3}{2}\right)^0}{0!} + \dfrac{\left(\frac{3}{2}\right)^1}{1!} + \dfrac{\left(\frac{3}{2}\right)^2}{2!}\right] + \cfrac{\left(\frac{3}{2}\right)^3}{3!\left(1 - \frac{3}{(2)(3)}\right)}}$$

$$= \cfrac{1}{\left[\dfrac{1}{1} + \dfrac{1.5}{1} + \dfrac{2.25}{2}\right] + \cfrac{3.375}{6\left(1 - \frac{1}{2}\right)}}$$

$$= \cfrac{1}{1 + 1.5 + 1.125 + \dfrac{3.375}{3}}$$

$$= \frac{1}{3.625 + 1.125}$$

$$\frac{1}{4.8}$$

$$P_0 = .208$$

1. $$A = \frac{\left(\dfrac{\lambda}{\mu}\right)^{M+1}}{(M-1)!\left(M - \dfrac{\lambda}{\mu}\right)^2} \times P_0$$

$$= \frac{\left(\dfrac{3}{2}\right)^{3+1}}{(3-1)!\left(3 - \dfrac{3}{2}\right)^2} \times .208$$

$$= \frac{(1.5)^4}{2(1.5)^2} \times .208$$

$$= \frac{5.06}{4.5} \times .208$$

$$= \frac{1.05}{4.5}$$

$$= .23 \text{ machines}$$

2. $$B = A + \frac{\lambda}{\mu} = .23 + \frac{3}{2}$$
$$= 1.73 \text{ machines}$$

3. $$C = \frac{A}{\lambda} = \frac{.23}{3}$$
$$= .08 \text{ hours}$$

4. $.08 + .50 = .58$ hours

5. Man-time available per hour = 3 man-hours
    Man-hours used   1.5 man-hours
    Excess man-hours   1.5 at \$2 per
                                    hour = \$3

B

Random numbers for Monte Carlo problems[*]

217	590	735	965	276	027	658	289	260	572
686	359	273	366	451	539	308	080	747	416
584	895	372	370	694	623	364	449	416	877
379	668	206	918	238	485	587	543	322	654
933	051	047	945	927	272	310	017	002	807
755	482	252	018	695	273	123	943	518	037
806	672	856	030	043	852	957	768	006	207
242	601	105	033	672	850	951	621	414	904
593	877	679	098	970	840	391	543	174	703
638	780	709	407	697	973	687	859	476	611
039	302	411	195	374	198	057	531	721	508
322	160	509	543	422	523	351	152	617	169
507	794	941	115	728	071	748	679	252	396
447	300	889	181	370	532	608	883	520	539
547	539	210	354	861	025	229	731	141	786
322	810	756	491	869	285	371	709	431	629
536	990	532	133	215	626	463	616	172	135
439	027	759	297	544	890	049	784	156	641
238	273	941	056	196	283	184	154	714	282
709	739	310	685	146	114	027	141	774	229
692	912	670	340	319	116	843	317	396	990
270	999	075	843	918	453	942	797	606	082
054	579	869	187	940	406	743	855	108	135
834	482	068	368	619	539	991	799	920	400
287	594	981	898	433	496	837	673	576	516
943	344	947	996	457	875	060	475	161	741
696	094	870	050	758	332	843	475	933	153
407	272	332	502	258	963	896	467	287	506
120	799	798	761	876	032	477	832	223	404
994	899	118	417	093	298	356	455	145	854

[*] On page 39.

C

Discount tables

Present Value of $1

	Percent						
	5	10	15	20	25	30	40
Today................	1.000	1.000	1.000	1.000	1.000	1.000	1.000
Year							
1...................	.952	.909	.870	.833	.800	.769	.714
2...................	.907	.826	.756	.694	.640	.592	.510
3...................	.864	.751	.657	.578	.512	.455	.364
4...................	.822	.683	.572	.482	.410	.350	.260
5...................	.784	.621	.497	.402	.328	.269	.186
6...................	.746	.564	.432	.335	.262	.207	.133
7...................	.711	.513	.376	.279	.210	.159	.095
8...................	.677	.466	.327	.233	.168	.123	.068
9...................	.645	.424	.284	.194	.134	.094	.048
10..................	.614	.386	.247	.161	.107	.084	.035
11..................	.585	.351	.215	.134	.086	.064	.025
12..................	.557	.319	.187	.112	.069	.049	.018
13..................	.530	.290	.163	.093	.055	.038	.013
14..................	.505	.263	.141	.078	.044	.029	.009
15..................	.481	.239	.123	.065	.035	.023	.006
20..................	.384	.149	.061	.026	.012	.005	.001
25..................	.303	.092	.030	.010	.004	.001	
30..................	.241	.057	.015	.004	.001		
35..................	.197	.040	.010	.003			
40..................	.153	.022	.004	.001			

Present value of $1 received annually for N years

	Percent						
	5	10	15	20	25	30	40
Today...............	1.000	1.000	1.000	1.000	1.000	1.000	1.000
Year							
1.................	.952	.909	.870	.833	.800	.769	.714
2.................	1.859	1.736	1.626	1.528	1.440	1.361	1.224
3.................	2.723	2.487	2.283	2.106	1.952	1.816	1.589
4.................	3.545	3.170	2.855	2.589	2.362	2.166	1.849
5.................	4.329	3.791	3.352	2.991	2.689	2.436	2.035
6.................	5.075	4.355	3.784	3.326	2.951	2.643	2.168
7.................	5.786	4.868	4.160	3.605	3.161	2.802	2.263
8.................	6.463	5.335	4.487	3.837	3.329	2.925	2.331
9.................	7.108	5.759	4.772	4.031	3.463	3.019	2.379
10.................	7.722	6.145	5.019	4.192	3.571	3.092	2.414
11.................	8.307	6.495	5.234	4.327	3.656	3.147	2.438
12.................	8.864	6.814	5.421	4.439	3.725	3.190	2.456
13.................	9.394	7.103	5.583	4.533	3.780	3.223	2.468
14.................	9.899	7.367	5.724	4.611	3.824	3.249	2.477
15.................	10.380	7.606	5.847	4.675	3.859	3.268	2.484
20.................	12.530	8.514	6.259	4.730	3.954	3.316	2.497
25.................	14.203	9.077	6.464	4.948	3.985	3.329	2.499
30.................	15.528	9.427	6.566	4.979	3.995	3.332	2.500
35.................	16.474	9.603	6.604	4.988	3.997	3.333	2.500
40.................	17.420	9.779	6.642	4.997	3.999	3.333	2.500

D

Solution to preventive repair problem[*]

THE generalized formula for calculating the number of breakdowns is:

$$B_n = N \sum_1^n p_n + B_{(n-1)}p_1 + B_{(n-2)}p_2 + B_{(n-3)}p_3 + \cdots + B_1 p_{(n-1)}$$

To show how this works, we will calculate the expected number of breakdowns if overhauls are scheduled on 1-, 2-, 3-, or 4-month bases. B is the number of breakdowns and N is the number of machines.

Scheduled overhaul every month:

$$B_1 = N p_1$$
$$B_1 = 50(.05) = 2.50$$

Scheduled overhaul every 2 months:

$$B_2 = N(p_1 + p_2) + B_1 p_1$$
$$B_2 = 50(.05 + .02) + 2.50(.05)$$
$$= 3.50 + .13 = 3.63$$

Scheduled overhaul every 3 months:

$$B_3 = N(p_1 + p_2 + p_3) + B_2 p_1 + B_1 p_2$$
$$B_3 = 50(.05 + .02 + .03) + 3.63(.05) + 2.50(.02)$$
$$= 5.00 + .18 + .05 = 5.23$$

Scheduled overhaul every 4 months:

$$B_4 = N(p_1 + p_2 + p_3 + p_4) + B_3 p_1 + B_2 p_2 + B_1 p_3$$
$$B_4 = 50(.14) + 5.23(.05) + 3.63(.02) + 3.50(.03)$$
$$= 7.00 + .26 + .07 + .11 = 7.44$$

We will not work out the remaining figures here. They are given in Figure 7–6. These figures (plotted in Figure 7–7) show that preventive maintenance should be used. The machines should be overhauled every 6 or 7 months. Such a policy would entail monthly costs of $3,130 and would save $1,027 a month, compared to the $4,157 monthly cost of following a breakdown and repair policy.

[*] On page 173.

E

For strength and stress discussion[*]

It is unnecessary to calculate the value for the intersecting point of the two curves. The probability of failure can be calculated directly by using this formula:

$$P = \frac{\text{Average strength} - \text{average stress}}{\sqrt{(\text{strength std. dev.})^2 + (\text{stress std. dev.})^2}}$$

$$= \frac{250 - 100}{\sqrt{35^2 + 20^2}}$$

$$= \frac{150}{\sqrt{1225 + 400}}$$

$$= \frac{150}{40.3}$$

$$= 3.72$$

This 3.72 is now used as the measure to show the probabilities of failure. It shows that the proportion of the cases which fall beyond 3.72 standard deviations are .0001, or 1 chance in 10,000.

The .0001 figure comes from Appendix F, which shows that a point out 3.7 standard deviations from the mean includes .99989 of the cases, leaving .00011 cases which are farther out.

---

[*] On page 269.

690

F

Areas under the normal curve

Section A

Rounded off numbers are cumulated from small to large by tenths of standard deviations (largely for use when using random numbers in simulation problems).

Standard deviations	Per-cent	Standard deviations	Per-cent	Standard deviations	Per-cent	Standard deviations	Per-cent
−3.0	.1	−1.4	8.3	+0.2	57.9	+1.7	95.3
−2.9	.2	−1.3	9.9	+0.3	61.7	+1.8	96.2
−2.8	.3	−1.2	11.7	+0.4	65.4	+1.9	96.9
−2.7	.4	−1.1	13.8	+0.5	69.0	+2.0	97.5
−2.6	.6	−1.0	16.1	+0.6	72.4	+2.1	98.0
−2.5	.8	−0.9	18.6	+0.7	75.6	+2.2	98.4
−2.4	1.0	−0.8	21.4	+0.8	78.6	+2.3	98.7
−2.3	1.3	−0.7	24.4	+0.9	81.4	+2.4	99.0
−2.2	1.6	−0.6	27.6	+1.0	83.9	+2.5	99.2
−2.1	2.0	−0.5	31.0	+1.1	86.2	+2.6	99.4
−2.0	2.5	−0.4	34.6	+1.2	88.3	+2.7	99.6
−1.9	3.1	−0.3	38.3	+1.3	90.1	+2.8	99.7
−1.8	3.8	−0.2	42.1	+1.4	91.9	+2.9	99.8
−1.7	4.7	−0.1	46.0	+1.5	93.1	+3.0	99.9
−1.6	5.7	0.0	50.0	+1.6	94.3	+3.1	100.0
−1.5	6.9	+0.1	54.0				

Section B

Sums of all areas from the left of the normal curve to the point indicated. At the mean, for example, the 0.0 point below, the areas to the left sum up to .50 of the whole area under the curve. At 1 standard deviation above the mean, the area enclosed to the left comes to .84134 of the whole area. The mean-plus-2 standard deviations determine a point which encloses a left-hand area which includes .97725 of the whole area.

To get areas for measures below the mean, use the complements of the numbers below. Thus the mean-minus-1 standard deviation encloses an area to its left of .15866 of the total area under the curve. The mean-minus-2 standard deviations enclose an area which includes .02275 of the total area.

	.00	.01	.02	.03	.04	.05	.06	.07	.08	.09
0.0	.50000	.50399	.50798	.51197	.51595	.51994	.52392	.52790	.53188	.53586
0.1	.53983	.54380	.54776	.55172	.55567	.55962	.56356	.56749	.57142	.57535
0.2	.57926	.58317	.58706	.59095	.59483	.59871	.60257	.60642	.61026	.61409
0.3	.61791	.62172	.62552	.62930	.63307	.63683	.64058	.64431	.64803	.65173
0.4	.65542	.65910	.66276	.66640	.67003	.67364	.67724	.68082	.68439	.68793
0.5	.69146	.69497	.69847	.70194	.70540	.70884	.71226	.71566	.71904	.72240
0.6	.72575	.72907	.73237	.73536	.73891	.74215	.74537	.74857	.75175	.75490
0.7	.75804	.76115	.76424	.76730	.77035	.77337	.77637	.77935	.78230	.78524
0.8	.78814	.79103	.79389	.79673	.79955	.80234	.80511	.80785	.81057	.81327
0.9	.81594	.81859	.82121	.82381	.82639	.82894	.83147	.83398	.83646	.83891
1.0	.84134	.84375	.84614	.84849	.85083	.85314	.85543	.85769	.85993	.86214
1.1	.86433	.86650	.86864	.87076	.87286	.87493	.87698	.87900	.88100	.88298
1.2	.88493	.88686	.88877	.89065	.89251	.89435	.89617	.89796	.89973	.90147
1.3	.90320	.90490	.90658	.90824	.90988	.91149	.91309	.91466	.91621	.91774
1.4	.91924	.92073	.92220	.92364	.92507	.92647	.92785	.92922	.93056	.93189
1.5	.93319	.93448	.93574	.93699	.93822	.93943	.94062	.94179	.94295	.94408
1.6	.94520	.94630	.94738	.94845	.94950	.95053	.95154	.95254	.95352	.95449
1.7	.95543	.95637	.95728	.95818	.95907	.95994	.96080	.96164	.96246	.96327
1.8	.96407	.96485	.96562	.96638	.96712	.96784	.96856	.96926	.96995	.97062
1.9	.97128	.97193	.97257	.97320	.97381	.97441	.97500	.97558	.97615	.97670
2.0	.97725	.97784	.97831	.97882	.97932	.97982	.98030	.98077	.98124	.98169
2.1	.98214	.98257	.98300	.98341	.98382	.98422	.98461	.98500	.98537	.98574
2.2	.98610	.98645	.98679	.98713	.98745	.98778	.98809	.98840	.98870	.98899
2.3	.98928	.98956	.98983	.99010	.99036	.99061	.99086	.99111	.99134	.99158
2.4	.99180	.99202	.99224	.99245	.99266	.99286	.99305	.99324	.99343	.99361
2.5	.99379	.99396	.99413	.99430	.99446	.99461	.99477	.99492	.99506	.99520
2.6	.99534	.99547	.99560	.99573	.99585	.99598	.99609	.99621	.99632	.99643
2.7	.99653	.99664	.99674	.99683	.99693	.99702	.99711	.99720	.99728	.99736
2.8	.99744	.99752	.99760	.99767	.99774	.99781	.99788	.99795	.99801	.99807
2.9	.99813	.99819	.99825	.99831	.99836	.99841	.99846	.99851	.99856	.99861
3.0	.99865	.99869	.99874	.99878	.99882	.99886	.99899	.99893	.99896	.99900
3.1	.99903	.99906	.99910	.99913	.99916	.99918	.99921	.99924	.99926	.99929
3.2	.99931	.99934	.99936	.99938	.99940	.99942	.99944	.99946	.99948	.99950
3.3	.99952	.99953	.99955	.99957	.99958	.99960	.99961	.99962	.99964	.99965
3.4	.99966	.99968	.99969	.99970	.99971	.99972	.99973	.99974	.99975	.99976
3.5	.99977	.99978	.99978	.99979	.99980	.99981	.99981	.99982	.99983	.99983
3.6	.99984	.99985	.99985	.99986	.99986	.99987	.99987	.99988	.99988	.99989
3.7	.99989	.99990	.99990	.99990	.99991	.99991	.99992	.99992	.99992	.99992
3.8	.99993	.99993	.99993	.99994	.99994	.99994	.99994	.99995	.99995	.99995
3.9	.99995	.99995	.99996	.99996	.99996	.99996	.99996	.99996	.99997	.99997

Index